DIVUS JULIUS

1. Marble head of Caesar wearing an oak wreath, found on Thasos, in the local Museum (Photograph: German Archaeological Institute, Rome); p. 167.

DIVUS JULIUS

STEFAN WEINSTOCK

OXFORD
AT THE CLARENDON PRESS
1971

Oxford University Press, Ely House, London W. 1

GLASGOW NEW YORK TORONTO MELBOURNE WELLINGTON
CAPE TOWN IBADAN NAIROBI DAR ES SALAAM LUSAKA ADDIS ABABA
DELHI BOMBAY CALCUTTA MADRAS KARACHI LAHORE DACCA
KUALA LUMPUR SINGAPORE HONG KONG TOKYO

PRINTED IN GREAT BRITAIN
AT THE UNIVERSITY PRESS, OXFORD
BY VIVIAN RIDLER
PRINTER TO THE UNIVERSITY

D.   M.

WILHELM KROLL

FRANZ CUMONT

HUGH LAST

S.

PREFACE

WHAT I had planned as an introductory chapter to a work on the religion of the age of Augustus has become a book in its own right. I had to change course when I realized the identity of the reformer about whom I wished to write: it was not Augustus but Caesar. This book is therefore primarily a search for a new synthesis of the evidence, rather than a straightforward presentation of it in the form of a handbook. Yet I have quoted the most important texts in full and added the relevant bibliography for the sake of those in need of information. My narrative is naturally much indebted to my predecessors, more to the general works of Drumann, Mommsen, Meyer, and Gelzer than to the specialized studies listed below in the Select Bibliography, which seldom go beyond the limited amount of evidence presented by Heinen in 1911; I have tried to be comprehensive and even yet may not have succeeded completely. The Caesar who thus emerges is not new. Nevertheless, some of his features may seem unfamiliar. This is due partly to additional evidence, partly to my reluctance to share the view that Caesar was a rationalist or that he and Roman religion can be judged in the light of puritan ideals. This view I believe to be modern prejudice. My successors no doubt will find that I am not free from prejudices either, and will make the necessary corrections. I am, of course, well aware of the provisional nature of my conclusions. A book of this kind is never finished. But now I begin to feel that I should not add much to its substance by withholding it any longer.

The page of dedication records old debts of gratitude; it is the fulfilment of a long-cherished hope. My first and foremost debt is to German scholarship and in particular to Wilhelm Kroll. I began my studies in the turbulent years after the break-up of my native land, the Austro-Hungarian Empire; a mere chance brought me ultimately to Breslau University where I became Kroll's pupil. He was not rated among the leading Latin scholars of his generation; he did not belong to any 'school' nor did he create one. He was what he wanted to be: a worthy servant of a great tradition. His profound learning, intellectual honesty (including the rare virtue of detachment), severe method, and sound judgement have guided me all through my life. As time has passed he is no longer under-rated in the world of scholarship; the publication in 1969 of his selected essays would have been a well-deserved memorial for the centenary of his birth.

My interest in Roman religion dates from my undergraduate days. There was nobody to guide me at that time or for many years to come, until good luck in adversity brought me into contact with Franz Cumont, the undisputed master. The study of his works on oriental religions and collaboration with him in the field of Greek astrology extended my horizon. But even more, the stimulation of watching a man so full of ideas and always driven by the spirit of the pioneer has had a lasting effect on my work.

In the end fortune guided me to Oxford and to Hugh Last, the leading Roman historian of his generation. His influence went far beyond his own field. He liked to inspire and to promote the work of others, and I became one of the many who benefited from his invaluable help and advice. We have learnt since his untimely death in 1957 how difficult it is to carry on without his warming presence. It was he who persuaded me to lecture on the religion of the first century B.C. rather than on that of early Rome, a fateful turn without which I could not have written this book. It is impossible to say how far he would have approved of it. But he would have noticed, I am sure, with great satisfaction that the scholar most frequently quoted in it is Theodor Mommsen, and he would perhaps have concluded—rightly—that I owe to him my rather belated conversion to Mommsen. In fact it is mainly due to Last's efforts that nowadays Mommsen's spirit is nowhere so much alive as in England.

It gives me great pleasure to record a further debt I owe to these three men, a personal one. They knew that I had been uprooted from early youth, and that therefore I was in need of more than scholarly help; they never tired of acting accordingly and of enlisting the sympathy of others. In the end, thanks to the generosity of Oxford University, Exeter College, and my friends amongst their members, I was able to find a home here and to devote my time to undisturbed research.

I have incurred further debts in connection with this book. The Faculty of Literae Humaniores made a grant to cover the expenses of typing. Professor H. Chadwick (now Dean of Christ Church) paved the way to its publication. The Delegates of the Oxford University Press accepted it, and their officials worked untiringly on its worthy presentation.[1] The English idiom has been much improved by Mr. D. J. Caslon, the learned and vigilant proof-readers of the Printer, and my friends Mr. P. G. McC. Brown, Mr. A. Drummond, Professor R. G. M. Nisbet, Mr. J. A. North, and Mr. P. J. Parsons. These friends also helped me

---

[1] On only one point did we disagree, and there we agreed to differ—as the reader may see if he compares the spelling of the title of this book with that adopted in the text.

in correcting the proofs, improved my argument at many points, and eliminated painful errors. In numismatic matters I greatly benefited from the valuable advice of Mr. M. H. Crawford and Dr. C. M. Kraay.

Finally, for the photographs and for permission to reproduce them, I gratefully acknowledge my debt to the following scholars and institutions: Mr. D. E. L. Haynes and the Trustees of the British Museum, London; the National Gallery, London; Mr. C. M. Daniels, Newcastle, and the Trustees of the Museum at Chesters; Staatliche Antikensammlung, Munich; Professor T. Dohrn and the Diözesenmuseum, Cologne; Sopraintendenza alle Antichità, Aquileia; Messrs. Giraudon, Paris, and Alinari, Rome; and above all Dr. H. Sichtermann and the Deutsches Archäologisches Institut, Rome. For the casts of coins and permission to reproduce them I am indebted to Dr. C. M. Kraay and the Coin Room of the Ashmolean Museum, Oxford; Mr. R. A. G. Carson and the Department of Coins and Medals of the British Museum, London; M. J. B. Giard, Cabinet des Médailles, Paris; Dr. H. D. Schultz, Münzkabinett der Staatl. Museen, Berlin; Dr. Küthmann, Staatl. Münzsammlung, Munich; Dr. A. Kromann, Kgl. Mønt- og Medaillesamling, Copenhagen; Dr. C. C. Vermeule, Boston, Mass., U.S.A.

S. W.

Oxford, June 1968–March 1971

CONTENTS

LIST OF PLATES

ABBREVIATIONS

AE	*L'année épigraphique*
BJ	*Bonner Jahrbücher*
BMC	*British Museum Catalogue of Greek Coins*
Broughton	T. R. S. Broughton, *The Magistrates of the Roman Republic*
Degr.	A. Degrassi, *Inscriptiones Latinae liberae rei publicae*
Degrassi	A. Degrassi, *Fasti anni Numani et Iuliani* (*Inscr. Ital. 13. 2*)
Drumann	W. Drumann, *Geschichte Roms* (2. Aufl. hrsg. v. P. Groebe)
E.–J.	V. Ehrenberg–A. H. M. Jones, *Documents illustrating the Reigns of Augustus and Tiberius*
Grueber	H. A. Grueber, *Coins of the Roman Republic in the British Museum*
Habicht	Chr. Habicht, *Gottmenschentum und griechische Städte*
Head, *HN*	B. V. Head, *Historia Numorum* (second edition)
Henzen, *AFA*	Guil. Henzen, *Acta fratrum Arvalium*
IGR	R. Cagnat *et alii*, *Inscriptiones Graecae ad res Romanas pertinentes*
ILS	H. Dessau, *Inscriptiones Latinae selectae*
Latte	K. Latte, *Römische Religionsgeschichte*
Mattingly	H. Mattingly, *Coins of the Roman Empire in the British Museum*
Mél.	*Mélanges d'archéologie et d'histoire*
Mommsen, *StR*	Th. Mommsen, *Römisches Staatsrecht*
Mommsen, *Strafr.*	Th. Mommsen, *Römisches Strafrecht*
Myth. Lex.	W. H. Roscher, *Ausführliches Lexikon der griechischen und römischen Mythologie*
Nash	E. Nash, *Pictorial Dictionary of Ancient Rome*
Nilsson	M. P. Nilsson, *Geschichte der griechischen Religion*
Or. gr.	W. Dittenberger, *Orientis Graeci Inscriptiones selectae*
PBSR	*Papers of the British School at Rome*
v. Premerstein	A. von Premerstein, *Vom Werden und Wesen des Prinzipats*
RAC	*Reallexikon für Antike und Christentum*
Ryberg	I. S. Ryberg, *Rites of the State Religion in Roman Art*
Sydenham	E. A. Sydenham, *The Coinage of the Roman Republic*
Syll.	W. Dittenberger, *Sylloge Inscriptionum Graecarum*
L. R. Taylor	L. R. Taylor, *The Divinity of the Roman Emperor*
Vittinghoff	F. Vittinghoff, *Römische Kolonisation und Bürgerrechtspolitik unter Caesar und Augustus*
Wissowa	G. Wissowa, *Religion und Kultus der Römer*

SELECT BIBLIOGRAPHY

H. HEINEN, *Klio* 11 (1911), 129–77.

W. W. FOWLER, *Roman Ideas of Deity*, 1914.

E. MEYER, *Caesars Monarchie u. das Principat d. Pompeius*, 1922 (1918).

L. R. TAYLOR, *The Divinity of the Roman Emperor*, 1931.

J. CARCOPINO, *Les étapes de l'impérialisme romain*, 1961 (1934), 118–73.

A. ALFÖLDI, *Studien über Caesars Monarchie*, 1952.

K. KRAFT, *Jahrb. f. Numismatik u. Geldgesch.* 3/4 (1952/3), 7–98.

F. TAEGER, *Charisma* 2 (1960), 3–88.

D. FELBER, *Caesars Streben nach der Königswürde* (Unters. zur röm. Gesch. hrsg. v. F. Altheim, 1, 1961), 209–84.

G. DOBESCH, *Caesars Apotheose zu Lebzeiten u. sein Ringen um den Königstitel*, 1966.

H. GESCHE, *Die Vergottung Caesars*, 1968 (*non vidi*).

I

INTRODUCTION

THE title 'Divus Iulius' conveniently sums up the two principal themes of this book: Caesar's religious reforms and his honours. Both had to be given a place within the ancestral tradition and must therefore be introduced with a brief sketch of this tradition.

The Romans had no sacred books on which one could base a discussion of their religion. What was due to the gods, the *ius divinum*, was laid down in continuous legislation and was to some extent reflected in the Calendar, fragments of which have survived. Had the Romans possessed a written constitution those laws would have been collected in it. And yet, although there was no early codification, no essential matter was ever forgotten and only what had become obsolete was neglected. There were the private cults of the individual citizen, of his household, and of his Gens; the local cults of the various communities; and the public cults of the State. There were also private beliefs based on genuine Roman tradition, on Greek philosophy, or on Etruscan, Greek, and Oriental religious doctrines. Nevertheless it is not correct to speak of a contrast between personal religion and the religion of the State, between a philosophy of life and the establishment. The gods of the State cared for the needs of the individual, and he was bound to them by ritual acts from birth to death. He made his vows to them, as well as to the gods of his own household, in personal troubles like illness and misfortune, and at important events like soldiering, travel, marriage. There were differences between individuals: one believed in *haruspicina*, another in astrology, a third in magic—there was no rule of exclusivism; but these were passing beliefs, whereas the ancestral tradition remained constant. Further, one could be pious by nature[1] or a sparing worshipper, infrequent and negligent; or one might abuse priestly office and the religious ritual in a struggle for political power. A man would also have his particular cults, the cults of those gods to whom his family was attached by long tradition; he would build them new temples or repair and improve the old. Strong emotions and feverish

---

[1] Pomponia, the mother of the elder Scipio, visited all temples to pray and sacrifice when her son Lucius was a candidate for the aedileship, Polyb. 10. 4. 4; Münzer, *Adelsp.* 162. 1; Meyer, *Kl. Schr.* 2. 429.

B

religious activities were the exception, caused by great national disasters like famine, pestilence, or the dangers of the Hannibalic War; or by great personal crises like Cicero's exile or the death of his daughter Tullia. On the whole religious fervour was not conspicuous; and yet the attachment of the Romans to their gods was strong and much acknowledged by observers like Polybius, Panaetius, and Posidonius.[1]

The religion of the State was based on the original cults of the city-state, and not on reflections about man and the universe, life and death, good and evil, and the like. This basis still remained after Rome had achieved mastery of the world and new cults had been introduced from Latium, Italy, and the Greek world with the gradual extension of the political horizon. A greater political consciousness too led to new religious needs and to the creation of the cults of personified values and virtues, such as Concordia, Salus, Pietas, Victoria, Honos, Virtus. The new cults were quickly accepted and assimilated. But the old cults were scrupulously observed, with their primitive ritual,[2] archaic prayers which few people understood,[3] and elementary methods of divination.[4] At the same time it was the duty of the statesman to build, to reform, and to reorganize, not in the sense of innovation but with due respect for the ancestral inheritance: Sulla, for example, was a great reformer and built or rebuilt many temples all over Italy. That is not to say that there were not exceptions and even long periods of decline. But we need not accept the frequent assertion that the piety of the ancestors led to the greatness of Rome and that the negligence, indifference, and abuse of their descendants led or could have led to its decline.[5]

Educated Romans were well aware of the Greek philosophical criticism of traditional religion and often took their share in the debate. But the effect should not be over-estimated. Lucretius' criticism, for instance, of what he calls *religio* does not concern religion or the gods of Rome at all, but Greek myths of the kind which prompted Plato to expel Homer from his State. Nor were the gods who lived far from the affairs of men and did not influence them the gods of Rome but the Epicurean gods; when Lucretius speaks of the gods of Rome he speaks differently. Similarly Varro adopted the Stoic doctrine in his great theological

[1] Polyb. 6. 56. 7; Posid., *FGrHist.* 87 F 59; Diod. 28. 3.

[2] Cic. *div.* 2. 148: 'maiorum instituta tueri sacris caerimoniisque sapientis est'; Livy 6. 41. 8.

[3] Quintil. 1. 6. 40: 'Saliorum carmina vix sacerdotibus suis satis intellecta. (41) sed illa mutari vetat religio et consecratis utendum est.'

[4] Many instances in Val. Max. 1. 1.

[5] Varr. *Ant. rer. div.* 1, frg. 2a Ag. (August. *CD* 6. 2).

work *Antiquitates rerum divinarum* and spoke of the threefold religion, of the poets, of the philosophers, and of the State, with a great deal of rational criticism.[1] But when he turned to the ancestral religion he forgot all he had learned from the philosophers.[2] Again, Cicero presented a great theological debate among Academics, Stoics, and Epicureans in his work *De natura deorum* and said all that was to be said about popular religion. But he also spoke of the Romans' approach to such debates: they opposed the *auctoritas* of the ancestors to rational argument, and the advice of the *pontifices* to that of the philosophers.[3] It is Cicero's great merit to have formulated this attitude for the first time with admirable clarity, and there is no doubt that this was always the principal feature of the Roman religious spirit. St. Augustine, an African who was brought up in the Roman world, became really conscious of it when he read Cicero; he consequently saw to it that authority was given a central position in the Church also.[4]

One of our two themes then will be the attitude of Caesar as citizen and statesman: was he 'pious' or sceptical, correct or negligent, and were his reforms and building activities as they should have been? The other theme, the religious honours paid to Caesar, will appear to be a paradoxical one from this point of view. And yet it will not be dismissed here as an irresponsible game by Caesar or by his friends and enemies, but considered a serious attempt at further reform. Religious honours for an individual were frequent in Greece, and not a novelty in Rome either. But hitherto they had not been lasting. They became a constitutional necessity from the moment when the real power passed from the annual magistrates to the single and permanent ruler. The ruler cult is a fact of history; 'Divus Iulius' is concerned with the Roman version of it and sets out to prove that it was conceived by Caesar.

---

[1] Varr. *Ant. rer. div.* 1, frgs. 6–8 Ag. (August. *CD* 6. 5; 4. 27); on the social 'usefulness' of religion see Polyb. 6. 56. 6 ff.; 18. 34. 7; Walbank, *JRS* 55 (1965), 8.

[2] Varr. *Ant. rer. div.* 1, frg. 2a Ag. (August. *CD* 6. 2).

[3] Cic. *ND* 3. 5: 'nec me ex ea opinione, quam a maioribus accepi de cultu deorum inmortalium, ullius umquam oratio . . . movebit. sed cum de religione agitur, Ti. Coruncanium, P. Scipionem, P. Scaevolam, pontifices maximos, non Zenonem aut Cleanthen aut Chrysippum sequor . . . (6) . . . a te enim philosopho rationem accipere debeo religionis, maioribus autem nostris etiam nulla ratione reddita credere . . . (7) . . . mihi quidem ex animo exuri non potest esse deos, id tamen ipsum, quod mihi persuasum est auctoritate maiorum, cur ita sit nihil tu me doces . . . (9) . . . mihi enim unum sat erat ita nobis maioris nostros tradidisse. sed tu auctoritates contemnis, ratione pugnas'; 1. 61; 2. 2; *har. resp.* 18 f.; *JRS* 51 (1961), 209.

[4] August. *c. ep. Manichaei* 5 (*CSEL* 25. 197 = *Patr. Lat.* 42. 176): 'ego vero evangelio non crederem, nisi me catholicae ecclesiae commoveret auctoritas'; Heinze, *Vom Geist des Römertums* 20. 1; K.-H. Lütcke, *Auctoritas bei Augustin* (1968), 144 ff.

II

THE ANCESTRAL TRADITION

INDIVIDUAL families had their own legends and cults. The legends
often referred to their origins, even divine origins, and to the achievements of their members.[1] The cults were those which they particularly
promoted either in their private shrines or in public temples built by
a member of the family; as instances the Claudii, Aemilii, Iulii, and
Cornelii are mentioned.[2] Some families had a special goddess named after
them, for instance Egeria, Hostia, Venilia, Feronia,[3] though not the great
families of Rome. They preserved the record of such cults by oral tradition, which was later used by historians and antiquarians whenever they
needed it. A specialist was M. Valerius Messalla Rufus (*cos.* 53), whose
work *De familiis* included the Aelii, Servilii, probably also the Porcii
Catones;[4] then came Atticus who wrote about the Iunii, Claudii, Cornelii, Fabii, Aemilii;[5] Varro and Hyginus who wrote about the 'Trojan'
families.[6] A great deal has survived, of odd fragments rather than exhaus-
tive information, which is not surprising. It is surprising, however, that the
direct information about Caesar and the Gens Iulia is equally meagre;
how meagre it is can be measured by the abundance of what is known
about Augustus' family and his early life.[7] This was not always the case.
A member of the family, L. Iulius Caesar, wrote about the traditions of
the Iulii in his work on the origins of Rome about the middle of the first
century B.C. or somewhat earlier.[8] There were also some biographies of
Caesar, for instance by his friends C. Oppius and L. Cornelius Balbus;[9]

---

[1] Cic. *Brut.* 62; Livy 8. 40. 4; Pliny 35. 7. The glory of the families was often advertised
on coins.—The Fabii and Antonii were descended from Hercules (Ov. *F.* 2. 237; *Pont.*
3. 3. 99 f.; App. *BC* 3. 16. 60; 19. 72; Plut. *Ant.* 4. 2; 36. 7), the Memmii from Venus (Lucr.
1. 26 ff.), the Vitellii from Faunus (Suet. *Vit.* 1. 2); W. F. Otto, *Rhein. Mus.* 64 (1909),
449 ff.; Wissowa 404.   [2] Macrob. 1. 16. 7; Tac. *A.* 15. 23. 3; Dion. Hal. 1. 70. 4.

[3] Wissowa 33; Latte 58 f.

[4] Pliny 7. 173; 34. 137; 35. 8 (Peter, *HRR* 2, p. LXVIII; 65); Gell. 13. 20. 17; Münzer,
Beitr. z. Quellenkritik d. Naturgesch. d. Plin. 351 f.; Hanslik, *RE* 8A. 169.

[5] Nep. *Att.* 18. 3 f.; Norden, *Kl. Schr.* 368 f.

[6] Serv. *Aen.* 5. 704 (2. 166); 5. 389; cf. Peter, *HRR* 1, p. XXXIX; Münzer, *Adelsp.* 133. 1;
Dahlmann, *RE* Suppl. 6. 1241 f.; Ch. Vellay, *Studies in Honor of D. M. Robinson* 2. 945 ff.

[7] Suet. *Aug.* 1 ff.; 94; Deonna, *RHR* 83/4 (1921), 1 ff.

[8] Serv. Dan. *Aen.* 1. 267 and nine further fragments in *Orig. gent. Rom.*; see below, p. 17. 6.

[9] Suet. *Caes.* 53; 81. 1 f.; Strasburger, *Caesars Eintritt in die Gesch.* 30 ff.; Münzer, *RE* 18. 1.
735. A further biographer seems to have been Q. Aelius Tubero, Suet. 56. 7(?); 83. 1; Gell.
6. 9. 11; Peter, *HRR* 1, pp. CCCLXVI ff.; 308 ff. Teuffel-Kroll 1. 497; Strasburger 35.

and there must have been some relevant poetry, historical works, and numberless political pamphlets. They are lost, but some of their evidence would have survived had the beginning of Caesar's biography in Suetonius and Plutarch not been lost also: the former begins with his sixteenth year, the latter with his eighteenth.[1] Nevertheless far more can be recovered than appears at first sight.

I. BOVILLAE

The Iulii belonged to the 'Trojan' families of Rome, that is, to those who traced their descent from Aeneas or one of his companions.[2] Their founder was Ascanius, son of Aeneas, who was also called Iulus.[3] Their home was Alba Longa, which Ascanius founded and chose as the seat of his kingship. Alba Longa was destroyed by 'Tullus Hostilius', and the Alban families, the Iulii among them, moved to Rome.[4] There they became a patrician family and were placed in the *tribus Fabia*, which was named after one of the most prominent families.[5] The Iulii too became prominent and held high office in the fifth and fourth centuries B.C., but then suffered an eclipse which lasted almost 200 years.[6] When Caesar was born the family was prominent again. His grandfather was married to a member of a distinguished family, the Marcii Reges,[7] mentioned by Caesar with pride in the funeral oration for his aunt Iulia, the wife of Marius;[8] his father reached the praetorship and Sex. Iulius Caesar, probably his uncle, was consul in 91 B.C.[9] Other Iulii too who were not closely related to his branch of the family had achieved prominence by that time. The Iulii were listed among the noble families who fought in 100 against Saturninus and Glaucia.[10]

[1] Strasburger, op. cit. 78 f.

[2] Serv. *Aen.* 2. 166; Livy 1. 30. 2 (below, n. 4); Dion. Hal. 3. 29. 7; *RE* 19. 446 f. (with bibliography).

[3] Serv. *Aen.* 1. 267; Verg. *Aen.* 1. 288: 'Iulius, a magno demissum nomen Iulo'; 6. 789: 'hic Caesar et omnis Iuli / progenies'; according to Fest. 340 M. (460 L.; below, p. 7. 3) Iulus was the son of Ascanius; Münzer, *RE* 10. 106; Kroll, ibid. 953.

[4] Livy 1. 30. 1: (Tullus Hostilius) 'Roma interim crescit Albae ruinis ... (2) principes Albanorum in patres, ut ea quoque pars rei publicae cresceret, legit: Tullios, Servilios, Quinctios, ⟨Iulios,⟩ Geganios, Curiatios, Cloelios' ('Tullios' of the MSS has been replaced in all editions by 'Iulios' since Sabellius; the MSS tradition is, however, supported by the inverted alphabetical order, also by the fact that there was at least one patrician Tullius, M'. Tullius, *cos.* 500 B.C.: Münzer, *RE* 7A. 1314 f.). The same list without the Tullii in Dion. Hal. 3. 29. 7; Tac. *A.* 11. 24. 2: (Claudius) 'neque enim ignoro Iulios Alba ... accitos.'

[5] Suet. *Aug.* 40. 2; cf. *AE* 1960, 26 ('Ti. Iulio Zoili f. Fab(ia) Pappo ...'; *PIR* 4. 3. 243 no. 447); Münzer, *RE* 6. 1741. On Kaeso (a special *praenomen* of the Fabii) and Caesar see below, p. 333; *luperci Fabiani* and *Iulii*, p. 332; *tribus Iulia*, pp. 158 ff.; Mommsen, *StR* 3. 788. 6 (no special relationship between the Alban Iulii and the Roman Fabii).

[6] Münzer, *RE* 10. 106.

[7] Münzer, *RE* 14. 1535 ff.; 1601.

[8] Suet. *Caes.* 6. 1 (below, p. 18. 1).

[9] Münzer, *RE* 10. 185 f.; 476.

[10] Cic. *Rab. perd.* 21.

Alba Longa was destroyed, but its cults were preserved,[1] and with them the cults of the Iulii, though not at Alba, which was not rebuilt, but at Bovillae, which had been founded from Alba and never broke the bond with it:[2] its inhabitants were still called Albani Longani Bovillenses in the imperial period.[3] It will be seen that Caesar was attached to both Alba and Bovillae, but that the family had stronger roots in Bovillae than in Alba. It is possible that it was Iulus-Ascanius who founded Bovillae when his half-brother Silvius became king of Alba.

Bovillae was said to have been founded on the spot where the bull was caught which, when about to be sacrificed on the Alban Mount, had escaped.[4] This story served a twofold purpose: it explained the name of Bovillae as derived from *bos*, and gave the reason why it was built in that particular spot. The animal which led the way to the place of a future settlement was a frequent feature of foundation-legends.[5] It is sufficient to mention the white sow which Aeneas wanted to sacrifice after landing in Latium; it escaped, however, and was found where Lavinium was later built.[6] Consequently the sow became a symbol of the sacred origins of the Romans, had a statue in Lavinium, and later was often reproduced in significant contexts.[7] Bovillae could not compare in importance with Lavinium; and yet the bull may have had a similar significance for its inhabitants, with similar statues and symbolism. This suggestion is prompted by a curious prodigy which occurred at the beginning of the Civil War, when Caesar was about to depart

[1] Cic. *Mil.* 85: 'Albani tumuli atque luci ... Albanorum ... arae, sacrorum populi Romani sociae et aequales'; Livy 1. 31. 3: 'visi etiam audire vocem ingentem ex summi cacuminis luco, ut patrio ritu sacra Albani facerent'; Strab. 5. 231: ἡ μὲν Ἄλβα κατεσκάφη πλὴν τοῦ ἱεροῦ, οἱ δ' Ἀλβανοὶ πολῖται 'Ρωμαίων ἐκρίθησαν; Doboşi, *Ephem. Dacorom.* 6 (1935), 257 ff.

[2] *Orig. gent. Rom.* 17. 6: 'regnante Latino Silvio (in Alba) coloniae deductae sunt . . . Bovillae ceteraque oppida circumquaque'; Diod. 7. 5. 9; listed among the thirty Latin cities by Dion. Hal. 5. 61. 3; cf. 6. 20. 3; Dessau, *CIL* 14, pp. 230 f.; Hülsen, *RE* 3. 798 f.; Nissen, *Ital. Landeskunde* 2. 585 f.; Gelzer, *RE* 12. 950; Ashby, *The Roman Campagna* 189 f.; Beloch, *Röm. Gesch.* 180; Doboşi, l.c. 240–366 (monograph).

[3] *ILS* 6188 f.; Wissowa, *Herm.* 50 (1915), 4.

[4] Schol. Pers. 6. 55: 'Bovillae ... quia aliquando in Albano monte ab ara fugiens taurus iam consecratus ibi comprehensus est, inde Bovillae dictae'; Non. 122 M. s.v. 'Hillas'; cf. Klausen, *Aeneas u. die Penaten* 1107 f. Another bull led the Sabini to the site of the later Bovianum, Strab. 5. 250; Mommsen, *Unterital. Dial.* 173; Wissowa 145; Eisenhut, *RE* 8a. 919. There was a Greek prototype which served to explain the name of Boeotia: Cadmus was led by a cow to the site where he was to found Thebes, 'Hellanicus', *FGrHist.* 4 F 51; Ov. *Met.* 3. 10 ff., etc.; Crusius, *Myth. Lex.* 2. 887.

[5] Eitrem, *RE* 6a. 913 ff.; Seston, *RAC* 7. 689 f.

[6] Lycophr. 1255 ff.; Fab. Pict. frg. 4 P.(Alba); Varr. *LL* 5. 144; etc.; Alföldi, *Early Rome and the Latins* 271 ff. (with bibliography). The ram seems to have been the sacred animal of Antium, Sydenham 128, no. 782 (on the Greek analogies see Usener, *Kl. Schr.* 4. 288; Nilsson, 1. 532 f.).

[7] Varr. *RR* 2. 4. 18; Dion. Hal. 1. 57. 1; *ILS* 6911; Beloch, op. cit. 180; cf. *JRS* 50 (1960), 57; pl. 6. 8–11; Alföldi, op. cit. 273; pls. 4–7.

to the war against Pompey and wanted to sacrifice a bull to Fortuna. The bull escaped, ran out of the city, and reaching a lake swam across it: this portended victory for him should he cross the sea.[1] It will be argued that this was the bull of Bovillae again in a new role, and moreover, that this same bull appeared later on the standards of Caesar's legions.[2] Here it is important only in so far as it shows Caesar's attachment to his home-town and its symbol. He may have intended to make the bull of Bovillae as popular as the she-wolf of Rome.

It was not Iulus who succeeded Aeneas in the kingship but Silvius, son of Aeneas by Lavinia; Iulus received a hereditary priestly office instead.[3] This was the legendary basis of the fact that a Iulius was always in charge of the public cults in and around Bovillae. But the Iulii also had their private shrines, special festivals, and games there.[4] Bovillae became a Roman *municipium*, probably under Sulla and certainly before the time of Cicero.[5] As to Caesar, it will be seen that in 45 he began to wear the dress and the shoes of the Alban kings,[6] and some further evidence will be found in connection with the celebration of the *Feriae Latinae* in 44 B.C.[7] What was done at Bovillae after his death is not recorded; certainly his statue must have been set up in the shrine.[8] When Augustus died his corpse was carried from Nola to Bovillae and thence to Rome.[9] In A.D. 16 Tiberius dedicated a public shrine at Bovillae and set up a statue of Augustus in it;[10] his priests, the *sodales Augustales*, had their seat there.[11]

[1] Dio 41. 39. 2 (below, p. 116. 5).　　　　　　　[2] See below, pp. 116 ff.

[3] Fest. 340 M. (460 L.): 'Silvi sunt appellati Albani reges a Laviniae filio, quem post excessum Aeneae . . . enixa est. qui restitutus in regnum est post mortem Ascani, praelatus Iulo, fratris filio, cum inter eos de regno ambigeretur'; Dion. Hal. 1. 70. 4 (below, p. 29. 4) Diod. 7. 5. 8 (below, p. 29. 5). On Silvius and Iulus see also *Orig. gent. Rom.* 17. 4; Schwegler, *Röm. Gesch.* 1. 337 ff.; Heinze, *Virgils epische Technik* 158. 1; Norden, *Vergils Aeneis B. VI*, pp. 316 f.; Zwicker, *RE* 3A. 130 f.; Bömer, *Ovidius, Die Fasten* 2. 209; Ogilvie ad Liv. 1. 3. 2 ff.

[4] Dion. Hal. 1. 70. 4; Macrob. 1. 16. 7: 'sunt . . . feriae propriae familiarum, ut familiae Claudiae vel Aemiliae seu Iuliae sive Corneliae'; Tac. *A.* 15. 23. 3 (A.D. 63): 'decretum, utque . . . ludicrum circense, ut Iuliae genti apud Bovillas, ita Claudiae Domitiaeque apud Antium ederetur'; the shrine is to be inferred from Tac. *A.* 2. 41. 1 (A.D. 16): 'sacrarium Genti Iuliae effigiesque Divo Augusto apud Bovillas dicantur'; see below, p. 10, on Vediovis and Aeneas; Mommsen, *Röm. Chronol.* 160. 316.

[5] *Liber colon.* p. 231 Lachm.; Cic. *Planc.* 23; *ILS* 4942.

[6] Dio 43. 43. 2 (below, p. 324. 26).　　　　　　　[7] See below, pp. 323 ff.

[8] This is an inference from Tac. *A.* 2. 41. 1 (above, n. 4).

[9] Suet. *Aug.* 100. 2: 'corpus decuriones . . . a Nola Bovillas usque deportarunt . . . a Bovillis equester ordo suscepit urbique intulit.'

[10] Tac. *A.* 2. 41. 1; Doboşi, l.c. 359 f.

[11] Fragments of the Fasti of the *sodales Augustales* have been found at Bovillae, *CIL* 14. 2388 ff.; R. Paribeni, *NSc.* 1926, 306 ff.; Doboşi, l.c. 273 ff.; M. W. H. Lewis, *The Official Priests of Rome* (1955), 133 ff.

2. VEDIOVIS AND IULUS

An altar found at Bovillae was set up about the end of the second century B.C. and, as its inscription states, was dedicated to Vediovis pater by the Gens Iulia in accordance with the laws of Alba (pl. 2. 1–2).[1] This inscription confirms the traditional relationship between the Gens Iulia, Alba, and Bovillae. But it is surprising to learn that Vediovis was the ancestral god of the Iulii, and this information, though rightly accepted, has never been explained. What is known of Vediovis[2] does not, at first sight, make him suitable for such a role: it is a link with the Trojan legend that is needed here. Our next task then is to search for this missing link.

Vediovis appeared relatively late in Rome.[3] Two temples were built for him at the beginning of the second century B.C., one on the island in the Tiber with a festival on 1 January, the other on the Capitol with a festival on 7 March. There was also an Agonium (or Agonalia) in his honour on 21 May;[4] no details have survived about this, and the ritual itself is obscure. This evidence is reliable, but does not reveal more than that Vediovis was considered to be an indigenous god who could receive a temple inside the *pomerium*; the location of the temples and the dates of the festivals do not help further. The other evidence which makes him a god of the Underworld[5] or identifies him with Apollo[6] is clearly not reliable: it rests on speculation, not on facts. One piece of evidence, however, which connects him with Iuppiter,[7] is valuable as it can be confirmed by linguistic considerations. His name appears in the same variations as does Iovis with the particle 've-' added at the beginning—Vediovis, Vedius, Veiovis:[8] Diovis, Dius, Iovis. One may

---

[1] *ILS* 2988 (Degr. 270): 'Vediovei patrei genteiles Iuliei'; (*in latere*): 'Vedi[ovei] aara'; (*in parte postica*): 'leege Albana dicata'; Münzer, *RE* 10. 106; Degrassi, *Imagines* 399; Doboşi, l.c. 266 ff.

[2] Wissowa 236 ff.; id. *Myth. Lex.* 6. 174 f.; Koch, *Der röm. Iuppiter* 61 ff.; E. C. Evans, *The Cults of the Sabine Territory* 189 ff.; Marchetti-Longhi, *Röm. Mitt.* 58 (1943), 32 ff.; Bömer's note on Ov. *F.* 3. 429 ff.; Latte 81 f.; G. Piccaluga, *Studi e materiali* 34 (1963), 229 ff.; V. L. Johnson, *TAPA* 91 (1960), 109 ff. and *Latom.* 26 (1967), 320 ff.

[3] According to Varr. *LL* 5. 74 Vediovis was one of the Sabine gods brought by Titus Tatius to Rome, which would imply an early cult. But Varro's assertion of the Sabine origin of many gods is open to doubt, and cannot be confirmed in the present case from any other source.

[4] Degrassi 388; 421; 460; Wissowa 236 f.; Latte 82. 1.

[5] Macrob. 3. 9. 10 (*devotio*): 'Dis pater, Veiovis, Manes, sive quo alio nomine fas est nominare'; Mart. Cap. 2. 166: 'Pluton, quem etiam Ditem Veiovemque dixere'; accepted by Wissowa and Koch, who further identify Dion. Hal. 2. 10. 3 τοῦ Καταχθονίου Διός and 1. 64. 5 Πατρὸς θεοῦ χθονίου with Veiovis without any justification; *contra*, Latte 81 f.

[6] Gell. 5. 12. 12 (below, p. 11. 1).

[7] Paul. 379 M. (519 L.); Ov. *F.* 3. 437 ff. (below, p. 9. 2).

[8] Vediovis: *ILS* 2988; Paul. 379 M. (519 L.); Gell. 5. 12. 8; Vedius: Varr. *LL* 5. 74(?); Mart. Cap. 2. 142; 166; Veiovis: Cic. *ND* 3. 62; Ov. *F.* 3. 430, etc.

PLATE 2

1

3

2

1–2. Altar of the Gens Iulia from Bovillae, in the Gardens of the Principi Colonna, Rome (From Degrassi, *Imagines* 399); p. 8.

3. Marble statue of Vediovis from the Capitol, in the Museo Capitolino, Rome (Photograph: German Archaeological Institute, Rome); p. 11.

add Vediovis pater and Iuppiter (allowing for the contraction of Iuppiter from 'Iovis pater'). The particle 've-' had either a privative or a diminutive force, as exemplified by 'vesanus' on the one hand and by 'vegrandis' on the other.[1] The conclusion is that Vediovis was the 'young Iuppiter', a view which was held by the antiquarian Verrius Flaccus and, probably on his authority, by Ovid,[2] and is further confirmed by usage: his temple on the island in the Tiber is ascribed to Iuppiter in the authors, to Vediovis in the Calendars.[3] What this young Iuppiter stood for in origin is not known;[4] what matters here is the question of his possible relationship to the Iulii.

There were many attempts to explain the name Iulus.[5] The chronicler of the family, L. Caesar, connected it with ἰοβόλος and ἴουλος, the good archer, or the youth whose first beard is growing, as was the case with Ascanius at the time of his victory over Mezentius; others derived it from king Ilus, the founder of Ilium.[6] These are the usual playful etymologies of no consequence. There is one more, which deserves serious consideration: that Iullus is a diminutive form of Iovis and therefore the name of a 'young' Iuppiter, his son.[7] In fact good

[1] Gell. 5. 12. 8 ff.; 16. 5. 5; Koch, op. cit. 68; Walde–Hofmann 2. 740; E. Polomé, *Hommages à M. Niedermann* (1956), 274 (against the connection of Veiovis with Umbr. Vofonio-); Latte 81. 3; see also the following note.

[2] Paul. 379 M. (519 L.): 'vesculi ... ve enim syllabam rei parvae praeponebant, unde Vediovem parvum Iovem et vegrandem fabam minutam dicebant'; Ov. *F*. 3. 437 (Veiovis on the Capitol): 'Iuppiter est iuvenis: iuvenalis aspice vultus ... (445) nunc vocor ad nomen. vegrandia farra coloni, / quae male creverunt, vescaque parva vocant. / vis ea si verbi est, cur non ego Veiovis aedem / aedem non magni suspicer esse Iovis?' But the identification of some youthful heads on Republican coins with Veiovis (Sydenham 76; 113 f.; 116; pls. 19. 564; 21. 732; Latte 82. 3; fig. 21a) is not justified; see also T. J. Luce, *AJA* 72 (1968), 25 f.

[3] Livy 31. 21. 12; 34. 53. 7; 35. 41. 8; Ov. *F*. 1. 293 (but 3. 430 Veiovis); Vitr. 3. 2. 3; *F. Praen*. 1 Jan. and 7 March; *F. Ant. Mai*. 7 March; *F. Venus*. 21 May (Degrassi 388; 421; 460).

[4] Cf. 'Iuppiter puer' at Praeneste (Cic. *div*. 2. 85; not accepted by Wissowa 260) and at Terracina (Serv. *Aen*. 7. 799); Koch, op. cit. 82; Latte 82. 3; 176. 2.—Rhomus son of Iuppiter according to Antigonus (third cent. B.C.?), *FGrHist*. 816 F 2 (Fest. 266 M. = 328 L.).

[5] The original form was Iullus, not Iulus: see *ILS* 92; Mommsen, *Ges. Schr*. 7. 187; Bücheler, *Kl. Schr*. 3. 146; 161. In the following, however, the traditional spelling will be adopted, Iullus only when needed for linguistic considerations.

[6] Serv. (and Dan.) *Aen*. 1. 267: 'occiso Mezentio Ascanium sicut L. Caesar scribit Iulum coeptum vocari, vel quasi ἰοβόλον, id est sagittandi peritum, vel a prima barbae lanugine quam ἴουλον Graeci dicunt, quae ei tempore victoriae nascebatur. sciendum est autem hunc primo Ascanium dictum ... deinde Ilum dictum a rege Ilo, unde et Ilium, postea Iulum occiso Mezentio: .... "at puer Ascanius cui nunc cognomen Iulo / additur, Ilus erat" ' (Verg. *Aen*. 1. 267); cf. App. *BC* 2. 68. 281; Livy 1. 3. 2: 'Ascanius ..., quem Iulum eundem Iulia gens auctorem nominis sui nuncupat' (Ogilvie ad loc.). This version of the story depends on Cato (frg. 9 P.) but the etymologies and the identification of Ascanius with Iulus were certainly later additions (when ἰοβόλος was pronounced 'iovolos').

[7] *Orig. gent. Rom*. 15. 5: 'Latini Ascanium ob insignem virtutem non solum Iove ortum crediderunt, sed etiam per diminutionem declinato paululum nomine primo Iolum, dein postea Iulum appellarunt.'

linguistic evidence has been produced in support of this etymology:
Iollus–Iullus could depend on a hypothetical *Iovilus which survived
in Oscan 'iovila', both deriving from Iovis.[1] This is formally correct,
and yet it has a flaw which renders it impossible for early Latin: the
early form of Iovis is Diovis and that of 'iovila' is 'diuvila',[2] whereas
there is no early Diollus or Diullus. Iullus therefore cannot have been
named after Iovis and does not prove an early relationship of the family
to the god. It was not, like Marcus from Mars, a theophoric name,[3]
but could have become one at a secondary stage, that is, when the
divine descent of the family was first claimed. The rest of the tradition
is correct: the Iulii were named after a Iullus as were the Marcii after
Marcus, the Tullii after Tullus, the Quin(c)tii after Quintus, and so
on;[4] and 'Iullus' was given as *cognomen* to some early members of the
family.[5]

Vediovis was a youthful Iuppiter; Iulus was assumed to be one. The
conclusion seems unavoidable that the Iulii created the gentilician cult
of Vediovis precisely because they believed him to be identical with
Iulus. If so, this identification was part of a wider issue. When Aeneas
died he became Iuppiter Indiges, Iuppiter the 'Ancestor', and Ascanius
instituted his cult and built him a temple.[6] There is no evidence to show
that this cult had any effect on Ascanius, that is, that he was ever called
a son of Iuppiter. But when the Iulii identified him with their ancestor
they accepted the consequences: Iulus, the son of Iuppiter-Aeneas,
became, under the name of Vediovis, their ancestral god and received
a cult at Bovillae.

One would expect that the Iulii, when they became more influential,
would have done something for their Vediovis in Rome as well. The
statue which stood in his temple on the Capitol is described as a youthful figure with bow and arrows and with a goat at his side, made first of

[1] Bücheler, op. cit.; accepted by Walde–Hofmann 1. 729.

[2] Vetter, *Handb. der italischen Dialekte* 1. 67 ff. (nos. 74 f.).

[3] Schulze, *Lat. Eigennamen* 464 ff. has not included it in his list of theophoric names.

[4] Schulze, op. cit.; Ernst Fraenkel, *RE* 16. 1668.

[5] Münzer, *RE* 10. 106; Broughton 2. 575.

[6] Livy 1. 2. 6: 'Iovem Indigetem appellant'; Serv. Dan. *Aen.* 1. 259: 'Ascanius . . . ei tem-
plum condidit et Iovem Indigetem appellavit'; cf. Dion. Hal. 1. 64. 4 f. (he was also called
Aeneas Indiges, 'Indiges pater', and Lar Aineias: *JRS* 50 (1960), 117, 58). An apparently rival
tradition asserted that King Latinus had become Iuppiter Latiaris (Fest. 194 M. = 212
L.: 'Latinus rex Iuppiter factus Latiaris'). The drawing on the Cista Pasinati, (Alföldi,
Early Rome and the Latins 257; pl. 17), which would provide additional evidence, is modern:
I am indebted for this verdict to Mr. D. E. L. Haynes, Professor C. M. Robertson, and
Professor D. E. Strong, who kindly examined the Cista on my behalf.—Cf. also Suet. *Aug.* 1. 1:
'ara Octavio consecrata' (Velitrae).

cypress-wood,[1] later also of marble (pl. 2. 3).[2] The bow and arrows have
been explained as the attributes of Apollo,[3] pointing to the identity of
the two gods,[4] or as an ancient misinterpretation of the thunderbolt
which Vediovis should have held;[5] the goat, on the other hand, was to
refer to the 'chthonic' character of the god.[6] Our argument leads to
another explanation. This Vediovis represented none other than the
young Iulus at the time when he killed Mezentius with his bow. As L.
Caesar said, he was at that time a good archer ($\iota o\beta \acute{o}\lambda o s$) and his beard
had just begun to grow ($\check{\iota} o v\lambda o s$).[7] This type was probably the cult-image
of Vediovis-Iulus at Bovillae; the same type was now set up in the
temple of Vediovis on the Capitol by a member of the family, perhaps
by Caesar himself. This does not mean that the cult of the family too
was established in Rome. It would have been possible: the Fabii, for
instance, used to perform their private sacrifice on the Quirinal.[8] There
is no such evidence about the Iulii for Caesar's time. Later, however,
perhaps under Tiberius, the Ara Gentis Iuliae was built on the Capitol,[9]
no doubt in the neighbourhood of the temple of Vediovis, and regular
sacrifices were then made there.[10]

The cult of this Vediovis-Iulus is a surprising feature of the Iulian
tradition. It was clearly not the connection with Iuppiter that Caesar
was after. He preferred the other genealogy, the descent from Venus,
which rested on the authority of Homer and was popular in his day
and long before at Rome, as it concerned more than one family and in
the end all the Romans.[11] Yet he was and remained attached to the

---

[1] Gell. 5. 12. 1: 'aedes Vediovis Romae inter arcem et Capitolium ... (11) simulacrum
igitur dei Vediovis quod est in aede ... sagittas tenet, quae sunt videlicet partae ad nocen-
dum. (12) quapropter eum deum plerumque Apollinem esse dixerunt; immolaturque ritu
humano capra, eiusque animalis figmentum iuxta simulacrum stat'; Pliny 16. 216: 'simulacrum in arce de cupresso durat a condita urbe anno DLXI dicatum'; Ov. *F*. 3. 437: 'Iuppiter
est iuvenis, iuvenalis aspice vultus. / aspice deinde manum: fulmina nulla tenet ... (443) stat
quoque capra simul: nymphae pavisse feruntur / Cretides; infanti lac dedit illa Iovi.'

[2] This statue has been found at the excavations on the Capitol, unfortunately without
head and hands: Marchetti-Longhi, *Röm. Mitt.* 58 (1943), 33, fig. 3; Latte 82. 3; fig. 19;
Nash 2. 495.

[3] Cf. Apollo's epithets $\dot{\epsilon}\kappa\eta\beta\acute{o}\lambda o s$, $\dot{a}\rho\gamma\upsilon\rho o\tau\acute{o}\xi o s$, $\kappa\lambda\upsilon\tau o\tau\acute{o}\xi o s$, etc.: Gruppe, *Griech. Mythologie*
1244. 2.   [4] Gell. l.c.   [5] Latte 82.

[6] Wissowa 238; *contra*, Latte 82. 4.

[7] Serv. *Aen.* 1. 267 (above, p. 9. 6).

[8] Livy 5. 46. 2: 'sacrificium erat statum in Quirinali colle genti Fabiae'; 5. 52. 3 f.; the
Lares Hostilii (Paul. 102 M. = 90 L.) originally represented the ancestral cult of the Gens
Hostilia; Fest. 238 M. (274 L.): '... in sacrificio gentis Claudiae.'

[9] *ILS* 1988–91 (military diplomas, the full list in Nesselhauf, *CIL* 16, p. 196; the earliest
is dated A.D. 68); Platner–Ashby 247.

[10] Henzen, *AFA* LIX (birthday of Augustus, A.D. 50–4): 'ad aram Gentis Iuliae vaccam.'

[11] See below, pp. 15 ff. The descent from Iuppiter still remained valid because Venus was
the daughter of Iuppiter, App. *BC* 2. 151. 633.

ancestral cult and even gave a new turn to it. The descent from Iuppiter was repeated later in a more general sense when the Iulii were masters of the world.[1] But what has always been startling is the fact that Caesar himself was called Iuppiter Iulius in the last months of his life.[2] It is no longer so startling if one connects it with the transformation of Iulus into young Iuppiter, Vediovis. This Alban background explains the choice of the name but not what Caesar may have had in mind: it was certainly not local folklore that he wanted to advertise but, as will be suggested later, a grand scheme of ruler cult for his empire.

3. APOLLO

Another ancestral god was Apollo, one of the first Greek gods to be accepted by the Roman State at the beginning of the fifth century B.C.[3] He was first the god of healing and of the Sibylline oracles,[4] in the Hannibalic War also the god of victory,[5] and under Augustus the great god of the State. At the time of his arrival in Rome the Iulii were already Roman citizens; how then did they form their attachment to the new god? It could have happened long before and outside Rome, as Apollo had been a popular god all over Italy; this is a possibility, but there is nothing to support it. It is on the other hand a fact that it was a member of the family, Cn. Iulius, who as consul in 431 B.C. dedicated the first temple of Apollo in Rome,[6] the only one until Augustus built the second on the Palatine. The special relationship therefore probably dates from this event, which was purely accidental. The next piece of information appears in connection with one of the many interpretations of the *cognomen* 'Caesar'. The Iulii, it was said, worshipped Apollo because he, as the god of medicine, protected those who were born by the 'Caesarian' operation, like that member of their family who subsequently assumed the name Caesar.[7] The aetiology is irrelevant, but not its date: it cannot be earlier than the middle of the third century B.C., the probable date of

---

[1] Verg. *Georg.* 3. 34: 'Assaraci proles demissaeque ab Iove gentis / nomina'; *Aen.* 1. 380: 'genus ab Iove summo'; Sil. Ital. 11. 178 f.   [2] Dio 44. 6. 4; see below, pp. 287 ff.; 305. 10.

[3] Arnob. 2. 73; Livy 3. 63. 7; Wissowa 293 ff.; Latte 221 ff.

[4] Varr. *Ant. rer. div.* 14, frg. 62 Ag. (August. *CD* 4. 21); Quintil. 3. 7. 8; Livy 4. 25. 3; Macrob. 1. 17. 15.   [5] Livy 25. 12. 15 (below, p. 13. 4).   [6] Livy 4. 29. 7.

[7] Serv. *Aen.* 10. 316: 'Caesarum etiam familia ideo sacra retinebat Apollinis, quia qui primus de eorum familia fuit, exsecto matris ventre natus est, unde etiam Caesar dictus est'; on other interpretations of the name see SHA *Ael.* 2. 3–5; Münzer, *RE* 10. 182; Alföldi, *Hist. Aug.-Colloquium* 1966/7 (1968), 9 ff. Originally it was, like Kaeso of the Fabii, a *praenomen* (*Auctor de praen.* 3) and apparently much preferred by the Iulii; see also below, pp. 332 f.; 334. 4.

the first Iulius who called himself Caesar, that is, Sex. Iulius Caesar (*pr.* 208).[1] But this relatively late date does not render the statement about the early bond between the Iulii and Apollo suspect. The bond is further confirmed by the assertion, however arbitrary it is, that Vediovis, the other ancestral god of the Iulii, was none other than Apollo.[2] What did Apollo mean to the Iulii? This is a legitimate question; a similar question concerning Vediovis has received a possible answer above. No such answer is available here. And if we turn to Caesar we find an imaginative scheme but no answer either.

Caesar was born on the principal day of the *ludi Apollinares*,[3] an accident which no doubt influenced his actions. But it cannot have been the decisive influence. It is important that by Caesar's time Apollo had emerged from his relative obscurity in Rome. The change was mainly due to Sulla, who successfully maintained in the face of rival claims that it was his great-grandfather, P. Cornelius Rufus, who founded the *ludi Apollinares* in 212 B.C. and adopted the *cognomen* 'Sulla' as an abbreviated form of Sibylla.[4] Sulla visited Delphi on his campaign in Greece, referred no doubt to the special relationship of his family to Apollo, and received an oracle. He went away with a silver image of Apollo and always carried it with him. He claimed that it helped him to win his victories and prayed to it before the decisive battle at the Porta Collina in 82 B.C.[5] But the story has an abrupt end. Sulla founded games in commemoration of his victory, the *ludi Victoriae*, and built a temple for Venus, his chief goddess; but Apollo received nothing. Above all, Sulla resigned and died, and Apollo was almost forgotten again. He is seldom mentioned by Catullus, Lucretius, and Cicero and then mostly as the Greek god; what this virtual neglect means can best be measured by his great popularity in the Augustan poets. Caesar was no doubt influenced by Sulla's precedent: it will be seen that this was not the only case, and also that he always made something different of it.[6]

One piece of further evidence is safe but not significant by itself: in 45 the *ludi Apollinares* were given at Caesar's expense.[7] Another piece of

---

[1] Münzer, *RE* 10. 464 f.; 475.　　　　[2] Gell. 5. 12. 11 (above, p. 11. 1).

[3] 13 July 100 B.C.: Dio 47. 18. 6 (below, p. 157. 3).

[4] Livy 25. 12. 9 ff.; 27. 23. 5; Macrob. 1. 17. 27 ff. His adversaries, L. Calpurnius Piso Frugi and C. and L. Marcius Censorinus, made the same claim on behalf of their ancestors, Macrob. ibid.; Fest. 326 M. (436 L.); Sydenham 97–104; 111; 117.

[5] Plut. *Sulla* 29. 11; Front. *Strat.* 1. 11. 11.

[6] It may or may not have been significant that an inscription was set up on Delos in honour of his father, later also of Augustus and Iulia, *Inscr. de Délos* 1701; 1588 f.; 1592.

[7] Dio 43. 48. 3.

evidence is significant but suspect at first sight. When considering his succession, Caesar decided in favour of adopting Octavius when Atia, his niece and Octavius' mother, declared that Octavius was a son of Apollo: once when she was taking part at a midnight festival in the temple of Apollo, she fell asleep, and the god in the form of a snake associated with her. This is the evidence of Dio and of his probable source, Asclepiades of Mendes,[1] a Greek writer, presumably of the age of Augustus. This evidence was rightly distrusted as long as it stood alone and seemed to be of a relatively late date. An epigram which referred to this divine descent was not helpful because it was anonymous.[2] It has now reappeared in the *Epigrammata Bobiensia* with the name of its author, Domitius Marsus,[3] and this has changed the situation completely. Domitius was a friend of Vergil and Horace, as well as of Octavian, for whom he wrote another epigram about Atia which was to be her epitaph after her death in 43. He must therefore have written this one either between 41 and 31 in support of Octavian's political and religious claims, or much earlier, even during Caesar's lifetime. At any rate, Dio's story about the reason for Octavian's adoption is no longer suspect. Not that Atia ever made such a statement; it must have been Caesar who inspired the story of Octavian's divine descent at the time when he decided to make him his heir. It was the divine legitimation of his succession, and the divine ancestor was Apollo, the god of the Gens Iulia. The god of the Octavii was Mars,[4] and not, as far as is known, Apollo.

That Apollo was brought to the fore again by Caesar is a probability, not a certainty. But it is further supported by the god's sudden popularity after the Ides of March. In July 44 it was Brutus' task as praetor to give the *ludi Apollinares*. He was absent, but they were given in his name and with great splendour, and they turned popular sentiment again in favour of the conspirators.[5] Later the conspirators issued coins with the bust of Apollo and his symbols in Greece, indicating that they were fighting with his support.[6] But the story has it that, when celebrating his birthday on Samos in the autumn of 42, Brutus anticipated disaster by quoting the line of the *Iliad*: 'but destructive fate by the hand of Leto's son has killed me'.[7] This is no doubt an anecdote; but

---

[1] Dio 45. 1. 2; *FGrHist.* 617 F 2 (Suet. *Aug.* 94. 4).   [2] Auson. p. 417 (VII) P.

[3] *Epigr. Bob.* 39: 'Domitii Marsi de Atia, matre Augusti: / ante omnes alias felix tamen hoc ego dicor, / sive hominem peperi femina sive deum'; Dahlmann, *Gymn.* 63 (1956), 561; Barigazzi, *Athen.* 52 (1964), 261.   [4] Suet. *Aug.* 1. 1.

[5] Cic. *Att.* 15. 18. 2; 26. 1; *Phil.* 1. 36; 2. 31; App. *BC* 3. 24. 90; Plut. *Brut.* 21. 3.

[6] Sydenham 202; 204; pls. 29. 1287; 30. 1290; 1293 f.; 1303; 1308.

[7] Hom. *Il.* 16. 849; App. *BC* 4. 134. 564.

it is a fact, and a significant one, that at Philippi the password of his enemies, Antony and Octavian, was 'Apollo'.[1] After the victory Octavian began to claim Apollo for himself. That much at least may be inferred from an apocryphal story, circulated by Antony, that Octavian dressed up as Apollo at a banquet held in 40 B.C.[2] Finally in 36, Octavian vowed that he would build a temple for Apollo on his private ground on the Palatine after the god had expressed, through a prodigy, his wish to have his sanctuary there.[3] The conclusion is that without Caesar's initiative Augustus would not have built that splendid temple on the Palatine, and Apollo would not have become the most popular god of his age.

4. VENUS

The principal cult belonged unquestionably to Venus. We must distinguish between the Italian goddess and her Hellenized version on the one hand, and the ancestral goddess of the Aeneadae on the other.[4] Of the first it is enough to say that she did not belong to the early gods of Rome: she did not appear in the early calendar or in the old prayers;[5] nor is there any trace of an old Venus Iovis, the 'grace' of Iuppiter, from which, it is asserted,[6] the independent goddess developed. Although she had long been worshipped in many places in Italy outside Rome, it was only during the Samnite Wars that her first temples were built in Rome.[7] We can therefore assume that neither was the other Venus, the ancestress, known before c. 300 B.C. in Rome.

The cult of the Venus of the Aeneadae naturally began outside Rome, on the coast of Latium. Aeneas had long been known there, as elsewhere in Italy—in Veii, for instance, already in the sixth century[8]—and it is possible, though it cannot be proved, that the cult was created as early as that, for there were some shrines in Latium which bear the mark of high antiquity. Cassius Hemina, the early historian, records that Aeneas brought an image of Venus Erucina with him from Sicily and dedicated it on the Laurentine shore to Venus Frutis.[9] The antiquarian Verrius Flaccus adds that there was in fact a temple of Venus Frutis, called Frutinal:[10] this will have contained the archaic image in question. The

---

[1] Val. Max. 1. 5. 7.   [2] Suet. *Aug.* 70.
[3] Suet. *Aug.* 29. 3; Dio 49. 15. 5; Vell. 2. 81. 3.
[4] Wissowa 288 ff.; R. Schilling, *La religion romaine de Vénus* (1954); Koch, *RE* 8A. 828 ff.; id. *Religio* 39 ff.; Latte 183 ff.   [5] Varr. *LL* 6. 33; Macrob. 1. 12. 12 f.
[6] Latte 183; cf. *JRS* 51 (1961), 208.   [7] Livy 10. 31. 9; Fest. 265 M. (322 L.).
[8] Alföldi, *Die trojanischen Urahnen* 17; pl. 13. 3; id. *Early Rome and the Latins* 286 ff.
[9] Cass. Hem. frg. 7 P. (Solin. 2. 14); Serv. Dan. *Aen.* 1. 720; Diod. 4. 83. 4.
[10] Paul. 90 M. (80 L.).

epithet Frutis is puzzling; the assumption that it is a local transliteration of Aphrodite cannot be proved,[1] nor would the Greek name as an epithet make sense. But her sanctuary could have been a very old one. Another, to be inferred from the place-name Aphrodisium,[2] may equally have been old because it preserved its Greek name. Two further temples are recorded, one at Lavinium, the other at Ardea,[3] both common temples of the Latins, and dating therefore from the time of Latin independence, that is, any time before the middle of the fourth century B.C.

The Roman evidence begins with the third century. At the beginning of the First Punic War Segesta, which was in charge of the temple of Aphrodite on Mount Eryx, took the side of the Romans because of their common descent from Aeneas.[4] The legend here served Roman politics,[5] as it did in the East whenever Roman intervention needed justification; and Ilium was always accorded preferential treatment on this account.[6] The first temple for the divine ancestress, the Venus Erucina, was built in Rome during the Second Punic War, the second in 181 B.C.,[7] probably because of the political importance of Sicily during the war; that is perhaps why she and not the Venus of Lavinium was chosen. The Trojan origin of the Romans was by then generally accepted, and Venus and Aeneas received their place in the poetry of Naevius and Ennius.[8]

The old Trojan families, the Iulii among them, had resided long since in Rome. Did they have their own private cult of Venus at Bovillae as they had that of Iulus? The common shrines of Venus at Lavinium and Ardea prove that the members of the independent Latin League worshipped her as their common ancestress; but it does not necessarily follow that individual families did the same. A public cult of Aeneas is known, but not a private one. From the beginning of the first century B.C. Venus was at the centre of extensive political propaganda; Sulla contributed his share towards it, although it is not certain that

---

[1] Walde–Hofmann 1. 554 (with bibliography); Schilling, op. cit. 79; Koch, *RE* 8A. 845 f.; *contra*, Latte 184. 2.

[2] Pliny 3. 56; Mela 2. 4. 71.

[3] Strab. 5. 232; Schilling, op. cit. 67. 2; Castagnoli, *Archeol. Class.* 19 (1967), 11.

[4] Dio 11, frg. 43 (Zonar. 8. 9. 12), 1, p. 150 B.; cf. Cic. *Verr.* 4. 72; Tac. *A.* 4. 43. 6; Suet. *Claud.* 25. 5 (founded by Aeneas: Fest. 340 M.= 458 L.).

[5] Kienast, *Herm.* 93 (1965), 483 ff.

[6] Plut. *Flamin.* 12. 12; *Syll.* 591. 18 f.; Livy 37. 37. 3; 38. 39. 10; Iustin. 31. 8; Suet. *Claud.* 25. 3.

[7] Livy 22. 9. 7 ff.; 10. 10; 23. 30. 13 ff.; 31. 9; 40. 34. 4; Strab. 6. 272; Norden, *Kl. Schr.* 366; Kienast, l.c. 478 ff.

[8] Macrob. 6. 2. 31; Serv. Dan. *Aen.* 1. 273; 6. 777; Enn. *A.* 52 V.; etc.

the Cornelii claimed to be 'Trojans';[1] and Pompey even built her a shrine,[2] although the Pompeii, a plebeian family, certainly did not.

Caesar, on the other hand, could rely on a long tradition of his family. The moneyer Sex. Iulius Caesar issued coins with Venus *c.* 130–125 B.C.,[3] as did L. Iulius Caesar *c.* 105 B.C. (pl. 3. 1–2).[4] Other members of the family were patrons of Ilium and much honoured for their benefactions; both sides stressed the common origin on solemn occasions.[5] And there was yet another member of the family, L. Iulius Caesar, who wrote about the origins of Rome and of the Aeneadae.[6] Next we can trace this tradition to the house of Marius. Plutarch records that the younger Marius was a son of Mars and Venus.[7] This is either a reference to Marius, the great warrior, and Iulia respectively, or to Iulia alone. For it could be argued that she was of divine descent on both sides, because on the maternal side she belonged to the Marcii Reges, whose theophoric name led back to Mars. At any rate Caesar picked up and varied this lore in 68 in his funeral oration for Iulia, who was his aunt, asserting that she was descended from the kings on the maternal side through the Marcii Reges and from the gods on the paternal side through

---

[1] Plut. *Sulla* 34. 4; App. *BC* 1. 97. 452 ff. (Sulla Epaphroditus; dedication to the Aphrodite of Aphrodisias in Caria); Balsdon, *JRS* 41 (1951), 8.

[2] See below, pp. 39, 81.

[3] Sydenham 56; Grueber, pl. 29. 17; Schilling, op. cit., pl. 29. 3; Koch, *RE* 8A. 858; Münzer, *RE* 10. 476, no. 150; Broughton 2. 442.

[4] Sydenham 82; Grueber, pl. 31. 11; Schilling, pl. 29. 4; Münzer, *RE* 10. 468 f.; Broughton 2. 442; 161.

[5] L. Iulius Caesar (*cos.* 90) exempted the land of Ilium from taxes as censor in 89 and was honoured with a statue (*ILS* 8770; Münzer, *RE* 10. 468), as was his daughter Iulia (*IGR* 4. 195; Münzer 892, no. 543). His son, L. Iulius Caesar, the moneyer of *c.* 94 (see the preceding note), took part as the quaestor of Asia in 87 at the festival of Athena at Ilium (*IGR* 4. 197; Münzer 469).

[6] He has not yet been identified. His *praenomen* is Lucius in three passages (*Orig. gent. Rom.* 15. 4; 18. 5; Serv. Dan. *Aen.* 1. 267; Fraenkel, *JRS* 38 (1948), 133); Gaius once (*Orig. gent. Rom.* 16. 4), and he is quoted seven times without *praenomen*. E. Meyer, *Caesars Monarchie* 511. 1, identified him, as was often done before, with the dictator. This led Carcopino, *Points de vue sur l'impérialisme romain* 113 f. (= *Les étapes . . .* 137 f.), to the suggestion that Caesar compiled this work (quoted in *Orig. gent. Rom.* 9. 6 as 'Pontificalium libro primo') in 63 immediately after his election as *pontifex maximus*; he justified his claim to this office by asserting that his ancestor Iulus had already held it, when, after the death of his father Ascanius, not he but his uncle Silvius became king (Dion. Hal. 1. 70. 4; Diod. 7. 8 [below, p. 29. 5]). His suggestion was accepted by J. Perret, *Les origines de la légende troyenne de Rome* (1942), 565 f. and Alföldi, *Studien über Caesars Monarchie* 34 (rejected by Felber, *Caesars Streben nach der Königswürde* 244 ff.). But the evidence quoted above does not favour the authorship of the dictator, and, in the work of this Caesar, Iulus was identical with Ascanius (Serv. Dan. *Aen.* 1. 267), not his son. All the fragments but one are found in the *Orig. gent. Rom.*; cf. Momigliano, *JRS* 48 (1958), 68 ff.; Bickel, *Rhein. Mus.* 100 (1957), 201 ff. (who suggests L. Iulius Caesar, *cos.* 64); Münzer, *RE* 10. 468 ff.

[7] Plut. *Mar.* 46. 8: ἐν ἀρχῇ παῖς Ἄρεως ὠνομάζετο, ταχὺ δὲ τοῖς ἔργοις ἐλεγχόμενος, αὖθις Ἀφροδίτης υἱὸς ἐκαλεῖτο.

Venus.[1] What he said was probably traditional on such occasions and did not mean much by itself: it did not concern his own person. He was thirty-two and still far away from mastery of the world: the highest office he had attained was that of quaestor. But soon he became more explicit. Dio quotes him for the astonishing assertion that he had received the bloom of youth from Venus.[2] A reference to this theme by Cicero is so close to the wording of Dio that a common source, a direct quotation from Caesar, must in fact be assumed. Cicero adds the malicious comment that this bloom of youth was lost long before in the company of King Nicomedes.[3] This special gift of Venus to Caesar must have been recorded in a legend about his birth or youth of which no other trace exists. It will be examined in its proper context.[4]

The narrative must be broken off here for the time being. When it is resumed in the context of the Civil War, victory, and mastery of the world,[5] the part of Venus will be described in great detail: how Caesar fought in her name, vowed and built her a temple, and how he made plans for her cult in Rome and in the provinces. It will conclude with an appreciation of the extent to which Caesar brought about the transformation of Venus into the national goddess of the Romans that she never had been before.

[1] Suet. *Caes.* 6 1: 'amitae meae Iuliae maternum genus ab regibus ortum, paternum cum diis inmortalibus coniunctum est. nam ab Anco Marcio sunt Marcii Reges, quo nomine fuit mater; a Venere Iulii, cuius gentis familia est nostra.'

[2] Dio 43. 43. 3: τό τε ὅλον τῇ τε Ἀφροδίτῃ πᾶς ἀνέκειτο καὶ πείθειν πάντας ἤθελεν ὅτι καὶ ἄνθος τι ὥρας ἀπ' αὐτῆς ἔχοι.

[3] Suet. *Caes.* 49 3: 'Cicero. . . non contentus in quibusdam epistulis scripsisse (frg. inc. 5 Watt) . . . "floremque aetatis a Venere ortae" in Bithynia contaminatum.' I have added the quotation marks and substituted 'ortae' (the reading of group X) for the generally accepted 'orti'; 'ortum' of cod. G would be another possibility. The same source may be detected behind the words of Vell. 2. 41. 1: 'ab Anchise ac Venere deducens genus, forma omnium civium excellentissimus.' 'Flos aetatis' or 'iuventae' means youth, or bloom of youth, or virginity (*Thes.L.L.* 6. 1. 934 f.): Caesar used it in the second sense, Cicero in the third, which nobody else did with regard to men; cf. Strasburger, op. cit. 46 f.; J.Klass, *Cicero u. Caesar* (1939), 81 ('59 B.C.': not convincing).—For another possible quotation from Caesar see below, p. 83. 3.   [4] See below, pp. 23 f.   [5] See below, pp. 80 ff.

III

THE RISE

IT was a widespread belief in Greece, and even in Rome, that kings and great men were descended from gods, Alexander from Zeus,[1] Seleucus I from Apollo,[2] Aeneas from Venus, Romulus from Mars, Servius Tullius from the *Lar familiaris* or Vulcanus,[3] Scipio Africanus Maior from Iuppiter.[4] Caesar was a descendant of Venus but not her son. The founder of Caesar's family, Iulus, was the son of Iuppiter in a special sense: his father Aeneas was worshipped as Iuppiter after his death.[5] If there was no manifestation of Iulus' divine descent at his birth, there was one later: when he was still a child a halo surrounded his head.[6] The circumstances of Caesar's birth must have been miraculous, to indicate his great destiny. With his early youth, they were no doubt described in the lost chapters of Suetonius and Plutarch.[7] A few fragments have survived: two of these, preserved by Sidonius Apollinaris and Servius respectively, refer to the moment of his birth; a third, already mentioned, to the intervention of Venus; one or two more to physiognomical signs.

Sidonius Apollinaris, writing in the fifth century A.D., says in his Panegyric in honour of Anthemius that Caesar was born whilst the laurel blazed.[8] Though brief and obscure the reference must have been

[1] Plut. *Alex.* 2. 5; Iustin. 11. 11. 3; 12. 16. 2; more in Pease on Cic. *div.* 2. 135; Taeger, *Charisma* 1. 191 f.

[2] Iustin. 15. 4. 3; Powell, *Coll. Alex.* 140; Sokolowski, *Lois sacrées de l'Asie Mineure* (1955), no. 24; 34 f. (p. 63); *Or. gr.* 212. 13 f.; 219. 26 f. (Stähelin, *RE* 2A. 1231 f.; Nilsson 2. 165 f.). Plato and Pythagoras sons of Apollo: Diog. Laert. 3. 1. 2; Porph. *v. Pythag.* 2 (Meyer, *Ursprung u. Anfänge d. Christentums* 1. 55. 4).

[3] Pliny 36. 204; Dion. Hal. 4. 1 f.; Ov. *F.* 6. 627 ff.; on further cases (Caeculus, Modius Fabidius) see *Studi in onore di Luisa Banti* (1965), 348 f.; Meyer, op. cit. 1. 55 f. and *Kl. Schr.* 2. 435. 2.

[4] Livy 26. 19. 7; Gell. 6. 1. 2 f.; Sil. Ital. 13. 637 ff.; Meyer, *Kl. Schr.* 2. 433 ff.; A. R. Anderson, *HSCP* 39 (1928), 32 ff.; Hubaux, *Les grands mythes de Rome* 78 f.; Classen, *Gymn.* 70 (1963), 319; below, p. 302.

[5] Livy 1. 2. 6; Serv. Dan. *Aen.* 1. 259 (above, p. 10. 6).

[6] Verg. *Aen.* 2. 682 ff.; cf. Theocr. 24. 22 (Heracles) and Gow ad loc.; Livy 1. 39. 1 f. (Servius Tullius) and Ogilvie ad loc.; Riess, *RE* 18. 1. 362.

[7] See above, p. 5.

[8] Sid. Apoll. *carm.* 2. 120: 'Iulius in lucem venit dum laurea flagrat.'

to a miraculous sign of Caesar's future greatness and divinity, because
the context is about similar signs concerning Iulus, Cyrus, Romulus,
Alexander, and Augustus.[1] Three interpretations are possible: one
would connect the sign with Apollo, the second with the use of the
laurel for prognostics, and the third with forecasts from a sudden
flame.

It is not arbitrary to think of Apollo in the first place. It will be recalled that the Gens Iulia was closely connected with him;[2] the laurel was
above all his plant; and Caesar was born on the principal day of the
ludi Apollinares, 13 July. The verse of Sidonius would then mean that
the coincidence of Caesar's birth with the festival of Apollo already
indicated his future greatness. But this would not be sufficient to explain
the inclusion of Caesar in that list of divine children. And we could not
go so far as to say that Caesar was descended from Apollo: there is
no evidence to justify this, and moreover, it is Augustus whom Sidonius
calls a son of Apollo.

The second possibility is to consider the meaning of the blazing
laurel. The laurel was often used in ancient ritual: its branches were
carried, wreaths of them were made and worn, and it was burnt.[3]
Its basic function was purification, which is not relevant here. Although
the birth of a child was always connected with purificatory rites,[4] the
blazing laurel here had another function, to reveal the future. This in
fact it often did:[5] it was the plant of Apollo, the great god of divination.
If it burnt with a bright flame and loud crackle on the altar, it indicated
good things to come, either for the whole year or after a festival like
the Parilia.[6] This belief was not limited to the laurel: the bright flame
on the altar was always a good omen,[7] its absence a bad one. The
conclusion could be that at the festival of Apollo in 100 B.C. the laurel
on the altar burnt with a particularly bright flame and loud crackle
to announce the future greatness of the newborn child. This interpretation sounds attractive, and yet it would be isolated: the other
relevant evidence always refers to the general welfare, not to the fate
of a single person.[8]

---

[1] Sid. Apoll. *carm.* 2. 115–28.   [2] See above, pp. 12 ff.
[3] Pliny 15. 127 ff.; Lyd. *mens.* 4. 4; Ogle, *AJP* 31 (1910), 287 ff.; Eitrem, *Opferritus* 206 ff.;
id. *Symb. Osl.* 12 (1933), 16; 29; Steier, *RE* 13. 1439 ff.
[4] *Festschr. Andreas Rumpf* (1952), 157.
[5] Porph. *de cultu simulacrorum,* frg. 8 Bidez (Euseb. *pr. ev.* 3. 11. 24); Lyd. *mens.* 4. 4 (p. 68 W.);
Ogle, l.c. 296.   [6] Tib. 2. 5. 81 ff.; Ov. *F.* 1. 344; 4. 742 (Parilia).
[7] Aesch. *Prom.* 498; Ps.-Aristot. *mir. ausc.* 122 (133); *Syll.* 1170. 24; Verg. *Georg.* 4. 385;
Prop. 3. 10. 19f.; Ov. *Pont.* 4. 9. 53; *Trist.* 3. 13. 15 f.; *F.* 1. 75 f.; Tib. 4. 1. 134; Eitrem, op. cit.
137 f.; Riess, *RE* 18. 1. 361 f.   [8] Soph. *Ant.* 1005 ff.; Eur. *Or.* 621; Prop. 2. 28b. 36.

The third possibility equally concerns divination, not by means of the laurel particularly but by fire in general. It was always a good omen, if the fire on the altar suddenly arose from the ashes by itself and came to a blaze. This announced Alexander's[1] and Seleucus I's kingship,[2] Augustus'[3] and Tiberius' future rule[4]—even Cicero's consulate.[5] Accordingly the verse of Sidonius would mean that when laurel was burnt on the altar at the festival of Apollo and its fire was already reduced to ashes, it came again to a bright flame at the moment when Caesar was born. This interpretation is preferable to the other two because it is supported by the Greek precedents and the later Roman instances.

What did the sudden flame announce? This question may be answered with the second fragment, a quotation from Suetonius' *Life of Caesar* preserved by Servius: the seers declared that the invincible ruler of the world was born.[6] It has been assumed that this forecast concerns Augustus, not Caesar, and refers to the passage in Suetonius' *Life of Augustus* where Nigidius Figulus makes a similar pronouncement on the day of Augustus' birth after examining his horoscope.[7] This assumption is attractive but cannot be right, unless Servius is guilty of negligence, which admittedly he often is. The words 'in vita Caesaris' refer to Caesar rather than to Augustus; Caesar can be called 'invincible ruler' with greater justification than Augustus;[8] the word 'responsa' does not aptly indicate Nigidius Figulus' learned horoscope. Above all, it would be strange if such a forecast had not been made for Caesar; Augustus inherited rather than inspired it.

[1] Suet. *Aug.* 94. 5 (below, n. 3).   [2] App. *Syr.* 56. 284; Paus. 1. 16. 1.

[3] Suet. *Aug.* 94. 5: 'Octavio postea, cum per secreta Thraciae exercitum duceret (60 B.C.), in Liberi patris luco barbara caerimonia de filio consulenti, idem (i.e. the mastery of the world as predicted by Nigidius Figulus) affirmatum est a sacerdotibus, quod infuso super altaria mero tantum flammae emicuisset, ut supergressa fastigium templi ad caelum usque ferretur, unique omnino Magno Alexandro apud easdem aras sacrificanti simile provenisset ostentum.'

[4] Dio 54. 9. 6 f. (20 B.C.); Suet. *Tib.* 14. 3. The same was observed at Misenum before his death (Suet. *Tib.* 74), a good omen, according to his enemies, not for him but for Rome.

[5] Serv. *Ecl.* 8. 105; according to Dio 37. 35. 4 and Plut. *Cic.* 20. 1 f. this omen occurred at the festival of the Bona Dea in 63 and prompted Cicero to action against Catilina on the Nones of December; cf. *RE* 5A. 711. The omen also served magic purposes, Verg. *Ecl.* 8. 104; cf. also Val. Max. 1. 1. 7.

[6] Serv. *Aen.* 6. 798: 'Suetonius ait in vita Caesaris responsa esse data per totum orbem nasci invictum imperatorem' (the *varia lectio* 'Caesarum' is impossible with 'vita' in the singular; the words 'per totum orbem' do not make sense in their place and ought to be moved next to 'invictum').

[7] Suet. *Aug.* 94. 5: 'dominum terrarum orbi natum'; Strasburger, *Caesars Eintritt in die Geschichte* 79.

[8] Cic. *Marc.* 12; Dio 43. 45. 3; App. *BC* 2. 145. 607; Nic. Dam. *v. Caes.* 80, *FGrHist.* 90 F 130; *HTR* 50 (1957), 233 f.; below, p. 188.

It was in fact repeated in another form. First at Gades in 67 B.C., when Caesar dreamt that he committed incest with his mother: the key to the dream is that not his own mother but the earth, the mother of all, is meant, and that the union meant mastery over it.[1] The dream is also recorded for 49 B.C. for the night before crossing the Rubicon,[2] an even more suitable occasion. Another version of the story is connected with the campaign of 47: he fell down when landing in Africa, which would have been a bad omen had he not turned it into a good one by embracing the earth and exclaiming 'teneo te, Africa':[3] the victory at Thapsus proved that he was right. The mastery of the world was finally demonstrated in 46 when his statue was set up on the Capitol with the globe at his feet.[4]

What is the real date of the omen at Caesar's birth? It is certainly not early, not earlier than the Civil War. It may have been an answer to Pompey's claim that he was the conqueror of three continents, even of the world.[5] And it may have been part of the same story which recorded another omen, the laurel branch dropped by a kite on the Forum at the time of Caesar's departure against Pompey in 49 B.C., thus forecasting his victory.[6] This prodigy certainly inspired the later one about another laurel branch, dropped into the lap of Livia, which was planted and provided all subsequent triumphators with their laurel wreaths.[7] Caesar's birth-omen is at any rate not posthumous evidence: it would not have made sense to invent such embellishments after his death. So it was part of a biography compiled in the last years of his life.

The official celebration of Caesar's birthday was first decreed in 44 B.C.,[8] but was not observed until 42, when it was decreed again after his consecration.[9] One of its special features was that everybody carried or wore laurel, or did both. This was the normal practice at supplications, which the new festival may have resembled; but it is possible that in this case it was prescribed to commemorate the omen at Caesar's birth.

---

[1] Suet. *Caes.* 7. 2; Dio 37. 52. 2; 41. 24. 2. The dream was preceded by a relevant experience: in the temple of Gades he noticed the statue of Alexander, who had conquered the world (*orbem terrarum*) and this reminded him of his own incapacity; Strasburger, op. cit. 94 ff.

[2] Plut. *Caes.* 32. 9; below, p. 343.   [3] Suet. *Caes.* 59; below, p 342.

[4] Dio 43. 14. 6; 21. 2; below, pp. 41 ff.; 50 ff.

[5] Cic. *Sest.* 129; *Balb.* 9; 16; Plut. *Pomp.* 45. 6 f.

[6] Dio 41. 39. 2 (followed by the bull-prodigy, above, pp. 6 f., and below, pp. 116 ff.).

[7] Dio 48. 52. 3 (37 B.C.); Pliny 15. 136 f.; Suet. *Galba* 1. A different version is recorded by Serv. *Aen.* 6. 230: 'nata erat laurus in Palatio eo die, quo Augustus: unde triumphantes coronari consueverant.' This is a birth-omen again and must somehow be related to that of Caesar. At any rate the laurel had become the plant of Augustus, the son of Apollo.

[8] Dio 44. 4. 4; below, pp. 206 f.   [9] Dio 47. 18. 5 f.

The birth-omen was one of the signs of great destiny; another was the bloom of youth which Caesar received, so he boasted, from Venus.[1] A similar claim, raised by one of the Memmii, helps us to understand it. Their ancestor was Mnestheus, a companion of Aeneas and a descendant of Assaracus.[2] That is to say, the Trojan genealogy was created with the help of an identification of the two names, Memmius and Mnestheus, on the basis of an adventurous derivation from *memor* and μνήμων respectively and in spite of the fact that the family was of plebeian origin. Members of the family put Venus on their coins about the beginning of the first century B.C. (pl. 3. 3–4),[3] not much later than the Iulii. It can be inferred from Lucretius that it was his patron, C. Memmius (*pr.* 58), who made the Trojan claim more conspicuous.[4] Lucretius began his poem with the invocation of Venus as 'genetrix', a term coined by Ennius for the mother of Aeneas:[5] Lucretius borrowed it from Ennius but made Venus the mother of all the Aeneadae, the Romans. After a few lines he singled out one of these Aeneadae, Memmius, and said that Venus adorned him with all her gifts and wanted him to excel always.[6] These lines are best understood as an allusion to what Memmius had said in greater detail in poem or speech. He must have done this before 60 B.C. because in that year Cicero called him the new Paris who had seduced the wife of M. Lucullus, the new Menelaus, and perhaps that of his brother, L. Lucullus-Agamemnon.[7] What Memmius said was in substance what Caesar must have said of himself. But it was invented by neither of them;

---

[1] Dio 43. 43. 3; Suet. *Caes.* 49. 3; above, p. 18.

[2] Verg. *Aen.* 12. 127; 5. 117; 184; 189 ff.; 493 ff.; cf. Tümpel, *Myth. Lex.* 2. 3080 f. It has been alleged that according to Probus this genealogy was already known to Naevius (see Heyne ad Verg. *Aen.* 5. 117). But I cannot find the evidence and believe it to be apocryphal.

[3] Venus in *biga* on coins of L. Memmius, *c.* 105 B.C., and of L. and C. Memmius, 87 B.C. (Sydenham 79; 110; cf. Münzer, *RE* 15. 607; 619 f.; Koch, *RE* 8A. 858; 860; Broughton 2. 446); for the date of these coins see M. H. Crawford, *Num. Chron.* 7/4 (1964), 143. Borghesi, *Œuvres* 1. 150, was the first to connect these coins with the evidence in Lucretius (Münzer, *RE* 15. 603, is sceptical and would ascribe the Trojan legend of the family to the C. Memmius of Lucretius). The genealogical connection of the Memmii with Venus is denied by Latte 186. 1.

[4] Münzer, *RE* 15. 609 ff.; A. Biedl, *Wien. Stud.* 49 (1931), 109; T. P. Wiseman, *Num. Chron.* 7/4 (1964), 157; id. *CQ* 61 (1967), 164 ff.

[5] Lucr. 1. 1: 'Aeneadum genetrix, hominum divomque voluptas, / alma Venus'; Enn. *A.* 52 V.: 'te, sale nata(?), precor, Venus et genetrix patris nostri.'

[6] Lucr. 1. 24: 'te sociam studeo scribendis versibus esse, / quos ego de rerum natura pangere conor / Memmiadae nostro, quem tu, dea, tempore in omni / omnibus ornatum voluisti excellere rebus'; cf. F. Giancotti, *Il preludio di Lucrezio* (1959), 92 ff.

[7] Cic. *Att.* 1. 18. 3; Münzer, *RE* 15. 611. Pompey called Caesar 'Aegisthus' for having seduced his wife Mucia, Suet. *Caes.* 50. 1.

nor did they apparently use it in their bitter political warfare against one another.[1]

This story of the divine grace had its origin in poetry, not in political propaganda. It first appeared in Homer: Athena gave Odysseus youth and charm in the land of the Phaeacians.[2] Vergil, or rather Naevius, borrowed it from Homer and substituted Venus and Aeneas for Athena and Odysseus, and Carthage for the land of the Phaeacians. And so it appeared in the *Aeneid*:[3]

> os umerosque deo similis; namque ipsa decoram
> caesariem nato genetrix lumenque iuventae
> purpureum et laetos oculis adflarat honores.

There are other versions of the story.[4] A god could pass on his gifts by a mere turn of his eyes towards his favourite. That is how the Muses provided the kings with eloquence at their birth; they were then honoured for their rulings like gods.[5] That too is how Melpomene passed the gift of poetry to Horace,[6] and Apollo or Charis splendour to the victors at the races.[7] The transformation can also be effected with ointment, bath, and magic, and may be the reward for a service given to the god.[8]

It is clear that the version of the story relevant here is that in which Aeneas is involved. Caesar and Memmius received the bloom of youth from Venus because Aeneas had received it before them. It is important to add that it was the Romans who stressed beauty in this context. The Greeks appreciated masculine beauty almost exclusively

---

[1] Suet. *Caes.* 23. 1; 49. 2; 73, etc.; Meyer, *Caesars Monarchie* 93 f.; Münzer, l.c.

[2] Hom. *Od.* 6. 229 ff.; 235; 237; cf. 8. 18 ff.; 69 f.; 23. 156 ff.; 24. 367 ff.; 16. 172 ff. (golden staff).

[3] Verg. *Aen.* 1. 589 ff.

[4] Athena gave it to Odysseus because she was his protector; and that is why she also gave it to Telemachus (*Od.* 2. 12 = 17. 63) and Penelope (*Od.* 18. 192 ff.). It was more natural that such a gift came from Aphrodite (Phaon: Serv. Dan. *Aen.* 3. 279; Aelian. *v.h.* 12. 18; Palaeph. 48; Lucian. *mort. dial.* 9. 2), Hebe, the Charites, Hera (Iason: Apoll. Rhod. 3. 922 f.; Val. Flacc. 5. 365), and in particular from Medea.

[5] Hes. *Theog.* 81 f.; 91 f.

[6] Hor. *c.* 4. 3. 1; Callim. *Aet.* frg. 1. 37 Pf.; *Epigr. Gr.* 403 (Kaibel).

[7] Pind. *Isthm.* 2. 18; *Olymp.* 7. 19; cf. Alciphr. 1. 36. 4.

[8] Medea (Aeson: *Epic. Gr. frg. Nosti* 6 K.; Ov. *Met.* 7. 215 f.; Dionysus' nurses: Aesch. *TGF* 50 N.; Ov. *Met.* 7. 294 f.); cf. Herzog–Hauser, *Soter* 160; Steuding, *Myth. Lex.* 6. 232. Once it is a 'god' (Hom. *Il.* 9. 445 f.), another time it is Ares (*Hymn. Hom.* 8. 9), the planet, not the god. A similar act was used to make someone immortal, Berenice by Aphrodite (Theocr. 15. 106), Aeneas (Ov. *Met.* 14. 605 ff.) and Caesar (Ov. *Met.* 15. 843 ff.) by Venus; cf. Eitrem, *Opferritus* 99 f. Another kind of change was performed by Zeus when before the battle Agamemnon received the head and eyes of Zeus, the waist of Ares, the breast of Poseidon (Hom. *Il.* 2. 475 ff.).

in an erotic context and often described it in their novels;[1] but not even
Alcibiades was considered a greater statesman or even superhuman for
his good looks. Neither Alexander nor his successors were made remarkable in this respect,[2] although their divine origin was stressed. In
Rome, on the other hand, Sulla was prominent because of his gold-
blonde hair,[3] Pompey had a particular charm,[4] Caesar's divine nature
was manifested in his good looks,[5] and so was Augustus' after
him.[6]

What Caesar attributed to Venus was used by others, perhaps also
by one of his biographers, for further prognostics. It was said that he
was a larger and more vigorous child at his birth than the average, and
that he had beautiful locks and bluish-grey eyes.[7] The first sign does
not require any comment; the latter two rest on the interpretation of
the name Caesar with the help of 'caesaries' and 'caesius' respectively.
There was an old belief that the hair was the source of life and power,
and that its loss can be fatal, as in the case of Nisus and Pterelaus whose
daughters caused their downfall and death by cutting their hair.[8] It is
particularly relevant here that Sulla too had golden locks like these
mythical heroes, and was therefore said to have been the man of
destiny,[9] probably by a physiognomist whom he met in the East.[10] There
is no comparable precedent for the power of Caesar's eyes;[11] they
may have had the same divine vigour and irresistibility which were

---

[1] Rohde, *Der griech. Roman* 160 ff.; Bieler, *ΘΕΙΟΣ ΑΝΗΡ* 1. 50 ff.

[2] There were some exceptions, Pythagoras (Porph. *v. Pyth.* 18 = Dicaearch. frg. 33
Wehrli; Iambl. *v. Pyth.* 2. 9; 5. 20; Apul. *Flor.* p. 21. 4 H.), Apollonius of Tyana (Philostr.
v. Apoll. 1. 7), and above all Demetrius Poliorcetes (Duris, *FGrHist.* 76 F 13. 7; Diod. 20. 92. 3;
Plut. *Dem.* 2. 2); cf. the attack by Philod. π. τ. καθ' Όμηρον ἀγ. βασ., col. xix (p. 55 Ol.);
O. Murray, *JRS* 55 (1965), 171 f.

[3] Plut. *Sulla* 6. 12 f.; cf. Livy 4. 19. 1: 'A. Cornelius Cossus eximia pulchritudine corporis.'

[4] Plut. *Pomp.* 2. 1 f.

[5] See below, n. 7; cf. Charax, *FGrHist.* 103 F 13 (Jo): θεὸς ἐνομίσθη διὰ τὸ κάλλος.

[6] See below, p. 26. 1.

[7] SHA *Ael.* 2. 4: '(Caesar) . . . vel quod cum magnis crinibus sit utero parentis effusus, vel
quod oculis caesiis et ultra humanum morem viguerit'; Lyd. *mens.* 4. 102 (p. 142 W.): Οὐάλης
δὲ ὅς καὶ αὐτὸς τὰ Καίσαρος ἔγραψε (*HRR* 2. 161 P.) φησὶν ἄριστον μὲν αὐτὸν καὶ πρεπωδέστατον
ἐν μεγέθει γενέσθαι, ἔτι μὴν καὶ κομήτην· τὴν γὰρ κόμην πατρίως οἱ Ῥωμαῖοι καισάριεν προσαγο-
ρεύουσι, καί φησιν, ὡς διὰ τὸ ἐξ αὐτῆς κάλλος Καῖσαρ προσηγορεύετο (Valens is otherwise not
known; cf. SHA *Alex.* 48. 6; Peter, *HRR* 2, p. CLXXXX; Strasburger, op. cit. 79).

[8] Aesch. *Choeph.* 613 f.; Schol. Eur. *Hipp.* 1200; *Ciris* 122 ff.; Hygin. *fab.* 198; Apollod.
2. 60; Schol. Lycophr. 650; 932; Kroll ap. Skutsch, *Aus Vergils Frühzeit* 2. 193 ff.; Sommer,
RE 7. 2105; Schmidt, *RE* 3A. 656 f.

[9] Plut. *Sulla* 6. 12 f.; Vell. 2. 24. 3.

[10] Plut. *Sulla* 5. 11.

[11] Diog. Laert. 5. 6. 86: (Heraclides Ponticus) πρᾷός τ' ἦν τὸ βλέμμα καὶ σεμνός; Bieler,
op. cit. 1. 54. On the various colours of the eyes of the gods see Cic. *ND* 1. 83; Min. Fel. 22. 5;
on 'caesius' (γλαυκῶπις) see J. André, *Étude sur les termes de couleur* (1949), 178; Niedermann,
Mus. Helv. 7 (1950), 150 ff.

ascribed to Augustus' eyes.[1] It is perhaps no coincidence that what
Vergil praises as gifts of Venus in Aeneas—youthful beauty, locks, and
eyes[2]—are the special features of Caesar too and they may have been recorded together in the lost biography.

2. THE INDIVIDUAL AND THE CITIZEN

One would expect to meet the military and political genius also in
the role of an imaginative religious reformer. This will in fact emerge in
the course of our narrative. Much of the evidence, however, shows the
features of an average Roman. Caesar had the best education of his
age and knew all about philosophy; but he was not a theorist. We have
seen, and shall see again and again, that he was closely attached to his
family and its ancestral cults without any mental reservation. We have
also seen how he advertised his good looks, which he received from his
ancestral goddess, Venus, and which marked him out as a man of
destiny. He had his horoscope like many of his contemporaries:[3] there
is no evidence to show that he believed or disbelieved in it. He certainly
did not anticipate the ideals of the Enlightenment in antiquity. He let
his hair and beard grow after a disaster in Gaul in 53 and did not cut
them until he had taken vengeance.[4] He invoked the vengeance of the
gods on those who started the Civil War, and later on himself should he
ever listen to slaves denouncing their masters.[5] He used to recite a magic
formula before departure, ever since his chariot had broken down on
a journey.[6] He believed that chance had a great share in human
matters, often spoke of good luck and bad luck, and promoted the
cult of Fortuna.[7] These are odd and insignificant fragments; but they
show that there was nothing particularly pious or profound or critical
in his approach to the supernatural or irrational.

As a citizen he always performed his religious duties, which were
numerous on his campaigns. It is, however, surprising to notice that
he never mentions them in his *Bellum Gallicum* and *Bellum Civile*. But
when Hirtius and the other continuators take over the narrative we
hear a great deal about his lustrations of the army, his prayers, vows,
and sacrifices, his gratitude to the gods for their help, and the like.[8]

---

[1] Suet. *Aug.* 79. 2; Serv. *Aen.* 8. 680; Pliny 11. 143; Iulian. *Caes.* 309 B; cf. Plut. *Mar.*
39. 3 (the flaming eyes of Marius); Suet. *Nero* 51.

[2] Verg. *Aen.* 1. 589 ff.; above, p. 24.   [3] Cic. *div.* 2. 99 f.

[4] Suet. *Caes.* 67. 2; Polyaen. 8. 23. 23.

[5] Dio 41. 15. 4; 41. 38. 3.   [6] Pliny 28. 21 (below, p. 77. 1).

[7] Caes. *BG* 4. 26. 5; 5. 58. 6; 6. 30. 2; *BC* 3. 68. 1, etc.; below, pp. 112 ff.

[8] *BG* 8. 43. 5; 52. 1; *B. Alex.* 70. 4; 75. 3; *B. Afr.* 74. 2; 75. 1; 82. 2; 86. 3; *B. Hisp.* 29. 4.

There is confirmation from other sources. He made his vows and offerings to Venus and Mars before the battle at Pharsalus.[1] When, in the battle at Munda, his soldiers got frightened and were reluctant to fight, he implored the gods in the traditional manner not to let him down after so many glorious deeds.[2] There were many occasions of this kind during his political career. He sacrificed when he left his house[3] and again before he entered the Senate, when he also took the auspices.[4] There is no need to quote further evidence: a great deal will be discussed later. The correct performance of religious duties does not, of course, prove much. But there is some odd evidence which shows that occasionally he was given to reflections about religious matters. The *Bellum Gallicum* contains an intelligent essay about the religion of the Gauls and Germans;[5] the *Bellum Civile* repeatedly refers to the sanctity of shrines and their treasures.[6] He intervened whenever an offence was committed against them. It cannot therefore be true that he plundered the temples of Gaul:[7] he will have borrowed some of their treasures to finance his wars, which had long been a traditional and lawful practice.[8] For his part he did not destroy the trophy of Mithridates at Zela in 47, although it commemorated a victory over the Romans, because it was dedicated to the gods of war;[9] but he set up his own at its side. That is perhaps why two years earlier he left Pompey's trophy in the Pyrenees intact and commemorated his own victory instead with an altar in the neighbourhood.[10]

There was, on the other hand, the charge of abuse and negligence. The charge of abuse is certainly true for the time of his consulate in 59, when he ignored the evil celestial signs reported by his colleague Bibulus and did not interrupt, as he should have done, his legislative activities.[11] But the abuse was begun by Bibulus with the alleged signs, and Caesar had to resist if he did not want to submit to sabotage. The charge of negligence is less well attested. It did not mean that he did less than he should have done:[12] he was the *pontifex maximus* and built and planned a great deal. He is said to have ignored the warning of evil signs found in the victims after sacrifice or to have given them

---

[1] App. *BC* 2. 68. 281; 2. 88. 368.

[2] App. *BC* 2. 104. 431; cf. Sulla's prayer to Apollo before the battle at the Porta Collina in 82 B.C., Plut. *Sulla* 29. 12.   [3] App. *BC* 2. 115. 480.

[4] App. *BC* 2. 116. 488; Suet. *Caes.* 81. 4; Mommsen, *StR* 3. 935. 2.

[5] Caes. *BG* 6. 16 ff.   [6] Caes. *BC* 1. 6. 8; 2. 21. 3; 3. 33. 2; 3. 105. 1.

[7] Suet. *Caes.* 54. 2.   [8] Stengel, *Griech. Kultusaltert.* 29.

[9] Dio 42. 48. 2.   [10] Dio 41. 24. 3.

[11] Cic. *har. resp.* 48; *dom.* 40 f.; Suet. *Caes.* 20. 1; Dio 38. 6. 5.

[12] Cf. Suet. *Tib.* 69: 'circa deos ac religiones neglegentior'; Hor. *c.* 1. 34. 1: 'Parcus deorum cultor et infrequens'; below, p. 181. 7.

a favourable interpretation on his own authority.[1] But such a charge
was often made without justification in contemporary political warfare
and may have been made up in his case too by his adversaries. But even
if it were true, it would not make Caesar a rebel or a cynic. When in 46
his adversaries, led by Metellus Scipio, broadcast an old oracle about
the invincibility of the Scipiones in Africa, Caesar did not contest the
validity of the oracle, but is said to have made it ineffective by having
a Scipio in his own camp.[2]

3. THE PRIESTHOODS

A Roman priest was the intermediary between his fellow citizens
and the gods of the State. His qualifications were Roman citizenship
and in certain cases patrician origin; and he must not have committed
any criminal offence.[3] He could not hold a priesthood if another member of his family was a member of the same priestly college[4] or if he
was already holding another priestly office: an *augur* could not as a rule
become a *pontifex* also.[5] Professional competence was not required but
it was an advantage if he was an expert in law.[6] His piety was the piety
of the citizen, not of the individual: he was scrupulous in performing
his duties towards the gods but nobody expected him to be a puritan.
Religious or philosophical conversion was frequent enough.[7] But the
case of C. Valerius Flaccus (*pr.* 183), who became a model of virtue
after his appointment as *flamen Dialis* in 209 B.C., was unique.[8] And it
was exceptional that at Caligula's election as *pontifex* his *pietas* and
character were praised.[9] Priesthoods were much coveted, as were the
political offices. Their holders gained in authority and influence, and
could in certain cases promote, obstruct, or even frustrate political
actions.[10] It was customary to co-opt a member of the same family on

---

[1] Suet. *Caes.* 59; 77; Cic. *div.* 2. 52; App. *BC* 2. 116. 488; Polyaen. 8. 23. 32 f.

[2] Dio 42. 57. 5.

[3] *ILS* 6087. 67; Cic. *Brut.* 127; Plut. *QR* 99; Mommsen, *StR* 2. 32; *Strafr.* 1002; Wissowa
491.

[4] Dio 39. 17. 1; Mommsen, *Röm. Forsch.* 1. 89 (restricts its validity to the *augures*); Bardt,
Priester der vier grossen Collegien 34 ff.; Wissowa 481. 2; Münzer, *Adelsp.* 251.

[5] Wissowa 493; Latte 394. 1; for exceptions see below, p. 32. 8.

[6] Cic. *leg.* 2. 47; *de or.* 1. 170; Livy 30. 1. 5.

[7] Cf. Nock, *Conversion* (1933) and *RAC* 2. 105 ff.; e.g. Hor. *c.* 1. 34 with A. Delatte, *Ant.
Class.* 4 (1936), 293 ff.; Fraenkel, *Horace* 253 ff.

[8] Livy 27. 8. 5 ff. Münzer, *Adelsp.* 188 f. and *RE* 8A. 6, is certainly right in denying the
authenticity of the story; but what matters here is that the story existed at all.

[9] Suet. *Cal.* 12. 1: 'ad pontificatum traductus est insigni testimonio pietatis atque indolis.'

[10] On politics and public priesthoods see L. R. Taylor, *Party Politics in the Age of Caesar* 90 ff.

the death of a priest:[1] this often limited the priesthood to a few families and perpetuated their political influence.

Caesar's ancestors did not hold many priestly offices, no doubt because of the long political eclipse of the family. C. Iulius Caesar Strabo, a second cousin of Caesar's father, was *pontifex* c. 99–87 B.C.,[2] and L. Iulius Caesar (*cos.* 64) was *augur* from 88 (or 80) to 40 B.C.[3] There will have been others of whom no record has survived. In addition the Iulii held a hereditary priesthood at Bovillae. It will be recalled that Ascanius was succeeded by his half-brother Silvius in the kingship of Alba, and that Iulus, who was in this tradition his son, received the highest priestly office instead, which his descendants, the Iulii, inherited from him and still held at the time when Dionysius of Halicarnassus was writing.[4] Diodorus adds that this office gave him a status as if he were a second king.[5] It has been assumed that this story was invented in 63 when Caesar became *pontifex maximus*, thus dating his claim to the office back to the time of his legendary ancestor.[6] But this interpretation introduces into the evidence what it does not contain. And what it contains is supported by facts. The Iulii were in charge of the local cults of Bovillae and probably of Alba, all concerned with the tradition of the Aeneadae. We have met the cults of Vediovis and of Venus.[7] There is nothing unusual in such a tradition: there were many cults which were reserved to certain families at the beginning or for ever.[8] Again, there were sacred offices which entitled their holders to the title of a king: a well-known instance is the 'rex Nemorensis'.[9] There is a strong tradition which points to the fact that the ritual of the *Feriae Latinae* on the Alban Mount too was administered by a 'king'; and this was not far away from Bovillae. Moreover we shall have to discuss the fact that in 45 Caesar began to wear the dress of the Alban kings, and we shall

---

[1] Suet. *Nero* 2. 1; Cic. *Phil.* 13. 12; Tac. *H.* 1. 77; Serv. *Aen.* 11. 768; Wissowa 484. 2; Münzer, *Adelsp.* 359 f.

[2] Gell. 4. 6. 2; Diehl, *RE* 10. 428; Broughton 2. 3.

[3] Macrob. 3. 13. 11; Broughton 2. 135; 255. Bickel, *Rhein. Mus.* 100 (1957), 202; 231, suggests that he was also a *pontifex*. This is impossible because he would have been the second Iulius in the college, which was against the rules; and so was the possession of the two priesthoods by the same man.

[4] Dion. Hal. 1. 70. 4: Ἰούλῳ δὲ ἀντὶ τῆς βασιλείας ἱερά τις ἐξουσία προσετέθη καὶ τιμή . . . ἣν ἔτι καὶ εἰς ἐμὲ τὸ ἐξ αὐτοῦ γένος ἐκαρποῦτο, Ἰούλιοι κληθέντες ἀπ' ἐκείνου.

[5] Diod. 7. 8 (Euseb. *Chron.* p. 138 Karst): 'Julios aber, verlustig gegangen des Fürstentums, wurde in das Hohepriestertum eingesetzt, und war wie ein zweiter König; von welchem her, sagen sie, noch bis auf heute bestehe zu Rom das Julische Geschlecht.'

[6] Meyer, *Caesars Monarchie* 511; see above, p. 17. 6.   [7] See above, pp. 8 ff.; 15 ff.

[8] The Aurelii were in charge of the cult of Sol (Paul. 23 M. = 22 L.), the Potitii and Pinarii of that of Hercules (Livy 1. 7. 14); Wissowa 404.

[9] Suet. *Cal.* 35. 3; Wissowa 248. The office of 'rex sacrorum' existed in many places, *ILS* 4942 (Bovillae); 4016; 6196 (Lanuvium); 6210 (Tusculum); 6607 (Florentia); Latte 405.

conclude that this also meant the sacred kingship.[1] This local priesthood, however, did not mean much as long as the Iulii were insignificant; Caesar changed the situation completely.

Caesar was designated *flamen Dialis* in 87 or in January 86 at the age of thirteen.[2] The previous holder of the office, L. Cornelius Merula, a follower of Sulla, committed suicide in 87,[3] and the victors Marius and Cinna hastened to choose a successor. Caesar was chosen because he was Marius' nephew and, as required, a patrician; the choice was in their interest, not in his. The *flamen Dialis* had great authority, political and religious, but was precluded from following a political career, in contrast to most other priests. When Caesar reached the age required for the administration of his priestly office, he could not be inaugurated because Sulla, after his victory, made all the appointments of Marius and Cinna invalid.[4] The office remained vacant until 11 B.C.[5] It is interesting, though idle, to speculate how far Caesar would have been able to live the life of a *flamen Dialis*, with all its cumbersome restrictions, and to renounce a political career. He should have been grateful to Sulla for having saved him from this predicament.

Caesar became a *pontifex* by co-optation in 73 in place of C. Aurelius Cotta (*cos.* 75), who had been *pontifex* from *c.* 91 until his death.[6] It was a remarkable appointment in many respects. Caesar himself was absent as a legate in the war against the pirates in Greece[7] and clearly owed his new office to the activities of his mother Aurelia and her political friends.[8] Formally the choice was in accordance with custom, in so far as he took the place of a relation, the cousin of his mother, although it was not customary to give the place of a plebeian, which Cotta was, to a patrician. The leading members of the college, Q. Caecilius Metellus Pius, Q. Lutatius Catulus, P. Servilius Vatia Isauricus,

---

[1] See below, pp. 323 ff.

[2] Suet. *Caes.* 1. 1: 'annum agens sextum decimum patrem amisit; sequentibusque consulibus flamen Dialis destinatus . . . a dictatore Sulla . . . sacerdotio . . . multatus'; Vell. 2. 43. 1: 'idem mox ad sacerdotium ineundum (quippe absens pontifex factus erat in Cottae consularis locum, cum paene puer a Mario Cinnaque flamen Dialis creatus victoria Sullae, qui omnia ab iis acta fecerat irrita, amisisset id sacerdotium) festinans in Italiam . . .'; Plut. *Caes.* 1. 3 (not correct); Strasburger, op. cit. 80; L. R. Taylor, *CP* 36 (1941), 113 ff.; Gelzer, *Caesar* 18. The *pontifex maximus*, Q. Mucius Scaevola (*cos.* 95), must have had his share in this designation. [3] Vell. 2. 20. 3; App. *BC* 1. 65. 296; 74. 341 f.

[4] Suet. *Caes.* 1. 1; Vell. 2. 43. 1; Plut. *Caes.* 1. 3 (above, n. 2).

[5] Dio 54. 36. 1; Tac. *A.* 3. 58. 2.

[6] Vell. 2. 43. 1 (above, n. 2); Broughton 2. 23; 113; L. R. Taylor, *AJP* 63 (1942), 393; 411.

[7] Vell. 2. 43. 1; *Syll.* 748. 22; Broughton 2. 113; 115. 6; id. *TAPA* 79 (1948), 63 ff. Raubitschek, *JRS* 44 (1954), 65, suggests that it was on this occasion that a statue was set up in Caesar's honour in the temple of Nike at Tralles (Caes. *BC* 3. 105. 6); below, p. 97.

[8] Gelzer, *Caesar* 22 f.

M. Terentius Varro Lucullus, were all followers of Sulla[1] whom one would
not have expected to vote for a nephew of Marius. His powerful supporters therefore must have made him somehow acceptable to the
nobility. And they were willing to overlook the fact that he had not
yet held any political office at the time of his election. His progress was
now made easier.

His mother was aiming at the promotion of his political career and
nothing else; at that time she was certainly not preparing his way to
the office of *pontifex maximus* although it is true that the holder had to be
a member of the pontifical college. When Q. Caecilius Metellus Pius
(*cos.* 80, *pont. max.* since 81) died in 63 B.C., Caesar became a candidate
and was elected in preference to elder and more deserving competitors,
P. Servilius Isauricus and Q. Lutatius Catulus, who had helped him
into the college ten years earlier;[2] both were consulars, whereas Caesar
had not even reached the praetorship. It was an election by 17 out of
the 35 tribes, not, like the pontificate, the result of a co-optation.

The normal activities of the *pontifex maximus* need not be described
here.[3] It was the most important religious office, which provided its holder
with great authority and power if he knew how to use it. Caesar was well
aware of this: the title *pontifex maximus* was never omitted on inscriptions set up in his honour in East and West except on those where he
was styled a god.[4] How desirable the office was emerges from an incident
during the Civil War. When Caesar suffered a defeat at Dyrrhachium
in 48, the members of three distinguished families began to argue in the
Pompeian camp about who should take his place as *pontifex maximus*;[5]
two of these contenders were dead a few months later and the third in
46. He lived after his election in a house belonging to the State on the
Sacra Via, the *domus publica*,[6] and his office was the Regia, which had
served as such since the regal period. He took part in numberless
State functions and presided over many consultations; and he always
conducted his office in the traditional manner. The verdict of the *pontifices* at the Bona Dea scandal, which closely concerned him, was correct,[7]
and he himself spoke about it in the Senate in his capacity as *pontifex
maximus*.[8] By divorcing his wife Pompeia he meant to protect his

---

[1] L. R. Taylor, *CP* 36 (1941), 117 f.; Broughton 2. 114.
[2] Sall. *Cat.* 49. 2; Suet. *Caes.* 13; Plut. *Caes.* 7. 1 ff.; Dio 37. 37. 1 ff.; Vell. 2. 43. 3; Strasburger, op. cit. 102; L. R. Taylor, *CP* 37 (1942), 422.   [3] Wissowa 508 ff.; Latte 400 ff.
[4] Degr. 406–8 (*ILS* 70 f.); Raubitschek, *JRS* 44 (1954), 73; D. Kienast, *Zeitschr. Sav.
Stift.* 78 (1961), 416 f.
[5] Caes. *BC* 3. 83. 1; App. *BC* 2. 69. 285; Plut. *Pomp.* 67. 6; *Caes.* 42. 1; Münzer, *Adelsp.*
360.   [6] Suet. *Caes.* 46.   [7] Cic. *Att.* 1. 13. 3.
[8] Schol. Bob. Cic. *Clod.* p. 85. 14 St.; Gelzer, *Caesar* 54. 131; Balsdon, *Hist.* 15 (1966), 67.

religious office as well as his personal reputation. But he did not break his political bond with the culprit Clodius: that was a different kind of relationship.

At the elections, too, Caesar exerted his influence in the traditional manner.[1] He did not forget his own family either. Sex. Iulius Caesar, who was probably his great-nephew, became *flamen Quirinalis c.* 58 B.C.;[2] and the *flamines maiores* were always created with the active participation of the *pontifex maximus*. His power became greater still through the co-operation of the other important priestly college, that of the *augures*. As *pontifex* he could not become an *augur*, but Pompey became one *c.* 61[3] and with his help Caesar overcame much resistance as long as the triumvirate lasted. The sabotage (*obnuntiatio*) of Bibulus in 59 shows how the augural doctrine could be used in political warfare.[4] Pompey no doubt saw to it that the augural college did not interfere with Caesar's further political activities. Caesar's long absence in Gaul was not in-compatible with his office: his predecessor Metellus spent eight years in Spain, 79–71, in the war against Sertorius.[5]

The Civil War created a new situation. Many priests left Rome with Pompey, and Caesar replaced them with others without observing the necessary rites;[6] but these may have been temporary replacements only. A new turn was taken after the victory at Pharsalus. Caesar became an *augur* in 47,[7] no doubt in order to make the co-operation of that college sure. He was not the first *pontifex* to hold the augurate as well, but it had not often been done before.[8] It was the first move towards the accumulation of priesthoods. Augustus followed his example,[9] and it be-came the general practice of the emperors. The victory created further problems. Varro dedicated his *Antiquitates rerum divinarum* to Caesar, and in it he urged the reform of religion; Granius Flaccus dedicated to him his *De indigitamentis*,[10] which was probably another antiquarian survey of prayers and ritual. Caesar would have tackled the problems even

---

[1] L. R. Taylor, *AJP* 63 (1942), 407 f.

[2] Cic. *har. resp.* 12; L. R. Taylor 397; Broughton 2. 199; Burkert, *Hist.* 11 (1962), 372 f.

[3] Cic. *Att.* 8. 3. 3; Dio 38. 12. 2; Sydenham 171; pl. 27. 1028; Broughton 2. 192; 255.

[4] See above, p. 27; on the power of the *augures* see e.g. Cic. *har. resp.* 8 f.; L. R. Taylor, *Party Politics* 83 f.   [5] App. *BC* 1. 108. 505 f.

[6] Dio 41. 36. 3: ἱερέας τε ἀντὶ τῶν ἀπολωλότων (read ἀπεληλυθότων?) ἀντικατέστησεν, οὐ πάντα τὰ κατ' αὐτοὺς ἐν τῷ τοιούτῳ νενομισμένα τηρήσας.

[7] Dio 42. 51. 4; Cic. *fam.* 13. 68. 2; Sydenham 170.

[8] e.g. C. Marcius Rutilus in 300 B.C. (Livy 10. 9. 2; *ILS* 9338), Q. Fabius Maximus in 216 B.C. (Livy 30. 26. 10; *ILS* 56), T. Otacilius Crassus in 211 (Livy 26. 23. 8; 27. 6. 15); Wissowa 493; Münzer, *Adelsp.* 63; 83; Latte 394. 1.

[9] *Mon. Anc.* 7. 3; Gagé, *Mél.* 48 (1931), 75 ff.

[10] Lact. *div. inst.* 1. 6. 7; Censor. 3. 2.

without such encouragements. There was a *lex Iulia de sacerdotiis* but its contents are not known; the only piece of evidence refers to the eligibility of absent candidates,[1] which recalls his own case in 73 B.C. It may have further ruled that the number of *pontifices*, *augures* and *quindecimviri* should be increased, as was done in 47.[2] The most important reform was the introduction of the Julian Calendar in 46,[3] of which something will have to be said later.

Our attention is turned in a different direction with the election of C. Octavius, his great-nephew and heir, as *pontifex* in 47 in place of L. Domitius Ahenobarbus (*cos.* 54), who died at Pharsalus.[4] It was not against the rules which excluded further members of the same family from the college: Octavius was not yet a member of the Gens Iulia. Nor was his youth a hindrance or unusual: he had just taken the *toga virilis*. Later, members of the imperial family too became *pontifices* in their youth, at the time when they received the position of 'crown-prince', Marcellus, Tiberius, C. Caesar.[5] Was the election of Octavius in 47 an indication that Caesar wanted to make him his successor then already, or did he just want to do a favour to his niece and Octavius' mother, Atia? The decree of 44 followed: Caesar's son or adopted son should become *pontifex maximus* after him.[6] This meant that his political heir should also inherit his supreme priesthood. The decree was planned for Octavian, and there was no formal hindrance as he was already a member of the college. After the murder Antony acted quickly. As he was an *augur* he could not become the *pontifex maximus*; but Lepidus was a member of the college and was elected to the office, though not in a wholly correct fashion.[7] Caesar's heir did not get the office until 12 B.C. It was offered him in 36 after the defeat of Lepidus but he

---

[1] Cic. *ad Brut.* 13 (1. 5). 3; cf. Mommsen, *StR* 2. 30. 3 (on Cic. *Phil.* 2. 4); Wissowa 73. 1; above, p. 30.

[2] Dio 42. 51. 3 f.; 43. 51. 9. He followed the precedent of Sulla who had also increased the number of *pontifices*, Livy, *Per.* 89. In 44 he added two to the existing two plebeian aediles and called them *aediles* (*plebis*) *Ceriales*, Dio 43. 51. 3; Suet. *Caes.* 41. 1; *Dig.* 1. 2. 2. 32; Dessau, *ILS* 3, pp. 350 f.; Mommsen, *StR* 1. 345. 6; 2. 480 f.; Wissowa 300.

[3] Suet. *Caes.* 40; below, pp. 197; 251.

[4] Vell. 2. 59. 3: 'pontificatusque sacerdotio puerum honoravit'; Nic. Dam. *v. Caes.* 4. 9 (*FGrHist.* 90 F 127): ἐνεγράφη εἰς τὴν ἱερωσύνην εἰς τὸν Λευκίου Δομιτίου τόπον τετελευτηκότος; Cic. *Phil.* 5. 46: 'C. Caesar, C. f., pontifex pro praetore'; L. R. Taylor, *AJP* 63 (1942), 406. 68; Broughton 2. 292.

[5] Tac. *A.* 1. 3. 1 (Marcellus); *ILS* 146 (Tiberius); Dio 55. 9. 4; *ILS* 106 f. (C. Caesar).

[6] Dio 44. 5. 3: τὸν δὲ δὴ υἱόν, ἄν τινα γεννήσῃ ἢ καὶ ἐσποιήσηται, ἀρχιερέα ἀποδειχθῆναι ἐψηφίσαντο; rejected by Mommsen, *StR* 2. 1106. 6; Adcock, *CAH* 9. 726; Schmitthenner, *Oktavian u. d. Testament Cäsars* 9; Syme, *Hist.* 7 (1958), 177; accepted by Meyer, *Caesars Monarchie* 524 f.; Münzer, *Adelsp.* 361; v. Premerstein 248; L. R. Taylor, *CP* 37 (1942), 423.

[7] Dio 44. 53. 6 f.; App. *BC* 2. 132. 552; Livy, *Per.* 117; Vell. 2. 63. 1.

refused to have it as long as Lepidus lived:[1] it was always an office for life. His successors were regularly elected to the office after him. It was traditional by then and does not answer the question why Caesar appointed an heir for that office too. One possible answer is that he was about to leave for Parthia and wanted to assure continuity for the time after his death.

Another of his last acts as *pontifex maximus* was the designation of his own *flamen*, the later *flamen Divi Iulii*:[2] this was to be one of the *flamines maiores* who were always chosen by the *pontifex maximus*. He was no doubt also involved in the detailed planning of his cult, about which the facts will be given later.[3] The decree concerning the succession was not itself so startling as it first appears. It will be recalled that it was customary to appoint a member of the same family into a vacancy in the college; also that the Iulii had a hereditary priesthood at Bovillae and perhaps even on the Alban Mount. This latter point may have been used for the justification of the new arrangement; but no doubt it was intended to be more than such a parochial, and more or less irrelevant, honour.

[1] *Mon. Anc.* 7. 3; 10. 2; Suet. *Aug.* 31. 1; Dio 49. 15. 3; App. *BC* 5. 131. 543; Sen. *clem.* I. 10. 1.   [2] Dio 44. 6. 4; below, pp. 305. 10; 306.

[3] See below, pp. 391 ff.

IV

THE CONQUEROR

It is possible to believe that Caesar knew from early youth that one day he would be the master of Rome, and also how he would achieve this: it would be a belief in the vision and omnipotence of genius, about which no rational argument could be conducted. But it is possible to argue that he foresaw already in Gaul that he would not be able to share his power with anyone, Pompey or the Senate, and that he made his plans accordingly. The decisive event would have been the death in 54 B.C. of his daughter, Iulia, who had been married to Pompey; the bond between the two men was thus broken. He virtually ruled alone for so many years in Gaul: now he would have planned his single rule for Rome, and his plans would have included the honours in question, human and divine. It is possible to argue; but there is not sufficient evidence. It is not enough to refer to the great political influence which he had built up in Rome with the help of his friends and his wealth in all those years, to his prospect of a spectacular triumph, to his claim of divine descent, to his plan to build his Forum with a temple of Venus in its centre. It is probable that had he been elected consul for 49 he would not have been a lesser autocrat than he was in his first consulate; but nothing is known about his plans for this contingency.

I. SCIPIO AND POMPEY

It is also possible to argue that Caesar had such plans at the beginning of the Civil War. There is in fact some evidence about Venus and Fortuna, about his role as liberator, and about his clemency, which also had their religious consequences later.[1] But even if there was more this would not point to a detailed plan. And yet it has been assumed that such a plan was made, not by Caesar but by his flatterers: to make him consul and dictator for life, to set up his statues in the Comitium, on the Rostra, in the Curia, on the Capitol, and in the temple of Iuppiter; to carry his image dressed in triumphal costume from the temple

[1] See below, pp. 80 ff., 112 ff., 133 ff.

of Iuppiter to the Circus in the *pompa circensis* in the company of the images of the gods. These were the honours which were once decreed, according to Livy, for the elder Scipio who, however, refused to accept them.[1] But as these were precisely the honours which were decreed for Caesar in the following years, it has been assumed that Livy, without knowing it, owed this list to a pamphlet written soon after Caesar's arrival in Rome in April 49 B.C., which attacked Caesar with the fiction about Scipio's refusal of the same honours.[2] If so, there was a detailed plan in 49 even though Caesar did not yet accept it. This is a brilliant theory, and it is hard to resist it. Scipio, always a celebrated hero, was at that time particularly in the news: Oppius, Caesar's friend, wrote about him[3] as he also wrote about Caesar,[4] and had opportunity enough to compare the two. One difficulty lies in the duplication of events: the honours would have been planned in 49 exactly as they were gradually executed in the following years, and Caesar would first have rejected and later accepted them.[5] The decisive objection, however, is that there is early evidence to show that those honours were in fact decreed for Scipio and that he accepted them. The similarity, which is undeniable and goes even beyond the evidence provided by Livy, is to be explained by the fact that, whenever Caesar was honoured, a precedent was sought, and that the precedent was often found in Scipio.[6] In sum, it is not proven that there was a detailed plan in 49 B.C.

And yet as time went on Caesar and his friends must have evolved a plan as to how he should be rewarded for his victories. As these victories were won over Pompey and his followers, the question arises whether Caesar's first honours were inspired by those granted to Pompey before. Pompey was the great contemporary whose example he first meant to emulate, who was later his ally and rival, and who lost in the end: he was more topical than any of the past heroes of Roman history. We

---

[1] Livy 38. 56. 12: 'castigatum . . . ab eo populum ait, quod eum perpetuum consulem et dictatorem vellet facere; prohibuisse statuas sibi in Comitio, in Rostris, in Curia, in Capitolio, in cella Iovis poni; (13) prohibuisse, ne decerneretur, ut imago sua triumphali ornatu e templo Iovis Optimi Maximi exiret.'

[2] Mommsen, *Röm. Forsch.* 2. 502 ff.

[3] Frgs. 1–3 P. (*HRR* 2, p. 46 ff.); Münzer, *RE* 18. 1. 729 ff.; Schanz–Hosius 1. 350.

[4] Frgs. 5–8 P.; Strasburger, op. cit. 30 ff.

[5] To avoid this difficulty E. Meyer, *Caesars Monarchie* 531 ff., changed the date of the pamphlet to February 44 B.C.; cf. also R. M. Haywood, *Studies on Scip. Afr.* (1933), 16 ff.; W. Hoffmann, *Livius u. der Zweite Punische Krieg* (1942), 77; Walbank, *Proc. Cambr. Phil. Soc.* N.S. 13 (1967), 56.

[6] Another hero whose example inspired some of the Caesarian honours was Camillus. He too was held to be a saviour of Rome, its new founder; he triumphed on a chariot of white horses, built a temple of Concordia, and added a day to the *ludi Romani*. They will be considered below in their proper context.

shall therefore survey the relevant features of Pompey's career first, and use them later for comparison in the detailed discussion of the Caesarian honours.

Pompey's dream was to become a second Alexander, and it was alleged in his youth and propagated later that there was a similarity even in their appearance.[1] Pompey proved his valour early, and Sulla acknowledged it when he greeted him in 83 B.C. at the age of twenty-three as *imperator*[2] and entrusted him with military expeditions. Pompey won his war in Africa in forty days;[3] his soldiers hailed him 'Magnus' on the battlefield,[4] as also did Sulla in Rome.[5] He was granted his first triumph at the age of twenty-six, against the rule which prescribed that the triumphator should have held the official rank of a consul or praetor.[6] On the day of his triumph, 12 March 79 B.C., he tried to enter Rome on a chariot drawn by elephants(?)[7]—another theme leading to Alexander and Alexander's mythical ancestors, Heracles and Dionysus, the divine conquerors of the world. He did not succeed because of the narrowness of the gate, and had to use the normal chariot with horses. He earned his second triumph in the war against Sertorius and the rebels in Spain. He set up a trophy in the Pyrenees with his statue on the top of it and with an inscription recording the conquest of 876 cities[8]— a further act which recalled his model, Alexander.[9] He held this triumph *de Hispania* on 29 December 71, which was again against the rules, but it was the day before his first consulate.[10] These two triumphs were extraordinary but not spectacular.

The third triumph held at the end of the long wars in the East, on the other hand, surpassed everything that had happened before.[11] He had been chosen for the conduct of these wars on account of his earlier victories and with the recommendation of Cicero. Cicero stressed that Pompey possessed both the valour and the good luck which were required for a successful general; and that he was destined for the task by the *Fortuna*

---

[1] Sall. *hist.* 3. 88 M.; Plut. *Pomp.* 2. 2; Pliny 7. 95; Cic. *Arch.* 24; *Att.* 2. 13. 2; *HTR* 50 (1957), 228; Balsdon, *Hist.* 1 (1950), 298 f.; Gelzer, *Pompeius* 134 ff.; Heuss, *Ant. u. Abendl.* 4 (1954), 81 f.

[2] Plut. *Pomp.* 8. 3; cf. Diod. 38/39. 10.   [3] Plut. *Pomp.* 12. 8.

[4] Plut. *Pomp.* 13. 8; Pliny 7. 96.   [5] Plut. *Pomp.* 13. 7.

[6] Pliny 7. 95; Livy, *Per.* 89; Drumann 4. 345. 4; Miltner, *RE* 21. 2074.

[7] Plut. *Pomp.* 14. 6; Pliny 8. 4; Gran. Licin. 36 (p. 31 Fl.); Drumann 4. 345.

[8] Sall. *hist.* 3. 89 M.; Pliny 3. 18; 7. 96; 37. 15; P. Goessler, *RE* 21. 2045 ff. After his victory over the Pompeians in 49, Caesar did not set up another trophy and statue in the neighbourhood, but an altar (for which god?), Dio 41. 24. 3.

[9] Arr. *Anab.* 5. 29; Diod. 17. 95. 1.

[10] Vell. 2. 30. 2; Drumann 4. 396 f.; Miltner, *RE* 21. 2089.

[11] On extravagant triumphal pomp see Bruhl, *Mél.* 46 (1929), 77 ff.

populi Romani.[1] Victory was won, and the triumph was prepared by decrees of 63 and 62, proposed by Cicero, granting Pompey supplications for ten and twelve days respectively,[2] and by a plebiscite, supported by Cicero and Caesar but opposed by Cato, also granting him the privilege of the triumphal dress and the golden crown in the Circus, and the *toga praetexta* and the laurel wreath in the theatre.[3] Both rewards, the supplications of excessive length and the special costumes, were extraordinary and will have to be explained together with the relevant Caesarian honours.[4] The triumph began on 28 September 61 with a long procession of treasures and other exhibits;[5] Pompey himself drove in on the following day, 29 September, his birthday.[6] This was clearly intentional: he had been back since February and yet delayed the triumph for almost seven months.[7] His chariot was set with precious stones, which was unusual; but he wore the normal triumphal dress and not, as is asserted, the cloak of Alexander.[8] His son Gnaeus was riding on one of the horses of his chariot,[9] which was significant but not an innovation. Some of the trophies carried in the procession represented the conquered countries, and one of them the whole world, the Oikoumene,[10] that is, either a personification or a globe with a trophy mounted on it.[11] It was said, and repeated many times later, that with his three triumphs he celebrated the conquest of three continents, so that Rome owed her mastery of the world to him.[12] A few

---

[1] Cic. *de imp.* 45; 47 f. [2] Cic. *prov. cons.* 27.

[3] Dio 37. 21. 4; Vell. 2. 40. 4; Cic. *Att.* 1. 18. 6 (below, p. 108. 6). Syme, *JRS* 28 (1938), 117, doubts whether Caesar in fact supported these proposals. [4] See below, pp. 270 f.

[5] Pliny 7. 97 f.; Plut. *Pomp.* 45; App. *Mithr.* 116. 568 ff.; Bruhl, l.c. 89 f.; Gelzer, *Pompeius* 132 ff. [6] Pliny 37. 13. [7] Cic. *Att.* 1. 14. 1.

[8] App. *Mithr.* 117. 577: αὐτὸς δὲ ὁ Πομπήιος ἐπὶ ἅρματος ἦν, καὶ τοῦδε λιθοκολλήτου (read: [καὶ] τὴν λιθοκόλλητον?) χλαμύδα ἔχων, ὥς φασιν, Ἀλεξάνδρου τοῦ Μακεδόνος, εἴ τῳ πιστόν ἐστιν· ἔοικε δ' αὐτὴν εὑρεῖν ἐν Μιθριδάτου, Κῴων παρὰ Κλεοπάτρας λαβόντων (cf. 23. 93; Gelzer, *Pompeius* 134; Miltner, *RE* 21. 2125). This story is supported by the fact that Caligula too wore Alexander's mantle and even his breastplate (Dio 59. 17. 3: τόν τε θώρακα τὸν Ἀλεξάνδρου, ὥς γε ἔλεγε, καὶ ἐπ' αὐτῷ χλαμύδα σηρικὴν ἀλουργῆ, πολὺ μὲν χρυσίον, πολλοὺς δὲ καὶ λίθους Ἰνδικοὺς ἔχουσαν ἐπενέδυ; Suet. *Cal.* 52: 'triumphalem quidem ornatum etiam ante expeditionem assidue gestavit, interdum et Magni Alexandri thoracem'). And yet it will be argued below, p. 335, that the story is apocryphal, invented to discredit Pompey.

[9] Sydenham 171; pl. 27. 1028. The coin is attributed by Eckhel, *Doctrina Numorum* 5. 281, to the third triumph; by Mommsen, *Röm. Münzwesen* 609, to the first: see the argument in Grueber 2. 464 n. For other instances see I. S. Ryberg pl. 6. 13; Ehlers, *RE* 7A. 508.

[10] Dio 37. 21. 2: τρόπαια δὲ ἄλλα τε πολλὰ καὶ καλῶς κεκοσμημένα καθ' ἕκαστον τῶν ἔργων καὶ τὸ βραχύτατον ἔπεμψε, καὶ ἐπὶ πᾶσιν ἓν μέγα, πολυτελῶς τε κεκοσμημένον καὶ γραφὴν ἔχον ὅτι τῆς οἰκουμένης ἐστίν. The other trophies may have represented the conquered countries, listed by Pliny 7. 98; Plut. *Pomp.* 45. 2; App. *Mithr.* 116. 568; see below, pp. 51 f.

[11] See below, pp. 42 f., 47 ff.

[12] Cic. *Sest.* 129: 'qui tripertitas orbis terrarum oras atque regiones tribus triumphis adiunctas huic imperio notavit'; *Balb.* 9: 'qui tot habet triumphos quot orae sunt partesque terrarum'; 16: 'cuius res gestae omnis gentes cum clarissima victoria terra marique

years later L. Vinicius (*cos.* 33) issued a coin showing a flying Victoria carrying a palm-branch to which four wreaths were attached (pl. 3. 5).[1] Three of these referred to Pompey's three triumphs, the fourth was the golden crown he was entitled to wear at the games in the Circus. Faustus Sulla, the son of the dictator and husband of Pompey's daughter, issued a coin *c.* 56 B.C. which propagated the same theme (pl. 3. 6): the globe in the centre, surrounded by the four wreaths, the fourth placed over the globe, jewelled and bound with a fillet, the golden crown again.[2] This was soon after the dedication of his theatre. He began to build it, and the shrines which were to be connected with it, for Venus Victrix, Hercules Invictus, Honos and Virtus, Victoria, and Felicitas, after his triumph of 61 B.C. He dedicated the theatre and apparently most of the shrines in his second consulate in 55 B.C.,[3] the shrine of Victoria and perhaps that of Felicitas in his third in 52.[4] His statue too stood there, surrounded by fourteen figures representing the conquered provinces,[5] which recalls the monument set up in the Pyrenees before his second triumph and even more the procession of these provinces in his third.[6] It will in turn be recalled in the discussion of the statue which was set up for Caesar in 46 on the Capitol.[7]

Such was Pompey, the conqueror before Caesar. His rewards were often excessive and contained a number of unusual features, but were not abnormal and did not constitute a menace to the State. Such excessive honours were granted to others before him, to Scipio for instance; it was an intermezzo which passed, though not always without difficulties, and the traditional way of life continued. It would be interesting

---

peragrassent, cuius tres triumphi testes essent totum orbem terrarum nostro imperio teneri, quem populus Romanus inauditis honoribus singularibusque decorasset'; Plut. *Pomp.* 45. 6: μέγιστον δ' ὑπῆρχε πρὸς δόξαν, καὶ μηδενὶ τῶν πώποτε 'Ρωμαίων γεγονός, ὅτι τὸν τρίτον θρίαμβον ἀπὸ τῆς τρίτης ἠπείρου κατήγαγεν. (7) ἐπεὶ τρίς γε καὶ πρότερον ἦσαν ἕτεροι τεθριαμβευ-κότες· ἐκεῖνος δὲ τὸν μὲν πρῶτον ἐκ Λιβύης, τὸν δὲ δεύτερον ἐξ Εὐρώπης, τοῦτον δὲ τὸν τελευταῖον ἀπὸ τῆς Ἀσίας εἰσαγαγών, τρόπον τινὰ τὴν οἰκουμένην ἐδόκει τοῖς τρισὶν ὑπῆχθαι θρίαμβοις; Diod. 40. 4; Cic. *Pis.* 16; cf. Manil. 1. 793: 'orbis domitor'; Lucan. 6. 595: 'dominus rerum'; 8. 553; 9. 1014: 'terrarum domitor'.

[1] Sydenham 155; pl. 26. 930a. Three trophies were carved on his ring, Dio 42. 18. 3.

[2] Sydenham 146; pl. 24. 882; Mommsen, *Röm. Münzwesen* 629; J. Cl. Richard, *Mél.* 75 (1963), 316 f.

[3] Dio 39. 38. 1; Vell. 2. 48. 2; Cic. *fam.* 7. 1. 2 f.; *Pis.* 65; Ascon. p. 1; 20 St.; Pliny 7. 158; 8. 20; *F. Amit.* and *F. Allif.* 12. Aug. (Degrassi 493).

[4] Gell. 10. 1. 7; *F. Allif.*

[5] Suet. *Nero* 46. 1: 'a simulacris gentium ad Pompei theatrum dedicatarum'; Pliny 36. 41: 'Varro ... et a Coponio quattuordecim nationes quae sunt circa Pompeium factas auctor est'; 8. 20: 'Pompei quoque altero consulatu, dedicatione templi Veneris Victricis'; cf. Serv. Dan. *Aen.* 8. 721: 'porticum ... Augustus fecerat in qua simulacra omnium gentium conlocaverat: quae porticus appellabatur "ad nationes" '; Pliny 36. 39; Platner–Ashby, s.v.

[6] See above, pp. 37. 8; 37. 10.

[7] See below, pp. 51 f.

to speculate what his rewards would have been like had he won the battle at Pharsalus, and whether they would have ended with another Ides of March; but it would be an idle speculation. Pompey was defeated, and Caesar had to be accommodated. We must examine how this was done.

2. THE STATUE ON THE CAPITOL

No precise information exists about the rewards voted for Caesar after the victory at Pharsalus;[1] more is known about those given after the victories at the Nile and at Zela, which will be dealt with later. But when the news of the victory at Thapsus was received, a statue and a chariot were set up in Caesar's honour on the Capitol,[2] an unusual action which requires a detailed comment.

In the early Republic, perhaps in contrast to the regal period, no statues of the living were set up on behalf of the State.[3] Statues of famous ancestors stood in private houses[4] and, by permission of the Senate, even in public places. It is not certain when the first exception was made. It is claimed for the hero of the fifth century, L. Minucius (*cos.* 458);[5] but, if it was not a cult image, he may have received it long after his death when exceptions became more numerous. Nor is it likely that Camillus' statue on the Rostra was set up while he was still alive; but it was an archaic statue, as it was dressed in a *toga* without *tunica*.[6] The instances at the turn of the fourth century to the third, Q. Marcius Tremulus (*cos.* 306 and 288) and Sp. Carvilius Maximus (*cos.* 293),[7] may be historical, as certainly are those of the end of the third century, Q. Fabius Maximus[8] and Scipio Africanus. Scipio is particularly relevant here because he often served as precedent for the Caesarian honours: his statues should have stood, and probably did, all over Rome, even on the Capitol.[9] There were, further, the statues

---

[1] Dio 42. 19. 3.   [2] Dio 43. 14. 6; 21. 2 (below, pp. 41. 6f.).

[3] Mommsen, *StR* 1. 447 f. The pretender (below, p. 134) Sp. Cassius (*cos.* 486) will have resumed the practice of the kings by setting up, as is asserted, his own statue (Piso frg. 37 P.; cf. Mommsen, *Röm. Forsch.* 2. 167. 1 and *StR* 1. 448. 1.; Ogilvie on Livy 2. 41 with bibliography).

[4] Iuven. 7. 125; 8. 3; Mart. 2. 90. 6; Verg. *Aen.* 7. 177; Mommsen, *StR* 1. 445. 1; *contra*, Rowell, *AJP* 62 (1941), 265 ff. (not convincing); see also below, p. 56. 2.

[5] Pliny 18. 15; 34. 21; Livy 4. 16. 2 with Ogilvie's note for further evidence and bibliography; below, p. 293. 9.   [6] Ascon. *Scaur.* p. 29 St.

[7] Cic. *Phil.* 6. 13; Livy 9. 43. 22; Pliny 34. 23; Münzer, *RE* 14. 1596; Vessberg, *Stud. zur Kunstgesch. d. röm Rep.* (1941), 19 ff.; Welin, *Stud. zur Topogr. des Forum Rom.* (1953), 136 ff.; 155 ff.; Becatti, *La colonna coclide istoriata* (1960), 33 ff.

[8] Plut. *Fab.* 22. 8; Münzer, *RE* 6. 1826.

[9] Enn. *V.* 1 V.; Livy 38. 56. 12 (above, p. 36. 1); 38. 56. 4; Mommsen, *Röm. Forsch.* 2. 475. 122 (statue on the burial monument of the family).

of Marius, Sulla, Pompey,[1] and also of lesser personalities like Q. Fabius Maximus (*cos.* 45), who placed his own, together with those of his distinguished ancestors, on the top of the Fornix Fabianus when he was aedile in 57 B.C.[2]

Caesar did not receive any statues for his achievements in Gaul; but in 48, after the victory at Pharsalus, he was decreed some.[3] It is not recorded where they were, or were to be, set up. In the East this was done at once, in accordance with Greek tradition, in temples and public places, and he was often styled a god on the inscriptions.[4] The majority will have been the usual standing figures on a platform; some may have been associated with the Dea Roma, others accompanied by Victoria or standing in chariots.[5]

The statue erected on the Capitol after the victory at Thapsus was different from all these antecedents. The evidence rests on two passages of Dio which are conflicting and make the interpretation difficult. The first records the decree: a chariot facing the statue of Iuppiter, and Caesar's bronze statue mounted on a globe and its inscription calling him a demigod, ἡμίθεος.[6] The second is found in the narrative of the triumph: when Caesar reached the Capitol, he did not notice the chariot and his statue, with the Oikoumene or the globe at his feet, and the inscription from which he later deleted the term ἡμίθεος.[7] The two passages agree that Caesar is connected with the globe but differ about the form of this connection. A single composition has been suggested: Caesar's statue in the chariot and the chariot mounted on the globe,[8] for which, however, no analogy could be produced; or again, Caesar in the chariot but the globe at his feet,[9] which would also be unique

---

[1] Plut. *Caes.* 6. 1; Vell. 2. 43. 4; Val. Max. 6. 9. 14; Suet. *Caes.* 11; Dio 42. 18. 2; 43. 49. 1; Polyaen. 8. 23. 31.   [2] *ILS* 43; cf. Cic. *Vatin.* 28.

[3] Dio 42. 19. 3.

[4] Caes. *BC* 3. 105. 5; *Syll.* 760, etc.; cf. Raubitschek, *JRS* 44 (1954), 65 ff.; below, p. 296.

[5] Many of the inscribed bases have survived (Raubitschek, l.c.); there is also some numismatic evidence and the evidence concerning the Hellenistic kings (Pliny 34. 78; Diog. Laert. 5. 5. 75; Diod. 20. 46. 2) and Augustus (*Mon. Anc.* 24. 2).

[6] Dio 43. 14. 6: ἅρμα τέ τι αὐτοῦ ἐν τῷ Καπιτωλίῳ ἀντιπρόσωπον τῷ Διὶ ἱδρυθῆναι καὶ ἐπὶ εἰκόνα αὐτὸν τῆς οἰκουμένης χαλκοῦν ἐπιβιβασθῆναι, γραφὴν ἔχοντα ὅτι ἡμίθεός ἐστιν; cf. Serv. Dan. *Ecl.* 9. 46: 'eique in Capitolio statuam, super caput auream stellam habentem, posuit: inscriptum in basi fuit "Caesari emitheo" ' (confusing it with the statue which was set up by Octavian for Caesar after his death in the Forum, Pliny 2. 94; Suet. *Caes.* 88; below, pp. 370. 5; 393. 7); cf. Dio 56. 36. 2 (Tiberius' funeral oration on Augustus, A.D. 14): τοῦ ἡμιθέου ἐκείνου Καίσαρος.

[7] Dio 43. 21. 2: μήτε τὸ ἅρμα τὸ πρὸς τὸν Δία ἀνιδρυθὲν αὐτῷ μήτε τὴν εἰκόνα τῆς οἰκουμένης τὴν ὑπὸ τοῖς ποσὶν αὐτοῦ κειμένην, μήτε τὸ ἐπίγραμμα αὐτῆς ὑπολογισάμενος, ὕστερον δὲ τὸ τοῦ ἡμιθέου ὄνομα ἀπ' αὐτοῦ ἀπήλειψεν.

[8] Mommsen, *Röm. Forsch.* 2. 504. 169.

[9] Gelzer, *Caesar* 257; Drumann 3. 549 is not clear.

and moreover without any support in the texts. The two texts must first be understood with the help of relevant analogies before a choice can be made. They have the globe in common, and therefore we take that first.

(a) The Globe

The celestial and terrestrial globe is often mentioned in Greek literature and represented in art, e.g. as the attribute of Urania,[1] but never as a political symbol, the symbol of the mastery of the world: this it became only at Rome. This fact was observed more than forty years ago[2] and yet ignored or underrated in later discussion. A representation of Demetrius Poliorcetes on a painting at Athens in 290 B.C. would prove the contrary, that is, a Greek origin, if he really had been mounted on the globe there. But this is not what the evidence says: he was driving his chariot towards Oikoumene,[3] a female personification[4] probably in a reclining posture, which is, as analogies show,[5] a possible composition. If so, the picture represented Demetrius' claim to the mastery of the world in succession to Alexander,[6] but it did that without the globe.

Now to the change of the Greek globe into a Roman symbol. It is first found on coins of Cn. Cornelius Lentulus Marcellinus (cos. 56) and of P. Cornelius Lentulus Spinther (cos. 57) respectively, about 75 B.C. (pl. 3. 7–8):[7] on the first it is among other symbols, wreath, sceptre, and rudder, suggesting victory and rule over land and sea; on the second it is placed under the foot of the seated Genius populi Romani. A few years later it was under the foot of Roma on a coin of Q. Fufius Calenus

---

[1] A. Schlachter, Der Globus (1927), 1 ff.; Brendel, Röm. Mitt. 51 (1936), 1 ff.; see also Cook, Zeus 1. 41 ff.; Mrs. Strong, JRS 6 (1916), 32 ff.; T. Hölscher, Victoria Romana (1967), 41 ff.; 180 ff.

[2] Schlachter, op. cit. 64 ff.; contra, Vogt, Vom Reichsgedanken der Römer 182. 2; Hommel, Antike 18 (1942), 128.

[3] Duris, FGrHist. 76 F 14: γινομένων δὲ τῶν Δημητρίων Ἀθήνησιν ἐγράφετο ἐπὶ τοῦ προσκηνίου ἐπὶ τῆς οἰκουμένης ὀχούμενος; Eustath. Il. 5. 449. Meyer, Caesars Monarchie 385, is ambiguous: '. . . eine eherne Statue im Iuppitertempel, der die Weltkugel zu Füssen lag, wie die Athener im Jahre 290 den Gott Demetrios malten'; Alföldi, Röm. Mitt. 50 (1935), 118 (D. sitting on the globe) and my interpretation, HTR 50 (1957), 232. 133, are wrong.

[4] See below, p. 47.

[5] It seems to have been created for the rising Sol (Helios) with the earth at his feet; cf. the medallion of Antoninus Pius (Gnecchi, I medaglioni romani 2, pl. 50. 6), another in the Vatican Museum (M. Guarducci, Rend. Pont. Accad. 30/1 (1957/9), 161, fig. 1; coins of Commodus, ibid. 165, fig. 3 f.), and the relief from Ephesus in Vienna (Toynbee, The Hadrianic School, pl. 32. 3); for later instances see E. Dinkler-v. Schubert, RAC 8. 78 f. It was also used by the artist of the breastplate of the statue of Augustus from Primaporta.

[6] Cf., e.g., Anth. Pal. 16. 120. 4: γᾶν ὑπ' ἐμοὶ τίθεμαι, Ζεῦ, σὺ δ' Ὄλυμπον ἔχε.

[7] Sydenham 122; 130; pl. 21. 752; 22. 791; cf. Fuhrmann, Mitt. Arch. Inst. 2 (1949), 38 f. (also for the following notes); see below, p. 206.

(*cos.* 47) and the otherwise unknown Cordus (pl. 3. 9).[1] This and later numismatic evidence leads to the postulate of a Greek work of art, preferably a seated Roma with the globe under her foot. The Roman mastery of the world had been recognized since their victory over Antiochus III at Magnesia in 190 B.C.,[2] was much debated and propagated in the second century, and may have inspired an artistic representation of this kind, if not at once, perhaps not later than Sulla's victories in the East. A quotation from a speech of Ti. Gracchus *c.* 133 B.C.[3] is our earliest datable evidence on the Roman side but he was certainly not the first to refer to this claim. It is due to the persistence of this claim that the globe first appeared on those coins in the seventies of the first century. Cicero often referred to it before and after Pompey's triumph, when the globe, as we have seen, received an even greater topicality. It was probably carried in his triumph of 61 and was reproduced on a coin of Faustus Sulla *c.* 54, commemorating Pompey's conquests and celebrating his rewards.[4]

Caesar adopted this symbolism soon after arriving in Rome in 49 B.C. One of his followers, C. Vibius Pansa (*cos.* 43), issued a coin with Roma seated on weapons, her foot on the globe, and crowned by Victoria (pl. 3. 10);[5] Caesar's own coins show Gallic trophies (pl. 3. 11).[6] This was clearly his answer to the Pompeian propaganda, past and present: his conquest of Gaul contributed no less than Pompey had done to Rome's mastery of the world. The same representation is found on a coin of T. Carisius issued after Caesar's triumph (pl. 3. 12);[7] he also issued a coin with a globe, a cornucopiae placed on it, and sceptre and rudder on either side (pl. 3. 13);[8] that is, rule over land and sea, a symbolism which we have met already on the coins of Cn. Cornelius Lentulus.[9] The claim was now, after the victories in East and West,

---

[1] Sydenham 131; pl. 23. 797; Münzer, *RE* 7. 204; below, pp. 96, 232.

[2] Livy 37. 45. 8: 'in hac victoria quae vos dominos orbis terrarum fecit'; Vell. 1. 6. 6; *Athen. Mitt.* 77 (1962), 313.

[3] *Or. Rom. frg.* 34. 13 Malc. (Plut. *Ti. Gr.* 9. 6): κύριοι τῆς οἰκουμένης (reference contributed by Professor R. G. M. Nisbet).

[4] See above, p. 39, and below, p. 272.

[5] Sydenham 159; Grueber, pl. 50. 6; below, pp. 61; 93.

[6] Sydenham 167 ff.; pl. 27. 1006 ff.; below, pp. 61. 6; 86. 3; 377. 3.

[7] Sydenham 164; Grueber, pl. 52. 9 (Victoria on the obverse); below, p. 99. 7.

[8] Sydenham 163 f.; Grueber, pl. 52. 4; 9.

[9] Similar issues followed: coin of C. Considius Paetus, showing the globe with two cornucopiae on it (Sydenham 165; Grueber, pl. 52. 22); of L. Aemilius Buca, showing the globe with caduceus and clasped hands, symbols of peace and concord (Sydenham 177; pl. 28. 1063); of P. Sepullius Macer, with the globe in the pediment of the (projected) temple of the Clementia Caesaris (Sydenham 179; pl. 28. 1076); of L. Mussidius Longus, issued after Caesar's death, with Caesar's head on the obv., the globe with the cornucopiae between rudder, caduceus, and the flamen's cap on the rev. (Sydenham 181; Grueber, pl. 56. 18–20).

PLATE 3

1. Denarius of Sex. Iulius Caesar, c. 130–125 B.C. (Sydenham 56. 476), London; obv.: head of helmeted 'Roma'; rev.: Venus crowned by Cupid in biga, legend 'Roma', 'Sex. Iuli(us) Caisar'; p. 17.

2. Denarius of L. Iulius Caesar, c. 105 B.C. (Sydenham 82. 593), Oxford; obv.: head of Mars, legend 'Caesar'; rev.: Venus in biga of Cupids, legend 'L. Iuli(us) L. f.'; p. 17.

3. Denarius of L. Memmius, c. 102 B.C. (Sydenham 79. 574), Oxford; obv.: head of Saturn, legend 'Roma'; rev.: Venus in biga, above, Cupid with wreath, legend 'L. Memmi(us) Gal(eria)'; p. 23.

4. Denarius of L. and C. Memmius, 87 B.C. (Sydenham 110. 712), London; obv.: head of Saturn, legend 'ex s.c.'; rev.: Venus in biga, above, Cupid, legend 'L. C. Memies L. f. Gal(eria)'; p. 23.

5. Denarius of L. Vinicius, c. 52 B.C. (Sydenham 155. 930), Oxford; obv.: head of Concordia, legend 'Concordiae'; rev.: Victoria with palm-branch, to which four wreaths are attached, legend 'L. Vinici(us)'; p. 39.

6. Denarius of Faustus Cornelius Sulla, c. 56 B.C. (Sydenham 146. 883), Oxford; obv.: head of Hercules, legend 's.c.'; rev.: four wreaths, one of which is jewelled, around a globe; p. 39.

7. Denarius of Cn. Cornelius Lentulus Marcellinus, c. 75 B.C. (Sydenham 122. 752), Oxford; obv.: head of the Genius populi Romani, legend 'G.p.R.'; rev.: globe between rudder and sceptre, legend 'ex s.c., Cn. Len(tulus) q(uaestor)'; p. 42.

8. Denarius of P. Cornelius Lentulus Spinther, c. 75 B.C. (Sydenham 130. 791), London; obv.: head of Hercules, legend 'q(uaestor) s.c.'; rev.: Genius p. R. seated and crowned by Victoria, his foot on globe, legend 'P. Lent(ulus) P. f. L. n.'; p. 42.

9. Denarius of Q. Fufius Calenus and of Cordus, c. 69 B.C. (Sydenham 131. 797), Oxford; obv.: heads of Honos and Virtus, legend 'Ho(nos), Virt(us), Kaleni'; rev.: Roma with foot on globe and Italia, legend 'Ro(ma), Ital(ia), Cordi'; p. 43.

10. Denarius of C. Vibius Pansa, c. 48 B.C. (Sydenham 159. 949), London; obv.: head of Libertas, legend 'Libertatis'; rev.: Roma seated on shields, crowned by Victoria, her foot on globe, legend 'C. Pansa C. f. C. n.'; p. 43.

11. Denarius of Caesar, 48 B.C. (Sydenham 167. 1009), Oxford; obv.: female head, legend 'LII (= 52)'; rev.: trophy, legend 'Caesar'; p. 43.

12. Quinarius of T. Carisius, c. 46 B.C. (Sydenham 164. 987), London and Paris; obv.: bust of Victoria; rev.: Roma seated on shields with her foot on a globe, legend 'T. Carisi(us)'; p. 43.

13. Denarius of T. Carisius, c. 46 B.C. (Sydenham 163. 984), Oxford; obv.: head of Roma, legend 'Roma'; rev.: globe with cornucopiae between sceptre and rudder, legend 'T. Carisi(s)'; p. 43.

14. Denarius of L. Staius Murcus, 44–43 B.C. (Sydenham 205. 1315), London; obv.: head of Neptune; rev.: a man extends his hand to a kneeling woman, trophy in the background, legend 'Murcus Imp.'; p. 46.

15. Aureus of Cossus Cornelius Lentulus (photo: C. Vermeule, cf. Numismatica 1 (1960), 1 ff.); obv.: head of Augustus, legend 'Augustus Divi f.'; rev.: man and kneeling woman, legend 'Cossus Lentulus, August(us), Res pub(lica)'; p. 46.

16. Sestertius of Galba, A.D. 68 (Mattingly 1. 358. 258), London; obv.: bust of Galba, legend 'Ser. Sulpi(cius) Galba Imp. Caesar Aug. p. m., tr. p.'; rev. Galba and kneeling woman, an Amazonian figure in the background, legend 'Libertas restituta, s.c.'; p. 46.

17. Sestertius of Vespasian, A.D. 71 (Mattingly 2. 118. 549), Paris; obv.: head of Vespasian, legend 'Imp. Caesar Vespasianus Aug. p. m., t. p., p. p., cos. III'; rev.: Vespasian and a kneeling woman with an Amazon between them in the background, legend 'Libertas restituta'; p. 46.

18. Sestertius of Hadrian, A.D. 117 (Mattingly 3. 397. 1101), London; obv.: head of Hadrian, legend 'Imp. Caes. Divi Traian(i) Aug(usti) f. Traian(us) Hadrian(us) Opt. Aug. Ger.'; rev.: Hadrian receiving a globe from a senator, legend 'Dac. Parthico p. m., tr. p., cos., p. p., s.c.'; p. 47.

PLATE 3

PLATE 4

Clay relief from the Via Cassia near Rome: 'Caesar' crowned by Victoria, trophy and prisoners (r.), globe and 'Oikoumene' (l.), wall at either end; Museo Nazionale, Rome (Photograph: German Archaeological Institute, Rome); p. 45.

more justified than ever.[1] The symbolism was resumed under Augustus and continued under his successors.[2] This survey shows that it was not a sudden whim of the Senate to connect Caesar with the globe. But it does not decide the question of the dedication on the Capitol: was Caesar mounted on the globe, or did he have it at his feet? To answer this question and to explain the function of the statue some further evidence is needed.

(b) The Relief from the Via Cassia

Fresh and important evidence is provided by a clay relief found in 1935 on the Via Cassia near Rome (pl. 4).[3] It has been dated to the age of Caesar, which is probable on account of its contents and of some analogies, but cannot be confirmed on stylistic grounds because of the low quality of the work.

In the centre a man in armour and with a spear in his left hand is facing a kneeling Amazon who wears a helmet and also holds a spear; a globe is between them on the ground, and a flying Victoria is about to crown them an; at his side there is a trophy with armour, shields, and two captives, and at either end a wall is being built. It has been suggested that the victorious general is Caesar and the kneeling woman Roma; further, that her extended hand means that she is handing over to Caesar either the diadem, which would recall the scene of the Lupercalia of 44 B.C.,[4] or a wreath, which might indicate the celebration of a victory.[5] These two interpretations are impossible because there is no trace of any object which she might have held in her hand.[6] It could have been painted; but to suppose this, one would first have to prove that it must have been there, and this is not the case. Moreover there is nothing on the relief to point to the scene at the Lupercalia, and in fact it would have been politically a perverse idea to commemorate it on a relief; and a second wreath, in addition to that held by Victoria, would not make sense either. Nor is the kneeling position explained by these assumptions: kneeling mostly means submission, of a man to

---

[1] On Victoria and the globe see below, pp. 50f.

[2] Schlachter, op. cit. 69 ff.

[3] Fuhrmann, Mitt. Arch. Inst. 2 (1949), 23 ff.; pl. 8; Alföldi, Studien über Caesars Monarchie 26f.; pl. 16; on the engines at either end see also J. W. Shaw, Hesperia 36 (1967), 395 ff. For the view that the relief represents Aurelian building a wall see G. Hafner, Atlantis 35 (1963), 781 f. (not accessible to me).

[4] Fuhrmann, l.c.; accepted by G. C. Picard, Les trophées romains (1957), 224.

[5] Alföldi, op. cit.

[6] This is the verdict of Prof. Luisa Banti, Mr. M. W. Frederiksen, and myself after an examination of the original.

the gods[1] or of the defeated enemy to the general or the emperor, asking for mercy.[2] But if the woman is Roma, this interpretation is impossible: she cannot kneel down, not even in front of Caesar.

Another interpretation seems more promising. Caesar is extending his hand to raise Roma from prostration, which was later a popular composition. A coin issued a few years later in 44 or 43 B.C. by L. Staius Murcus (pr. 45?), in commemoration of his victory over the adventurer Q. Caecilius Bassus at Apamea, shows a man raising a kneeling woman, and a trophy in the background (pl. 3. 14).[3] The composition is reminiscent of the central part of our relief even though it has the trophy in the centre and not at the side of the general; it might therefore support the Caesarian date of the relief. The woman on the coin, who is apparently neither helmeted nor turreted, would be for this alternative not a personification of Asia or Syria, nor of Apamea, as is suggested, but of Roma again, whom Murcus saved from rebellion.[4] A unique *aureus* of Cossus Cornelius Lentulus (*cos.* 1) shows Augustus facing another kneeling woman, who is, according to the legend, the 'Res publica' (pl. 3. 15);[5] she further appears on coins of Galba and Vespasian and is called 'Roma resurge(n)s', even if the legend is changed sometimes to 'Libertas restituta' (pl. 3. 16–17).[6]

This numismatic evidence proves that the resurgent Roma was a frequent theme in Roman art after Caesar. But it does not prove by itself that the kneeling figure on the relief too is Roma. This identification ought to find support in its context: there is more on the relief than the general and the kneeling woman. The other items, however, turn our attention to a different theme, to victory and the mastery of the world: the globe, the trophy, Victoria with the wreath, even the scene at either end, the building of a wall. Taken together they all suggest that this clay relief is a copy, albeit a very poor one, of a triumphal relief which commemorated Caesar's achievements. There used

---

[1] Soph. *Trach.* 900; Plaut. *Rud.* 695, etc.; Bolkestein, *Theophrastos' Charakter d. Deisidaimonia* (1929), 25 ff.; Alföldi, *Röm. Mitt.* 49 (1934), 46 ff.

[2] Cf., e.g., Caes. *BC* 3. 98. 2; Suet. *Caes.* 20. 4; Cic. *fam.* 6. 14. 2; Plut. *Cato min.* 66. 1 f.; Sydenham 145; pl. 24. 879; 168; pl. 27. 1011; etc.

[3] Sydenham 205; pl. 30. 1315; Grueber, pl. 112. 10; Münzer, *RE* 3A. 2138; Broughton 2. 330; 349.

[4] A different composition is found on the coin of M'. Aquillius issued *c.* 68 B.C., where the general, an earlier Aquillius, is raising the kneeling Sicilia (Sydenham 132; pl. 23. 798); repeated by L. Aquillius Florus in 18 B.C. (Mattingly 1. 9; pl. 2. 7).

[5] It was published by C. Vermeule, *Numismatica* 1 (1960), 1 ff.; the date of the issue is not certain, see below, p. 102 (on the date of the alleged fellow moneyer L. Cornelius Lentulus).

[6] Mattingly 1. 358; pl. 59. 1; Kraay, *The Aes Coinage of Galba* (1956), 41 f.; pl. 33 P 191; Mattingly 2. 118; 121; pls. 21. 1; 9; 22. 1; Alföldi, *Röm. Mitt.* 49 (1934), 52; Fuhrmann, l.c. 39 f.

to be a temporary record of such achievements in the triumphal procession, trophies in great number, representations of conquered cities,
even of their sieges in pictorial form.[1] What could be the function of the
general and the Amazon on a triumphal relief?

The general as the principal figure needs no justification. The globe
is supported by its precedents in Rome, the most important being that
of Pompey's triumphal procession, to which we shall have to return
again. But Roma will not fit in, and the globe between her and Caesar
could not be explained in a satisfactory manner. It would be at first
sight an attractive suggestion that she is about to hand it over to Caesar.
Coins of Trajan and Hadrian show a *togatus*, that is, a senator, handing
it over to the new emperor (pls. 3. 18; 5. 2);[2] Hadrian also receives it
from Iuppiter (pl. 5. 1):[3] but these are standing male figures. The
kneeling woman with the globe in front of the emperor is found again on
Trajan's coins with the legend 'Italia rest(ituta)' (pl. 5. 3–4).[4] But this
Italia is holding the globe apparently as her symbol and is not handing
it over—she could not possibly do so because Trajan is grasping her
other hand in the act of raising her up. The conclusion is that it could
be Roma, resurgent with Caesar's help, if it were not a triumphal relief
with a different theme, and above all if the globe were not there.

The alternative is Oikoumene.[5] We met this personification as a reclining figure in the company of Demetrius Poliorcetes on a painting
at Athens.[6] It is further known from the relief of Archelaos of Priene
in the British Museum[7] and from the Arch of Galerius at Salonika:[8]
on the former she is a standing figure, surmounted by a basket (*kalathos*),
and is attending the apotheosis of Homer in the company of Chronos;
on the latter she is without a basket, in the company of Eirene,
Homonoia(?), Galerius, and Diocletian. The two representations differ
from each other, and neither is, like the Caesarian figure, an Amazon.
This then is not in favour of the identification. Another obstacle can

---

[1] Quint. 6. 3. 61; Livy 41. 28. 10; Tac. *A.* 2. 41. 5; Ov. *Pont.* 3. 4. 105; *Ars Amat.* 1. 220 ff.;
Claudian, *Cons. Stil.* 3. 22; Jahn ad Pers. 6. 47.

[2] Mattingly 3. 157; 236 f.; 397 f.; pls. 46. 1 f.; 76. 1; 6; Strack, *Unters. z. röm. Reichsprägung*
1. 48; pls. 4. 343; 2. 43 f.   [3] Mattingly 3. 269; pl. 51. 8.

[4] Mattingly 3. 186; 195; 203; pl. 35. 10; Strack, op. cit. 1. 190; pls. 2. 162; 7. 412; Toynbee,
The Hadrianic School 109; pl. 15. 27–9; Hamberg, *Studies in Roman Imperial Art* (1945), 31.

[5] Cf. Giesinger–Schmidt, *RE* 17. 2173 f.; Toynbee, op. cit., 24 f.

[6] See above, p. 42. 3.

[7] Lippold, *Die griech. Plastik* 373; pl. 131. 3 (with bibliography); D. Pinkwart, *Das Relief
d. Archelaos* (1965), 34 ff.; pl. 1. 10a.

[8] Kinch, *L'Arc de triomphe de Salonique* (1890), 36; pl. 5; Reinach, *Rép. rel.* 1. 389; L'Orange,
Stud. z. Gesch. d. spätant. Porträts (1933), fig. 61; Toynbee, op. cit. 25. 1; pl. 21. 3. On a further,
very doubtful, representation of Oikoumene (a marble statue at Porto Raphti in Attica)
see C. Vermeule, *Hesp.* 31 (1962), 77 ff.

PLATE 5

1. Aureus of Hadrian, A.D. 119–138 (Mattingly 3. 269. 242), London; *obv.*: bust of Hadrian, legend 'Imp. Caesar Traian. Hadrianus Aug.'; *rev.*: Hadrian receives the globe from Iuppiter who holds a thunderbolt and has an eagle at his feet, legend 'p. m., tr. p., cos. III'; p. 47.

2. Sestertius of Trajan, A.D. 101–2 (Mattingly 3. 157*), Paris; *obv.*: bust of Trajan, legend 'Imp. Caes. Nerva Traian(us) Aug. Germ. p. m.'; *rev.*: Trajan receiving a globe from a senator, legend 'tr. pot, cos. IIII, p. p., s.c.'; p. 47.

3. Dupondius of Trajan, A.D. 104–11 (Mattingly 3. 195. 920), London; *obv.*: bust of Trajan, legend 'Imp. Caes. Nervae Traiano Aug. Ger. Dac., p. m., tr. p., cos. V, p. p.'; *rev.*: Trajan raising up Roma who holds a globe; between them two children stretching out their hands, legend 'S.P.Q.R. optimo principi Roma rest(ituta)'; p. 47.

4. Sestertius of Trajan, A.D. 104–11 (Mattingly 3. 186*), Paris; *obv.*: bust of Trajan, legend 'Imp. Caes. Nervae Traiano Aug. Ger. Dac., p. m., tr. p., cos. V, P. p.'; *rev.*: Trajan raising up kneeling Italia who holds a globe; between them two children stretching out their hands, legend 'S.P.Q.R. optimo principi, rest(ituta) Italia, s.c.'; p. 47.

5. Denarius of Vespasian, A.D. 71 (Mattingly 2. 96. 459), Oxford; *obv.*: head of Vespasian, legend 'Imp. Caesar Vespas. Aug. cos. III, tr. p., p. p.'; *rev.*: female bust with turreted crown, legend 'Paci orb(is) terr(arum) Aug., Ephe(sus)'; p. 50.

6. Sestertius of Hadrian, A.D. 119–21 (Mattingly 3. 418. 1211), Oxford; *obv.*: head of Hadrian, legend 'Imp. Caesar Traianus Hadrianus Aug. p. m., tr. p., cos. III, p. p.'; *rev.*: Hadrian raising kneeling, turreted woman, legend 'Restitutori Orbis terrarum, s.c.'; p. 50.

7. Denarius of Augustus, 31–29 B.C. (Mattingly 1. 99. 602), Oxford; *obv.*: head of Octavian; *rev.*: Victoria on globe holding palm and wreath, legend 'Caesar Divi f.'; p. 51.

8. Denarius of Augustus, 29–27 B.C. (Mattingly 1. 103. 631), Oxford; *obv.*: head of Octavian; *rev.*: Curia Iulia with Victoria mounted on globe on its pediment, legend on architrave 'Imp. Caesar'; p. 51.

9. Denarius of Augustus 31–29 B.C. (Mattingly 1. 100. 615), Oxford; *obv.*: bust of Victoria; *rev.*: male figure with foot on globe, legend 'Caesar Divi f.'; p. 51.

10. Coin of M. Maecilius Tullus, 7 B.C. (Mattingly 1. 42. 217), London; *obv.*: head of Augustus on a globe, behind, Victoria, legend 'Caesar August. pont. max. tribunic. pot.'; *rev.*: legend 'S.C., M. Maecilius Tullus IIIvir a.a.a.f.f.'; p. 51.

11. Aureus of Augustus, c. 22–19 B.C. (cf. Mattingly 1. 56. 307), Oxford; *obv.*: head of Augustus; *rev.*: Capricorn holding a globe and rudder, above, cornucopiae, legend 'Augustus'; p. 51. 8.

12. Denarius of C. Fundanius, c. 101 B.C. (Sydenham 81. 583), Oxford; *obv.*: helmeted head of 'Roma'; *rev.*: triumphator (Marius?) holding laurel-branch and staff in quadriga, rider on near horse, legend 'Q(uaestor?), C. Fundan(ius)'; p. 56.

13. Aureus of Sulla, 82–81 B.C. (Sydenham 123. 756), London; *obv.*: helmeted head of 'Roma', legend 'L. Manli(us) pro. q(uaestor)'; *rev.*: Sulla in triumphal quadriga with caduceus, above, Victoria with wreath, legend 'L. Sulla im(perator)'; p. 56.

14. Aureus of Pompey, 61 B.C.(?) (Sydenham 171. 1028), London; *obv.*: head of Africa wearing elephant's skin, legend 'Magnus'; *rev.*: Pompey in triumphal quadriga holding branch, rider on near horse, above, Victoria with wreath, legend 'pro. cos.'; p. 56.

15. Aureus of Augustus, 31–29 B.C. (Mattingly 1. 97. 590), London; *obv.*: head of Octavian; *rev.*: triumphal quadriga surmounted by four miniature horses, legend 'Caesar Divi f.'; p. 56.

16. Denarius of Augustus, 29–27 B.C. (Mattingly 1. 101. 617), Oxford; *obv.*: Victoria on prow with palm and wreath; *rev.*: Augustus in quadriga, legend 'Imp. Caesar'; p. 57.

17. Denarius of Augustus, 29–27 B.C. (Mattingly 1. 102. 624), Oxford; *obv.*: head of Octavian; *rev.* Augustus on triumphal quadriga mounted on an arch, legend on architrave 'Imp. Caesar'; p. 57.

PLATE 5

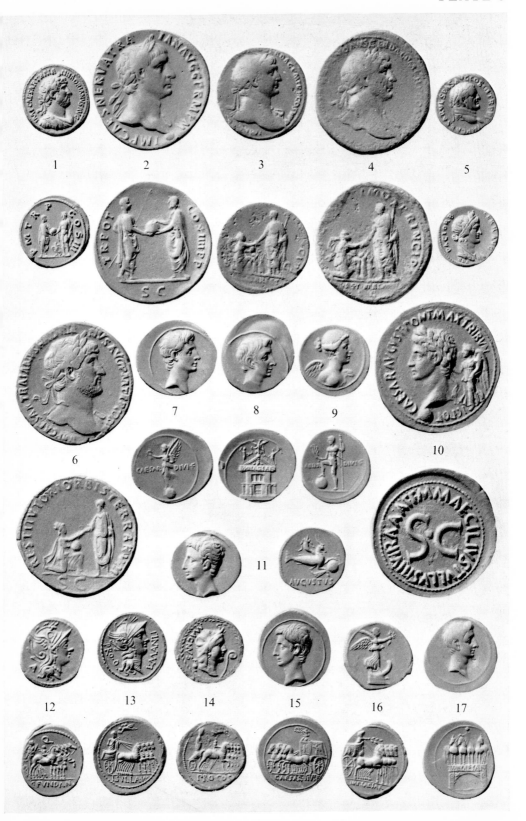

1

2

3

4

5

6

7

8

9

10

11

12

13

14

15

16

17

PLATE 6

PLATE 6

1. Denarius of Augustus, 19–15 B.C. (Mattingly 1. 68. 392), Oxford; *obv.*: head of Augustus, legend 'Caesari Augusto'; *rev.*: triumphal quadriga with an aquila in it and surmounted by four miniature horses, legend 'S.P.Q.R.'; p. 57.

2. Denarius of Augustus, 19–15 B.C. (Mattingly 1. 69. 397), Oxford; *obv.*: toga picta over tunica palmata between aquila and wreath, legend 'S.P.Q.R. Parenti Cons(ervatori) suo'; *rev.*: quadriga, in front four miniature horses, legend 'Caesari Augusto'; p. 57.

3. Denarius of Augustus, 19–15 B.C. (Mattingly 1. 67. 385), Oxford; *obv.*: head of Augustus, legend 'Caesari Augusto'; *rev.*: shrine with a triumphal chariot surmounted by four miniature horses, and an aquila in it, legend 'S.P.Q.R.'; p. 57.

4. Denarius of T. Carisius, c. 46 B.C. (Sydenham 164. 985), Oxford; *obv.*: bust of Victoria, legend 'S.C.'; *rev.*: Victoria with wreath in quadriga, legend 'T. Carisi'; p. 59.

5. Denarius of C. Considius Paetus, c. 46 B.C. (Sydenham 165. 994), London; *obv.*: bust of Minerva; *rev.*: Victoria in quadriga with palm and wreath, legend 'C. Considi'; p. 59.

6. Denarius of C. Vibius Pansa, c. 48 B.C. (Sydenham 159. 949), London; *obv.*: head of Libertas, legend 'Libertatis'; *rev.*: Roma seated on shields, crowned by Victoria, her foot on globe, legend 'C. Pansa C. f. C. n.; p. 61.

7. Sestertius of Hadrian, A.D. 119–38 (Mattingly 3. 433. 1310?), Oxford (original and cast); *obv.*: head of Hadrian, legend 'Hadrianus Augustus'; *rev.*: Hadrian on the Rostra of the temple of Divus Iulius addresses citizens; on the platform of the temple quadrigae right and left of the colonnade, legend 'cos. III, s.c.'; p. 59.

8. Denarius of L. Papius Celsus, c. 45 B.C. (Sydenham 161. 965), Oxford; *obv.*: laureate male head and trophy, legend 'TRIMPVS' (instead of TRIVMPVS); *rev.*: she-wolf placing brand on a brazier, an eagle, legend 'Celsus IIIvir, L. Papius'; pp. 64 f.

9. Denarius of Cn. Cornelius Blasio, c. 110 B.C. (Sydenham 75. 561e), Oxford; *obv.*: helmeted head of Mars with a star above it, legend 'Cn. Blasio Cn. f.'; *rev.*: Iuppiter between Iuno and Minerva, legend 'Roma'; p. 67.

10. Denarius of Caesar, 47 B.C. (Sydenham 168. 1013), Oxford; *obv.*: head of Venus; *rev.*: Aeneas with Anchises and the Palladium, legend 'Caesar'; p. 86.

11. Denarius of Caesar, 46 B.C. (Sydenham 168. 1014), Oxford; *obv.*: bust of Venus with Cupid; *rev.*: trophy with weapons, at foot a male and a female prisoner, legend 'Caesar'; p. 86.

12. Denarius of Caesar, 46 B.C. (Sydenham 168. 1015), London; *obv.*: bust of Venus with Cupid; her hair is ornamented with a star; on l. Cupid and lituus, on r. sceptre; *rev.*: trophy with weapons and prisoners, legend 'Caesar'; p. 86.

13. Aureus of Hadrian, A.D. 128–32 (Mattingly 3. 307. 529), London; *obv.*: bust of Hadrian, legend 'Hadrianus Augustus, p. p.'; *rev.*: Venus holding Victoria, with sceptre and shield, legend 'Veneri Genetrici'; p. 86.

14. Aureus of Marcus Aurelius, A.D. 161–76 (Mattingly 4. 407. 171), London; *obv.*: head of Faustina II, legend 'Faustina Augusta'; *rev.*: Venus holding Victoria, with shield set on captive, legend 'Venus Genetrix'; p. 86.

15. Aureus of Marcus Aurelius, A.D. 161–76 (Mattingly 4. 407. 174), London; *obv.*: bust of Faustina II, legend 'Faustina Augusta'; *rev.*: Venus holding Victoria, with shield on which she-wolf and twins, legend 'Venus Victrix'; p. 86.

16. Medallion of Hadrian, A.D. 119–38 (Gnecchi 3. 19), Paris; *obv.*: head of Hadrian, legend 'Hadrianus Augustus cos. III, p. p.'; *rev.*: Venus holding Victoria, with shield on which Aeneas with Anchises and Ascanius, legend 'Veneri Genetrici'; p. 86.

17. Denarius of C. Vibius Pansa, c. 48 B.C. (Sydenham 159. 949), Oxford; *obv.*: head of Libertas, legend 'Libertatis'; *rev.*: Roma seated on shields, crowned by Victoria, her foot on a globe, legend 'C. Pansa C. f. C. n.'; p. 93.

18. Denarius of C. Terentius Lucanus, c. 145 B.C. (Sydenham 49. 425), Oxford; *obv.*: helmeted head of 'Roma' crowned by Victoria; *rev.*: Dioscuri on horseback, legend 'C. Ter. Luc, Roma'; p. 93.

easily be removed. One might think that Oikoumene's Latin equivalent, *Orbis terrarum*, ought to be a male figure, but strangely enough it is not. It is a woman on the Gemma Augustea, wearing a mural crown and about to place a wreath on the head of Augustus,[1] which, however, could be ascribed to the fact that this is a Greek piece of art; one could add that the identification of the figure is not certain. The first certain evidence is found on coins of Vespasian, a turreted female bust with the legend 'Paci Orb(is) terr(arum) Aug(ustae)' (pl. 5. 5).[2] She next appears on coins kneeling in front of Hadrian, identified by the mural crown, the globe which she holds, and the legend 'Restitutori Orbis terrarum' (pl. 5. 6).[3] She is helped up by Hadrian and is, like Italia on the coins of Trajan, holding the globe and not handing it over: it is her symbol. This is the closest analogy to the Caesarian group, even if there the woman is an Amazon and has the globe at her side, not on her lap. If the analogy holds, she too is the Oikoumene rather than Roma. But she does not make Caesar a 'restitutor' of the Oikoumene but its master: she is kneeling in front of him in submission.[4]

(c) Dominus Terrarum

These conclusions are relevant for the interpretation of the statue of 46 to which we now return. The first question concerns its relation to the globe. On the relief Caesar is not standing on it but has it at his side. In fact there is no pre-Caesarian evidence of a figure, divine or human, Greek or Roman, mounted on the globe: the earliest dates from Augustus and concerns Victoria. He placed the Victoria, brought in 209 B.C. from Tarentum to Rome, in the Curia Iulia when it was completed in 29 B.C.[5] She stood there on the globe, as we learn from the similar

---

[1] Furtwängler, *Ant. Gemmen* 2. 257; *CAH Plates* 4. 156; J. H. Oliver, *Demokratia, the Gods and the Free World* (1960), 164, would identify her with Demokratia (turreted?).

[2] Mattingly 2. 91 ff.; 96; 98 f.; 105; pls. 15. 16; 16. 2 f.; 11 f.; 17. 3; 5; 18. 13.

[3] Mattingly 3. 418; pl. 79. 2; Strack, op. cit. 2. 61; Toynbee, op. cit. 24; pl. 1. 1–4; Hamberg, op. cit. 31; cf. the two turreted kneeling figures on either side of Venus on a relief of the Villa Medici in Rome, P. Veyne, *REL* 38 (1960), 306 ff.

[4] The coin of Murcus (above, p. 46), the closest analogy to the relief, is not against the identification of Oikoumene on the relief. She is not the figure on the coin, because there the globe is missing; she could be Roma, as suggested above, but she could equally be Asia or Syria or Apamea liberated by Murcus. It is possible that the model of the relief also influenced the Pompeians to use its symbolism for their own ends. A coin issued by M. Minatius Sabinus in Spain shows a kneeling turreted figure (a city in Spain?) who hands a shield over to Cn. Pompeius Magnus, the son (Sydenham 173; pl. 27. 1037a = our pl. 10. 9). It may mean surrender or an award of a *clupeus Virtutis* or a request to carry on the struggle for freedom.

[5] Dio 51. 22. 1 f.; cf. *RE* 8A. 2521. I would no longer accept the view (as I did ibid. 2507) that the Nike of Pergamum was already mounted on the globe (Bulle, *Myth. Lex.* 3. 349; Woelcke, *BJ* 120. 169 f.); cf. also T. Hölscher, *Victoria Romana* (1967), 6 ff.

representation of her on the apex of the pediment of the Curia (pl. 5. 7–8),[1] which also explains her great popularity in the imperial period. Then other winged deities like Eros, later also some without wings, were mounted on the globe;[2] human figures not at all, except Christ in late antiquity.[3] It is true that Augustus and his successors occasionally had their busts on a globe on coins (pl. 5. 10);[4] but this is symbolism and does not reflect an artistic composition: no full figure of an emperor is known in this posture. Consequently the statement of the first passage in Dio about Caesar to this effect[5] cannot be right. There remains the second passage: the οἰκουμένη is at his feet,[6] that is, either at his side or under his foot. There is comparable evidence for both, more for the second than for the first. We have met the globe under the foot of the *Genius populi Romani* and of Roma, and could find it under the foot of Iuppiter and other gods,[7] though not of men of the Republican period. But the emperors had it, beginning probably with Augustus (pl. 5. 9),[8] so that the innovation may belong to Caesar; if it was not this statue, it will have been another. The relief, however, supports the other alternative,[9] to which Dio's wording too is closer, but adds the personification. It is possible to assume that Oikoumene was kneeling in front of Caesar's statue on the Capitol also, asking for mercy; but this would be without any support from the tradition and would not in fact be necessary.[10] The globe at his feet was alone sufficient to convey the same idea.

It was a startling innovation but not a baseless improvisation. To assess its significance it is necessary to return once more to Pompey's triumph of 61 B.C.[11] The globe appeared there for the first time in a relevant

---

[1] Mattingly 1. 99; 101; 111 f.; pls. 14. 14; 18 f.; 15. 1; 17. 16 ff.

[2] Schlachter, op. cit. 87.

[3] Mosaic in the Cathedral of S. Gennaro at Naples, fifth century A.D., L'Orange, *Studies in the Iconography of Cosmic Kingship* 169, fig. 119.

[4] Mattingly 1. 41 ff.; pl. 20. 6 (Augustus). The evidence is collected by Mrs. Strong, *JRS* 6 (1916), 27 ff. (the most notable is the bust of Commodus in the Museo dei Conservatori at Rome, ibid., pl. 4).

[5] Dio 43. 14. 6 (p. 41. 6).

[6] Dio 43. 21. 2 (p. 41. 7).

[7] Schlachter, op. cit. 95 ff.

[8] The 'Neptune' on coins of *c.* 31–29 B.C. (Mattingly 1. 100; pl. 15. 5) could be Augustus (Schlachter, op. cit. 70): see his representation on the relief of Ravenna (*CAH Plates* 4. 160a; Ryberg, pl. 28. 42c). The Capricorn, his natal star, holding the globe, was represented on coins soon after 27 (Mattingly 1. 107; pl. 16. 9; cf. 56; 62; 80; pls. 5. 15; 7. 1–3; 11. 13); Victoria seated on the globe *c.* 11–6 B.C. (Mattingly 1. 80; 85; pls. 11. 12; 12. 16 f.; 20 f.); see our pl. 5. 17.

[9] Cf. also Schlachter, op. cit., pls. 1. 2; 15; 28; 2. 54; 56.

[10] A recumbent Oikoumene is assumed by Brendel, *Gnom.* 36 (1964), 503. 2.

[11] See above, p. 38.

context but probably not yet with the personification of the Oikoumene;[1] there were the personifications of the fourteen conquered provinces instead. And later these personifications surrounded his statue, which he set up at his theatre in 55; we shall see later that Cicero praised him as 'victor omnium gentium', which was a friendly exaggeration. The praise passed, the statue with its attendants no doubt remained but lost all its significance except that it served as a contrast to the Caesarian honour of 46.[2] The fourteen provinces were replaced by the globe: formerly Roma, that is, the Roman people, was its ruler;[3] now an individual Roman, Caesar.

It will be recalled that his anonymous biographer, on whom Suetonius ultimately depends, mentioned a prodigy at Caesar's birth which pointed to his future mastery of the world, probably also the later dreams at Gades and at the Rubicon which further confirmed his destiny.[4] The statue on the Capitol proved that the prodigy had come true in 46, or rather it inspired a biographer or a poet to make it appear as the fulfilment of a birth-omen and of later prodigies. Such adornments were required by the tradition of ancient biography. That Caesar in fact claimed mastery of the world is confirmed by Cicero and Lucan,[5] even though they were not impartial authors. It is further confirmed by the evidence about Augustus, who inherited the prodigy[6] and made it true again; he, however, wanted to return the title to the Roman people.[7] But Horace[8] and Ovid,[9] and also the inscription of the Ara Narbonensis (A.D. 11),[10] renewed the Caesarian claim.[11] Domitian

---

[1] Cf. the trophy mounted on a prow (Woelcke, *BJ* 120 (1911), pl. 8; frequent on coins) on the one hand, and the frequent Augustan antefix with Victoria holding the trophy and mounted on the globe (Woelcke, l.c. 161 f.; Schlachter, op. cit. 83; pl. 2. 30) on the other.

[2] Pliny 7. 99 (Pompey's conquests) : 'si quis e contrario simili modo velit percensere Caesaris res, qui maior illo apparuit, totum profecto terrarum orbem enumeret, quod infinitum esse conveniet.'

[3] Iustin. 43. 3. 2 : (Romulus) 'finitimisque populis armis subactis primo Italiae, mox orbis imperium quaesitum'; Livy 1. 16. 7 : 'ut mea Roma caput orbis terrarum sit' (Norden on Verg. *Aen.* 6. 782; *Thes.L.L.* 3. 426. 29) ; Cic. *leg. agr.* 2. 22 : 'vobis omnium gentium dominis'; *Planc.* 11 : 'huius principis populi et omnium gentium domini atque victoris'; *Phil.* 6. 12 ; cf. (also for the following notes) *Thes.L.L.* 5. 1922; F. Christ, *Die röm. Weltherrschaft in der ant. Dichtung* (1938), 115 ff.   [4] See above, p. 22.

[5] Cic. *off.* 3. 83 : 'rex populi Romani dominusque omnium gentium esse concupiverit'; Lucan 9. 20 : 'quem dominum mundi facerent civilia bella'; 8. 553 : 'domitor mundi'.

[6] Suet. *Aug.* 94. 5 : 'dominum terrarum orbi natum'.

[7] Suet. *Aug.* 40. 5 ; Verg. *Aen.* 1. 282; 6. 851.

[8] Hor. *c.* 1. 12. 57 : 'latum reget aequus orbem' (1. 1. 6 : 'terrarum dominos evehit ad deos').   [9] Ov. *Pont.* 2. 8. 26 (1. 9. 36) ; cf. 3. 3. 61.

[10] *ILS* 112 : 'orbi terrarum rectorem; . . . imperium orbis terrarum auspicatus est.'

[11] Augustus also refused to be called 'dominus' (Suet. *Aug.* 53. 1 ; Tiberius: Suet. *Tib.* 27) but was called, like a Hellenistic ruler, κύριος in the East: *Or. gr.* 606. 1 ; Caligula, *Acts* 25. 26 ; Claudius, *P.Oxy.* 37. 6 ; Wilcken, *Ostr.* 2. 1038. 6.

was explicitly called 'master of the world' by his flatterers,[1] and later emperors were often so styled on inscriptions.[2]

'Dominus terrarum' would have been a fitting term for the inscription of the statue; but it was inscribed instead that he was a ἡμίθεος.[3] This was even more startling: it lifted Caesar officially for the first time to the divine sphere. It is possible that it was an answer to Pompey's much advertised *cognomen* 'Magnus', which no doubt was also inscribed on the statue at his theatre: it is recorded that Caesar made a slighting reference to that *cognomen* on the battlefield of Zela.[4] But when he arrived at Rome he removed his own startling epithet from the inscription.

The original wording of the inscription cannot be recovered with certainty; it was unquestionably in Latin.[5] 'Hemitheus' is impossible because it is first found at Rome in late antiquity, in Servius and Martianus Capella;[6] so is 'semideus', because it seems to have been coined by Ovid.[7] 'Heros' would be suitable, as it was known to Cicero and Varro;[8] but, had it been used, Dio would not have replaced it with another Greek term. 'Deo Caesari', on the other hand, is possible: the Greeks often styled him θεός,[9] people in Italy called him 'Deus Caesar',[10] and even in Rome an official inscription, set up in the following year, had the wording 'Deo Invicto'.[11] Other possibilities are 'Divo Iulio', as he was called after his death,[12] or 'Genio Caesaris', which would be an attractive but highly hypothetical antecedent of the 'Numen Augusti'.[13] But these are mere guesses. What is not a guess is that the problem of Caesar's divinity was then raised for the first time in public; and it never disappeared again.

---

[1] Mart. 1. 4. 2; 7. 5. 5; 8. 2. 6; 8. 32. 6; Stat. *Silv.* 3. 4. 20; cf. *P. Oxy.* 1021 (Smallwood, *Documents* 47) Nero: ὁ δὲ τῆς οἰκουμένης . . . αὐτοκράτωρ; Sauter, *Der röm. Kaiserkult b. Martial u. Statius* (1934), 31 ff.; Christ, op. cit. 116.

[2] *IGR* 1. 1015 (Marcus Aurelius); *Syll.* 906A; *ILS* 751; 754 (Julian); cf. *CIL* 8. 19852; 13. 8895; Firmic. *Math.* 2. 30. 5.—Euseb. *pr. ev.* 9. 27. 22 (God): ὁ τῆς οἰκουμένης δεσπότης.

[3] The inscription of his statue at Karthaia on Keos stated that he was a θεός and σωτὴρ τῆς οἰκουμένης (*IG* 12. 5. 557); below, p. 166. 3.

[4] App. *BC* 2. 91. 384: ὦ μακάριε Πομπήιε, τοιούτοις ἄρα κατὰ Μιθριδάτην . . . πολεμῶν ἀνδράσι μέγας τε ἐνομίσθης καὶ Μέγας ἐπεκλήθης (popular criticism of the *cognomen* in 59: Cic. *Att.* 2. 19. 3). And yet a plan seems to have existed c. 55 that Caesar too should be called 'Magnus': Catull. 11. 10 (below, p. 181. 1).

[5] The Greek wording has been suggested by L. R. Taylor 65. 13; Taeger, *Charisma* 2. 80.

[6] Serv. *Ecl.* 4. 24; 9. 46; *Aen.* 8. 314; Mart. Cap. 2. 156; 160.

[7] Ov. *Ib.* 82; *Met.* 14. 673; *Her.* 4. 49.

[8] Cic. *ND* 2. 166; Varr. *Ant. rer. div.* 15, frg. 8 Ag. (Arnob. 3. 41); *Thes.L.L.* 6. 2661 ff.; cf. Verg. *Ecl.* 4. 16: 'deum vitam accipiet divisque videbit / permixtos heroas'.

[9] *Syll.* 760; *IG* 12. 5. 165b; 557; 12. 2. 35 (*IGR* 4. 33).

[10] *ILS* 6343; *CLE* 964 (below, p. 300. 7).   [11] Dio 43. 45. 3 (below, p. 175. 4).

[12] Cic. *Phil.* 2. 110; *ILS* 71 ff.; below, p. 391.

[13] Cf. *JRS* 39 (1949), 166 f. (in need of revision and elaboration); below, pp. 213. 7; 304. 3.

3. THE CHARIOT

The other votive offering was a chariot. But again Dio does not explain why it was made. The answer must be attempted with the help of other relevant evidence, in the first place with the help of some features of the history of the chariot.[1]

The use of the chariot was always restricted: gods and kings had it, warriors in battle, and athletes at the races. Of the gods, Zeus and Helios had it most frequently;[2] in Rome, Iuppiter[3] but also Sol,[4] Apollo, Mars, Minerva, and others. Iuppiter's first chariot was made at Veii, when the Capitoline temple was built, and placed on its pediment.[5] As to the royal privilege, there is evidence about the Persian kings,[6] the tyrants of Syracuse,[7] Philip, Alexander, and the Diadochs;[8] also about the kings of Rome.[9] In republican Rome its use was forbidden; the exceptions will be discussed in another context,[10] but the principal inheritor of the royal privilege, the triumphator, should at least be mentioned here. This category of chariots is otherwise not relevant for the present argument.

Chariots were frequent votive offerings, originally dedicated by those who were entitled to use them. Most of the Greek evidence concerns the victors in the races at Olympia.[11] But there are also instances of real victory. A chariot was dedicated to Athena on the Acropolis of Athens to commemorate a victory over the Boeotians and Chalcidians in 505 B.C. ;[12]

[1] Wahle–Unger, *Eberts Reallexikon* 14. 231 ff.; Wilke, ibid. 243 ff.; Wiesner, *Fahren u. Reiten* (*Der Alte Orient* 38. 2–4 (1939)), 24 ff.; 44 ff.; G. Hafner, *Viergespanne in Vorderansicht* (1938), 48 ff.; 82 ff.

[2] Zeus: Hom. *Il.* 8. 438; Eur. frg. 312 N.; Plat. *Phaedr.* 246 e; Athen. 5. 202 a.—Helios: Paus. 2. 3. 2; Pliny 34. 63; *Epigr. gr.* 618. 7 (Kaibel), etc.; C. C. Hense, *Poetische Personifikation in griech. Dichtungen* (1868), 150; often in art, e.g. *Myth. Lex.* 1. 2006 ff.

[3] e.g. Hor. *c.* 1. 12. 58; 1. 34. 8; below, pp. 67; 71.   [4] See below, pp. 71 f.

[5] Fest. 274 M. (342 L.); Plut. *Poplic.* 13; Pliny 28. 16; 35. 157; K. Gross, *Die Unterpfänder der röm. Herrschaft* (1935), 43 ff. A similar chariot was placed there (?) by the Ogulnii in 296 B.C. (below, p. 58. 1), and it later became customary to represent Iuppiter riding a chariot alone (Sydenham 48 f.; 52 ff.; 62; 68 f., etc.; Grueber, pls. 26. 18 f.; 27. 1; 7 f.; 28. 18; 92. 1 ff.; 9 f.; 15 ff., etc.; Paul. 98. M.= 87 L.: 'nummi quadrigati et bigati a figura caelaturae dicti'; Mattingly, *JRS* 35 (1945), 73 f.), or accompanied by Victoria (Sydenham 5 f.; 61; pl. 13. 64–7), or Victoria alone (Sydenham 33 f.; 54; 56; 67; 70; 115; 119; 121; pls. 18. 466; 21. 729; 748; on Caesarian specimens see below, p. 99. 4). These coins were issued in commemoration of victories and depended on a Greek composition, not of Zeus but of victors in racing contests, see R. Thomsen, *RE* 24. 691.

[6] Hdt. 7. 40; 140; Aesch. *Pers.* 84; 1000; Xen. *Cyrop.* 6. 1. 50 f.; *Anab.* 1. 7. 20; Sen. *de ira* 3. 21. 2.   [7] Livy 24. 5. 4; Pliny 7. 110; Theop. frg. 187; Diod. 14. 44. 8.

[8] Pliny 34. 78; Diog. Laert. 5. 5. 75; Kallixeinos, frg. 2.

[9] Dion. Hal. 5. 47. 3; Flor. 1. 5. 6.   [10] See below, p. 273.

[11] Paus. 6. 1. 6; 4. 10; 9. 4, etc.; W. W. Hyde, *Olympic Victor Monuments* (1921), 264 ff.; Hafner, op. cit. 82 ff.; G. B. Waywell, *BSA* 62 (1967), 19 ff.

[12] Hdt. 5. 77; Paus. 1. 28. 2; *Anth. Pal.* 6. 343; *P.Oxy.* 31, no. 2535; Meiggs–Lewis, *Greek Hist. Inscr.* 15; Judeich, *Topogr. Athens* 236 ff.; M. Treu, *Gnom.* 40 (1968), 350.

a Rhodian dedication at Delphi probably also followed a victory.[1]
Other chariots were set up in honour of gods and of kings, for instance
of Philip and Alexander with their statues in them;[2] of the 360 statues
which Demetrius of Phaleron allegedly had in Athens many were
in chariots;[3] chariots of Antigonus and Demetrius Poliorcetes, who
saved Athens from the tyranny of Demetrius of Phaleron, stood near
the statues of the tyrannicides.[4] Other rulers followed, also Roman
generals: Cicero protested against the plan of setting up a chariot in
Cilicia in his honour.[5] Others did not protest, and Caesar may have
been honoured in this way, for example after his victories at Pharsalus
and Zela.

The Roman evidence begins with Romulus, who dedicated a chariot to
Vulcanus after the conquest of Cameria and his second triumph, a
captured chariot; he added his own statue and that of Victoria crowning him, with an inscription recording his achievements.[6] This cannot
be an old dedication: Victoria was not known at Rome before the
Samnite Wars.[7] But it need not be very much later either; at any rate
the existence of these sculptures, whatever their date, cannot be doubted.
The dedication to Vulcanus in the Forum, instead of to Iuppiter on the
Capitol, is at first sight surprising.[8] But captured weapons were often
dedicated to Vulcanus and burnt in his honour.[9] It was a convenient
form of disposal and at the same time an honour for the god of fire.
Further, Romulus seems to have had a special relationship to Vulcanus:
he was said to have been the founder of his cult,[10] and Vulcanus appears
in his company on a Caesarian relief at Città Castellana (pl. 14),[11] if it is

[1] Syll. 441; 614. 35; Pomtow, RE Suppl. 4. 1413 f.; Hafner, op. cit. 98 f.
[2] Pliny 34. 78: (Euphranor) 'fecit et quadrigas bigasque ... item Alexandrum et Philip-
pum in quadrigis'; Hafner, op. cit. 94 f.; Lippold, Die griech. Plastik 260.
[3] Diog. Laert. 5. 5. 75.   [4] Diod. 20. 46. 2.
[5] Cic. Att. 5. 21. 7: 'ob haec beneficia ... nullos honores mihi nisi verborum decerni sino,
statuas, fana, τέθριππα prohibeo.' But his and his brother's statues stood in the Heraeum of
Samos (Dörner, Ath. Mitt. 68 (1953), 63), and at least his brother received a cult (Q. fr. 1. 1.
31: 'tuas virtutes consecratas et in deorum numero conlocatas vides'); below, p. 289.
[6] Plut. Rom. 24. 5: ἐν δὲ τοῖς ἄλλοις λαφύροις καὶ χαλκοῦν ἐκόμισε τέθριππον ἐκ Καμερίας·
τοῦτο δ' ἀνέστησεν ἐν τῷ ἱερῷ τοῦ Ἡφαίστου, ποιησάμενος ἑαυτὸν ὑπὸ Νίκης στεφανούμενον;
Dion. Hal. 2. 54. 2: ἐκ ταύτης τῆς στρατείας καὶ δεύτερον θρίαμβον κατήγαγε καὶ ἀπὸ τῶν
λαφύρων τέθριππον χαλκοῦν ἀνέθηκε τῷ Ἡφαίστῳ καὶ παρ' αὐτῷ τὴν ἰδίαν ἀνέστησε εἰκόνα
ἐπιγράψας Ἑλληνικοῖς γράμμασι τὰς ἑαυτοῦ πράξεις. According to another tradition (Solin.
1. 20), Romulus held his second triumph de Antemnatibus.
[7] Dio 8, frg. 36 (1, p. 105 B.); RE 8A. 2505.
[8] Romulus dedicated the spolia opima to Iuppiter Feretrius on the Capitol after killing
Acro, King of Caenina, on the occasion of his first triumph (ILS 64).
[9] Serv. Aen. 8. 562; Livy 1. 37. 5; Wissowa 230. 1.
[10] Plut. QR 47; Pliny 16. 236.
[11] Herbig, Röm. Mitt. 42 (1927), Beil. 15; CAH Plates 4. 90; Ryberg, pl. 7. 16; cf. RE 8A.
2504; 2515.

right to identify as Romulus the general who is sacrificing to Mars and is being crowned by Victoria. There are some common features but also differences between the dedications of Romulus and Caesar, to which we shall have to return. No other analogies are found until the time of the Second Punic War. Gilded chariots used to be set up on the Capitol at the end of the third and the beginning of the second century B.C.;[1] but why this was done and why it was not done again later is not known. Finally there were chariots with statues of triumphators kept in their houses[2] and also set up by permission of the Senate in public places.[3] It is important to note that, according to contemporary coins, Marius, Sulla, and **Pom**pey were granted this honour (pl. 5. 12–14).[4]

We must add the post-Caesarian evidence before returning to the dedication of 46 B.C. In 35 Octavian set up a chariot at the Rostra in honour of Antony when he received the news of the execution of Sex. Pompeius.[5] This leads to the inference that another chariot already stood in Octavian's honour, perhaps on the Capitol, commemorating the victories at Mylae and Naulochus: he was at that time resolved to grant Antony whatever was granted him. Far more was done after the victory at Actium, so much so that Augustus a few years later re-moved some 80 silver statues which represented him on foot, on horseback, and in chariots, melted them down, and made votive offerings from the money in the new temple of Apollo on the Palatine.[6] It was not the statues that Augustus objected to but the precious metal, which was due only to the gods.[7] There were and remained others which were made of bronze and marble. There were also empty chariots. Coins issued after the battle at Actium in the East show empty four-horse chariots with four miniature horses on the apex of the pediment of the chariot (pl. 5. 15), no doubt a copy of the arrangement on the temple of Iuppiter Capitolinus.[8] Another coin of the East shows Octavian in a

---

[1] Livy 29. 38. 8 (204 B.C.): 'quadrigae aureae eo anno in Capitolio positae ab aedilibus curulibus C. Livio et M. Servilio Gemino'; 35. 41. 10 (192 B.C.): 'de multa damnatorum quadrigae inauratae in Capitolio positae'; 38. 35. 4 (189 B.C.): 'eo anno . . . seiuges in Capitolio aurati a P. Cornelio positi: consulem dedisse inscriptum est.' On *quadrigae* in the temple of Fortuna at Praeneste, first century B.C., see H.-G. Kolbe, *Epigr. Stud.* 5 (1968), 169.

[2] Iuven. 7. 125: 'huius enim stat currus aeneus alti / quadriiuges in vestibulis'; 8. 3: 'stantis in curribus Aemilianos'; Mart. 2. 90. 6: 'atriaque inmodicis artat imaginibus'; Mommsen, *StR* 1. 445. 1; Vessberg, *Stud. z. Kunstgesch. d. röm. Rep.* (1941), 104.

[3] Pliny 34. 19: 'nostri currus nati in iis qui triumphavissent'; Prudent. *c. Symm.* 2. 556: 'frustra igitur currus summo miramur in arcu / quadriiugos stantesque duces in curribus altis / Fabricios, Curios, hinc Drusos, inde Camillos'; Mommsen, *StR* 1. 448.

[4] Sydenham 81; 123; 171; pls. 22. 756; 27. 1028; Grueber, pl. 32. 7.

[5] Dio 49. 18. 6.   [6] *Mon. Anc.* 24. 2.

[7] K. Scott, *TAPA* 62 (1931), 108 = *ARW* 35 (1938), 124 f.

[8] Mattingly 1. 97; pl. 14. 10 f.

quadriga holding a branch, which commemorates his Actian triumph (pl. 5. 16)[1] and recalls the similar representations of Marius, Sulla, and Pompey: this chariot must have existed at Rome in some public place. A third coin of the East shows the triumphal arch which was decreed for the Actian victory, surmounted by a *quadriga*, in which stands Augustus (pl. 5. 17).[2] Other chariots followed later. When he returned from the East in 19 B.C. he did not hold a triumph although it was expected.[3] A golden crown was given to him and a chariot which, however, he refused to mount.[4] Contemporary coins issued in Spain show the head of Augustus on the obverse, and a chariot, with a military standard surmounted by an eagle inside and with the four miniature horses on the reverse (pl. 6. 1);[5] or the same reverse without the standard, and on the obverse the *toga picta* and the *tunica palmata*, that is, the triumphal dress, between a standard and a wreath, and the legend 'S.P.Q.R. Parenti Conservatori suo' (pl. 6. 2).[6] Another coin shows a domed shrine containing the chariot without the horses but with the miniature horses and the standard (pl. 6. 3).[7] The conclusion is that these illustrations commemorate two related honours of 19 B.C. One was that Augustus was entitled to use a chariot in Rome wearing the triumphal dress, which he declined: we shall return later to this decree.[8] The other was to set up a chariot, probably on the Capitol in a shrine of its own, given by the Senate and the Roman people and inscribed with the name of Augustus and, *inter alia*, with the words 'Parenti Conservatori suo'. When Augustus finally accepted the title of 'pater patriae' in 2 B.C. this was also inscribed not only in his house and the Curia Iulia, but on a chariot which stood in the Forum Augustum.[9]

We have surveyed the chariots of the gods and kings; the chariots as votive offerings for victories, including those of Romulus and of the Second Punic War and after; the chariots with generals as triumphal monuments in the Republic and under Augustus; and the empty chariot of Augustus. To which category should Caesar's chariot be assigned?

---

[1] Mattingly 1. 101; pl. 15. 6 f. (*c.* 29 B.C.).

[2] Mattingly 1. 102; pl. 15. 8 (29–27 B.C.); also on issues of Rome in 16 B.C., ibid. 1. 14 f.; pl. 3. 4; cf. *RE* 8A. 2524.

[3] Prop. 3. 4. 13 ff.; Dio 54. 8. 3 wrongly states that he held an *ovatio*.

[4] *Chron. Min.* 2, p. 135 Mms. (below, p. 274. 6).

[5] Mattingly 1. 68 f.; pl. 8. 15–19; Alföldi, *Ant. Class.* 8 (1939), pl. 26. 2 (enlarged).

[6] Mattingly 1. 69 f.; pls. 8. 20; 9. 1–3.

[7] Mattingly 1. 67 f.; pl. 8. 10–14; cf. the *quadriga* with a palm-branch in it, 13 B.C. (ibid. 1. 20; pl. 3. 20), and the *quadriga* with elaborate decoration under Tiberius (1. 134; 136; 139; pls. 24. 10; 13; 25. 3).   [8] See below, p. 274.

[9] *Mon. Anc.* 35. 1: 'et in Foro Aug. sub quadrigis, quae mihi ex s.c. positae sunt'; cf. Mommsen, *Res gestae* 154.

A preliminary question is first to be settled, its location. Dio says that it was facing Iuppiter. This cannot have been the cult image which was in the *cella*, whereas the chariot stood in the open on the Area Capitolina; nor the statue in the chariot placed on the pediment by the two Ogulnii in 296 B.C.:[1] for the word 'facing' requires a statue on the ground. There were various statues on the Area. One, the statue of Iuppiter Imperator brought to Rome from Praeneste by the dictator T. Quinctius Cincinnatus in 380 B.C., must be excluded, because it stood on the podium of the temple between the *cellae* of Iuppiter and Minerva.[2] But another statue stood in the open so that it was visible even from the temple of Iuppiter Latiaris, the bronze colossus set up by Sp. Carvilius Maximus (*cos.* 293 and 272), with his own statue at its feet.[3] A further statue stood on a column at the time of the Catilinarian conspiracy.[4] There was also, as may be inferred from later imitations, a seated statue somewhere, with the globe at its feet;[5] and there will have been others. A safe choice clearly cannot be made. But one would give preference to the seated statue because of the globe, and even more to the colossus because Carvilius' statue was in its company, perhaps 'facing' it. A comparable dedication was made on the Area by Q. Fabius Maximus in 209, a colossus of Hercules together with his own equestrian statue.[6] These analogies, if they are analogies, do not necessarily imply that Caesar's statue and chariot had to be facing a statue of Iuppiter dedicated by Caesar himself; nothing is known of such a dedication, but it is not impossible.

Caesar's chariot was not his triumphal chariot, because it was set up before he triumphed, although no doubt in anticipation of his triumph. It was certainly not, like that of Romulus, a trophy. The two had, it is true, the statue and the inscription in common but probably nothing else; there was no Victoria with Caesar and no globe with Romulus;

---

[1] Livy 10. 23. 11: 'Cn. et Q. Ogulnii aediles curules . . . in Capitolio . . . Iovemque in culmine cum quadrigis . . . posuerunt'; Sydenham 187; pl. 29. 1149; Mattingly 2. 210; pl. 41. 4; relief of M. Aurelius, *CAH Plates* 5. 104a.

[2] Livy 6. 29. 8: 'signum Praeneste devectum Iovis Imperatoris in Capitolium tulit. (9) dedicatum est inter cellam Iovis ac Minervae'; *contra*, Cic. *Verr.* 2. 4. 129: 'Iovem autem Imperatorem . . . signum illud, quod ex Macedonia captum in Capitolio posuerat T. Flamininus' (194 B.C.); Cicero's evidence is accepted by Beloch, *RG* 356, Livy's by Vessberg, op. cit. 17 f.; both versions are accepted by Combès, *Imperator* 38 ff. Iuppiter Imperator is also found in Pliny *Paneg.* 6. 1; Degr. 192.

[3] Pliny 34. 43: 'fecit et Sp. Carvilius Iovem, qui est in Capitolio, victis Samnitibus . . . e pectoralibus eorum ocreisque et galeis. amplitudo tanta est, ut conspiciatur a Latiari Iove. e reliquiis limae suam statuam fecit, quae est ante pedes simulacri eius.'

[4] Dio 37. 9. 1; Cic. *Cat.* 3. 19 f.; Vessberg, op. cit. 68.

[5] Schlachter, op. cit. 93 f.; 110 f.; pl. 1. 28; Jones, *Catal. Mus. Cap.* pl. 66. 3 A 4; Cook, *Zeus* 1. 42 ff.; pl. 6 f.   [6] Plut. *Fab.* 22. 8.

one was in the Forum, the other on the Capitol. Next, the gilded chariots of the third–second century too are relevant, at least in so far as they were equally empty chariots; no more can be said because nothing else is known about them. Sulla, Pompey, and Augustus were, in contrast, riding in their chariots. Caesar was not riding in his even on coins: his place is taken by Victoria (pl. 6. 4–5).[1] The empty chariot is further confirmed by those set up in honour of Augustus after the victories at Mylae and Naulochus, after Actium, and after the return of the standards in 19 B.C. It is also supported by coins of Hadrian, which show the temple of Divus Iulius with two chariots in front of it (pl. 6. 7):[2] an obvious conjecture is that one of these was the chariot of 46 which was transferred from the Capitol to the temple after this was completed in 29 B.C.

The final question is whether the statue and the chariot were not only set up at the same time but also belonged together, as for example Romulus' statue stood at the side of his chariot. We have seen that what has been proposed so far does not stand up to scrutiny, viz. that Caesar stood in the chariot with the globe at his feet or with the chariot mounted on the globe. If it was a single composition, only one explanation seems possible: it represented the end of the triumph, in anticipation, Caesar having just descended from his chariot on the Area Capitolina, with the globe at his feet. There are some analogies for such a descent[3] but they cannot prove the case for Caesar; it remains only a possibility.

---

[1] Coins of T. Carisius and C. Considius Paetus, Sydenham 164 f.; pl. 26. 985; 994; below, p. 99.

[2] Mattingly 3. 433; the *quadrigae* on a few specimens only: Strack, op. cit. 2. 114; Stucchi, *I monumenti della parte meridionale del Foro Romano* (1958), 43; fig. 16; below, p. 400.

[3] Tiberius on the Gemma Augustea, *CAH Plates* 4. 156a (cf. Suet. *Tib.* 20); cf. F. E. Brown, *Excav. at Dura, Prelim. Rep.* 7/8 (1933/5), 197 (painting in the temple of Zeus Theos: Zeus standing in front of two white and two red horses and being crowned by two flying Victories). The closest analogy seems to be that of Demetrius Poliorcetes, who received an altar as θεὸς καταιβάτης in 307 in Athens on the spot where he descended from his chariot on arrival, Plut. *Demetr.* 10. 5; *Mor.* 338 a; Clem. Alex. *protr.* 4. 54. 6; Habicht 48 ff.; below, pp 289; 297.

V

THE TRIUMPHATOR

THE triumph was the privilege granted to victorious generals of entering Rome in a chariot and wearing a special costume.[1] When victory was won, the army was the first to acknowledge it by acclaiming the general as *imperator* on the battlefield. He then sent his report to the Senate, which, after considering it, decreed that thanksgivings (*supplicatio*) should be held. On arrival the general made his request for a triumph at a meeting of the Senate held outside the *pomerium*. He had to prove that he had fulfilled the conditions laid down for it, above all that the battle was fought under his auspices and his command, that is, at a time when he was in legitimate possession of power. His request was often rejected and sometimes the minor triumph (*ovatio*) was granted instead. If the triumph was granted, he drove into Rome in a chariot, wore the triumphal dress, was wreathed, his face painted red, and he held a sceptre. He was preceded by the prisoners, booty, and other exhibits and was followed by his army. The procession ended on the Capitol, where the triumphator made his thank-offering to Iuppiter. Simple in early days, it gradually became under Greek influence an elaborate pageantry.

Caesar did not celebrate a triumph before 46 B.C. He had been granted one in 60 B.C. for his victories in Spain, after his soldiers had acclaimed him *imperator*[2] and supplications too had been held at Rome.[3] But when he arrived he could not remain outside Rome as long as was necessary for the preparation of his triumph, because he wanted to be a candidate for the consulate of 59. For this he had to be in Rome in person unless he was granted dispensation by the Senate, for which he asked in vain. Facing the choice, he chose the prospect of the consulate and abandoned the triumph.[4] It was the year after Pompey's memorable

[1] Ehlers, *RE* 7A. 493 ff. with evidence and bibliography.

[2] Dio 44. 41. 3; App. *BC* 2. 8. 27; Plut. *Caes.* 12. 4.

[3] There is no explicit evidence about these supplications. But they were normally held after the acclamation and before the triumph, and are in addition implied by Cic. *Pis.* 59: 'quid est, Caesar, quod te supplicationes totiens iam decretae . . . delectent?' For the word 'totiens' must refer to at least three occasions, i.e. not only to 57 and 55 (below, p. 63) but also to 60 B.C.; cf. Nisbet, in his edition, p. 201.

[4] Dio 37. 54. 1 ff.; 44. 41. 3; App. l.c.; Plut. *Caes.* 13. 1 ff.; Mommsen, *StR* 1. 127. 2; Gelzer, *Caesar* 57.

third triumph in 61—a triumph which Caesar had not seen, because
he was in Spain. And even if it was wrong to say that he intentionally
provoked the war in Spain to gain glory and to emulate Pompey,[1] it
would be equally wrong to deny that he wanted to promote his career
by showing himself victorious in that war.

He had to wait fourteen years for the next opportunity. He had deserved a triumph by his achievements in Gaul: this was acknowledged
by imperatorial acclamations in Gaul and by supplications in Rome.[2]
But on his arrival from Gaul he could not ask for a triumph: the Civil
War had begun. Moreover, when he reached Rome, he again forsook his
right to the triumph by entering Rome in April 49. Not for the meeting
of the Senate, which was held outside the *pomerium*,[3] but for the opening
of the Aerarium by force (if it is correctly recorded that he took part
in it).[4] Even if he did not, he unquestionably spent eleven days in Rome
in December 49[5] and was in Rome again from October to December 47.
And yet he did not give up his claim to have deserved a triumph. He
issued coins after his return from Gaul which show trophies of Gallic
arms, prisoners with hands tied behind their backs,[6] the proper stuff
for a triumphal procession. C. Vibius Pansa (*cos.* 43) issued coins with
Roma and Victoria (pl. 6. 6):[7] another reference to the conquest of
Gaul. However, he had to go to war again. He won. But he did not
report his victory at Pharsalus and did not ask for a triumph;[8] although
some honours were decreed, no supplications were held either. But
when he reported his victories at the Nile and at Zela, victories over
foreign enemies, supplications were held,[9] and the triumph too must
have been decreed. It was done in his absence, which was unusual; it
must have included a special exemption because against the rules he

[1] Dio 37. 42. 1; cf. Cic. *Pis.* 59; Sall. *Cat.* 54. 4; Gelzer, *Caesar* 83. 120; Balsdon, *Julius
Caesar and Rome* (1967), 50 (the Spanish campaign as the turning-point in Caesar's life).

[2] See below, pp. 63 f.

[3] Dio 41. 15. 2.

[4] Caesar himself does not mention the opening of the Aerarium: he left for Spain after the
meeting of the Senate (*BC* 1. 32 f.) and still called himself 'Imperator' in April 49 (Cic.
Att. 10. 8B), wrongly if meanwhile he had entered the city. Cicero (*Att.* 10. 4. 8) does not
explicitly say that Caesar was in Rome, but App. *BC* 2. 41. 163 f.; Plut. *Caes.* 35. 6 ff.; Flor.
2. 13. 21, do; cf. O. E. Schmidt, *Der Briefwechsel des Cicero* 167; Drumann 3. 399; Gelzer,
Caesar 192. 82.

[5] Caes. *BC* 3. 2. 1.

[6] Sydenham 167 ff.; pl. 27. 1008; 1010 f.; 1016; above, p. 43; below, p. 377. 3.

[7] Sydenham 159; Grueber, pl. 50. 6; above, p. 43; below, pp. 93; 96.

[8] Dio 42. 18. 1; Plut. *Caes.* 56. 9. Pompey did not send reports about his successes to Rome
either, Dio 41. 52. 1; 3. On the principle see Val. Max. 2. 8. 7.

[9] Cic. *Phil.* 14. 23: 'num misit ullas . . . litteras de illa calamitosissima pugna Pharsalia,
num te de supplicatione voluit referre? profecto noluit. at misit postea de Alexandria, de
Pharnace: Pharsaliae vero pugnae ne triumphum quidem egit.'

had already been in Rome.[1] At any rate this decree must have existed before April 46 because, when the news of the victory at Thapsus was received, supplications were decreed again, and reference was made to the triumph already decreed.[2] Caesar landed in Italy in July 46 and was met by distinguished citizens, whom he reassured, as he reassured the Senate when he arrived at Rome, by promising clemency, the rule of law, and the like.[3]

This was the prelude. Already it presents a number of unusual features; we can only discuss the more significant of them, in the first place the supplications.

I. THE SUPPLICATIONS

The supplications of 46 were not the first to be decreed for Caesar; but now they became much more important and were also decreed for events other than victory, so that a brief survey of this institution is necessary.[4]

Supplications were prayers and sacrifices performed in an emergency such as war, pestilence, or famine, and were the exception to a religious rule. The rule was that at public festivals a limited number of people, priests, magistrates, and attendants, took part in the sacrifice at the altars in front of the temples. These were open for a short while but generally closed. At the supplications, on the other hand, all temples were opened, special images of the gods were exhibited on couches, and the whole community took part, the men wreathed and carrying a laurel branch, the women with loosened hair.[5] A similar ritual was performed at the end of the emergency, especially when victory was won, in gratitude, *gratulatio*, also, and more frequently, called *supplicatio*.[6] It is with this thanksgiving that we are concerned here. It was decreed by the Senate when the general's report about his victory was received and found to deserve it.[7] Although it was due to the gods, it was at the same time an honour for the general in whose name it was held.[8] And

---

[1] He may have already received dispensation in October 49 when he was made dictator (Caes. *BC* 2. 21. 5); for the rule see Cic. *fam.* 8. 6. 1: 'Appius . . . introierat in urbem triumphique postulationem abiecerat.'

[2] Dio 43. 14. 3: τεσσαράκοντά τε γὰρ ἡμέρας ἐπὶ τῇ νίκῃ αὐτοῦ θύειν ἔγνωσαν καὶ τὰ ἐπινίκια τὰ προεψηφισμένα . . . πέμψαι οἱ ἔδοσαν.

[3] Plut. *Cic.* 39. 4; Cic. *fam.* 14. 23 f.; *Att.* 11. 20. 2; 21. 2.

[4] Wissowa 423 ff. and *RE* 4A. 942 ff.; A. K. Lake [Michels], *Quantulacumque, Studies pres. to K. Lake* (1937), 243 ff.; L. Halkin, *La supplication d'action de graces chez les Romains* (1953), 9 ff.; Latte 245.   [5] Livy 3. 7. 7 f.; 40. 37. 3; 43. 13. 8.

[6] Livy 45. 2. 6 ff.; 5. 23. 3; 27. 51. 7 ff.

[7] Cic. *fam.* 15. 13. 3; *Att.* 7. 2. 6; *Phil.* 14. 29; 37.

[8] Livy 34. 42. 1; Cic. *Cat.* 3. 15; *Phil.* 14. 29.

if the achievement deserved more, the *supplicatio* lasted more than one day.

In the first century B.C. it was acknowledged that the thanksgiving was an honour much desired by the general and that the number of days was increased against precedent and without any regard for the requirements of the ritual.[1] The change came suddenly in 63 B.C., when ten days of supplications were decreed for Pompey's victory over Mithridates, to which another twelve days were added in the following year. The decree was proposed by Cicero, the consul, and he bore the principal responsibility for the change.[2] How exceptional the decision was may be assessed by the fact that soon afterwards supplications were also decreed for Cicero, but only for one day. Yet Cicero's supplication was in itself a novelty, because it was for the suppression of the Catilinarian conspiracy, not for a victory over an enemy: he never ceased to refer to this distinction.[3]

Caesar received fifteen days of supplications for his successes in Gaul in 57:[4] the proposal was made again by Cicero, and the number of days was based on the precedent of Pompey.[5] And whereas Pompey received supplications twice for successes in the war against Mithridates, Caesar received them three times for Gaul: the second time in 55 for twenty days,[6] the third time in 52 for another twenty days.[7] These decrees were made after long debates in the Senate and against the strong opposition first of Cato, later also of Pompey.[8] Bibulus

---

[1] Cic. *prov. cons.* 26: 'supplicationem quindecim dierum decrevi sententia mea. rei publicae satis erat tot dierum quot C. Mario; dis immortalibus non erat exigua eadem gratulatio quae ex maximis bellis; ergo ille cumulus dierum hominis est dignitati tributus. (27) ... ergo in illa supplicatione quam ego decrevi res ipsa tributa est dis immortalibus et maiorum institutis et utilitati rei publicae, sed dignitas verborum, honos et novitas et numerus dierum Caesaris ipsius laudi gloriaeque concessus est.'

[2] Cic. *prov. cons.* 27: 'ego, quo consule referente primum decem dierum est supplicatio decreta Cn. Pompeio Mithridate interfecto et confecto Mithridatico bello et cuius sententia primum duplicata est supplicatio consularis—mihi enim estis adsensi, cum eiusdem Pompei litteris recitatis, confectis omnibus maritimis terrestribusque bellis supplicationem dierum duodecim (*codd.*: 'decem' Manutius, Klotz) decrevistis ...'; Drumann 4. 482.

[3] Cic. *Cat.* 3. 15: 'supplicatio dis inmortalibus pro singulari eorum merito meo nomine decreta est, quod mihi primum post hanc urbem conditam togato contigit'; *Pis.* 6: 'mihi togato senatus, non ut multis bene gesta, sed ut nemini conservata re publica singulari genere supplicationis deorum immortalium templa patefecit'; *Phil.* 2. 13: 'qui honos post conditam hanc urbem habitus est togato ante me nemini'; Nicolet, *REL* 38 (1960), 236 ff. (on the influence of his terminology on Livy, esp. 4. 10. 8).

[4] Caes. *BG* 2. 35. 4; Dio 39. 5. 1; Plut. *Caes.* 21. 1.

[5] Cic. *prov. cons.* 26 f.

[6] Caes. *BG* 4. 38; Dio 39. 53. 2; Plut. *Caes.* 22. 4; cf. Cic. *Pis.* 59 (above, p. 60. 3).

[7] Caes. *BG* 7. 90. 8; Dio 40. 50. 4 (who wrongly speaks of 60 days).

[8] Cato suggested in the debate of 55 that Caesar should be handed over to the Germans for punishment because of breach of faith (see below, p. 245); Halkin, op. cit. 44 f.; Gelzer, *Caesar* 118 f.

followed in 50 with another twenty days for his successes in the East:[1] this was Cato's work and aimed against Caesar. Such generosity was not shown towards Cicero, who got his brief, no doubt one-day, supplications for his victories in Cilicia after a long struggle.[2] Caesar did not ask for supplications after his victory at Pharsalus, but received them —their length is unknown—after the victories at the Nile and at Zela. He was awarded forty days after the victory at Thapsus in 46[3] and fifty days after the victory at Munda in 45.[4] This inflation of supplications was continued after Caesar's death.[5] They were held after the victory at Philippi, for instance, for almost a whole year,[6] and Augustus recorded that they were decreed for him fifty-five times and lasted for 890 days.[7] By then the supplications had become almost a formality, but this was not yet the case under Caesar. His three supplications in Gaul lasting 55 days, and the four in the last two years of his life lasting for more than a hundred days, each established a record for its time. Together with the other honours they enhanced his status in Rome.

They also prepared the ground for a more ambitious scheme. It was decreed in the following year, 45, that, whenever a victory was reported, supplications should be held in Caesar's name on a special day, even if he had no share in that victory.[8] We shall see later that this was part of a new doctrine, which proclaimed that all victories were Caesar's victories; also that the decree was made valid even after Caesar's death, apparently in order to preserve continuity and to prevent the factions in the Civil War from asserting themselves at the expense of the State. It was renewed for Augustus soon after the victory at Actium.[9]

2. TRIUMPHUS

We now turn to the triumph and to its special features in 46 B.C. It will be convenient to begin with a *denarius*, issued by L. Papius Celsus

---

[1] Cic. *Att.* 7. 2. 6 f.; Meyer, *Caesars Monarchie* 262. 3; Halkin, op. cit. 47 f.

[2] Cic. *fam.* 15. 10; 15. 13. 3; 3. 9. 4; 15. 4. 11–16; 8. 11. 1; 2. 15. 1; *Att.* 7. 1. 7 f.; Halkin, op. cit. 48 ff.; Meyer, op. cit. 221.

[3] See above, p. 62. 2. Soon afterwards P. Sulpicius Rufus too received supplications (Cic. *fam.* 13. 77. 1), no doubt just for a single day, and in the following year (45) P. Vatinius (Cic. *fam.* 5. 9. 1; 10a. 3; 10b. 11). [4] Dio 43. 42. 2.

[5] In 44 for Lepidus because he had restored the peace with Sex. Pompeius (Cic. *Phil.* 3. 23); in 43 fifty days for Hirtius, Pansa, and Octavian for their victory over Antony (Cic. *Phil.* 14. 29; 37), a few days later another fifty days for D. Iunius Brutus for his share in that victory (Cic. *fam.* 11. 18. 3; App. *BC* 3. 74. 302; Dio 46. 39. 3 speaks of 60 days); in November 43 for Octavian, Antony, and Lepidus for the creation of the triumvirate (Dio 47. 2. 2). [6] Dio 48. 3. 2. [7] *Mon. Anc.* 4. 2.

[8] Dio 43. 44. 6 (below, p. 107. 8).

[9] Dio 57. 15. 5.

before or after the triumph (pl. 6. 8), showing the laureate head of 'Triumpus' with a trophy at his side on the obverse, and a scene on the reverse which refers to the Lanuvian origin of the otherwise unknown moneyer and is therefore irrelevant here.[1] It is an unexpected piece of evidence, because this is the first and last appearance of the personification on a coin; so we need an explanation of its origin and its relevance to Caesar's triumph.

The origin of the term 'triumphus' need not detain us here. Even if it depends on Θρίαμβος, an epithet of Dionysus,[2] this relationship is not helpful because the early triumph had nothing to do with Dionysus. When the word first appeared in Rome in the fivefold exclamation 'triumpe' of the Carmen Arvale,[3] it did not refer to a triumph or, again, to Dionysus or his Roman 'equivalent', Liber pater, and it is not certain whether it could be considered as the vocative of the personification. The conclusion is that this 'triumpe' had lost its Dionysiac connotation when it reached Rome, and became a ritual cry, also used at the celebration of victories; further, that the noun 'triumphus' and the personification Triumphus came into being in consequence of this cry, just as the wedding-cry, ὑμήν, led to the creation of the god Hymenaeus[4] or in Rome 'talassio' to that of the youth Talassius.[5]

The personification must have existed at an early date. One may dismiss the evidence of the prodigies of 218 and 214 B.C., when a newborn, or yet unborn, child shouted 'Triumphus' or 'io Triumphe',[6] as anachronistic, because the source is Livy, who in turn does not seem to depend here on contemporary recording. But the exclamation of the 'victorious' slave in Plautus' *Pseudolus* (first performed in 191 B.C.), 'Triumphe', is a certain and important instance,[7] and therefore Livy may be right in reporting that in the triumph of Aemilius Paullus in 167 B.C. the soldiers invoked Triumphus.[8] Consequently Varro's assertion that 'io Triumphe' was a permanent feature of the triumphal

---

[1] Sydenham 161; pl. 26. 965. Another coin of this moneyer shows the bust of Victoria (ibid.). His colleague, C. Antius Restio, reproduced Hercules, his ancestor, with a trophy, ibid. 162; pl. 26. 970 f.

[2] For the evidence and discussion see Ehlers, l.c. 493 f.; Walde–Hofmann, s.v.

[3] *ILS* 5039 (Degr. 4); Norden, *Aus altröm. Priesterbüchern* 228.

[4] e.g. Theocr. 18. 58; Catull. 61; Maas, *Philol.* 66 (1907), 590 ff.; id. *RE* 9. 131.—Cf. ἰά-"Ιακχος, Nilsson, *Opuscula* 3. 237. 18.

[5] Catull. 61. 134; Livy 1. 9. 12; Plut. *QR* 31; *Rom.* 15. 2 f. (Iuba, *FGrHist.* 275 F 90); Serv. *Aen.* 1. 651; Marbach and Münzer, *RE* 4A. 2064 f.; Ribezzo, *Studi e materiali* 23 (1951/2), 44 ff.

[6] Livy 21. 62. 2 (Val. Max. 1. 6. 5); 24. 10. 10.

[7] Plaut. *Pseud.* 1051: 'ite hac, Triumphe, ad cantharum recta via.'

[8] Livy 45. 38. 12: (milites) 'laureati . . . Triumphum nomine cient.'

procession[1] is valid not only for the first century but even earlier. There is no Caesarian evidence for the personification besides the coin; in Augustan poetry Triumphus became a popular figure. Horace appealed to him after the Actian victory not to delay the triumph;[2] he turned to him again *c.* 15 B.C., at the time of Augustus' victory in Gaul.[3] The god was no doubt often addressed at that time,[4] especially in poems inscribed 'Triumphus'.[5] A painting of Apelles, with which Augustus decorated the Forum Augustum, showing Alexander on a chariot and a prisoner with his hands tied behind his back, was now called 'Triumphus and Bellum'[6] and inspired the prophecy in the first book of the *Aeneid* about Augustus ending all wars;[7] under Claudius the head of Alexander was replaced by that of Augustus. Here Triumphus need not be the personification; but if it is, it is due to reinterpretation of the Augustan age, providing it with the individual features of Alexander and Augustus. How such speculations were anticipated under Caesar, it is impossible to say. But the coin of L. Papius Celsus and the Augustan evidence lead to the suggestion that there was some poetry about Caesar's campaigns before and after the triumph in which the personification already had such a role.

An analysis of the term 'triumphus', then, does not help: its derivation from the Greek Θρίαμβος would lead to the conclusion that the triumph was the procession of a new Dionysus, which it certainly was not; nor does its probably correct derivation from the cry 'triumpe' assist us. The decisive question therefore is: whom else could the triumphator impersonate? He did not appear like his normal self, a soldier or a

---

[1] Varr. *LL* 6. 68: 'cum imperatore milites redeuntes clamitant per urbem in Capitolium eunti "io Triumphe".'

[2] Hor. *epod.* 9. 21: 'io Triumphe, tu moraris aureos / currus et intactas boves? / io Triumphe, nec Iugurthino parem / bello reportasti ducem.'

[3] Hor. *c.* 4. 2. 49: 'teque, dum procedis, io Triumphe, / non semel dicemus, io Triumphe, / civitas omnis.'

[4] Tib. 2. 5. 118; Ov. *am.* 1. 2. 25: 'populo clamante Triumphum'; 34; *Met.* 1. 560: 'cum laeta Triumphum / vox canet'; *Trist.* 4. 2. 52.

[5] Ovid wrote such a poem for the Pannonian triumph of Tiberius, A.D. 12, *Pont.* 3. 4. 3: 'utque suo faveas mandat, Rufine, Triumpho'.

[6] Pliny 35. 27: 'Divus Augustus in Foro suo celeberrima in parte posuit tabulas duas, quae Belli faciem pictam habent et Triumphum, item Castores et Victoriam'; 35. 93: (Apelles) 'Romae Castorem et Pollucem cum Victoria et Alexandro Magno, item Belli imaginem restrictis ad terga manibus, Alexandro in curru triumphante. (94) quas utrasque tabulas Divus Augustus in Fori sui celeberrimis partibus dicaverat...; Divus Claudius pluris existimavit utrisque excisa Alexandri facie Divi Augusti imagines addere'; Serv. Dan. *Aen.* 1. 294; cf. *RE* 8A. 2526 f.; 2539 f.; Wissowa, *Myth. Lex.* 1. 777 f.; Matz, *Festschr. f. Weickert* (1955), 52; below, p. 375.

[7] Verg. *Aen.* 1. 294: 'claudentur Belli portae; Furor impius intus / saeva sedens super arma et centum vinctus aenis / post tergum nodis fremet horridus ore cruento.'

civilian, but wore a special dress and had special equipment.[1] The tradition provides us with two different answers, and both have found their modern supporters.

One is that the triumphator represented Iuppiter: he wore Iuppiter's dress, which was kept in the Capitoline temple: a purple cloak first, an embroidered one, the *toga picta*, later, and the *tunica palmata* under it; he also had the attributes of Iuppiter, the sceptre and the golden crown,[2] and his face was painted red as was the image of the Capitoline Iuppiter;[3] his chariot too was a symbol of divinity, because as a rule no mortal was allowed to use one inside Rome.[4] We have to supplement this evidence with what is known in this respect about Iuppiter. The statue in the *cella*, as well as that in the pediment, was in fact painted red,[5] and it was the duty of the censors to put the renewal of this paint periodically out to contract.[6] Both statues probably wore the triumphal dress.[7] That in the *cella* was a standing figure holding a sceptre and the thunderbolt, as can be seen on the coins of Cn. Cornelius Blasio issued *c.* 110 B.C. (pl. 6. 9).[8] This statue was destroyed by the fire of 83 B.C.,[9] and the new temple had a sitting Iuppiter as the cult image.[10] But there must have been another standing figure as well, because the seated figure was not suitable for triumphal dress. It is also relevant that two other statues seem to have been modelled on such a standing figure, the ivory statues of Scipio and Caesar which were kept in the same *cella* and, dressed in the triumphal costume, were carried in the procession of the gods in the *pompa circensis*.[11] The standing figure of Iuppiter too, similarly dressed, will have been carried in that procession. This

---

[1] Mommsen, *StR* 1. 411 f.; Marquardt, *Staatsverw.* 2. 586; Ehlers, *RE* 7A. 504 f.

[2] Livy 10. 7. 10: 'Iovis Optimi Maximi ornatu decoratus'; Iuven. 10. 38: 'in tunica Iovis'; Serv. *Ecl.* 10. 27: 'omnia Iovis insignia'; SHA *Alex. Sev.* 40. 8: 'pictam togam . . . de Iovis templo sumptam'; SHA *Prob.* 7. 4 f.: 'Capitolina palmata'; Suet. *Aug.* 94. 6 (below, p. 69. 2); see also the following note.

[3] Serv. *Ecl.* 10. 27: 'aether autem est Iuppiter. unde etiam triumphantes, qui habent omnia Iovis insignia, sceptrum, palmatam, . . . faciem quoque de rubrica inlinunt instar coloris aetherii'; Serv. Dan. *Ecl.* 6. 22: 'quod robeus color deorum sit: unde et triumphantes facie miniata, et in Capitolio Iuppiter in quadrigis miniatus'; Pliny 35. 157; 33. 111 f. (below, p. 73. 4); Plut. *QR* 98. 287 d.

[4] See p. 273.

[5] Pliny 35. 157: 'Vulcam Veis accitum, cui locaret Tarquinius Priscus Iovis effigiem in Capitolio dicandam; fictilem eum fuisse et ideo miniari solitum; fictiles in fastigio templi eius quadrigas'; Cic. *fam.* 9. 16. 8: 'polypum miniati Iovis similem' (= coloured red); above, p. 54. 5.

[6] Pliny 33. 112; Plut. *QR* 98. 287 d.

[7] For the pediment only the crown is attested, Plaut. *Tri.* 83 ff.; *Men.* 941.

[8] Sydenham 75; pl. 19. 561e; cf. Ov. *F.* 1. 201 f.

[9] Plut. *Is.* 71.

[10] Dio 54. 25. 4; Eckhel, *Doctrina Numorum* 6. 327 f.; Platner–Ashby 299 f.; Mattingly 2, p. lii; A. Zadoks-Jitta, *JRS* 28 (1938), 50 ff.   [11] See below, p. 185.

is additional evidence for the first alternative because of the connection between triumph and *pompa circensis*.[1]

According to the other view, all the attributes mentioned above belonged to the equipment of the kings of Rome, who had received it from Etruria;[2] the Etruscan kings in turn would have borrowed it from their 'Iuppiter'. If so, the triumphator represented the king for that single day,[3] that is, he was a man, not a god. In fact the choice is not as simple as these alternatives would suggest.[4] There are some difficult points,[5] and the greatest difficulty is caused by one of the Caesarian privileges. When the news of the victory at Thapsus was received, it was decided that Caesar should use a chariot with white horses in his triumph.[6] The horses used were normally dark, but there were a few real or alleged exceptions, the most famous being that of Camillus. The chariot with white horses also belonged to Iuppiter, and the question arises why Caesar was to share its use with the heroes of the legendary past.

3. THE WHITE HORSES

We shall find that the chariot with white horses was first used by gods and kings in Greece and Persia; but it will be convenient to begin with the Western tradition. When Aeneas reached Italy, he saw four white horses grazing on the pasture, an omen of the coming wars and of their successful end,[7] but also probably of his right to a chariot. Later

[1] Mommsen, *Röm. Forsch.* 2. 42 ff.; Wissowa 127.

[2] Dion. Hal. 3. 61. 1; 62. 2; 5. 47. 3; Flor. 1. 5. 6.

[3] The Romans used to send sceptre, crown, *toga picta*, and *tunica palmata* as presents to foreign kings whom they recognized, to Porsenna (Dion. Hal. 5. 35. 1), Masinissa (Livy 30. 15. 11), Ariovistus (Caes. *BG* 1. 43. 4), Ptolemy of Mauretania (Tac. *A.* 4. 26. 4); cf. Mommsen, *StR* 3. 592. 3.

[4] On the controversy see Deubner, *Herm.* 69 (1934), 316 ff., who rejected the traditional identification of the triumphator with Iuppiter, as did before him Reid, *JRS* 6 (1916), 177 ff., and Warde Fowler, *CR* 30 (1916), 153 ff.; most scholars still accept the other view, e.g. Wallisch, *Philol.* 99 (1955), 254 ff.; Latte 152. 3.

[5] The red paint was given great significance in the controversy (see the various, not always convincing, explanations listed by Deubner, l.c. 321; further E. Wunderlich, *Bedeutung d. roten Farbe* (1925), 63; 85; Wagenvoort, *Roman Dynamism* 166 f.; Bömer, *Gnom.* 21 (1949), 358; id. *RE* 21. 1979 f.). No sides need be taken because the fact is here more important than its explanation. But it must be added that the red paint was not an exclusive characteristic of Zeus-Iuppiter. It is also recorded for the statue of Artemis (?Paus. 2. 2. 6), of Pan (Verg. *Ecl.* 10. 26), of Priapus (Tib. 1. 1. 17; *Priap.* 1. 5; Ov. *F.* 1. 400; 415; 6. 333), and above all of Dionysus (Paus. 2. 2. 6; 7. 26. 11; 8. 39. 6). In Italy his worshippers too painted their faces on his festivals, Tib. 2. 1. 55: 'agricola et minio subfusus, Bacche, rubenti'; cf. Verg. *Georg.* 2. 385 ff.

[6] Dio 43. 14. 3: τὰ ἐπινίκια τὰ προεψηφισμένα ἐπί τε λευκῶν ἵππων . . . πέμψαι οἱ ἔδοσαν.

[7] Verg. *Aen.* 3. 537: 'quattuor hic, primum omen, equos in gramine vidi / tondentis campum late, candore nivali.'

King Latinus rode such a chariot and wore a crown of twelve rays, the attribute of his grandfather, Sol.[1] The source in both cases is Vergil, but this is valuable antiquarian evidence of a kind which was not invented by Vergil. It is supported by the dream of Octavius, Augustus' father: he saw that his son wore a radiate crown and his chariot was drawn by twelve, not four, white horses; he had the dress and the attributes of Iuppiter, sceptre and thunderbolt.[2] This is late again, in so far as it comes from Suetonius, but is also certainly not a late invention. The twelve horses correspond to the twelve rays in the crown of Latinus: that much is solar symbolism peculiar to Latinus because of his descent from Sol. Otherwise, as king, he would have appeared like Aeneas and the Augustus of the dream with the attributes of Iuppiter. All this was, it must be repeated, not mere poetical fancy: it will be recalled that Aeneas was worshipped as Iuppiter Indiges at Lavinium, and Latinus as Iuppiter Latiaris at Alba Longa.[3] At least Iuppiter Latiaris will have been represented in a chariot of white horses in the pediment of his temple on the Alban Mount. About the date of this evidence nothing can be said at first except that it is pre-Vergilian; but one feels that it is of greater antiquity, and two odd passages lend strong support to this feeling.

Plautus speaks of a missed opportunity in the present which cannot be attained later, even with a chariot of white horses;[4] Horace of someone who with his white horses would surpass the greatest slanderers of his age in their art.[5] Plautus' Greek original, a play of the otherwise unknown Demophilus, obviously meant that not even a god could recover such a lost chance. Plautus' audience certainly understood the symbolism, because some of their temples were decorated with such chariots of gods. The phrase in Horace is probably a parodistic quotation from earlier poetry, presumably from Ennius.[6] In Horace it indicates superiority, the king of slanderers; in Ennius it will have referred

---

[1] Verg. Aen. 12. 161: 'Latinus / quadriiugo vehitur curru, cui tempora circum / aurati bis sex radii fulgentia cingunt, / Solis avi specimen, bigis it Turnus in albis' (12. 84); Galinsky, AJP 90 (1969), 454 ff. (with bibliography); cf. PGM 4. 750 (1, p. 98 Pr.): λαβὼν κάνθαρον ἡλιακὸν τὸν τὰς ιβ´ ἀκτῖνας ἔχοντα; 1109 (p. 110): τὸν δὲ θεὸν ὄψῃ κιβωρίου καθήμενον, ἀκτινωτόν ... βασταζόμενον ὑπὸ β´ ἀγγέλων ταῖς χερσὶν καὶ, κύκλῳ αὐτῶν ἀκτῖνας ιβ´; Dolger, Ant. u. Christ. 6 (1940/50), 39 ff.; 49; below, p. 383. 5.

[2] Suet. Aug. 94. 6: 'nocte videre visus est filium mortali specie ampliorem, cum fulmine et sceptro exuviisque Iovis Optimi Maximi ac radiata corona, super laureatum currum, bis senis equis candore eximio trahentibus.'   [3] See above, p. 10.

[4] Plaut. Asin. 278: 'nam si occasioni huic tempus sese supterduxerit, / numquam edepol quadrigis albis indipiscet postea'; cf. Amph. 450: 'quadrigas si nunc inscendas Iovis / atque hinc fugias, ita vix poteris ecfugere infortunium.'

[5] Hor. sat. 1. 7. 8: 'Sisennas, Barros ut equis praecurreret albis.'

[6] This was suggested by Heinze ad loc.

to the procession of a king of divine descent, Latinus or Romulus, rather than an insolent one like Tullus Hostilius. At any rate, the passage in Plautus proves that the symbolism of white horses was known in Rome about 200 B.C.

Aeneas and Latinus did not hold triumphs, but Romulus did and was the first to use the chariot with white horses. The evidence comes from Propertius, is brief and uninstructive.[1] It conflicts with the other evidence, according to which the triumphal chariot, like the whole ritual of the triumph, was introduced from Etruria by Tarquinius Priscus.[2] It is impossible to say how old the tradition about Romulus is, except that it is certainly not older than that about Camillus to which we shall turn presently. No other early hero was granted this privilege until A. Postumius Tubertus, who as dictator of 431 B.C. held a triumph over the Aequi and Volsci.[3] The triumph is well attested by the Fasti, but his white horses are mentioned only by Ovid and ignored in the long narrative of Livy and elsewhere.[4] It does not go well with another incident, namely that, shortly before, he executed his son because of insubordination in the decisive battle at the Algidus.[5] It is impossible to say why Postumius was singled out for this honour. It was in the same battle that Camillus, the next hero, first fought and proved his valour,[6] and it is therefore possible that the case of Postumius was created to serve as precedent for Camillus. The next instances, of Aemilius Paullus and Marius, can be dismissed because the source is the poet Claudian:[7] they were clearly added to the list in the imperial period.

The post-Caesarian instances are somewhat puzzling. It is not known whether Caesar used the white horses again in his triumph over Spain in 45. They are nowhere recorded for Augustus' Actian triumph of 29 B.C. The probability is that he did not use them; the historians and poets would not have remained silent about such a detail. Had he used them, one could better understand other contemporary evidence. Messalla held a triumph with white horses in 27 B.C. according to Tibullus,[8] and Ovid predicted them for Tiberius for his triumph over

---

[1] Prop. 4. 1. 32: 'quattuor hinc albos Romulus egit equos.'   [2] See above, p. 68.

[3] Ov. F. 6. 723: 'unde suburbano clarus, Tuberte, triumpho, / vectus es in niveis, Postume, victor equis.'   [4] Livy 4. 26 ff.; 29. 4.   [5] Livy 4. 29. 5.

[6] Plut. Cam. 2. 1 f. It is worth adding that in that year (431) C. (or Cn.) Iulius Mento (who dedicated the temple of Apollo, above, p. 12) was one of the consuls and L. Iulius Iullus the master of horse, that is, two members of the Gens Iulia.

[7] Claudian. 26. 126 f.

[8] Tib. 1. 7. 7: 'at te victrices lauros, Messalla, gerentem / portabat nitidis currus eburnus equis.'

Germany[1] and for C. Caesar, Augustus' grandson, when he left for Parthia in 2 B.C.[2] There is, however, no evidence that Tiberius had them in his Pannonian triumph,[3] and C. Caesar died before he could hold one at all. The antiquarian assertion that the triumph was generally held in a chariot with white horses[4] is certainly not justified, not even for the late imperial period.

4. CAMILLUS AND CAESAR

When the news of the conquest of Veii in 396 B.C. reached Rome, thanksgiving was decreed for four days, for the first time for so many days; and the matrons began it before it was decreed. The population went out of the city to meet Camillus and gave him an unprecedented welcome.[5] He then entered Rome in a triumphal chariot drawn by four white horses.[6] This was, according to Livy, resented because it was not what a citizen and a mortal should do: it encroached on the privileges of the gods, Iuppiter and Sol.[7] Plutarch speaks only of Iuppiter and adds that this was never done before or after,[8] which is either a mistake or else it points to a pre-Caesarian source; according to Dio it was the cause of Camillus' exile.[9] This is all: a rather uniform and meagre tradition. It differs from what we have learnt about Aeneas, Latinus, and Romulus: in their case the white horses represented a privilege, not an abuse. We must therefore first investigate the history of this privilege and of its abuse, and then return to Camillus.

We begin with the gods. The chariots of Zeus and Helios were drawn by white horses in Persia[10] and in Greece;[11] accordingly their

---

[1] Ov. *Pont.* 2. 8. 50: 'purpureus niveis filius instet equis.'

[2] Ov. *Ars amat.* 1. 214: 'quattuor in niveis aureus ibis equis.'   [3] Ov. *Pont.* 3. 4. 35; 100.

[4] Serv. *Aen.* 4. 543: 'qui autem triumphat, albis equis utitur quattuor'; cf. Pliny *Paneg.* 22. 1: 'quadriiugo curru et albentibus equis'; Claudian. *Cons. Stil.* 3. 20: 'ipse albis veheretur equis'; 24. 20; 28. 369; Apul. *Apol.* 22; Lact. *de mort. pers.* 16. 6; Marquardt, *Staatsverw.* 2. 586; Ehlers, *RE* 7A. 504.   [5] Livy 5. 23. 3 f.; below, p. 289 n. 9.

[6] Diod. 14. 117. 6; Dio–Zonar. 7. 21. 3 (1, p. 72 B.); Dio 52. 13. 3; Plut. *Cam.* 7. 1; *vir. ill.* 23. 4.

[7] Livy 5. 23. 4: 'triumphusque omnem consuetum honorandi diei illius modum aliquantum excessit. (5) maxime conspectus ipse est curru equis albis iuncto urbem invectus; parumque id non civile modo sed humanum etiam visum. (6) Iovis Solisque equis aequiperatum dictatorem in religionem etiam trahebant, triumphusque ob eam unam maxime rem clarior quam gratior fuit.'

[8] Plut. *Cam.* 7. 1: σοβαρῶς ἐθριάμβευσε καὶ τέθριππον ὑποζευξάμενος λευκόπωλον ἐπέβη καὶ διεξήλασε τῆς Ῥώμης, οὐδενὸς τοῦτο ποιήσαντος ἡγεμόνος πρότερον οὐδ' ὕστερον. ἱερὸν γὰρ ἡγοῦνται τὸ τοιοῦτον ὄχημα τῷ βασιλεῖ καὶ πατρὶ τῶν θεῶν ἐπιπεφημισμένον; Klotz, *Rhein. Mus.* 90 (1941), 290.   [9] Dio 52. 13. 3; *vir. ill.* 23. 4.

[10] Hdt. 7. 40; Xen. *Cyrop.* 8. 3. 12; Curt. 3. 3. 11; cf. Bidez–Cumont, *Les Mages hellénisés* 2. 142. 2. Sacrifice of white horses to Helios: Hdt. 1. 216. 4; Philostr. *v. Apoll.* 1. 31; id. *Heroic.* 10. 2; Heliod. 10. 6. 5; probably also on Rhodes, Fest. 181 M. (190 L.); Reinach, *Cultes, mythes et religions*, 4. 48; Cumont, *Ét. syr.* 100. 1; id. *JRS* 27 (1937), 69. 33.

[11] Ov. *am.* 2. 1. 24: 'niveos Solis equos'; *Pap. Giess.* 3 (Wilcken, *Chrest.* no. 491 = Smallwood,

descendants, the Dioscuri[1] as well as Eos and Hemera,[2] rode on white horses. There is corresponding Roman evidence: both Iuppiter and Sol are mentioned by Livy. In fact, a chariot of Sol stood on the apex of the pediment of his temple in the Circus;[3] another probably on the temple of Sol Indiges on the Quirinal, as may be inferred from the representation of the chariot on the relief of his *pulvinar* which stood in front of the temple;[4] and there was a third on the temple of Apollo Palatinus.[5] The chariots of Iuppiter are even more relevant: it is enough to mention the two of the Capitoline temple, one made by Vulca when the temple was built, and the other dedicated by the Ogulnii in 296 B.C.[6]

The kings of the Greek heroic age do not seem to have had such a chariot, with the exception of Amphiaraus and Rhesus,[7] whereas the Persian kings always had one.[8] It was probably from them that the tyrants of Syracuse borrowed it when they wanted to represent Zeus: first Dionysius I (430–367), who also borrowed the Persian diadem and purple cloak[9] and was followed by Dionysius II,[10] Nysaeus,[11] and Hieronymus.[12] Two further imitators of Zeus were inspired by the example of the first Dionysius: Clearchus, tyrant of Heraclea of Pontus, 364 B.C., called himself son of Zeus, painted his face red, wore a red

---

Documents . . . of Hadrian, no. 519): Ἅρματι λευκοπώλῳ . . . ἥκω . . . Φοῖβος θεός; Verg. *Aen.* 12. 161; Suet. *Aug.* 94. 6 (above, p. 69 n. 2); often on vase-paintings (Schauenburg, *Ant. Kunst* 5 (1962), 51 ff.); *quadriga* with white horses on the mosaic of the Ninfeo Bergantino at Castelgandolfo, A. Balland, *Mél.* 79 (1967), 453 ff.; 498 f.

[1] Pind. *Pyth.* 1. 66; Iustin. 20. 3. 8; Wilamowitz, *Euripides' Herakles* 222 f.; also in the Roman tradition: Flor. 1. 11. 4; 1. 28. 15; Val. Max. 1. 8. 1; cf. *Studi e materiali* 13 (1937), 15 f. That is perhaps why Domitian rode on a white horse in the triumph of Vespasian and Titus, Suet. *Dom.* 2. 1.

[2] Bacchyl. frg. 20 C 22; Theocr. 13. 11; Aesch. *Pers.* 386; Soph. *Ai.* 673; Ov. *Met.* 15. 189; *Trist.* 3. 5. 56. [3] Tert. *spect.* 8; Tac. *A.* 15. 74. 1.

[4] Quintil. 1. 7. 12; cf. *RE* 8A. 1714 f. [5] Prop. 3. 31. 11; Hor. *c.s.* 9.

[6] See above, p. 54. 5; p. 58. 1.

[7] Hom. *Il.* 10. 437 (in Ov. *Met.* 13. 252 captured by Ulixes and used for his 'triumph'); Pind. *Ol.* 6. 14; Stat. *Theb.* 6. 330; [Eur.] *Rhes.* 616 f.; Catull. 58a. 4; cf. G. Radke, *Die Bedeutung der weissen u. schwarzen Farbe* (1936), 8 f.

[8] Sen. *de ira* 3. 21. 2: 'unus ex iis equis, qui trahere regium currum albi solebant, abreptus vehementer commovit regem'; above, p. 54. 6.

[9] Livy 24. 5. 4: (Hieronymus) 'purpuram ac diadema . . . quadrigisque etiam alborum equorum interdum ex regia procedentem more Dionysii tyranni'; Baton, *FGrHist.* 268 F 4: Σῶσις . . . τὸν Ἱερώνυμον ἀνέπεισεν διάδημά τε ἀναλαβεῖν καὶ τὴν πορφύραν καὶ τὴν ἄλλην πᾶσαν διασκευὴν ἣν ἐφόρει Διονύσιος ὁ τύραννος; Diod. 14. 44. 8: ἐμνηστεύσατο δὲ καὶ τῶν πολιτικῶν τὴν ἐπισημοτάτην Ἀριστομάχην, ἐφ' ἣν ἀποστείλας λευκὸν τέθριππον ἤγαγεν εἰς τὴν ἰδίαν οἰκίαν; Stroheker, *Dionysios I* (1958), 159. Exaenetus, an Olympic victor of 412 B.C., entered his home-town, Acragas, in a *quadriga*, followed by 300 youths in *bigae* with white horses, Diod. 13. 82. 7.

[10] Pliny 7. 110: 'Dionysius tyrannus . . . quadrigis albis egredientem (Platonem) in litore excepit.'

[11] Theop., *FGrHist.* 115 F 187: Νυσαῖος ὁ Διονυσίου τοῦ προτέρου υἱὸς κύριος τῶν ἐν Συρακούσαις γενόμενος πραγμάτων κατεσκευάσατο τέθριππον καὶ τὴν ἐσθῆτα τὴν ποικίλην ἀνέλαβεν.

[12] Livy 24. 5. 4; Baton 4.

mantle and a golden crown, and had an eagle carried in front of him;[1] the chariot with white horses may be added, although it is not explicitly mentioned. About the same time the physician Menecrates of Syracuse called himself Zeus, wore a purple mantle, a golden crown, and sandals, held a sceptre, and was accompanied by men dressed up as gods.[2]

This list provides us with all the necessary help, although the evidence is not uniform: one piece is missing here, another there. But on the whole it proves that the chariot belonged in the first place to Zeus and Helios, and that rulers who claimed divine status for themselves liked to appear in the dress and with the attributes of Zeus.[3] It further proves that Camillus did not invent the chariot with white horses but followed Greek precedents; and that he did it because he too wanted to liken himself to Iuppiter. He had to do this in many respects—provided that it was really Iuppiter whom the triumphator represented—and it could not have been resented, as is asserted in our sources. What was arrogance at Syracuse was a religious privilege at Rome, although only for the day of the triumph. Camillus did nothing wrong by adding the white horses to the ritual: it rendered the connection with Iuppiter even closer. But there may have been more. Pliny quotes the antiquarian Verrius Flaccus, who in turn quoted earlier authorities, for the custom of painting both the statue of Iuppiter and the face of the triumphator red, and for the fact that Camillus so appeared in his triumph.[4] This special mention of Camillus is puzzling as it stands; it is not if one infers from it that Camillus was the first to paint his face red.[5] Consequently one could further assume that he brought about a change in the history of the triumph.

The development of the triumph would have to be revised as follows. One would have to accept again that part of the tradition which

---

[1] Iustin. 16. 5. 8: 'obliviscitur se hominem, interdum Iovis se filium dicit. (9) eunti per publico aurea aquila velut argumentum generis praeferebatur, (10) veste purpurea et cothurnis regum tragicorum et aurea corona utebatur. (11) filium quoque suum Ceraunon vocat'; Memnon, *FGrHist.* 434 F 11; Suid. s.v. Κλέαρχος; Isocr. *ep.* 7. 12 f.; cf. Weinreich, *Menekrates* 17; Balsdon, *Hist.* 1 (1950), 364. 5; Wallisch, *Philol.* 99 (1955), 250; P. R. Franke, *Arch. Anz.* 81 (1966), 131.

[2] Athen. 7. 289 c: αὐτὸς δ᾽ ὁ Ζεὺς (= Menecr.) πορφύραν ἠμφιεσμένος καὶ στέφανον χρυσοῦν ἐπὶ τῆς κεφαλῆς ἔχων καὶ σκῆπτρον κρατῶν κρηπῖδάς τε ὑποδεδεμένος περιῄει μετὰ τοῦ θείου χόρου; cf. Weinreich, op. cit. 9; Nilsson 2. 138.

[3] Statues of Dionysius I were also provided with the attributes of Dionysus ([Dio Chrys.] *or.* 37. 21 : 2, p. 22 A.), and his son, Dionysius II, called himself son of Apollo (Plut. *de Alex. fort.* 2. 5. 338 b; cf. Plat. *epist.* 3. 315 b; 13. 361 a).

[4] Pliny 33. 111: 'enumerat auctores Verrius, quibus credere necesse sit Iovis ipsius simulacri faciem diebus festis minio inlini solitam triumphantiumque corpora; sic Camillum triumphasse'; cf. above, p. 67. 3.

[5] For a different view see Münzer, *RE* 7. 327 f.

ascribed the equipment of the triumphator to the kings.[1] It was Camillus who made a god of him by using the white horses and the red paint and by reinterpreting the rest: the chariot, the dress, the sceptre, and the crown were no longer regal but divine attributes, as they were for the Greek pretenders. One of Camillus' innovations, the red paint, was incorporated in the ritual, the other, the white horses, was not. His reinterpretation too was accepted, but the old one also remained valid: the triumphator represented Iuppiter, and yet made his offerings to him[2] and was warned during the procession that he was a mortal and had to be protected against evil influences.[3]

Who was this innovator, the Camillus of history or of the legend? Such behaviour would have been much too early for the historical Camillus, perhaps even earlier than our first Greek example, Dionysius I, who became tyrant of Syracuse in 405 B.C., that is, nine years before Camillus held his triumph. The example of the Persian kings, which was earlier still, does not seem to help, because the Romans will have had it not from the Persians but from the Greeks, and Dionysius was the first Greek to wear the dress of Zeus. But even if there had been earlier Greek examples, unknown to us, some mythical king for instance, the historical Camillus would still remain unacceptable because it would imply that a Roman general transformed the triumph under Greek influence as early as the beginning of the fourth century B.C.

It was, then, the Camillus of the legend; but in this case the date becomes crucial again, though in a different sense: was this transformation created before or after Caesar?[4] The pre-Caesarian date would lead to the suggestion that a Greek historian reinterpreted the Roman triumph in the light of what he knew of the Greek imitators of Zeus. He added features of this kind to Camillus' triumph, and these would have attracted the attention of Caesar and his friends. The post-Caesarian date would lead to an even simpler explanation: a friend justified, or an adversary condemned, Caesar's triumph by creating Camillus' precedent either as an exceptional privilege or as a sign of arrogance; Caesar's real precedents could have been either the ancestral heroes or the Sicilian tyrants or the Persian kings.

The ancestral heroes were Aeneas, Latinus, and Romulus, who in turn inherited the white horses from Iuppiter and Sol. It is clear that

[1] See above, p. 68.   [2] Iuven. 10. 41; Epict. 3. 24. 85; Tert. *Apol.* 33.
[3] Macrob. 1. 6. 9; cf. Deubner, l.c. 322 f.
[4] The tradition was created before Caesar according to Schwegler, *Röm. Gesch.* 3. 228. 1; Bömer on Ov. *F.* 6. 724 (2, p. 384); Ogilvie on Livy 5. 23 (pp. 679 f.); after Caesar according to Hirschfeld, *Kl. Schr.* 278; Münzer, *RE* 7. 328; Momigliano, *CQ* 36 (1942), 113, is undecided.

these gods did not get their white horses because of the example of mortals, Greeks or Persians or Camillus, but from their Greek relations, Zeus and Helios—Iuppiter certainly, Sol probably, long before Camillus and the tyrants. The Dioscuri who, riding on their white horses, fought in the sixth century at the river Sagras on the side of the Locrians, fought at the beginning of the fifth at Lake Regillus (and later at Pydna) on the side of the Romans.[1] Aeneas and Latinus had the horses by right and not as an exceptional privilege for a single day. Romulus is a borderline case: he had them, like Camillus, for the triumph only, but was, like Aeneas, of divine descent and worshipped after his death. The charge of arrogance could not have been made in his case. One could assert that Caesar's horses too were those of Aeneas, his ancestor, but again restricted to the single day and not incurring the charge of arrogance.[2]

The second alternative, the Sicilian tyrants, could be the real precedents even behind the ancestral example. For them the horses were part of their monarchic symbols which created a close link with Zeus. In this case it would have been the first manifestation of Caesar's similar aspirations, even if this time it was restricted to a single day.

The third alternative, that of the Persian kings, appears rather farfetched. But it is a fact that ever since the disaster of Crassus revenge on Parthia much occupied the minds of the Romans. We shall see that in 44, when the Parthian campaign was prepared, Caesar was to be invested with the insignia of the Persian kings so as to make him appear the legitimate ruler there.[3] The chariot with white horses, then, could have been part of this scheme—provided that Caesar planned his campaign as early as 46 and that he used his triumph as a prelude to the relevant honours, regal and divine, of the last weeks of his life. The advantage of this interpretation is that the issue of the chariot would no longer be isolated; its shortcoming is that it is much too startling.

A clear decision cannot be made here. The chariot was followed by other honours which could equally be applied to a triumphator or a king or a god. The question then must be re-examined when all these honours are discussed together.[4]

---

[1] Iustin. 20. 3. 8; *vir. ill.* 16. 3; Flor. 1. 11. 4; 1. 28. 15; Val. Max. 1. 8. 1; *Studi e materiali* 13 (1937), 15.

[2] Drumann 3. 548. 10 and Alföldi, *Mus. Helv.* 9 (1952), 230, assume that in spite of the decree of the Senate Caesar did not use the chariot with white horses.

[3] See below, pp. 338 ff.

[4] See below, pp. 270 ff.

5. THE TRIUMPH OF 46 B.C.

The triumph, long expected, long delayed and long prepared, was held in August 46 B.C., a fourfold triumph, Gallicus, Alexandrinus, Ponticus, Africanus, on four, not consecutive, days.[1] Some of its unusual features have already been mentioned. First it conflicted with the rule which prescribed that a general must not enter Rome before the triumph. Caesar had been in Rome repeatedly, so that the Senate must have granted him dispensation from the rule.[2] Pompey, on the other hand, had stuck to the rule. In 61 he arrived in Italy in February but did not enter Rome until his triumph almost seven months later.[3] Again, in some earlier cases one day was not sufficient for the triumph: the triumph of Aemilius Paullus lasted three days,[4] that of Pompey two days. But the former entered Rome only on the third day,[5] the latter on the second,[6] whereas Caesar drove in on all four days. His example was followed by Augustus, who held a threefold triumph on three consecutive days after the Actian victory, 13–15 August 29 B.C.[7] This was another innovation, the background of which is obscure: Pompey triumphed over fourteen nations and the pirates, and yet it was a single triumph.

The triumphal procession surpassed in length, wealth, and variety Pompey's last triumph, as also any other triumph ever held before.[8] There were now the exhibits of the four triumphs, and there was the chariot with white horses, which was, as we have seen, a claim to superhuman status. Two incidents may be connected with this claim. On the first day, the triumph over Gaul, Caesar's chariot broke down at the temple of Felicitas so that he had to continue in another chariot.[9] If this were true reporting, it would mean a warning against human arrogance. It recalls the fate of Aemilius Paullus, who lost two sons at the time of his great triumph.[10] But the story is no doubt apocryphal; according to Pliny, the chariot broke down on an ordinary journey, and Caesar later protected himself against a recurrence by reciting a

---

[1] Suet. *Caes.* 37. 1: 'quater eodem mense, sed interiectis diebus . . . diverso quemque apparatu et instrumento.'   [2] See above, pp. 61 f.   [3] See above, p. 38.

[4] Plut. *Aem. Paul.* 32. 4; *Fasti triumph.* 167 B.C.; Diod. 31. 8. 10.

[5] Plut. *Aem. Paul.* 33. 1; 34. 6; Diod. 31. 8. 12.

[6] Pliny 37. 13; Plut. *Pomp.* 45. 1.   [7] Dio 51. 21. 5 ff.

[8] Suet. *Caes.* 37; Dio 43. 21–22. 1; App. *BC* 2. 101. 418; Drumann 3. 550 ff.; Bruhl, *Mél.* 46 (1929), 90 ff.

[9] Suet. *Caes.* 37. 2: 'Gallici triumphi die Velabrum praetervehens paene curru excussus est axe diffracto'; Dio 43. 21. 1: ἐν δ' οὖν τῇ πρώτῃ τῶν νικητηρίων τέρας οὐκ ἀγαθὸν αὐτῷ ἐγένετο· ὁ γὰρ ἄξων τοῦ ἅρματος τοῦ πομπικοῦ παρ' αὐτῷ τῷ Τυχαίῳ . . . συνετρίβη, ὥστε ἐφ' ἑτέρου αὐτὸν τὰ λοιπὰ ἐπιτελέσαι.   [10] Plut. *Aem. Paul.* 35. 2; Livy 45. 40. 7.

magical formula before setting out.[1] The temple of Felicitas was of course a suitable place for staging such a breakdown: she represented the divine help which all generals needed,[2] and was particularly topical just then because a new temple was being built for her to be dedicated by Lepidus in the following year or the year after.[3] The incident can best be understood in retrospect: it was a warning of the coming disaster.

The other incident is said to have occurred when Caesar reached the Capitol and descended from the chariot: he then climbed up the steps of the Capitoline temple on his knees.[4] This was not done before, though it is asserted that it was part of the ritual;[5] and it is recorded that Claudius did it in A.D. 41 'according to precedent'.[6] Nevertheless it is probable that here the fictitious precedent of Caesar is meant, which in turn may have been invented by one of his apologists to show his humility at a time when he had just descended from the chariot with white horses and was facing his own statue with the inscription that he was a demigod. Here was now the proof: he was a mortal who approached the supreme god with due humility even on the day of his triumph.

An incident of a different kind occurred on the fourth day at the end of the banquet which was normally held after the triumph. Caesar, garlanded and wearing slippers, entered the Forum Iulium and was escorted home by the populace by the light of torches carried by elephants.[7] Another version of this story is recorded by Suetonius: the elephants, forty of them, carried the torches on the first day of his triumph, when he was ascending the steps of the temple of Iuppiter Capitolinus (clearly not on his knees).[8] This version can easily be dismissed. There was no need for torches in daylight, and the appearance of elephants on the Capitol seems bizarre. The story may somehow have been inspired by Pompey's first triumph in 79, when he vainly attempted to enter Rome on a chariot of elephants;[9] or by the other story about

[1] Pliny 28. 21: 'Caesarem dictatorem post unum ancipitem vehiculi casum ferunt semper, ut primum consedisset, id quod plerosque nunc facere scimus, carmine ter repetito securitatem itinerum aucupari solitum.'   [2] See below, p. 113.   [3] Dio 44. 5. 1 f.

[4] Dio 43. 21. 2: τοὺς ἀναβασμοὺς τοὺς ἐν τῷ Καπιτωλίῳ τοῖς γόνασιν ἀνερριχήσατο; Meyer, Caesars Monarchie 388; Gelzer, Caesar 265. 53.   [5] Dio 1, p. 75 B.

[6] Dio 60. 23. 1: τά τε ἄλλα κατὰ τὸ νομιζόμενον πράξας καὶ τοὺς ἀναβασμοὺς τοὺς ἐν τῷ Καπιτωλίῳ τοῖς γόνασιν ἀναβάς, ἀναφερόντων αὐτὸν τῶν γαμβρῶν ἑκατέρωθεν.

[7] Dio 43. 22. 1: ἐπειδὴ ἐκ τοῦ δείπνου ἐγένοντο, ἔς τε τὴν ἑαυτοῦ ἀγορὰν ἐσῆλθε βλαύτας ὑποδεδεμένος καὶ ἄνθεσι παντοδαποῖς ἐστεφανωμένος, καὶ ἐκεῖθεν οἴκαδε παντὸς μὲν ὡς εἰπεῖν τοῦ δήμου παραπέμποντος αὐτόν, πολλῶν δὲ ἐλεφάντων λαμπάδας φερόντων ἐκομίσθη. It is remarkable that Caesar kept on his slippers into which he had changed for the banquet (cf. Cic. Pis. 13; Marquardt, Privatleben 595 f.; Balsdon, Life and Leisure in Anc. Rome (1969), 41; 51).

[8] Suet. Caes. 37. 2: 'ascenditque Capitolium ad lumina quadraginta elephantis dextra sinistraque lychnuchos gestantibus'; criticism by Drumann 3. 554. 2.

[9] See above, p. 37.

Cn. Domitius Ahenobarbus (*cos.* 122), who after his victory in Gaul
rode through the province on an elephant followed by his soldiers in
a kind of triumphal procession.[1] But even if this evidence is dismissed,
the elephants must have acquired a special significance. They reappeared
under Augustus, and later in an important context[2] which must have
been inspired by a Caesarian precedent, whatever it was. The other
version, the torchlight procession after the banquet, can be supported
by two analogies. C. Duilius (*cos.* 260) returned from the banquet held
after his triumph by the light of torches and led by musicians;[3] it is also
recorded that he used to do this after all public banquets, and even that
this privilege was officially granted him,[4] which is not likely. There is
no mention of the elephants. One elephant reappears in the case of
L. Cornificius (*cos.* 35) who fought as Octavian's legate against Sex.
Pompeius and saved his troops in 36: he was so proud of this that he
used to return home from banquets on the back of an elephant,[5] which
he may well have acquired after his African campaign and triumph of
33 B.C. These analogies are relevant but do not really explain the
Caesarian incident. It seems certain that there was in fact a torchlight
procession with musicians and populace, also that elephants formed
a part of the procession, and that their use was a special privilege, not
created for the moment. But its real meaning remains obscure. It may
well be that he, like Cornificius, did it because he had saved the life
of citizens; but it may equally have been some sort of a superhuman
honour. If it had been an established practice, one would call this procession a κῶμος or even a Dionysiac revel, which would suit well the end
of the triumph; but for this further evidence would be needed.

An incident which took place at the end of all the festivities may be
appended here. When some of Caesar's soldiers were rioting because of
the great expenses of the triumph and the games, Caesar himself seized
one of them and handed him over to the authorities for execution. Two
others were slaughtered on the Campus Martius by the *pontifices* and

---

[1] Suet. *Nero* 2. 1, not accepted by Münzer, *RE* 5. 1323; but such festivals were often held
in the provinces, see below, pp. 289; 293; 299.

[2] Suet. *Claud.* 11. 2; Dio 61. 16. 4; Pliny 34. 15; *Anth. Pal.* 9. 285; *Greek Lit. Pap.* 113
(Page); Mattingly 1. 3; 7; 10; 75; 134 f.; 138; Cichorius, *Röm. Stud.* 344 ff.; Rumpf, *BJ*
155/6 (1955/6), 129 ff.

[3] Dio 6 (1, p. 75 B. = Zonar. 7. 21. 11): καὶ παρὰ ταῖς ἐκεῖ (Capit.) δειπνήσας στοαῖς, πρὸς
ἑσπέραν οἴκαδε μετ' αὐλῶν καὶ συρίγγων ἀπήρχετο; *vir. ill.* 38. 4: 'Duellio concessum est, ut
praelucente funali et praecinente tibicine a cena publice rediret'; Ehlers, *RE* 7A. 510.

[4] Val. Max. 3. 6. 4; Flor. 1. 18. 10.

[5] Dio 49. 7. 6: τοσοῦτον γάρ που ὁ Κορνουφίκιος ἐπὶ τῇ τῶν στρατιωτῶν σωτηρίᾳ ἐφρόνει ὥστε
καὶ ἐν τῇ Ῥώμῃ ἐπὶ ἐλέφαντος, ὁσάκις ἔξω τῆς οἰκίας ἐδείπνει, ἀνακομίζεσθαι; Groag, *PIR* 2. 373,
no. 1503.

the *flamen Martialis*, and their heads were set up at the Regia.[1] The rioting is certainly a fact, even if the reason given for it may not be the correct one: nor can the punishment be doubted. But what the priests did is without analogy. It was probably an archaic form of execution[2] rather than a sacrifice,[3] and the *flamen Martialis* had his part in it because it took place on the Campus Martius. The fixing of the heads at the Regia has been compared with the fixing of the head of a horse, the *equus October*, annually either at the Sacra Via or at the Subura;[4] but this would lead to a human sacrifice instead of the animal sacrifice, whereas here we are dealing with punishment, not a ritual. The whole case remains obscure. It cannot have anything to do with the execution of the prisoners at the end of the triumph or with the punishment of defaulting soldiers during the campaign.

The celebrations did not end with the four days of the triumph. A few weeks later the dedication of the temple of Venus Genetrix followed, and games instituted in her honour. Caesar also created the cult of the Victoria Caesaris, again to be connected with games. Further, he probably planned a cult of the Fortuna Caesaris and certainly that of Mars Ultor. These cults will be considered in the following chapter.

---

[1] Dio 43. 24. 3: οὐ πρότερόν γε ἐπαύσαντο ταραττόμενοι πρὶν τὸν Καίσαρα ἄφνω τε αὐτοῖς ἐπελθεῖν καὶ κρατήσαντά τινα αὐτοχειρίᾳ πρὸς τιμωρίαν παραδοῦναι. (4) οὗτος μὲν οὖν διὰ ταῦτα ἐδικαιώθη, ἄλλοι δὲ δύο ἄνδρες ἐν τρόπῳ τινὶ ἱερουργίας ἐσφάγησαν. καὶ τὸ μὲν αἴτιον οὐκ ἔχω εἰπεῖν (οὔτε γὰρ ἡ Σίβυλλα ἔχρησεν, οὔτ' ἄλλο τι τοιοῦτο λόγιον ἐγένετο), ἐν δ' οὖν τῷ Ἀρείῳ πεδίῳ πρός τε τῶν ποντιφίκων καὶ πρὸς τοῦ ἱερέως τοῦ Ἄρεως ἐτύθησαν, καὶ αἵ γε κεφαλαὶ αὐτῶν πρὸς τὸ βασίλειον ἀνετέθησαν. This evidence is rejected as not trustworthy by Reid, *JRS* 2 (1912), 41.   [2] Mommsen, *Strafr.* 913.

[3] Wissowa 421. 2; Schwenn, *Menschenopfer* 166; Gelzer, *Caesar* 265.

[4] Wissowa 144 f.

VI

THE NEW CULTS

MANY a temple at Rome owed its origin to the initiative of an individual who was prompted in war or peace to make a vow. It was then his task to build the temple, and that of his family to care for it later and to repair or rebuild it if necessary. It was a civic duty generally accepted by the Romans long before they were reminded of it by writers like Cicero and Horace or even by philosophers.[1] In the first century B.C. Sulla was a great builder of temples and so was Pompey after him. Now it was the turn of Caesar.

I. VENUS GENETRIX

(a) The Forum Iulium

The temple of Venus Genetrix was an organic part of the Forum Iulium: we must therefore begin with the history of this Forum[2] as far as it is relevant here. It was not to be a market, which was the original function of the fora[3] and always remained so, for example, for the Forum Boarium, the Forum Holitorium, and to some extent also for the Forum Romanum, but like the last it was to be a seat of the law courts.[4] The earliest information dates from 54 B.C. when Caesar was still in Gaul: in that year his friends bought ground on his behalf which was to be used for the extension of the Forum Romanum.[5] The word 'extension' clearly alludes to its special purpose: it was to relieve the Forum Romanum by creating further space for the courts. This special purpose was expressly stated when the next forum, the Forum Augustum, was built.[6] Caesar must have thought of the architectural

---

[1] Cic. *Cat.* 4. 24; Hor. *sat.* 1. 6. 34 f.; 2. 2. 103 with Heinze's notes; Antiochus of Ascalon ap. Stob. 2. 152 W.; Nock, *CAH* 10. 458.

[2] Platner–Ashby 225 f.; R. Thomsen, *Opusc. Archaeol.* 2 (1941), 195 ff.; Nash 1. 424 ff.; Th. Hastrup, *Anal. Rom. Inst. Dan.* 2 (1962), 45 ff.; B. Tamm, *Auditorium and Palatium* (1963), 120 ff. [3] Paul. 84 M. (74 L.); Varr. *LL* 5. 145.

[4] App. *BC* 2. 102. 424 (below, p. 81. 9).

[5] Cic. *Att.* 4. 16. 8: 'in monumentum illud quod tu tollere laudibus solebas, ut forum laxaremus et usque ad Atrium Libertatis explicaremus, contempsimus sescenties HS ...; efficiemus rem gloriosissimam'; cf. Suet. *Caes.* 26. 2: 'forum de manubiis incohavit, cuius area super sestertium milies constitit'; Pliny 36. 103.

[6] Suet. *Aug.* 29. 1: 'fori extruendi causa fuit hominum et iudiciorum multitudo, quae videbatur non sufficientibus duobus etiam tertio indigere.'

features of his Forum when he bought the ground: the Basilica Iulia, which was built at the same time, was based on a definite plan. If so, it was his original intention to separate it from the Forum Romanum by means of the colonnades. And it was to be the first Forum named after its builder at Rome;[1] outside Rome there were some precedents, the Forum Appi, Clodi, Aureli and the like. Caesar himself had founded such 'market'-places, a Forum Iulium (Iliturgis) in Spain,[2] a Forum Iulii (Fréjus) in Gallia Narbonensis[3] and elsewhere.[4] The new Forum, while serving the community, also served Caesar: like any other public building or temple it was a memorial of its builder. Moreover it not only bore his name but also contained his statues, an equestrian and a standing one,[5] and above all the temple of Venus was there.

The temple of Venus is not mentioned with the plans of 54, and Appian says that Caesar vowed it in 48 on the battlefield of Pharsalus.[6] Those who accept this evidence[7] have to face some difficult points. We have seen that, since Pharsalus was a battle in a civil war, Caesar did not report his victory to the Senate, the Senate did not decree supplications and a triumph, and Caesar refused to have many other honours suggested by them.[8] And yet on this theory the temple was built to commemorate this victory. Next, Caesar's attachment to Venus was not of recent date. It rested on the tradition of his family and, as we have seen, he had made ample use of it before. The plan of a temple must long have been in his mind. Sulla probably built one for Venus Felix, and Pompey dedicated one of the shrines which he built together with his theatre to Venus Victrix. That was in 55, and Caesar bought the site in Rome in the following year when Iulia, Pompey's wife, was dead and thus the bond between the two men broken. Caesar had a much stronger reason to build a temple for Venus than Pompey or even Sulla; and with it the Forum Iulium was a more suitable memorial of the conquest of Gaul than without it. Finally, Appian compares the Forum Iulium with the squares of the Persians,[9] not only because these

---

[1] It is generally called Forum Caesaris, also in the Fasti (Degrassi 514), Forum Iulium only by Augustus (*Mon. Anc.* 20. 3).   [2] Pliny 3. 10; Schulten, *RE* 9. 1068.

[3] Pliny 3. 35; Mela 2. 77; Ihm, *RE* 7. 69. It was a market-place without municipal rights and became a colony *c.* 36 B.C.; Syme, *CQ* 32 (1938), 40 f.; Vittinghoff 100. 2.

[4] See *RE* 7. 70; *Diz. epigr.* 3. 212 f.; Bömer, *Gymn.* 72 (1965), 8. 3.   [5] See below, p. 86 f.

[6] App. *BC* 2. 68. 281: νεών τε αὐτῇ Νικηφόρῳ χαριστήριον ἐν Ῥώμῃ ποιήσειν εὔχετο κατορθώσας; 2. 102. 424: ἀνέστησε καὶ τῇ Γενετείρᾳ τὸν νεών, ὥσπερ εὔξατο μέλλων ἐν Φαρσάλῳ μαχεῖσθαι.

[7] It is accepted by Platner–Ashby 226; R. Thomsen, *Opusc. Archaeol.* 2 (1941), 218; P. Gros, *Mél.* 79 (1967), 519.   [8] See above, pp. 40; 61; 64.

[9] App. *BC* 2. 102. 424: καὶ τέμενος τῷ νεῷ περιέθηκεν, ὃ ʽΡωμαίοις ἔταξεν ἀγορὰν εἶναι οὐ τῶν ὠνίων, ἀλλ᾽ ἐπὶ πράξεσι συνιόντων ἐς ἀλλήλους, καθὰ καὶ Πέρσαις ἦν τις ἀγορὰ ζητοῦσιν ἢ μανθάνουσι τὰ δίκαια.

too were used for the judiciary but probably also because of its architectural plan. The Forum in its final form was a square, enclosed on
three sides by the two colonnades and the temple between them (pl. 7):[1]
this plan is often found in the East, for example in Pergamum and
Priene, and that is presumably what Appian had in mind.[2] It is more
probable that Caesar adopted this plan right from the beginning than
only on the battlefield of Pharsalus. The fact that part of the temple
stood on the old city-wall does not render the suggestion of this early
planning impossible. It is certainly right to say that Caesar could not
have afforded to ignore the wall as long as he was not the undisputed
ruler; but it is not necessary to assume that it was part of the original
plan to extend the Forum as far as the city-wall.

The temple was dedicated on 26 September 46,[3] but the Forum was
not yet ready; it was completed by Augustus.[4] As so often, Caesar laid
the foundations for a new development. The architectural scheme of
a closed square with a temple became the model for the imperial fora.[5]
As early as 29 B.C. Augustus authorized C. Cornelius Gallus, incidentally a native of Forum Iulii in Gaul and first prefect of Egypt,[6] to
build a Forum Iulium in Egypt.[7] If he built it at Alexandria at the
Caesareum,[8] he is likely to have reproduced the plan of the Forum
Iulium in Rome. It was certainly reproduced when, in Rome, the Forum
Augustum was built with the temple of Mars Ultor and dedicated in
2 B.C. Those of Vespasian, Nerva, and Trajan followed.

[1] See the reconstruction by Thomsen, l.c. 195 ff.; 215; the remains in Nash 1. 424 ff.
D. F. Brown, *Temples of Rome as Coin Types* (1940), 15, assumes that it is reproduced on coins
of Trajan (Mattingly 3. 182 f.; 193; 202; pl. 32. 8; Strack, op. cit. 1. 149 f.); accepted by
F. Panvini-Rosati, *Riv. ital. numism.* 57 (1955), 81 f. This identification could be justified by
the fact that the temple was rebuilt and dedicated by Trajan on 12 May 113 (Degrassi,
F. Ost. p. 203). But the coins are of earlier date (A.D. 104–11), the seated image cannot be
the original Venus Genetrix, and above all the frequency of the plan in the imperial period
(see n. 5) renders such an identification hazardous.
[2] App. *BC* 2. 102. 424; Gjerstad, *Opusc. Archaeol.* 3 (1944), 42 ff.; 57 f.; 70 ff.
[3] Dio 43. 22. 2; App. *BC* 2. 102. 424; 3. 28. 107; *F. Arv.* etc. (Degrassi 514).
[4] *Mon. Anc.* 20. 3: 'Forum Iulium et basilicam . . . coepta profligataque opera a patre
meo perfeci.'
[5] Gjerstad, l.c. 40 ff.; P. H. v. Blanckenhagen, *Journ. of the Soc. of Architectural Historians*
13/14 (1954), 21 ff. (I owe the reference to this important article to Professor F. Rakob).
According to B. Tamm, op. cit. 122 f., the plan was developed from the Greek peristyles
known in Italy since the second century B.C.
[6] Hieron, *Chron.* p. 164 H.; Syme, *CQ* 32 (1938), 39 ff. (Fréjus, Gall. Narb.); Boucher,
C. Cornelius Gallus (1966), 11 (Voghera, Gall. Cisalp.); Bömer, *Gymn.* 72 (1965), 8 f. (near
Aquileia).
[7] *AE* 1964, 255 (inscription on an obelisk for which, as discovered by Magi, Caligula
substituted another, *ILS* 115): 'C. Cornelius Cn. f. Gallus, praef. fabr. Caesaris Divi f.,
Forum Iulium fecit'; J. P. Boucher 33 f.; Volkmann, *Gymn.* 74 (1967), 501 ff. (with bibliography); G. Guadagnant, *Opusc. Rom.* 6 (1968), 21 ff.
[8] See below, p. 297.

PLATE 7

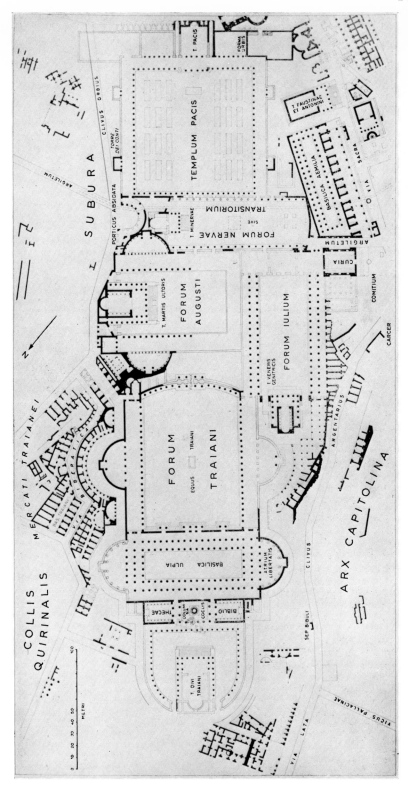

The Forum Iulium and the imperial Fora (From *Enciclopedia dell'arte antica* 6. 838); p. 82.

(b) Victrix and Genetrix

Caesar's attachment to Venus has been discussed in great detail up to the beginning of the Civil War, but for the rest only briefly.[1] The account has now to be completed. There is no evidence about the years Caesar spent in Gaul; but, as we have seen, he must have planned to build a temple as a memorial of the conquest of Gaul. When the Civil War broke out he propagated the tradition of his family anew. He spoke about his divine ancestry to his soldiers,[2] and his adversaries called him 'the descendant of Venus' among themselves without mentioning his name,[3] which shows how strongly he stressed his claim. But she was now more than the ancestress: she was also the goddess of war, in fact no other than Pompey's Venus Victrix. She had appeared in armour already in Sulla's dream, helping him in a battle, and in gratitude Sulla sent a golden crown and an axe with an explanatory inscription to the Aphrodite of Aphrodisias in Caria.[4] Pompey's Venus Victrix must have been similar: a figure either in armour or surrounded by weapons or holding a trophy.[5] Appian says that it was to this Venus Victrix that Caesar vowed the temple on the battlefield of Pharsalus, allegedly inspired by a dream of which no details are given.[6] Pompey too is said to have dreamt before the battle: he was decorating her temple with trophies,[7] which, however, he did, it emerged later, as the loser, in Caesar's honour. 'Venus Victrix' was Caesar's watchword in the battle—Pompey's was 'Hercules Invictus'[8]—and her figure was later engraved on his finger-ring.[9] What she may have been like can be seen on contemporary coins: Venus standing and holding

---

[1] See above, pp. 17 f.

[2] Dio 41. 34. 1: τί μὲν ἀπό τε τοῦ Αἰνείου καὶ ἀπὸ τοῦ 'Ιούλου γέγονα...; cf. Callisth., FGrHist. 124 F 36 = Plut. Alex. 33. 1 (Alexander's prayer before the attack on Arbela, 331 B.C.): εἴπερ ὄντως Διόθεν ἐστὶν γεγονώς ...

[3] Caelius ap. Cic. fam. 8. 15. 2 (March 49): 'Venere prognatus'; cf. Schol. Gronov. Cic. Marc. 1, p. 296 St.: 'constat Caesarem se iactare divina origine a Venere esse natum.' Caesar himself may have used the solemn word 'prognatus', which is also found in BG 2. 29. 4; 6. 18. 1, but before him only in poetry; see Fraenkel, Horace 82. 4; see also above, p. 18.   [4] App. BC 1. 97. 452 ff.

[5] She is found on Caesarian coins and later; the only relevant earlier coin was issued c. 54 B.C. by Faustus Sulla, Sulla's son and Pompey's son-in-law, with the bust of Venus on the obverse and trophies on the reverse, Sydenham 146; pl. 24. 884; cf. Wissowa, Myth. Lex. 6. 199.

[6] App. BC 2. 68. 281; Serv. Dan. Aen. 1. 720: 'ipsa et Victrix et Genetrix ex Caesaris somnio sacrata'.   [7] Plut. Pomp. 68. 2 f.; cf. App. BC 2. 69. 284.

[8] App. BC 2. 76. 319; 'Venus' without epithet is recorded for the battle at Munda (2. 104. 430). If Servius' (Aen. 7. 637) 'Venus Genetrix' refers to this battle, he may be right; if to the battle at Pharsalus, probably wrong.

[9] Dio 43. 43. 3: γλύμμα αὐτῆς ἔνοπλον ἐφόρει καὶ σύνθημα αὐτὴν ἐν τοῖς πλείστοις καὶ μεγίστοις κινδύνοις ἐποιεῖτο.

a sceptre, and Victoria, with a shield at her side,[1] the reproduction of an important statue. There was later a temple of Venus Victrix on the Capitol,[2] built by Augustus or at least provided by him with a cult image. It is possible that it was built in execution of a Caesarian plan.

Caesar's devotion to Venus Victrix was thus not a passing mood which ended when Pompey was defeated; in fact, as we shall see later, she was probably the goddess to whom the new goddess, the Victoria Caesaris, was first attached.[3] It is, on the other hand, true that after victory was won the other Venus, Caesar's ancestress, became the stronger again. He went to Asia, visited Ilium, like the earlier members of the family, and granted it new privileges.[4] The cities of the province of Asia, which had now to make amends to Ceasar for their support of Pompey, set up his statue at Ephesus, calling him a descendant of Ares and Aphrodite.[5] There will have been similar dedications in many other places, especially at centres of the cult of Aphrodite like Aphrodisias in Caria.[6] Meanwhile the temple was built and completed at Rome: it became the temple of Venus Genetrix. This was a new epithet, never given to Venus or any other goddess before, and was said to have been suggested to Caesar by another dream;[7] in fact he borrowed the word from Lucretius (who had it from Ennius) and made an epithet of it.[8]

New epithets were created whenever a god received a new function. They can reveal a great deal about the character of the cult and have therefore always been considered with great care. But the meaning of Venus Genetrix has seemed so obvious that only cursory attention has been paid to the epithet. And yet that obvious meaning does not fit into the traditional pattern. A god could be called 'pater', a goddess 'mater', but not, as was done by the Greeks, in a genealogical sense.[9] Iuppiter was often, it is true, called 'genitor' under Greek influence,[10] that is, father of the gods and men, but this never became

---

[1] See below, pp. 86; 99.

[2] *F. Amit.* 9. Oct.: 'Genio publico, Faustae Felicitati, Veneri Victrici in Capitolio' (Degrassi 518); Wissowa, *Myth. Lex.* 6. 199 (on the cult image); cf. *RE* 8A. 2498.

[3] See below, p. 99.

[4] *IGR* 4. 199; Strab. 13. 594; Lucan 9. 950 ff.; Norden, *Kl. Schr.* 370 (*N. Jahrb.* 7 (1901), 259 f.). This was the basis of the later rumour that he intended to transfer the capital to Ilium, Suet. *Caes.* 79. 3; Nic. Dam. *v. Caes.* 20. 68. [5] *Syll.* 760 (below, p. 296. 9).

[6] L. Robert, *Ant. Class.* 35 (1966), 415 f.; below, pp. 140f.

[7] Serv. Dan. *Aen.* 1. 720 (above, p. 83. 6).

[8] See above, p. 23. In the age of Caesar it was not a rare word, Catull. 63. 50; Lucr. 2. 599; 708; Val. Sor. 4 M., etc.; *Thes.L.L.* 6. 1821. [9] Wissowa 26.

[10] Enn. *A.* 456 V.; Cic. *carm.* frg. 3; Verg. *Aen.* 7. 306, etc.; *Thes.L.L.* 6. 1818 f.; Carter, *Epitheta deorum* 51 f.; also other gods: see Carter's Index.

an epithet, which would imply cult.[1] There was a public as well as private cult of the *Di patrii*, but these were different: the gods inherited from the ancestors. It is the divine ancestors who are relevant here, and these too were in fact worshipped by the Romans, not the great gods, as was done by the Greeks, but the *Lares*, the *Di Indigetes*, the *Di parentes* or *parentum*. They were, however, private gods; we shall have to say more about them later.[2] They had their public equivalents, but outside Rome. It will be recalled that Aeneas was worshipped as Lar Aeneas or Aeneas Indiges or Iuppiter Indiges, and that Iulus became Vediovis pater.[3] Caesar now added Venus Genetrix as the most important of all, and at Rome. It was not an innovation, and yet it was startling; nor was he the first to call her a mother but the first to create a public cult for her as mother. The ambiguity of the term well served his purpose: she belonged not only to the Gens Iulia but to all Aeneadae. The temple will have been inscribed with his, the builder's, name: that was the normal practice. It no doubt stated that he was *pontifex maximus*, *augur*, dictator, and consul for the third time, and, perhaps, that he built the temple *de manubiis*. It was certainly no coincidence that the Senate decreed in the same year that his name should also be inscribed on the Capitoline temple in place of that of Q. Lutatius Catulus (*cos.* 78), because it was he who had completed that temple, and Catulus had to account for some embezzlement.[4] This was the new version of an old story[5] but it was not successful: the name of Catulus remained.[6] It is possible that Caesar did something for the Capitoline temple in those years of feverish building activities; but he did not like this kind of change and was clearly satisfied that only the temple of Venus Genetrix should bear his name. The temple would have become an important religious centre, had Caesar lived longer—if it is right to make an inference from the temple of Mars Ultor built in the Forum Augustum: this temple was particularly favoured by the imperial family and received many functions which had hitherto been reserved for Iuppiter Capitolinus.[7]

The cult image, not finished in time, was by the Greek sculptor Arcesilaus;[8] it is not known what it was like. One suggestion is that it

---

[1] There was one exception in the Greek world, the cult of Apollo Genetor on Delos, Aristot. frg. 489 R.; Censor. 2. 3 (Timaeus); Macrob. 3. 6. 2.   [2] See below, pp. 290 ff.
[3] See above, p. 10.   [4] Dio 43. 14. 6.
[5] In 62 Caesar as praetor called Catulus to account and proposed that Pompey should be charged with what was still to be done on the temple; and that in the end Pompey's name should be inscribed on it (Dio 37. 44. 1 f.).
[6] Val. Max. 6. 9. 5; Tac. *H.* 3. 72.
[7] Dio 55. 10. 2–5 (lex templi).   [8] Pliny 35. 156.

was a fully dressed standing figure with Cupid on her shoulder,[1] as she is often found, for example on a relief at Città Castellana (pl. 14), on another in the Villa Medici at Rome, or on the Claudian relief at Ravenna (pl. 8. 1–2).[2] In fact coins issued by Caesar himself in 47 and 46 (pl. 6. 10–12) and a relief found at Sperlonga (pl. 8. 3), showing the bust of Venus with Cupid, point to such a statue.[3] There may have been one in his house or in the shrine of the Gens Iulia at Bovillae and he may have asked Arcesilaus to create another. The other view is that the statue on coins with Victoria in her hand was the cult image.[4] It is impossible to decide the case because this type is inscribed on later imperial coins as Venus Victrix as well as Venus Genetrix (pl. 6. 13–14).[5] It would be possible if the decoration of the shield of 'Venus Genetrix' with Aeneas, Anchises, and Ascanius on a medallion of Hadrian (pl. 6. 16)[6] were not a later addition. But this must be the case, because on coins the shield is decorated with the head of Medusa only,[7] and on a coin of Marcus Aurelius ('Venus Victrix') with the she-wolf and the twins (pl. 6. 15),[8] which is another later addition.

In front of the temple Caesar's equestrian statue was erected, about which there is a twofold tradition. The horse was the likeness of his own horse, which was born in 60 when he first stood for the consulate, had almost human feet, and would not endure any other rider: it was declared to be an omen of his future mastery of the world.[9] But the statue was also said to have been that of Alexander by Lysippus with

---

[1] Weickert, *Festschr. f. Arndt* (1925), 52 ff.; Bieber, *Röm. Mitt.* 48 (1933), 261 ff.; Schiller, *La religion romaine de Vénus* 311 f.

[2] P. Hommel, *Stud. zu den röm. Figurengiebeln* (1954), pl. 2 f.; *CAH Plates* 4. 160a; Ryberg, pl. 28. 42. M. Borda, *Bull. Comun.* 73 (1949/50), 197, prefers another version, represented on coins of M'. Cordius Rufus, Sydenham 162; pl. 26. 976.

[3] Sydenham 168; Grueber, pl. 101. 9 f., above, p. 61. 6; Iacopi, *L'Antro di Tiberio a Sperlonga* (1963), 118 ff.

[4] Coin of P. Sepullius Macer, Sydenham 178; Grueber, pl. 54. 20 f.; Goethert, *Zur Kunst d. röm. Rep.* (1931), 19 ff.; Hommel, op. cit. 28; Ryberg 23 ff.; see below, p. 99.

[5] Mattingly 4. 407; pl. 56. 11; 14 (Marcus Aurelius); cf. 3. 307; 334; pl. 57. 12; Strack 2, pl. 6. 277 (Hadrian, 'Venus Genetrix' only).

[6] Gnecchi, *I medaglioni romani* 3. 19; pl. 146. 2; cf. Kekulé, *Arch.-epigr. Mitt.* 3 (1879), 20; Toynbee, *Rom. Med.* 141.

[7] Mattingly 3. 307; pl. 57. 12; Strack 2. 178 f.; pl. 6. 277.

[8] Mattingly 4. 407; pl. 56. 14; a coin of Nero already shows them on the shield of Roma, Mattingly 1. 217; pl. 41. 4.

[9] Dio 37. 54. 2: ἵππος τις αὐτῷ διαφυὰς ἐν ταῖς τῶν προσθίων ποδῶν ὁπλαῖς ἔχων ἐγεννήθη, καὶ ἐκεῖνον μὲν γαυρούμενος ἔφερεν, ἄλλον δὲ ἀναβάτην οὐδένα ἀνεδέχετο; Suet. *Caes.* 61: 'quem natum apud se, cum haruspices imperium orbis terrae significare domino pronuntiassent, magna cura aluit ... cuius etiam instar pro aede Veneris Genetricis postea dedicavit.' Caesar's horse was followed by Caligula's even more fabulous horse, Incitatus (below, pp. 173; 213), and in a contrary sense perhaps by that of Cn. Seius (Münzer, *RE* 2A. 1120 f.), which brought destruction to its subsequent owners, Dolabella, Cassius, and Antony (Gell. 3. 9. 1–6).

PLATE 8

I

2

3

1. Marble relief in the Villa Medici, Rome: Pediment of the temple of Mars Ultor, with Mars between Venus and Fortuna; pp. 86, 129.

2. Marble relief at Ravenna: Augustus, Livia, imperial prince as heros, another as general, seated female figure; p. 86.

3. Marble relief found at Sperlonga, in the local Museum: Venus with Cupid; p. 86.
(Photographs: German Archaeological Institute, Rome).

Caesar's head substituted for that of Alexander.[1] These two versions, it is clear, belong together. It was originally Alexander's horse, Bucephalas, which would not take any other rider than Alexander; and as an omen this too pointed to Alexander's rule.[2] As the features of Bucephalas were transferred to Caesar's horse,[3] the Lysippian statue too was adapted to Caesar. He was often compared with Alexander[4] and his mastery of the world too was, as we have seen, a topical theme at that time.[5] The next step was to date the omen back to the time of his first consulate. The statue bore no doubt a suitable inscription. There was the recent precedent of Sulla, who was honoured on his victorious return to Rome with a gilded equestrian statue at the Rostra, also with an inscription.[6] Caesar's statue was appropriately placed in front of the temple of Venus: he had achieved victory with her help.

There was a second statue in the Forum Iulium, about which nothing is known except that it wore a cuirass.[7] It was therefore the type which we met on the relief from the Via Cassia,[8] and the statue which was set up on the Capitol in 46 may have been similar too. This is how the ancestral heroes Aeneas and Romulus[9] were represented, and, after Caesar's example, Augustus and his successors, though it may not have been so elaborate as the statue of Augustus from Primaporta. But it became a site of great distinction: official documents were fastened to it[10] as military *diplomata* were later to the Ara Gentis Iuliae on the Capitol.[11]

---

[1] Stat. *Silv.* 1. 1. 84: 'cedat equus, Latiae qui contra templa Diones / Caesarei stat sede fori; quem traderis ausus / Pellaeo, Lysippe, duci, mox Caesaris ora / mirata cervice tulit.'

[2] Diod. 17. 76. 6; Plut. *Alex.* 6; Curt. 6. 5. 18; Pliny 8. 154; Gell. 5. 2; *Hist. Alex. Magni* 1. 15; A. R. Anderson, *AJP* 51 (1930), 17 ff.

[3] Pliny 8. 155: (Bucephalas) 'nec Caesaris dictatoris quemquam alium recepisse dorso equus traditur, idemque similes humanis pedes priores habuisse, hac effigie locatus ante Veneris Genetricis aedem.'

[4] Cic. *Att.* 12. 40; 13. 28. 3; App. *BC* 2. 149–154. 620–649; below, p. 188.

[5] See above, pp. 50 ff.

[6] App. *BC* 1. 97. 451; Vell. 2. 61. 3 (who also mentions equestrian statues of Pompey and Caesar). [7] Pliny 34. 18: 'Caesar quidem dictator loricatam sibi dicari in foro suo passus est.'

[8] See above, p. 45. [9] Romulus, for instance, on the altar at Cività Castellana (pl. 14).

[10] Pliny *ep.* 8. 6. 13: 'senatusque consulta de iis rebus facta in aere inciderentur, idque aes figeretur ad statuam loricatam Divi Iulii.' It is generally assumed that Pliny refers to a statue in front of the temple of Divus Iulius (cf. Sherwin-White ad loc.) and in fact the statue which stood on its site on a column after the Ides of March for a while (below, pp. 365 ff.), and no doubt again later, may have worn a cuirass. But express evidence exists only for the Forum Iulium, which leads to the conclusion that the office of the *fiscus* too, to which reference is made on inscriptions with 'procurator a loricata' (*CIL* 6. 8690–2; *AE* 1913, 143a; 1924, 81; Hirschfeld, *Kais. Verwaltungsb.* 4. 4; Platner–Ashby 103. 1; 498; Pflaum, *Les carrières procuratoriennes équestres* (1960), 1. 57), was located in the Forum Iulium, and not at the temple of Castor. It is to be assumed that this statue was not removed and destroyed with the others after the Ides of March (below, p. 365) or, if it was, it was soon re-erected.

[11] See above, p. 11. 9. Documents were deposited in the Caesareum of Smyrna (*IGR* 4. 1480) and of Gytheum (*IG* 5. 1208. 45).

(c) Lusus Troiae and the Funeral Games

The dedication of the temple was followed by games, the *ludi Veneris Genetricis*, in the Circus, which again surpassed all that was done before in splendour and expense.[1] A great deal of information is available about this feature of the games, which, however, need not detain us. Important information is more scarce: that the games were to become annual and that for their performance a special college was created;[2] that they were also called *ludi Victoriae Caesaris*; and that the *lusus Troiae*[3] and the funeral games for Iulia[4] were held at the same time. The alternative names of the games are of considerable interest and will be discussed in connection with the new goddess, the Victoria Caesaris.[5] The two special games require some comment here, the *lusus Troiae* held in the Circus and the funeral games held in the Forum.

The *lusus Troiae* were equestrian exercises performed by noble youths and consisted of complicated manœuvres, one of the various means to prepare young men for military service and to make them known as future citizens. These games were instituted, according to Vergil, who gives a long description of them, by Aeneas at the funeral games of his father Anchises, Iulus having a leading part in them.[6] They were later renewed by Ascanius-Iulus when he founded Alba Longa.[7] In fact originally the games had no connection with Troy and Aeneas[8] and had been obsolete when they were first revived by Sulla.[9] This is a strange fact, and it is impossible to say how he came to do it, by himself or on the advice of the learned antiquarians of his age. He clearly did it with the intention of putting the games into the service of the Trojan legend. The second revival by Caesar certainly served this purpose, and the festival of Venus Genetrix was a suitable occasion for it. The role of Iulus was no doubt created and stressed then for the first time: it cannot have been invented by Vergil or Varro. It is even possible that Iulus' role was now given to young Octavius as it was given later in 29 B.C., after the Actian triumph, to Tiberius, and later still to Augustus' grandsons, C. Caesar and Postumus Agrippa.[10] Those taking part were

[1] Dio 43. 22. 2–23.

[2] Pliny 2. 93: 'ludis, quos faciebat Veneri Genetrici non multo post obitum patris Caesaris in collegio ab eo instituto'; Obs. 68: 'ludis Veneris Genetricis, quos pro collegio fecit.'

[3] Dio 43. 23. 6; Suet. *Caes.* 39. 2.

[4] Dio 43. 22. 3 f.; Plut. *Caes.* 55. 4; Vell. 2. 56. 1; App. *BC* 2. 102. 423.

[5] See below, pp. 91 ff.

[6] Verg. *Aen.* 5. 545 ff.; H. v. Petrikovits, *Klio* 32 (1939), 209 ff.; Mehl, *RE* Suppl. 8. 888 ff.

[7] Verg. *Aen.* 5. 596 ff.

[8] Paul. 367 M. (504 L.): 'lusus puerorum equestris'; Marquardt–Wissowa, *StV* 3. 525 f.; issowa 450; L. R. Taylor, *JRS* 14 (1924), 160; Latte 115 f.   [9] Plut. *Cat. min.* 3. 1.

[10] Suet. *Tib.* 6. 4; Dio 54. 26. 1; 55. 10. 6.

sons of patricians.[1] This was not the case at Sulla's games, where the plebeians Sex. Pompeius and the younger Cato had a leading role. It was then an innovation by Caesar—a logical one as the games celebrated the Trojan origins—due no doubt to his general policy of restoring the patrician families to prominence again.[2] These games were often repeated in the following decades, for example in 29 when the temple of Divus Iulius was dedicated;[3] they were popular under Augustus and later.[4] This they could not have been, had Caesar not revived them as one of the means to demonstrate and celebrate the Trojan origins.

The funeral games for Iulia were held at the same time, but not in the same place. They were gladiatorial contests which were performed by tradition in the Forum.[5] Such games were often held in honour of distinguished men by members of their family, for example for Aemilius Paullus and Sulla.[6] Caesar himself gave such games as aedile in 65, in memory of his father, who had died long before, in 85:[7] it was an act of piety rather than a political demonstration, one of the many signs of family pride so apparent in Caesar's character. Moreover he was a great friend of gladiatorial combats,[8] so much so that the Senate decreed in 44 to hold such combats in Rome and in Italy annually on a special day in his honour.[9] When Iulia died in 54 he announced that funeral games and a banquet would be held in her memory.[10] It increased their significance that he made them coincide with the *ludi Veneris Genetricis*: this was an innovation which was followed by Octavian when he held the funeral games of Caesar in 44, again on the day of the games of Venus Genetrix.[11] Caesar built a temporary amphitheatre in the Forum for the occasion;[12] his example was again followed under Augustus: T. Statilius Taurus (*cos.* 37 and 26) built a permanent one in 29 B.C. on

---

[1] Dio 43. 23. 6; 48. 20. 2; 51. 22. 4; 53. 1. 4; 54. 26. 1; Mommsen, *StR* 3. 31. 3; Kübler, *RE* 18. 2. 2230. Octavius could have taken part in the games only if the rule was waived in his case or if he had already been made a patrician.

[2] Cf. Syme, *Roman Revolution* 68 ff.   [3] Dio 51. 22. 4.

[4] Suet. *Aug.* 43. 2: 'Troiae lusum edidit frequentissime maiorum minorumque puerorum, prisci decorique moris existimans clarae stirpis indolem sic notescere' (Dio 48. 20. 2; 49. 43. 3; 53. 1. 4; 54. 26. 1; 55. 10. 6; 59. 7. 4, etc.).   [5] Cf. K. Schneider, *RE* Suppl. 3. 760 ff.

[6] Didasc. Ter. *Ad.*; Dio 37. 51. 4.   [7] Dio 37. 8. 1; Pliny 33. 53.

[8] Suet. *Caes.* 31. 1; 39. 1; Caes. *BC* 1. 14. 4; Cic. *Att.* 7. 14. 2; 8. 2. 1.

[9] Dio 44. 6. 2: κἂν ταῖς ὁπλομαχίαις μίαν τινὰ ἀεὶ ἡμέραν καὶ ἐν τῇ ῾Ρώμῃ καὶ ἐν τῇ ἄλλῃ ᾽Ιταλίᾳ ἀνέθεσαν.

[10] Suet. *Caes.* 26. 2: 'munus populo epulumque pronuntiavit in filiae memoriam, quod ante eum nemo'; Dio 43. 22. 3: ἐπὶ τῇ θυγατρὶ καὶ θηρίων σφαγὰς καὶ ἀνδρῶν ὁπλομαχίας ἐποίησεν; Plut. *Caes.* 55. 4: θέας δὲ καὶ μονομάχων καὶ ναυμάχων ἀνδρῶν παρασχὼν ἐπὶ τῇ θυγατρὶ ᾽Ιουλίᾳ πάλαι τεθνεώσῃ; App. *BC* 2. 102. 423; Gelzer, *Caesar* 134; 161; 264.

[11] Serv. *Aen.* 8. 681; 1. 287; 6. 790; *Ecl.* 9. 47; below, p. 368.   [12] Dio 43. 22. 3.

the Campus Martius.[1] The details about the games may be omitted here, but Caesar's intention is obvious and must be stressed: the public festival was at the same time a festival of his family.

(d) The Cult

Caesar's close link with Venus remained. The games were held again in 45, not in September, as will be seen later, but in July in his absence, then in 44 after his death, and later also.[2] This link was also demonstrated at his funeral: the bier was placed on the Rostra in a shrine made on the model of the temple of Venus Genetrix.[3] His statue was set up in her temple after the comet appeared at the games of 44.[4] In 42, after his consecration, the Senate decreed that his image should be carried at the *pompa circensis* together with that of Venus.[5] Later Augustus transferred Apelles' painting of the Aphrodite Anadyomene from Cos to the temple of Divus Iulius in Rome, with the argument that she was the founder of his family.[6]

Caesar established the cult of his Venus outside Rome also. Some of the colonies founded or planned by him were named after his goddess.[7] The precedent here again was Sulla, who had founded the Colonia Veneria Cornelia Pompeii in 80 B.C.[8] The principal cult of such colonies naturally belonged to Venus. The Colonia Genetiva Iulia Ursonensis in Spain, founded in 44, deserves particular mention, not only because its name recalls Genetrix,[9] but because, according to its constitution, a special day was reserved for the games to be held in honour of Venus.[10] This will have been the rule in the other colonies too. The cult spread to many other places in Italy and the provinces: dedications to Venus Genetrix have been found at Praeneste, Beneventum, Spain, Dalmatia, and elsewhere;[11] dedications to Venus Victrix and Venus Erucina[12] too may refer to Caesar's goddess. Her popularity declined under Augustus: Apollo was in the ascendant. Vergil did much to stem this decline; but Venus now had to share her care of Aeneas with Apollo.[13]

---

[1] Dio 51. 23. 1; Suet. *Aug.* 29. 5.

[2] See below, pp. 111; 156; 368.

[3] Suet. *Caes.* 84. 1; below, p. 361.

[4] Dio 45. 7. 1, below, pp. 363; 393.

[5] Dio 47. 18. 4; below, p. 393. 10.

[6] Strab. 14. 657; Pliny 35. 91.

[7] Most of these, called Colonia Veneria Iulia, like Sicca, Rusicade, Dyrrhachium, were probably founded under Augustus, see Grant, *From Imperium to Auctoritas* 276 f.; Vittinghoff 112. 4; 113. 2; 126. 9.

[8] Mommsen, *Ges. Schr.* 5. 208.

[9] Genetiva: Genetrix = genetivus: genitor.

[10] *ILS* 6087 § LXXI; cf. Vittinghoff 59. 2.

[11] *ILS* 3172; 3171a; 5513; Koch, *RE* 8A. 883 (where the reference to Veii is to be omitted).

[12] See Koch's list, l.c.

[13] Verg. *Aen.* 3. 80 ff.; 154 f.; 251 f.; 369 ff.; 6. 56 ff.; Hor. *c.* 4. 6. 21 ff.; Heinze, *Virgils epische Technik* 84; above, pp. 14 f.

2. VICTORIA CAESARIS

(a) Venus and Victoria

The *ludi Veneris Genetricis* were instituted as annual games. But when they were first repeated in 45 they were no longer held on 26 September but from 20 to 30 July, and were now called *ludi Victoriae Caesaris*.[1] The change of date will be discussed together with the change of the name of the month Quintilis to Iulius.[2] Here the change of the name of the games is relevant. It has been explained by the close relationship, even identity, between Venus and Victoria.[3] But this explanation cannot be right. It is true that Sulla, a devotee of Venus, created the *ludi Victoriae*,[4] though not that Pompey's Venus Victrix could also be called Victoria;[5] further, that there are dedications to Venus Victrix and Felicitas on the one hand,[6] and to Victoria and Felicitas on the other;[7] later also to Venus Victrix Parthica Augusta and Victoria Parthica Augusta.[8] All this proves that Venus, especially Venus Victrix, could be, like Victoria, a goddess of victory, but not more. Venus never had wings, and Victoria was never without them; Venus and Victoria can appear together, Victoria even, as we shall see presently, in a subordinate position in the hand of Venus. Further, the festival of Venus Genetrix remained on the old date, 26 September; on the new date of the games, 20–30 July, Caesar's statue was carried in the company of Victoria,[9] not of Venus. And ultimately there was a Victoria Caesaris but no Venus Caesaris. The conclusion is that Victoria Caesaris was by no means another name for Venus Genetrix or Victrix but was created to be a personal goddess of Caesar, comparable to the Fortuna Caesaris, Felicitas Caesaris, Clementia Caesaris, and the like. What she stood for requires examination, which is best begun with a brief history of the cult of Victoria at Rome.

(b) Victoria

Victoria was not one of the old deities:[10] the Romans had prayed and

---

[1] Suet. *Aug.* 10. 1; Cic. *fam.* 11. 28. 6; *ILS* 9349; Mommsen, *CIL* 1, pp. 322 f.; Degrassi 486.　　　　　　　　　　　　　　　　　　　　　[2] See below, p. 156.

[3] Mommsen, *CIL* 1, pp. 322 f.; Wissowa 292 and *Myth. Lex.* 6. 192 ff. (I accepted this view in *RE* 8A. 2514 and *HTR* 50 (1957), 226); *contra*, A. Baudrillart, *Les divinités de la victoire* (1894), 79 ff.　　　　　　　　　　　　　　　　　　[4] See below, p. 102.

[5] Gell. 10. 1. 7; see below, p. 93. 5.

[6] There was a shrine of Venus Victrix and Felicitas on the Capitol (*F. Amit.* 9 Oct.): above, p. 84. 2.

[7] A cult of the Victoria et Felicitas Caesaris at Ameria, *ILS* 6631 f.

[8] *ILS* 305; 3177.　　　　　　　　　　　　　　　　　　　　　[9] Cic. *Att.* 13. 44. 1.

[10] *RE* 8A. 2501 ff.; Graillot, Daremb.–Sagl. 5. 836 ff.; 850 ff.; Wissowa 139 ff.; Latte 234 f. and *Myth. Lex.* 6. 294 ff.; T. Hölscher, *Victoria Romana* (1967), 173 ff.

given thanks for victory to other gods, especially to Iuppiter and Mars, before they felt the necessity to create the personification. They were inspired by the Greek Nike, with whom their Victoria was always identical in appearance, though not in substance, and the occasion was the Samnite Wars towards the end of the fourth century B.C. It was at the time when the tale about Alexander's empire, his invincibility, and about the successors who claimed to emulate him, had reached Rome[1] that the Romans wanted to have their own goddess of victory.[2] Her first temple was dedicated in 294 B.C., and about the same time other gods, Iuppiter, Mars, Hercules, for instance, began to receive the epithets Victor and Invictus.[3] She grew in significance as the Roman power grew; her frequent appearance on early coins[4] shows that in the third century she, the new goddess, was as popular in Rome as the most prominent of the old gods. The time of the great generals followed, Scipio, Marius, Sulla, Pompey, who carried the cause of Victoria further in various ways;[5] in the end she was the great symbol of the empire of the world, built by the invincible generals, legions, and people.[6] Scipio was rewarded with statues for his victories, was called 'invictus', and was said to have celebrated the anniversaries of his victory of Zama.[7] Marius set up his own statue between two Victoriae on the Capitol and statues of Victoria probably in many other places.[8] Sulla followed. He claimed that to commemorate his victories one of his ancestors founded in 212 B.C. the *ludi Apollinares*, which soon became annual games.[9] Sulla now founded his own games, the *ludi Victoriae*, which also became annual.[10]

Pompey, as always, requires closer attention in this context. It is generally assumed that he did nothing for the cult of Victoria. And yet she must have appeared in his third triumph in one form or another; Cicero called him 'victor omnium gentium' and 'invictissimus civis',[11] and L. Vinicius (*cos.* 33) issued a coin *c.* 55 showing the flying Victoria carrying a palm-branch to which four wreaths were attached (pl. 3. 5).[12]

[1] *HTR* 50 (1957), 246 f.   [2] Livy 10. 33. 9; cf. Dio 8, frg. 36 (1, p. 105 B.).
[3] Livy 10. 29. 14; Val. Max. 1. 8. 6; *RE* 8A. 2486 f.; Mattingly, *JRS* 35 (1945), 73 f.
[4] Cf. the *quadrigati, victoriati, denarii*: Mattingly, l.c.; Wolters, *Festschr. f. Wölfflin* 17.
[5] *HTR* 50, 221 ff.; *RE* 8A. 2487 ff.
[6] Cornif. 4. 66: 'urbs invictissima'; Cic. *Cat.* 2. 19: 'huic invicto populo'; *Planc.* 11: 'huius principis populi et omnium gentium domini atque victoris'; *Pis.* 20: 'invictis legionibus'; more in *RE* 8A. 2496 f.
[7] Enn. *V.* 3 V.; Cic. *rep.* 6. 9; Livy 38. 51. 5; Gell. 4. 18. 3; App. *Syr.* 40. 208.
[8] Suet. *Caes.* 11; Plut. *Caes.* 6. 1; Obs. 70.   [9] Livy 25. 12. 15; Macrob. 1. 17. 25 ff.
[10] Vell. 2. 27. 6; Cic. *Verr.* 1. 31 with Ps.-Ascon. (p. 216; 338 St.); Mommsen, *Röm. Münzwesen* 625. 464; Degrassi 525 f.; below, p. 96 n. 5.
[11] Cic. *Pis.* 16; 34; Plut. *Cat. min.* 53. 3.
[12] Sydenham 155; pl. 26. 930a; above, pp. 38f.

That was about the time of the dedication of his theatre and its shrines. The Fasti Allifani has the following relevant entry: 'V(eneri) V(ictrici) H(onori) V(irtuti) V(ictoriae) Felicita[ti in theatro marmoreo]'.[1] The obvious conjecture that the fourth 'V' stands here for 'Victoria' has been rejected on the grounds of her assumed identity with Venus Victrix, and 'Valentia' or 'Vesta' or 'Valetudo' have been suggested instead,[2] which are as improbable as 'Victoria' is convincing. She goes as well together with Felicitas as does Honos with Virtus: there is evidence of common cult and common dedications to Victoria and Felicitas.[3] Again, it is recorded that Pompey dedicated the theatre and the shrine of Venus Victrix in his second consulate in 55;[4] but Tiro speaks of the dedication of the temple of Victoria in his third consulate in 52.[5] If he makes no mistake in this dating, and does not mean Venus Victrix by Victoria, there is no reason to doubt that Pompey created a cult of Victoria, presumably a common cult of Victoria and Felicitas in his theatre, and was followed in this respect by Caesar and Augustus.

(c) Caesar and Victoria

Caesar followed the example of his predecessors and yet transformed it completely. The evidence will be discussed under four headings, Roma, Victoria, Venus, and Caesar. The first theme is the earliest. Soon after Caesar's arrival from Gaul in 49, C. Vibius Pansa (*cos.* 43) issued a coin showing Roma seated on shields, her foot on a globe, and crowned by Victoria (pl. 6. 17).[6] This may be a combination of two earlier motifs, Roma with Victoria, and Roma with the globe. In the second century the head of Roma crowned by Victoria appeared on the coins of C. Terentius Lucanus, who was perhaps the patron of Terence (pl. 6. 18),[7] followed in the first decade of the first century by the full figure of Roma seated on weapons and crowned again by

---

[1] Degrassi 493 f. (12 Aug.).

[2] Mommsen, *CIL* 1. 1, p. 324; Hanson, *Roman Theatre-Temples* (1959), 52. 51; for the interpretation adopted above see A. Baudrillart, op. cit. 89 ff.; T. Hölscher, op. cit. 148. 922.

[3] See above, p. 91. 7.

[4] Pliny 8. 20; cf. Dio 39. 38. 1; Vell. 2. 48. 2; Cic. *Pis.* 65; Ascon. p. 1; 20 St.; Pliny 7. 158.

[5] Gell. 10. 1. 7: 'cum Pompeius ... aedem Victoriae dedicaturus foret ... nomenque eius et honores scriberentur, quaeri coeptum est, utrum "consul tertio" inscribendum esset an "tertium".' A statue of Victoria is mentioned by Dio 50. 8. 3 (32 B.C.).

[6] Sydenham 159; Grueber, pl. 50. 6; Münzer, *RE* Suppl. 5. 371; H. G. Gundel, *RE* 8A. 1963 f.; above, pp. 43; 61.

[7] Sydenham 49; Grueber, pl. 23. 8; Alföldi, *Die trojanischen Urahnen* 36; cf. Münzer, *RE* 5A. 664 f. (copied in the Social War for Italia, Sydenham 92 f.; pl. 19. 630; 632; Alföldi, pl. 11. 3).

PLATE 9

1. Stater of Aetolia, c. 279–168 B.C. (*BMC Thessaly to Aetolia* 194), Oxford; *obv.*: head of Athena; *rev.*: Aetolia with sword and spear sits on shields and holds Nike, legend Αἰτωλῶν; p. 96.

2. Aes of P. Papirius Carbo from Nicomedia 61–59 B.C. (*BMC Pontus* 152), London; *obv.*: head of Roma(?), legend Νικομηδέων; *rev.*: Roma sits on shields and holds Nike, legend Ἐπὶ Γαΐου Παπειρίου Καρβῶνος, Ῥώμη; p. 96.

3. Denarius of M. Nonius Sufenas, c. 60 B.C. (Sydenham 146. 885), Oxford; *obv.*: head of Saturn with sickle, legend 'S.C, Sufenas'; *rev.*: Roma sits on arms and is crowned by Victoria, legend 'Sex. Noni(us) pr(aetor) l(udos) V(ictoriae) p(rimus) f(ecit)'; p. 96.

4. Denarius of L. Hostilius Saserna, 48 B.C. (Sydenham 159. 951), Oxford; *obv.*: female head wearing an oak-wreath; *rev.*: Victoria carrying caduceus, trophy and palm-branch, legend 'L. Hostilius Saserna'; p. 96.

5. Quinarius of A. Licinius Nerva, 47 B.C. (Sydenham 146. 956), London and Paris; *obv.*: helmeted female head, legend 'Nerva'; *rev.*: Victoria with wreath and palm-branch, legend 'A. Liciniu(s)'; p. 96.

6. Denarius of L. Plautius Plancus, 47 B.C. (Sydenham 160. 959), Oxford; *obv.*: mask of Medusa, legend 'L. Plautius'; *rev.*: Victoria with palm-branch leads the four horses (of the triumphal chariot), legend 'Plancus'; pp. 96 f.

7. Denarius of M. Porcius Cato, 47 B.C. (Sydenham 176. 1053a), Oxford; *obv.*: female bust, legend 'M. Cato pro. pr(aetore), Roma'; *rev.*: seated Victoria with palm-branch and wreath, legend 'Victrix'; p. 97.

8. Denarius of Q. Caecilius Metellus Pius Scipio, 47 B.C. (Sydenham 175. 1050), London; *obv.*: female figure with head of a lion surmounted by a disk, legend 'G(enius) T(utelaris?) A(fricae), Scipio imp., Q. Metel. Pius'; *rev.*: Victoria with caduceus and shield, legend 'leg(atus) pro pr(aetore), P. Crassus Iun(ianus)'; p. 97.

9. Denarius of Q. Caecilius Metellus Pius Scipio, 47 B.C. (Sydenham 175. 1049), London; *obv.*: turreted head of city-goddess between corn-ear and caduceus, legend 'leg(atus) pro pr(aetore), Crass(us) Iun(ianus)'; *rev.*: trophy between lituus and jug, legend 'Scip. imp., Metel. Pius'; p. 97.

10. Denarius of M. Mettius, 44 B.C. (Sydenham 176. 1055), Oxford; *obv.*: head of Caesar, legend 'Caesar Imper(ator)'; *rev.*: Venus holding Victoria and sceptre, her arm rests on shield placed on globe, legend 'M. Mettius'; p. 99.

11. Denarius of L. Aemilius Buca, 44 B.C. (Sydenham 177. 1061), Oxford; *obv.*: head of Caesar, legend 'Caesar dict. perpetuo'; *rev.*: Venus holding Victoria and sceptre, legend 'L. Buca'; p. 99.

12. The same (Sydenham 177. 1062), London; but Venus is seated on *rev.*; p. 99.

13. Denarius of C. Cossutius Maridianus, 44 B.C. (Sydenham 178. 1067), Oxford; *obv.*: head of Caesar, legend 'Caesar dict. perpetuo'; *rev.*: Venus holding Victoria, resting her arm on shield placed on globe, legend 'C. Maridianus'; p. 99.

14. The same (Sydenham 178. 1068), London, but *obv.* legend: 'Caesar dict. in perpetuo'; p. 99.

15. Denarius of P. Sepullius Macer, 44 B.C. (Sydenham 178. 1070), London; *obv.*: head of Caesar, legend 'Caesar Imper(ator)'; *rev.*: Venus holding Victoria and sceptre which rests on star, legend 'P. Sepullius Macer'; p. 99.

16. Denarius of P. Sepullius Macer, 44 B.C. (Sydenham 178. 1074a), London; *obv.*: head of Caesar, legend 'Caesar dict. perpetuo'; *rev.*: Venus holding Victoria and sceptre which rests on star, legend 'P. Sepullius Macer'; p. 99.

17. Aureus of Nero, A.D. 64–8 (Mattingly I. 211. 82), London; *obv.*: head of Nero, legend 'Nero Caesar Augustus'; *rev.*: Roma seated on cuirass holds Victoria, legend 'Roma'; p. 100.

18. Denarius of C. Vibius Varus, 42 B.C. (Sydenham 186. 1139), Oxford; *obv.*: head of Hercules; *rev.*: Minerva holding Victoria, legend 'C. Vibius Varus'; p. 100.

19. Tetradrachm of Alexander I Bala of Syria, 147 B.C. (*BMC Syria* 52), Oxford; *obv.*: diademed head of Alexander; *rev.*: Zeus seated holding Nike and sceptre, legend Βασιλέως Ἀλεξάνδρου Θεοπάτορος Εὐεργέτου εξρ (= 165 = 147 B.C.); p. 100.

20. Tetradrachm of Lysimachus, c. 306–281 B.C. (Head, *HN* 284), Oxford; *obv.*: diademed head of Alexander with horn; *rev.*: Athena seated holding Nike, legend Βασιλέως Λυσιμάχου; p. 100.

21. Tetradrachm of Seleucus VI, 96–95 B.C. (*BMC Syria* 95), Oxford; *obv.*: diademed head of Seleucus VI; *rev.*: Athena standing and holding Nike, legend Βασιλέως Σελεύκου Ἐπιφανοῦς Νικάτορος; p. 100.

22. Denarius of C. Vibius Varus, 42 B.C. (Sydenham 186. 1144), London; *obv.*: bearded head of M. Antony; *rev.*: goddess holds Victoria and cornucopiae, legend 'C. Vibius Varus'; p. 100.

23. Denarius of C. Vibius Varus, 42 B.C. (Sydenham 186. 1145), London; *obv.*: bearded head of Octavian; *rev.*: goddess holds Victoria and cornucopiae, legend 'C. Vibius Varus'; p. 100.

PLATE 9

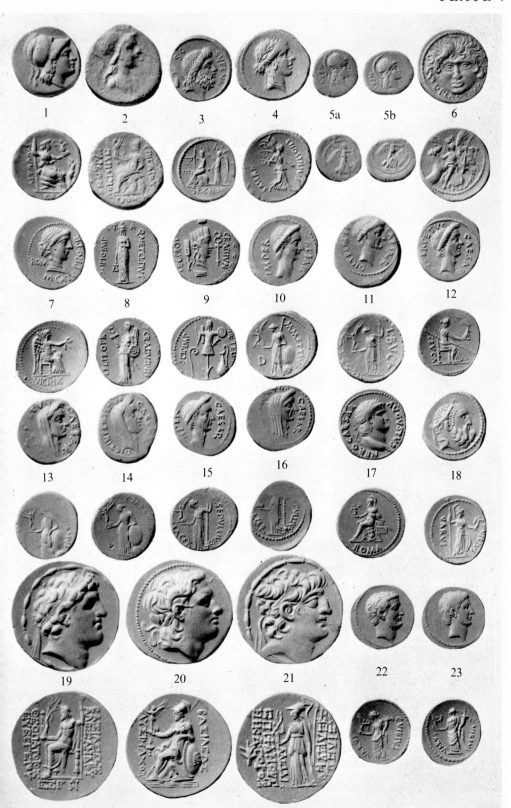

PLATE 10

PLATE 10

1. Denarius of Augustus, 29–27 B.C. (Mattingly 1. 104. 637), London; *obv.*: bust of Octavian (top of a herm), behind, thunderbolt; *rev.*: Octavian seated holds Victoria, legend 'Imp. Caesar'; p. 101.

2. Aureus of Nero, A.D. 64–8 (Mattingly 1. 208. 56), Oxford; *obv.*: head of Nero, legend 'Nero Caesar'; *rev.*: Nero radiate holds branch and Victoria, legend 'Augustus Germanicus'; p. 101.

3. Sestertius of Galba, A.D. 68 (Mattingly 1. 359. 206 §), Oxford; *obv.*: head of Galba, legend 'Ser. Sulpi. Galba Imp. Caesar Aug. p. m., tr. p.'; *rev.*: Senatus with branch crowns Galba who holds Victoria and branch, legend 'Senatus Pietati Augusti, S.C.'; p. 101.

4. Sestertius of Vespasian, A.D. 69–70 (Mattingly 2. 180†), Paris; *obv.*: head of Vespasian, legend 'Imp. Caesar Vespasianus Aug.'; *rev.*: Vespasian with sceptre receives Victoria from Roma, legend 'Roma et Augustus, cos. iterum, tribun. pot., s.c.'; p. 101.

5. Aureus of Titus, A.D. 79–80 (Mattingly 2. 242. 107), London; *obv.*: bearded head of Titus, legend 'Imp. Titus Caes. Vespasian. Aug., p. m.'; *rev.*: Vespasian radiate seated holds sceptre and Victoria, legend 'Divus Vespasian(us)'; p. 101.

6. Sestertius of Titus, A.D. 80–1 (Mattingly 2. 269. 222), Oxford; *obv.*: legend 'S.C., Imp. T. Caes. Divi Vesp. f. Aug., p. m., tr. p., p. p., cos. VIII'; *rev.*: Vespasian radiate seated on a quadriga of elephants with riders, legend 'Divo Aug. Vesp., S.P.Q.R.'; p. 101.

7. Sestertius of Trajan, A.D. 103 (Mattingly 3. 159. 757), London; *obv.*: bust of Trajan, legend 'Imp. Caes. Nerva Traian. Aug. Germ. Dacicus, p. m.', *rev.*: Roma seated on cuirass with spear receives Victoria from Trajan, legend 'tr. p. VII, imp. IIII, cos. V, p. P., s.c.'; p. 101.

8. Denarius of L. Lentulus, 12 B.C. (?) (Mattingly 1. 26. 124), London; *obv.*: head of Augustus, legend 'Augustus'; *rev.*: Augustus with shield inscribed c(lupeus) v(irtutis) places a star over the head of Caesar who holds Victoria, legend 'L. Lentulus flamen Martialis'; p. 102.

9. Denarius of Cn. Pompeius Magnus and M. Minatius Sabinus, 46 B.C. (Sydenham 173. 1037a), London; *obv.*: head of Pompey, legend 'Cn. Magnus Imp.'; *rev.*: turreted personification (of a city in Spain?), Cn. Pompeius receiving shield from turreted, kneeling personification, legend 'M. Minat. Sabi., pr. q.'; pp. 50. 4; 104.

10. Denarius of Cn. Pompeius Magnus and M. Minatius Sabinus, 46 B.C. (Sydenham 173. 1036c), Oxford; *obv.*: head of Pompey, legend 'Cn. Magnus Imp. f.'; *rev.*: turreted personification (of a city of Spain?) standing on pile of arms, holding spear and grasping hand of Cn. Pompeius who disembarks from ship, legend 'M. Minat. Sabin pr. q.'; p. 104.

11. Denarius of Sex. Pompeius, 45 B.C. (Sydenham 174. 1042), Paris; *obv.*: head of Pompey, legend 'Sex. Magn. Imp., Sal(pensa)'; *rev.*: Pietas with sceptre and branch, legend 'Pietas'; p. 104.

12. Denarius of Sex. Pompeius, 45 B.C. (Sydenham 174. 1043), London; *obv.*: head of Pompey, legend 'Sex. Magnus Sal(pensa) Imp.'; *rev.*: Pietas with sceptre and branch, legend 'Pietas'; p. 104.

13. As of Sex. Pompeius, 45 B.C. (Sydenham 174. 1044a), Oxford; *obv.*: head of Ianus (Pompey), legend 'Magn'.; *rev.*: prow, legend 'Pius, Imp.'; p. 104.

14. Denarius of Sex. Pompeius, c. 42 B.C. (Sydenham 210- 1344), Oxford; *obv.*: head of Pompey between jug and lituus, legend 'Mag. Pius Imp. iter. *rev.*: Neptune with his foot on prow stands between Anapias and Amphinomus who carry their parents, legend 'praef. clas. et orae marit. ex. s.c.'; p. 104.

15. Aureus of Sex. Pompeius, c. 42 B.C. (Sydenham 210.¶ 1346a), London; *obv.*: head of Sex. Pompeius, bearded, legend 'Mag. Pius Imp. iter.'; *rev.*: heads of Pompey and Cn. Pompeius, with lituus and tripod, legend 'praef. clas. et orae marit. ex s.c.' p. 104.

16. Denarius of Sex. Pompeius, c. 40 B.C. (Sydenham 210. 1347), Oxford; *obv.*: head of Neptune, legend 'Mag. Pius Imp. iter.'; *rev.*: naval trophy, legend 'praef. clas. et orae marit. ex. s.c.'; p. 104.

17. Denarius of Sex. Pompeius, c. 40 B.C. (Sydenham 211. 1348), Oxford; *obv.*: Pharos of Messana surmounted by Neptune, legend 'Mag. Pius Imp. iter.'; *rev.*: Scylla, legend 'praef. clas. et orae marit. ex s.c.'; p. 104.

Victoria.[1] It is clear that there was a statuary model for these coin issues. The Greeks had such goddesses seated on weapons in many places, for instance in Aetolia (pl. 9. 1).[2] They also had had a cult of the Dea Roma from the beginning of the second century B.C.[3] and represented her in the same manner as those other goddesses. Thus she appeared on coins issued by C. Papirius Carbo (*pr.* 62) in 61–59 B.C. and by C. Caecilius Cornutus (*pr.* 57) in 56 in various cities of Pontus and Bithynia: Amisus, Bithynium, Nicaea, and Nicomedia (pl. 9. 2),[4] though there she is not crowned by Victoria but is holding her in her hand, a difference which will become important later. Such statues will have existed in many Greek cities before one of them was set up at Rome. This type was then represented on the Roman coins mentioned above and repeated on those issued by M. Nonius Sufenas *c.* 60 B.C. (pl. 9. 3),[5] which were to commemorate Sulla's *ludi Victoriae.* The second motif too, the globe under Roma's foot, is found on pre-Caesarian coins, first on those of Q. Fufius Calenus and Cordus (pl. 3. 9),[6] but it is a standing Roma and without Victoria. The seated version, which is needed here, is vouched for by the somewhat earlier coin of P. Cornelius Lentulus with the seated *Genius populi Romani* being crowned by Victoria, and with his foot on the globe (pl. 3. 8):[7] it must depend on a corresponding figure of Roma, which we met on the coin of C. Vibius Pansa (pl. 3 10), and which was repeated shortly before Caesar's death by T. Carisius (pl. 3 12.[8]

As the war went on, Victoria became, as the numerous coin-issues show, more and more important. L. Hostilius Saserna, one of three brothers and followers of Caesar, represented her with caduceus, symbol of peace, trophy, and palm-branch (pl. 9. 4):[9] this may still refer to the victory in Gaul and offer a promise of peace; A. Licinius Nerva with wreath and palm (pl. 9. 5);[10] L. Plautius Plancus, the brother of L. Munatius Plancus (*cos.* 42), represented her in her *quadriga*

---

[1] Sydenham 87 f.; Grueber, pl. 96. 3; 14 f. (again Italia of the rebels, Sydenham 91; pl. 19. 622; 624; cf. Alföldi, pl. 14. 2).
[2] *BMC Thessaly to Aetolia* 194; pl. 30. 3 f.; Head, *HN* 334 (mentioned by Grueber 2. 307 n.). According to Crous, *Corolla L. Curtius* (1937), 220, it did not precede but followed the Roma-type.
[3] Latte 312. 1; cf. *Ath. Mitt.* 77 (1962), 311.
[4] *BMC Pontus* 117; 152; 179; pls. 26. 1; 31. 10; 34. 1; Head, *HN* 497; see below, p. 100.
[5] Sydenham 146; pl. 24. 885; Crous, l.c. 218 (also for the following); above, p. 92. 10.
[6] Sydenham 131; pl. 23. 797; Münzer, *RE* 7. 204; above, pp. 42 f.; below, p. 232.
[7] Sydenham 130; pl. 22. 791; Münzer, *RE* 4. 1393; above, p. 42.
[8] Sydenham 164; Grueber, pl. 52. 9.
[9] Sydenham 159; Grueber, pl. 50. 9; Münzer, *RE* 8. 2512 ff.; Syme, *Roman Rev.* 79. 4.
[10] Sydenham 160; Grueber, pl. 50. 14.

(pl. 9. 6),[1] Lollius Palicanus in her *biga*,[2] perhaps in expectation of further victories. They may have been well-known monuments; there was a Victoria in the *biga* on the Capitol.[3] It is surprising to see that Caesar himself, contrary to his normal habit, recorded the prodigies preceding the battle: in the temple of Athena at Elis the statue of Nike, probably held by Athena in her hand, turned towards the door, and a tree of laurel shot up from the stone pavement in her own temple at Tralles, where a statue of Caesar stood.[4] We may add that at Mytilene offerings for Roma Nikophoros were decreed to commemorate the victory.[5] After the victory at Zela (2 August 47) Caesar set up a trophy in the neighbourhood,[6] which recalls Pompey's trophy in Spain; it is possible that some of the relevant coins refer to this trophy. He announced his victory to the Senate with the words 'veni, vidi, vici', which were later inscribed on a tablet and carried in the triumphal procession.[7] Supplications were decreed for his victories at the Nile and Zela, and Eastern rulers sent him golden crowns.[8]

Those who survived, organized resistance in Africa, prayed for victory, and also chose Victoria as their symbol.[9] Cato placed her seated figure, the cult-image of the temple built by one of his ancestors, on his coins (pl. 9. 7).[10] Scipio, who was in command, issued others with a trophy or Victoria holding a caduceus (pl. 9. 8–9), thus promising victory and peace.[11] The latter coin shows a mysterious personification of Africa on the obverse; another coin, her well-known head,[12] which had already been borrowed by Pompey from indigenous coinage to commemorate his African victory;[13] it was also used later. This reference of Scipio to both victory and Africa is clearly intentional, and not only in the obvious sense. It is recorded that Scipio invoked an ancient oracle, according to which the Scipios were destined to be lucky and

---

[1] Sydenham 160; pl. 26. 959b: the palm-branch proves that she cannot be 'Aurora', as she is called by the numismatists.   [2] Sydenham 161; Grueber, pl. 50. 20.

[3] Tac. *H.* 1. 86. 1; Plut. *Otho* 4. 8; *RE* 8A. 2512.

[4] Caes. *BC* 3. 105. 3 : 'item constabat Elide in templo Minervae . . . quo die proelium secundum Caesar fecisset, simulacrum Victoriae . . . ad valvas se templi limenque convertisse . . . (6) item Trallibus in templo Victoriae, ubi Caesaris statuam consecraverant, palma per eos dies inter coagmenta lapidum ex pavimento exstitisse ostendebatur'; Obs. 65a; Plut. *Caes.* 47. 1 f.; Val. Max. 1. 6. 12; Dio 41. 61. 4.

[5] *IG* 12. 2. 25. 5 (*IGR* 4. 27); below, p. 100. 8.   [6] Dio 42. 48. 2; see above, p. 37.

[7] Plut. *Caes.* 50. 3; Dio 42. 48. 2; Suet. *Caes.* 37. 2; Cichorius, *Röm. St.* 245 ff.

[8] Cic. *Phil.* 14. 23; Dio 42. 49. 3.

[9] Cic. *fam.* 6. 7. 2 (Aulus Caecina, Dec. 46) : 'nemo nostrum est, . . . quin vota victoriae suae fecerit, nemo quin, etiam cum de alia re immolaret, tamen eo quidem ipso tempore, ut quam primum Caesar superaretur, optaret.'

[10] Sydenham 175 f.; Grueber, pl. 121. 8–12; Livy 35. 9. 6; *RE* 8A. 2512.

[11] Sydenham 175; pl. 28. 1049 f.

[12] Sydenham 175; pl. 28. 1051.   [13] Sydenham 171; pl. 27. 1028.

invincible in Africa.[1] The oracle was probably created for Scipio Maior during the Second Punic War and was used again in 147 B.C. for Scipio Aemilianus, when the task of the conquest of Carthage was transferred to him.[2] It is recorded that to nullify the effect of that prophecy Caesar had a member of the Gens Cornelia, Scipio Salvitto, in his camp.[3] But he had to fight against other evil signs as well. He was warned not to sail at the time of the winter solstice because it was inauspicious:[4] he ignored this warning. A second warning came when the victim escaped at the sacrifice, an evil sign,[5] and yet he did not delay his departure but mastered the winds. When he reached Africa he fell down on the shore, an evil sign again: he turned it into a good one by embracing the earth and exclaiming 'teneo te, Africa',[6] thus anticipating the coming victory. Needless to say, this is not normal historical recording but a mixture of facts and fancy. It is a fact that Caesar did delay his departure because of the unfavourable winds;[7] also that they could not possibly have been the storms of the solstice, because, according to the Julian Calendar, it was only about 8 October. Again it is likely that Scipio invoked the ancient oracle in his favour, because this seems to be confirmed by his coins; one may not be so sure whether Caesar really had the other Scipio in his camp. But it is a good story, which best belongs to a literary work, even poetry, perhaps a contemporary epos entitled *Bellum Africum*.[8] It will have contained many other incidents as well, presented the Caesarian version of the struggle, no doubt without the high drama of Cato's death, and demonstrated that Victoria was on his side and made him victorious.[9]

---

[1] Suet. *Caes.* 59; Dio 42. 57. 5; Plut. *Caes.* 52. 4; Münzer, *Adelsp.* 100; Weber, *Der Prophet u. sein Gott* 68. 2.

[2] Flor. 1. 31. 12. The oracle about the third Cornelius who was to rule over Rome (Cic. *Cat.* 3. 9; 4. 2 (below, p. 193. 1); Sall. *Cat.* 47. 2, etc.) was a later version of it, which is not relevant here.

[3] Suet. *Caes.* 59: 'ad eludendas autem vaticinationes, quibus felix et invictus in ea provincia fataliter nomen Scipionum ferebatur, despectissimum quendam ex Corneliorum genere, cui ad opprobrium vitae Salvitoni cognomen erat, in castris secum habuit'; Dio 42. 48. 1; Plut. *Caes.* 52. 5; Pliny 35. 8; Münzer, *RE* 4. 1505 f.

[4] Auspicia: Min. Fel. *Oct.* 25. 4; haruspex: Cic. *div.* 2. 52 (cf. Ter. *Phorm.* 709: 'haruspex vetuit, ante brumam autem novi / negoti incipere'); Dio 42. 56. 1: ἐς τὴν Ἀφρίκην καίτοι τοῦ χειμῶνος ἐνεστηκότος ἐπεραιώθη; B. *Afr.* 1. 3; 2. 4; Plut. *Caes.* 52. 2.

[5] Suet. *Caes.* 59; cf. below, pp. 118. 8 f.; 342. 5.

[6] Suet. *Caes.* 59; above, p. 22. [7] B. *Afr.* 1. 3. 44.

[8] See below, p. 123, for the suggestion that the whole Civil War was treated in epic poetry.

[9] Cic. *Lig.* 18: 'tuus invictus exercitus'; 19: 'nunc melior ea (pars) iudicanda est, quam etiam di adiuverunt'; Lucan 1. 128: 'victrix causa deis placuit, sed victa Catoni.' Colonia Victrix Iulia was a frequent name of Caesarian colonies; there was also the *legio VI Victrix*, *RE* 8A. 2489 f.; Vittinghoff 67. 3; 80.

It was after the victory at Thapsus (6 April 46) that the Senate decreed a number of honours in connection with the expected triumph. They need not be discussed here again, nor the clay relief[1] closely reflecting those honours. But the flying Victoria of the relief, about to crown Caesar, deserves a brief mention: it is the only instance of this kind not found on contemporary coins. There were many allusive issues before and after the triumph. The coin of L. Papius Celsus with the unique head of Triumphus has already been mentioned; he also issued a coin with the bust of Victoria.[2] This bust was repeated by other moneyers, T. Carisius, L. Valerius Acisculus, but also by the *praefectus urbi* of 45, L. Munatius Plancus, and by C. Clovius, who was a *praefectus* with another function.[3] Its constant repetition suggests that it had a special meaning in addition to the celebration of Caesar's victory. Carisius and Considius also reproduced Victoria in the act of riding in the triumphal *quadriga*,[4] an old and frequent theme which does not require comment by itself. Here, however, it stands for Caesar's chariot but without Caesar, although before him Marius, Sulla, and Pompey were represented in their triumphal chariots.[5] Carisius further issued coins with Victoria in the *biga*, Considius with Victoria walking,[6] again old and frequent themes; Carisius also Victoria on the obverse and Roma with her foot on the globe on the reverse, which was mentioned above.[7]

We turn to the third theme, Victoria's association with Venus. Four moneyers, M. Mettius, L. Aemilius Buca, C. Cossutius Maridianus, and P. Sepullius Macer, issued the coins in question while Caesar was still alive (pl. 9. 10–16): the fully-dressed Venus holding Victoria in her right hand, a sceptre in her left, and having a shield at her side, with some variations which need not be mentioned here.[8] This is clearly the reproduction of a statue. The question whether it was the cult-image of Venus Genetrix has already been considered.[9] But another question is more relevant here: how is it to be interpreted? It provides us with one of the decisive proofs that Victoria and Venus were not identical. But it shows a close attachment, as was not shown before at Rome,

[1] See above, pp. 45 ff.

[2] Sydenham 161; Grueber, pl. 51. 3; see above, pp. 64 f.

[3] Sydenham 164; 166; 169 f.; pl. 26. 985; Grueber, pl. 53. 11; 13; 17; S. L. Cesano, *Rend. Pont. Accad.* 23/4 (1947/9), 129 ff.

[4] Sydenham 164 f.; pl. 26. 985; 994.

[5] Sydenham 81; 123 f.; 171; above, pp. 38; 56.   [6] Sydenham 163; 165.

[7] Sydenham 164; Grueber, pl. 52. 9; above, p. 43.

[8] Sydenham 176–8; pl. 28. 1063; 1076; Grueber, pls. 54. 5 f.; 8 f.; 15 ff.; Cesano, l.c. 136 ff.; Alföldi, *Studien üb. Caesars Monarchie*, pls. 3–14 (valuable collection).

[9] See above, pp. 85 f.

Victoria being placed in the hand of Venus. We have met her already
on earlier Greek coins in the hand of Roma.[1] If we want to understand
the significance of this composition we have to examine its history in
Greece.

(d) Victoria Caesaris

This history begins with Phidias and his Athena Parthenos at Athens
and his Zeus at Olympia, both holding a Nike, Athena standing,[2] Zeus
seated.[3] These two statues inspired many others, standing or seated,
which are reflected on the coinages of the Hellenistic kings, particularly
on that of the Seleucids (pl. 9. 19–21):[4] they became symbols of victory
and of invincibility. Further, Nike was placed in the hand of other
deities as well, of Dionysus, Artemis, Demeter; they were then often
called Nikephoroi.[5] The next to receive a Nike was the Dea Roma,
represented as an Amazon seated on shields, a version of the seated
Athena.[6] We have already seen this Roma on some coins of Pontus and
Bithynia and assumed that it existed in many other places.[7] The Roma
Nikophoros of Mytilene who received a sacrifice after the victory at
Pharsalus[8] was no doubt such a Roma. In the West she is first found on the
relief of the Gens Augusta at Carthage (pl. 11. 1),[9] at Rome on coins,
seated or standing, from Nero, Galba, and Vespasian onwards, often
with the legend 'Roma Victrix' (pl. 9. 17).[10]

This is a clear line from Phidias to the Dea Roma of the Greek cities.
But the change from Roma to Venus in 45 B.C. is abrupt, which suggests that it was due to Caesar's personal intervention. It was an independent creation, even if there is some isolated, and therefore irrelevant,
evidence about an Aphrodite Nikephoros and Stratonikis in the Greek
world.[11] It was not continued. After Caesar's death Minerva—no doubt
the Athena Parthenos—followed on Roman coins (pl. 9. 18; 22–3),[12] but

---

[1] See above, p. 96.

[2] Epict. 2. 8. 20; Richter, Scritti in onore di Calderini–Paribeni 3 (1956), 147 ff.; G. P.
Stevens, Hesp. 30 (1961), 1 ff.

[3] Cornut. 9 (p. 10 L.); Schrader, Arch. Jahrb. 56 (1941), 7 ff.

[4] Lacroix, BCH 73 (1949), 163 ff.

[5] Höfer, Myth. Lex. 3. 358 ff.; gr. Kruse, RE 17. 310 f.

[6] Athena: e.g. Head, HN 284.   [7] See above, p. 96.

[8] IGR 4. 27; Sherk, Greek, Roman and Byz. Stud. 4 (1963), 145 ff.

[9] CAH Plates 4. 134; Ryberg, pl. 27. 41b.

[10] Mattingly 1. 211; 232 ff.; 353; 381; 2. 154; 195, etc.; C. C. Vermeule, The Goddess
Roma in the Art of the Rom. Emp. (1959), 29 ff.; pls. 1 ff.

[11] Aphrodite Nikephoros at Argos (Paus. 2. 19. 6), Stratonikis at Smyrna, BMC Ionia
239 ff.; pl. 25. 9 (second–first cent. B.C.); 266 ff.; pl. 28. 7 (Augustus); Head, HN 593;
Gebhard, RE 4A. 325 f.

[12] Coin of C. Vibius Varus, c. 42 B.C., Sydenham 186; Grueber, pl. 58. 11.

PLATE 11

1

1. Marble altar of the Gens Augusta from Carthage in the Musée du Bardo, Tunis, front face: Roma holding Victoria, in front of her an altar with globe, cornucopiae and caduceus (Photograph: German Archaeological Institute, Rome); p. 100.

2. Silver cup from Boscoreale, destroyed, formerly Coll. Rothschild, Paris: Augustus seated and holding a globe receives Victoria from Venus who is accompanied by Cupid (From *Mon. Piot* 5, pl. 31.); p. 101.

2

3

3. Bronze relief on a swordsheath from Mainz, British Museum, London: Tiberius receives Victoria from Germanicus, between them Mars in the background; at the side of Tiberius a shield inscribed 'Felicitas Tiberi', behind him Victoria with a shield inscribed 'Vic. Aug.' (Photograph: British Museum); p. 101.

why she took the place of Roma and Venus is not clear. After a long and puzzling interval, Iuppiter, Mars, and Virtus, with Victoria, appeared during the Civil Wars.[1]

Caesar went even further. It was not enough that he gave Victoria as attribute to his ancestress Venus: he too was going to hold her in his hand. This had not happened before; it was always Zeus and not the ruler, a human being, on the coins of the Hellenistic kings. There is no direct Caesarian evidence. It is on coins of the East issued *c*. 29–27 B.C. that Victoria first appears in the hand of Augustus, who is seated on a curule chair (pl. 10. 1).[2] The next piece of evidence is provided by one of the silver cups from Boscoreale: Augustus, seated on a throne, holds a globe in his hand, and Venus, accompanied by Cupid, is handing the statue of Victoria over to him (pl. 11. 2).[3] On the sword-sheath of 'Tiberius', found at Mainz, Augustus is seated and is receiving Victoria from Tiberius (pl. 11. 3).[4] It would not matter if, as has been suggested, they were rather Tiberius and Germanicus:[5] one could still claim that the composition depended on an Augustan model. But that model was not created for Rome. It was coins of the East that showed Augustus holding Victoria, but not the coins issued at Rome. They did not have it until Nero, who was the first, as we have seen, to represent the seated Roma with Victoria on his coins: now he too was holding her, but he was standing (pl. 10. 2).[6] So was Galba, who in addition is being crowned by the personified Senatus (pl. 10. 3).[7] Vespasian too appears in the company of the Senatus, but also of Roma, who is handing Victoria over to him (pl. 10. 4); he is further represented with Victoria by Titus as Divus Vespasianus, seated and on a throne or on a chariot with elephants (pl. 10. 5–6).[8] On coins of Domitian only Iuppiter Victor is found with Victoria,[9] on those of Nerva and Trajan, the seated Roma; once she is receiving Victoria from Trajan, who is standing facing her (pl. 10. 7).[10]

This development shows that the theme was firmly established at the end of the first century A.D., after its first appearance in Augustan

[1] Mattingly 1. 371; 376; 293; 342; 351.   [2] Mattingly 1. 104; pl. 15. 16.
[3] H. de Villefosse, *Mon. Piot.* 5 (1899), 34 ff.; pl. 31. 1; *CAH Plates* 4. 128a; Rostovtzeff, *Social and Economic Hist. of the Rom. Emp.* 1. 76; pl. 13; T. Hölscher, op. cit. 181; pl. 3. 1.
[4] *CAH Plates* 4. 140a; Lippold, *Festschr. d. röm.-germ. Zentralmus. in Mainz*, 1 (1952), 5; cf. *RE* 8A. 2527; T. Hölscher, op. cit. 112 ff.; pl. 15. 1.
[5] Gagé, *Rev. arch.* 5e. sér. 32 (1930), 9.
[6] Mattingly 1. 208; pl. 39. 13; above, p. 100. 10.   [7] Mattingly 1. 359; pl. 59. 3.
[8] Mattingly 2. 180; 242; 269; pls. 31. 1; 46. 19; 51. 5.
[9] Mattingly 2. 369, etc.; pl. 72. 10.
[10] Mattingly 3. 15; 18; 71; 159; pls. 14. 5; 27. 4; also standing: 164; pl. 28. 1, etc.; on later emperors see Schlachter, *Globus* 85, 1.

art and after what seems to be a reverse under the Julio-Claudian emperors. One would not hesitate to ascribe the initiative here too, as so often elsewhere, to Caesar. This is initially no more than a hypothesis but it is supported by a *denarius* of L. Cornelius Lentulus (*cos.* 3) of uncertain date (pl. 10. 8):[1] 20–15, 12, and *c.* 6 B.C. have been proposed.[2] The obverse shows the head of Augustus, the reverse two figures standing; the one has a shield at his side, inscribed 'C(lupeus) V(irtutis)', and is crowning the other, who has a star over his head and holds Victoria in his right hand: Augustus and Caesar. Augustus is identified by the shield, which he received from the Senate and the Roman people in 27 B.C.,[3] and Caesar by the star, which was placed on his statues after the appearance of the comet in July 44 and after his consecration in 42 B.C.[4] Agrippa has also been proposed instead of Caesar, but without any justification and against all probability, mainly, as it seems, in order to get support for the attribution of some moneyers to the year 12 B.C.[5] Here, then, there is explicit evidence for Caesar; but whether he was responsible, or Augustus after his death, cannot be decided on the evidence of this coin. The silver cup from Boscoreale helps. It makes better sense if it depends on a Caesarian composition: Venus handing over Victoria to Caesar is natural, to Augustus only if it follows the Caesarian precedent. She was his ancestress and received the Victoria for the first time under his rule. It is clear that the silver cup reflects monumental representations of this handing over. They inspired later variations, the creation of the groups of Roma and Vespasian and of Roma and Trajan: on the former Roma is giving, on the latter receiving.

Our next contention is that all this was not mere artistic fancy but served to interpret the new goddess, Victoria Caesaris. It is certain that there was a statue of Venus holding Victoria; it is almost certain that there was another of Caesar, and in addition a group of the two, Venus handing Victoria over to Caesar. At any rate the Victoria Caesaris was created, a personal goddess, which was an innovation. There was no Sullan precedent: his festival was called at first 'ludi Victoriae', and 'Sullae' or 'Sullanae' was added later,[6] probably when it was to be distinguished from Caesar's festival without implying the existence of a personal Victoria of Sulla. Moreover Sulla's victory

---

[1] Mattingly 1. 26; pl. 4. 14.

[2] Mommsen, *Zeitschr. f. Num.* 11, 80 (25–15 B.C.); Mattingly 1, p. cvii (12 B.C.); Grueber 2. 102 (6 B.C.); cf. Groag, *PIR* 2. 336 f.; Gagé, *Congr. Internat. Numism. Paris 1953*, 2 (1957), 222 ff.   [3] *Mon. Anc.* 34. 2; below, p. 229.

[4] Pliny 2. 94; Suet. *Caes.* 88; Obs. 68; below, p. 371.

[5] Mattingly 1, pp. xcvii; cvii.   [6] See above, p. 92.

acquired an evil connotation of tyranny, proscription, and the like in
the course of time,[1] whereas Caesar meant to build a different political
programme on his victory which promised generosity and clemency towards his fellow citizens.[2]

(e) Imperator

One is bound to assume that Victoria Caesaris must have concerned
Caesar himself even more as a divine symbol of a change in his status.
What this change could have been may be reconstructed with the help
of some of the honours which the Senate decreed in the following
year when the news of the victory at Munda reached Rome (20 April
45).[3] The following seem relevant here:[4] Caesar should receive the
'praenomen Imperatoris'; he should always wear the laurel wreath; his
lictors should have laurel on their fasces; supplications should be held
on his behalf after every victory; he should wear the triumphal garb
at all functions; and his ivory statue should be carried in the *pompa
circensis*. All these honours were—so it will be argued—to celebrate
Caesar's new status, that of the permanent Imperator.

An imperator was anyone who could give orders, a ruler, an official
or a private citizen; there is no need to recapitulate the history of the
term.[5] It is a strange usage that matters here, the acclamation of the
military commander as imperator by his soldiers on the battlefield after
victory was won.[6] It became his title, which he kept until his return to
Rome. It was recorded, for example, on inscriptions and coins during
its tenure, but often also later.[7] Successful generals like Sulla and Pompey
were naturally acclaimed more than once, and the iteration too was duly
recorded.[8] It is important to add that Pompey was also acclaimed

[1] Sall. *Cat.* 21. 4; 37. 6; 9.

[2] Caes. ap. Cic. *Att.* 9. 7c. 1 (March 49): 'temptemus hoc modo . . . omnium voluntates
recuperare et diuturna victoria uti, quoniam reliqui crudelitate odium effugere non potuerunt,
neque victoriam diutius tenere praeter unum L. Sullam, quem imitaturus non sum. haec nova
sit ratio vincendi, ut misericordia et liberalitate nos muniamus'; cf. *RE* 8A. 2509.

[3] See below, pp. 175 ff.

[4] For references and discussion see below, pp. 106 ff.

[5] See *Thes.L.L.* 7. 1. 553 ff.; Rosenberg, *RE* 9. 1139 ff.; R. Combès, *Imperator* (1966, with
bibliography).

[6] Tac. *A.* 3. 74. 6: 'Tiberius . . . Blaeso tribuit ut imperator a legionibus salutaretur prisco
erga duces honore, qui bene gesta re publica gaudio et impetu victoris exercitus conclama-
bantur'; Dio 43. 44. 2; 52. 41. 3; App. *BC* 2. 44. 176 f.; Mommsen, *StR* 1. 124; Rosenberg
1141 f.

[7] D. McFayden, *The History of the Title Imperator under the Roman Empire* (1920), 7 ff.;
Kienast, *Zeitschr. Sav. Stift.* 78 (1961), 403 ff.; Combès, op. cit. 452 ff.

[8] Sulla: *ILS* 870; *Or. gr.* 441. 101; 442. 8; *Syll.* 747. 39; Sydenham 756–61; 767. Pompey:
ILS 876 f.; 8776; 9459; Degr. 380–2; *Syll.* 751 f.; 762; *IGR* 3. 869; 4. 49 f.; 79 f.; 1710;
AE 1957. 18; Cic. *fam.* 5. 7; Pliny 7. 97; Plut. *Pomp.* 8. 3; Diod. 39. 10; Sydenham 1035–9.

Magnus, which thus became his *cognomen*;[1] and that Cicero when praising his abilities and achievements stated that the Roman people wanted him alone, 'unum imperatorem', for the conduct of the war against Mithridates.[2] This was a non-technical usage and yet symptomatic of the change of times. In 61, after his third triumph, he was granted the exceptional privilege of wearing the triumphal dress and crown in the Circus:[3] we shall return to this later. His sons inherited the *cognomen* Magnus from their father and earned the title imperator for themselves by their own achievements. The elder issued coins in Spain in 46 with the head of his father and the legends 'Cn. Magnus imp.' and 'Cn. Magnus imp. f.' (pl. 10. 9–10),[4] the former referring to the father, the latter to himself. He had probably been acclaimed shortly before and used this opportunity for an advertisement of his father's glory as well. He could not do more, because he was murdered in April 45 after the defeat at Munda. His brother Sextus followed in 45 with issues showing his father's head again and the legend 'Sex. Magn. Pius imp. Sal.' (pl. 10. 11–13),[5] thus implying that he had just been acclaimed. In 42 and 40 his second acclamation was commemorated: 'Mag. Pius imp. iter.' (pl. 10. 14–17).[6] Here he replaced his original *praenomen* by the *cognomen* Magnus which is already attested by Cicero for March 43;[7] and he used as his sole *cognomen* Pius, which he had assumed in 45. The behaviour of Pompey and his sons shows that the title, though provisional, had gained in importance and was finally used almost like the permanent *cognomen* Magnus.

Caesar was first acclaimed in 61 in Spain.[8] While he was in Gaul he was called by Catullus ironically 'imperator unicus'.[9] By this he will have meant little more than 'the successful general'; and yet one is reminded of Cicero's similar praise of Pompey and of the latter's subsequent exceptional status, especially as Catullus too had both of them in mind. It is safe to assume—there is no explicit evidence—that in Gaul Caesar was acclaimed three times, in 57, 55, and 52, because in these years supplications were decreed for him in Rome.[10] Cicero addressed him as imperator in a letter written in 54,[11] and Caesar himself used this

---

[1] Livy *Per.* 103; Plut. *Pomp.* 13. 7 f.; Mommsen, *StR* 3. 213. 1.

[2] Cic. *imp. Cn. Pomp.* 44: 'universus populus Romanus . . . unum sibi ad . . . bellum Cn. Pompeium imperatorem depoposcit.'

[3] See below, p. 108. 6.   [4] Sydenham 1036–8.

[5] Sydenham 1041–44; 1045 ('Magnus Pius imp. f.').   [6] Sydenham 1344–8.

[7] Cic. *Phil.* 13. 50 (draft of SC): 'Magnum Pompeium, Gnaei filium'; cf. *ILS* 8891 (Lilybaeum): 'Mag. Pompeio Mag. f. Pio imp. augure . . .'; Syme, *Hist.* 7 (1958), 174; 182.

[8] Plut. *Caes.* 12. 4; Dio 44. 41. 3; App. *BC* 2. 8. 27; Cic. *Pis.* 59.

[9] Catull. 29. 11; 54. 7.

[10] Caes. *BG* 2. 35. 4; 4. 38; 7. 90. 8; Dio 39. 5. 1; 53. 2; 40. 50. 4.

[11] Cic. *fam.* 7. 5; cf. *prov. cons.* 32 (56 B.C.).

title in 49 in his letters to Cicero.[1] The title further appeared on inscriptions in the East[2]—here in the form αὐτοκράτωρ—and West [3]in the same
manner as in the case of Pompey but without the numeral of iteration;[4]
also after 46,[5] although through the triumph he had ceased to be imperator until the next acclamation.

Caesar thus followed tradition and was no doubt particularly influenced
by Pompey's precedent. But he soon went further, although he made his
innovation appear less new than it in fact was. We learn of a plan
through Cicero's *Paradoxa Stoicorum*,[6] written about May 46, that is, at
the time when the victory of Thapsus was known in Rome but the
triumph not yet held. Cicero, without mentioning Caesar by name, indicates that there were three versions of a plan in circulation: Caesar
should be praised as imperator, or called so, or should be thought worthy
of this name. Cicero was, of course, opposed to all this. But a few months
later he changed his mind, after the triumph and the extensive celebrations that followed it. In his speech *Pro Ligario* he now acknowledged that
Caesar was the one real imperator in the Roman empire and yet had
written the year before to say that he was willing to share this title with
Cicero.[7] We remember what Cicero had said about Pompey twenty
years earlier, and Catullus about Caesar ten years earlier. But here the
imperator is no longer just the ideal commander. Cicero's reference to

---

[1] Cic. *Att.* 9. 6A (March 49): 'Caesar imp. s. d. Ciceroni imp.'; 9. 16; 10. 8B.

[2] Jos. *AJ* 14. 10. 2. 190 (48 B.C.): Γάιος Ἰούλιος Καῖσαρ αὐτοκράτωρ καὶ ἀρχιερεὺς δικτάτωρ
τὸ δεύτερον; 14. 10. 2. 192; 3 f. 196; 199; 7. 211. On inscriptions set up in many places
after the victory at Pharsalus and later (collected by Raubitschek, *JRS* 44 (1954), 65 ff.)
αὐτοκράτωρ, unless it precedes the name (see below p. 106. 4 f.), always follows it immediately before or after ἀρχιερεύς; the office of consul or dictator comes only after that;
Kienast, l.c. 415 f.

[3] *ILS* 70 (Degr. 406, Bovianum, 48 or 46 B.C.): 'C. Iulio Caesari imperatori dictatori
iterum pontufici maximo . . .'; A. Panuccio, *Athen.* 45 (1967), 158 f. (*AE* 1967. 107, Vibo
Valentia, 46 B.C.): 'C. Caesari pontif. max. imp. cos. tert. ex s.c. populus patrono'; *ILS* 5320
(Degr. 580, Corubis, 45 B.C.): 'C. Caesare imp. cos. IIII . . .'; Lex Urson., *ILS* 6087, CIIII
(44 B.C.): '. . . iussu C. Caesaris dict. imp.'

[4] This fact renders the interpretation of the legend ⅃ II on some coins of Caesar (Sydenham 1008–12)—commonly believed to be a numeral indicating his age, 52—as 'I(mperator)
IT(erum)' by Eckhel 6. 15 and Carcopino, *Mél. Bidez* 1. 38; *Les étapes de l'impérialisme
romain* 150. 1, most unlikely. In Jos. *AJ* 14. 10. 2. 192 and 6. 202 αὐτοκράτωρ τὸ δεύτερον is
an error for αὐτ. δικτάτωρ τὸ δεύτ., see 190 (above, n. 2).

[5] L. Gasperini, *Seconda Miscellanea* (1968), 382 (Tarentum): 'C. Iulio C. f. Caesare patre
patr. imperatore dict. rei publicae constituendae . . .'

[6] Cic. *Parad.* 33: 'laudetur vero hic imperator aut etiam appelletur aut hoc nomine
dignus putetur! quo modo aut cui tandem hic libero imperabit, qui non potest cupiditatibus
imperare?' 37; 41: 'ille videat, quo modo imperator esse possit, cum eum ne liberum quidem
esse ratio et veritas ipsa convincat'; Gelzer, *RE* 7A. 1011.

[7] Cic. *Lig.* 7: qui ad me ex Aegypto litteras misit, ut essem idem qui fuissem, qui, cum
ipse imperator in toto imperio populi Romani unus esset, esse me alterum passus est; a quo
hoc ipso C. Pansa mihi hunc nuntium perferente concessos fasces laureatos tenui, quoad
tenendos putavi.

this previous correspondence, in which 'Caesar imp.' will have addressed 'Cicero imp.', shows that the technical term is meant.[1] The conclusion therefore is that here Cicero has the same plan in mind which he alluded to in the *Paradoxa*; but this time he refers to it with favour.

The plan was realized by the Senate in 45 when, according to Suetonius and Dio, it granted Caesar, his sons, and descendants the *praenomen Imperatoris*.[2] The validity of this evidence is, however, much contested[3] and it has been assumed that it was invented by Augustus in order to support his own claim to that *praenomen*. It is tempting to accept this view. For on coins of 44 the title does not precede but follows his name, as it does on earlier Caesarian coins and inscriptions and on those of Pompey and everybody else. Yet it is not true to say that no evidence for the *praenomen* exists[4] or that in some cases where *imperator* follows the name[5] it could not be part of the nomenclature. Nonetheless it must be admitted that the few instances that there are and the two passages in Cicero are not sufficient to convert the sceptic.

A new defence of the authenticity of the decree can be attempted with the help of the other honours voted at the same time and mentioned at the beginning of this section.[6] We comment on them in the traditional order of the events[7] to which they belonged. They all depended on the

---

[1] See the letters of 49, above, p. 105. 1 ; that from Egypt has not survived. The reference to the *fasces laureati* points to the same conclusion: see below, p. 107.

[2] Suet. *Caes.* 76. 1 : 'non enim honores modo nimios recepit: . . . praenomen Imperatoris, cognomen Patris patriae . . .' ; Dio 43. 44. 2 (45 B.C.) : τό τε τοῦ αὐτοκράτορος ὄνομα οὐ κατὰ τὸ ἀρχαῖον ἔτι μόνον . . . ἀλλὰ καθάπαξ τοῦτο δὴ τὸ καὶ νῦν τοῖς τὸ κράτος ἀεὶ ἔχουσι διδόμενον ἐκείνῳ τότε πρώτῳ τε καὶ πρῶτον, ὥσπερ τι κύριον, προσέθεσαν. καὶ τοσαύτη γε ὑπερβολῇ κολακείας ἐχρήσαντο ὥστε καὶ τοὺς παῖδας τούς τε ἐγγόνους αὐτοῦ οὕτω καλεῖσθαι ψηφίσασθαι, μήτε τέκνου τι αὐτοῦ ἔχοντος καὶ γέροντος ἤδη ὄντος ; 52. 41. 3 ; App. *BC* 2.110. 461 does not seem relevant.

[3] It is rejected by Mommsen, *StR* 2. 767. 3 (basis of all later discussion) ; McFayden, op. cit. 23 ff. ; Syme, l.c. 176 ; Felber, *Caesars Streben nach der Königswürde* (*Unters. z. röm. Gesch.*, hrsg. v. F. Altheim 1. 1961), 233 ff. ; Combès, op. cit. 123 ff. ; it is accepted by Rosenberg 1143 ; v. Premerstein, 246 f. ; Alföldi, *Studien über Caesars Monarchie* 29 ; Kraft, *Jahrb. f. Num. u. Geldgesch.* 3/4 (1952/3), 65 ; Kienast, l.c. 417.

[4] Jos. *AJ* 16. 6. 2. 162 (document of Augustus') : ἐπὶ τοῦ ἐμοῦ πατρὸς Αὐτοκράτορος Καίσαρος ; *Syll.* 763 (Cyzicus, 46 B.C.) : . . . τῷ Αὐτοκράτορι Γαΐῳ Ἰουλίῳ, Γαΐου νεἱῷ, Καίσαρι ; so also *IGR* 4. 929 ; *IG* 12. 5. 557. These epigraphical instances are valid only if one assumes that the old praenomen Γάιος was kept by error. On the other hand, the entry, *Fast. Vall.*, 2 Aug. (Degrassi 491) : 'Feriae quod hoc die Imp. Caesar Hispaniam citeriorem vicit', is clearly due to a confusion with Augustus: the other Calendars have 'C. Caesar' or 'Caesar'.

[5] App. *BC* 4. 8. 34 (edict of proscriptions, 43 B.C.) Γάιον μὲν δὴ (Καίσαρα) καὶ αὐτοκράτορα ὄντα καὶ ἄρχοντα ἱερῶν ; *Syll.* 764. 10 (SC de Mytilen., 45 B.C.) : . . . Γάιος Καῖσαρ αὐτοκράτωρ ; *Or. gr.* 455 = E.-J. 299 (SC de Aphrodis., 42 B.C.) : . . . ὡς ἔκρινε Γάιος Καῖσαρ αὐτοκράτωρ.

[6] It is not a new attempt in so far as most of this evidence has already been mentioned by v. Premerstein 248 in its proper context.

[7] For the sequence acclamation, supplication, triumph see Cic. *Pis.* 97 ; Val. Max. 2. 8. 7. It did not rest on an ancestral or later law but on the practice of the second and first centuries B.C. A list of the acclamations is provided by Combès, op. cit. 452 ff. ; of the supplications by Halkin, *La supplication d'action de grâces chez les Romains* (1953), 19 ff. ; of the triumphs by the

victory: the acclamation took place after it was won. A permanent imperator therefore would be the permanent victor: in fact all victories had now become Caesar's victories, as—so it was decided—others fought and won under his auspices.[1] Next, after the acclamation the imperator put on a laurel wreath, which he wore until his return to Rome: Caesar was now entitled to wear it always.[2] After the acclamation the fasces of the imperator were decorated with laurel branches[3] and so was the spear of his messenger,[4] who took his report, again decorated with laurel, the *laureatae litterae*,[5] to the Senate at Rome. The laurel of the fasces used to be deposited by the imperator in the lap of the Capitoline Iuppiter on his return:[6] Caesar has now received the privilege of having the fasces of his lictors always decorated with laurel.[7] After the *laureatae litterae* had been received, the Senate decreed supplications for the victor in question:[8] henceforth supplications were to be held in Caesar's name, as well as in the victor's name, even if he had not taken part in that campaign.[9] Finally, the imperator, if he was granted the triumph, wore the triumphal dress and crown on that single day:[10] Caesar was granted the permanent use of the triumphal dress for all functions.[11] This honour requires some further comment, which, however, will lead us back to the central issue.

Anyone was entitled to wear military rewards and symbols of past office at the games:[12] military decorations like the *corona aurea*[13] (to be

Fasti Triumphales and by Degrassi, who in his commentary produces all the evidence that is missing in the Fasti.

[1] See the evidence about the supplications below, n. 9; see also below, p. 112. 4 f.

[2] Dio 43. 43. 1: καὶ τῷ στεφάνῳ τῷ δαφνίνῳ ἀεὶ καὶ πανταχοῦ ὁμοίως ἐκοσμεῖτο; Suet. *Caes*. 45. 2: 'ius laureae coronae perpetuo gestandae'; Mommsen, *StR* 1. 428. 1.

[3] Obs. 61a; Caes. *BC* 3. 71. 3; Dio 54. 25. 4; 55. 5. 2; *Mon. Anc*. 4. 1; Mommsen ad loc. and *StR* 1. 374; Samter, *RE* 6. 2005 f.

[4] Pliny 15. 133 f.; Plut. *Pomp*. 41. 4; Sen. *Ag*. 390; Mart. 7. 6. 6; v. Premerstein, *RE* 12. 1014; Halkin, op. cit. 81 ff.

[5] Livy 5. 28. 13; 45. 1. 6; Pliny 15. 133, etc.; v. Premerstein, *RE* 12. 1014.

[6] Pliny 15. 134; Obs. 61a.

[7] Dio 44. 4. 3: καὶ τοῖς ῥαβδούχοις δαφνηφοροῦσιν ἀεὶ χρῆσθαι.   [8] See above, p. 62.

[9] Dio 43. 44. 6: ἱερομηνίαν τε ἐξαίρετον ὁσάκις ἂν νίκη τέ τις συμβῇ καὶ θυσίαι ἐπ' αὐτῇ γίγνωνται, κἂν μήτε συστρατεύσηται μηθ' ὅλως ἐπικοινωνήσῃ τῶν καταπραχθέντων; 45. 7. 2: ἱερομηνίαις τισὶν ἐπινικίοις ἰδίαν ἡμέραν ἐπὶ τῷ ὀνόματι αὐτοῦ ἐβουθύτησαν; 47. 18. 4: εἴ τε νίκη τις ἠγγέλθη ποθέν, χωρὶς μὲν τῷ κρατήσαντι, χωρὶς δὲ ἐκείνῳ καὶ τεθνεῶτι τιμὴν ἱερομηνίας ἔνεμον; 57. 15. 5; Cic. *Phil*. 1. 12: 'de supplicationibus referebatur . . . (13) an me censetis . . . decreturum fuisse, ut Parentalia cum supplicationibus miscerentur, . . . ut decernerentur supplicationes mortuo?' 5. 19.   [10] See above, pp. 66 f.

[11] Dio 43. 43. 1: αὐτὸς δὲ τήν τε στολὴν τὴν ἐπινίκιον ἐν πάσαις ταῖς πανηγύρεσι κατὰ δόγμα ἐνεδύετο; App. *BC* 2. 106. 442: θύειν μὲν αὐτὸν αἰεὶ θριαμβικῶς ἠμφιεσμένον; cf. Dio 60. 6. 9 (Claudius); Mommsen, *StR* 1. 414. 4.

[12] Polyb. 6. 39. 9; Mommsen, *StR* 1. 438. 2.

[13] Gell. 2. 11. 2; Pliny 7. 102; 22. 6; Livy 3. 29. 3; 7. 10. 14; 7. 26. 10; 7. 37. 1 (Fest. 190 M. = 208 L.); 26. 48. 14; Marquardt, *StV* 2. 576 f.; Steiner, *BJ* 114 (1905), 38 ff.; 47 ff. (epigraphical list); 82 ff.

distinguished from the golden crown of the triumphators), even the
corona civica if one had saved the life of a citizen in battle;[1] the *toga
praetexta* if one had been a magistrate.[2] Accordingly, past triumphators
were entitled to the laurel wreath[3] which they, in common with their
soldiers, had worn in the triumphal procession,[4] to the *toga praetexta*
of their past consulship, but not to the golden crown decorated with
gems which had been held over their head in the procession nor to the
triumphal dress. One might therefore say that Caesar's privileges were
not new in spite of the fact that they were not restricted to the games.
Even the triumphal dress and golden crown had already been granted
to L. Aemilius Paullus in 167[5] and Pompey in 61[6]; they were entitled
to wear the golden crown and the triumphal dress in the Circus, and
the laurel wreath and the *toga praetexta* in the theatre. Here again the
privilege was now extended: Caesar, as the permanent triumphator,
could wear crown and dress without such restrictions. Yet we are bound
to ask why such exceptions were made at all.

The answer may be found if attention is turned to the paradox and the
early history of the acclamation. The paradox is that it makes the victor
what he already is, a 'commander'; as to the history, there is no certain
evidence of early cases, which means that the numberless early victors
had not been so acclaimed. These two problems are solved if one
assumes that the Roman custom was created under the influence of the
acclamation of the Hellenistic kings by their armies.[7] The first example
known to us is that of the elder Scipio. He was saluted king by the
native princes on his victorious campaign in Spain in 209; he rejected this
name because it was impossible in Rome and asked them to call him, as

---

[1] Pliny 16. 13; below, p. 163.

[2] Cic. *Phil.* 2. 110; Livy, *Per.* 19; Mommsen, *StR* 1. 437. 1.

[3] Dio 48. 16. 1; Mommsen, *StR* 1. 438; cf. Zonar. 7. 21 (2, p. 150 Dd. = Dio 6: 1,
p. 74 B.).

[4] Pliny 33. 11; Iuven. 10. 39; App. *Pun.* 66. 297; Zonar. 7. 21; Mommsen, *StR* 1. 427. 2;
Alföldi, *Röm. Mitt.* 50 (1935), 39.

[5] *Vir. ill.* 56. 5: 'ei a populo et a senatu concessum est, ut ludis circensibus triumphali
veste uteretur'; Mommsen, *StR* 1. 439. 1.

[6] Dio 37. 21. 4: δαφνηφορεῖν τε αὐτὸν κατὰ πάσας ἀεὶ τὰς πανηγύρεις, καὶ τὴν στολὴν τὴν μὲν
ἀρχικὴν ἐν πάσαις αὐταῖς, τὴν δὲ ἐπινίκιον ἐν τοῖς τῶν ἵππων ἀγῶσιν ἐνδύνειν, ταῦτα γὰρ αὐτῷ
συμπράσσοντος ἐς τὰ μάλιστα τοῦ Καίσαρος, καὶ παρὰ τὴν τοῦ Κάτωνος ... γνώμην, ἐδόθη;
Vell. 2. 40. 4: 'absente Cn. Pompeio T. Ampius et T. Labienus tribuni pl. legem tulerant,
ut is ludis circensibus corona aurea(laurea *coni.* Kraft, l.c. 34) et omni cultu triumphan-
tium uteretur, scaenicis autem praetexta coronaque laurea(aurea *cod.*: *corr.* Lipsius, *contra-
dixit* Mommsen, *StR* 1. 427. 2). id ille non plus quam semel, et hoc sane nimium fuit, usurpare
sustinuit'; Cic. *Att.* 1. 18. 6.

[7] Curt. 10. 7. 7; Iustin. 15. 2. 10 f.; 24. 5. 14; App. *Syr.* 54. 275 f.; Plut. *Demetr.* 18. 1;
37. 2; Aymard, *Études d'histoire ancienne* (1967), 152 (= *REA* 52 (1950), 125). On Radin
and Coli, who pleaded for an indigenous origin of the acclamation, see Combès, op. cit. 33 ff.

did his soldiers, imperator.[1] The latter will have called him so—if they did it formally at all—after the conquest of Carthago Nova, which was subsequently celebrated in Rome with supplications,[2] though not with a triumph on his return in 206 because he had been *sine magistratu* on that campaign.[3] It is odd that Scipio contrasted the Greek and Roman terms at the very time when the Roman term was about to receive an official meaning. It may therefore be suggested that the practice of acclamation had grown out of this incident. This, of course, cannot be proved and in fact does not matter here because Scipio's case undoubtedly served as precedent for his successors. Whether Scipio ever made use of his title is not certain.[4] The next imperator, L. Aemilius Paullus, certainly did: he was acclaimed in 189 in Spain[5] and again in 168 in Macedonia after the victory at Pydna.[6] In 189 supplications too were held,[7] but there is no certainty about the triumph;[8] in 168 both were granted.[9] It was on this occasion that the triumphal dress was also granted to him for the Circus.[10] If this was the official reward for the 'imperator', we must assume that Scipio too had received it, if not immediately, perhaps after the triumph of 201. But this privilege was certainly not lasting; it was still a novelty. It must be added that many victories were won, supplications held, triumphs celebrated in the decades after Scipio but, as far as we know, no other general was acclaimed. In 155 Scipio Nasica Corculum (*cos.* 162) refused to accept an acclamation after his victory in Dalmatia:[11] he would have been the next imperator. He perhaps felt that this honour was not desirable for the 'perfect citizen'. But after him the acclamation gradually became an accepted institution, and was even considered to be a lesser honour than the triumph.[12] The special distinction of the triumphal dress for the games was not granted again to anyone except Pompey in 61. He did not like it and wore it only once.[13]

---

[1] Livy 27. 19. 4; Polyb. 10. 40. 5 (with Walbank's note); *ILS* 66(?); cf. Aymard, op. cit. 387 ff.; Étienne, *Le culte impérial dans la Péninsule Ibérique* (1958), 85 ff.; Kienast, l.c. 405 ff.; Combès, op. cit. 55 ff.   [2] Livy 27. 7. 4; App. *Iber.* 23. 92.

[3] Livy 28. 38. 4; App. *Iber.* 38. 156 (wrong); cf. Mommsen, *StR* 1. 126 ff.

[4] *ILS* 66 (omitted by Degrassi) is not sufficiently reliable.

[5] *ILS* 15 (Degr. 514).   [6] *ILS* 8884 (Degr. 323).   [7] Livy 37. 58. 5.

[8] Cf. Vell. 1. 9. 3; *ILS* 43; Sydenham 926; Degrassi, *Fasti Triumph.* 553. Instead of the triumph a further acclamation is assumed for 181, which does not seem likely.

[9] Livy 45. 2. 1; 45. 35 ff.; *F. Triumph.*, etc.

[10] *Vir. ill.* 56. 5 (above, p. 108. 5).

[11] *Vir. ill.* 44. 4: 'consul Delminium urbem Dalmatarum expugnavit. (5) imperatoris nomen a militibus et a senatu triumphum oblatum recusavit.' The triumph was in fact held in 155 (*F. Triumph.*).

[12] The acclamations were by then far more numerous than the triumphs.

[13] See above, p. 108. 6.

This is the place to append a further item to Caesar's imperatorial privileges because it can be seen only now that it was one of them: his ivory statue was placed in the cella of the Capitoline Iuppiter and, wearing the triumphal dress, taken hence in the *pompa circensis* to the Circus.[1] This becomes part of those privileges if one assumes that the statue was to represent Caesar in his absence; if he was present, he was to wear the triumphal dress himself. The statue was used at the Parilia and the *ludi Victoriae Caesaris* in 45;[2] and presumably it would have been used during his long absence in Parthia. This was not an innovation either: the same honour had been granted to the elder Scipio,[3] and that is why it seems probable that he too was entitled to wear the triumphal dress when he was in Rome, at least for a while. This is not all that has to be said about the ivory statue;[4] but no more is needed here.

It would be wrong to conclude that Caesar and the Senate were influenced by the origin of the acclamation when they decided that he should become a permanent imperator. Taken over in Rome, the acclamation had ceased to be part of the ritual of king-making, and many centuries had passed since the regal dress had become the triumphal dress.[5] Caesar had his plans for a monarchy, but he meant to achieve it by other means.[6]

Returning to the report of Suetonius and Dio about the *praenomen Imperatoris*, we may say that its authenticity has now been vindicated. If the evidence discussed in the last few pages is trustworthy—and hitherto it has never been doubted—so must theirs be: they all belong together. This does not mean that Caesar intended to break with the past at once. He would have allowed the acclamation of some temporary *imperatores*, as he had allowed Cicero to keep his own title as long as he wanted to. He would have allowed the *laureati fasces* for others, as he again did in the case of Cicero.[7] He may have wished to discontinue the triumphs of others eventually; but we shall see that his legates celebrated triumphs after his own in the same year.[8] Yet in spite of these, perhaps temporary, concessions, the *praenomen Imperatoris* was not a mere decoration nor, like Pompey's *cognomen* Magnus, just a reward, but an indication

---

[1] Dio 43. 45. 2: ἀνδριάντα αὐτοῦ ἐλεφάντινον, ὕστερον δὲ καὶ ἅρμα ὅλον (below, p. 285. 6) ἐν ταῖς ἱπποδρομίαις μετὰ τῶν θείων ἀγαλμάτων πέμπεσθαι ἔγνωσαν; Cic. *Att.* 13. 28. 3; for the details see also the evidence about Scipio, below, n. 3.

[2] See below, p. 185.

[3] Livy 38. 56. 12: 'prohibuisse statuas sibi in Comitio, . . . in cella Iovis poni; prohibuisse, ne decerneretur, ut imago sua triumphali ornatu e templo Iovis Optimi Maximi exiret'; Val. Max. 4. 1. 6: 'voluerunt imaginem eius triumphali ornatu indutam Capitolinis pulvinaribus adplicare.' On this alleged refusal see above, p. 36.

[4] See below, pp. 185; 271.   [5] See above, p. 68.

[6] See below, pp. 270 ff.   [7] Cic. *Lig.* 7 (above, p. 105. 7).   [8] See below, p. 198.

of the fact that he was to be the permanent supreme commander. And that is probably why the iteration was no longer recorded. Octavian inherited this *praenomen* with everything else. But when he assumed it and how he made it acceptable to everyone cannot be part of this narrative. It is enough to say that in this sense Caesar, not Augustus, was the first Roman 'emperor'.

(f) Victoria and Augustus

The festival of the Victoria Caesaris was first held in July 45; Caesar's statue was carried in the company of Victoria in the *pompa circensis*.[1] It was repeated in 44, in spite of the murder,[2] and later: chance preserved explicit evidence for A.D. 15 and for the age of Trajan.[3] The Curia Iulia, which was begun by Caesar in 44 and dedicated by Augustus in 29, had an altar and a statue of Victoria, who thus became the goddess of the Curia.[4] Whenever the Senate met there, its prayers, which became obligatory under Augustus,[5] were directed to her.[6] The statue mounted on the globe has already been mentioned;[7] it was the prototype of numberless representations of a similar kind. But, although she stood in the Curia Iulia, she was never called Victoria Caesaris or, for that matter, Victoria Augusta,[8] apparently because Augustus destined her to be the goddess of Rome, not only of the dynasty. What Caesar would have called her may be asked but cannot be answered. The temple of Divus Iulius, which was dedicated about the same time, had a frieze decorated with Victoriae.[9]

The Victoria Caesaris was succeeded by the Victoria Augusti and Victoria Augusta.[10] It was part of Augustus' religious policy to change the character of Caesar's deities. Caesar made them personal through the addition of his name in the genitive; Augustus made them more general by replacing the genitive with the adjectival Augusta. He was successful on the whole, but the Caesarian tradition survived and became effective again under the later emperors. There were exceptions even under Augustus. An altar at Capua was dedicated to the Victoria

---

[1] Cic. *Att.* 13. 44. 1 (below, p. 185. 11); cf. Ov. *am.* 3. 2. 45.
[2] Pliny 2. 93; Obs. 68; below, p. 368.   [3] *ILS* 9349; *CIL* 6. 37834. 36.
[4] *Fast. Maff.* 28 Aug. (Degrassi 504): 'hoc die ara Victoriae in Curia dedicata est'; Herodian 7. 11. 3: τὸν ἱδρυμένον βωμὸν τῆς Νίκης; Dio 51. 22. 1: ἐνέστησε δὲ ἐς αὐτὸ τὸ ἄγαλμα τὸ τῆς Νίκης, τὸ καὶ νῦν ὄν.   [5] Suet. *Aug.* 35. 3; Dio 54. 30. 1 (12 B.C.).
[6] Herodian 5. 5. 7: τοῦ ἀγάλματος τῆς Νίκης, ᾧ συνιόντες ἐς τὸ βουλευτήριον λιβανωτόν τε θυμιῶσιν ἕκαστος καὶ οἴνου σπένδουσι.   [7] See above, pp. 50 f.
[8] *ILS* 495 (A.D. 258, Africa): 'Victoriae sen(atus) Rom(ani)'; Philocal. 4 Aug. (Degrassi 492): 'Victoria senati'; see also the preceding notes.
[9] M. F. Squarciapino, *Rend. Linc.* (1957), 270 ff.; cf. *RE* 8A. 2516 f.
[10] Cf. *RE* 8A. 2519.

Caesaris Augusti and so were some games at Iguvium.[1] The inscription on the sword-sheath of 'Tiberius' was, as the corresponding inscription 'Felicitas Tiberi' shows, 'Vic(toria) Aug(usti)', not 'Aug(usta)'.[2] There is ample evidence for the Victoria Claudii, Galbae, Othonis, Vespasiani, and so on.[3] Augustus meant to change the form but not the substance. The victories were always his and his successors' victories. The wars were fought under his auspices, even if under the leadership of someone else.[4] The sword-sheath from Mainz records his victory achieved by Tiberius; an inscription of Lepcis, another by Cossus Cornelius Lentulus (cos. 1 B.C.) in A.D. 6;[5] Tacitus, a victory of Tiberius won by Germanicus in A.D. 16.[6] It was now the emperor who was acclaimed imperator on the battlefield in his absence, not the general who was present.[7] Nobody could hold a triumph except the emperor or the imperial princes to whom he delegated it.

3. FORTUNA CAESARIS

Caesar claimed that he began to fight the Civil War for the restoration of liberty and that his cause received divine support, particularly from Venus and Fortuna. We have seen that he built a temple for Venus Genetrix; there is no conclusive evidence for plans about Fortuna, but the circumstantial evidence seems overwhelming. It consists of long-established and current beliefs, of beliefs about the related Felicitas, and of some Caesarian and Augustan evidence, fact and fiction.

(a) Fortuna

Fortuna was an old and popular goddess in Rome and Italy.[8] No other deity, perhaps not even Iuppiter, had as many dedications and shrines at Rome as she had. She helped the fortunes of individual citizens, for instance, farmers and merchants; she assisted women, especially in child-birth, and she was goddess of many oracles. She received a number of further features under the influence of the Greek Tyche and Greek theory. Philosophers, statesmen, and historians had much to say about τύχη and often wrote περὶ τύχης.[9] Many common-

---

[1] CIL 10. 3816; 11. 5820 (ILS 5531); 12. 2389 (Augustum, Gall. Narb.).

[2] CIL 13. 6796; above, p. 101. It is therefore not correct to ascribe coins of Philippi, because of the legend 'Vic(toria) Aug(usti)', to the age of Claudius, Durry, REA 42 (1940), 413.

[3] Thes.L.L. 2. 1402. 9; 44–54; Graillot, Daremb.–Sagl. 5. 840. 5–7; Mattingly (Index).

[4] Mon. Anc. 4. 2: 'ob res a me aut per legatos meos auspicis meis . . . gestas'; Suet. Aug. 21. 1; Mommsen, StR 1. 94. 1; 130; above, p. 107.

[5] ITR 301 (E.-J. 43): 'auspiciis Imp. Caesaris Augusti . . . ductu Cossi Lentuli consulis.'

[6] Tac. A. 2. 41. 1: 'ductu Germanici, auspiciis Tiberii.'   [7] Tac. A. 2. 18. 2.

[8] W. F. Otto, RE 7. 12 ff.; Wissowa 256 f.; Latte 176 ff.; I. Kajanto, RAC 8. 182 ff.

[9] Nilsson 1. 756; 2. 200 ff. (with bibliography).

place views reached Rome at an early date. Plautus and Ennius said that Fortuna was able to help, to do harm, to make things appear uncertain, to influence the course of a war, to humble the powerful, and the like.[1] But the Romans never accepted her absolute rule, and certainly not the blind chance which Tyche so often represented; they contended that she liked to help the valiant.[2] Nor did they remain in the sphere of theory but turned to her with vows and dedications. At the beginning of the second century B.C. M. Furius Crassipes (pr. 187) repaid her help in war with an offering from the booty.[3] In the war against the Celtiberi in Spain, Q. Fulvius Flaccus (cos. 179) vowed a temple for Fortuna Equestris in a difficult equestrian battle in 180 B.C. and dedicated it in 173 B.C.[4] In 101 Q. Lutatius Catulus (cos.102) vowed another for *Fortuna huiusque diei* to commemorate his good fortune in the battle at Vercellae;[5] he will have given details in his Memoirs.

The favours of Fortuna led to *felicitas*, and it was an early belief that a successful general must possess it.[6] In 201 the Senate granted a triumph to Scipio Africanus because he won the victory with his *virtus* and *felicitas*.[7] Again, when the temple of the Lares Permarini was dedicated in 179 B.C. to commemorate the victory of L. Aemilius Regillus (pr. 190) over Antiochus III in 190, it was recorded on its inscription that the victory was won 'auspicio, imperio, felicitate ductuque eius'.[8] That is why Felicitas too became a goddess, and her first temple was built by L. Licinius Lucullus (cos. 151) after 146 B.C., apparently vowed during his campaign in Spain in 151/150 B.C.[9]

Marius' great successes led to reflections in the Greek and Roman manner. Historians, including Posidonius, agreed that he was a favourite

[1] Plaut. *Capt.* 304; Enn. *A.* 312 V.; cf. Philemon frg. 111 K.: ἅπαντα νικᾷ καὶ μεταστρέφει Τύχη; Menand. frg. 482. 9 K. (but see frg. 417 n. K.–Th.): Τύχη κυβερνᾷ πάντα.

[2] Plaut. *Poen.* 1328: 'e virtute vobis fortuna optigit'; Enn. *A.* 257 V.: 'fortibus est fortuna viris data'; 199: 'quorum virtuti belli fortuna pepercit'; Cato *Orig.* frg. 83 P.: 'dii immortales tribuno militum fortunam ex virtute eius dedere.'

[3] *CIL* 1². 48 (Degr. 100). He made a similar dedication to Mars, *ILS* 3142 (Degr. 221); Münzer, *RE* 7. 353.

[4] Livy 40. 40. 10; 44. 9; 42. 10. 5; Wissowa 262. 4; Latte 179. 3.

[5] Plut. *Mar.* 26. 3; cf. Eutrop. 5. 2. 1: 'iterum a C. Mario et Q. Catulo contra eos dimicatum est, sed a Catuli parte felicius.'

[6] Cic. *div.* 1. 102: 'maiores nostri . . . omnibus rebus agendis "quod bonum, faustum, felix fortunatumque esset" praefabantur'; *de imp.* 28: 'ego enim sic existimo in summo imperatore quattuor has res inesse oportere: scientiam rei militaris, virtutem, auctoritatem, felicitatem'; H. Erkell, *Augustus, Felicitas, Fortuna* (1952), 43 ff. (with bibliography); Bömer, *Gymn.* 73 (1966), 73 ff.; R. Combès, *Imperator* (1966), 408 ff.; Hellegouarc'h, *Homm. M. Renard* (1969), 1. 421 ff.   [7] Cic. *fin.* 4. 22.   [8] Livy 40. 52. 5.

[9] Strab. 8. 381; Dio frg. 76. 2 B.

of Fortuna,[1] in spite of the fact that a few days before his death he declared that a thinking man could not trust Fortuna.[2] Cicero wrote an epic poem *Marius*,[3] Varro a Logistoricus, *Marius aut de fortuna*,[4] and allusions to the theme often appear.[5] His adversary Sulla was even more successful, but there is nothing to suggest that he was particularly devoted to the Roman Fortuna or even believed, as is often asserted, in an all-powerful Tyche.[6] But he stressed his *felicitas*, called himself 'Felix', and probably built a temple of Venus Felix.[7] The principal theme of his Memoirs was to show that his victories, as well as the defeats of his adversaries, were due to his *felicitas* rather than to his *virtus*.[8] Pompey's early successes too were considered under this aspect, and Cicero had much to say about it in his speech, *De imperio Cn. Pompei*. Generals, he said, used to be chosen not only for their bravery but also for their good luck.[9] It was the *Fortuna populi Romani* who chose Pompey to bring an earlier campaign to a successful conclusion.[10] Pompey's *felicitas* brought about the support of the citizens, the allegiance of the allies, the submission of the enemy, even the favour of the winds and storms.[11] Friendly historians like Theophanes of Mytilene no doubt elaborated this theme.[12] But again, it did not remain mere talk. In 55 Pompey created a new cult of Felicitas, together with that of Venus Victrix, Victoria, Honos, and Virtus.[13]

[1] Norden, *Kl. Schr.* 105 ff. (*Rhein. Mus.* 48 (1893), 542 ff.).

[2] Posid., *FGrHist.* 87 F 37 (Plut. *Mar.* 45. 9): οὐκ ἐστι νοῦν ἔχοντος ἀνδρὸς ἔτι τῇ τύχῃ πιστεύειν ἑαυτόν.

[3] *FPL* 67 f. M.; W. W. Ewbank, *The Poems of Cicero* 78; 124 ff.; E. Malcovati, *Cicerone e la poesia* (1943), 266; Dahlmann, *Varronische Studien* 2 (1959), 15 f. Archias too wrote about Marius, Cic. *Arch.* 19 ff.

[4] It is, however, not certain that it is concerned with this Marius, see Dahlmann, op. cit. 5 ff. Varro also wrote a Menippean Satire Ἔχω σε περὶ τύχης (frgs. 169–72 B.).

[5] e.g. Ov. *Pont.* 4. 3. 45: 'ille Iugurthino clarus Cimbroque triumpho, / quo victrix totiens consule Roma fuit, / in caeno Marius iacuit cannaque palustri, / pertulit et tanto multa pudenda viro.'

[6] e.g. Latte 279 f.; *contra*, Erkell, op. cit. 72 ff. (with bibliography).

[7] Vell. 2. 27. 5; Pliny 22. 12; App. *BC* 1. 97. 451; Plut. *Sulla* 34. 3; Wissowa 291; Balsdon, *JRS* 41 (1951), 1 ff.   [8] Plut. *Sulla* 6. 8 f.

[9] Cic. *de imp.* 47: 'magnis imperatoribus non solum propter virtutem, sed etiam propter fortunam saepius imperia mandata atque exercitus esse commissos.'

[10] Cic. *de imp.* 45: 'amisissetis Asiam, Quirites, nisi ad ipsum discrimen eius temporis divinitus Cn. Pompeium ad eas regiones Fortuna populi Romani attulisset'; cf. Cic. *Cat.* 1. 15 (in 65 she frustrated the plot of the Catilinarians against the consuls).

[11] Cic. *de imp.* 48: 'non sum praedicaturus, quantas ille res ... quantaque felicitate gesserit, ut eius semper voluntatibus non modo cives adsenserint, socii obtemperarint, hostes oboedierint, sed etiam venti tempestatesque obsecundarint.'

[12] Cicero himself recalled Pompey's good fortune once more at the end of his life, *Phil.* 13. 12: 'Cn. Pompei filius posset ... fortunas patrias recuperare.'

[13] F. *Allif.* 12 Aug. (Degrassi 493): 'Veneri Victrici, Honori, Virtuti, Victoriae, Felicitati in theatro marmoreo'; Wissowa 291; above, p. 93.

This survey shows that statesmen always depended on the help of Fortuna, which became manifest in their *felicitas*, and that they liked to pay their debt by building temples for the new goddess Felicitas also. Thus Caesar did not break fresh ground when he ascribed a considerable power to Fortuna in all matters, especially in war.[1] This he often repeated in his *Commentarii*,[2] and there is no doubt that he meant what he said; he liked to add that Fortuna was always helping him. It is remarkable that Caesar, who has so little to say in his writings about religion and the irrational, makes this exception with Fortuna. He must have done this in his official reports and private utterances from the beginning of his campaigns in Gaul, because Cicero referred to it in 56 as if it had been a generally accepted fact,[3] and in 54 Vatinius asserted that Cicero had become friendly towards Caesar because of his good fortune and luck.[4]

The principal figures, then, in the Civil War were the two proven favourites of Fortuna in the recent past. One question occupied the minds of all: whom would she favour now? At the beginning of 49 Q. Sicinius, a follower of Pompey, issued a *denarius* with a female head and the legend 'Fort(una) p(opuli) R(omani)' (pl. 13. 1),[5] the earliest coin with her representation. It was no doubt a reminder of Pompey's Eastern campaigns, which he had won with her help,[6] and an expression of the hope that she would help him again. But he left Rome; those who remained behind, like Cicero, hesitated and were inclined to leave the decision to Fortuna in a more fatalistic manner.[7] Caesar took up the challenge immediately. He wrote a letter to Cicero on 16 April on his way to Spain and claimed the favours of Fortuna for himself: for all was going well for him and badly for his adversaries.[8] This he

---

[1] Caes. *BG* 6. 30. 2: 'multum cum in omnibus rebus, tum in re militari potest Fortuna . . . (4) sic et ad subeundum periculum et ad vitandum multum Fortuna valuit.'

[2] Caes. *BG* 4. 26. 5; 5. 58. 6; 6. 35. 2; *BC* 3. 68. 1 (followed by the author of the *B. Alex.* 25. 4; 43. 1; 43. 4); cf. Rambaud, *L'art de la déformation historique dans les Commentaires de César*, 1966 (1952), 256 ff.; Gelzer, *Caesar* 177. 401; G. Schweicher, *Schicksal u. Glück in den Werken Sallusts u. Caesars* (Diss. Köln 1963), 94 ff.

[3] Cic. *prov. cons.* 35: 'sit in eius tutela Gallia, cuius fidei virtuti felicitati commendata est. qui . . . Fortunae muneribus amplissimis ornatus . . .'; *Pis.* 81 f.; G. Schweicher, op. cit. 130. 2.

[4] Cic. *fam.* 1. 9. 7: 'me fortuna et felicitate C. Caesaris commotum illi amicum esse coepisse.' It was at that time that Cicero wrote his epic poem about Caesar's British expedition, *Q.fr.* 2. 16 (15). 5; 3. 1. 11; W. Allen jr., *TAPA* 86 (1955), 143 ff.

[5] Sydenham 157; Grueber, pl. 47. 10; Richard, *Mél.* 75 (1963), 322; Münzer, *RE* 2A. 2198.   [6] Cic. *de imp.* 45 (above, p. 114. 10).

[7] Cic. *Att.* 10. 2. 2 (6 Apr. 49): 'res sunt inexplicabiles. Fortunae sunt committenda omnia; sine spe conamur ulla. melius si quid acciderit, mirabimur.'

[8] Caes. ap. Cic. *Att.* 10. 8B. 1: 'si non Fortunae obsecutus videberis—omnia enim secundissima nobis, adversissima illis accidisse videntur'; Gelzer, *Caesar* 193; on the Caesarian propaganda against Pompey see Dio 41. 13. 1–4.

proved once more in Spain: he defeated the best army of the Pompeians in a campaign of forty days[1]—once Pompey's campaign against the pirates too had lasted only forty days[2]—and returned to Rome to prepare for the war against Pompey himself. He became master of Italy without difficulty, or, as he later told his soldiers, without bloodshed, through the help of Fortuna.[3] On the other hand Cato was reported as saying that he did not defend Sicily because Fortuna had deserted Pompey.[4]

(b) Caesar's Sacrifice

Caesar offered a sacrifice to Fortuna before he left Rome in December 49. It was on this occasion that the prodigy of the escaped bull occurred which we have connected with the foundation legend of Bovillae.[5] The prodigy was explained as a sign of the coming victory which Caesar would achieve overseas. The sacrifice to Fortuna was not in vain: according to one version of the tradition she helped him when he crossed the sea in January 48 from Brundisium by delaying the storms of winter.[6] Caesar's own version provides the confirmation, even if it is more rational. A sudden south wind made the quick crossing possible and at the same time protected his ships against hostile attack; it helped again when they reached port by changing into a southwest wind. But even Caesar stressed that the safe crossing was due to the favour of Fortuna,[7] and later, in a speech to his soldiers, he referred once more to her help in safely transporting them all in the presence of a

[1] Caes. BC 2. 32. 5.

[2] Plut. Pomp. 26. 7; App. Mithr. 95. 438; Livy, Per. 99; vir. ill. 77. 5.

[3] Caes. BC 3. 73. 3: 'habendam Fortunae gratiam, quod Italiam sine aliquo vulnere cepissent'; Gelzer, Caesar 216 f.

[4] Plut. Cat. min. 53. 3: Πομπήιον . . . προλέλοιπε τὸ εὐτυχεῖν; cf. Dio 41. 13. 1: Πομπήιος . . . καὶ τὴν τύχην καὶ τὴν δόξαν ἀντίπαλον ἐκτήσατο.

[5] Dio 41. 39. 2: τῇ Τύχῃ θύοντος ὁ ταῦρος ἐκφυγὼν πρὶν τιτρώσκεσθαι, ἔξω τε τῆς πόλεως ἐξεχώρησε καὶ πρὸς λίμνην τινὰ ἐλθὼν διενήξατο αὐτήν. (3) κἀκ τούτων ἐπὶ πλέον θαρσήσας ἠπείχθη, καὶ μάλισθ' ὅτι οἱ μάντεις μένοντι μὲν αὐτῷ οἴκοι ὄλεθρον, περαιωθέντι δὲ τὴν θάλασσαν καὶ σωτηρίαν καὶ νίκην ἔσεσθαι ἔφασαν; see above, pp. 6 f. and below, p. 323.

[6] Plut. fort. Rom. 6: τῆς Τύχης τὸν καιρὸν ὑπερθεμένης; App. BC 2. 53. 217: τῷ μὲν χειμῶνι τύχην ἀγαθὴν ἀντιθέντες; contra, 2. 54. 221: he was held up by a storm of the winter solstice; again, 2. 58. 241: ἀντὶ λογισμῶν ὁ Καῖσαρ ἐπεποίθει τῇ Τύχῃ. Both versions are wrong: it was only nominally winter, but in fact, according to the Julian Calendar, October.

[7] Caes BC 3. 26. 1: 'illi . . . nacti austrum . . . altero die Apolloniam . . . praetervehuntur. (2) . . . cum Coponius . . . nostris remissiore vento adpropinquasset, idem auster increbruit nostrisque praesidio fuit . . . (4) nostri usi Fortunae beneficio . . . nacti portum . . . eo naves introduxerunt (qui portus ab Africo tegebatur, ab austro non erat tutus) . . . (5) quo simul atque intro est itum, incredibili felicitate auster, qui per biduum flaverat, in Africum se vertit. (27. 1) hic subitam commutationem Fortunae videre licuit'; App. BC 2. 59. 245: αἱ μὲν δὴ μεγάλοις αὖθις ἱστίοις ἐξ ἀέλπτου τὸ πνεῦμα ἐδέχοντο καὶ διέπλεον ἀδεῶς.

hostile navy.[1] He attempted to return to Brundisium in a fishing boat to supervise the transport of the second half of his troops personally. The sea was stormy and the fisherman frightened. Caesar exhorted him: 'do not be afraid, you carry Caesar and the Fortuna Caesaris.'[2] This attempt ended in failure, and the situation became unfavourable, although all his ships reached him in the end. Now he tried once more to come to terms with Pompey and became more modest in his claims. He reminded him of the great harm Fortuna was able to cause in war; of the good opportunity for making peace as long as the prospects of the two adversaries were equal. If Fortuna gave some advantage to either of them, the favoured would not be prepared to talk about peace.[3]

As the war went on Rome was disturbed by various prodigies. One concerned Fortuna and Caesar jointly: a thunderbolt hit the temple of Fortuna Publica and the *horti Caesaris* nearby at the Porta Collina; the temple of Fortuna opened of its own accord, and blood flowed thence to the temple of Fortuna Respiciens.[4] It is not recorded how these prodigies were explained and purged; clearly they reflected the fortunes of the war. There is less evidence from later years; but Fortuna is said to have been in Caesar's company everywhere.[5] That is why, it was said, Pompey did not dare to risk a battle at Pharsalus.[6] Caesar ascribed his victory at the Nile in 47 to his luck,[7] and Felicitas was his battle-cry at Thapsus in 46.[8] A temple of Felicitas was being

---

[1] Caes. *BC* 3. 73. 3: 'denique recordari debere, qua felicitate inter medias hostium classes ... omnes incolumes essent transportati'; Vell. 2. 51. 2: 'sua et celeritate et fortuna C. Caesar usus.' A less favourable account is given by Dio: Caesar succeeded in crossing with part of the troops but when he sent the ships back for the rest, Bibulus intercepted them and caused much damage. Caesar then saw that his own crossing was more lucky than prudent, εὐτυχέστερον τὸν πλοῦν ἢ εὐβουλότερον ἐπεποίητο (41. 44. 4); cf. Chaeremon frg. 2 (*TGF* 782 N.): τύχη τὰ θνητῶν πράγματ' οὐκ εὐβουλία.

[2] Plut. *Caes.* 38. 5: ἴθι, ἔφη, γενναῖε, τόλμα καὶ δέδιθι μηδέν· Καίσαρα φέρεις καὶ τὴν Καίσαρος Τύχην συμπλέουσαν; *fort. Rom.* 6; *reg. et imp. apophth. Caes.* 9; App. *BC* 2. 57. 236: θαρρῶν ἴθι πρὸς τὸν κλύδωνα· Καίσαρα φέρεις καὶ τὴν Καίσαρος Τύχην; Lucan. 5. 510 ff. (*Fortuna comes*); on the other version of the story see below, p. 121.

[3] Caes. *BC* 3. 10. 6: '... quantum in bello Fortuna posset, iam ipsi incommodis suis satis essent documento. (7) hoc unum esse tempus de pace agendi, dum sibi uterque confideret et pares ambo viderentur; si vero alteri paulum modo tribuisset Fortuna, non esse usurum condicionibus pacis eum, qui superior videretur.' [4] Dio 42. 26. 3.

[5] Vell. 2. 55. 1: 'sequens Fortunam suam Caesar pervectus in Africam est ... (3) sua Caesarem in Hispaniam comitata Fortuna est.'

[6] App. *BC* 2. 66. 275: ἐπικίνδυνον μὲν ἡγεῖτο ... τύχῃ Καίσαρος λαμπρᾷ περὶ τῶν ὅλων συνενεχθῆναι; 2. 69. 287: τοσοῦτον ἀνδρὶ μεγαλουργῷ καὶ παρὰ πᾶν ἔργον ἐς ἐκείνην τὴν ἡμέραν εὐτυχεστάτῳ γενομένῳ τὸ δύσθυμον ἐνεπεπτώκει; 2. 86. 363: ἀηττήτῳ καὶ εὐτυχεστάτῳ ἐξέτι νέου γενομένῳ; Lucan. 2. 727: 'lassata triumphis / descivit Fortuna tuis.'

[7] *B. Alex.* 32. 1; cf. Cic. *Phil.* 2. 64.

[8] *B. Afr.* 83. 1; cf. App. *BC* 2. 97. 405: τὸ τοῦ Καίσαρος κλέος ἐς ἄμαχον εὐτυχίαν ἐδοξάζετο, οὐδὲν ἔτι τῶν ἡσσωμένων ἐς ἀρετὴν αὐτοῦ μεριζόντων, ἀλλὰ καὶ τὰ σφέτερα αὐτῶν ἁμαρτήματα τῇ Καίσαρος τύχῃ προστιθέντων; cf. 2. 88. 270 f. (Cassius' surrender at the Hellespont).

built and dedicated in 44;[1] at Ameria the cult of the Victoria et Felicitas Caesaris was created.[2]

This narrative is not convincing in all its parts. It is certain that Fortuna had a prominent share in the war: Caesar's own words, coins, prodigies, and the cult of Felicitas prove it. But a great deal, especially in Greek writers, may have been coloured by a comparison with Alexander.[3] One is inclined to dismiss at least two incidents as fictitious: the sacrifice to Fortuna[4] and Caesar in the fishing boat.[5] The sacrifice to Fortuna was unusual: before departure it was generally offered to Iuppiter on the Capitol.[6] The special sacrifice could only have taken place if Caesar had intended to build a temple of Fortuna at the end of the campaign and made a vow before departure accordingly. The sacrifice of the bull was irregular, a male animal to a female deity.[7] And the escape of the victim could not portend victory: it was always of evil significance.[8] Another tradition attributed it to a later campaign, to the departure to Africa in 47, as an evil omen which Caesar, however, ignored.[9] And yet it may be asserted that it is valuable evidence even if it is not a correct historical record. The bull as victim is justified if, as has already been suggested,[10] it was to create a link with the bull of Bovillae, the home-town of the Iulii: when it first escaped it led to the foundation, its present escape portended victory. The bull portended victory, so to speak, by leading the way for Caesar's legions. This may give an even deeper significance to the incident.

It was customary to carry the picture of an animal in front of the

---

[1] Dio 43. 21. 1; 44. 5. 2; below, p. 127.

[2] ILS 6631 f.; CIL 11. 4367; HTR 50 (1957), 226.

[3] App. BC 2. 149. 620: ἀνὴρ ἐπιτυχέστατος ἐς πάντα καὶ δαιμόνιος καὶ μεγαλοπράγμων καὶ εἰκότως ἐξομοιούμενος Ἀλεξάνδρῳ; cf. Curt. 10. 5. 35: 'fatendum est tamen, cum plurimum Virtuti debuerit, plus debuisse Fortunae, quam solus omnium mortalium in potestate habuit'; Cic. Marc. 19: 'tantus est enim splendor in laude vera, . . . ut haec a Virtute donata, cetera a Fortuna commodata esse videantur'; Balsdon, Gnom. 37 (1965), 583.

[4] Dio 41. 39. 2 (see above, p. 116. 5); below, p. 323.

[5] Plut. Caes. 38. 5; App. BC 2. 57. 236 (above, p. 117. 2).

[6] Livy 45. 39. 11, etc.; Mommsen, StR 1. 64; Wissowa 126; 383.

[7] Arnob. 7. 19; Wissowa 413; Bömer, Gymn. 73 (1966), 75. 36. Accordingly Fortuna used to receive a cow (Henzen, AFA 86; 122; 124). But at Praeneste, as Mr. A. Drummond points out to me, a male calf was sacrificed to her (Degrassi 438); cf. the unique sacrifice of a bull to Salus, Henzen, AFA, p. LXII.

[8] Paul. 247 M. (287 L.): 'Piacularia auspicia appellabant, quae sacrificantibus tristia portendebant, cum . . . hostia ab ara aufugisset'; Livy 21. 63. 13 (218 B.C.): 'immolantique ei vitulus iam ictus e manibus sacrificantium sese cum proripuisset, multos circumstantes cruore respersit . . . id a plerisque in omen magni terroris acceptum'; Serv. Dan. Georg. 2. 395; Serv. Aen. 9. 624; Thulin, Etr. Disc. 2. 16 f.

[9] Suet. Caes. 59 (above, p. 98). It was of evil significance for Pompey in Thessaly, App. BC 2. 68. 283; Lucan. 7. 165 ff.; for Galba, Suet. Galba 18. 1; see also below, p. 342.

[10] See above, pp. 6 f..

army, above all an eagle; the custom came from the East to Greece and Rome.[1] The Roman legions had five animal symbols before Marius: eagle, wolf, 'Minotaurus' (that is, man-headed bull), horse, boar. Marius kept the eagle and abolished the others.[2] The next innovator was Caesar: his legions had a bull on their standard (pl. 12. 1–3).[3] It has been assumed that this bull was the Taurus of the zodiac,[4] just as Augustus' legions adopted the Capricorn, his natal star.[5] But as Caesar was not born in the sign of Taurus, it was argued that he chose this sign because Venus, his ancestress, was its protecting goddess.[6] This is a conjecture prompted by the belief that all animal symbols of the legions were, like that of Augustus, astrological in origin, which is demonstrably wrong.[7] Moreover the doctrine about the tutelary deities did not mean so much to Caesar and his contemporaries as to make him decide in its favour instead of his own natal star.[8] But if the bull was not the sign of the zodiac, it must have been again the bull of Bovillae.[9]

The innovation can be dated only approximately. It is most unlikely that Caesar's legions already had the bull on their standards in Gaul: the bull was not a symbol of the Roman State but his own, and he was still no more than a proconsul. The proper date would rather be the beginning of the Civil War, when he reasserted the ancestral tradition of the Iulii by claiming that he was fighting with the help of Venus,[10] that is, the time of the prodigy of the bull. The bull may have been

[1] Sarre, *Klio* 3 (1903), 333 ff.; Kubitschek, *RE* 2A. 2327 ff.; Merkelbach, *Studi in onore di U. E. Paoli* (1956), 514 ff.; Rumpf, *Ath. Mitt.* 77 (1962), 233 ff.; Seston, *RAC* 7. 689 ff.

[2] Pliny 10. 16: 'Romanis eam (aquilam) legionibus Gaius Marius in secundo consulatu suo (104 B.C.) proprie dicavit. erat et antea prima cum quattuor aliis: lupi, minotauri, equi, aprique singulos ordines anteibant. paucis ante annis sola in aciem portari coepta erat, reliqua in castris relinquebantur. Marius in totum ea abdicavit'; Paul. 148 M. (135 L.); 235 M. (267 L.); Veget. *Epit.* 3. 6. Mommsen, *Ges. Schr.* 6. 136, saw that the 'Minotaurus' can be no other than the man-headed bull often represented on Campanian coins (Head, *HN* 38 f.).

[3] The *leg. IV Macedonica, V Macedonica*(?), *VI Victrix, VII Claudia, VIII Augusta, X Pratensis, X Gemina*: Ritterling, *RE* 12. 1549; 1599; 1614; 1643; 1671; 1678 (with reference to the archaeological evidence); Drumann 3. 708 ff. The bull on Babylonian standards: Sarre, l.c. 366.

[4] v. Domaszewski, *Abhandl. z. röm. Rel.* 5 f.

[5] Ritterling, *RE* 12. 1373 ff.

[6] Manil. 2. 439: 'Taurum Cytherea tuetur'; Vett. Val. 1. 2 (p. 7. 2 Kr.); *Men. rust.* (Degrassi 286 ff.); Mommsen, *Röm. Chronol.* 305 ff.; Wissowa, *Apophoreton d. Graeca Halensis* (1903), 35 ff.

[7] See the criticism of v. Domaszewski by Ritterling, *RE* 12. 1373 and Housman, *Manilius* 1², p. 96 n.

[8] This was Leo, if his horoscope was based on the position of the Sun.

[9] A bull could also be a symbol of power (Dio Chrys. *de regno* 2. 68).

[10] Dio 41. 34. 1; Cic. *fam.* 8. 15. 2 (above, p. 83. 3).

put on the standards before he left for the war against **Pompey**. The reason for the innovation is not far to seek. It may have been a frequent idea already, as it was later, that the legionary eagle represented the real eagle that would fly as a good augury in advance of the legions on their march.[1] Now it was Caesar's symbol that led the way. It was not a meaningless use of symbols, but should be compared with Constantine's vision in daylight of the cross which was to make him victorious, and even more with his dream before the battle against Maxentius at the Milvian Bridge in A.D. 312.[2] He was advised in this dream to mark the shields of his soldiers with the monogram of Christ to achieve victory; the monogram was later attached to the Christian standard, the Labarum (pl. 13. 2).[3] Needless to say, the similarity is so close as to suggest that Caesar's innovation must have been the ultimate precedent for Constantine's dream and subsequent action, probably with intermediary versions of the prodigy or miracle. If so, it was Caesar who first received the divine advice to use his symbol and the prophecy: 'hoc signo victor eris' or τούτῳ νίκα. It was an effective way to reassure his soldiers in case they were hesitating to go overseas to fight Pompey; it is possible that he even decorated his ships with the bull.[4] There is no certainty about what really happened. Caesar's idea may have been presented in the form of a dream, in which the divine advice would have come from Fortuna: we know of important dreams of Sulla, Pompey, and of Caesar himself.[5] Or else it may have been presented in connection with the prodigy of the bull as its natural consequence. At any rate, once the precedent was established, Augustus followed with his Capricorn and his successors with other animal symbols. It was probably this bull that L. Livineius Regulus reproduced on the reverse of a *denarius* in 42, with Caesar's head on the obverse (pl. 13. 3);[6] so too, under Augustus, the mint of Lugdunum in Gaul, where many old legionaries will have been settled

---

[1] Tac. *A.* 2. 17. 2 (A.D. 16): 'pulcherrimum augurium, octo aquilae (for eight legions) petere silvas et intrare visae imperatorem adverteret. exclamat irent, sequerentur Romanas aves, propria legionum numina'; *H.* 1. 62: 'laetum augurium Fabio Valenti exercituique . . . ipso profectionis die aquila leni meatu, prout agmen incederet, velut dux viae praevolavit'; App. *BC* 4. 101. 425; 128. 532.

[2] Lact. *de mort. pers.* 44. 5 f.; Euseb. *v. Const.* 28 f.; Baynes, *Constantine the Great and the Christian Church* (1929), 58 ff. (with bibliography); Egger, 'Das Labarum, die Kaiserstandarte der Spätantike', *Sitz.-Ber. Wien* (1960), 234. 1.

[3] Bruun, *Rom. Imp. Coin.* 7. 572.

[4] Later Taurus was the name of some ships at Misenum (*CIL* 10. 3447; 3648), Capricornus that of others (*CIL* 10. 3597).

[5] See above, p. 83. 6, and below, pp. 346; 357.

[6] Sydenham 183; Grueber, pl. 57. 18. His other coins too show a close relation between obv. and rev.

PLATE 12

1

2

1. Tombstone in the Museum at Chesters: a legionary soldier holds a standard surmounted by a bull (Photograph: Mr. C. M. Daniels, Newcastle); pp. 119; 121. 2.

2–3. Bronze shield from the river Tyne, British Museum: an eagle in the centre; the four seasons in the corners; above, Mars; below, a bull; r. and l. standards and the inscription: 'Leg. VIII Aug.' (Photographs, original and drawing: British Museum); p. 119.

3

(pl. 13. 4).[1] The bull or its head on the military standard is often found on legionary or other coinage (pl. 13. 5–6), and on other representations in metal or stone.[2]

(c) Fortuna in the Fishing Boat

The other incident which is open to doubt is Caesar's journey with his Fortuna in the fishing boat on the stormy sea.[3] Greeks and Romans had had to face the storms of the sea innumerable times before. They used to turn with prayers and sacrifices to the gods for help, to Zeus, Apollo, Hera, Poseidon, or to the special gods of the winds like Boreas and Zephyrus, and created the cult of the winds in many places.[4] Experts like Medea in mythical times, certain priests in historical times, too, could help with incantations and other magical practices.[5] The first great man who had a miraculous passage was Alexander in Pamphylia in 334/3 B.C., at least according to Callisthenes and those who followed him.[6] It was no longer the prayers, sacrifices, or magic that helped him but a special divine favour.[7] Among Romans Scipio was

---

[1] Mattingly 1. 78 ff.; pl. 11. 1–6; 14–20; Grant, *From Imperium to Auctoritas* 124; 211 f. (Spain); 216; 379. The traditional interpretation is an alleged play on the words 'taurus' and Augustus' early *cognomen* 'Thurinus' (Suet. *Aug.* 7. 1; A. Stein, *RE* 6a. 646; Mattingly 1, p. cxv).

[2] Mattingly–Sydenham 5. 1. 94 ff.; 5. 2. 388; 468 f.; 488; Kubitschek–Frankfurter, *Führer durch Carnuntum*[6] (1923), 76, fig. 36 (*CIL* 3. 11244); Domaszewski, *Fahnen* 75, fig. 90 (Chesters, above, pl. 12. 1); id. *Abhandlungen z. röm. Rel.* 4 (Cremona: *Not. Scavi* (1887), 209; *ILS* 2283); cf. Domaszewski, *Abh.* 4 ff.; Ritterling, *RE* 12. 1313; 1599; 1614; 1643; 1671.

[3] Plut. *Caes.* 38. 5; App. *BC* 2. 57. 236; etc. (above, p. 117. 2). It is, as a story about Caesar's 'luck', a popular theme in modern research (e.g. W.-H. Friedrich, *Thesaurismata . . . für Ida Kapp* (1954), 1 ff.; Brutscher, *Mus. Helv.* 15 (1958), 75 ff.; G. Schweicher, op. cit. 140 ff.; Bömer, *Gymn.* 73 (1966), 63 ff. with bibliography). But if it were right to take Τύχη as a simple noun meaning 'luck', the story would become irrelevant. An exception is Wilamowitz, *Glaube d. Hell.* 2. 307, who connects this Tyche with the Tyche of the Hellenistic kings (see below, pp. 126 f.), also Bömer, l.c. 69 ff. A different, and even more important, aspect of the story, that of the divine *comes*, is stressed by Nock, *JRS* 37 (1947), 113.

[4] Stengel, *Opferbräuche d. Griechen* 146 ff.; Fiedler, *Antiker Wetterzauber* (1931), 5 ff.; Steuding, *Myth. Lex.* 6. 511 ff.; Cook, *Zeus* 3. 103 ff.; Nilsson 1. 116 f.; D. Wachsmuth, Πόμπιμος ὁ δαίμων (Diss. Berlin 1967), 466 ff.

[5] Paus. 2. 12. 1; Ov. *Met.* 7. 197 ff.; cf. Hdt. 7. 191; Hesych. s.v. ἀνεμοκοῖται. Orpheus too could help (Diod. 4. 43. 1; 4. 48. 6) and even Empedocles, e.g. frg. 111 D.-K.; Stengel, op. cit. 149; Fiedler, op. cit. 21. Certain gems had the same power, Zoroastr. frg. 59; 62; 66 B.–C. (Pliny 37. 142; 155); see further the texts in Fiedler 74 ff.

[6] FGrHist. 124 F 31; his followers are listed by Jacoby ad loc. Arr. *Anab.* 1. 26. 2, on the other hand, gives a rational account of the passage from Phaselis to Perge. App. *BC* 2. 149. 622 compares Caesar with Alexander, who τὸν Παμφύλιον κόλπον τῆς θαλάσσης ἀνακοπείσης διέτρεχε δαιμονίως, καὶ τὸ πέλαγος αὐτῷ τοῦ Δαίμονος κατέχοντος ἔστε παρέλθοι; for Caesar, on the other hand, the Adriatic Sea became navigable in midwinter (πλώτη καὶ εὔδιος γενομένη) and he sailed to Britain safely, which no Roman had done before, and ventured to travel in the small boat under the protection of his Fortuna (2. 150. 625).

[7] Antiochus IV Epiphanes may have boasted of a similar achievement, 2 Maccab. 9. 8: ὁ δ' ἄρτι δοκῶν τοῖς τῆς θαλάσσης κύμασιν ἐπιτάσσειν διὰ τὴν ὑπὲρ ἄνθρωπον ἀλαζονείαν; cf.

PLATE 13

1. Denarius of Q. Sicinius, 49 B.C. (Sydenham 157. 938), Oxford; obv.: head of Fortuna, legend 'Fort(una) p(opuli) R(omani)'; rev.: palm, caduceus, wreath, legend 'Q. Sicinius IIIvir'; p. 115.

2. Bronze coin of Constantine, A.D. 327 (Bruun, Roman Imp. Coin. 7. 572. 19), Oxford; obv.: head of Constantine, legend 'Constantinus Max. Aug.'; rev.: standard surmounted by the Christian monogram ☧, legend 'Spes Publica, cons.'; p. 120.

3. Denarius of L. Livineius Regulus, 42 B.C. (Sydenham 183. 1106), London; obv.: head of Caesar between laurel-branch and caduceus; rev.: bull, legend 'L. Livineius Regulus'; p. 120.

4. Aureus of Augustus, 15–12 B.C. (Mattingly I. 78. 450), London; obv.: head of Augustus, legend 'Augustus Divi f.'; rev.: bull, legend 'imp. X'; pp. 120 f.

5. Antoninianus of Gallienus, A.D. 258 (Mattingly–Sydenham, Roman Imp. Coin. 5. 1. 94), London and Paris; obv.: radiate head of Gallienus, legend 'Gallienus Aug.'; rev.: bull, legend 'Leg. X Gem. VI P(ia?) VI F(idelis?)'; p. 121.

6. Antoninianus of Carausius c. A.D. 288 (P. H. Webb, Roman Imp. Coin. 5. 2. 468), London; obv.: radiate head of Carausius, legend 'Imp. Carausius P(ius) F(elix) Aug.'; rev.: bull, legend '(Leg. VII?) Cl(audia), M(oneta) L(ondiniensis)'; p. 121.

7. Quinarius of P. Sepullius Macer, 44 B.C. (Sydenham 179. 1078), Berlin; obv.: bust of Victoria; rev.: Fortuna with rudder and cornucopiae, legend 'P. Sepullius Macer'; p. 124.

8. Denarius of M. Arrius Secundus, 41 B.C. (Sydenham 180. 1083), London; obv.: bust of Fortuna, legend 'F(ortuna) p(opuli) R(omani), M. Arrius Secundus'; rev.: spear between wreath and a square object; p. 125.

9. Aureus of Ti. Sempronius Graccus, c. 40 B.C. (Sydenham 184. 1126), London; obv.: head of Octavian, legend 'Divi Iuli f.'; rev.: Fortuna with rudder and cornucopiae, legend 'Ti. Sempron(ius) Graccus IIIIvir, q(uaestor) d(esignatus)'; p. 125.

10. Aureus of Antony, 41 B.C. (Sydenham 190. 1173), London; obv.: head of Antony, legend 'Ant(onius) aug(ur), Imp(erator), IIIv(ir) r(ei) p(ublicae) c(onstituendae)'; rev.: Fortuna with rudder and cornucopiae, at her foot, stork, legend 'Pietas, cos.'; p. 125.

11. Denarius of Q. Rustius, 19 B.C. (Mattingly I. 1. 2), Oxford; obv.: two busts of Fortuna on bar, legend 'Q. Rustius, Fortunae Antiat(i)'; rev.: altar inscribed with 'For(tunae) Re(duci)', legend 'Caesari Augusto, ex s.c.'; p. 126.

12. Aureus of Augustus, 19–15 B.C. (Mattingly I. 64. 361), London; obv.: head of Augustus; rev.: altar, inscribed 'Fortun(ae) Redu(ci)', Caesari Aug(usto), S.P.Q.R.'; p. 126.

13. Denarius of Galba, A.D. 68 (Mattingly I. 314. 39), Oxford; obv.: head of Galba, legend 'Imp. Ser. Galba Caesar Aug.'; rev.: Fortuna with rudder and patera and with her foot on a globe is sacrificing at an altar, legend 'Salus generis humani'; p. 127.

14. Aureus of Galba, A.D. 68 (Mattingly I. 352. 241), London; obv.: head of Galba, legend 'Imp. Galba Caesar Aug., p. p.'; rev.: Fortuna with rudder and cornucopiae, legend 'Fortuna Aug.'; p. 127.

15. Denarius of Augustus, 31–29 B.C. (Mattingly I. 98. 599), Oxford; obv.: head of Octavian; rev.: Venus with spear and helmet leans on a column at which a shield with a star, legend 'Caesar Divi f.'; p. 129.

16. Aureus of L. Mussidius Longus, 42 B.C. (Sydenham 182. 1098), London; obv.: head of Octavian, legend 'C. Caesar IIIvir r(ei) p(ublicae) c(onstituendae)'; rev.: Mars helmeted with spear and sword and with his foot on shield, legend 'L. Mussidius T. f. Longus IIIIvir a(uro) p(ublico) f(eriundo)'; p. 131.

17. Denarius of P. Clodius, 42 B.C. (Sydenham 184. 1121), London; obv.: head of Antony, legend 'M. Antonius IIIvir r(ei) p(ublicae) c(onstituendae)'; Mars with spear and sword, legend 'P. Clodius M. f.'; p. 131.

18. Denarius of Octavian, 42 B.C. (Sydenham 206. 1320), Oxford; obv.: bust of helmeted Mars and spear, legend 'Caesar IIIvir r(ei) p(ublicae) c(onstituendae)'; rev.: aquila surmounted by trophy between two standards, legend 'S.C.'; p. 131.

19. Aureus of Augustus, 18–17 B.C. (Mattingly I. 58. 315), London; obv.: head of Augustus, legend 'Augustus'; rev.: Mars in circular domed shrine with aquila and standard, legend 'Martis Ultoris'; pp. 131 f.

20. Denarius of Augustus, 18–17 B.C. (Mattingly I. 60. 332), London; obv.: head of Augustus, legend 'Caesar Augustus'; rev.: Mars with aquila and standard, legend 'signis receptis'; pp. 131 f.

21. Denarius of Augustus, 18–17 B.C. (Mattingly I. 71. 415 n.), Oxford; obv.: head of Augustus, legend 'Caesar Augustus'; rev.: Mars with aquila and standard, legend 'signis receptis'; pp. 131 f.

PLATE 13

1   2   3   4   5a   5b

6   7   8   9   10   11

12   13   14   15   16   17

18   19   20   21

said to have mastered the storms and winds of the sea when he reached Africa safely with his troops,[1] and so later did Pompey, not only in his youth,[2] but as recently as 57. He was then in charge of the corn-supply (*cura annonae*), and was once setting out on a stormy sea and had to reassure the frightened seamen. He did it by his example and with the words: 'to sail is necessary, to live is not'; and he was success-ful.[3] One version of the story about Caesar belongs to this tradition, when he reassures the fisherman with the words: 'Caesarem vehis'.[4] This version reappeared in a different form two years later when he set out for the campaign in Africa.[5] But the other version is relevant here: it is not Caesar but his Fortuna that would save the boat. Fortuna always favoured Caesar, before and afterwards: has she now become the Fortuna Caesaris? This is the only evidence that she has: should one accept it?

Fortuna had not hitherto been a goddess of seafarers: the ultimate source of the story is Greek poetry. Although Tyche was not a goddess of seafarers either,[6] once in Aeschylus and twice in Pindar she sat at the ship's helm and saved it.[7] Our story is therefore not a normal record of a historical event but a literary, more or less poetical, version of it. But it is not in its proper setting. It would make sense only if the crossing had been successful. And it was successful once before, from Brundisium to Greece, and Fortuna was helping there.[8] It may be assumed that the incident originally belonged to this crossing and was transferred by a hostile writer to an unsuccessful attempt.

These observations are relevant, and yet they do not make the cause

5. 21. The power of calming the storm was then ascribed to Jesus (Mc. 4. 37 ff.; cf. Kloster-mann ad loc.) and to Andreas (*Acta Andreae* 9, p. 141 Tischend.); cf. Psalm 88(89). 10: σὺ δεσπόζεις τοῦ κράτους τῆς θαλάσσης, τὸν δὲ σάλον τῶν κυμάτων αὐτῆς σὺ καταπραΰνεις; 64(65). 8; 106(107). 29.

[1] Livy 29. 27. 6 ff. (204 B.C.).

[2] Cic. *de imp.* 48 (above, p. 114.11); Petron. 123. 241: 'quem fracto gurgite Pontus / et veneratus erat submissa Bosporus unda'; E. Pfeiffer, *Stud. z. ant. Sterngl.* 101 f.

[3] Plut. *Pomp.* 50. 2: ἀνάγεσθαι δὲ μέλλων, πνεύματος μεγάλου κατὰ θάλασσαν ὄντος, καὶ τῶν κυβερνητῶν ὀκνούντων, πρῶτος ἐμβὰς καὶ κελεύσας τὴν ἄγκυραν αἴρειν, ἀνεβόησε· πλεῖν ἀνάγκη, ζῆν οὐκ ἀνάγκη; Meyer, *Caesars Monarchie* 118. 1.

[4] Flor. 2. 13. 37: 'quid times? Caesarem vehis'; Dio 41. 46. 3; cf. *Paneg. lat.* 8. 14. 5: 'quid est quod timere possimus? Caesarem sequimur' (= the emperor Constantius).

[5] This power was later ascribed to Augustus (Philo *leg. ad Gai.* 21. 145: οὗτός ἐστιν ὁ Καῖσαρ ὁ τοὺς καταρράξαντας πανταχόθι χειμῶνας εὐδιάσας) and to Nero (Calp. *Ecl.* 4. 100: 'deus hinc, certe deus expulit euros'); cf. Apul. *Met.* 5. 9. 8: 'deam spirat mulier, quae . . . ventis ipsis imperat'.

[6] Cf., e.g., Wilamowitz, *Glaube d. Hell.* 2. 300 ff.

[7] Aesch. *Ag.* 664: Τύχη δὲ σωτὴρ ναῦν θέλουσ' ἐφέζετο; Pind. *Olymp.* 12. 2: σώτειρα Τύχα. / τὶν γὰρ ἐν πόντῳ κυβερνῶνται θοαί / νᾶες; frg. 40 Sn.: Τύχα . . . δίδυμον στρέφουσα πηδάλιον; cf. for the wording Thuc. 5. 112: τῇ . . . σῳζούσῃ τύχῃ ἐκ τοῦ θείου . . . πιστεύοντες.

[8] See above, pp. 116 f.

of the Fortuna Caesaris sufficiently convincing. She is in need of further support. It will be remembered that Pompey had long had a reputation of being the man of good fortune and that at the beginning of the Civil War the Pompeians issued the first coin with the representation of Fortuna. Caesar had to make his counter-claim, which he did by broadcasting the incident in the fishing boat. During the years that followed, his good fortune began to play an ever-increasing role.[1] Finally P. Sepullius Macer issued a *quinarius* with Victoria on the obverse and Fortuna with rudder and cornucopiae on the reverse (pl. 13. 7).[2] This was the first representation of Fortuna with her symbol, so popular in the imperial period.[3] This is strange, because Tyche was represented differently, often as an Amazon, often with a turreted crown, best known from the Tyche of Antioch and her many variants;[4] but never with the rudder. It was therefore suggested that Fortuna with the rudder was created at Rome, but this was not accepted.[5] The same suggestion must now be renewed in the form that it was Caesar who vowed and dedicated the first Fortuna with the rudder to commemorate that successful crossing.[6] But that single dedication could not explain why this new Fortuna-type became so popular later. Caesar must have planned more. The Fortuna-coin of Sepullius Macer shows Victoria on the obverse: this leads to the conjecture that the coin was issued with

[1] App. *BC* 2. 88. 370 f.; 2. 97. 405 (above, p. 117. 8); Cic. *Marc.* 19 (above, p. 118. 3); *Lig.* 38: 'nihil habet nec fortuna tua maius quam ut possis, nec natura melius quam ut velis servare quam plurimos'; *Deiot.* 19; 21; Vell. 2. 55. 1; 3 (above, p. 117. 5); G. Schweicher, op. cit. 131; 134.

[2] Sydenham 179; Grueber 1. 550; J.-C. Richard, *Mél.* 75 (1963), 327.

[3] R. Peter, *Myth. Lex.* 1. 1503 ff.; [Dio Chrys.] *or.* 64. 5: τῇ μὲν δεξιᾷ χειρὶ πηδάλιον κατέχει καὶ . . . ναυτίλλεται. τί δὲ ἄρα τοῦτο ἦν; πότερον ὡς μάλιστα τῶν πλεόντων τῆς τύχης δεομένων, ἢ διότι τὸν βίον ἡμῶν ὥς τινα μεγάλην ναῦν κυβερνᾷ καὶ πάντας σῴζει τοὺς ἐμπλέοντας; 63. 7; C. C. Hense, *Poetische Personification* (1868), 166; Gruppe, *Gr. Myth.* 2. 1087 n.

[4] Waser, *Myth. Lex.* 5. 1357 ff.; T. Dohrn, *Tyche von Antiochia* (1960).

[5] Furtwängler, *Collection Sabouroff*, 1 (1883–7), text to pl. 25; *contra*, Hiller v. Gaertringen, *Ath. Mitt.* 36 (1911), 358; Nilsson 2. 207. 6. The objection rests on a doubtful Greek precedent (*Syll.* 183: 'stela anaglypho Fortunae, quae sinistra gubernaculum tenet'). But even if it really existed, it would not make much difference. In that case Caesar would have made a rare representation of Tyche popular to serve his own ends.

[6] The alternative would be a symbolical interpretation of the rudder (see Dio Chrys. above, n. 3). Governing was compared with the steering of a ship at an early date, and that is why κυβερνάω could also mean 'to govern' and κυβερνήτης not just the steersman but also a guide or governor (the same applies to Latin 'gubernare'). When the belief in Tyche's power grew, it was possible to say that she had her share in this government (Plat. *leg.* 4. 709 b: μετὰ θεοῦ τύχη καὶ καιρὸς τἀνθρώπινα διακυβερνῶσι σύμπαντα; Menand.(?) frg. 482. 9 K. = 417. 8 K.–Th.: Τύχη κυβερνᾷ πάντα), or to speak of her oar, *Epigr.* 491. 5 K. (attributed to the second or first century B.C.): τύχης δ' οἴακι. But all this does not prove that as a goddess she also had the rudder as her attribute: in poetry the Moirai too held an oar (Aesch. *Prom.* 515), as did Eros (*Hymn. Orph.* 58. 8) and Mithras (*Pap. Gr. Mag.* 3. 103: 1, p. 36 Pr.); cf. Hense, op. cit. 166.

regard to the imminent Parthian expedition and in the hope of Caesar's safe departure and victorious return in the company of his Fortuna. He would then have built a temple or may even have begun it already.[1] The coin clearly renders the story about the Fortuna Caesaris more probable; but this again is not enough to be fully conclusive.

It is more decisive that the Fortuna of the fishing boat came to new life under Augustus. But it did not come all of a sudden. The debate about Caesar's luck did not cease after his death. Cicero, who had acknowledged as recently as 46 B.C. in his speech *Pro Marcello* that Caesar was favoured by Fortuna, delivered his verdict, now denying that Caesar, with his evil intentions, could lay claim to *felicitas* and *fortuna*.[2] An *aureus* was issued by M. Arrius Secundus in 41 with a female bust identified by the legend as the 'F(ortuna) p(opuli) R(omani)' (pl. 13. 8),[3] the same representation as that found on the coin of the Pompeian Q. Sicinius in 49 B.C.,[4] not necessarily with the same anti-Caesarian tendency. But the debate was turning again in Caesar's favour. An *aureus* issued by Antony in 41 with his own head on the obverse (pl. 13. 10),[5] another by Ti. Sempronius Gracchus in 40 after the peace of Brundisium with the head of Octavian (pl. 13. 9), show Fortuna with rudder and cornucopiae on the reverse,[6] that is, the new Fortuna first represented under Caesar on the coins of Sepullius Macer. They clearly indicate that Caesar's plans were now adopted by both Antony and Octavian.

No evidence can be found for more than ten years. But some time after the victory at Actium Augustus must have resumed the old plans. They are reflected in Horace's Ode to the Fortuna of Antium,[7] written in 26 B.C. while Augustus was in Spain and was preparing for further expeditions. After describing her various functions in the manner of his Pindaric model, Horace turns to Fortuna as the mistress of the sea,

[1] It was the temple of Fors Fortuna, built under Augustus, completed and dedicated in A.D. 17 by Tiberius at the Porta Portuensis in the *horti Caesaris*, left by Caesar to the Roman people, Tac. *A.* 2. 41. 1; Plut. *fort. Rom.* 5; *Brut.* 20. 3; Platner–Ashby 213; Bömer, *Unters. üb. d. Religion d. Sklaven* 1. 147.

[2] Cic. *Marc.* 19 (below, p. 232. 7); *ep. ad Nep.* frg. 5 (Watt): 'neque enim quicquam aliud est felicitas, nisi honestarum rerum prosperitas; vel . . . felicitas est fortunae adiutrix consiliorum bonorum, quibus qui non utitur felix esse nullo pacto potest. ergo in perditis impiisque consiliis quibus Caesar usus est nulla potuit esse felicitas.'

[3] Sydenham 180; Grueber, pl. 55. 17.

[4] See above, p. 115. 5.

[5] Sydenham 190; Grueber, pl. 104. 6–8. Liegle, *Zeitschr. f. Num.* 42 (1935), 82, rightly suggested that this was again Fortuna in spite of the legend 'Pietas' and of the stork, the symbol of Pietas, at her feet (on the Pietas of L. Antonius see below, p. 255).

[6] Sydenham 184; pl. 28. 1126.

[7] Hor. *c.* 1. 35; cf. Pind. *Ol.* 12 (above, p. 123. 7).

domina aequoris: she should protect Augustus and his warriors on three
overseas expeditions, against the Britons, Parthians, and Arabs:

29   serves iturum Caesarem in ultimos
                      orbis Britannos et iuvenum recens
                         examen Eois timendum
                    partibus Oceanoque rubro.

This is the first explicit evidence that Fortuna, even if only the Fortuna
of Antium, was the goddess of seafarers. She comes from the Pindaric
model, where Tyche as Σώτειρα sits at the ship's helm. But there this
is only one of Tyche's many functions: in Horace it is the relevant
function which gives topicality to the prayer. Augustus must have made
a vow to the Fortuna of Antium before his departure, some time before
26 B.C. when Horace wrote his Ode, a vow for the event of his safe
return. But more than seven years passed before he fulfilled that vow,
and then not for the expeditions to Britain and Arabia but for his return
from the East after the Parthian question had been settled peacefully.
In 19 B.C. he founded the altar of Fortuna Redux,[1] in form the Roman
version of the Fortuna of Antium (pl. 13. 11–12),[2] in essence, however,
none other than the Fortuna Caesaris in the fishing boat.[3] She is the
protecting companion who safely brings her protégé back.[4] The only
difference is that her name no longer expresses a personal attachment.[5]

(d) Fortuna Caesaris

This Fortuna Caesaris was not wholly a new creation. Tyche could
have in the Greek world a similar function. She could be, like the
Daemon,[6] the divine companion of man;[7] and the Tyche of a king

---

[1] *Mon. Anc.* 11: 'Aram Fortunae Reducis ante aedes Honoris et Virtutis ad Portam
Capenam pro reditu meo senatus consacravit, in qua pontifices et virgines Vestales anni-
versarium sacrificium facere iussit eo die quo consulibus Q.Lucretio et M. Vinicio in urbem
ex Syria redieram, et diem Augustalia ex cognomine nostro appellavit'; *F. Amit.* 12 Oct.;
15 Dec.; *Fer. Cum.* 15 Dec. (Degrassi 519 f.; 538).

[2] See the coins with two female busts and the legend 'Q.Rustius Fortunae Antiat(i)' on
the obverse, and with an altar inscribed 'For(tunae) Re(duci) Caesari Augusto' on the
reverse, Mattingly 1. 1 f.; pl. 1. 1 f.; the altar alone, ibid. 1. 63; pl. 7. 10–12. Rustius himself was a member of an Antiate family: Syme, *Hist.* 13 (1964), 120.

[3] I propose to discuss the history of this cult elsewhere.

[4] This is not an isolated idea, cf. Cic. *ND* 2. 165: 'et nostra civitas et Graecia tulit singu-
lares viros, quorum neminem nisi iuvante deo talem fuisse credendum est. (166) quae ratio
poetas maxumeque Homerum . . . inpulit ut principibus heroum . . . certos deos discriminum
et periculorum comites adiungeret'; Nock, *JRS* 37 (1947), 105 ff.

[5] This change was often made by Augustus, see above, p. 111; below, pp. 171; 174; 253;
255 f.

[6] Plat. *Phaed.* 107 d; Rohde, *Psyche* 2. 316. 1; Nilsson 2. 210 ff.

[7] Aeschin. *in Ctesiph.* 157: τὸν δαίμονα καὶ τὴν τύχην τὴν συμπαρακολουθοῦσαν τῷ ἀνθρώπῳ
φυλάξασθαι; Demosth. 18. 258: ἐγὼ μὲν δὴ τοιαύτῃ συμβεβίωκα τύχῃ; 266; 42. 21; Philemon
frg. 10 K.; Nilsson 2. 209 f.

could receive public worship. An inscription from Mylasa was dedicated to the Tyche of the Persian king;[1] another recorded an oath by the Tyche of Seleucus II Callinicus (246–226 B.C.),[2] and Strabo referred to such an oath in Pontus.[3] An inscription set up in Susa about the end of the first century B.C. mentions the Daemon of Phraates and the Tyche of Tiridates.[4] This Tyche was known in Rome at an early date. Ennius mentions the Fortuna Hectoris and that of Thyestes,[5] and legend ascribed one to Servius Tullius.[6] He owed his kingship to her help and was said to have been the founder of most of her temples.[7] One might argue that this is not a fact of history, and that no Roman worshipped a personal Fortuna until Seianus took a statue, dedicated by Servius Tullius, into his house.[8] Later Galba and other emperors too had their personal Fortuna in their houses, known as Fortuna Augusti or Τύχη Σεβαστοῦ.[9] And what she was like we learn from coins of Galba: the Fortuna with the rudder (pl. 13. 13–14)[10] which was claimed above for the Fortuna Caesaris.

The incident in the fishing boat, then, served as the aetiological basis for the introduction of the new goddess. Fortuna, who favoured him before and now again in preference to Pompey, was to become his companion. Caesar had already built a temple for Felicitas, who was called outside Rome 'Felicitas Caesaris';[11] and he was going to have other related goddesses like Clementia Caesaris, Victoria Caesaris, Salus Caesaris.[12] She was advertised on coins and realized, in a modified form, in the Fortuna Redux of Augustus. She was to be like the Tyche of the kings and served with these as the model of the Fortuna Augusti of the emperors from Galba onwards.

---

[1] *CIG* 2693b: Ὁ δῆμος Τύχῃ Ἐπιφανεῖ βασιλέως.

[2] *Or. gr.* 229. 60: ὀμνύω Δία, Γῆν, Ἥλιον . . . καὶ τὴν τοῦ βασιλέως Σελεύκου Τύχην.

[3] Strab. 12. 557: τὸν βασιλικὸν καλούμενον ὅρκον τοῦτον ἀπέφηναν "Τύχην βασιλέως" καὶ "Μῆνα Φαρνάκου". In Egypt it was the oath by the Daemon of the king, *PSI* 361. 6 (251/250 B.C.): ὀμνύω δέ σοι τὸν βασιλέως δαίμονα καὶ τὸν Ἀρσινόης; *Zenon Pap.* 3. 59462. 9: ὀμνύω δέ σοι τὸμ βασιλέως (= Ptolemaeus Euergetes) δαίμονα καὶ Βερενίκην βασιλίσσαν; cf. E. Seidl, *Der Eid im ptolem. Recht* (1929), 14; 18; 50 f.; Kunkel, *Zeitschr. f. Sav. St.* 51 (1931), 244. 2.

[4] Cumont, *CRAI* (1930), 212; 216 ff.; *SEG* 7. 12 f.; cf. *Syll.* 1044. 34 f.; Wilamowitz, *Glaube d. Hell.* 2. 307.

[5] Enn. *Sc.* 172 V.: 'ubi Fortuna Hectoris nostram acrem aciem inclinatam'; 353: 'eheu, mea Fortuna (= Thyest.), ut omnia in me conglomeras mala.'

[6] Val. Max. 3. 4. 3: 'in Tullio vero Fortuna praecipue vires suas ostendit.'

[7] Varr. *LL* 6. 17; Dion. Hal. 4. 27. 7; Plut. *QR* 74; *fort. Rom.* 10: ἄλλαι τε μυρίαι Τύχης τιμαὶ καὶ ἐπικλήσεις, ὧν τὰς πλείστας Σερούιος κατέστησεν.   [8] Dio 58. 7. 2.

[9] Suet. *Galba* 4. 3; 18. 2; Dio 64. 1. 2; cf. Hellegouarc'h, *Hommages M. Renard* (1969), 1. 421 ff.

[10] Mattingly 1. 314 f.; 350; 352; pls. 52. 18 ff.; 54. 25; 55. 6.

[11] See above, pp. 76 f.; 91; 117 f.

[12] See above, pp. 91 ff.; below, pp. 169 ff.; 241 ff.

4. MARS ULTOR

This title requires justification. It is a fact that Caesar announced after his triumph in 46 that he would build a temple for Mars on the Campus Martius, his largest temple in the world;[1] but it is a conjecture that he meant to call the god Ultor. It is another fact that it was Augustus who built the temple of Mars Ultor in the Forum Augustum and dedicated it in 2 B.C.;[2] and it is recorded that he vowed it in 42 in the battle at Philippi to avenge the murder of Caesar, *pro ultione paterna*.[3] Our task then is to show that this record is not correct and that Augustus only executed the plan conceived by Caesar. But before we do so we must consider the question why Caesar wanted to honour Mars with a temple.

Mars was worshipped all over Italy and was originally perhaps more popular than Iuppiter. At Rome too he was, with Iuppiter and Quirinus, one of the principal gods, even though there he became in the first place the god of war. He had many festivals but just an altar on the Campus Martius for a long time.[4] His first temple was built at the Porta Capena and dedicated in 388 B.C.;[5] another, that of Mars Invictus, built perhaps after the Samnite Wars, is of unknown location;[6] a third was dedicated in 138 B.C. in the neighbourhood of the old altar.[7] Caesar's temple would have been the next, again on the Campus Martius. But was it to be just for the god of war? What we have learned about Venus Genetrix turns our attention to another aspect of Mars: as father of Romulus he too was an ancestral god.

The pair Mars and Venus was Greek in origin and known at Rome since the *lectisternia* of 217 B.C.[8] It soon became popular at Rome precisely because it was connected with the 'Trojan' and Roman origins. It was in this sense that the younger Marius was called a son of Mars and Venus;[9] that Sulla set up an inscription on the battlefield of Chaeronea in 86 to Mars, Venus, and Victoria,[10] in the following year to

---

[1] Suet. *Caes.* 44. 1: 'destinabat in primis Martis templum, quantum nusquam esset' extruere repleto et conplanato lacu, in quo naumachiae spectaculum ediderat.'

[2] *Mon. Anc.* 21. 1: 'in privato solo Martis Ultoris templum forumque Augustum ex manibiis feci'; 22. 2; Vell. 2. 100. 2; Dio 55. 10. 2 ff.; 60. 5. 3; cf. Wissowa 146 f.; Keune, *Myth. Lex.* 6. 28 ff.; Gagé, *Mél.* 49 (1932), 82 ff.; Schilling, *Rev. phil.* 68 (1942/3), 44 ff.; E. Buchner, *RE* 9A. 572 ff.; Latte 302 f.

[3] Ov. *F.* 5. 573: 'si mihi bellandi pater est Vestaeque sacerdos / auctor et ulcisci numen utrumque paro: / Mars ades et satia scelerato sanguine ferrum, / stetque favor causa pro meliore tuus! / templa feres et, me victore, vocaberis Ultor'; Suet. *Aug.* 29. 2: 'aedem Martis bello Philippensi pro ultione paterna suscepto voverat.'

[4] Fest. 189 M. (204 L.); Livy 35. 10. 12; 40. 45. 8.   [5] Livy 6. 5. 8; Ov. *F.* 6. 191 f.

[6] *F. Venus.* 14 May (Degrassi 457).

[7] Corn. Nep. ap. Prisc. 8. 4. 17 (p. 383 H.); Pliny 36. 26.

[8] Livy 22. 10. 9.   [9] Plut. *Mar.* 46. 8; above, p. 71.   [10] Plut. *Sulla* 19. 9.

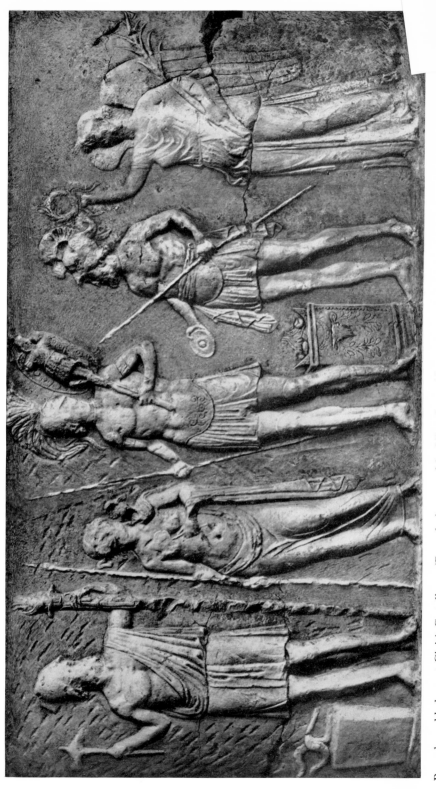

Round marble base at Cività Castellana: 'Romulus' crowned by Victoria sacrifices to Mars who holds a spear and a trophy, and has Venus and Vulcanus at his side (Photograph from the cast in the Museo della Cività Romana); pp. 86, 129.

Mars alone at Sicyon;[1] that Caesar sacrificed at Pharsalus to Mars and
Venus[2] and was hailed after the victory in Asia as a son of Ares and
Aphrodite.[3] A Caesarian relief at Cività Castellana shows Romulus being
wreathed by Victoria while sacrificing to Mars, who is in the company
of Venus and Vulcanus (pl. 14).[4] Coins issued in the East c. 31–29 B.C.
show a statue of Venus, probably the Venus Victrix of the Capitol,
which may have stood in the company of Mars (pl. 13. 15).[5] About
the same time Horace too brought them together.[6] In the Pantheon,
dedicated by Agrippa in 25, there were statues of Mars and Venus.[7] On
one of the short sides of the Augustan base of Sorrento[8] the background
is represented by the Augustan palace. In front of it there is Mars with
helmet and armour, with raised right hand holding a spear; beside
him Cupid and some remains of a seated figure with cornucopiae. The
presence of Cupid suggests that the missing figure on the left was Venus.
They appeared together again on the pediment of the temple of Mars
Ultor (pl. 8. 1)[9] as well as inside the temple.[10] According to the Feriale
Cumanum, which was set up in A.D. 4 or later, a common offering was
made to Mars Ultor and Venus (Genetrix) at Cumae,[11] and no doubt
elsewhere. On a post-Augustan relief at Algiers are found Venus with
Cupid, Mars in the centre, and, on the right, a member of the imperial
family with a hole in his forehead where a star was fitted in (pl. 27. 3).[12]
On the Claudian relief at Ravenna Augustus appears as Mars, Livia
with Cupid as Venus (pl. 8. 2),[13] closely resembling the types used on
the pediment of the temple of Mars.

This survey shows that Mars and Venus were intimately connected
before and after Caesar as the two ancestral gods of the Romans. We shall
see later that not only Aeneas but also Romulus was popular at that time
because statesmen, including Caesar, liked to play the role of a new

---

[1] CIL I². 2828 (Degr. 224): 'L. Cornelius L. f. Sulla imper(ator) Martei.'

[2] App. BC 2. 68. 281: θυόμενός τε νυκτὸς μέσης τὸν Ἄρη κατεκάλει καὶ τὴν ἑαυτοῦ πρόγονον Ἀφροδίτην.

[3] Syll. 760 (below, p. 296. 9).

[4] R. Herbig, Röm. Mitt. 42, Beil. 15; Rostovtzeff, Soc. and Econ. Hist. of the Hell. World 2, pl. 104; Ryberg, pl. 7. 16; cf. RE 8A. 2504.

[5] Mattingly 1. 98; Wissowa, Myth. Lex. 6. 199; cf. RE 8A. 2498.

[6] Hor. c. 1. 2. 33 ff.   [7] Dio 53. 27. 2.

[8] Rizzo, 'La base di Augusto', BC 60 (1932), 77 ff.; pl. 4; Stucchi, I monumenti della parte meridionale del Foro Romano 11 ff. (temple of Divus Iulius); Th. Kraus, Festschr. f. Mercklin (1964), 73.

[9] P. Hommel, Stud. zu den röm. Figurengiebeln (1954), 22 ff.; pl. 2; Ryberg 69 f.; pl. 21 bis, 36d; P. Zanker, Forum Augustum (1969), 18 f.

[10] Ov. Trist. 2. 295 f.; Kraus, l.c. 72.   [11] ILS 108 (12 Iul.?).

[12] CAH Plates 4. 136; Kraus, l.c. 72.

[13] Ryberg, pl. 28. 42c; Hommel, op. cit., pl. 3.

founder.[1] And an ancestral tree which led from Aeneas through Ascanius-Iulus to Romulus and Remus also existed.[2] If, therefore, Caesar built and dedicated a temple for Venus it was only natural that he should vow another for Mars.

The Parthian campaign was then imminent. In fact the need for action had not ceased to be urgent since the defeat of Crassus in 53 B.C.[3] In the following years Cassius and Bibulus successfully resisted the Parthian onslaught. In 51 it was suggested that the new expedition should be led either by Pompey or Caesar or by the consuls;[4] in 50 Caesar made two legions available for the campaign, but in the end they were not sent.[5] It is a fair conjecture that the war would have taken place had the Civil War not intervened.[6] But the Romans did not lose sight of it and the Parthians too were active all the time. They promised Pompey help for the battle at Pharsalus, though they did not keep their promise.[7] For a while after his defeat Pompey himself considered taking refuge in their country.[8] Caesar intended to turn at once against them and would have done so but for the war in Africa.[9] And it is possible to argue that that is why he sacrificed at Pharsalus not only to Venus but also to Mars: it could have been the vow for the coming war and victory. Mars moved even more to the foreground, if it is right to assume that it was about that time that Caesar named one of his legions *Martia* for its bravery,[10] an unprecedented distinction which apparently inspired the similar honorific names of later legions. Caesar did not give up the campaign but left two legions with his cousin Sex. Caesar in Syria.[11] He resumed the plan in 45,[12] and when he assembled his sixteen legions in 44, his task was to avenge the death of Crassus and his men and to conquer Parthia.[13]

The long planning of the campaign and the theme of revenge, the

---

[1] See below, pp. 177 ff.   [2] See above, p.183.

[3] Dio 40. 28–30; Cic. *Att.* 5. 18. 1; Timpe, *Mus. Helv.* 19 (1962), 108 ff.

[4] Cic. *fam.* 8. 10. 2 (Caelius to Cic., Nov. 51): 'alius enim Pompeium mittendum . . ., alius Caesarem cum suo exercitu, alius consules'; 8. 14. 4.

[5] [Caes.] *BG* 8. 54; Dio 40. 65. 2 ff.; App. *BC* 2. 29. 114 f.

[6] Cf. Cic. *Att.* 6. 1. 14 (Febr. 50): 'Parthicum bellum impendet.'

[7] Dio 41. 55. 4; Timpe, l.c. 111.

[8] Dio 42. 2. 5; App. *BC* 2. 83. 349 f.

[9] Dio 45. 46. 3; App. *BC* 3. 77. 312; 4. 58. 250; Meyer, *Caesars Monarchie* 474. 1; Adcock, *CAH* 9. 713; Timpe, l.c. 114 f.

[10] Val. Max. 3. 2. 19; App. *BC* 3. 45. 185; 66 ff. 272 ff.; 4. 115 f., 479 ff.; Dio 45. 13. 3.

[11] Dio 47. 26. 3; B. *Alex.* 66. 1; Gelzer, *Caesar* 282 f.

[12] Cic. *Att.* 13. 27. 1; 31. 3 (May 45).

[13] Dio 43. 51. 1: ἐπιθυμία τε πᾶσι τοῖς Ῥωμαίοις ὁμοίως ἐσῆλθε τιμωρῆσαι τῷ τε Κράσσῳ καὶ τοῖς σὺν αὐτῷ φθαρεῖσι, καὶ ἐλπὶς τότε, εἴπερ ποτέ, τοὺς Πάρθους καταστρέψεσθαι; App. *BC* 2. 110. 459: Παρθυαίους δὲ τινύμενος τῆς ἐς Κράσσον παρασπονδήσεως; Iustin. 42. 4. 6.

sacrifice to Mars at Pharsalus, and the promise of the temple later, lead us to the suggestion that the temple was to commemorate the Parthian victory (as the temple of Venus commemorated the conquest of Gaul) and was to be dedicated to Mars Ultor. To uphold this suggestion it is necessary to show that the tradition according to which it was Octavian who vowed the temple of Mars at Philippi in 42 to avenge the death of Caesar, cannot be right. We have therefore to consider the theme of vengeance, the situation at Philippi, the subsequent propaganda for the Parthian campaign, and the temple of Mars.

When Octavian accepted the adoption he accepted the obligation of vengeance with it.[1] The *lex Pedia* was created for this purpose in 43, a trial was held, the murderers exiled, and their property confiscated.[2] With this the legal form of vengeance was ended. The war followed only because of the attack of the conspirators on the authorities of Rome, and that is why they had to die.[3] Nevertheless it is understandable that Antony and Octavian spoke at Philippi to their soldiers about vengeance,[4] and that after the victory supplications were decreed because Caesar's murder was now avenged.[5] These two pieces of evidence seem to provide strong support for the third about Octavian's vow of the temple in the battle. And yet it cannot be right. It was not his private battle, but conducted by the *triumviri* together, and among these Antony was far more powerful than he was, and was in fact the real victor; in contrast, Octavian was ill and unlucky during the battle.[6] Next, the supplications had to be decreed for something other than victory, because it was a victory in a civil war. For the same reason Octavian could not have vowed the temple for the event of victory.

It is nevertheless probable that the temple was vowed, but collectively by the *triumviri* and in expectation of the Parthian war. Mars appeared on their coins in the following years (pl. 13. 16–18),[7] and at Brundisium Antony was charged with the war with the express purpose of avenging the death of Crassus.[8] A long but unsuccessful war followed,[9] and later Augustus was urged again and again to resume it, and reference was made again to vengeance.[10] It is significant that the name Mars Ultor is

---

[1] App. *BC* 3. 11. 37; Dio 46. 48. 1; 47. 22. 4; Kunkel, *Unters. zur Entwicklung des röm. Kriminalverfahrens* (1962), 127 ff.

[2] Vell. 2. 69. 5; Livy, *Per.* 120.   [3] *Mon. Anc.* 2. 2; Ov. *F.* 3. 709 f.

[4] Dio 47. 42. 3 ff.   [5] Dio 48. 3. 2.

[6] App. *BC* 4. 110 f. 463 ff.; Dio 47. 41. 3; 45 f.; Suet. *Aug.* 13. 1, etc.; cf. Fitzler-Seeck, *RE* 10. 280.   [7] Sydenham 182; 184; 206; Grueber, pls. 56. 7–9; 57. 20; 105. 4 f.

[8] App. *BC* 5. 65. 275.

[9] H. Buchheim, *Die Orientpolitik d. Triumvirn M. Antonius* (1960), 74 ff.

[10] Verg. *Georg.* 3. 31; 4. 560; Hor. *sat.* 2. 5. 62; 2. 1. 15; *c.* 1. 2. 21; 51: 'ne sinas Medos equitare inultos'; 3. 5. 3 ff.; 2. 9. 18; 1. 35. 29 ff.

first found on coins of 19 after the Parthian settlement and the return of
the standards lost by Crassus (pl. 13. 19–21);[1] also that these were deposited in the temple of Mars Ultor when it was completed.[2] Ovid, who
wrote after the dedication of the temple, was, on the other hand, the first
to speak of Octavian's alleged vow at Philippi, although he certainly did
not invent it;[3] but he called Mars the twofold avenger,[4] which shows that
he was well aware of the original function of the temple and that it was
now pushed to the background. The temple was suitably dedicated in
the year when C. Caesar, Augustus' grandson and heir, was about to
set out for a new Parthian expedition and to avenge the past again; and
Mars was asked again for his help.[5] The temple served many purposes:
this Mars was the god of military training, of war and victory, and also
supported dynastic interests.[6] But he was not Caesar's avenger.

If then it was the *triumviri* and not Octavian alone who vowed the
temple at Philippi to take revenge, not on the murderers of Caesar, but
on the Parthians, they can only have renewed Caesar's vow. It was
he who meant to build the temple on his return from Parthia; and it
was then he who chose the strange epithet which no other god bore at
Rome.[7] What made him choose it is not clear. A Greek god could be
called Timoros, Zeus in the first place, then Dike, Helios, and others.[8]
This Mars was still the god of war and victory, but also the ancestral
god, the father of Romulus. The next step was to represent the emperors
and empresses as Mars and Venus—so already Augustus and Livia
on the Claudian relief of Ravenna[9]—and to honour a young prince
with the name of a New Ares in Greece.[10]

[1] Mattingly 1. 58; 60; 65; 71 f.; 114; Kraus, l.c. 66 ff.; pl. 35.

[2] *Mon. Anc.* 29. 2; cf. Dio 55. 10. 4.

[3] Ov. *F.* 5. 573 ff.; above, p. 128. 3.

[4] Ov. *F.* 5. 579: 'nec satis est meruisse semel cognomina Marti: / persequitur Parthi signa
retenta manu'; 595: 'rite deo templumque datum nomenque bis ulto, / et meritus voti
debita solvit honor.'

[5] Ov. *Ars amat.* 1. 178: 'Parthe, dabis poenas: Crassi gaudete sepulti / signaque barbaricas
non bene passa manus! / ultor adest'; 203: 'Marsque pater Caesarque pater, date numen
eunti.'

[6] Dio 55. 10; P. Zanker, *Forum Augustum* (1969), 10 ff.

[7] Iuppiter Ultor on an inscription after the death of Nero (?)—an improvisation?—
ILS 9239, and on coins beginning with Commodus, Bernhart, *Handbuch d. Münzkunde* 189.
In the Greek version of *Mon. Anc.* 21. 2; 29. 2 the epithet is Ἀμύντωρ, which is not found elsewhere (Hom. *Il.* 15. 610 ἀμύντωρ Ζεύς; cf. 18. 98 quoted by App. *BC* 3. 13. 47) and comes from
poetry (Pfeiffer ad Callim. frg. 635).

[8] Preisendanz, *Myth. Lex.* 5. 965 f.; Ziegler, *RE* 6A. 1308 f.; cf. Cumont, *Mem. Pont.
Accad.* 3. 1 (1923), 65 ff. (Sol).

[9] See above, p. 129.

[10] *IG* 2–3². 3250 (E.–J. 64, C. Caesar); 3257 (E.–J. 136, Drusus); Curtius, *Mitt. Arch. Inst.*
1 (1948), 61 f.; Orlandos, *Arch. Ephem.* (1965), 111 (ll. 11 ff.).

VII

THE LIBERATOR

POMPEY's sons began the war anew in Spain. Caesar left Rome in November 46 and won the decisive victory at Munda on 17 March 45. When the news of this victory reached Rome on 20 April, the Senate decreed supplications for fifty days; further, that on the following day, the day of the Parilia, games should be held; that Caesar should be called 'Liberator' and a temple of Libertas should be built; that two statues should be set up on the Rostra, one wearing the *corona civica*, the other the *corona obsidionalis*, a third on the Capitol among the kings of Rome, a fourth in the temple of Quirinus with the inscription 'Deo Invicto'; that an ivory statue should be carried in the procession of the gods in the *pompa circensis*; that supplications should be held on his behalf after every victory; that the anniversaries of his victories should become public festivals; and that he should wear a laurel wreath always and the triumphal garb at the games in the Circus. A triumph was also decreed and held in October.[1]

This is a long and puzzling list; it is given without comment, and modern research has not done much about it. A more detailed interpretation may begin with the question as to the general aim of these honours. Those of 46 were mainly chosen with the purpose of surpassing all that was ever granted to Pompey. Now Caesar's supremacy was firmly established: the fresh honours had to surpass those of 46 and to be a commensurate expression of his unique political standing in religious terms. The honours suggest that the conqueror has now also become a liberator, saviour, and founder: these then should be the central themes of this and the following two chapters.

I. LIBERTAS

The modern critic might feel that it was not an auspicious time to call Caesar a liberator and to want to build a temple for Libertas,[2] when he had been dictator for some years and was about to found his

---

[1] Dio 43. 42. 1–43. 1; 44. 1; 6; 45. 3 f.; App. *BC* 2. 106. 440 ff.; Vell. 2. 56. 3.

[2] Dio 43. 44. 1: αὐτόν τε Ἐλευθερωτὴν καὶ ἐκάλουν καὶ ἐς τὰ γραμματεῖα ἀνέγραφον καὶ νεὼν Ἐλευθερίας δημοσίᾳ ἐψηφίσαντο.

monarchy. And yet he could not have justified his past and present actions by any other means than by the requirements of freedom. So strong was the power of tradition.

Libertas was the principal characteristic of the Roman republic which distinguished it from the regal period.[1] It was due to it that the citizens possessed and exercised political rights in contrast to the slaves who obeyed their masters and to the conquered who were ruled by their conquerors.[2] The regal period ended in tyranny, and the founder of the republic, L. Iunius Brutus, made the Romans swear not to tolerate kings in Rome again.[3] It was a crime and was punished accordingly.[4] Three 'pretenders' were often quoted, Sp. Cassius of 486 B.C., Sp. Maelius of 439 B.C., and M. Manlius of 386 B.C.: they were condemned to death and executed.[5] The charge was probably true, even if the details were more or less legendary and partly impossible. There was, on the other hand, the great hero, the elder Scipio, who refused the kingship in Spain in 209 B.C. because it was intolerable at Rome.[6]

The restoration of freedom became a political slogan in the age of the Gracchi. Ti. Gracchus was accused in 133 by his enemies of aiming at kingship,[7] and Scipio Nasica (*cos.* 138) murdered him for the sake

---

[1] Kroll, *Kultur der ciceronischen Zeit* 1. 10 ff.; 124 ff.; H. Kloesel, *Libertas*, Diss. Breslau 1935 (valuable); Ch. Wirszubski, *Libertas as a Political Idea*, 1950 (Momigliano, *JRS* 41 (1951), 146 ff.); Wickert, *RE* 22. 2080 f.; A. Dermience, *Ét. class.* 25 (1957), 157 ff. (Cicero); J. Bleicken, *Hist. Zeitschr.* 195 (1962), 1 ff.; J. Hellegouarc'h, *Le vocabulaire latin des relations . . .* (1963), 542 ff.; M. A. Giua, *Studi class. e orientali* 16 (1967), 308 ff. On the corresponding Greek term see Schlier, *Theol. Wörterb. z. N.T.* 2. 484 ff.; D. Nestle, *Eleutheria* 1, 1967 (with bibliography); id. *RAC* 8. 269 ff.; Pohlenz, *Griech. Freiheit* (1955), 113 ff. (*Inschr. v. Priene* 19. 18: οὐθὲν μεῖζόν ἐστιν ἀνθρώποις Ἕλλησιν τῆς ἐλευθερίας; Philo, *Quod omnis probus liber* 139).

[2] Cic. *Parad.* 34: 'quid est enim libertas? potestas vivendi ut velis'; *Dig.* 1. 5. 4 pr.: 'libertas est naturalis facultas eius quod cuique facere libet, nisi si quid vi aut iure prohibetur. servitus est constitutio iuris gentium, qua quis dominio alieno contra naturam subicitur'; Epict. 4. 1. 1: ἐλεύθερός ἐστιν ὁ ζῶν ὡς βούλεται. On the various degrees of freedom in international relations see *Dig.* 49. 15. 7. 1 (Proculus); A. H. M. Jones, *Anatol. Studies pres. to W. H. Buckler* (1939), 109 ff.

[3] Livy 2. 1. 9: 'Brutus . . . populum . . . iure iurando adegit neminem Romae passuros regnare'; App. *BC* 2. 107. 444 (45 B.C.): εἰσὶ δ' οἳ καὶ βασιλέα προσειπεῖν ἐπενόουν, μέχρι μαθὼν αὐτὸς ἀπηγόρευσε καὶ ἠπείλησεν ὡς ἀθέμιστον ὄνομα μετὰ τὴν τῶν προγόνων ἀράν; 2. 119. 499 (after the murder): ἐβοηδρόμουν βασιλέα καὶ τύραννον ἀνελεῖν; Béranger, *REL* 13 (1935), 85 ff.

[4] Mommsen, *Strafr.* 551.

[5] Cic. *rep.* 2. 49; *Phil.* 2. 114; Mommsen, *Röm. Forsch.* 2. 153 ff. (with further evidence and discussion).

[6] Livy 27. 19. 3: 'multitudo Hispanorum . . . regem eum ingenti consensu appellavit. (4) tum Scipio . . . sibi maximum nomen imperatoris esse dixit, quo se milites sui appellassent; regium nomen alibi magnum, Romae intolerabilem esse'; Polyb. 10. 40. 4; Dio 16, frg. 57. 48 (1, p. 245 B.); Münzer, *Adelsp.* 100 f.; D. Kienast, *Zeitschr. f. Sav. Stift.* 78 (1961), 406 f.; Michelfeit, *Philol.* 108 (1964), 262; Aymard, *Études d'hist. anc.* (1967), 390 f.

[7] Cic. *Lael.* 41; Sall. *Iug.* 31. 7; 'tyrant': Diod. 34. 33. 6 f.; Plut. *Tib. Gr.* 19. 3 (Meyer, *Kl. Schr.* 1. 408. 1); demanded even the diadem: Plut. *Tib. Gr.* 19. 3; Flor. 3. 14. 7; *vir. ill.* 64. 6 (below, p. 335). But Gracchus himself spoke of freedom and of the expulsion of the kings, Plut. *Tib. Gr.* 15. 5 = *Or. Rom. frg.* p. 151 Malc.

of freedom on the Capitol, allegedly at the statues of the kings;[1] it was said that Scipio Nasica should have received a statue as a tyrannicide.[2] But C. Gracchus brought in the *lex Sempronia*, which forbade murder without the authority of the Roman people;[3] Caesar referred to it in 63 B.C. when pleading against the capital punishment of the Catilinarians.[4] Although Cicero proved that this law was not applicable and very much hoped that he would be honoured as a liberator,[5] the tribune Q. Caecilius Metellus Nepos tried to bring in a bill as early as January 62 to the effect that Cicero should be prosecuted for murder, and that Pompey should be called back to liberate Rome from Cicero's tyranny.[6] Others called Cicero a king, even a foreign king like Tarquinius Superbus, because he was not a native of Rome but of Arpinum.[7] The charge of his tyranny was later often repeated.[8] Where Metellus failed, Clodius succeeded: his bill of 58 was a repetition of the *lex Sempronia* and led to Cicero's exile[9] and other consequences, which will be discussed presently. Any man who was more powerful and successful than the rest was exposed to the same charge, in the first place Pompey[10] and Caesar.[11]

2. THE PERSONIFICATION

However old the idea was, there was no early cult of the goddess Libertas.[12] It was probably Iuppiter Capitolinus who was the custodian of political and social freedom until a special temple of Iuppiter Liber or Iuppiter Libertas, later often called just Libertas, was built by Ti. Sempronius Gracchus (*cos.* 238) on the Aventine;[13] the cult was also established outside Rome in many places.[14] There is little evidence about the history of the cult. In the Second Punic War Ti. Sempronius

---

[1] Cic. *Brut.* 212 (written in 46 B.C.): 'ex dominatu Ti. Gracchi privatus in libertatem rem publicam vindicavit'; App. *BC* 1. 17. 70.   [2] Cic. *rep.* 6. 8.

[3] Schol. Gronov. Cic. *Cat.* p. 289 St.; Cic. *Rab. perd.* 12; Bleicken, *RE* 23. 2453.

[4] Cic. *Cat.* 4. 7; 10.   [5] Cic. *Cat.* 3. 14; *Sulla* 33.

[6] Plut. *Cic.* 23. 4; Gelzer, *Kl. Schr.* 2. 272; Classen, *Philol.* 104 (1962), 189 f.

[7] Cic. *Sulla* 21 f.; *Att.* 1. 16. 10; Iuven. 8. 237 f.

[8] Cic. *Sest.* 109; *Vatin.* 23; Ps.-Sall. *in Cic.* 5.

[9] Livy, *Per.* 103; Vell. 2. 45. 1; Dio 38. 14. 4; Cic. *dom.* 47; Gelzer, *RE* 7A. 914; 917.

[10] Cic. *Att.* 2. 17. 1; Suet. *Caes.* 49. 2; Val. Max. 6. 2. 7 (below, p. 335. 5); O. Murray, *JRS* 55 (1965), 180. 95.

[11] Cic. *ep. ad Q. Axium* frg. 5 (p. 171 Watt); Suet. *Caes.* 49. 2 (edict of Bibulus, 59 B.C.); Strasburger, op. cit. 108; Gelzer, *Caesar* 35. 39; W. Allen jr., *TAPA* 84 (1953), 227 ff.; Brunt, *CR* 71 (1957), 195. 1.—Cic. *Att.* 7. 20. 2 (49); 13. 37. 2 (45); 14. 14. 2; 15. 20. 2; *Deiot.* 33; *Phil.* 2. 114; *off.* 3. 83.

[12] Wissowa 120; 138 f.; id. *Herm.* 58 (1923), 388; Latte 70; 256; Degrassi 440; 504.

[13] Livy 24. 16. 19; Paul. 121 M. (108 L.).

[14] *ILS* 3065–7; 4906; Degr. 29.

Gracchus (*cos.* 215) achieved victory at Beneventum in 214 with the help of slaves. He set them free, and they celebrated the victory wearing the *pileus*, the cap which slaves used to receive after manumission. This scene was commemorated in a painting which Gracchus placed in the temple of Libertas built by his father.[1] This shows that Libertas was the goddess of former slaves also and that is why, as we learn from coins, she received the liberty-cap as her attribute.[2] The cap soon acquired a new significance. At the end of the Second Punic War Scipio liberated many Roman citizens from Carthaginian captivity; these followed him in his triumphal procession of 201 B.C.,[3] and at least one of them, the senator Q. Terentius Culleo (*pr.* 187), wore the liberty-cap.[4] In 197 B.C. it was the colonists of Placentia and Cremona who, rescued from the captivity of the Gauls, wore it in the triumphal procession of C. Cornelius Cethegus (*cos.* 197),[5] and in 194 two thousand more former prisoners of the Second Punic War, found in Greece, at the triumph of T. Quinctius Flamininus.[6] All this happened within a decade after the Second Punic War; there is no evidence of further instances.[7] But the cap had become a symbol of political freedom also. It was in this sense that King Prusias II of Bithynia wore it in 167 B.C.: he owed his freedom to the Roman people.[8]

Libertas first appears on the coins of M. Porcius Laeca and C. Cassius Longinus (*cos.* 96) *c.* 125 B.C. (pl. 15. 1–2):[9] she is riding a triumphal chariot and holding a sceptre and the cap; on the coin of Porcius she is also crowned by Victoria. And yet neither refers to liberation through war and victory, but to laws of their ancestors which protected civic liberties: Porcius to the *lex Porcia de provocatione*,[10] as did later another

[1] Livy 24. 16. 18 f.; Latte 256 (believes it to have been a painting of the goddess).

[2] See below, n. 9 ; Mattingly 1. 185, etc.; Strack, op. cit. 1. 176. 761. The cap was also worn at the Saturnalia (Sen. *ep.* 18. 3; Mart. 11. 6. 4; 14. 1. 2).

[3] Dio 17, frg. 57. 86 (1, p. 272 B.); Zonar. 9. 14. 13.

[4] Livy 30. 45. 5. He also wore it at Scipio's funeral, Livy 38. 55. 2; Plut. *Apophth. Scip. Mai.* 7; Ps.-Quintil. *decl.* 9. 20; Val. Max. 5. 2. 5 (generally done by slaves who were set free by the testament of the deceased, App. *Mithr.* 2. 4; Dion. Hal. 4. 24. 6; *Cod. Iust.* 7. 6. 5; below, p. 361. 2).

[5] Livy 33. 23. 1; Degrassi, *Scritti* 214. This incident is not recorded for the triumph of L. Furius Purpurio (*cos.* 196), Livy 31. 21. 18; 48. 11; 49. 3, although his campaign of 200 with its incidents is so similar that it has been assumed to be apocryphal and made up on the model of Cethegus' campaign, Münzer, *RE* 7. 362 f.; *contra*, De Sanctis, *Storia dei Romani*, 4. 1. 412. 11; Broughton 1. 326. 1.

[6] Livy 34. 52. 12; Val. Max. 5. 2. 6; Plut. *Flamin.* 13. 9.

[7] For a different view see Gagé, 'Les clientèles triomphales de la République Romaine', *Rev. hist.* 218 (1957), 1–31.

[8] Livy 45. 44. 19; Polyb. 30. 19. 3; Dio 20, frg. 69 (1, p. 302 B.); Habicht, *RE* 23. 1111.

[9] Sydenham 63; 61; Grueber, pl. 28. 3 f.; 11.

[10] Mommsen, *Röm. Münzwesen* 526; H. Gundel, *RE* 22. 213 (no. 17); Bleicken, *RE* 23.

member of the family, P. Porcius, who issued a coin with the legend 'Provoco';[1] Cassius to the *lex Cassia tabellaria* of L. Cassius Longinus Ravilla (*tr. pl.* 137),[2] also commemorated by a coin of Q. Cassius Longinus (*tr. pl.* 49) *c.* 56 with the bust of Libertas (pl. 15. 3).[3] The moneyer C. Egnatius Maximus issued a coin with Libertas in the *biga*, crowned by Victoria; another with her bust, and a third with the temple of Iuppiter Libertas on the Aventine, with Iuppiter and Libertas standing in it, and with their symbols, thunderbolt and cap, in the pediment (pl. 15. 4–6).[4] These coins must reflect important events, perhaps a victory and offerings to the temple in consequence of it, or a rebuilding. But nothing is known of the moneyer or of the time of the issues; they may belong to the years after Sulla's death.[5]

Libertas, then, has become the goddess of freedom, of the citizens as well as of the freedmen, who protected the Romans against servitude threatened by the enemy, but also against political tyranny. The latter theme became more and more topical and is best illustrated by a coin of Q. Caepio Brutus, issued *c.* 55 B.C. (pl. 15. 7) (and again after Caesar's murder), with the head of Libertas on the obverse and his 'ancestor', L. Iunius Brutus, on the reverse.[6] In 58 when Cicero was exiled as a tyrant, his property was confiscated, his house destroyed, like those of the ancient 'pretenders',[7] and a shrine of Libertas erected in its place.[8] This shrine did not last long; Cicero returned and received his property back. While he was in exile, people acclaimed him in Rome as a champion of freedom and applied a reference to (Servius) Tullius at a performance of Accius' *Brutus* to him.[9]

2448 f.; cf. Cic. *de or.* 2. 199: 'provocationem, patronam illam civitatis ac vindicem libertatis'; Livy 3. 45. 8: 'tribunicium auxilium et provocationem . . ., duas arces libertatis tuendae.'

[1] Sydenham 78; Grueber, pl. 95. 13; Mommsen, op. cit. 552 f.; H. Gundel, *RE* 22. 214 (no. 21); Bleicken, l.c.

[2] Münzer, *RE* 3. 1726 f.; 1742.

[3] Sydenham 153; Grueber, pl. 48. 12; Mommsen, op. cit. 635 f.; Münzer, *RE* 3. 1740 f.

[4] Sydenham 129; pl. 22. 786–8.

[5] Sulla was both tyrant and liberator. His followers accompanied him in his triumph of 81 with their families but called him saviour and father, not liberator, and wore a wreath, not the cap, Plut. *Sulla* 34. 2; Alföldi, *Mus. Helv.* 10 (1953), 104.

[6] Sydenham 150; pl. 25. 906.

[7] Cic. *dom.* 101; cf. Livy 2. 41. 11; for further instances see Ogilvie's note ad loc.

[8] Plut. *Cic.* 33. 1: ὁ δὲ Κλώδιος ἐξελάσας αὐτὸν κατέπρησε μὲν αὐτοῦ τὰς ἐπαύλεις, κατέπρησε δὲ τὴν οἰκίαν καὶ τῷ τόπῳ ναὸν Ἐλευθερίας ἐπῳκοδόμησε; Dio 38. 17. 6: ἥ τε οὐσία αὐτοῦ ἐδημεύθη, καὶ ἡ οἰκία ὥσπερ τινὸς πολεμίου κατεσκάφη, τό τε ἔδαφος αὐτῆς ἐς νεὼν Ἐλευθερίας ἀνέθηκαν; Cic. *dom.* 108: 'ista tua pulchra Libertas deos Penatis et familiaris meos Lares expulit, ut se ipsa tamquam in captivis sedibus conlocaret . . . (110) . . . Libertatis simulacrum in ea domo conlocabas'; *leg.* 2. 42; W. Allen, *TAPA* 75 (1944), 1 ff.; B. Tamm, *Auditorium and Palatium* (1963), 37 ff.; G.–Ch. Picard, *REL* 43 (1965), 229 ff.

[9] Cic. *Sest.* 123: 'nominatim sum appellatus in Bruto: "Tullius, qui libertatem civibus stabiliverat".'

PLATE 15

1. Denarius of M. Porcius Laeca, c. 125 B.C. (Sydenham 63. 513), Oxford; obv. helmeted head of 'Roma', legend 'Laeca'; rev.: Libertas with pileus and sceptre in quadriga crowned by Victoria, legend 'M. Porc(ius), Roma'; p. 136.

2. Denarius of C. Cassius, c. 125 B.C. (Sydenham 61. 502), Oxford; obv.: helmeted head of 'Roma' and voting urn; rev.: Libertas with pileus and sceptre in quadriga, legend 'C. Cassi(us), Roma'; p. 136.

3. Denarius of Q. Cassius, c. 56 B.C. (Sydenham 153. 918), Oxford; obv.: head of Libertas, legend 'Libert., Q. Cassius'; rev.: domed temple of Vesta with sella curulis, between voting urn and tabella inscribed 'A(bsolvo) C(ondemno)'; p. 137.

4. Denarius of C. Egnatius Maxsumus, c. 75 B.C. (Sydenham 129. 786), London; obv.: bust of Venus with Cupid, legend 'Maxsumus'; rev.: Libertas (with pileus behind her) in biga crowned by Victoria, legend 'C. Egnatius Cn. f. Cn. n.'; p. 137.

5. Denarius of C. Egnatius Maxsumus, c. 75 B.C. (Sydenham 129. 787), Oxford, obv.: bust of Libertas and pileus, legend 'Maxsumus'; rev.: helmeted Roma with spear and her foot on the head of a wolf, and Venus with Cupid and sceptre, right and left rudder on prow, legend 'C. Egnatius Cn. f. Cn. n.'; p. 137.

6. Denarius of C. Egnatius Maxsumus, c. 75 B.C. (Sydenham 129. 788), London; obv.: bust of Cupid with bow and quiver, legend 'Maxsumus'; rev.: distyle temple with Iuppiter and Libertas, in pediment, thunderbolt and pileus, legend 'C. Egnatius Cn. f. Cn. n.'; p. 137.

7. Denarius of M. Iunius Brutus, c. 55 B.C. (Sydenham 150. 906), Oxford; obv.: head of Libertas, legend 'Libertas'; rev.: L. Brutus between two lictors and preceded by an attendant, legend 'Brutus'; p. 137.

8. Denarius of C. Vibius Pansa, 48 B.C. (Sydenham 159. 949), Oxford; obv.: head of Libertas, legend 'Libertatis'; rev. Roma with sceptre and sword, seated on shields, her foot on globe, is crowned by Victoria, legend 'C. Pansa C. f. C. n.'; p. 140.

9. Denarius of L. Lollius Palicanus, 45 B.C. (Sydenham 161. 960), Oxford; obv.: head of Libertas, legend 'Libertatis'; rev.: Rostra with a chair, legend 'Palikanus'; p. 140.

10. Bronze of Aphrodisias, c. A.D. 238-44 (Inv. Waddington 2220), Paris; obv.: radiate head of Gordian III, legend Αὐτ(ο)κ(ράτωρ) Μ. Ἀν(τώνιος) Γορδιανὸς Σε(βαστός); rev.: Demos at sacrifice is crowned by Eleutheria, legend Δῆμος, Ἐλευθερία Ἀφροδισιέων; p. 140.

11. Bronze of Aphrodisias, imperial period (BMC Caria 30), London; obv.: bearded head, legend Δῆμος; rev.: goddess with sceptre and patera, legend Ἐλευθερία Ἀφροδισιέων; p. 140.

12. Denarius of M. Iunius Brutus, 43 B.C. (Sydenham 202. 1287), Oxford; obv.: head of Libertas, legend 'Leibertas'; rev.: lyre between plectrum and laurel-branch, legend 'Caepio Brutus pro cos.'; p. 142.

13. Denarius of C. Cassius Longinus and P. Cornelius Lentulus Spinther, 42 B.C. (Sydenham 204. 1305), Oxford; obv.: bust of Libertas, legend 'Leibertas, C. Cassi(us) imp.'; rev.: jug and lituus, legend 'Lentulus Spint.'; p. 142.

14. As of Claudius, A.D. 41 (Mattingly 1. 185, 145), Oxford; obv.: head of Claudius, legend 'Ti. Claudius Caesar Aug., p. m., tr. p., imp.'; rev.: Libertas with pileus, legend 'Libertas Augusta, S.C.'; p. 142.

15. Denarius of Galba, A.D. 68 (Mattingly 1. 312. 24), Oxford; obv.: head of Galba, legend 'Imp. Ser. Galba Aug.'; rev.: Libertas with pileus, r. and l. a corn-ear, legend 'Libertas p(opuli) R(omani)'; p. 142.

16. Bronze of Patrai (Achaea), c. A.D. 67 (Cohen 1. 308. 418), Paris; obv.: radiate head of Nero, legend 'Nero Caesar Aug. Germ.'; rev.: Iuppiter with eagle(?) and sceptre(?), legend 'Iuppiter Liberator, C(olonia) P(atrensis)'; p. 144.

17. Copper of Sicyon, c. A.D. 67 (Cook, Ζεύς 2. 97), London; obv.: head of Nero, legend Νέ(ρων) καὶ Ζεὺς Ἐλευθέριος; rev.: Nero(?) on horseback, legend ἐπὶ Γ(αίου) Ἰου(λίου) Πολυαίνου, Σι(κυωνίων); p. 144.

18. Denarius of M. Iunius Brutus and L. Plactorius Cestianus, 42 B.C. (Sydenham 203. 1301), London; obv.: head of Brutus, legend 'L. Plaet. Cest., Brut. imp.'; rev.: pileus between two daggers, legend 'Eid(ibus) Mar(tiis)'; p. 148.

19. Denarius of M. Iunius Brutus and P. Servilius Casca Longus, 42 B.C. (Sydenham 203. 1298), Paris; obv.: head of Neptune with trident, legend 'Casca Longus'; rev.: Victoria with palm and broken diadem, under her feet broken sceptre, legend 'Brutus imp.'; p. 148.

PLATE 15

1   2   3   4   5   6

7   8   9   10   11

12   13   14   15   16

17   18   19

3. CAESAR AND LIBERTY

Caesar has much to say about *libertas* in his *Bellum Gallicum*, especially in Book 7, in connection with the rising of Vercingetorix, where he uses the term more often than in all the other books put together;[1] but it was the freedom the Gauls were fighting for against the Romans, which is not relevant here. In the *Bellum Civile* there is just one passage,[2] which is, however, relevant and very important. In addition the second *Epistula ad Caesarem*, often attributed to Sallust,[3] which describes the situation at Rome as it was before the outbreak of the Civil War, praises the value of *libertas*[4] and reminds Caesar of what he did for it in his youth.[5] The villain is Pompey, and Caesar should come to the rescue of the State and restore liberty.[6] Caesar came, and justified his armed intervention, as we learn from his *Bellum Civile*, in almost the same terms,[7] with the addition of the phrase 'in libertatem vindicare', which was not new and was often repeated later.[8] Pompey in turn asserted, or was said to have asserted, that he left Rome to fight for liberty as the Athenians did at the time of the Persian invasion; Rome too lost it once before at the time of the Gallic invasion but Camillus came and recovered it.[9] Both Pompey and Caesar, when addressing their soldiers before the battle at Pharsalus, referred to tyranny and liberty but probably did not call themselves liberators, as Dio asserts.[10] It was for Caesar more than

---

[1] Caes. *BG* 7. 1. 5: 'Galliam in libertatem vindicent'; 7. 1. 8: 'libertatemque quam a maioribus acceperint recuperare'; 7. 4. 4: 'hortatur ut communis libertatis causa arma capiant'; 37. 2; 4; 64. 3; 76. 2; 77. 13 f.; 89. 1.   [2] Caes. *BC* 1. 22. 5 (below, n. 7).

[3] The value of the evidence is not impaired by the doubts over the authorship, provided that it is based on more than the one passage in *BC* 1. 22. 5.

[4] 'Sall.' *ep. ad Caes.* 2. 5. 7: 'additis novis civibus magna me spes tenet fore, ut omnes expergiscantur ad libertatem: quippe cum illis libertatis retinendae, tum his servitutis amittendae cura oritur'; 11. 4: 'libertas iuxta bonis et malis, strenuis atque ignavis optabilis est'; 12. 5: 'libertatem gloria cariorem habeo'; 10. 5.

[5] Ibid. 2. 2. 4: 'sin in te ille animus est, qui iam a principio nobilitatis factionem disturbavit, plebem Romanam ex gravi servitute in libertatem restituit.'

[6] Ibid. 2. 3. 1: 'Cn. Pompeius . . . rem publicam conturbavit . . . eisdem tibi restituendum est'; 4. 3: 'optatius habent ex tua calamitate periculum libertatis facere, quam per te populi Romani imperium maximum ex magno fieri'; 13. 3: (patria atque parentes) 'non flagitium a te neque malum facinus petimus, sed utei libertatem eversam restituas'; Kroll, *Herm.* 62 (1927), 380 f. Cf. also Antony's *accusatio Pompei* in December 51, Cic. *Att.* 7. 8. 5: 'quid censes . . . facturum esse ipsum, si in possessionem rei publicae venerit . . .?' Gelzer, *Caesar* 173.

[7] Caes. *BC* 1. 22. 5: 'se non maleficii causa ex provincia egressum, sed uti se a contumeliis inimicorum defenderet . . . et se et populum Romanum factione paucorum oppressum in libertatem vindicaret'; Dio 41. 17. 3: τούς τε γὰρ ἀντιστασιάζοντάς σφισι πολεμίους ἑκάτεροι τῆς πατρίδος ὀνομάζοντες, καὶ ἑαυτοὺς ὑπὲρ τῶν κοινῶν πολεμεῖν λέγοντες; Kroll, *Herm.* 62 (1927), 381; Gelzer, *Caesar* 176. 399.

[8] See below, p. 143. 2.   [9] App. *BC* 2. 50. 205.

[10] Dio 41. 57. 2: ἀλλήλους τε τυράννους καὶ αὑτοὺς ἐλευθερωτὰς αὐτῶν ὀνομάζοντες; App.

a temporary weapon. His followers C. Vibius Pansa (*cos.* 43) and
Lollius Palicanus reproduced the head of Libertas on their coins in
48 and 45 B.C. respectively (pl. 15. 8–9),[1] which suggests that his claim
was officially accepted and that the honours decreed by the Senate after
the victory at Pharsalus, but rejected by him,[2] may have included plans
for a new shrine of Libertas connected with his name. But there was
still opposition, and at the *ludi Victoriae Caesaris* in 46 the poet Laberius
spoke in the theatre of the loss of liberty and suffered no harm for it.[3]

Caesar brought liberty to the Greek world also. It was important
for the Greek cities ever since they were no longer able to uphold it
by themselves. It first depended on the Hellenistic rulers, then on the
Roman generals, beginning with Titus Flamininus, who solemnly restored it at Corinth in 196 B.C.[4] It was often in danger, for instance at
the time of Mithridates, when Sulla saved it.[5] But whenever those
cities expressed their gratitude to the Senate, they never referred to the
divine personification, although they often spoke of the restoration of
their ancestral freedom.[6] They had a Zeus Eleutherios, the 'equivalent'
of Iuppiter Liber, but no cult of an Eleutheria.[7] Caesar will have followed the established tradition when he went to Asia after the victory
of Pharsalus. Important traces of his activities have been found at
Aphrodisias in Caria. Its temple of Aphrodite had already under Sulla
favoured the Romans as the descendants of Aeneas.[8] Caesar, himself an
Aenead in a special sense, achieved even more: the cult of Eleutheria,
clearly the Greek version of Caesar's Libertas, was created for the first
time (pl. 15. 10–11). C. Iulius Zoilos, as his name suggests a protégé of
Caesar, was her priest, also the priest of Aphrodite.[8] This new cult

BC 2. 72. 301 (Pomp.): ὑπὲρ γὰρ ἐλευθερίας καὶ πατρίδος ἀγωνιζόμεθα. Pompey as liberator in
his youth, *B. Afr.* 22. 2.

[1] Sydenham 159; 161; pl. 26. 960; Grueber, pl. 50. 6.   [2] Dio 42. 19. 3.

[3] Laber. frg. 125 R. (Macrob. 2. 7. 4): 'porro Quirites, libertatem perdimus'; Cic. *fam.*
12. 18. 2; W. Schulze, *Kl. Schr.* 179.

[4] See below, p. 143; *Or. gr.* 222. 17; 'patrocinium libertatis': Livy 34. 58. 9; cf. Mommsen,
StR 3. 726; Heuss, *Die völkerrechtl. Grundlagen d. röm. Aussenpolitik* 94 ff.; Magie, *Roman Rule*
944 f.; 954 f.; 965 f.; Larsen, *CP* 40 (1945), 88.

[5] App. *Mithr.* 61. 250; *ILS* 31; 34; 38 (Degr. 174 f.); Degrassi, *Scritti* 434 ff. (with bibliography).   [6] See the inscriptions mentioned in the preceding note.

[7] As a personification she is found on coins of Tium, Bithynia *c.* 282 B.C. and of Cyzicus
c. 450–300, Head, *HN* 518; 526; Waser, *RE* 5. 2346 f.; Deubner, *Myth. Lex.* 3. 2133; L.
Robert, *Ant. Class.* 35 (1966), 414. 1. There was the goddess Demokrateia instead. She was
painted by Euphranor in the Stoa of Zeus Eleutherios in Athens (Paus. 1. 3. 2); her statue
stood in the Agora (*CIG* 1. 95; Wilhelm, *Österr. Jahresh.* 35 (1943), 160. 1; 13 f.; Raubitschek,
Hesp. 31 (1962), 242; L. Moretti, *Iscrizioni storiche ellenistiche* 7. 13) and her cult is attested
for the fourth century B.C. (*Syll.* 1029. 67), later also at Pergamum (*Syll.* 694. 31); cf. Mommsen, *StR* 3. 726; Nilsson 1. 733. 2; 2. 144. 2; Habicht 230. 29; Raubitschek, 238 ff.

[8] App. *BC* 1. 97. 453; above, p. 83.

[9] Th. Reinach, *REG* 19 (1906), 128: Ἡ βουλὴ καὶ ὁ δῆμος ἐτίμησεν | Γάιον Ἰούλιον Ζωίλον

implies that Caesar also restored the freedom of the city.[1] This act will have been the subject of a lost letter, Γράμματα Καίσαρος, mentioned in a document of Antony in 39 B.C.[2] Caesar restored the liberty of many other cities of the East and West,[3] and some of them, for instance Amisus in Pontus, may have instituted a similar cult.[4] A personal bond too was no doubt created between Caesar and these cities. The inhabitants of Nicopolis in Epirus, a free city founded by Augustus after the victory at Actium, used to acknowledge their debt for their freedom to his Genius;[5] and other cities worshipped him as Zeus Eleutherios.[6] Their gratitude may have found such a cultic expression already under Caesar.

The theme received a new urgency at Rome through the campaign in Africa. Before the battle at Thapsus Scipio distributed pamphlets among Caesar's soldiers exhorting them to liberate the Senate and the Roman people from Caesar's tyranny, in answer to Caesar's pamphlets which offered Scipio's soldiers clemency and financial rewards.[7] The climax came with Cato's suicide at Utica in 46 and his subsequent public and literary glorification in Rome. Those who wrote special works in his praise included Cicero, Brutus, M. Fadius Gallus, and Munatius Rufus.[8] Caesar was in Spain conducting the war against the last Pompeians. His friends made plans in the winter of 46/45 to counteract the adverse effect of Cato's posthumous popularity and to represent Caesar instead as the man of liberty. This is an inference from the

τὸν ἱερέα τῆς Ἀφροδίτης καὶ τῆς | Ἐλευθερίας διὰ βίου; cf. L. Robert, l.c. If it were the same Zoilos who is represented on a relief of the Hadrianic age or of the end of the first century A.D. (Giuliano, Annuario 37/8 (1959/60), 389 ff.), the Caesarian date of the inscription would be impossible. But it is not necessary to assume this. An inscription, AE 1960. 26, mentions another distinguished member of the family, 'Ti. Iulius Zoili f. Fab(ia) Pappus', a comes and librarian of Tiberius, which makes it probable that the rise of the family was in fact due to the patronage of Caesar; cf. Panciera, Epigr. 31 (1969), 117 ff.—Eleutheria on later coins, BMC Caria 30; pl. 5. 12; (our pl. 15. 11; cf. 10); Ἐλεύθερος Δῆμος ibid. 38; L. Robert, l.c. 418. 2.

[1] Cf. Tac. A. 3. 62. 2: 'Aphrodisienses . . . dictatoris Caesaris ob vetusta in partis merita . . . decretum adtulere'; listed among the free cities by Pliny 5. 109.

[2] Or. gr. 453 f.; cf. ILS 8780; Magie, op. cit. 1282; L. Robert, l.c. 409 ff. (with bibliography).

[3] On the political significance of this privilege, often granted also by Augustus, see Grant, From Imperium to Auctoritas 338 ff.; 401 ff.; Vittinghoff 8 ff.; 82. 5; 110. 3.

[4] Amisus (Dio 42. 48. 4; Strab. 12. 547) was called Eleuthera (Pliny 6. 7; Head, HN 497; IGR 4. 1586; cf. 3. 96; Magie, op. cit. 1450. 3; Sherwin-White on Pliny ep. 10. 92) and had an era of its Eleutheria, dating from its second liberation in 31 B.C., IGR 4. 1586 (Or. gr. 530). Other cities, like Laodicea in Syria (Macrob. 2. 3. 12), Antiochia on the Orontes or Aegeae in Cilicia, introduced Caesarian eras, Head, HN 779; 716; for further evidence see Dio 44. 53. 3; Head, HN 945; Kubitschek, RE 1. 650; Magie, op. cit. 1261. 9; below, p. 197.

[5] Epict. 4. 1. 14: Νικοπολῖται ἐπιβοᾶν εἰώθασι "νὴ τὴν Καίσαρος Τύχην ἐλεύθεροί ἐσμεν"; Schober, RE 17. 516; W. Schulze, Kl. Schr. 179. 1.

[6] See below, p. 144. 1.

[7] Dio 43. 5. 3 f.; below, p. 238.

[8] Cic. Or. 35; fam. 6. 7. 4; Brutus: Cic. Att. 12. 21. 1; 13. 46. 2; Fadius: Cic. fam. 7. 24. 2; 7. 25; Munatius: Plut. Cat. min. 37. 1; Meyer, Caesars Monarchie 434 ff.; Gelzer, RE 7A. 1024; id. Caesar 279 f.; Strasburger, Caesars Eintritt in die Gesch. 42 f.

fact that Cicero now accepted the position, writing about the new servitude as the alternative to the victory of the Pompeians, which would have meant catastrophe.[1] Hirtius (*cos.* 43) wrote in Caesar's defence,[2] and to Caesar himself the theme was important enough for him to spend time writing his *Anticato* at the time of the battle at Munda,[3] an angry work about which, however, little else is known. And the decree to build a new temple for Libertas and to call him officially 'Liberator' was made when the news of the victory at Munda was received.[4] It was clearly no chance decision.

The temple was never built; it seems that the conspirators meant to build it, because the goddess now appeared on their coins (pl. 15. 12–13),[5] and 'Libertas' was their watchword at Philippi.[6] Later Augustus claimed to have restored liberty,[7] and yet did not build a temple, but rebuilt the old one of Iuppiter Libertas.[8] The next tyrant was Seianus, and after his death in A.D. 31 statues and dedications were set up for Libertas,[9] probably with the cap in her hand. She was the 'Libertas restituta' as indicated on inscriptions,[10] and was reproduced in this posture after the death of the subsequent new tyrants on coins of Claudius, Galba, Vitellius, Vespasian, Nerva (pl. 15. 14–15).[11]

4. 'LIBERATOR'

There is no real analogy to Caesar's new title 'Liberator'. The two Scipiones were honoured for their victories with the *cognomen* 'Africanus'; a Caecilius Metellus became 'Numidicus', another 'Macedonicus', a third 'Creticus', a fourth 'Delmaticus'; P. Servilius Vatia was called 'Isauricus'. Another type of *cognomen* was represented by Sulla's 'Felix', Pompey's 'Magnus', Metellus' (*cos.* 80) 'Pius'.[12] Caesar was called 'Invictus' and 'Imperator', now also 'Liberator'.

---

[1] Cic. *fam.* 4. 14. 1; 6. 21. 1; Macrob. 2. 3. 12; Gelzer, *Caesar* 279.

[2] Cic. *Att.* 12. 40. 1.

[3] Suet. *Caes.* 56. 5, etc.; cf. Augustus' *Rescripta Bruto de Catone* (Suet. *Aug.* 85. 1).

[4] Demetrius Poliorcetes was similarly honoured at Athens for his victory in 307 B.C. His equestrian statue was set up in the Agora at the side of the statue of Demokrateia, an altar was built, and sacrifices instituted for him as Soter, Wilhelm, *Österr. Jahresh.* 35 (1943), 157 ff.

[5] Sydenham 202; 204; pl. 29. 1287; 1303; Mattingly, *Ant. Class.* 17 (1948), 448 f.

[6] Dio 47. 43. 1; cf. 47. 39. 1: περί τε τῆς ἐλευθερίας καὶ τῆς δημοκρατίας τότε ὡς οὐπώποτε ἐπολέμησαν; 47. 42. 3: οἱ μὲν περὶ τὸν Βροῦτον τήν τε ἐλευθερίαν καὶ τὴν δημοκρατίαν τό τε ἀτυράννευτον καὶ τὸ ἀδέσποτον τοῖς σφετέροις προεβάλλοντο.   [7] *Mon. Anc.* 1. 1.

[8] *Mon. Anc.* 19. 2.   [9] Dio 58. 12. 4; *ILS* 157; Degrassi, *Scritti* 3. 277 ff.

[10] *ILS* 238 (Galba); 274 (Nerva); Wissowa, *Myth. Lex.* 2. 2033.

[11] Mattingly 1. 185; 312; 319 f.; 333; 339; 344; 370 f.; 386; 389; 2. 71; 118; 127; 132, etc.; cf. Wickert, *RE* 22. 2080 ff.—Eleutheria on coins of Galba, *BMC Alexandria*, pl. 8. 192.

[12] Mommsen, *Röm. Forsch.* 1. 52 ff.

'Liberator', though not a new word,[1] was a new and surprising title: no god and no man had received it before. 'Libertatis vindex', given later to Augustus, would have been a more obvious choice, because the struggle for freedom was often expressed, also by Caesar, with the words 'in libertatem vindicare'.[2] Iuppiter was called 'Liber' and 'Libertas',[3] and Zeus was 'Eleutherios'.[4] Kings and statesmen often became in Greece 'Saviours' and 'Benefactors', none of them an Ἐλευθερωτής.[5] Antigonus and his son Demetrius Poliorcetes were 'Soteres' in Athens for their act of liberation,[6] and when Titus Flamininus proclaimed the freedom of Greece at Corinth in 196 B.C., he too was honoured as a Soter.[7] The Roman generals who freed fellow citizens from captivity were not called liberators either; the evidence to the contrary is clearly anachronistic.[8]

But Caesar had his successors: so strongly was the title, hitherto an almost non-existent word, attached to his person. After the murder efforts were made to transfer it to Brutus and Cassius. Cicero, who never used the word before, applied it now ten times to them, for the first time as early as April 44;[9] and liberty became an important theme of his *Philippic Orations*. Their statues were set up at Athens beside those of the tyrannicides,[10] which was, as will be seen later, an exceptional distinction. A long pause followed after their death. Augustus recorded the restoration of liberty by his victories over Caesar's murderers and over Antony in the same terms as Caesar used in justification of his march on Rome in 49.[11] But he was called 'libertatis populi Romani vindex' after his victory at Actium,[12] not a liberator. In Egypt, however,

---

[1] Plaut. *Pers.* 419: 'scortorum liberator' is the only piece of pre-Caesarian evidence: it must have been a rare word.

[2] Cic. *Flacc.* 25; *rep.* 1. 48; *fam.* 2. 5. 2; Caes. *BC* 1. 22. 5 (above, p. 139. 7); *Mon. Anc.* 1. 1; for further evidence see the valuable collection of Weber, *Princeps* 137* ff., n. 557.

[3] See above, p. 135. 12 f.   [4] Fehrle, *Myth. Lex.* 6. 619 ff.

[5] The word did exist: it is used once of Heracles (Max. Tyr. 15. 6d) and Diogenes (Lucian, *Vit. Auct.* 8); see also above, p. 139. 10.

[6] Diod. 20. 46. 2. Annual festivals, Soteria, were later celebrated in commemoration of a liberation in many places, e.g. at Priene from the tyranny of Hieron in 297 B.C., Paus. 7. 2. 10; Pfister, *RE* 3A. 1223; Nilsson 2. 88.

[7] Plut. *Flamin.* 10. 7; 16. 7; *Syll.* 592 (*ILS* 8766, Gytheum); cf. Alcaeus of Messene, *Anth. Pal.* 16. 5. 4; Plut. *Flamin.* 12. 11.

[8] Livy 34. 50. 9 (Flamininus); Zonar. 9. 14. 3; Dio 17, frg. 57. 86: 1, p. 272 B. (Scipio).

[9] Cic. *Att.* 14. 12. 2: 'quid censes cum Romam puer (Octavian) venerit, ubi nostri liberatores tuto esse non possunt?'; *ad Brut.* 24 (1. 16). 2; *Phil.* 1. 6; 1. 36; 2. 89; 2. 114; 10. 8; 14. 12; Dio 44. 1. 2; 19. 2; 21. 1.

[10] Dio 47. 20. 4: εἰκόνας σφίσι χαλκᾶς παρά τε τὴν τοῦ Ἁρμοδίου καὶ παρὰ τὴν τοῦ Ἀριστογείτονος, ὡς καὶ ζηλωταῖς αὐτῶν γενομένοις, ἐψηφίσαντο; below, pp. 145 f.

[11] *Mon. Anc.* 1. 1: '... rem publicam a dominatione factionis oppressam in libertatem vindicavi'; Caes. *BC* 1. 22. 5; Syme, *Roman Revolution* 155; 516.

[12] Mattingly 1. 112; pl. 17. 4.

he was identified with Zeus Eleutherios,[1] the Greek equivalent of Iuppiter Libertas.

The term lost its force for some time to come: a few passages without any particular significance are found in Livy.[2] It was Nero who returned to it.[3] He instituted the cult of Iuppiter Liberator—an epithet which Iuppiter never had before—with whom he apparently wished to be identified.[4] This wish was known at least to Seneca and Thrasea Paetus, who had formerly been his counsellors. When they were forced to commit suicide and offered their blood to Iuppiter Liberator, they implied by this choice that it was Nero who was the recipient god.[5] Nero did not mean to be the hero of freedom in Rome only. The institution of the new cult was in anticipation of his declaration of freedom in Greece,[6] an intentional repetition of Titus Flamininus' feat;[7] in gratitude the Greeks called him Zeus Eleutherios (pl. 15. 16–17).[8] After his death the Romans wore the liberty-cap[9] and referred again to Iuppiter Liberator,[10] who was of course no longer Nero. Even now 'liberator' remained a rare word. If we except Tacitus' singular and solemn reference to Arminius as the liberator of Germany,[11] we do not meet it again in a suitable context[12] until the age of Diocletian and Constantine, when it became one

[1] The earliest evidence is perhaps an undated epigram (*Gr. Lit. Pap.* 113, p. 470 Page); then a document of 12 B.C. (Preisigke, *Sammelbuch* 3. 7257); another epigram, of 7 B.C. (*IGR* 1. 1295 = Kaibel 978); cf. *IGR* 1. 1117; 1163; 1322; *P. Oslo.* 26; Wilcken, *Chrest.* no. 111. It is found outside Egypt also at Mytilene (*IGR* 4. 62), Kys in Caria (*BCH* 11 (1887), 306, no. 1), Gytheum (E.–J. 102. 5); cf. P. Riewald *,De imperatorum Romanorum cum certis dis et comparatione et aequatione* (1912), 286 ff.; Fehrle, *Myth. Lex.* 6. 622; Barbieri, *Diz. Epigr.* 4. 889.

[2] Two refer to L. Brutus (1. 56. 8; 60. 2), one to Valerius Publicola (2. 7. 8), two to Flamininus and the Romans (34. 50. 3; 9), one to the Romans alone (35. 17. 8); cf. also 6. 14. 5.

[3] The two inscriptions, *CIL* 5. 5509; 6963, probably belong to a much later period.

[4] Calp. Sic. *Ecl.* 4. 142: 'tu quoque mutata seu Iuppiter ipse figura, / Caesar, ades'; Nock, *CR* 40 (1926), 18.

[5] Tac. *A.* 15. 64. 4; 16. 35. 2; Dio 62. 21. 4; Schol. Iuven. 5. 36; Mattingly, *JRS* 10 (1920), 38.

[6] See the bronze coin issued in Greece with Nero's head on the obv., Iuppiter and the legend 'Iuppiter Liberator c(olonia) P(atrensis)' on the rev., Cohen 1. 308, no. 418; Eckhel 2. 256 (obv.: Nero in temple, legend Νέρωνι Πατρέων; rev.: Libertas with *pileus*). The *aureus*, Mattingly 1. 214; pl. 40. 15, is a forgery, see Mattingly, ibid., p. clxxxiv. 1; cf. Barbieri, *Diz. Epigr.* 4. 886; E. Meyer, *RE* 18. 2. 2213.

[7] *Syll.* 814; 796A (Momigliano, *JRS* 34 (1944), 115 f.).

[8] *ILS* 8794 = *Syll.* 814 (Boeotia); coin of Sicyon with Nero as Zeus Eleutherios, Cook, *Zeus* 2. 97. 3 (fig. 55); *CAH Plates* 4. 205h; Barbieri, l.c. 889 f.; Nock, l.c. (coin of Dios Hieron with Zeus and Nero, *BMC Lydia* 75).

[9] Suet. *Nero* 57. 1; Dio 63. 29. 1; Mattingly 1. 292.

[10] Coin of the Civil Wars issued in Gaul, A.D. 68, with Iuppiter seated and the legend 'Iuppiter Liberator', Mattingly 1. 295; pl. 50. 9.

[11] Tac. *A.* 2. 88. 3 (on 15. 64. 4 and 16. 35. 2 see above, n. 5).

[12] The inscription of M. Sulpicius Rufus, set up in A.D. 144 in Mauretania, *AE* 1931, 36: '. . . lib(eratori?) et patr(ono) . . .' (Carcopino, *Le Maroc antique* 205; Gagé, *Rev. hist.* 218 (1957), 14; M. Burzachechi, *Arch. Class.* 13 (1961), 180 f.), is not a certain instance.

of the regular titles of the emperors.[1] This is the history of the term which was created by Caesar himself, rather than by his friends, in 45, if not already at the beginning of the Civil War in 49 B.C.

5. CAESAR AND BRUTUS

The title was not all that Caesar got. Dio records in a different context but for the same year, 45 B.C., that his statue was set up on the Capitol beside the kings of Rome.[2] No satisfactory explanation has been found for this honour. That it should have indicated that Caesar was, or was going to be, another king, as was already assumed in antiquity,[3] is clearly absurd. But his was not the first statue that was added to those of the kings: Brutus, who had liberated Rome from the tyranny of Tarquinius Superbus, already stood there.[4] One may therefore suggest that Caesar was placed there as the new liberator from tyranny; and in support of this suggestion it is necessary first to investigate the case of Brutus.

Brutus was not always the great hero of the Roman Republic. Even if he was a person of history,[5] which implies that once there was a patrician Gens Iunia, founded by 'Iunius', a companion of Aeneas,[6] it is certain that his legend cannot have been popular before the end of the fourth century B.C. That was the time when the plebeian Iunii achieved power and influence and claimed the founder of the Republic for themselves as their ancestor.[7] It was no doubt one of them who set up his statue on the Capitol, but not too early: he cannot have done it before the statues of the kings stood there, that is, in the third, rather than the fourth, century B.C.[8] Brutus may have joined the kings even later, because his case also depends on Greek influence, on the idea

---

[1] *AE* 1939, 58: 'Liberatori orbis Romani . . . Gaio Aurel. Valerio Diocletiano'; *ILS* 694 (Const.) : '. . . liberatori urbis'; Barbieri, l.c. 887 f.

[2] Dio 43. 45. 3: καὶ ἄλλην (εἰκόνα) ἐς τὸ Καπιτώλιον παρὰ τοὺς βασιλεύσαντάς ποτε ἐν τῇ ῾Ρώμῃ ἀνέθεσαν. (4) . . . ὀκτὼ γὰρ ἅμα αὐτῶν (ἑπτὰ μὲν ἐκείνοις, ὀγδόης δὲ τῷ γε Βρούτῳ τῷ τοὺς Ταρκυνίους καταλύσαντι) οὐσῶν παρὰ ταύτην τότε τὴν τοῦ Καίσαρος ἔστησαν.

[3] Cic. *Deiot.* 33: 'te in invidia esse, tyrannum existimari, statua inter reges posita animos hominum vehementer offensos'; Suet. *Caes.* 76. 1: 'statuam inter reges'; 80. 3: 'subscripsere quidam . . . statuae . . . Caesaris (*FPL* p. 92 M.): "Brutus, quia reges eiecit, consul primus factus est: hic, quia consules eiecit, rex postremo factus est." '

[4] Plut. *Brut.* 1. 1: ὃν ἀνέστησαν ἐν Καπιτωλίῳ χαλκοῦν οἱ πάλαι ῾Ρωμαῖοι μέσον τῶν βασιλέων ἐσπασμένον ξίφος, ὡς βεβαιότατα καταλύσαντα Ταρκυνίους; Dio 43. 45. 4.

[5] Broughton 1. 4. 1; Ogilvie, *Livy* 216 f.; *contra*, Schur, *RE* Suppl. 5. 360; Gjerstad, *Legends and Facts of Early Roman History* (1962), 45 f.

[6] Dion. Hal. 4. 68. 1; according to the Schol. Townl. *Il.* 5. 412 he was an autochthon, son of King Daunus.

[7] Münzer, *RE* 10. 961; Schur, l.c. 356 ff.

[8] Pliny 33. 9; 33. 24; 34. 22 f.; Vessberg, *Stud. z. Kunstgesch. d. röm. Rep.* 83 ff.

of honouring a liberator with a statue in a public place, as had been done for Harmodius and Aristogiton in the Agora of Athens[1] and later for Antigonus and Demetrius[2] in the same place, although by then it was forbidden by law.[3] The Greek example is evident: the tyrannicides were represented with sword drawn (pl. 16. 1), and so was Brutus[4] although he did not kill anyone; it was also asserted, wrongly, that Brutus expelled the kings in the same year in which the tyranni- cides freed Athens from the Pisistratids.[5]

The literary evidence began, as so often, later, and poetry probably preceded historiography. The earliest evidence comes from the *Greek Annals* of A. Postumius Albinus (*cos.* 151) and suggests that the story already existed more or less in the same form as is known from Livy.[6] About the same time or not much later Accius wrote his Praetexta *Brutus* in honour of his patron, D. Iunius Brutus Callaicus (*cos.* 138).[7] This is even more important. Accius probably added some specific Greek features to the story, such as the analogy of the tyrannicides, which will have inspired Callaicus to set up the statue on the Capitol, if it was not there already. It is known that Callaicus built a great deal at Rome, and that Accius provided these buildings with suitable in- scriptions.[8] The statue must have existed about 133 B.C. when Laelius demanded a statue for Scipio Nasica because he had murdered the 'tyrant' Ti. Gracchus—provided that this is an authentic story.[9]

The later Iunii kept the memory of their 'ancestor' alive. Both M. and D. Brutus had his mask in their houses.[10] M. Brutus put him on

---

[1] Aristot. *Rhet.* 1. 9, p. 1368ª18; Paus. 1. 8. 5 (with the notes of Hitzig–Blümner for further evidence); Pliny 34. 17; Judeich, *Topogr. v. Athen* 340; A. J. Podlecki, *Hist.* 15 (1966), 129 ff. (with bibliography).

[2] Diod. 20. 46. 2 (golden statues on chariots and nearby an altar for the Soteres); Habicht 46. In addition Demetrius' soldiers erected another statue on horseback nearby, next to the statue of Demokrateia, L. Moretti, *Iscriz. storiche ellenistiche* 7. 13; Habicht 230. 29; above, p. 140. 7.

[3] *Syll.* 320. 30; *IG* 2². 646. 37; Ps.-Plut. *X or.* 852 D; another exception was made with Brutus and Cassius in 42 B.C., Dio 47. 20. 4; above, p. 143. On the cult of the tyrannicides Aristot. *Ath. Pol.* 58. 1; Demosth. 19. 280.

[4] Cf. S. Brunnsäker, *The Tyrant-Slayers of Kritias and Nesiotes* (1955); Plut. *Brut.* 1. 1 (above, p. 145. 4); Rumpf, *Festschr. v. Mercklin* (1964), 131 ff.; Coarelli, *Mél.* 81 (1969), 137 ff.

[5] Pliny 34. 17: 'Atheniensis nescio an primis omnium Harmodio et Aristogitoni tyran- nicidis publice posuerint statuas. hoc actum est eodem anno (in fact in 514 B.C.), quo et Romae reges pulsi.'   [6] Frg. 2 (*HRR* 1. 53 P.); Livy 1. 56. 7 ff.

[7] Acc. frg. 39 R. (Varr. *LL* 5. 80); cf. Münzer, *RE* 10. 1024; id. *Adelsp.* 336. 1. Brutus' pretence of stupidity (Postum. Albin. frg. 2 P. [Macrob. 3. 20. 5]; Livy 1. 56. 8; 59. 8) and all that resulted from it was inspired by the etymology of the adj. *brutus* = 'stupid'. But, as we learn from *Hamlet*, it was also a magnificent dramatic device: it must come from Accius. See also below, p. 319.

[8] Cic. *Arch.* 27 (Schol. Bob. p. 179 St.); Val. Max. 8. 14. 2; Münzer, *RE* 10. 1024.

[9] Cic. *rep.* 6. 8; above, p. 135; Coarelli, l.c. 143 ff.   [10] Cic. *Phil.* 2. 26.

his coins *c.* 59 B.C.(pl. 15. 7)[1] and asked Atticus to write a history of his family with the proper ancestral tree.[2] Even after he became Caesar's follower and trusted friend, he remained true to the tradition of his family. When Cato died at Utica he was one of those who wrote a eulogy in his memory.[3] To him turned Caesar's adversaries with their hopes. They wished the first Brutus back and inscribed the statue on the Capitol to that effect;[4] they also inscribed on M. Brutus' *tribunal* that he was not a real Brutus or that he was asleep.[5] Eventually he took the lead, was celebrated as a tyrannicide, and intended to perform Accius' *Brutus* again at the *ludi Apollinares* in 44 B.C.[6]

Needless to say, the statue of Caesar on the Capitol was a great provocation to his adversaries. The dictator was not only called 'Liberator' but stood at the side of the great hero of the Republic. A passage in Cicero is illuminating. When pleading before Caesar for King Deiotarus at the end of 45 B.C., he referred to this statue and to the gossip that it represented the new tyrant,[7] and retorted that Caesar was not a tyrant but the clement guide of his free fellow citizens.[8] That is what Brutus and the Greek tyrannicides stood for; Caesar now joined their company.

The liberty-cap too must have had a role in these honours. Caesar's statue or a provisional statue of Libertas may have held one; but there is no evidence to suggest that Roman citizens wore it in the triumphal procession of October 45, as they did at the time of Scipio, Cornelius Cethegus, and Flamininus. And yet it is not impossible that they did, considering that people wore it again when rejoicing after Nero's death. At any rate the cap must have been used by Caesar in one way or another as a political symbol. The conspirators, carrying their blood-covered swords, boasted that they had killed a tyrant and a king. One of them fixed the cap on the end of a spear; they called for the restoration of government and reminded the people of the Brutus of the heroic age and of the oath against kings.[9] And Brutus, his 'descendant', now placed

---

[1] Sydenham 150; pl. 25. 906.

[2] Nep. *Att.* 18. 3; Cic. *Att.* 13. 40. 1; Gelzer, *RE* 10. 988.

[3] Cic. *Att.* 12. 21. 1; 13. 46. 2; Gelzer, *RE* 10. 984 f.; above, p. 141.

[4] Suet. *Caes.* 80. 3: 'subscripsere quidam Luci Bruti statuae: "utinam viveres!"'

[5] Plut. *Brut.* 9. 7: "Βροῦτε, καθεύδεις", καὶ "οὐκ εἶ Βροῦτος ἀληθῶς"; cf. Cic. *Brut.* 331 (46 B.C.); Balsdon, *Hist.* 7 (1958), 91; see also below, p. 319.

[6] Cic. *Att.* 16. 5. 1.   [7] Cic. *Deiot.* 33 (above, p. 145. 3).

[8] Ibid. 34: 'quem nos liberi, in summa populi Romani libertate nati, non modo non tyrannum sed etiam clementissimum in victoria ducem vidimus, is Blesamio, qui vivit in regno, tyrannus videri potest?'

[9] App. *BC* 2. 119. 499: τὰ ξίφη μετὰ τοῦ αἵματος ἔχοντες ἐβοηδρόμουν βασιλέα καὶ τύραννον ἀνελεῖν. καὶ πῖλόν τις ἐπὶ δόρατος ἔφερε, σύμβολον ἐλευθερώσεως· ἐπί τε τὴν πάτριον πολιτείαν

the cap between two daggers on a coin;[1] on another he reproduced
Victoria with a broken sceptre and broken diadem (pl. 15. 18–19).[2]

6. THE *CORONA OBSIDIONALIS*

Caesar as liberator received a third reward. Two statues were set
up on the Rostra, one wearing an oak wreath, the *corona civica*, for
having saved the lives of the citizens, the other with a grass wreath, the
corona obsidionalis, because he had liberated Rome from siege.[3] It is this
wreath that we are concerned with here; it will be found that the oak
wreath had a different function[4] and does not represent a duplication
of the same honour. The justification of the wreath is at first sight surprising: Rome was not besieged during the Civil War. A history of the
wreath will help to explain what was meant by this reward.

The grass wreath was a greater and rarer distinction than the oak
wreath; it was in fact the greatest.[5] It was given by the soldiers
themselves to those who saved the whole army or part of it.[6] The
grass was taken from the battlefield, and its handing over was in
origin a symbol of surrender.[7] The list of its holders is short and not
entirely trustworthy. It is certainly a late invention that L. Siccius

παρεκάλουν καὶ Βρούτου τοῦ πάλαι καὶ τῶν τότε σφίσιν ὀμωμοσμένων ἐπὶ τοῖς πάλαι βασιλεῦσιν
ἀνεμίμνησκον.

[1] Dio 47. 25. 3: Βροῦτος . . . ἐς τὰ νομίσματα ἃ ἐκόπτετο εἰκόνα τε αὐτοῦ καὶ πιλίον ξιφίδιά
τε δύο ἐνετύπου, δηλῶν ἔκ τε τούτου καὶ διὰ τῶν γραμμάτων ὅτι τὴν πατρίδα μετὰ τοῦ Κασσίου
ἠλευθερωκὼς εἴη; Sydenham 203; pl. 30. 1301; H. A. Cahn, *Actes, Congr. Internat. Numism.,
Paris 1953* (1957), 213 ff.; Mattingly, *Ant. Class.* 17 (1948), 448.

[2] Sydenham 203; pl. 30. 1298.

[3] Dio 44. 4. 5 (44 B.C.): ἐπί γε τοῦ Βήματος δύο (ἀνδριάντας), τὸν μὲν ὡς τοὺς πολίτας σεσωκότος,
τὸν δὲ ὡς τὴν πόλιν ἐκ πολιορκίας ἐξῃρημένου, μετὰ τῶν στεφάνων τῶν ἐπὶ τοῖς τοιούτοις νενο-
μισμένων ἱδρύσαντο; App. *BC* 2. 106. 441 (45 B.C. [below, p. 163. 1], mentions only the
oak wreath explicitly). As to the difference in dating, Appian is right because Cicero referred to the statue in 45, *Deiot.* 34.   [4] See below, pp. 163 ff.

[5] Fest. 193 M. (208 L.): 'inter obsidionalem et civicam hoc interesse quod altera singularis
salutis signum est; altera diversorum civium servatorum'; Pliny 22. 8: 'quod si civicae
honos uno aliquo ac vel humillimo cive servato praeclarus sacerque habetur, quid tandem
existimari debet unius virtute servatus universus exercitus?'

[6] Gell. 5. 6. 8: 'obsidionalis est, quam ii qui liberati obsidione sunt dant ei duci qui
liberavit. ea corona graminea est, observarique solitum ut fieret e gramine, quod in eo loco
gnatum esset, intra quem clausi erant qui obsidebantur'; Fest. 190 M. (208 L.); Pliny 22. 7;
Steiner, *BJ* 114 (1905), 44 ff.; Alföldi, *Mus. Helv.* 9 (1952), 215 f. On a doubtful representation of the wreath on a pan see Zahn, *Arch. Anz.* 24 (1909), 559 ff.; that on the relief from the
Via Cassia (Fuhrmann, *Mitt. Arch. Inst.* 2 (1949), 28. 3; above, p. 45) is certainly a laurel
wreath; Kraft, *Jahrb. f. Numism.* 3/4 (1952/3), 16. 51.

[7] This is suggested by the analogy of 'herbam do', by which defeat was acknowledged,
Paul. 99 M. (88 L.): 'herbam do cum ait Plautus (frg. inc. 28) significat victum me fateor;
. . . qui in prato cursu aut viribus contendebant, cum superati erant, ex eo solo, in quo
certamen erat, decerptam herbam adversario tradebant'; Serv. *Aen.* 8. 128 (Varro); Pliny
22. 8; A. Otto, *Sprichwörter d. Röm.* 161; Eitrem, *Opferritus* 73. The handing over of a lump of
earth (Gell. 20. 10. 9; Nilsson, *Opuscula* 1. 330 ff.) was a related form of surrender.

Dentatus (*tr. pl.* 454), the Roman Achilles, was the first to receive it *c.* 450 B.C.[1] The next hero was P. Decius Mus (*cos.* 340) some hundred years later, and in fact his award may be authentic. He earned the wreath as a military tribune in the First Samnite War in 343 B.C., not perhaps, as is recorded, two at once, one from the whole army, the other from his own soldiers.[2] He was followed by the military tribune M. Calpurnius Flamma in 258 B.C.,[3] an unexceptionable case, because he is otherwise unknown. The next holder of the wreath, Q. Fabius Maximus, will require a detailed discussion at the end of the list because his story has some unusual features. There is no doubt that Scipio Aemilianus received the wreath in 149 B.C. during the Third Punic War[4] and Cn. Petreius in 102 B.C. in the war against the Cimbri:[5] the former is supported by good evidence, the latter is again a little-known man. Sulla received it from his soldiers in 89 B.C. at Nola after the battle against the Samnites, and the scene was painted later in his villa at Tusculum.[6] The fact cannot be disputed; but it is probable that Sulla created the occasion somewhat artificially in order to make himself appear like the great hero of the Samnite Wars, P. Decius Mus.

Caesar too, like Sulla, could have received the wreath from his soldiers; there were many dangerous situations in the Civil War, for instance in Egypt, when the army survived only owing to Caesar's initiative. The statue on the Rostra could then have commemorated such an incident. But it was set up by the Senate, not by the soldiers or Caesar himself, and because he liberated Rome from a siege, not as a memorial for a single episode in the war; his other statue on the Rostra did not stand for a single episode either. The instances we have met so far do not help here, but that of Q. Fabius Maximus does. It was in 217 B.C., during the Second Punic War, that Fabius as dictator saved the army of his *magister equitum* (or co-dictator) M. Minucius Rufus, the reluctant general saving the army of the daring one. Fabius was called 'pater' by Minucius, and his soldiers 'patroni' by those whom they saved;[7]

---

[1] Pliny 22. 9; 7. 102; Fest. 190 M. (208 L.); Gell. 2. 11. 2; Münzer, *RE* 2A. 2189.

[2] Fest. 190 M. (208 L.); Livy 7. 37. 2; Pliny 16. 11; 22. 9; *vir. ill.* 26. 2; Münzer, *RE* 4. 2279.   [3] Pliny 22. 11; Münzer, *RE* 3. 1373.

[4] Pliny 22. 13 (quoting Varro and Augustus); Vell. 1. 12. 4; *vir. ill.* 58. 4; cf. Livy, *Per.* 49.

[5] Pliny 22. 11; Münzer, *RE* 19. 1189; Mommsen, *StR* 1. 437. 2.

[6] Pliny 22. 12: 'scripsit et Sulla dictator (frg. 10 P.) ab exercitu se quoque donatum apud Nolam legatum bello Marsico, idque etiam in villa sua Tusculana . . . pinxit.'

[7] *ILS* 56: 'Q. Fabius Q. f. Maximus . . . exercitui profligato subvenit et eo nomine ab exercitu Miniciano pater appellatus est'; Livy 22. 29. 10: 'ego eum parentem appellavero . . . vos, milites, eos, quorum vos modo arma dexterae texerunt, patronos salutabitis'; 30. 2: 'cum patrem Fabium appellasset, circumfususque militum eius totum agmen patronos consalutasset, (3) parentibus, inquit, meis, dictator, quibus te modo nomine . . . aequavi,

but he was not given the wreath. He received it, according to another version of the story, which sounds like the record of an inscription, after the war from the Senate and the Roman people because he had saved Rome from the siege of the enemy.[1] Two contradictory stories stand here side by side. The earlier one must have recorded originally that Fabius received the wreath from Minucius on the battlefield as the other heroes did before and after him. The later one recorded that Fabius received it from the Senate and the Roman people when the war was over. When this version was created, the wreath had to be omitted from the earlier one. We cannot vouch for the veracity of either version, nor is it necessary to do so. The first is in accordance with the other cases; the second clearly depends on an inscription belonging to a statue, and, what is important here, it is an exact analogy to Caesar's honour in 45, even though the enemy was Hannibal, a real enemy, not Pompey, a fellow citizen.

The rescue of Minucius and his army is well attested. Polybius mentions it,[2] though not the wreath; this was no doubt added by Fabius Pictor and Ennius.[3] There is also indirect evidence in so far as this incident served as the model when the liberation of another Minucius, the consul of 458 B.C., by the dictator L. Quinctius Cincinnatus in the Volscan War was invented: he called him 'patron' and gave him, in addition to the *corona obsidionalis*, a golden wreath which was a frequent military reward.[4] The other version, the rescue of Rome from siege, is not so well attested. It does not rest on early evidence and is not supported by analogies: no other liberator, Camillus, or Scipio, Fabius' rival, or Marius, received that wreath.[5] Nor had the *corona civica*, which was, as will be seen, a close analogy in another respect, so extended a function before the age of Cicero.[6] The probability is

vitam tantum debeo, tibi cum meam salutem tum omnium horum'; Plut. *Fab.* 13. 6 ff.; Val. Max. 5. 2. 4; Sil. 7. 732 ff. (below, p. 168. 1); cf. W. Hoffmann, *Livius u. der Zweite Punische Krieg*, 27 ff. (with bibliography).

[1] Pliny 22. 10: 'data est et a senatu populoque Romano ... Fabio ... nec data, cum magistrum equitum exercitumque eius servasset, ... sed quo dictum est consensu honoratus est Hannibale Italia pulso, quae corona adhuc sola ipsius Imperii ⟨Romani⟩ ('imperii' *edd.*; 'Romani' *addidi*) manibus inposita est et quod peculiare ei est, sola a tota Italia data'; Gell. 5. 6. 10: 'hanc coronam gramineam senatus populusque Romanus Q. Fabio Maximo dedit bello Poenorum secundo, quod urbem Romam obsidione hostium liberasset.'

[2] Polyb. 3. 105. 8.

[3] Cf. Enn. *A.* 370 V.: 'unus homo nobis cunctando restituit rem.' Münzer, *RE* 6. 1828 f., is sceptical about Fabius' honours because they correspond to those granted to Augustus, but admits the possibility that they were later attached to a statue (Plut. *Fab.* 22. 8).

[4] Livy 3. 29. 3; Ogilvie ad loc. (?); *vir. ill.* 17. 2 ('corona aurea et obsidionali': 'et' should not be bracketed); Hirschfeld, *Kl. Schr.* 246; Münzer, *RE* 15. 1951.

[5] See also below, p. 165; Cic. *Cat.* 4. 21: 'sit aeterna gloria Marius, qui bis Italiam obsidione et metu servitutis liberavit'; *Rab. perd.* 29: 'cum ... obsidione rem publicam liberasset.'

[6] See below, p. 165.

that this version was created long after Fabius' death (203 B.C.) and the end of the war. What matters here is the choice between a pre- and post-Caesarian date. A pre-Caesarian date could be justified by the assumption that it was the Fabii who created this version in opposition to Scipio's claim that he was the hero of the Second Punic War, the saviour of Rome and liberator of its citizens.[1] It could have been argued that the episode of 217, not Scipio's victories, was the turning-point of the war: by saving Minucius, Fabius saved Rome. The rivalry between Fabius and Scipio is a fact,[2] but the Fabii may not have pressed their claim to this extent. Even if they did, the controversy must have ceased at the time when the two families became allied and each of them adopted a son of L. Aemilius Paullus. The arch built by Q. Fabius Maximus Allobrogicus in commemoration of his victory over the Allobroges in 121 B.C., bore statues of his ancestors, L. Aemilius Paullus and the younger Scipio,[3] though not that of our Fabius. But there were certainly many statues of his, kept by the family as well as in public places. In addition it is probable that all the real and fictitious heroes listed above had their statues with their grass wreath at Rome; at least the younger Scipio had one,[4] also Sulla, if this may be inferred from the painting at Tusculum, and one would naturally expect one of Fabius. But even if there was one, it is not what we are looking for. We need a group of two statues, the personification of the Imperium Romanum placing the wreath over the head of Fabius. This unique personification, apparently a male figure, cannot have been an early product, not of the time of our Fabius, not even of that of Allobrogicus.[5] After him a decline of the Fabii followed,[6] until a Q. Fabius Maximus, his grandson, became *aedilis curulis* in 57 and, after a praetorship *c.* 48, consul in 45 B.C. as Caesar's successor. It is known that as aedile he restored the Fornix Fabianus and did much for the glory of his family.[7] He asked Atticus to write about the Fabii, Aemilii, and Cornelii.[8]

[1] Polyb. 23. 14. 3; Livy 38. 51. 5; 38. 55. 2, etc.; above, p. 92. 7.

[2] Livy 28. 40 ff.; etc.; W. Hoffmann, op. cit. 88 ff. [3] *ILS* 43 (Degr. 392).

[4] Pliny 22. 13: 'donatum obsidionali in Africa . . . quod et statuae eius in foro suo Divus Augustus inscripsit.'

[5] The *Feriale Cumanum* of *c.* A.D. 4 (*ILS* 108) lists for 30 January a 'supplicatio Imperio Caesaris Augusti'; a coin of Corinth of the age of Nero has the legend 'Romae et Imperio' (*BMC Corinth* 71, nos. 572 f.; pl. 18. 7; Head, *HN* 405); an inscription of A.D. 246 is dedicated to the 'Genius imperii dd. nn.', that is, of Philippus Arabs and his son (*CIL* 8. 814 = *ILS* 508); cf. *JRS* 50 (1960), 49. [6] Cic. *Tusc.* 1. 81; Val. Max. 3. 5. 2; Münzer, *RE* 6. 1742.

[7] *ILS* 43; 43a; Cic. *Vatin.* 28; Münzer, *RE* 6. 1791.

[8] Nep. *Att.* 18. 4; Münzer, *Herm.* 40 (1905), 95. Others were similarly active about the same time. Q. Caecilius Metellus Scipio (*cos.* 52) set up equestrian statues of his ancestors on the Capitol, perhaps in 57 (Cic. *Att.* 6. 1. 17), and the Basilica Aemilia with ancestral portraits was also restored (Münzer, *Adelsp.* 317 f.; Coarelli, *Mél.* 81 (1969), 145 f.).

He must have set up the group[1] in question and provided it with an inscription recording Fabius' achievements and his reward, the grass wreath in its new function. The question thus arises: to whom does the priority belong, to Fabius or to Caesar? If the group dates from Fabius' aedileship, it was he who gave a new meaning to the wreath; if it belongs to 45, Caesar's statue was the earlier one, and Fabius was inspired by him to make the same claim for his ancestor. In this case he must have acted at once, because he died on the last day of that year. The new version of the story of Fabius was accepted, perhaps even promoted, by Varro, the probable source of Pliny and Gellius, but not by the historians: Livy still kept the earlier version.

The new function of the grass wreath was created at any rate in the age of Caesar, probably with the help of a corresponding extension in the use of the *corona civica*, which, however, will have taken place somewhat earlier. It was then granted by the Senate to Augustus in 30 B.C. when the death of Antony was reported, again for liberating the State from grave danger as in 45 B.C.;[2] there was no doubt a statue too. It was not given again to anyone, whereas the *corona civica* became a permanent reward for the emperors 'ob cives servatos'. The explanation may be that the State had been liberated for ever by the founder of the dynasty and was constantly secured by his successors.

7. *MENSIS IULIUS*

It was decreed in 44 B.C. that the month Quintilis should be called Iulius because Caesar was born in that month, and that one of the tribes selected by lot should become the *tribus Iulia*.[3] Our next task is to show that these two honours belonged together and that they were conceived, even if not executed, in 45[4] because they too were created in honour of Caesar the liberator.

---

[1] One person crowning another was, as we learn from coins, a frequent statuary composition; see, e.g., Sydenham, pls. 19. 605; 24. 831; 27. 1038; 30. 1353; Mattingly 1, pl. 59. 3; 2, pl. 20. 3, etc.

[2] Pliny 22. 13: 'ipsum Augustum M. Cicerone filio consule Idibus Septembribus senatus obsidionali donavit; adeo civica non satis videbatur. nec praeterea quemquam invenimus donatum'; Dio 51. 19. 5: προσεψηφίσαντο τῷ Καίσαρι καὶ στεφάνους καὶ ἱερομηνίας πολλάς; Plut. *Cic.* 49. 6; Hanslik, *RE* 7A. 1285 f.; cf. *Fast. Arv.* 1 Aug. (Degrassi 489): 'Feriae ex s.c. quod eo die Imp. Caesar rem publicam tristissimo periculo liberavit.'

[3] Dio 44. 5. 2 (44 B.C.): τόν τε μῆνα ἐν ᾧ ἐγεγέννητο Ἰούλιον κὰκ τῶν φυλῶν μίαν τὴν κλήρῳ λαχοῦσαν Ἰουλίαν ἐπεκάλεσαν; Macrob. 1. 12. 34: 'Quintilis . . . in honorem Iulii Caesaris dictatoris, legem ferente M. Antonio, M. filio consule, Iulius appellatus est, quod hoc mense a.d. quartum Idus Quintilis procreatus sit'; Censor. 22. 16; Plut. *Num.* 19. 6; Degrassi 321.

[4] App. *BC* 2. 106. 443 (45 B.C.): ἔς τε τιμὴν τῆς γενέσεως αὐτοῦ τὸν Κυιντίλιον μῆνα Ἰούλιον ἀντὶ Κυιντιλίου μετωνόμασαν εἶναι.

(a) The Honorific Months

It is probable that originally all the Roman months were named by numerals and that at a secondary stage some of them were renamed after a god.[1] This change then led to a link between the names of these months and certain families.[2] The month Martius was named after Mars but so were the Marsi, Marcii, and others; Maius after Maia and, though there was, apart from the *praenomen* 'Maius', no family of such name, there were the Maesii,[3] bearing the same name which the Oscan month Maesius,[4] the equivalent of the Roman Maius, bore, depending on an apparently forgotten god Maesius. And Iuno was the goddess of both the month Iunius and the family of the Iunii.[5] We could add the *mensis Iulius* here by asserting that it bore the name of the god Iulus and of the family of the Iulii. But we would have to admit that Iulus was an ancestral god of the Iulii[6] and not a public god of the Roman State; further, that even if this obstacle was ignored, the fact that a month was renamed in honour of a man, not of a god, requires an explanation. Part of this explanation could be found in the precedent of Brutus. It is recorded that the month Iunius was named after him when he liberated Rome from the tyranny of Tarquinius.[7] This evidence is of course open to doubt. It could have been invented when Caesar wanted to create his *mensis Iulius*, and historians often invented precedents for contemporary innovations. But nothing else could be said in favour of this late date, and the probability is against it. The second alternative is that the story about Brutus' *mensis Iunius* was created before Caesar and that Caesar followed his precedent, and nothing else. The story, however, is not a true one: both the *mensis Iunius* and the Gens Iunia were named after Iuno. It must then have been inspired by the Greeks, who used to name months in honour of men. We must therefore turn to the Greeks and consider the possibility that Caesar too was inspired by the Greek practice, even if he formally followed the alleged precedent of Brutus.

The Greeks had a great variety of calendars with months named after gods and festivals,[8] and in general they did not change these names.

---

[1] Mommsen, *Röm. Chronol.* 217 ff.; Sontheimer, *RE* 16. 66; Whatmough, *HSCP* 42 (1931), 157 ff.; Bömer, *Ovidius, Die Fasten* I, pp. 40 ff.

[2] Schulze, *Lat. Eigennamen* 469 f.   [3] Schulze, op. cit. 469. 7; *RE* 14. 281 f.

[4] Paul. 136 M. (121 L.): 'Maesius lingua Osca mensis Maius.'

[5] See above, p. 145.   [6] See above, pp. 9 f.

[7] Macrob. *Sat.* I. 12. 31: 'non nulli putaverunt Iunium mensem a Iunio Bruto, qui primus Romae consul factus est, nominatum, quod hoc mense, id est Kalendis Iuniis, pulso Tarquinio sacrum Carnae deae in Caelio monte voti reus fecerit.'

[8] Cf. Bischoff, *RE* 10. 1590 ff.

The exceptions began with Alexander, who changed the month Daisios into a Second Artemisios before the battle at the Granicus in 334 B.C. because Daisios was not a propitious month for fighting.[1] This was a religious, not a political change and is therefore not relevant here by itself. But it may have been due to this initiative of Alexander's that others felt free to introduce changes in honour of statesmen.[2] The first to be so honoured was Demetrius Poliorcetes after he liberated Athens from the tyranny of Demetrius of Phaleron in 307 B.C.: the month Munichion became Demetrion, and the festival of the Dionysia Demetria;[3] it was not a passing inspiration of the moment because such a month was also adopted in Euboea.[4] Later there were months called Seleuceus after Seleucus I Nicator, Antiocheon after Antiochus II, Eumenius after Eumenes I, and so on.[5] The Greeks also extended this honour to Roman generals: it is probable that at Mytilene a month was called after Pompey.[6] This was followed by a Iulios or Kaisareios in some places;[7] the evidence, it is true, is not earlier than the age of Augustus,[8] but there seems to be no reason to doubt their existence at an earlier date. At Rome Augustus followed Caesar's precedent: in 27 rather than in 8 B.C. the month Sextilis was renamed Augustus. He chose this month because, so it was asserted, his great achievements belonged to it; others proposed September, the month of his birth.[9] After his death in August A.D. 14 it was proposed again that September should become his honorific month because his death rendered August ominous;[10] but it was not done. More was done in the Greek world. Two calendars were created on Cyprus c. 15 and 9 B.C. with new names of the months, all pointing to the divine and Trojan descent of Augustus: Aphrodisios, Anchisaios, Romaios, Aineiadaios, Kapetolios, Sebastos, etc.; and Apogonikos, Aineios, Iulios, Kaisareios, Sebastos, etc.[11] This development was stopped for a while by Tiberius: he resisted the proposal that September should be called Tiberius and October, after his mother, Livius.[12] But Caligula called September Germanicus

---

[1] Plut. *Alex.* 16. 2.

[2] See for the following K. Scott, *YCS* 2 (1931), 201 ff.; Habicht 148. 43; 155.

[3] Philochor., *FGrHist.* 328 F 166 (Schol. Pind. *Nem.* 3. 4); Plut. *Dem.* 12. 2; Nock, *HSCP* 41 (1930), 60.   [4] Scott, l.c. 201 f.; Habicht 76 f.

[5] Scott 202 ff.; Habicht 148. 43; 155.   [6] *IG* 12. 2. 59. 18; Scott 206; Nilsson 2. 179. 13.

[7] Iulios (Bischoff, *RE* 10. 103), Iulaios (ibid. 7), Iulieos (98), Kaisar (1522 f.), Kaisarios (1523 f.).

[8] e.g. the month Kaisar began at Priene with the 23 September, the birthday of Augustus, *Or. gr.* 458. 54 (with Dittenberger's note).

[9] Suet. *Aug.* 31. 2; Dio 55. 6. 6 (8 B.C.); below, p. 157.   [10] Suet. *Aug.* 100. 2.

[11] Boll, *CCAG* 2. 139 ff.; Scott, l.c. 207 ff.; cf. *Ath. Mitt.* 77 (1962), 311.

[12] Suet. *Tib.* 26. 2; Dio 57. 18. 2.

after his father,[1] and Nero, Domitian, and others made even more radical changes.[2] The Greek influence was by then strong. A calendar of Caligula, in Egypt, for instance, contained the following months: Θεογέναιος, Σωτήρ, Γαῖος, Ἰουλιεύς, Γερμανίκειος, Δρουσιεύς, Νερώνειος, Καισάρειος.[3] There will have been such short-lived calendars in other provinces also. All culminated in Commodus' calendar, in which all the months were renamed after his own epithets as the Roman Hercules.[4] It did not differ in principle from the other Greek calendars. What was new was that he dared to introduce it at Rome; but it did not last.

This survey shows that the honorific month became in East and West a superhuman, often even an extravagant honour, but also that its origin was forgotten. To this we must return. Demetrius was so honoured because he and his father Antigonus liberated Athens from tyranny. It was one of the many honours with which he was rewarded.[5] His example inspired the alleged reward for Brutus, the liberator, and the example of Brutus, so we must conclude, the real reward for Caesar, the next liberator. Demetrius' statue stood at the side of the tyrannicides at Athens, Brutus' statue in the posture of a tyrannicide at the side of the kings on the Capitol, and now next to him the statue of Caesar. In the Calendar his month was followed by Caesar's month.

(b) Mensis Iulius

The new month at Athens, Demetrion, was devoted to the festivals of Demetrius, and the months of Seleucus and others were no doubt created with similar intentions. This was in accordance with old tradition. Many Greek months were named after their principal festival or after a god closely connected with it. This applies at Rome at least to March, May, and June, with their festivals of Mars, Maia, and Iuno respectively.[6] This rule does not apply to the month of Brutus: all he did was to dedicate a shrine to Carna on the Caelius on the first day of the month, that is, to an obscure goddess without any importance[7] and certainly without any relation to the founder.

---

[1] Suet. *Cal.* 15. 2.

[2] Suet. *Nero* 55; Tac. *A.* 15. 74. 1; 16. 12. 3; Suet. *Dom.* 13. 3; Dio 67. 4. 4, etc.; Scott, l.c. 230 ff.; Latte 320. 1.

[3] Scott, l.c. 245 f.   [4] SHA *Comm.* 11. 8; Dio 73. 15. 3; Herodian. 1. 14. 9.

[5] Diod. 20. 46. 1 f.; Plut. *Dem.* 10. 3 ff.; cf. *FGrHist.* 328 F 66 and 166, with Jacoby's comment (3 B Suppl. 1. 340 ff.; 542 ff.); Ferguson, *Hesp.* 17 (1948), 131. 43; Nilsson 2. 151; Habicht 44 ff.; on the honours of the later kings as saviours see Habicht 156. 76.

[6] The festival was on the first day of the month in question. There were in March in addition many other festivals of Mars, Wissowa 144.

[7] Macrob. 1. 12. 31 (above, p. 153. 7); Wissowa 236; Bömer on Ov. *F.* 6. 101; Latte 71.

The rule applies, however, to Caesar. He was born in July, and his birthday, as we shall see later,[1] was to become, against tradition, a public festival. This was to lend a personal aspect to the month. But however splendid the celebration was to be, it lasted only a single day and could not therefore compare with the *ludi Apollinares* of the same month, which lasted eight days.[2] This preponderance of Apollo in July was reduced by the festival of the *ludi Victoriae Caesaris*. These *ludi* were created in 46 and celebrated after the dedication of the temple of Venus Genetrix on 26 September. In 45 they were transferred to July and were held then and later always from 20 to 30 July.[3] This transfer has always been a puzzle; it was explained as due to a desire to hold the games on their real anniversary, which would not have been the case on their old date because sixty-seven days were added to the year 46 on the introduction of the Julian Calendar.[4] But it was rightly objected that no other festival changed its date in consequence of the reform of the calendar.[5] The new explanation would be that Caesar changed the date in order to have that long and splendid festival which was connected with his person in the month which was to bear his name. If so, the solution of another puzzle is also found. These games were called as often 'ludi Veneris Genetricis' as they were 'ludi Victoriae Caesaris'.[6] This twofold nomenclature was explained by the close relationship between Venus and Victoria, which, as we have seen,[7] did not exist to the extent that is usually assumed. It is therefore more probable that Caesar made use of that relationship in order to connect the festival with his own name, just as Demetrius changed the Dionysia into Demetria. The month now belonged more to Caesar than to Apollo: the *ludi Victoriae Caesaris* lasted eleven days, the *ludi Apollinares* only eight. The legal date of the new name of the month was 44, as it was proposed by the consul Antony. But it must have been planned in 45 when the *ludi Victoriae Caesaris* were first held in July; perhaps even in 46 when the Julian Calendar was created.[8]

The change met with resistance. It was felt that the month was now named after another divinity,[9] present or future, and it was ignored after the Ides of March but was brought back by Antony. He announced

---

[1] See below, pp. 206 ff.
[2] From 6 to 13 July, Degrassi 477 f.
[3] See above, p. 91.
[4] Mommsen, *CIL* 1², p. 322.
[5] Gagé, *Res gestae* 175 (who was the first to suggest that the change was made because of the *mensis Iulius*).
[6] See above, pp. 88. 2; 91. 1; below, p. 368. 9 f.
[7] See above, p. 110.
[8] 'Annus Iulianus': Censor. 20. 11; 21. 7; 23. 16.
[9] Suet. *Caes.* 76. 1: 'sed et ampliora etiam humano fastigio decerni sibi passus est ... appellationem mensis e suo nomine'; Flor. 2. 13. 91: 'mensis in caelo'.

that the *ludi Apollinares* of 44 were to be given 'Nonis Iuliis'.[1] The conspirators and Cicero were shocked. They wished to retain Quintilis; but the other side prevailed and the new name became legal soon after the appearance of the comet in July 44.[2] A further sign of this resistance is that the two names of the games were in use all the time. A third is probably the unusual Sibylline oracle of 42 which ordered that the celebration of Caesar's birthday should be transferred from 13 to 12 July in order to avoid a clash with the principal day of the *ludi Apollinares*:[3] this may have been an attempt to compensate Apollo for the damage he suffered in 45 B.C.

The new name of the month was not a meaningless formality: it retained Caesar's spell for a long time to come. In 36 Octavian set out from Puteoli for the expedition against Sex. Pompeius on 1 July because this was the month of Caesar, who had always been victorious; it was therefore a propitious beginning.[4] This kind of reasoning influenced Augustus' choice later. It was said that he chose Sextilis as his month because it contained the anniversary of his first consulate, which began on 19 August 43 B.C., and because it was the month of his great victories.[5] The latter is true of Caesar but not of him: Ilerda and Zela, 2 August 49 and 47, and Pharsalus, 9 August 48, which were by then all celebrated annually;[6] only 1 August was the day of his own conquest of Alexandria. He was, then, apparently more influenced in his choice by Caesar's than his own victories, and may already have planned the change when he held his triumph on 13–15 August 29, dedicated the temple of Divus Iulius on 18 August 29, and the altar of Victoria in the Curia Iulia on 28 August 29.[7] Later, in 2 B.C., he made 1 August the festival of Mars Ultor and of the *ludi Martiales*:[8] this was, besides the Apollo Palatinus, the most important new cult instituted by Augustus.

Demetrius as liberator had his statue, his month, and his festival, and so had Caesar; but Brutus only the statue and the month. The

---

[1] Cic. *Att.* 16. 1. 1 (8 July 44): 'itane? "Nonis Iuliis"? di hercule istis! sed stomachari totum diem licet. quicquamne turpius quam Bruto "Iuliis"?' 16. 4. 1 (10 July 44): 'quam ille (Brutus) doluit de "Nonis Iuliis"! mirifice est conturbatus. itaque sese scripturum aiebat ut venationem eam quae postridie ludos Apollinaris futura est proscriberent in "II Idus Quintilis"'; below, p. 369.

[2] Dio 45. 7. 2: καὶ ἄλλα τινὰ τῶν ἐς τὴν τοῦ Καίσαρος τιμὴν προδεδογμένων ἐγένετο· τόν τε γὰρ μῆνα τὸν Ἰούλιον ὁμοίως ἐκάλεσαν.

[3] Dio 47. 18. 6: συνέβαινε γὰρ ἐν τῇ αὐτῇ ἡμέρᾳ καὶ τὰ Ἀπολλώνια γίγνεσθαι, ἐψηφίσαντο τῇ προτεραίᾳ τὰ γενέσια ἀγάλλεσθαι, ὡς καὶ λογίου τινὸς Σιβυλλείου ἀπαγορεύοντος μηδενὶ θεῶν τότε πλὴν τῷ Ἀπόλλωνι ἑορτάζεσθαι.

[4] App. *BC* 5. 97. 404.   [5] Suet. *Aug.* 31. 2; Dio 55. 6. 6 f.

[6] Wissowa 445.   [7] Dio 51. 21. 5; 22. 1–3; Degrassi 496 f.; 504.

[8] Dio 60. 5. 3; Degrassi 490.

probability is therefore in favour of Demetrius as the real precedent. This conclusion is strengthened by a further honour, the creation of the *tribus Iulia*, which leads again to Demetrius but not to Brutus. Needless to say, it was the example of Brutus alone that mattered for political warfare. Demetrius was unknown to the public at large and of little importance to the educated; but to the planners it was his example that provided the lasting substance for the new honours.

8. *TRIBUS IULIA*

One of the tribes, selected by lot, was to be called *tribus Iulia*. Dio mentions this together with the *mensis Iulius*,[1] and in fact the two honours have some common features. He mentions it without comment, and there is no other evidence, except that the same honour was decreed for Octavian in 29 B.C.;[2] but here again there is no comment. Moreover this second decree raises the question: how could a *tribus Iulia* have been decreed for Octavian, if there was already another bearing that name? A *tribus Augusta* was not possible in 29 but could have been later. This difficulty does not inspire confidence in Dio's isolated evidence, and that is perhaps why it has never been the subject of a scholarly discussion. And yet it cannot be dismissed, because it is supported by Caesar's and Augustus' interest in the problems of citizenship in general and by the institution of such tribes in their colonies in particular; also by some relevant later evidence and interesting Greek analogies.

The citizens of the regal period were said to have been organized in three tribes, the Ramnes, Titienses, and Luceres, named after Romulus, T. Tatius, and Lucumo.[3] In the course of time this number was increased. They numbered 35 in Caesar's time and long before, if we ignore the short-lived ten new tribes created after the Social War; and this number remained constant through the imperial period.[4] Their names were not changed either: they were either territorial or gentilician names like Esquilina or Publilia. It is not probable that Caesar just wanted to include his name in the list of the 'family'-tribes—the addition of the *luperci Iulii* to the *luperci Fabiani* and *Quinctiales* rests on different considerations[5]—

---

[1] Dio 44. 5. 2 (above, p. 152. 3).
[2] Dio 51. 20. 2: καὶ φυλὴν ᾿Ιουλίαν ἐπ᾿ αὐτοῦ ἐπονομάζεσθαι . . . προσκατεστήσαντο.
[3] Varr. *LL* 5. 55; 89; 91; Livy 1. 13. 8, etc.; Mommsen, *StR* 3. 97.
[4] Mommsen, *StR* 3. 173; L. R. Taylor, *Party Politics in the Age of Caesar* 50 ff.
[5] See below, pp. 332 f.

but he may have referred to Romulus, whose alleged precedent he often followed. In fact, the inspiration came again from the Greeks.

The corresponding Greek organizations were the *phylae*, first three Dorian, four Ionian *phylae*, later a great variety in numbers and in names.[1] The first relevant piece of evidence would concern Alexander, with a *phyle Alexandris* at Ilium,[2] if it had not been created, as is probable, long after his death. If so, the new trend originated at Athens where, in 307 B.C., two new *phylae*, *Demetrias* and *Antigonis*, were added to the existing ten *phylae* in honour of Demetrius Poliorcetes and his father Antigonus.[3] It was in gratitude for the liberation of Athens from the tyranny of Demetrius of Phaleron, and was, like the honorific month, one of the many, mostly superhuman, honours decreed for them.[4] Other *phylae* of this type followed all over the Greek world: *Antiochis*, *Ptolemais*, *Eumenis*, *Attalis*, etc.[5] These new *phylae* received a preferential position; the *phylae Demetrias* and *Antigonis* of Athens were the first to vote, the first to supply the *prytanes* of the year, and so on.[6]

The Greeks created such *phylae* for Roman generals also. The evidence begins, it is true, with the imperial period, but there must have been republican, also Caesarian, precedents. There was at Cyzicus a *phyle Sebasteis* and a *Iouleis*,[7] at Prusias a *Sebastiane*, *Tiberiane*, *Iuliane*, *Antoniane*, etc.;[8] at Alexandria a *phyle Claudiane*;[9] the *phylae* of Antinoopolis in Egypt, a foundation of Hadrian, were named after, among others, Nerva, Trajan, Hadrian, and Hadrian's mother, wife, and sister.[10]

It is then probable that the Caesarian honour was inspired by Greek precedents. But Caesar had to accommodate the Greek example to Roman conditions—the *phylae* and tribes were corresponding but not identical institutions, nor were their functions identical—and had to put it into the service of his own plans. His plans included a considerable extension of Roman citizenship. He had been active for years in filling up the depleted tribes with new citizens, with men serving in his army, with the inhabitants of foreign cities and of provinces like Gaul and Spain.[11] And to improve the lot of many citizens he founded colonies.[12] We learn from the *lex Ursonensis* that his colonies, in addition

---

[1] Latte, *RE* 20. 994 ff. [2] *CIG* 3615; Habicht 21.
[3] Diod. 20. 46. 2; Plut. *Dem.* 10. 6; Latte, l.c. 1003; Habicht 45.
[4] See above, pp. 146; 153 f. [5] Latte 1003; Habicht 153 f.
[6] Latte 1007. [7] *IGR* 4. 153; 155.
[8] *IGR* 3. 1422; A. Koerte, *Ath. Mitt.* 24 (1899), 435 f. (partly reprinted in *IGR* 3. 65).
[9] *Pap. Lond.* 1912. 42 (Smallwood, *Documents . . . of Gaius, Claudius and Nero* 370).
[10] Kenyon, *APF* 2 (1902), 70 ff.; Weber, *Unters. z. Gesch. d. Kaisers Hadrians* 250.
[11] 'Sall.' *ep. ad Caes.* 2. 6. 1; Dio 43. 39. 5, etc.; Sherwin-White, *Roman Citizenship* 176 f.
[12] Vittinghoff 51 ff.

to being assigned to one of the Roman tribes, were organized in local
tribes: the inhabitants were citizens both of Rome and of their new
community.[1] Corinth, the Colonia Laus Iulia, belonged to the Roman
tribe Aemilia, but also had local tribes such as Aurelia and Calpurnia,
named after Caesar's mother and wife respectively; under Augustus
also Atia, Agrippia, Livia.[2] Caesar will have created or planned the
same kind of nomenclature for other colonies as well, and Augustus
followed his example. Augustus founded the colony Lilybaeum with
twelve tribes, one of which was called *tribus Iovis Augusti*;[3] at Iconium
there was later a *tribus Hadriana*.[4] It is clear that the Greek example had
its effect on the choice of the new names in Roman colonies, but also
that these in turn influenced the later names of the Greek *phylae*. It is
important to add that these names were chosen as were those for the
honorific months, embracing the emperors, their families, their epithets;
and both were to create a closer relationship to the dynasty. But that
was at a later stage. When Caesar took the initiative he must have
intended more: his tribe at Rome cannot have been just a ceremonial
frill.

The Julian tribe was not a new tribe, as were the ten tribes created
at the time of the great extension of citizenship in 90 B.C. and abolished
again:[5] it was an old one, selected by lot from the 35 tribes and perhaps
called, if we may apply Greek analogies,[6] by a double name, say,
tribus Fabia Iulia. It certainly had, like its Greek antecedents, a preferential position. It could have been the first to vote at the *comitia tributa*
at the election of the minor magistrates,[7] and thus have the initiative
and to some extent an influence on the results of the election. It could
have had an even more decisive role at the *comitia centuriata*, when the
consuls and praetors were elected. The first of its *centuriae* would
have been the first to announce its candidates, becoming the *centuria
praerogativa*, which by tradition had a great influence on the outcome
of the election.[8] These are the possibilities suggested by the provisions

---

[1] *ILS* 6087, CI.

[2] A. B. West, *Corinth* 8. 2: *Latin Inscriptions*, nos. 68; 86; 97; J. H. Kent, ibid. 8. 3,
p. 23.

[3] *ILS* 6770–6770b.   [4] *ILS* 9415.

[5] App. *BC* 1. 49. 214; Sisenna, frg. 17 P.; Vell. 2. 20. 2; Mommsen, *StR* 3. 179. 1; Kornemann, *RE* 16. 587; Sherwin-White, op. cit. 131 ff.

[6] At Nysa there was a 'phyle Octavia Apollonis' (*CIG* 2984), and a 'phyle Sebaste Athenais'
(*BCH* 7 (1883), 269); at Iconium a 'tribus Hadriana Herculana' (*ILS* 9415); Latte 1003
(with further instances).   [7] Cf. Mommsen, *StR* 3. 411 f.

[8] Livy 24. 7. 12; 26. 22. 2; 27. 6. 3; Cic. *Mur.* 38; *div.* 1. 103; 2. 83 (with Pease's notes);
L. R. Taylor, *Party Politics* 56; Chr. Meier, *RE* Suppl. 8. 567 ff. Or was there to be a link
with the reform of elections (Suet. *Caes.* 41. 2; Drumann 3. 612; Mommsen, *StR* 2. 731. 2)?

of a later law, the *lex Valeria Cornelia* of A.D. 5 as recorded on the Tabula Hebana.[1] It prescribed that ten voting *centuriae* should be named after the grandsons of Augustus, C. and L. Caesar, five for each, in their memory; after the death of Germanicus in A.D. 19 five further *centuriae* were named after Germanicus.[2] These fifteen *centuriae* were composed of senators and the *equites* of the judicial *decuriae*, belonging to 33 of the 35 tribes, and voted first at the *destinatio* of the consuls and the praetors; the senators and the *equites* of the two remaining tribes, Sucusana and Esquilina,[3] followed, and the other 160 *centuriae* came at the end. The advantage of the 'princely' *centuriae* was that their votes could already create a majority of the tribes for certain candidates, in which case the voting was broken off before the other *centuriae* were called up.[4]

The inference from one law to the possible contents of another must not be carried too far. They were certainly not identical. The 'Julian' law may not have had any provision for special *centuriae*; and even if it had, the first *centuria* of the Julian tribe cannot have been composed of men of distinction, as were the *centuriae Caesarum*, because it was selected by lot. But this examination of similarities and differences is possible only if it is right to say that there was a relationship between the two laws, that is, that the *lex Valeria Cornelia* ultimately depended on a *lex Iulia*, and that therefore Caesar's initiative must have had much more far-reaching consequences than can be inferred from Dio's meagre report. The *tribus Iulia*, and for that matter the *tribus Iulia Augusta* (?), may not have lasted for long; but they must have existed.[5]

The *tribus Iulia* was created, as its name shows, in honour of Caesar; that it was for the liberator is not found in Dio's evidence but is explicitly stated about the *phyle* of Demetrius, and this is sufficient. It may be added that his interest in such a voting organization was to be another sign that he meant to restore and preserve liberty. This intention received further support from the side of religion. It was decreed in 45

[1] E.-J. 94a. 10: 'ex lege quam L. Valerius Messalla Volesus Cn. Cornelius Cinna Magnus consules tulerunt suffragi ferendi causa.'

[2] Ibid. 5 ff. In A.D. 23 five further *centuriae* were probably created in honour of the younger Drusus, E.-J. 94b.

[3] Ibid. 23; 32.

[4] On the controversy concerning this law see Tibiletti, *Principe e magistrati repubblicani* (1953), 28 ff.; *Athen.* 37 (1949), 210 ff.; Nesselhauf, *Hist.* 1 (1950), 105 ff.; A. H. M. Jones, *JRS* 45 (1955), 13 f.; Syme, *Tacitus* 757 ff.; Brunt, *JRS* 51 (1961), 71 ff.

[5] It is possible that they survived in the 'corpus Iulianum' and 'corpus Augustale' of three urban tribes, *ILS* 6052 (Rome): 'Victoriae . . . sacrum trib(us) Suc(usanae) corp(oris) Iuliani C. Iulius Hermes . . . de suo fecit'; 6058: 'D.M. . . . viatori trib(us) Pal(atinae) corpore August(ali)'; 6060: '. . . tribu Esq(uilina) corpore Aug(ustali)'; Mommsen, *StR* 3. 190. 1; 277. There is, however, the difficulty that we do not know which part of the tribe was represented by such a 'corpus'.

that all the tribes should offer him sacrifices, hold games, and set up statues,[1] perhaps also present him with golden crowns.[2] The *tribus Iulia* may have been destined to have a leading part in such activities.

---

[1] App. *BC* 2. 106. 440: τιμαὶ πᾶσαι . . . θυσιῶν τε πέρι καὶ ἀγώνων καὶ ἀναθημάτων ἐν πᾶσιν ἱεροῖς καὶ δημοσίοις χωρίοις, ἀνὰ φυλὴν ἑκάστην; cf. the statues set up by the tribes in honour of Seianus in A.D. 29, Dio 58. 2. 7.

[2] This follows from the evidence concerning L. Antonius' triumph in 41 B.C., provided we ignore the boast that it had never happened before, Dio 48. 4. 6: αὐτὸς δὲ ἄλλους τε (στεφάνους) καὶ παρὰ τοῦ δήμου κατὰ φυλήν, ὃ μηδενὶ τῶν προτέρων ἐγεγόνει . . ., ἔλαβεν; cf. the banquets and libations of the tribes, families, and *vici* on Vespasian's arrival in Rome, A.D. 70, Jos. *BJ* 7. 73; for similar celebrations by the φυλαί in the Greek world see, e.g., *Or. gr.* 332. 40; *Syll.* 1027; L. Robert, *Essays in Honor of C. Bradford Welles* (1966), 185 f.

VIII

THE SAVIOUR

Two statues of Caesar stood on the Rostra, one of which, decorated with the grass wreath, has been discussed in the preceding chapter. The second wore an oak wreath, the *corona civica*, representing Caesar as the saviour of his fellow citizens.[1] It was not a duplication but a different honour. Its history too is different, and so are its associations: whereas the first statue leads to Libertas, the second leads to Salus and even prepares the ground for further honours, for the vows for Caesar's welfare and for the oath by it.

I. THE *CORONA CIVICA*

The oak wreath was the reward of a citizen who had saved the life of another in battle, and was originally given by the saved man,[2] who in addition accepted the obligation to honour his saviour like his father.[3] A man so honoured was entitled to wear this wreath at the games in the Circus, and everybody rose when he entered to take his privileged seat next to the senators;[4] he also had other privileges. Two such heroes may be mentioned here, a fictitious and a real one. The elder Scipio was said to have saved the life of his father in the battle at the Ticinus in 218 B.C. at the age of seventeen, was greeted by his father as his saviour, and yet refused to accept the *corona civica*: the feat was pure invention, and the saviour was, as stated in another source, a slave.[5] The other, and real, hero was Caesar, who received

---

[1] App. *BC* 2. 106. 441: στέφανος ἐκ δρυὸς ἦν ἐπ' ἐνίαις (εἰκόσι) ὡς σωτῆρι τῆς πατρίδος, ᾧ πάλαι τοὺς ὑπερασπίσαντας ἐγέραιρον οἱ περισωθέντες; Dio 44. 4. 5 (above, p. 148. 3).

[2] Gell. 5. 6. 11: 'civica corona appellatur, quam civis civi, a quo in proelio servatus est, testem vitae salutisque perceptae dat. ea fit e fronde quernea'; Paul. 42 M. (37 L.); Serv. *Aen.* 6. 772; Comm. Lucan. 1. 357 f.; Plut. *QR* 92; Steiner, *BJ* 114 (1905), 40 ff.; K. Kraft, *Jahrb. f. Num. u. Geldgesch.* 3/4 (1955), 26 ff.

[3] Polyb. 6. 39. 7: σέβεται δὲ τοῦτον καὶ παρ' ὅλον τὸν βίον ὁ σωθεὶς ὡς πατέρα, καὶ πάντα δεῖ τούτῳ ποιεῖν αὐτὸν ὡς τῷ γονεῖ; Cic. *Planc.* 72: 'milites faciunt inviti, ut coronam dent civicam et se ab aliquo servatos esse fateantur ... onus beneficii reformidant, quod permagnum est alieno debere idem quod parenti'; Alföldi, *Mus. Helv.* 9 (1952), 214.

[4] Pliny 16. 13: 'accepta (corona) licet uti perpetuo ludis. ineunti semper adsurgi etiam ab senatu in more est, sedendi ius in proximo senatui, vacatio munerum omnium ipsi patrique et avo paterno'; Mommsen, *StR* 1. 438. 2 (change of punctuation).

[5] Polyb. 10. 3. 6; Livy 21. 46. 7; Pliny 16. 14; Meyer, *Kl. Schr.* 2. 428; 430.

the wreath in 80 B.C. at the age of twenty from the propraetor M. Minucius Thermus at the siege of Mytilene.[1] Minucius, as a follower of Sulla, was not a political friend: so Caesar must have well deserved the distinction.

Caesar was given the wreath for the second time in 45 B.C. because he saved a great number of the citizens, not just one, and not by personal bravery on the battlefield. This means a change of function and turns our attention to the Greek analogy which might have inspired the change. The Greeks always had their θεοὶ σωτῆρες,[2] but kings too were acclaimed and honoured as Soteres: Ptolemy I, Antiochus I, Antigonus, and Demetrius Poliorcetes,[3] and later Roman generals like T. Quinctius Flamininus.[4] King Prusias greeted the senators in 167 B.C. as saviour gods,[5] and dedications were often set up in Rome out of gratitude to the Roman people.[6]

The Roman evidence begins with a coin of Q. Lutatius Cerco (*quaestor c.* 110 B.C.), which shows a galley within an oak wreath: it has rightly been assumed that the moneyer thus commemorated the victory of his ancestor C. Lutatius Catulus at the Aegates Islands in 241 B.C., which ended the First Punic War.[7] This coin does not suggest that he had received the wreath on that occasion but that his descendant held that he had deserved it. If so, this new turn of thought existed at the beginning of the first century B.C.: a *corona civica* could now be awarded to a general for a victory which saved Rome. But this view cannot have been formed much earlier. Camillus became the hero of Roman history because he saved Rome from the Gauls in 390 B.C.[8] This is an

[1] Suet. *Caes.* 2. H. E. Russell suggested (ap. L. R. Taylor, *Greece and Rome* 4 (1957), 12; cf. Gelzer 20. 25; 22. 40) that Caesar as owner of the *corona civica* was even granted membership of the Senate by Sulla (cf. Livy 23. 23. 6).

[2] Nock, 'Soter and Euergetes', *Papers . . . presented to honor F. C. Grant* (1951), 127 ff.; Nilsson 2. 184 f.; 390 f. (with bibliography).

[3] *Syll.* 390; 426, etc.; Wilcken, *Sitz. Ber. Berlin* (1938), 316; Nock, l.c. 130; Habicht 156. 76; above, p. 143. 6.

[4] Plut. *Flamin.* 10. 7; 16. 7, etc.; above, p.143. 7.

[5] Polyb. 30. 18. 5: χαίρετε, θεοὶ σωτῆρες; Livy 45. 44. 20: 'deos servatores suos senatum appellasse.'　　[6] Degrassi, *Inscr.* 176 f.; id. *Scritti* 418 f.

[7] Sydenham 75 (*c.* 106 B.C.?); pl. 19. 599; on another coin the name 'Q. Lutati(us)' is within an oak wreath, Grueber 2. 298 (*c.* 110 B.C.). A contemporary coin of L. Memmius shows a head wearing an oak wreath on the *obv.*, the Dioscuri with their horses on the *rev.* (Sydenham 74; Grueber, pl. 95. 10): this refers, according to Grueber 2. 299. 2, to King Menestheus, the alleged ancestor of the Memmii, who had saved Athens with the help of the Dioscuri from the tyranny of Theseus (accepted by Alföldi, l.c. 218). There remains the difficulty that the 'ancestor' of the Memmii was Mnestheus and a Trojan, not a Greek.

[8] Livy 5. 19. 2: 'fatalis dux . . . servandaeque patriae'; 5. 49. 8: 'servatam deinde bello patriam iterum in pace haud dubie servavit'; Manil. 1. 784: 'et Iove qui meruit caelum Romamque Camillus / servando posuit'; cf. Münzer, *RE* 7. 332; Momigliano, *CQ* 36 (1942), 113.

old tradition, as it is attested in the fourth century by Aristotle.[1] It is supported by a statue on the Rostra recording, probably by its inscription, what he had done.[2] Even if it was set up long after Aristotle, it was still an archaic statue, because it was dressed in the old manner with a *toga* without the *tunica*.[3] And yet there is no evidence that it wore the oak wreath. Another saviour was the elder Scipio; he too probably received a statue on the Rostra:[4] but here again there is no mention of an oak wreath. Nor is it mentioned for Marius[5] and Sulla,[6] the next saviours. The first real instance was Cicero, and that is why it was necessary to consider possible precedents. L. Gellius Poplicola (*cos.* 72) suggested in the Senate, no doubt in vain, that Cicero should receive the *corona civica* because he discovered and frustrated the conspiracy of Catilina.[7] Accordingly Cicero kept on repeating that he was the saviour of Rome and of its citizens from ruin.[8] Even if one accepts the inference from the coin of Lutatius Cerco that the wreath had received a new and extended function, it remains strange that Gellius made the proposal: Cicero was not a general, and there was no war and no battlefield where the *corona civica* was earned. It is stranger still that the senators acclaimed him 'parens patriae' or 'pater patriae'.[9] They followed the example of the single citizen who honoured his saviour with an oak wreath and called him 'father'. But they called Cicero 'father of the country', 'father of all'. This was a new departure, which will be examined in its proper place.[10]

Caesar was the next. He had been a saviour of the Gauls by virtue

---

[1] Aristot. frg. 610 R. (Plut. *Cam.* 22. 4); cf. Memnon, *FGrHist.* 434 F 1. 18; Plut. *Cam.* 30. 2.

[2] Ascon. *Scaur.* 46, p. 29 St.; Pliny 34. 23; Pliny, *Paneg.* 55. 6; Vessberg, *Stud. z. Kunstgesch. d. röm. Rep.* (1941), 22; 92 f.

[3] Cf. Marquardt–Mau, *Privatleben* 2. 550 f.

[4] Polyb. 23. 14. 3; cf. Gell. 4. 18. 12: 'cui salus imperii ac rei publicae accepta ferri deberet'; Livy 38. 56. 12 (above, p. 36. 1); Enn. *V.* 1 V.

[5] Cic. *Cat.* 3. 24: 'custos huius urbis'; *p. red. Quir.* 9: 'custos civitatis atque imperii vestri'; *Pis.* 43: 'Italia servata ab illo'; *Sest.* 37: 'conservatorem patriae'; 50: 'natus ad salutem imperii'; 116: 'conservatoris huius imperii'; *Cat.* 4. 21 (above, p. 150. 5).

[6] Plut. *Sulla* 34. 2 (below, p. 168. 5).

[7] Cic. *Pis.* 6: 'mihi . . . L. Gellius . . . civicam coronam deberi a re publica dixit'; Gell. 5. 6. 15: 'hac corona civica L. Gellius, vir censorius, in senatu Ciceronem consulem donari a re publica censuit, quod eius opera esset atrocissima illa Catilinae coniuratio detecta vindicataque.' Or was this just a rhetorical phrase suggesting that the Res Publica ought to crown Cicero (as the Imperium Romanum once crowned Fabius Maximus, above, pp. 149 f.)?

[8] Cic. *Att.* 9. 10. 3 (below, p. 202. 4); *Vatin.* 7: 'si ego te perditorem et vexatorem rei publicae fero, tu me conservatorem et custodem feras'; *Cat.* 3. 15; 25 f.; 4. 20; *Sulla* 22; *fam.* 5. 7. 3; *p. red. Quir.* 17; *dom.* 72; 94; 132; *Pis.* 6; 23; 94; *Sest.* 38; Graff, *Ciceros Selbstauffassung* (1963), 27; below, p. 169. 2.

[9] Cic. *Pis.* 6; *Sest.* 121; Plut. *Cic.* 23. 6 (below, p. 202. 2).

[10] See below, p. 202.

of his clemency before[1] and was going to save the Greeks too, as did
their kings and generals, for which they then called him 'Soter' on
their dedications in many places,[2] and even a god at Ephesus and at
Carthea on Keos.[3] But what happened at Rome is more relevant. The
Civil War began with a Last Decree because of the danger to the safety
of the citizens; Caesar first wanted to meet Pompey to restore this safety.[4]
Later he granted it to all who asked for it, explained it to P. Lentulus
Spinther (*cos.* 57) in February 49 at Corfinium[5] and after the battle of
Pharsalus to those who surrendered:[6] they were all surprised and impressed by his magnanimity. It was clemency, another innovation. It
was traditional to exercise clemency towards the defeated enemy and
Caesar often did so in Gaul; but he was the first to apply it to his
fellow citizens at Rome.[7] Even Cicero was converted. In 46 he began
to echo Caesar's statements and to confirm them in his speeches *Pro
Marcello* and *Pro Ligario*.[8] He admitted that he was one of the many
whose life Caesar had saved and pleaded with him to save more.[9] He
called Caesar a saviour in the same terms as he had called himself before,
a saviour in the Civil War.[10] He expressly asked for monuments to this

---

[1] Caes. *BG* 2. 28. 3: 'quos Caesar, ut in miseros ac supplices usus misericordia videretur,
diligentissime conservavit'; 2. 31. 4: 'si forte pro sua clementia ... statuisset Atuatucos esse
conservandos'; 7. 41. 1: 'Caesar nuntiis ad civitatem Haeduorum missis, qui suo beneficio
conservatos docerent quos belli iure interficere potuisset'; below, p. 236. 6.

[2] Pergamum (*IGR* 4. 303; 1677), Megara (*IG* 7. 62), Chios (*IGR* 4. 929, with the readings
of Raubitschek, *JRS* 44 (1954), 67), Athens (*IG* 2². 1222); Mytilene (*IGR* 4. 57), perhaps
also Phocaea (L. Robert, *Hell.* 10 (1955), 257 ff.); for further information and comment see
Raubitschek, l.c. 65 ff.; below, p. 258. 3.

[3] *Syll.* 760 (Ephesus; see below, p. 296. 9); *IG* 12. 5. 557: Ὁ δῆμος ὁ Καρθαιέων τὸν
θεὸν καὶ αὐτοκράτορα καὶ σωτῆρα τῆς οἰκουμένης Γάιον Ἰούλιον Καίσαρα ... ἀνέθηκεν.

[4] Caes. *BC* 1. 5. 3: 'decurritur ad illud extremum atque ultimum senatus consultum,
quo nisi paene in ipso urbis incendio atque desperatione omnium salutis ... numquam ante
descensum est'; 1. 24. 5: 'interesse rei publicae et communis salutis se cum Pompeio con-
loqui.'

[5] Caes. *BC* 1. 22. 3: '(Lentulus Spinther) cum eo de salute sua agit. orat atque obsecrat,
ut sibi parcat ... (6) cuius (Caes.) oratione confirmatus Lentulus, ut in oppidum reverti
liceat, petit: quod de sua salute impetraverit, fore etiam reliquis ad suam spem solacio.'

[6] Caes. *BC* 3. 98. 2 (below, p. 237. 7).

[7] See below, pp. 236 ff.

[8] Cic. *Marc.* 21: 'qui magis sunt tui quam quibus tu salutem insperantibus reddidisti?'
Lig. 34: 'quos tu tamen salvos esse voluisti'; 19.

[9] Cic. *Marc.* 12; 17.

[10] Cic. *Marc.* 22: 'quis est omnium tam ignarus rerum, ... tam nihil umquam nec de sua
nec de communi salute cogitans, qui non intellegat tua salute contineri suam, et ex unius tua
vita pendere omnium?' (cf. *dom.* 73: 'ostenditque (senatus) nec stare potuisse rem publicam,
si ego non fuissem'); *Marc.* 32: 'nisi te, C. Caesar, salvo ... manente salvi esse non possumus.
quare omnes te qui haec salva esse volumus, et hortamur et obsecramus, ut vitae, ut saluti
tuae consulas' (cf. *Vatin.* 8: 'quid ... praestantius mihi potuit accidere, quid optabilius
ad immortalitatem gloriae atque ad memoriam mei nominis sempiternam quam omnes hoc
cives meos iudicare, civitatis salutem cum unius mea salute esse coniunctam?'); cf. Graff,
op. cit. 35; 114.

clemency,[1] and a year later, in 45, in his speech *Pro rege Deiotaro*, he already referred to such monuments and in particular to the statue on the Rostra.[2] Such statues will have existed in many places. The head of one, wearing the oak wreath, was discovered on Thasos some years ago (pl. 1).[3] The title of 'parens patriae' also followed.[4] It is certainly not too bold to conclude that it was Cicero who inspired the Senate to grant Caesar in 45 the *corona civica* which should have been granted to him in 63 B.C. The influence of the Greek Soteres, gods and kings, can be felt but what was made of it was due to another influence, that of an old Roman tradition.

2. SALUS

The gods of Rome too were often honoured as saviours, and one of them, Salus, had no other function than this.[5] The word *salus* meant welfare, safety, private and public, not just health like *valetudo* (pl. 16. 2–3).[6] The goddess Salus was worshipped all over Italy and received a temple at Rome at the end of the fourth century B.C., representing the *salus publica*.[7] It was one of the many foundations prompted by the hazards of the Samnite Wars. The private Salus will have been much older, may have inspired hyperbolical expressions of gratitude from man to man, and thus become the first Roman equivalent of the Greek Soter:[8] *custos*[9] and *conservator*[10] came later. A 'saviour' is addressed in Comedy as 'Salus mea',[11] and he claims a statue, altar, and sacrifice

---

[1] Cic. *Lig.* 6: 'o clementiam admirabilem atque omnium laude praedicatione litteris monumentisque decorandam!'

[2] Cic. *Deiot.* 40: 'multa sunt monimenta clementiae tuae, sed maxima eorum incolumitates quibus salutem dedisti' (the word 'monimenta' is used here both in its original and metaphorical sense); 34: 'nullus locus est ad statuam quidem Rostris clarior.'

[3] Chamoux, *Mon. Piot* 47 (1953), 131 ff.; F. S. Johansen, *Anal. Rom. Inst. Dan.* 4 (1967), 43; pl. 27.

[4] See below, pp. 200 ff.   [5] Wissowa 131 ff. and *Myth. Lex.* 4. 295; Latte 234.

[6] *RE* 8A. 264 ff.

[7] It was vowed and built by C. Iunius Bubulcus, Livy 9. 43. 25; 10. 1. 9. The head of Salus appeared on coins of a later member of the family, D. Iunius Silanus, Sydenham 96; Grueber, pl. 32. 17–20.

[8] On the terminological difficulties see Cic. *Verr.* 2. 2. 154: 'is enim . . . Soter, qui salutem dedit'; *ILS* 33 (Degr. 177: 84 B.C.): 'Populus Laodicensis ab Lyco populum Romanum, quei sibei salutei fuit . . ' 'Ὁ δῆμος ὁ Λαοδικέων τῶν πρὸς τῷ Λύκῳ τὸν δῆμον τῶν 'Ρωμαίων γεγονότα ἑαυτῷ σωτῆρα; cf. A. Oxé, *Wien. Stud.* 48 (1930), 38 ff.; Dornseiff, *RE* 3A. 1219.

[9] Enn. *A.* 111 V.: (Romulus) 'qualem te patriae custodem di genuerunt'; Iuppiter Custos (Hor. *c.* 1. 12. 49) = Ζεὺς Σωτήρ; Hercules Magnus Custos (*F. Venus.*, 4 June, Degrassi 465) since 218 B.C. in the Circus Flaminius) = 'Ηρακλῆς Μέγας Σωτήρ.

[10] Cic. *Sest.* 53: 'pro di immortales, custodes et conservatores huius urbis atque imperii.'

[11] Plaut. *Bacch.* 879: 'ah, Salus mea, servavisti me'; *Cist.* 644: 'o Salute mea Salus salubrior'; *Pseud.* 709: 'dic utrum Spemne an Salutem te salutem, Pseudole?'

from his devotee for himself.[1] The expression was often reduced, like 'mea vita', to a term of endearment,[2] but it also kept its original meaning. A woman whose son was murdered by Verres called Cicero in Sicily her Salus and threw herself at his feet.[3] Cicero called P. Cornelius Lentulus Spinther (cos. 57) a god and Salus among other things because he helped him to return from exile.[4] This usage did not remain limited to the private sphere. It is probable that Sulla was called their Salus by his followers on his return to Rome,[5] and Caesar by his own as early as the beginning of the Civil War.[6] Before following up this trend, we must mention a different function of Salus: she was also a goddess of oath, certainly under Caesar but perhaps even earlier. It may have been in this function that she received the epithet Semonia.[7] It points to an old relationship with Semo Sancus, who was a god of oath[8] and in turn used to be connected with another god of oath, Dius Fidius.[9] Salus Semonia would then be the female version of Semo Sancus as was Fides of Dius Fidius. There was an early oath 'pro tuam fidem',[10] first

---

[1] Plaut. Asin. 712: 'si quidem mihi statuam et aram statuis / atque ut deo mi hic immolas bovem: nam ego tibi Salus sum'; Capt. 863: 'ego nunc tibi sum summus Iuppiter, / idem ego sum Salus, Fortuna, Lux, Laetitia, Gaudium'; Merc. 867: 'Spes, Salus, Victoria'; cf. Sil. 7. 734: (soldiers of M. Minucius Rufus, 217 B.C.) 'Fabiumque decus, Fabiumque salutem / certatim et magna memorabant voce parentem'; 747: 'caespite de viridi surgunt properantibus arae. / nec prius aut epulas aut munera grata Lyaei / fas cuiquam tetigisse fuit, quam multa precatus / in mensam Fabio sacrum libavit honorem'; see above, pp. 149 f.; below, p. 289.

[2] Plaut. Cas. 801: 'quid agis, mea salus?' Poen. 421: 'mea commoditas, mea salus'; cf. Asin. 614: 'certe enim tu vita's mihi'; Stich. 584: 'o mea vita, o mea voluptas, salve'; Tru. 391: 'o mea vita'; Wissowa 132. 5: Hofmann, Lat. Umgangssprache 195 f.

[3] Cic. Verr. 5. 129: 'me suam Salutem appellans . . . mihi ad pedes misera iacuit.'

[4] Cic. p. red. Quir. 11: 'parens, deus, Salus nostrae vitae, fortunae, memoriae, nominis'; cf. Planc. 25; Sest. 38: 'C. Marium, terrorem hostium, spem subsidiumque patriae'; below, p. 179.

[5] Lucan. 2. 221: 'hisne (= murder of citizens) Salus rerum, Felix his Sulla vocari, / his meruit tumulum medio sibi tollere Campo?' Plut. Sulla 34. 2: οἱ γὰρ . . . ἐστεφανωμένοι παρείποντο, σωτῆρα καὶ πατέρα τὸν Σύλλαν ἀποκαλοῦντες, ἅτε δὴ δι' ἐκεῖνον εἰς τὴν πατρίδα κατιόντες καὶ κομιζόμενοι παῖδας καὶ γυναῖκας; Alföldi, Mus. Helv. 10 (1953), 104.

[6] This is an inference from Cic. Att. 9. 7 B. 3 (Balbus to Cic., March 49): 'te (ita incolumi Caesare moriar!) tanti facio, ut paucos aeque ac te caros habeam.' This parenthesis recalls the popular oath when the swearer is willing to die for the truth of his assertion, Cic. Att. 5. 20. 6: 'moriar, si quicquam fieri potest elegantius'; 4. 17. 5: 'ne vivam, si scio' (Hofmann, op. cit. 28 ff.; 31): Balbus too is willing to die for what he says, provided that Caesar remains safe. His 'oath' then is a combination of the popular oath 'May I die' with the oath officially introduced in 44 'by Caesar's welfare (Salus)' (below, p. 212), but apparently anticipated by his followers at the beginning of the Civil War.

[7] Macrob. 1. 16. 8: 'qui nominasset Salutem Semoniam . . . ferias observabat'; ILS 3090 (A.D. 1); '. . . Salus Semonia, populi Victoria'; Fest. 309 M. (404 L.); Wissowa 131 f.; Norden, Aus altröm. Priesterbüchern 212 f.; Latte 51. 2.

[8] Wissowa 130; Norden, op. cit. 209 ff.; Latte 127.

[9] ILS 3472–6.

[10] Plaut. Amph. 373; 376; Men. 999; Rud. 615, etc.; W. Schulze, Kl. Schr. 174; Hofmann, op. cit. 28; 30; Heinze, Vom Geist d. Römertums 43.

without implying the goddess Fides: similarly there may have been another early oath 'per tuam salutem'. But whatever the origins, these two functions of Salus would have remained insignificant without the initiative of Caesar.

3. SALUS CAESARIS

What Caesar's followers felt about their own security at the beginning of the Civil War was later shared by many others who were at first his adversaries. It had often happened before that the welfare of the State depended on the life of a single man;[1] in 63 for instance on Cicero, as he boasted, adding that this was acknowledged by Pompey and others.[2] He expressed himself similarly in his *De re publica* about the younger Scipio[3] and in the following years often about Pompey.[4] Now in 46 he said the same about Caesar in his speech *Pro Marcello*.[5] The immediate cause of his protestations was the discovery of a plot against Caesar. But even without it he would not have spoken differently: we shall see that the annual vows for Caesar's welfare which were decreed later may have been inspired by Cicero's speech.[6]

It was talk without any consequence in all earlier cases, but now action was taken. The statue with the *corona civica* was one form of recognition, the future vows for his welfare were another. But there was even more. Cicero, recording the setting up of Caesar's statue in the temple of Quirinus on the Quirinal in 45, comments that it is better that Caesar shares a temple with Quirinus than with Salus.[7] Two explanations of this passage have been offered. It should either allude to the murder of Romulus-Quirinus by the senators for his tyranny,

---

[1] See below, pp. 219 f.; for the traditional view see Cic. *Rab. perd.* 20: 'omnes ... in salute rei publicae salutem suam repositam esse arbitrabantur.'

[2] Cic. *p. red. Quir.* 16; *Sest.* 129; *Phil.* 2. 12; *off.* 1. 78; above, p. 165. 8.

[3] Cic. *rep.* 6. 12 (below, p. 219. 6).

[4] Cic. *Mil.* 19 (52 B.C.): 'cuius in vita nitebatur salus civitatis'; *Att.* 6. 3. 4 (June 50): 'non quo ullum periculum videam stante Pompeio vel etiam sedente, valeat modo'; 8. 2. 3 (Febr. 49): 'in unius hominis quotannis periculose aegrotantis anima positas omnis nostras spes habemus'; Meyer, *op. cit.* 262; 268.

[5] Cic. *Marc.* 22 (above, p. 166. 10); 25: 'omnium salutem civium cunctamque rem publicam res tuae gestae complexae sunt'; 32: 'nisi te, C. Caesar, salvo ... salvi esse non possumus. quare omnes te qui haec salva esse volumus, et hortamur et obsecramus, ut vitae, ut saluti tuae consulas'; 24; 29; 33; above, p. 166. This was an old claim, often made, and was sometimes even true, see, e.g., Isocr. (3) *Nicocl.* 56; Baynes, *Byz. Studies and other Essays* 150. On the other 'plots' to kill Caesar see Balsdon, *Hist.* 7 (1958), 82.

[6] See below, p. 219.

[7] Cic. *Att.* 12. 45. 3 (17 May 45): 'de Caesare vicino scripseram ad te ... eum σύνναον Quirini malo quam Salutis'; see below, pp. 186 ff..

PLATE 16

1. Marble statues of the tyrannicides, Harmodios and Aristogeiton, copy of the bronze original by Kritios and Nesiotes, in the National Museum, Naples (*Photo*: German Archaeol. Inst., Rome); p. 146.

2. Denarius of D. Iunius Silanus, *c.* 91 B.C. (Sydenham 96. 645), Oxford; *obv.*: head of Salus, legend 'Salus'; *rev.*: Victoria in biga with palm-branch, legend 'Roma, D. Silanus L. f.'; p. 167.

3. Denarius of M². Acilius, 49 B.C. (Sydenham 154. 922), Oxford; *obv.*: head of Salus, legend 'Salutis'; *rev.*: Valetudo with serpent, a column at her side, legend 'Valetu(dinis)', M². Acilius IIIvir'; p. 167.

4. Sestertius of T. Quinctius Sulpicianus, 21 B.C. (Mattingly I. 36. 181), Oxford; *obv.*: oak wreath between two laurel-branches, legend 'ob civis servatos'; *rev.*: legend 'S.C., T. Quinctius Crispin. Sulpic. III vir a(uro) a(rgento) a(ere) f(lando) f(eriundo)'; p. 171.

5. Denarius of L. Mescinius Rufus, 16 B.C. (Mattingly I. 17. 90), London; *obv.*: bust of Augustus, legend (not legible here) 's.c. ob r(em) p(ublicam) cum salut(e) Imp. Caesar(is) Augus(ti) cons(ervatam)'; *rev.*: Mars on pedestal with spear and sword, legend 'S.P.Q.R. v(ota) p(ublica) s(olvit) pr(o) s(alute) et red(itu) Aug(usti)', L. Mescinius Rufus IIIvir'; p. 172.

6. Denarius of L. Mescinius Rufus, 16 B.C. (Mattingly I. 17. 91), London; *obv.*: legend in oak wreath 'I(ovi) O(ptimo) M(aximo) S.P.Q.R. v(otum) s(olvit) pr(o) s(alute) Imp. Cae(saris) quod per eu(m) r(es) p(ublica) in amp(liore) atq(ue) tran(quilliore) s(tatu) e(st)'; *rev.*: cippus inscribed 'Imp. Caes(ar) Augu(stus) comm(uni) cons(ensu)', legend 'S.C., L. Mescinius Rufus IIIvir'; p. 172.

7. Dupondius of Tiberius, A.D. 22–3 (Mattingly I. 131. 81), Oxford; *obv.*: legend 'S.C., Ti. Caesar, Divi Aug. f. Aug., p.m., tr. pot. XXIIII'; *rev.*: bust of Livia as Salus, legend 'Salus Augusta'; p. 172.

8. Aureus of Nero, A.D. 64–8 (Mattingly I. 212. 87), London; *obv.*: head of Nero, legend 'Nero Caesar Augustus'; *rev.*: Salus seated with patera, legend 'Salus'; p. 173.

9. Denarius of the Civil Wars, A.D. 68 (Mattingly I. 300. 43), London; *obv.*: helmeted goddess with spear and shield, legend 'Salus et Libertas'; *rev.*: aquila between two standards, and altar, legend 'signa p. R.'; p. 173.

10. Denarius of the Civil Wars, A.D. 68 (Mattingly I. 297. 31), Oxford; *obv.*: Victoria on globe with wreath and palm, legend 'Salus generis humani'; *rev.*: oak wreath, legend 'S.P.Q.R.'; p. 173.

11. Sestertius of Galba, A.D. 68 (Mattingly I. 328. 119), Paris; *obv.*: head of Galba, legend 'Ser. Galba Imp. Caesar Aug., tr. p.'; *rev.*: Salus seated with sceptre and patera, legend 'Salus Augusta, S.C.'; p. 174.

12. As of Galba, A.D. 68 (Mattingly I. 361. 265), Paris; *obv.*: head of Galba, legend 'Ser. Sulpi. Galba Imp. Caesar Aug., p.m., tr. p.'; *rev.*: Salus leaning on a column and feeding a snake, legend 'Salus Augusti, S.C.'; p. 174.

PLATE 16

implying the hope that Caesar would end similarly.[1] Or else the passage has nothing to do with the statue in the temple but with the decree of the Senate to build a house for Caesar, which, on the strength of this passage in Cicero, would have been planned on the Quirinal nearer to the temple of Quirinus than to that of Salus.[2] This second interpretation has nothing to recommend it, the religious term σύνναος is against it, and it has not found many supporters. The other, with the malicious innuendo, is the more popular one: it requires reading between the lines, cannot be proved, but is not impossible. A third interpretation may be proposed. Cicero's words, taken as they are, suggest that there was an alternative plan, to set up Caesar's statue in the temple of Salus but that finally, because of the Parilia,[3] Quirinus was chosen, the course favoured by Cicero. If so, Caesar was already associated with Salus. It is confirmed by the explicit evidence that later the oath 'per Salutem Caesaris' was introduced;[4] this evidence, until now isolated and more or less ignored, in turn receives substantial support. It is further confirmed by her successors, the Salus Augusti and Salus Augusta.

Salus Caesaris would have been the public version of the private *Salus mea*, comparable to the Clementia Caesaris for whom a temple was decreed about the same time, and to the Victoria Caesaris for whom games were instituted in the year before.[5] It is probable that a temple of the Salus Caesaris too was planned, vowed perhaps when the plot against Caesar's life was discovered, just as another temple of Salus was vowed in A.D. 65 after the failure of the Pisonian conspiracy.[6] The setting up of the statue in the old temple of Salus would have been a provisional measure until the completion of the new temple. It would have been a statue decorated with the *corona civica*, like the one on the Rostra.

4. SALUS AUGUSTA

Augustus too became a saviour and was rewarded with the *corona civica* 'ob civis servatos' and the golden shield in 27 B.C. (pl. 16. 4).[7] The Caesarian theme was resumed with all its consequences. Vows

---

[1] Meyer, op. cit. 449; L. R. Taylor, 65 f.; Nock, *HSCP* 41 (1930) 1. 1; Classen, *Philol.* 106 (1962), 183 ff.; 197; Burkert, *Hist.* 11 (1962), 358.

[2] Meyer, op. cit. 447. 3; Gelzer 285. 175.

[3] See below, p. 188. A statue of the elder Cato stood in the temple of Salus (Plut. *Cat. mai.* 19. 4) but only as a memorial of his achievements (below, p. 187) without any religious functions, and it cannot therefore be considered a precedent for the Caesarian honour.

[4] Dio 44. 50. 1: οὖ τήν τε Ὑγιείαν τήν τε Τύχην ὤμνυσαν; below, pp. 212 f.

[5] See above, p. 111, and below, p. 241.   [6] Tac. *A.* 15. 74. 4; below, p. 173. 7.

[7] *Mon. Anc.* 34. 2; Dio 53. 16. 4; Mattingly 1. 2; 7; 29 ff., etc.

were fulfilled in 16 B.C., apparently after his recovery from an illness, because with his life the State too was preserved (pl. 16. 5–6).[1] Ovid called him the Salus of the country,[2] and, what is more important, oaths too were performed by the Salus Augusti.[3] Her cult therefore must have existed in some form in Rome as well as in the provinces; in fact it is known that she had a priest at Alabanda.[4] In addition there is indirect evidence, provided by the Salus Augusta, which, though first found under Tiberius, must have been created under Augustus and was more general than the personal Salus. Augustus also dedicated a statue to *Salus publica*, the republican goddess, in 11 B.C.[5]

Tiberius was called by Valerius Maximus the Salus of the country,[6] but there was no Salus Tiberii, and 'Salus Augusta' was the legend on coins issued in A.D. 22/23 with the bust of Livia (pl. 16. 7).[7] She was ill at that time and vows were made for her recovery:[8] so her recovery was a matter of importance for the State. Salus Augusta appeared for the second time in A.D. 31, when she received dedications together with the *Libertas publica*, the local Genius, and the Providentia of Tiberius.[9] The occasion was the death of Seianus and the consequent rejoicing that Rome was saved from ruin: for this thanks were due to the Salus Augusta.

There is no direct evidence about Caligula, but the indirect is strong.

---

[1] *Denarius* of L. Mescinius Rufus with the legend 'S.C. ob rem publicam cum salute Imperatoris Caesaris Augusti conservatam', Mattingly 1. 17; pl. 3. 13; Strack, op. cit. 1. 172; v. Premerstein 125.

[2] Ov. *Trist.* 2. 574: 'o pater, o patriae cura (or 'Cura': *ILS* 2960; Verg. *Aen.* 6. 74; Hor. *c.* 3. 1. 40; *Thes.L.L. Onom.* 2. 753) Salusque tuae.'

[3] *Inst.* 2. 23. 1: 'Divus Augustus . . . per ipsius Salutem rogatus'; Mommsen, *StR* 2. 103. 3; 810. 4; v. Premerstein 207. 1.

[4] E.–J. 114: . . . ἱερέα διὰ γένους Ὑγιείας τε καὶ Σωτηρίας Αὐτοκράτορος Καίσαρος καὶ Ἡλίου.

[5] Dio 54. 35. 2: εἰκόνας . . . Ὑγιείας δὲ δημοσίας . . . καὶ Ὁμονοίας Εἰρήνης τε ἔστησεν; Ov. *F.* 3. 881: 'Ianus adorandus cumque hoc Concordia mitis / et Romana Salus araque Pacis erit.' The legend 'Salutis' on a provincial coin (which implies local cult): Grant, *From Imperium to Auctoritas* 271; cf. Mattingly 1. 308; pl. 51. 24.

[6] Val. Max. 1, *praef.*: 'te igitur . . . certissima Salus patriae, Caesar, invoco'; cf. *CIL* 6. 92: 'pro salute Ti. Caesaris Augusti . . . Concordiae'; 93; 91 (*ILS* 153).

[7] Mattingly 1. 131; pl. 24. 2; on local coins of Emerita in Spain, Vives, *La moneda Hispánica* 4. 67, no. 66 f.; pl. 145. 4 f.; an altar on a coin of Ilici, Spain, inscribed 'Sal. Aug.': Grant, *Aspects of the Principate of Tiberius* 114. 169; pl. 6. 7.

[8] Tac. *A.* 3. 64; 71. 1.

[9] *ILS* 157 (Interamna): 'Saluti perpetuae Augustae Libertatique publicae populi Romani, Genio municipi . . . Providentiae Ti. Caesaris Augusti, nati ad aeternitatem Romani nominis' (cf. Cic. *Sest.* 50: 'virum . . . natum ad salutem huius imperi, C. Marium'). A statue of Libertas was set up in the Roman Forum on this occasion (Dio 58. 12. 4): there may have been another for Salus Augusta. There is also other relevant evidence, *CIL* 13. 4635 (E.–J. 137, Nasium, Belgica): 'Tib. Caesari . . . et pro perpetua salute divinae domus'; West, *Corinth* 8. 2: *Lat. Inscr.* 90, no. 110: '. . . sacerdoti in perpetuum Providentiae Augustae et Salutis publicae'; cf. no. 15.

It was alleged that he swore by the Salus and Genius of his horse Incitatus:[1] this grotesque allegation could not have been made had there not been a Salus of Caligula. But when the annual *vota pro salute* of the emperor were made on 3 January A.D. 38, the Arvals sacrificed to, among others, Salus,[2] by which the *Salus publica* will have been meant. There is no evidence for a Salus of Claudius; but the *Salus publica* received public offerings from the Arvals during his illness,[3] which does not seem to have happened before and may have been inspired by the prayers to the Salus Augusta for Livia.

Nero's birthday, 15 December, was celebrated in A.D. 55 by the Arvals with an offering to his Salus and Genius besides the Capitoline triad,[4] an innovation in more than one respect. This Salus Neronis, inspired probably by Caligula's example, must have met with opposition, as may be inferred from the fact that on Nero's following birthdays her place was taken by Salus without epithet, although the offering to his Genius remained.[5] Nero's coins show Salus, without epithet, for the first time in the imperial period (pl. 16. 8):[6] it was probably because of the failure of the Pisonian conspiracy in A.D. 65, which was to be commemorated with a temple of Salus.[7] The Caesarian evidence, especially Cicero's speech *Pro Marcello*, comes back to mind.

Coins of the Civil Wars are inscribed with, among others, 'Salus et Libertas' (pl. 16. 9–10),[8] which recalls dedications under Tiberius after the death of Seianus, and 'Salus generis humani':[9] they represent the hopes raised by the rebellion of C. Iulius Vindex.[10] When Galba emerged, and with him new hopes for peace, he too was hailed as 'Salus generis humani',[11] which was more than 'Salus patriae', the title given

---

[1] Dio 59. 14. 7 (below, p. 213. 12).   [2] Henzen, *AFA* XLII; 102; below, p. 219.

[3] Henzen, *AFA* LVIII.

[4] *CIL* 6. 32352. 10: 'Saluti eius b(ovem) m(arem) (?), Genio ipsius taurum.' Henzen LXII refused to accept this wording, which is preserved only in a MS. copy ('neque .. immolari solet Saluti imperatoris . . .') and printed instead: 'Saluti [publicae vaccam]'.

[5] Henzen LXX; LXXVI. She began to receive offerings on many other occasions from Nero onwards, see Henzen 216; J. M. Reynolds, *PBSR* 30 (1962), 35.

[6] Mattingly 1. 212 f.; pl. 40. 2–9.

[7] Tac. *A.* 15. 74. 4: 'templum Saluti extrueretur.' When the Libonian conspiracy failed in A.D. 16 offerings were made to various deities but not to Salus, Tac. *A.* 2. 32. 4; Degrassi 509.

[8] Mattingly 1. 297; 300; pl. 50. 16 f.; 27.   [9] Mattingly 1. 297 f.; pl. 50. 18–22.

[10] Pliny 20. 160: 'Iulium Vindicem, adsertorem illum a Nerone libertatis'; Dio 63. 22. 6 (speech of Vindex): ἐλευθερώσατε πᾶσαν τὴν οἰκουμένην; cf. Pliny 16. 8: 'Augustus coronam . . . civicam a genere humano accepit ipse'; Strack, op. cit. 1. 191 f.; Mommsen, *Ges. Schr.* 4. 347 ff.; Bickel, *BJ* 133 (1928), 25 f.; P. A. Brunt, *Latom.* 18 (1959), 531 ff.

[11] Mattingly 1. 314; 350; pl. 52. 18–20; 54. 25; Suet. *Galba* 9. 2: 'supervenerunt et Vindicis litterae hortantis, ut humano generi assertorem ducemque se accommodaret'; cf. Pliny, *ep.* 10. 52: 'diem, domine, quo servasti imperium, dum suscipis, quanta mereris laetitia, celebravimus precati deos, ut te generi humano, cuius tutela et securitas saluti tuae innisa est, incolumem florentemque praestarent.' Trajan too was called 'Salus generis humani'

to Augustus and Tiberius. Under Galba, Salus Augusta appeared on coins for the second time[1] and Salus Augusti for the first time (pl. 16. 11–12),[2] the latter distinguished from the former as a goddess of health, that is, of the health of the emperor. The numismatic evidence suggests that the two goddesses were worshipped separately under the Flavians[3] although they were never mentioned in the prayers of the Arvals, who now always turned to the *Salus publica*.

There is no need to go further. It is enough to refer to the coin-legends, which show how popular the Salus of the emperors was during the imperial period.[4] The Christians preferred the oath by the Salus of the emperor to that by his Genius,[5] apparently because in contrast to the Genius they did not consider Salus a deity in this context. The oath was still in use in the Christian period of the fourth century:[6] this Salus definitely ceased to be a pagan goddess and remained only as a symbol of the welfare of the emperor.

This survey confirms the evidence of the two isolated passages: there was at the beginning a Salus Caesaris, followed by the Salus of Augustus, Caligula, Nero. It was also followed by vows, games, oaths; even the cult of the Genius Caesaris is relevant. But not much was done about these because of the murder, and about a cult of the Salus Caesaris nothing is known.

(Mattingly 3. 87; pl. 16. 1; Strack, op. cit. 1. 191) but no other emperor after him. As a goddess she is found on an inscription from Gaul, *ILS* 3827. The expression *genus humanum* originated earlier, see Livy 37. 45. 9: 'parcere vos generi humano oportet.'

[1] Mattingly 1. 328; pl. 57. 2 (seated as on Nero's coins, above, p. 173. 6).

[2] Mattingly 1. 361; pl. 59. 7 (standing and feeding a snake as does the Greek Hygieia).

[3] Mattingly 2. 476; Strack 1. 171 ff. The Salus Augusti seems to have received an altar or a temple under Titus, Mattingly 2. 261; 367; 375; 385; 400; 412; pls. 50. 1; 70. 7; 72. 1; 74. 4; cf. *CIL* 8. 12247: 'Saluti Augustorum' (M. Aurelius and L. Verus); 13. 8017: 'Saluti Imp. Severi Alexandri.'

[4] See the survey in Bernhart, *Handb. der Münzkunde d. röm. Kaiserzeit* 229 ff.

[5] Tert. *Apol.* 32. 2: 'iuramus sicut non per Genios Caesarum ita per Salutem eorum, quae est augustior omnibus Geniis'; cf. 35. 10: 'omnes . . . sacra faciebant pro salute imperatoris et Genium eius deierabant, alii foris, alii intus'; *Passio SS. Scilitanorum* 3 (v. Gebhardt, p. 23): 'et iuramus per Genium domini nostri imperatoris et pro salute eius supplicamus.'

[6] *Cod. Theod.* 2. 9. 3 (A.D. 395): 'qui nomina nostra (Arcadius and Honorius) placitis inserentes salutem principum confirmationem initarum esse iuraverint pactionum.'

IX

THE FOUNDER

MANY of the honours of 45 were decreed on 20 April, when the news of the victory at Munda was received in Rome.[1] That is why some of them were granted with regard to the character of the following day, the festival of the Parilia: that special games should be held on this Parilia in Caesar's honour;[2] that his ivory statue should be carried in the procession of the gods preceding the games, in the company of Romulus-Quirinus, the founder;[3] and that another statue should be set up in the temple of Romulus-Quirinus with the inscription 'Deo Invicto'.[4] These honours reflect another central theme: Caesar's relationship to Romulus, the foundation of Rome and its festival.

I. ROMULUS

It has been assumed that these honours owe their origin to the co-incidence of the arrival of the news with the Parilia. This assumption would be justified, if the coincidence had not been so timely and were not therefore so suspect.[5] It becomes even more suspect when some calculations are made. The messenger, who will have been a parti-cularly fast one, needed 34 days this time for the distance from Munda to Rome in the spring, whereas Caesar needed only 24 or 27 days in the winter before for the same distance, although he travelled with his troops.[6] A fast messenger reporting the death of Nero to Galba in June A.D. 68 needed only seven days for the somewhat shorter journey from Rome

---

[1] See above, p. 133.

[2] Dio 43. 42. 3: τά τε Παρίλια ἱπποδρομίᾳ ἀθανάτῳ, οὔτι γε καὶ διὰ τὴν πόλιν, ὅτι ἐν αὐτοῖς ἔκτιστο, ἀλλὰ διὰ τὴν τοῦ Καίσαρος νίκην, ὅτι ἡ ἀγγελία αὐτῆς τῇ προτεραίᾳ πρὸς ἑσπέραν ἀφίκετο, ἐτιμήθη.

[3] Dio 43. 45. 2 (above, p. 110. 1); Cic. Att. 13. 28. 3: 'hunc de pompa Quirini con-tubernalem.'

[4] Dio 43. 45. 3: ἄλλην τέ τινα εἰκόνα ἐς τὸν τοῦ Κυρίνου ναὸν Θεῷ Ἀνικήτῳ ἐπιγράψαντες . . . ἀνέθεσαν.

[5] Drumann 3. 580. 3. His suspicions have not been followed up so far.

[6] Suet. Caes. 56. 4; App. BC 2. 103. 429; O. E. Schmidt, Ciceros Korrespondenz 257; Fried-länder, Sittengesch. 1. 331; Riepl, Nachrichtenwesen 198; cf. Magie, Roman Rule 1263. 18. In 58 Caesar arrived with his troops in Geneva from Rome in a week (Plut. Caes. 17. 5; Caes. BG 1. 7. 1), which means a daily average of 100 miles (160 km.). On 'Caesariana celeritas' (Cic. Att. 16. 10. 1; App. BC 2. 47. 192; 53. 216) see Drumann 3. 723.

to Spain.[1] The messenger may of course have been delayed by the hazards of the weather or of the hostile territory or by some other unexpected event. But it is more probable that the delay was intentional, contrived by Caesar's friends who wanted to create a cultic basis for the relationship between Caesar and Romulus at the festival of the Parilia. They would have created it another time had the opportunity not arisen then. This assumption will become more probable when the origin and significance of that relationship is investigated and is shown to have been at that time an important political issue.

Romulus was the earliest hero of Rome.[2] Many details of his life and of his achievements were disputed, but not the principal one, the foundation of Rome. He was of divine descent[3] like the Greek founders or like Caeculus, the founder of Praeneste,[4] or Modius Fabidius, the founder of Cures.[5] He became, according to Ennius, a god in the end and assumed the name of Quirinus,[6] who had been, with Iuppiter and Mars, one of the principal gods of Rome. It has often been held that what Ennius says is not evidence but the creation of his own poetical fancy without any consequence, and that the apotheosis and the identification with Quirinus had not been part of the story before the middle of the first century B.C.[7] No evidence has ever been produced to prove this contention;[8] it is not probable in itself, and there is a

---

[1] Plut. *Galba* 7. 1. C. Laelius (*cos.* 190), Scipio's legate, needed 34 days from Tarraco to Rome (Livy 27. 7. 1) : but he travelled with captives and ships.

[2] Cf., e.g., Alföldi, *Mus. Helv.* 8 (1951), 203 ff. (with bibliography) ; id. *Early Rome and the Latins* 131 ff.; Classen, *Philol.* 106 (1962), 174 ff.; H. J. Krämer, *Synusia . . . W. Schadewaldt* (1965), 355 ff.; Gabba, *Entretiens . . . Fond. Hardt* 13 (1967), 143 ff.

[3] Enn. *A.* 113 V.: 'o sanguen dis oriundum'; 115; Promathion, *FGrHist.* 817 (Plut. *Rom.* 2. 4) ; Classen, l.c. 179.

[4] Serv. *Aen.* 7. 678; Schol. Veron. *Aen.* 7. 681 (Cato); cf. *Studi in onore di Luisa Banti* (1965), 348.   [5] Dion. Hal. 2. 48 (Varro).

[6] Serv. *Aen.* 6. 777: (Romulus) 'secundum Ennium referetur inter deos cum Aenea'; Enn. *A.* 65 V.: 'unus erit quem tu tolles in caerula caeli / templa'; 115: 'Romulus in caelo cum dis genitalibus aevum / degit'; 117: '⟨te⟩, Quirine pater, veneror Horamque Quirini'; accepted by Elter, *Donarem pateras* 40. 31 ff.; Bömer, *Ahnenkult* 75. 2; Latte 113; R. Schilling, *REL* 38 (1960), 186.

[7] Wissowa 155 f. and *Myth. Lex.* 4. 15; Koch, *Religio* 30; id. *RE* 24. 1318; Weber, *Princeps* 86*. 398; Kornemann, *Gnom.* 14 (1938), 496; Classen, l.c. 196 ff.; Burkert, *Hist.* 11 (1962), 358; 373; O. Skutsch, *Studia Enniana* (1968), 130 ff.

[8] The coin of C. Memmius issued *c.* 56 B.C. with the head of Quirinus (Sydenham 153; pl. 25. 921) and considered to be the principal piece of evidence for the contemporary identification of Romulus with Quirinus, cannot represent Romulus because the head is without diadem. Romulus, like all kings, was supposed to wear it (Iuven. 8. 259: 'diadema Quirini'), and Numa and Ancus Marcius are so represented on coins (Sydenham 172; 111; 149). Other heads on coins, claimed by Alföldi, *Mus. Helv.* 8 (1951), 190–203, for Romulus (Sydenham 133; 152), but rightly rejected by Classen, l.c. 185 f., on general grounds, are also without the diadem; cf. H. W. Ritter, *Diadem u. Königsherrschaft* (1965), 13. 2. In fact Romulus was not represented on coins, if we except the type with the she-wolf and the twins, before the age of Hadrian.

Greek and a Latin analogy against it. The Greek one is the generally
accepted cult of the founder in the Greek cities,[1] the Latin one is an
archaic inscription in Latium set up in honour of the deified Aeneas,[2]
thus confirming the antiquarian tradition according to which he was
worshipped after his death at the river Numicus as Iuppiter Indiges.[3]
This analogy renders it even more probable that the deification of
Romulus and his identification with Quirinus was believed and accepted long before Ennius. Further evidence is found in an oath of
allegiance of 91 B.C., which is addressed to, among others, the divine
founders,[4] who cannot be other than Aeneas and Romulus, and in
Cicero, who in 63 B.C. explicitly referred to Romulus' apotheosis.[5] There
must have been others who did the same at that time and even earlier.

2. THE SUCCESSORS OF ROMULUS

The Greeks used to call a benefactor or a saviour a new κτίστης of
their city.[6] That is how Romulus acquired a political topicality at
Rome: whoever saved it from ruin and rebuilt it became a 'new founder', another Romulus. But this was a late development. If the tradition
is to be trusted, Camillus was thesecond founder of Rome[7] and
Marius the third.[8] Camillus saved it from the Gauls, rebuilt it, re-
organized its constitution and some of its cults; and yet it is certain
that he was not called a 'new founder' in his time.[9] The elder Scipio
was not so honoured either, although he too was a saviour of Rome:[10]
this makes it probable that the Scipionic tradition was fixed before the
idea about the new founders became popular in Rome. Marius' name
in the list, on the other hand, cannot be called anachronistic. It was

---

[1] Hdt. 6. 38; Callim. *Aetia* 2, frg. 43. 78 ff. Pf.; Strab. 8. 5. 5, p. 366; Diod. 20. 102. 3;
Preisigke, *Sammelbuch* 6611; Höfer–Drexler, *Myth. Lex.* 2. 1580 ff.; Pfister, *Reliquienkult*
295 ff.; 445 f.; Eitrem, *RE* 8. 1136; Prehn, *RE* 11. 2083; Habicht 36 f.; 40; 105 ff.; 123;
162; 168.

[2] Degr. 1271: 'Lare Aineia d(onom)'; cf. *JRS* 50 (1960), 114 ff.; 118.

[3] Livy 1. 2. 6; Serv. Dan. *Aen.* 1. 259, etc.; above, p. 10.

[4] Diod. 37. 11: ἔτι δὲ τοὺς κτίστας γεγενημένους τῆς Ῥώμης ἡμιθέους καὶ τοὺς συναυξήσαντας
τὴν ἡγεμονίαν αὐτῆς ἥρωας.

[5] Cic. *Cat.* 3. 2: 'illum qui hanc urbem condidit ad deos immortales benevolentia famaque
sustulimus.'

[6] Eitrem, *RE* 8. 1136; Habicht 204 f.

[7] Livy 5. 49. 7: 'Romulus ac parens patriae conditorque alter urbis . . . appellabatur';
7. 1. 10: 'quem secundum a Romulo conditorem urbis Romanae ferrent'; Plut. *Cam.* 1. 1:
κτίστης δὲ τῆς Ῥώμης ἀναγραφεὶς δεύτερος; 31. 2: κτίστης λέγηται παρώσας Ῥωμύλον; Eutrop.
1. 20. 3: 'appellatus secundus Romulus, quasi et ipse patriae conditor'; Iulian. *Caes.* 323a.

[8] Plut. *Mar.* 27. 9: οἱ πολλοὶ κτίστην τε Ῥώμης τρίτον ἐκεῖνον ἀνηγόρευον.

[9] Münzer, *RE* 7. 338 f., suggests that this tradition was created in the age of Sulla and under
the influence of Sulla's restoration of the State.

[10] See above, p. 165.

equally a just claim: he had saved Rome from the Germans and was another great legislator. Moreover his son was said to have been a descendant of Mars and Venus,[1] which shows that Marius was in fact connected with Rome's origins. There remains, however, the difficulty that Cicero, his eloquent admirer, never calls him explicitly a 'founder' or 'Romulus'.[2]

Sulla was even more suitable for such a role: his victories, his dictatorial rule, and his new constitution must have created the feeling of a new beginning. Sallust calls him a 'left-handed Romulus';[3] his historians will have chosen a different epithet. Pompey was the next, when, in 67/66 B.C., the Senate provided him with the supreme command for the war against the pirates and Mithridates, and in addition with exceptional power in many respects, especially in the provinces. His quasi-monarchic power provoked comparison with Romulus, of which only the unfavourable version has survived: like Romulus he would be killed by the people for his tyranny.[4] The other version will have praised him and compared him with Romulus the founder; the tyrant was an exceptional though not isolated feature of the tradition.[5] After his third triumph the charge of tyranny was renewed and again when the triumvirate was founded, this time with the spectre of the diadem added.[6] Later his adversaries even asserted that he not only failed to live up to the role of a new Romulus but was bent on destroying the work of his model. For at the beginning of the Civil War the destruction of the temple of Quirinus was listed among the prodigies.[7] This was an exaggeration:[8] it will have been damaged by fire, but only to such an extent that the damage could quickly be repaired. The temple was in use again at the latest in 45, when it received Caesar's statue.[9] The conclusion therefore is that the prodigy was intended to create the belief that Pompey's war against his fellow citizens was bound to destroy not only the temple of the founder but also his foundation. If so, he was given the role of the late barbarian who would destroy Rome

[1] See above, p. 17.

[2] He calls him 'custos', 'conservator', 'parens patriae' (e.g. *Rab. perd.* 27; see also above, pp. 150. 5; 165. 5; below, p. 201. 10).

[3] Sall. *hist.* 1. 55. 5 M.: 'scaevus iste Romulus'; M. A. Giua, *Studi class. e orientali* 16 (1967), 320.

[4] Plut. *Pomp.* 25. 9: (the consul) εἰπὼν πρὸς αὐτὸν ὅτι ʽΡωμύλον ζηλῶν οὐ φεύξεται ταὐτὸν ἐκείνῳ τέλος, ἐκινδύνευσεν ὑπὸ τοῦ πλήθους διαφθαρῆναι.

[5] Cf. Classen, *Philol.* 106 (1962), 183 ff.

[6] See above, p. 135, and below, p. 335.

[7] Dio 41. 14. 3: καὶ ἕτερον (πῦρ) ἄλλα τε καὶ τὸν τοῦ Κυρίνου ναὸν κατέφλεξεν.

[8] Noticed by Koch, *Religio* 32; id. *RE* 24. 1316 f.

[9] Dio 43. 45. 3 (above, p. 175. 4, and below, pp. 186 ff.).

and disperse the ashes of Quirinus.[1] But Caesar intervened, saved Rome, and was rewarded with a statue in the restored temple of Quirinus. This is not mere fancy built on the prodigy and later poetry. The theme existed and had been used in a different form to predict Caesar's death and disaster for Italy in consequence of his agrarian law of 59, which settled Roman colonists in the territory of Capua.[2] It was the outcome of a hostile reaction to this law, but was created much later and incorporated in Balbus' biography of Caesar.[3] Caesar's colonists destroyed many tombs in Capua, even the tomb of the founder Capys. Here they found a Greek inscription on a bronze tablet announcing the murder of his descendant Caesar,[4] should his tomb be disturbed.[5] This is clearly a different story; and yet some of its features seem to vouch for the existence of the Pompeian version suggested above.

3. CICERO

These instances show that the Romans had their new founders before Caesar. But the issue was nowhere important enough to suggest that the idea had taken deep root in the political thought of the time. The change was brought about, as so often, by Cicero. His consulate inspired him to creative reflections about Roman history. He made a hero of Marius,[6] who was a fellow Arpinate[7] and another *homo novus*, and later even treated of him in an epic poem.[8] As consul he asserted that Marius deserved to be called a 'pater patriae' for his victories over the enemy;[9] he also spoke about the divine spirit that was acting in Marius and other saviours.[10] This was still before the discovery of the Catilinarian conspiracy. After its suppression Cicero referred to Romulus and his apotheosis as the reward for founding Rome, and to himself

---

[1] Hor. *epod.* 16. 13: 'ossa Quirini / ... dissipabit insolens.'

[2] On the law see Gelzer, *Caesar* 73 ff.   [3] See above, p. 4.

[4] Capys was held to be a cousin of Aeneas on his mother's side by Coelius Antipater, a relation through marriage by others (Serv. Dan. *Aen.* 10. 145); cf. Scherling, *RE* 10. 1922.

[5] Suet. *Caes.* 81. 1 (from Balbus, *HRR* 2. 46 P.); below, p. 342. According to Serv. Dan. *Aen.* 2. 35 the inscription was found on a bronze heifer at Capua. On desecration of tombs see Mommsen, *Strafr.* 812 ff.; A. Parrot, *Malédictions et violations de tombes* (1939), 153 ff.

[6] Gnauk, *Die Bedeutung d. Marius u. Cato Maior für Cicero* (1936), 38 ff.; Carney, *Wien. Stud.* 73 (1960), 121 f.

[7] Cic. *Sulla* 23: 'ex eo municipio, unde iterum iam salus huic urbi imperioque missa est'.

[8] *PLF* frgs. 10–18 M.; Büchner, *RE* 7A. 1245 ff.; Malcovati, *Cicerone e la poesia* (1943), 254 ff.; Benario, *CP* 52 (1957), 177 ff.

[9] Cic. *Rab. perd.* 27 (below, p. 201. 10).

[10] Cic. *Rab. perd.* 30: 'equidem et C. Mari et ceterorum ... mentes quae mihi videntur ex hominum vita ad deorum religionem et sanctimoniam demigrasse testor me pro illorum fama gloria memoria non secus ac pro patriis fanis atque delubris propugnandum putare.'

who had now saved Rome from ruin.[1] He did not say that he therefore
deserved the title of a 'new founder' but he meant it. He himself declared not very much later that the Nones of December 63, the day of
the decisive meeting of the Senate, was to be the new birthday of Rome,
a theme to which we shall have to return.[2] Ten years later, when he
wrote his theoretical work *De re publica*, he had much to say about
Romulus the founder and his apotheosis.[3] He even made a general
rule of it by stating that human creative activity never comes so close
to divine power as it does in the foundation of cities or in saving them
from ruin.[4] Again, he did not say so, but there is no doubt that he thought
that he too was such a man. He was less discreet in his speeches, correspondence, and other personal writings.[5]

4. CAESAR

A few years after Cicero, Caesar was consul. His membership of
the triumvirate and his sweeping legislation had provoked resentment
and the charge that he had behaved like a king.[6] Caesar certainly did
not fail to defend himself, and it is probable that he asserted in his
answer that his actions qualified him to become another Romulus.
That much can be recovered by inference from Catullus, who abused

---

[1] Cic. *Cat.* 3. 2: 'quoniam illum qui hanc urbem condidit ad deos immortales benevolentia
famaque sustulimus, esse apud vos posterosque vestros in honore debebit is qui eandem hanc
urbem conditam amplificatamque servavit'; R. Klein, *Königtum u. Königszeit bei Cicero* (Diss.
Erlangen 1962), 42 ff.

[2] Cic. *Flacc.* 102, etc.; below, p. 189.

[3] Cic. *rep.* 1. 64 (after quoting Enn. *A.* 111 f. V.): 'non eros nec dominos appellabant eos
quibus iuste paruerant, denique ne reges quidem, sed patriae custodes, sed patres et deos';
2. 17: 'Romulus . . . tantum est consecutus, ut cum subito sole obscurato non conparuisset,
deorum in numero conlocatus putaretur'; 6. 13. He had already alluded to the same doctrine
in 56, *Sest.* 143: (with regard to the heroes of the past, Brutus, Camillus, Fabius Maximus,
Scipio, etc.) 'qui hanc rem publicam stabiliverunt; quos equidem in deorum immortalium
coetu ac numero repono.'

[4] Cic. *rep.* 1. 12: 'neque enim est ulla res in qua propius ad deorum numen virtus accedat
humana, quam civitatis aut condere novas aut conservare iam conditas'; for the Greek
version of the doctrine see Euryphemus Pythagor. ap. Stob. 39. 27 (5, p. 915 H.); L. Delatte,
Les traités de la Royauté (1942), 261; 276.

[5] He soon created a myth about his consulate (cf. J. Graff, *Ciceros Selbstauffassung* (1963),
26 ff.), asked Archias to write an epic about it (Cic. *Arch.* 28; 31; *Att.* 1. 16. 15), himself wrote
a *Commentarius* in Greek for the use of Greek historians and intended to write one in Latin
as well (Cic. *Att.* 1. 19. 10; 2. 1. 2; Bömer, *Herm.* 81 (1953), 236 f.). He then wrote an epic
de consulatu in Latin (*PLF* frgs. 10–18 M.; Büchner, *RE* 7A. 1245 ff.; Malcovati, *Cicerone e la
poesia*, 254 ff.) and Greek (Cic. *Att.* 1. 19. 10; 2. 1. 1 ff.; Plut. *Crass.* 13. 4; Dio 46. 21. 4),
later also *de temporibus meis* (*PLF* frgs. 19–21 M.; Jachmann, *Miscell. Acad. Berol.* 2 (1950),
245 f.), and tried in 56 to persuade L. Lucceius to write an encomiastic history of his consulate,
exile, and rehabilitation (Cic. *fam.* 5. 12. 1; 6; 9; Reitzenstein, *Hellenist. Wundererzählungen*
84 ff.; Münzei, *RE* 13. 1557; Ullman, *TAPA* 73 (1942), 44 ff.; Graff, op. cit. 22).

[6] Cic. *ep. ad Q. Axium* frg. 5 (p. 171 Watt); Suet. *Caes.* 49. 2; above, p. 135. 11.

him *c.* 55 as a shameless Romulus, conqueror of Spain, Gaul, and Britain, *imperator* and lawgiver.[1] Caesar's answer will have been more an angry retort than a political programme: he was still allied to Pompey, and, with Iulia alive, he did not yet mean to follow an independent line. There is no further relevant evidence for the following years of his governorship in Gaul.

The Civil War brought Rome near ruin, and after the victories at Pharsalus and Thapsus the work of reconstruction had to begin. Caesar's reform of the State, like that of Sulla, had to include religious reforms. Reform had long been in the air. Cicero made many suggestions *c.* 53 in his work *De re publica*, and later in *De legibus*, in the latter with samples of legislation in archaistic style.[2] About 47 Varro, a former adversary, published his *Antiquitates rerum divinarum* and dedicated it to Caesar, the *pontifex maximus*.[3] At the beginning Varro expressed the fear that the gods might perish not by hostile attack but through the negligence of the Romans, and his book was to serve the purpose of saving them. This would be a greater service to the gods than what L. Caecilius Metellus (*cos.* 251) did in 241 when he saved the *sacra* from the burning temple of Vesta, or Aeneas when he saved the Penates from the ruins of Troy.[4] Clearly Varro wanted Caesar to take action. In a further fragment[5] he represented the view, commonly shared then and later,[6] that it was due to their piety that the Romans became masters of the world, implying that the empire could only survive if the gods received what was due to them.[7]

It seems certain that many contemporary pamphlets discussed the problems of reform. One of them can be recovered with great probability with the help of the second book of Dionysius of Halicarnassus.[8] It deals with Romulus, the four political virtues on which he based his work, *pietas, moderatio, iustitia, virtus*, and then describes his political and religious institutions at some length, with details about the cults of the gods, festivals, priests, sacrifices. It has been observed that this all-embracing role given to Romulus was in contrast to the accepted tradition of a gradual development of the constitution under the kings;

---

[1] Catull. 29. 5: 'cinaede Romule,... (11) imperator unice... (24) socer generque, perdidistis omnia' (Verg. *Aen.* 6. 826 ff.); cf. 11. 10: 'Caesaris visens monimenta magni' (or Magni?).

[2] Cic. *leg.* 2. 19–22.   [3] Lact. *div. inst.* 1. 6. 7: 'ad C. Caesarem pontificem maximum.'

[4] Varr. *Ant. rer. div.* 1, frg. 2a Ag. (Aug. *CD* 6. 2).

[5] Ibid. frg. 36 Ag. (Tert. *Apol.* 25); cf. Min. Fel. 25. 1.

[6] Cic. *har. resp.* 19; Hor. *c.* 3. 6. 5; Livy 44. 1. 11.

[7] The complaint of negligence was equally frequent, Varr. *sat. Men.* 181 B.; Livy 3. 20. 5 (Ogilvie ad loc.); 6. 41. 8; 10. 40. 10; 25. 1. 7 (in a different sense); Hellmann, *Livius-Interpretationen* 30 f.   [8] Dion. Hal. 2. 18–23.

and that these institutions of Romulus very much resembled the reforms Caesar intended, or was being advised, to introduce. These observations led to the conclusion that the book rests on a political pamphlet which meant to promote Caesar's plans by disguising them as institutions of Romulus.[1]

It is tempting to see another, a Greek, pamphleteer in the Epicurean philosopher Philodemus, who in his book on kingship[2] added the features of the ideal king as found in Homer to those of Romulus.[3] Philodemus was close to Caesar: his patron was L. Calpurnius Piso (*cos.* 58), Caesar's friend and father-in-law, to whom he dedicated his book.[4] There is, it is true, no explicit reference to contemporary history in this book but in another one[5] there is: to Antony's tyranny after the Ides of March. But the book does not contain a real political message;[6] it is not a serious work, gives much space to irrelevant matter, and does not discuss really important political topics. This verdict could be reversed if one were prepared to read between the lines; by this method, however, some attractive conjectures, but not one piece of solid proof, could be produced.[7]

There were no doubt many other, mostly unsolicited, pamphlets. There was one by Cicero, solicited by his and Caesar's friends, but it was not completed, and Caesar never saw anything of it.[8] Nevertheless we have a fairly clear idea of its contents. It will have attributed the same tasks and achievements to Caesar which Cicero used to record about his own consulate in his speeches and writings, demanded later from the true statesman in his works *De re publica* and *De legibus*, and already ascribed to, or expected from, Caesar in his speeches *Pro*

---

[1] Pohlenz, *Herm.* 59 (1924), 157 ff.; cf. Classen, l.c. 194; Klein, op. cit. 60 ff. This anonymous pamphlet was dated by v. Premerstein, 8 ff., Kornemann, *Klio* 31 (1938), 83 f., and J.-C. Richard, *Mél.* 75 (1963), 344 f., in the age of Augustus; by Gabba, *Athen.* 38 (1960), 175 ff., in that of Sulla. On pamphlets in general see Dio 43. 47. 6; H. Peter, *Die geschichtl. Litteratur über die röm. Kaiserzeit* 1. 164 ff.

[2] Philod. Περὶ τοῦ καθ' Ὅμηρον ἀγαθοῦ βασιλέως, ed. A. Olivieri (1909); cf. Philippson, *RE* 19. 2474; O. Murray, *JRS* 55 (1965), 161 ff.

[3] It was Momigliano, *JRS* 31 (1941), 152 f. (*Secondo Contributo* 380 f.), who first attached a political significance to this book and dated it to the period of Caesar's dictatorship.

[4] Philod., op. cit., col. 25. 16 ff.; Sudhaus, *Rhein. Mus.* 64 (1909), 476.

[5] Philod. Περὶ θεῶν 1. 25. 22 ff. (Diels, *Abh. Akad. Berl.* (1915), Nr. 7, p. 44); Momigliano, l.c. 154 (*Secondo Contributo* 383).

[6] This is the verdict of O. Murray, l.c. 177 ff., who in turn assumes that Philodemus wrote it for Piso and for his consulate in 58 (181 f.). Grimal, *REL* 44 (1966), 254 ff., returns to the Caesarian date, to the time after the victory at Munda in 45 (281), and assumes that Philodemus meant Caesar by the good king, and Antony by the bad one (273 ff.; not convincing).

[7] See additional note below, pp. 198 f.

[8] Cic. *Att.* 12. 40. 2; 51. 2; 13. 7. 1; 26. 2; 27. 1; 28; Meyer, op. cit. 438 ff.; Gelzer, *RE* 7A. 1024; cf. *HTR* 50 (1957), 233 f. (with bibliography); Pasoli, *Riv. fil.* 33 (1955), 337 ff.

Marcello and *Pro Ligario*. Caesar after his victories would now become the new founder and law-giver of Rome.

Caesar was also qualified for the new role through his legendary link with Romulus. The Trojan legend was always connected with Rome's beginnings: the gap between Aeneas and Romulus in time and relationship was variously filled.[1] The Gens Iulia had its own share in this procedure, and the family historian, L. Iulius Caesar, brought the genealogical tale from Aeneas and Iulus down to Romulus and Remus.[2] He probably also mentioned that Proculus Iulius, a member of the family, witnessed Romulus' apotheosis.[3] This version of the legend existed before Caesar's ascendancy. For his own time two pieces of evidence can be quoted. His statue at Ephesus set up in 48 bore the inscription that he was a descendant of both Ares and Aphrodite;[4] and later he proposed to build a temple for Mars, the father of Romulus.[5]

It is probable that Caesar was called κτίστης in many places of the East when he became the new founder of Rome, and even earlier.[6] There was no corresponding Latin term. It seems that first *creator* was tried out: this was used once by Cicero for Romulus.[7] Another was *conditor*[8] which had hitherto been the name of the god of the granary,[9] an obvious choice because, in contrast, the verb *condere* was always used for founding. There is no direct Caesarian evidence for *conditor* in the new sense. And yet it must have been coined for Caesar and under Caesar because it is found in authors who wrote soon after his death, Sallust, Varro, and Nepos;[10] it then occurs once in Vergil[11] and often

---

[1] Schwegler, *Röm. Gesch.* 1. 337 ff.; Mommsen, *Röm. Chronol.* 151 ff.; Alföldi, *Early Rome and the Latins* 125 ff. (with the assertion that the dynasty of the Alban kings was invented by Fabius Pictor; *contra*, Gabba, *Entretiens* 13 [*Les origines de la Rép. rom.*, 1967], 139 ff.).

[2] See above, pp. 17; 129 f.

[3] Cic. *rep.* 2. 20; *leg.* 1. 3: 'post excessum suum Romulus Proculo Iulio dixerit se deum esse et Quirinum vocari, templumque sibi dedicari in eo loco iusserit'; Livy 1. 16. 5 (with Ogilvie's note and bibliography); Ov. *F.* 2. 499 (with Bömer's note), etc.

[4] *Syll.* 760 (below, p. 296. 9).   [5] Suet. *Caes.* 44. 1; above, pp. 128 ff.

[6] At Mytilene, *IG* 12. 2. 165 (Pompey before him: ibid. 163; 165; *IGR* 4. 49 f.; 54 f.; *Archaiol. Delt.* 22 (1969), 461; A. Donati, *Epigr.* 27 (1965), 42 f.).

[7] Cic. *Balb.* 31: 'princeps ille creator huius urbis Romulus'; *Thes.L.L.* 4. 1114.—Of other terms, 'auctor' was not used in this sense before Vergil (*Thes.L.L.* 2. 1204. 66 ff.), *Georg.* 3. 36: 'Troiae Cynthius auctor'; *Aen.* 8. 134; Livy 5. 24. 11: 'Romulo . . . parente et auctore urbis Romae' (cf. Cic. *leg. agr.* 2. 100: 'auctores generis mei'). Another term, 'fundator' (*Thes.L.L.* 6. 1155), seems to have been first used by Vergil (*Aen.* 7. 678).

[8] Cf. *Thes.L.L.* 4. 146; Skard, *Festskrift til H. Koht* (1933), 57 ff. (who, however, wrongly assumes that Cicero was already called 'conditor'); Classen, l.c. 181; 187. 6.

[9] Fab. Pict. frg. 3 P. (Serv. Dan. *Georg.* 1. 21): '. . . Conditorem, Promitorem'; Cic. *Cluent.* 71; *p. red. sen.* 15 (Plaut. *Epid.* 523 is doubtful).

[10] Sall. *Iug.* 89. 4 (*c.* 40 B.C.): 'Capsa, cuius conditor Hercules'; Varr. *RR* 3. 1. 6 (37 B.C.): 'non a conditore nomen ei (Thebes) est impositum'; Nep. *Timol.* 3. 2.

[11] Verg. *Aen.* 8. 313: 'Euandrus, Romanae conditor arcis.'

in Livy.[1] It is an anachronism if Livy says that Camillus was called the second 'conditor' of Rome, or if Plutarch's Roman source applies the same term to Marius and Cicero.[2] But Caesar only experimented with this term; ultimately he adopted another, 'parens patriae'.[3] Augustus was no 'conditor' either, but 'parens patriae' or 'pater patriae', though officially not before 2 B.C.[4] He was κτίστης in many places in the East,[5] and so were Tiberius, Nero, and Domitian.[6] It was Hadrian who brought Caesar's ideas to new life. He renewed the games at the Parilia of A.D. 121,[7] issued coins at Rome with the legend 'Romulo conditori',[8] and was called outside Rome κτίστης and 'conditor' more often than anyone before or after him.[9]

5. THE PARILIA

Now to the festival of 45. We have seen that Caesar had long been prepared for the role of a new Romulus; that is why the coincidence of the festival and the arrival of the news about the victory was manipulated. The day began with the celebration of the Parilia proper, an archaic festival of the shepherds.[10] Some of its rites are known, but not in whose honour they were performed: not in honour of Pales, as was asserted in antiquity and long believed by modern scholars. The ritual must have received new features when the day became the anniversary

---

[1] Livy 5. 53. 8: 'casa illa conditoris est nostri'; 7. 30. 19: 'conditorum parentium deorum immortalium numero nobis eritis'; 10. 23. 12; 10. 27. 9. Romulus' statue in the Forum Augusti was inscribed: 'Ro[mulo] M[artis f(ilio)] ur[bis conditori]': Degrassi, Scritti 217.

[2] Livy 5. 49. 7; 7. 1. 10; Plut. Mar. 27. 9; Cic. 22. 5.

[3] See below, pp. 200 ff. 'Parens' and 'conditor' were later interchangeable, Quintil. 3. 7. 26: 'laudantur autem urbes similiter atque homines. nam pro parente est conditor'; Vittinghoff 52.

[4] Mon. Anc. 35. 1; Suet. Aug. 58. 2. He was called 'parens' at Bononia (ILS 5674), 'parens coloniae' at Iader in Dalmatia (ILS 5336); an exception is ILS 6773 (after his death): 'Divo Augusto conditori Siccenses.'

[5] Pompey was called κτίστης in 63 B.C. at Mytilene (Syll. 751 f.; above, p. 183. 6; ibid. 753 Theophanes κτίστης δεύτερος τῆς πατρίδος), which suggests that Caesar was the next and Augustus followed him. Augustus was called κτίστης at Nicopolis (Head, HN 321), Clazomenae (ibid. 569), Teos (BMC Ionia 319), etc., see Prehn, RE 11. 2086. But the title was far from general: the heading 'Augustus as κτίστης' in Grant, From Imperium to Auctoritas, 356, is misleading, and the title 'κτίστης τῆς οἰκουμένης' wrong (this is not found before Trajan and Hadrian).

[6] Or. gr. 471 (Tiberius): κτίστην ἐνὶ καιρῷ δώδεκα πόλεων (translated, CIL 3. 7096, 'conditor . . .'); Head, HN 653. On Nero and Domitian see Prehn, l.c.

[7] Mattingly 3. 282; 422 f.: '. . . Nat(ali) Urb(is) P(arilibus) Cir(censes) con(stituti)'; cf. Athen. 8. 361 F; Strack, op. cit. 2. 103 f.

[8] Mattingly 3. 306; 329 f.; 442 f.; Strack, op. cit. 2. 181.

[9] CIL 3. 3279; ILS 6779; Syll. 839; AE 1938. 140, etc.: see the list in Prehn, l.c.

[10] Paul. 222 M. (248 L.); Ov. F. 4. 721 ff.; 775 ff.; Dion. Hal. 1. 88. 3, etc.; Wissowa 199 f.; Latte 87 f.; Degrassi 443 ff.

of Rome's foundation. It is not known when this happened; the pre-Julian Calendar of Antium already has the entry 'Roma condita', but the anniversary may have been much older, perhaps as old as the belief in Romulus' apotheosis. Its own part in the ritual was no doubt an offering in honour of Romulus-Quirinus on the Quirinal.[1] Now a further offering in Caesar's honour must have been made, in addition to the supplications which began on that day and were to last for fifty days.[2]

The games followed, which had hitherto been no part of the Parilia. People wore wreaths in Caesar's honour,[3] and these were retained at the Parilia after the Caesarian part of the festival lapsed.[4] The games were introduced, as usual, by a procession of the gods from the Capitol to the Circus, among these an ivory statue of Caesar in the company of Romulus-Quirinus.[5] It was dressed in the triumphal garb and was to be kept in the *cella* of Iuppiter Capitolinus.[6] We have already connected the triumphal garb with the imperatorial privileges and also referred to the precedent of the elder Scipio.[7] Here some further comment about the statue is needed. It was a startling honour: Caesar received the privilege of the gods. It was not so startling in Greece: the statue of Philip was carried in the procession of the Twelve Gods, later probably also that of Alexander.[8] Caesar's statue was carried in a festival instituted in his honour. Attendants carried it on a hand-barrow, like the images of the gods,[9] and placed it in the Circus on the *pulvinar*, the couch of the gods.[10] This happened again in July during the *ludi Victoriae Caesaris*, with the difference that this time the procession was led by Victoria, immediately followed by the statue of Caesar.[11] The procession in the

---

[1] See above, p. 177.   [2] See above, p. 64.

[3] Cic. *Att.* 14. 14. 1; 14. 19. 3 (below, p. 367. 5). The citizens of Priene and Samothrace were wreathed at an annual festival in honour of Lysimachus, *Or. gr.* 11; *Syll.* 372; Nilsson 2. 153.

[4] *F. Caer.*: 'Parilia. Roma condita. Feriae coronatis omnibus'; the same in the *F. Esqu.*, both Augustan calendars (Degrassi 443 ff.).

[5] Dio 43. 45. 2; Cic. *Att.* 13. 28. 3 (above, p. 175. 3). Gelzer 285 dates this decree in May, which was the date of Cicero's letter; but Cicero's words clearly refer to the procession.

[6] These details are provided by the evidence concerning Scipio.   [7] See above, p. 110.

[8] Diod. 16. 92; Aelian, *v.h.* 5. 12; cf. *HTR* 50 (1957), 235. 143. It was continued under the Ptolemaic kings, Callixeinus, *FGrHist.* 627 F 2 (p. 175. 17); cf. also *Or. gr.* 332. 27.

[9] Such barrows, *fercula*, were frequent in funeral (Serv. *Aen.* 6. 861) and triumphal processions (Ryberg 99 ff.; 146 f., etc.; pls. 31 f.; 51–5): Augustus' statue at his funeral (Dio 56. 34. 1), statue of Victoria (on a sarcophagus at S. Lorenzo: *Ann. dell'Ist.* (1839), pl. N 1; Matz–Duhn, *Ant. Bildw.* no. 2245), of Cybele (Tillyard, *JRS* 7 (1917), pl. 8; Cumont, *Rel. or.* 53, fig. 3).

[10] This is an inference partly from Scipio (Val. Max. 4. 1. 6: 'voluerunt imaginem eius Capitolinis pulvinaribus adplicare', partly from the identical honour of 44 (below, p. 367).

[11] Cic. *Att.* 13. 44. 1 (20/21 July 45): 'acerba pompa . . . populum vero praeclarum, quod propter malum vicinum ne Victoriae quidem ploditur!' (above, p. 111).

company of Quirinus was repeated at the Parilia of 44, five weeks after the murder,[1] but apparently never again. And yet Caesar's precedent did not disappear completely. Although Augustus' statue was never carried in the *pompa circensis*, those of Germanicus and Britannicus were.[2] But it had become an honour for the dead, not a divine honour.

The games proper need not have had any unusual features. Many games were instituted to celebrate a victory; such was the origin of the *ludi Magni* or *Romani*, of the *ludi Apollinares* of 212 B.C., of the *ludi Victoriae* of Sulla in 81 B.C. and of Caesar's own *ludi Veneris Genetricis*, also called *ludi Victoriae Caesaris*, in 46 B.C.[3] But whereas these games were held in honour of the gods, Iuppiter, Apollo, Venus, and Victoria, those of the Parilia were held in honour of Caesar. It was a Greek custom to hold games for their rulers, later in honour of the Dea Roma and of Roman generals,[4] no doubt also of Caesar. At Rome it had not been done before; later the Augustalia followed in 19 B.C.

6. *DEUS INVICTUS*

It was soon after the festival that Caesar's statue was set up in the temple of Quirinus with the inscription 'Deo Invicto'. Cicero referred to it in two letters written after the middle of May 45.[5] This was not, like the ivory statue in the Capitoline temple, to be carried in the *pompa circensis*, and therefore requires some comment. It was the Greeks who used to set up the statue of a king or a general in a temple: through this association he became a σύνναος θεός,[6] Marcellus, for instance, in the temple of Athena at Lindos;[7] Titus Flamininus will have received such a place in many temples. At Rome, as we have seen, statues of distinguished men had long been allowed to stand in public places, though not in temples.[8] But in 181, when dedicating the temple of Pietas vowed by his father, M'. Acilius Glabrio set up a gilded equestrian statue of his father there.[9] This was clearly an act of filial piety

---

[1] Dio 45. 6. 4 (below, p. 367. 3); Cic. *Att.* 14. 14. 1; 14. 19. 3 (below, p. 367. 5).

[2] Tac. *A.* 2. 83. 2: 'ludos circenses eburna effigies (of Germanicus) praeiret'; Suet. *Tit.* 2: 'statuam ei (= Britannicus) auream in Palatio posuit et alteram ex ebore equestrem, quae circensi pompa hodieque praefertur, dedicavit prosecutusque est.'

[3] See above, p. 88.   [4] See below, p. 314.

[5] Dio 43. 45. 3; Cic. *Att.* 12. 45. 3(2); 13. 28. 3 (above, p. 175. 3).

[6] Nock, *HSCP* 41 (1930), 3 ff.; e.g. Attalus III's statue was set up in the temple of Asclepius Soter in Pergamum, ἵνα ᾖ σύνναος τῷ θεῷ, *Or. gr.* 332. 7; v. Domaszewski, *Abh.* 193; Nock 22; Habicht 142. 17; id. *Die Inschriften des Asklepieions* (1969), 3.

[7] Posid., *FGrHist.* 87 F 44 = Plut. *Marc.* 30. 7.

[8] See above, pp. 40 f.

[9] Livy 40. 34. 5 f.; Val. Max. 2. 5. 1; below, p. 250.

and did not imply cult. Again, Cato Censorius was rewarded by the
Roman people with a statue in the temple of Salus for having saved the
State from decline during his censorship through his concern for discipline and moral standards.[1] It is not known when this was done,
whether soon after his censorship (184 B.C.) or after his death (149 B.C.),
at a time when another member of the family had become influential.
That temple was chosen intentionally: not because the Gens Porcia had
any special relationship to Salus—as far as is known, it had not—but
probably because it was appropriate that he should be so honoured in
the temple of the goddess whose concern was the welfare of the Roman
people. However, he certainly did not have any share in the cult as
Caesar had later.[2] Next, Ap. Claudius Pulcher (*cos.* 79) dedicated the
portraits of his ancestors reproduced on shields (*imago clipeata*) in the
temple of Bellona, which Ap. Claudius Caecus (*cos.* 296) had vowed
and built at the beginning of the third century B.C.[3] Here again there
is no question of cult; it was rather a reproduction in metal of the ancestral images, which were kept in the Atrium of the Claudii.[4] Thus all
this evidence is not really relevant. But there were exceptions. We shall
see later that there were old cults of distinguished ancestors with statues,
even with shrines.[5] Nonetheless these are not relevant either, because
they were private cults and were not lasting. Scipio was among these;
but he also had many statues in public places.[6] The ivory statue in
the Capitoline temple excepted, there is no evidence for his statue in
a temple. And yet it may have existed; if it did, it would have been
the precedent for Cato's statue, although the latter was not intended
to have a share in the cult.[7] It would also have been the Roman precedent for Caesar's statue in the temple of Quirinus, even if it had lost
its religious significance long before. The real precedent for Caesar was
of course the practice of the Greeks. This new privilege was soon further
extended. It was decreed in the same or following year that his statues
should stand in all temples of Rome and Italy;[8] we know of a statue in

---

[1] Plut. *Cato mai.* 19. 4; cf. Pliny 34. 19 (Accius' statue in the temple of the Camenae).

[2] See above, p. 171.

[3] Pliny 35. 12; Livy 10. 19. 17; Ov. *F.* 6. 199 ff.; Vessberg, op. cit. 78 f.; W. H. Gross,
Convivium . . . K. Ziegler (1954), 67 ff.

[4] Mommsen, *StR* 1. 448. 4.

[5] See below, pp. 293 ff.

[6] Enn. *V.* 1 V.; Livy 38. 56. 12; above, p. 36.

[7] They both had the further privilege that their masks, which were taken to the funerals of
members of their families, were not kept at home, but Scipio's in the Capitoline temple,
Cato's in the Curia, Val. Max. 8. 15. 1 f.; *vir. ill.* 47. 9; Fronto, p. 129 N. (123 v. d. H.);
Mommsen, *Röm. Forsch.* 2. 503. 164.

[8] App. *BC* 2. 106. 440 (45 B.C.); Dio 44. 4. 4 (44 B.C.): below, p. 309. 3.

the temple of Venus Genetrix,[1] but it may have been set up after his death. Octavian's statues stood in the temples of the Italian cities from 36 B.C.[2] but not in Rome; he resisted whenever that was attempted.[3]

The dedication 'Deo Invicto' indicated that Caesar was the successor of Alexander, the prototype of all 'invincible' generals,[4] whose statue at Athens bore the same inscription.[5] Alexander's fame had reached Rome long before Caesar. Scipio was already called 'Invictus', perhaps even so inscribed on a statue, just as a dedication of his grandson included the words 'invictissimus imperator';[6] Pompey, a conscious imitator of Alexander, was called by Cicero 'invictissimus civis' and 'victor omnium gentium'.[7] Caesar was often compared with Alexander,[8] and it was about the time of the inscription that Cicero was working on his memorandum about government for Caesar, intentionally following the example of similar works written by Aristotle and Theopompus for Alexander.[9] The earlier Roman emulators of Alexander were called invincible, Caesar alone the invincible god.

This dedication does not fit well into the whole picture. The statue of a new 'Alexander' is not a suitable offering for the temple of Quirinus, nor is the festival of the foundation of Rome the right time for it. We remember that the original intention was that the statue should stand in the temple of Salus;[10] the change was necessary because of the 'co-incidence'. The inscription was even more objectionable than the 'demigod' of the preceding year. And the other statue in the procession of the gods was a symbol of divinity too. It was done in Caesar's absence and presumably without his approval. He could erase the inscription of 46, but he could not do it this time; the statue stood in a temple and was thus protected.

7. ROMA RESURGENS

This new version of the Parilia was not an episode without precedent or consequence. It was to be a new beginning of Rome, based

---

[1] Dio 45. 7. 1 (below, pp. 363. 5; 371. 5).

[2] App. BC 5. 132. 546; L. R. Taylor, TAPA 51 (1920), 116 ff.

[3] Dio 53. 27. 3; Suet. Aug. 52; for Tiberius see Suet. Tib. 26. 1.

[4] Plut. Alex. 14. 7; Tarn, Alexander the Great 2. 338 ff.; cf. HTR 50 (1957), 212 ff.

[5] Hyperid. or. 1, col. 32. 3: στῆσαι εἰκόνα Ἀλεξάνδρου βασιλέως τοῦ Ἀνικήτου Θεοῦ; cf. Dinarch. or. 1. 94: οὐ δεῖ τὸν δῆμον ἀμφισβητεῖν τῶν ἐν τῷ οὐρανῷ τιμῶν Ἀλεξάνδρῳ.

[6] Enn. V. 3 V.; Cic. Verr. 4. 82; above, p. 92.

[7] Cic. Pis. 16; 34; above, p. 38. 12.

[8] App. BC 2. 149–54; Stat. Silv. 1. 1. 86 (above, p. 87. 1); Meyer, Caesars Monarchie 472 ff. Cf. also [Sen.] Oct. 500: (Caesar) invictus acie, gentium domitor, Iovi / aequatus.

[9] Cic. Att. 12. 40; 13. 28. 3, with explicit reference to Alexander; above, p. 182.

[10] See above, p. 171.

on Caesar's rule and legislation. The precedent was Cicero's. He claimed that the Nones of December 63, when the Senate decided to take action against the Catilinarians, was to be the new birthday of Rome: it received a new life on that day.[1] He managed to give a symbolic significance to the Nones of December through endless repetition;[2] it even inspired the 'Ides of March'. The conspirators wanted their Ides to become the new birthday of Rome;[3] and Brutus complained that Cicero spoke far more of his Nones than they did of their Ides.[4] For a while Cicero had been planning another era, based on the death of his old enemy, Clodius, 18 January 52; he used it for dating for a year or so[5] and then dropped it. It is difficult to say how serious he was about it, but it seems certain that it influenced the plans about the Ides of March.

There was a great deal of loose talk of such rebirths,[6] based on some religious rituals on the one hand[7] and on the double birthday of the Hellenistic rulers on the other, the day of their physical birth and that of their accession.[8] Lesser mortals too could claim the beginning of a new life through some good news or benefaction. Cicero himself claimed such a new birthday, 4 August 57 B.C., when the Senate granted him his return from exile: he was now reborn as a statesman.[9] It is of course

---

[1] Cic. *Cat.* 3. 2: 'si non minus nobis iucundi atque inlustres sunt ii dies quibus conservamur quam illi quibus nascimur, quod salutis certa laetitia est, nascendi incerta condicio, et quod sine sensu nascimur, cum voluptate servamur'; *Flacc.* 102 (59 B.C.): 'o Nonae illae Decembres, quae me consule fuistis! quem ego diem vere natalem huius urbis aut certe salutarem appellare possum'; *de cons.*, *FPL* frg. 17 M.: 'o fortunatam natam me consule Romam!' (cf. Hor. *epist.* 2. 1. 256; W. Allen jr., *TAPA* 87 (1956), 130 ff. with bibliography). The same achievement was then ascribed to Camillus, Livy 6. 1. 3: 'clariora deinceps certioraque ab secunda origine velut ab stirpibus laetius feraciusque renatae urbis gesta domi militiaeque exponentur.'

[2] Cic. *Att.* 1. 19. 6 (March 60): 'ego autem ut semel Nonarum illarum Decembrium iunctam invidia ac multorum inimicitiis eximiam quandam atque immortalem gloriam consecutus sum'; *p. red. sen.* 12; *Planc.* 90; *fam.* 1. 9. 12; Dio 46. 21. 4.

[3] See below, p. 190.

[4] Cic. *ad Brut.* 25 (1. 17). 1 (Brutus to Atticus, June 43): 'non omnibus horis iactamus Idus Martias similiter atque ille Nonas Decembres suas in ore habet.'

[5] Cic. *Mil.* 98; *Att.* 5. 13. 1; 6. 1. 26; Drumann 2. 553 f.; M. Maclaren, *AJP* 87 (1966), 198 f.

[6] Plaut. *Capt.* 891: 'iterum gnatus videor, si vera autumas'; *Poen.* 1077: 'iterum mihi gnatus videor, quom te repperi'; Sall. *hist.* 2. 47. 3: 'si parricida vostri sum et bis genitus (on return from exile, 82 B.C.) hic deos Penatis meos patriamque . . . vilia habeo'; *B. Afr.* 90. 3: 'se eo demum die natos praedicantes laeti gratias agunt Caesari.'

[7] Jos. *AJ* 3. 16; Leisegang, *RE* 18. 2. 147; Wagenvoort, *Studies in Roman Literature* (1956), 132 ff.

[8] *Or. gr.* 56. 6; 90. 47; 383. 84; Iustin 37. 2. 1; Jos. *AJ* 15. 11. 6 (the Persian kings: Hdt. 1. 131. 1; 9. 110. 2); W. Schmidt, *Geburtstag im Altert.* 75 f.; Habicht 156; cf. *PBSR* 19 (1951), 136.

[9] Cic. *p. red. sen.* 27: 'ille dies, quem P. Lentulus mihi . . . natalem constituit'; *Att.* 3. 20. 1 (Thessalonica, Oct. 58): 'diemque natalem reditus mei cura ut in tuis aedibus . . . agam

a different proposition to talk of the rebirth of a city. But it was possible, since cities like human beings celebrated their birthday, as Rome did probably long before the time of Cicero.[1] But it was Cicero who first spoke of Rome's rebirth and its new birthday, though he may have known some Greek precedents. The numerous new κτίσται must have been celebrated somehow.

What Caesar's Parilia might have become can only vaguely be indicated with the help of what followed. After the murder Dolabella suggested that the birthday of Rome should be transferred to the Ides of March.[2] He did not succeed; in the end they were not called Parilia but Parricidium,[3] chosen no doubt as an intentional riposte, which was at the same time a convenient allusion to Caesar's title as 'pater patriae'; and it contained an implication that the liberators were just 'parricidae'.[4] On its fourth anniversary in 40 B.C. many senators and knights were slaughtered at the altars set up in Caesar's honour at Perusia.[5]

Augustus followed. He wanted, or others wanted him, to assume the name Romulus in 27 B.C. but he became 'Augustus' instead.[6] His rule dated from 7 January 43 when he first received an official position at Rome, or, as the colonists of Narbo put it, 'quo die imperium orbis terrarum auspicatus est'.[7] Its anniversary became a public festival. His rule was a new beginning, a new golden age, when, as Vergil once put it, Quirinus would be the lawgiver again together with his brother Remus.[8]

tecum et cum meis' (cf. Shackleton Bailey ad loc.); 4. 1. 8 (Sept. 57): 'alterius vitae quoddam initium ordimur'; *p. red. Quir.* 5: 'a parentibus . . . parvus sum procreatus, a vobis natus sum consularis'; *Att.* 6. 6. 4 (Rhodes, Aug. 50): 'amicorum litterae me ad triumphum vocant, rem a nobis . . . propter hanc παλιγγενεσίαν nostram non neglegendam'; L. Bösing, *Mus. Helv.* 25 (1968), 172.

[1] Accordingly cities too had their horoscopes, Seleucia (App. *Syr.* 58. 300 f.), Rome (by Tarutius Firmanus: Cic. *div.* 2. 98; Plut. *Rom.* 12. 2), even the world (Macrob. *Somn.* 1. 21. 23; Firmic. 3. 1. 1); cf. *CCAG* 9. 2. 176 f. (with further evidence and bibliography).

[2] App. *BC* 2. 122. 511: εἰσὶ δ' οἳ καὶ λέγουσιν αὐτὸν εἰσηγήσασθαι τὴν ἡμέραν θέσθαι τῇ πόλει γενέθλιον; 3. 35. 141: τὴν ἡμέραν τοῦ φόνου γενέθλιον τῇ πόλει τιθέμενος.

[3] Suet. *Caes.* 88 (below, p. 398. 1); Dio 47. 19. 1 (42 B.C.); Flor. 2. 17. 1; Val. Max. 1. 8. 8; cf. *F. Ost.* (Degrassi, *Inscr. It.* 13. 1. 183): 'Caesar parens patriae occisus.'

[4] Cic. *fam.* 12. 3. 1 (below, p. 385. 6). Cicero in turn accused Caesar of 'parricidium patriae' (an expression coined earlier: Cic. *Sulla* 6), *off.* 3. 83: 'potest . . . cuiquam esse utile . . . parricidium patriae, quamvis is (Caes.) qui se eo obstrinxerit, ab oppressis civibus parens nominetur?' *Phil.* 2. 17; 2. 31; 13. 23; cf. also *Verr.* 5. 170; *Cat.* 1. 29; 33; *Vatin.* 35, etc.

[5] Suet. *Aug.* 15 (below, p. 398. 9); Dio 48. 14. 4; Sen. *clem.* 1. 11. 1; Drumann 1. 475 ff.; below, pp. 398 f.

[6] Suet. *Aug.* 7. 2; Dio 53. 16. 7; Flor. 4. 12. 66; Serv. *Aen.* 1. 292.

[7] *ILS* 112 = E.-J. 100 (A.D. 12/13); *Fer. Cum., ILS* 108 (c. A.D. 4): 'eo die Caesar primum fasces sumpsit, supplicatio Iovi Sempiterno'; Pliny 11. 190.

[8] Verg. *Aen.* 1. 292: 'Remo cum fratre Quirinus / iura dabunt'; Mommsen, *StR* 2. 745. 2; *Ges. Schr.* 4. 18; cf. *Georg.* 3. 27: 'victoris arma Quirini'.

Later the accession of the emperors was often compared with the beginning of a new golden age, of Caligula,[1] Nero,[2] Domitian.[3] Caligula
even wanted to call the day of his accession, 18 March 37, Parilia.[4]
This brings us back to Caesar. It is clear that a new development began
with the Parilia of 45. But it is impossible to make conjectures about
the details with the help of later events. Nevertheless, the action of
Caligula, who liked to adopt ideas and actions of Caesar, may suggest
that Caesar too believed that Rome would be reborn under his rule.[5]

8. *SAECULUM IULIUM*

This title is suggested by a proposal made in the Senate after the
death of Augustus: the period from the day of his birth to that of his
death should be called 'saeculum Augustum' and so recorded in the
Calendar,[6] which, however, was not done. There was no 'saeculum
Iulium' either, and this could not of course have been proposed after
the Ides of March. And yet, after having dealt with the rebirth of Rome,
one is bound to ask the question whether the closely related idea
of a coming millennium was not propagated under Caesar. It must be
said and stressed at once that there is no explicit evidence. But there
are some curious precedents of the age of Sulla and later, important
facts of Caesar's own time, and an outbreak of strong millennial speculations immediately after his death, all culminating in Augustus' *ludi
saeculares* of 17 B.C. These facts justify an examination of the question,
which must be preceded by a short history of the idea of the *saeculum*.

It has been a source of great confusion in modern research that we
so readily assume that *saeculum* meant 'century' from the beginning.[7]
It did not. In Plautus and Terence,[8] and again in Lucretius,[9] who often
uses it, it means just 'generation', *genus*, Greek γενεά. Censorinus, an

---

[1] *Syll.* 797 (Assus) : . . . ὡς ἂν τοῦ ἡδίστου ἀνθρώποις αἰῶνος νῦν ἐνεστῶτος.

[2] Sen. *Apocol.* 4. 9: 'aurea formoso descendunt saecula filo'; Calp. Sic. *Ecl.* 1. 42: 'aurea secura cum pace renascitur aetas'; 63 ff.; Sauter, *Der röm. Kaiserkult bei Martial u. Statius* 20.

[3] Stat. *Silv.* 1. 6. 39: 'i, nunc saecula compara, Vetustas, / antiqui Iovis aureumque tem-pus'; Mart. 5. 19. 1 f.; 8. 55. 1 f.; Sauter, op. cit. 21.

[4] Suet. *Cal.* 16. 4: 'decretum . . . ut dies quo cepisset imperium Parilia vocaretur velut argumentum rursus conditae urbis'; cf. the annual sacrifice of the Arvals, 'quod hoc die . . . a senatu imperator appellatus est', Henzen, *AFA* 63; Pasoli, *Acta fratr. Arv.* (1950), 81.

[5] That Caligula liked to adopt Caesarian plans is a hypothesis which will be supported by further relevant evidence, see below, pp. 217; 241; 281; 283; 287; 325; 336; 382.

[6] Suet. *Aug.* 100. 3; cf. Hor. *c.* 4. 15. 4: 'tua, Caesar, aetas'.

[7] Cf. Nilsson's valuable discussion of the *ludi saeculares*, *RE* IA. 1696 ff., with full documenta-tion and bibliography. Only a few problems are relevant here, and even these must be treated as briefly as possible.

[8] Plaut. *Trin.* 283; *Mil.* 1079; Ter. *Ad.* 304; *Eun.* 246.   [9] Lucr. 1. 20; 1. 467; 5. 791.

intelligent writer of the third century A.D., who depends on a good antiquarian, no doubt Varro, first gives a correct definition: *saeculum* is the span of human life.[1] He then records its use by the Etruscans to measure history: a *saeculum* begins with the foundation of cities and communities and ends with the death of the eldest of those men whose birth coincided with the foundation. Then another *saeculum* begins and lasts as long as the oldest man of the new period is alive, and so forth. The end of a *saeculum* is announced by special portents, which are recorded in the ritual books of the *haruspices*. The Etruscans were granted ten *saecula*, after which their rule would come to an end.[2] This is a combination of two schemes. One was about the four ages of the world, first recorded by Hesiod, beginning with peace and happiness on earth;[3] the other about the four empires, one following the other, the Assyrians, Medes, Persians, and Greeks. Later the place of the Greeks was given to the Macedonians, and from the second century B.C. onwards the last empire was that of the Romans.[4] Claims and counterclaims followed, also prophecies announcing that the Roman empire would perish as the others had perished before.[5]

The Etruscan doctrine became influential at Rome in two forms: one was more speculative, at first without any lasting consequence, the other became the basis of a new festival. The former is first found in the age of Sulla. A great number of portents were recorded in 88 B.C., among them the sound of a trumpet from heaven. The Senate consulted the *haruspices*, who explained that those portents announced the beginning of a new *saeculum* and with it the Civil War.[6] In 65 frightening portents occurred again, and the *haruspices* declared that this time the portents indicated not just the end of a *saeculum* but the end of Rome altogether unless the gods intervened.[7] Divine intervention meant the appearance of an exceptional man, which was a new feature of the saecular doctrine, though an old theme elsewhere. The year before, Cicero recommended Pompey as such a heaven-sent man for the war against Mithridates, and even for the task of finishing all wars.[8] In 63

---

[1] Censor. 17. 2: 'saeculum est spatium vitae humanae longissimum partu et morte definitum.'   [2] Censor. 17. 5 f.   [3] Hes. *Erg.* 109 ff.

[4] Hdt. 1. 95; 130; Diod. 2. 21. 8; 28. 8; 32. 5–33. 6; *Or. Sib.* 3. 158 ff.; Lycophr. 1229; Vell. 1. 6; Swain, *CP* 35 (1940), 1 ff.

[5] Phleg. Mirab. 3 (*FGrHist.* 257 F 36); Daniel 2. 44; 7. 27; Hystasp. frg. 13 ff. (Bidez–Cumont).   [6] Plut. *Sulla* 7. 7.

[7] Cic. *Cat.* 3. 19: 'haruspices ... totius urbis atque imperi occasum appropinquare dixerunt, nisi di ... fata ipsa flexissent.'

[8] Cic. *de imp.* 41: 'omnes ... Cn. Pompeium sicut aliquem non ex hac urbe missum, sed de caelo delapsum intuentur'; 42: 'ad omnia nostrae memoriae bella conficienda divino quodam consilio natus.'

P. Cornelius Lentulus Sura (*cos.* 71) asserted, with reference to earlier saecular portents and their interpretation by the *haruspices*, that he too was such a man of destiny, the third Cornelius of an earlier prophecy.[1] Cicero in turn tried hard to interpret the signs of his consulate as pointing to himself and Pompey as the saviours of Rome.[2] The next saecular portents concerned Caesar and his age and will be discussed presently.

The other and earlier Roman version of the Etruscan doctrine was the sequence of the Roman *saecula* as constructed by Roman historians. They were all baseless with one exception. Varro and Verrius Flaccus recorded that in 249 B.C. during the First Punic War grave portents occurred, the *libri Sibyllini* were consulted, and it was decided to institute the *ludi Tarentini* on the Campus Martius in honour of Dis pater and Proserpina, and to repeat them every hundred years.[3] This was clearly a combination of the Etruscan doctrine with the traditional Greek advice to institute cultic performances. The games were also called, because of their periodic performance, 'ludi saeculares' and were in fact repeated in 146 though not, as the new meaning of *saeculum*, 'century', would have demanded, in 149 B.C.[4] It was the time when Scipio Aemilianus was victorious and destroyed Carthage.

The next games were due in 49 or 46 B.C., and this brings us to Caesar. But first we turn to the saecular portents of his age. Those which occurred after his death and are often discussed were not the first. One would expect such portents for the beginning of the Civil War and in fact one can be found among the prodigies recorded by Dio for 49 B.C. Such lists of prodigies are frequent and in general without any particular significance. But here the list includes an event which in normal circumstances was not a prodigy at all: M. Perperna (*cos.* 92), the last man of his generation, died, which pointed, so it was explained, to the beginning of a new era.[5] It was then a saecular portent, as envisaged by the Etruscan doctrine, and, as we shall see presently, occurred again after Caesar's death in the case of Vulcanius and an anonymous *haruspex*. What Perperna's death was further supposed to

[1] Cic. *Cat.* 3. 9: 'Lentulum autem sibi confirmasse ex fatis Sibyllinis haruspicumque responsis se esse tertium illum Cornelium, ad quem regnum huius urbis atque imperium pervenire esset necesse; Cinnam ante se et Sullam fuisse. eundemque dixisse fatalem hunc annum esse ad interitum huius urbis atque imperi, qui esset annus decimus post virginum absolutionem, post Capitoli autem incensionem vicesimus'; 4. 2; above, p. 98. 1.

[2] Cic. *Cat.* 3. 26: 'unoque tempore ... duos cives exstitisse, quorum alter finis vestri imperi non terrae sed caeli regionibus terminaret, alter huius imperi domicilium sedesque servaret.'

[3] Censor. 17. 8; Ps.-Acro ad Hor. *c.s.*   [4] Censor. 17. 11; Livy, *Per.* 49 (for 149).

[5] Dio 41. 14. 5: ὁ Περπέρνας ... ἀπέθανεν ... τελευταῖος πάντων τῶν ἐν τῇ τιμητείᾳ αὐτοῦ βουλευσάντων, καὶ ἐδόκει καὶ τοῦτό τι νεοχμώσειν.

portend is a matter of speculation, certainly nothing good: the new *saeculum* would be the age of civil war. It is possible that the burning of the temple of Quirinus, which appeared in the same list of prodigies, belonged to the same theme:[1] we have assumed that it indicated that Pompey's campaign threatened Rome with destruction. In contrast to these portents of gloom there must have been pro-Caesarian prophecies, especially when the Civil War took a turn in his favour. The prodigy of his birth which indicated that he was to be the master of the world,[2] the man of the new *saeculum*, may have been produced at that time. It was said about the same time that Rome had received new life under him, that he was its new founder.[3] We have seen that this claim was often made before and after him. We now add a further instance, that of Numa. Numa was said to have been born on the day when Rome was founded,[4] a stray notice but of particular significance. It can only be part of a wider issue which, in accordance with the Etruscan doctrine, let the *saecula* of Rome begin with its foundation and made Numa the first child of this first *saeculum*. It was in accordance with the same doctrine, and in contrast to Augustus and his republican predecessors, that Claudius, an expert in the Etruscan discipline, calculated the *saecula* of Rome from its foundation and celebrated his saecular games on its 800th anniversary in A.D. 47.[5] There must have been more about the *saeculum* of Numa than we can trace. He too was called a new founder,[6] and it is possible that his example influenced the speculations about the *saeculum Iulium*. This is certain for the *saeculum Augustum*. The *saeculum* of Numa lasted 76 years, consisting of 37 of the rule of Romulus and 39 of his own.[7] It was probably due to the coincidence that Augustus too lived 76 years that the term *saeculum Augustum* was suggested in the Senate. Needless to say, this suggestion could only have been made because, the coincidence apart, the idea of a *saeculum* of Numa as well as of Augustus was popular at that time. This in turn lends additional support to our conjectures about a *saeculum Iulium*. Finally further evidence about the saecular doctrine is provided by the events after Caesar's death. A new portent, a comet, appeared

[1] Dio 41. 14. 3 (above, p. 178. 7).

[2] Serv. *Aen.* 6. 798; above, p. 21. 6.   [3] See above, pp. 188 ff.

[4] Plut. *Numa* 3. 6: ἡμέρᾳ δὲ γεγονὼς κατὰ δή τινα θείαν τύχην ἐν ᾗ τὴν ῾Ρώμην ἔκτισαν οἱ περὶ ῾Ρωμύλον; Dio 1, frg. 6. 5 (pp. 13 f. B.).

[5] Tac. *A.* 11. 11. 1; Suet. *Claud.* 21. 2.

[6] Livy 1. 19. 1: 'urbem novam, conditam vi et armis, iure eam legibusque ac moribus de integro condere parat'; Liebeschütz, *JRS* 57 (1967), 48.

[7] Cic. *rep.* 2. 17; 27 (Polybius). According to Livy 1. 21. 6 and Plut. *Numa* 21. 7 Numa lived 80 years.

in July 44 at the *ludi Victoriae Caesaris*. The *haruspex* Vulcanius declared it to be the sign of the end of the ninth and of the beginning of the tenth *saeculum*. But because he revealed a secret against the will of the gods he would die, and in fact he died there and then.[1] We must of course correct his argument: he died because he was the last member of his generation, of the past *saeculum*. A similar story is reported for the following year, the time of the triumvirate with its proscriptions. Many fearful signs were observed and the *haruspices* consulted; the oldest of them, whose name is not given, said that the age of the kings would return and all would be slaves except himself, because he would, and did immediately, die.[2] It is possible that this prophecy was first made for Caesar's rule but in a favourable sense, comparable to the birth-omen, which announced his mastery of the world.

We return to the *ludi saeculares* which were due in 49 or 46 and were not held in spite of the younger Scipio's precedent, which must have attracted the attention of Caesar. But they were not forgotten: this is clearly a safe inference from all the portents and prophecies which we have just surveyed. It may therefore be conjectured that the games were in fact planned but were postponed, perhaps until the end of the Parthian campaign. Such a plan would in fact go well with the other plan to bring about a regeneration of Rome, for which we have found more tangible evidence.[3]

The conjecture is moreover almost a necessity. It alone accounts satisfactorily for the later development. It might be asserted that without Caesar's saecular role Vergil could not have written his *Fourth Eclogue*, nor could the belief have grown up that Augustus was the man of the new *saeculum*, nor the decision been taken to renew the *ludi saeculares* in 17 B.C. The conjecture receives further support from Vulcanius and the anonymous *haruspex*, whose hostile prophecies, as we have seen, were probably preceded by a favourable one. The *Cumaeum carmen*, a poem by an anonymous Greek who wrote under the guise of the Sibyl of Cumae and combined Greek and Etruscan doctrines about the ages of the world, is equally relevant. He again spoke of ten *saecula*, each with a divine ruler and a characteristic metal, reminiscent of the

---

[1] Serv. Dan. *Ecl.* 9. 46: 'Vulcanius aruspex in contione dixit cometen esse, qui significaret exitum noni saeculi et ingressum decimi; sed quod invitis diis secreta rerum pronuntiaret, statim se esse moriturum: et nondum finita oratione in ipsa contione concidit'; below, pp. 370 f.; 379. Bidez–Cumont, *Les Mages hellénisés* 1. 234 f. (on divine secrets).

[2] App. *BC* 4. 4. 15: ἡ μὲν βουλὴ θύτας καὶ μάντεις συνῆγεν ἀπὸ Τυρρηνίας· καὶ ὁ πρεσβύτατος αὐτῶν, τὰς πάλαι βασιλείας ἐπανήξειν εἰπὼν καὶ δουλεύσειν ἅπαντας χωρὶς ἑαυτοῦ μόνου, τὸ στόμα κατέσχε καὶ τὸ πνεῦμα, ἕως ἀπέθανεν.

[3] See above, pp. 181 ff.; 188 ff.

ages of Hesiod; the last, the tenth, *saeculum* was that of the Sol.[1] This
poem was used by Vergil in his *Fourth Eclogue* to announce a new *saeculum*
for Rome with the birth of a child of divine descent. This would be the
golden age, the *Saturnia regna*, and the child would grow up to rule over
the whole, now peaceful, world.[2] There is no need to go into further
detail or to quote other evidence. There are in fact just a few, not
very significant, traces of the saecular idea in the following fifteen years
or so.[3] But when Vergil wrote the first and sixth books of the *Aeneid*,
that is, *c.* 23 B.C., there must have been a plan to celebrate a new
saeculum as was done in 249 and 146: Iuppiter and Anchises prophesy
the coming of the new golden *saeculum* under Augustus with peace and
happiness.[4] The celebration was long delayed, perhaps until the
settlement of the Parthian problem was achieved, and that is why
it was suggested above that Caesar had postponed his own festival
until the end of his Parthian campaign. When it was held in 17, coins
were issued with the head of Divus Iulius and a comet over it (pl. 28. 8)[5]
—as if it were those games which Caesar had intended to hold but could
not. But for the rest they were Augustan games and were to commemorate the *saeculum Augustum*. It will be enough to quote one of the many
pieces of relevant evidence. His birthday was celebrated at the Ara
Numinis Augusti at Narbo (set up in A.D. 12/13) to commemorate the
saeculi felicitas in producing him as its ruler.[6] Such sentiments could
be ascribed to the age of Caesar but cannot be proved to have really
existed.

Caesar may or may not have wanted to use the term *saeculum* for
his age. This is not what is of primary importance here. He certainly
had ambitious plans and began to execute them: what followed after
his death and under Augustus shows the effect of his plans. Even before
this new eras, new time-reckonings, had been created to rival the old
olympiads. Such eras, begun with the rule of a dynasty, were in use

---

[1] Verg. *Ecl.* 4. 4: 'ultima Cumaei venit iam carminis aetas'; Serv. ad loc.: '. . . saecula per
metalla divisit, dixit etiam quis quo saeculo imperaret, et Solem ultimum, id est decimum,
voluit.'

[2] Verg. *Ecl.* 4. 6: 'redeunt Saturnia regna, / iam nova progenies caelo demittitur alto';
15: 'ille deum vitam accipiet divisque videbit / permixtos heroas, et ipse videbitur illis, /
pacatumque reget patriis virtutibus orbem.'

[3] Verg. *Georg.* 1. 500; 3. 16 ff.; Hor. *sat.* 2. 5. 62 f.

[4] Verg. *Aen.* 1. 286: 'nascetur pulchra Troianus origine Caesar, / imperium Oceano,
famam qui terminet astris'; 291: 'aspera tum positis mitescent saecula bellis: / cana Fides et
Vesta, Remo cum fratre Quirinus / iura dabunt'; 6. 789 ff.; Mommsen, *Ges. Schr.* 8. 568. 3.

[5] Mattingly 1. 13; pls. 2. 19 f.; 3. 1; below, p. 379.

[6] *ILS* 112 (E.–J. 100): 'qua die eum saeculi felicitas orbi terrarum rectorem edidit';
cf. E.–J. 98a (Halicarnassus).

in the Greek East.[1] Later there was also a Sullan era introduced in 85/84 B.C. in Asia[2] and a Pompeian era in some Greek cities from 64/63 B.C.[3] A Caesarian era dating from the victory at Pharsalus or his subsequent visit to the cities in question[4] is attested for Syria[5] and Lydia.[6] Augustus followed with the Actian[7] and Alexandrinian eras.[8] Caesar certainly did not plan such an era for Rome. And yet he reformed the Calendar in 46,[9] which was followed by decrees to record his victories[10] and his birthday[11] in the Calendar and to call a month Iulius.[12] Ultimately it would have been a calendar in which his and his gods' festivals would have had a considerable share. The Christian calendar, which is the realization of similar plans, shows what it would have been like.

9. THE TRIUMPH OF 45 B.C.

What was decreed and executed after the victory at Munda was done in Caesar's absence.[13] Other honours followed which were destined for his presence: the special wreaths and dress which decorated the statues set up in his honour were also to decorate his person. He was now entitled to wear a golden crown and the triumphal dress at the games, and a laurel wreath everywhere.[14] We have already explained them as part of the honour of the *praenomen Imperatoris*.

The triumph was again long delayed. Caesar was already in Italy in July, and people, including Cicero, putting their resentment aside, intended to go and meet him,[15] as they did the year before at Brundisium;[16] but nobody knew about his plans. Balbus, his friend, expected him back in August;[17] he himself announced later that he would be

---

[1] Kubitschek, *RE* 1. 632 ff. and *Grundriss d. ant. Zeitrechnung* 66 ff.; Bickermann, *Chronologie* 32 ff.; Head, *HN* 944 f.   [2] Kubitschek, *RE* 1. 638 and *Grundriss* 76.

[3] Head, *HN* 945; Seyrig, *Syria* 31 (1954), 73 ff.; 36 (1959), 71 ff.

[4] Kubitschek, *RE* 1. 650.

[5] Antioch (Newall, *Num. Chron.* 4. 19 (1919), 77 ff.; Seyrig, *Syria* 27 (1950), 6 ff.), Laodicea (*CIG* 4472; Seyrig, l.c. 26 ff.), Gabala (Lederer, *Zeitschr. f. Num.* 34 (1924), 179 ff.; *BMC Galatia* 243 f.), Scythopolis (Alt, *Zeitschr. Pal. Ver.* 55 (1932), 128).

[6] Dios Hieron (Keil–v. Premerstein, *Denkschr. Wien. Akad.* 57. 1 (1914), 63), Hypaepa (ibid. 65), 'Tire' (ibid. 87 f., with comment), an unknown town (P. Herrmann, 'Neue Inschriften ... von Lydien', *Denkschr. Wien. Akad.* 77. 1 (1959), 9); Magie, op. cit. 1261. 9.

[7] See below, p. 315.

[8] Dating from the conquest of Alexandria, 1 August 30 B.C., *RE* 8A. 2518 (with bibliography).   [9] Dio 43. 26; Suet. *Caes.* 40.

[10] App. *BC* 2. 106. 442; Wissowa 445; above, p. 157.

[11] Dio 44. 4. 4; 47. 18. 5; below, pp. 206 ff.

[12] Dio 44. 5. 2; App. *BC* 2. 106. 443; Macrob. 1. 12. 34; above, pp. 155 ff.

[13] See above, p. 133.

[14] Dio 43. 43. 1; Suet. *Caes.* 45. 2; App. *BC* 2. 106. 442; above, p. 107.

[15] Cic. *Att.* 13. 50. 3; Drumann–Groebe 3. 590.

[16] See above, p. 62; below, p. 289.   [17] Cic. *Att.* 13. 21a. 3.

present at the *ludi Romani* in September, which he wanted to be particularly splendid.[1] And yet in September he went to his estate near Labicum and wrote his testament.[2] It is not clear why he changed his plans, nor why he wanted to be present at the *ludi Romani*. Did he already plan the additional day of games which was decreed in his honour in the following year?[3] He held his triumph in early October[4] and this time respected the rule not to enter Rome beforehand. It is not reported, and not likely, that he used his chariot with white horses again,[5] and the pageantry was less splendid than the year before. There was an exhibition of spoils, different from those of his earlier triumph,[6] but they concerned only one campaign, not four. It was the first triumph ever held at Rome for a victory in a civil war and was therefore resented in some quarters.[7] Another unusual event was that his triumph *ex Hispania* was repeated soon afterwards by two of his legates, by Q. Fabius Maximus (who had been consul since the beginning of October) on 13 October and Q. Pedius (*pr.* 48), Caesar's nephew, on 13 December, although they were not entitled to it because they had fought under his command.[8] We have seen that this innovation was part of a plan to make Caesar the permanent imperator. Augustus followed his example for a while by allowing his legates to hold triumphs but later granted them only to members of the imperial family, and even to them exceptionally.[9] Caesar's further plans may have been different; doubtless he would have revealed them at his Parthian triumph.

ADDITIONAL NOTE

(to p. 182. 7)

None the less, the possibility of contemporary allusions should not be dismissed without due consideration. Philodemus mentions with disapproval that Demetrius Poliorcetes boasted of his beauty and refers to Paris who ended in disaster (9. 2 ff.); but he adds that beauty can make kings godlike, θεοειδεῖς and θεοείκελοι (19. 24; 31). This could be relevant on two counts. On the one hand the honours of Demetrius

[1] Cic. *Att.* 13. 45. 1; 46. 2.

[2] Suet. *Caes.* 83. 1; Gelzer, *Caesar* 284; cf. Cic. *fam.* 7. 25. 1.

[3] Cic. *Phil.* 2. 110; below, pp. 265; 385.

[4] Vell. 2. 56. 3: 'cum mense Octobri in urbem revertisset'; Livy, *Per.* 116: 'Caesar ex Hispania quintum triumphum egit.'

[5] See above, p. 68.

[6] Suet. *Caes.* 37. 1: 'novissimum Hispaniensem (triumphum), diverso quemque apparatu et instrumento'; 38. 2; Vell. 2. 56. 2: 'Hispaniensis argento rasili constitit'; Pliny 14. 97.

[7] Plut. *Caes.* 56. 7 ff.; Dio 43. 42. 1; on the incident with C. Pontius Aquila see Suet. *Caes.* 78. 2; below, p. 276.

[8] *Fasti triumph.* (Degrassi, *Inscr. Ital.* 13. 1. 86 f.; 567); Quintil. 6. 3. 61; Dio 43. 42. 1; Mommsen, *StR* 1. 128. 3; 130. 2.

[9] Dio 54. 24. 8; Mommsen, *StR* 1. 135.

often inspired those for Caesar (above, pp. 155 ff.); on the other the same boast was made in Rome by Caesar and Memmius, claiming that Venus provided them with the bloom of youth (above, p. 23), and moreover, Memmius was in fact nicknamed 'Paris' (Cic. *Att.* 1. 18. 3). Caesar could then be the other type, the man of godlike beauty, which in fact he wanted to be. Again, Philodemus mentions Nestor settling the quarrel between Achilles and Agamemnon (10. 27 ff.): Cicero here comes to mind and his attempt to restore the concord between Pompey and Caesar (below, p. 264). Identifications and comparisons with Homeric heroes were always fashionable. We have just met Memmius as Paris; in the same context M. Lucullus is 'Menelaus' and L. Lucullus 'Agamemnon' (Cic. *Att.* 1. 18. 3). Elsewhere Pompey is 'Agamemnon' and Caesar 'Aegisthus' (Suet. *Caes.* 50. 1). There had been many incarnations of Nestor (J. Schmidt, *RE* 17. 120): Pericles (Plat. *Symp.* 221 c), Gorgias (Plat. *Phaedr.* 261 b), Antiphon (*Biogr. Gr.* 231; 235 f. W.), Isocrates (Syrian. *in Hermog.* 1, p. 94 R.). Clearly Cicero too would have played the role of a new Nestor with great pleasure in the Civil War. Thirdly, one could find an allusion to Caesar's virtues (below, pp. 228 ff.) in the passages where the ἐπιείκεια (*clementia*) of the king is mentioned, and also where he is πολεμικός (= *virtus*), 6. 6 ff.; 7. 20 ff. (πολεμικόν is a convincing new reading and supplement in 9. 14 by O. Murray, l.c. 169): but here one could doubt that an allusion was really intended. It is even less likely that King Nicomedes is mentioned because of his alleged scandalous behaviour in Caesar's company (4. 30 ff.; suggested by O. Murray, l.c. 180; see above, p. 18). He is quoted for shortcomings of a different kind, and Philodemus, a friend of Caesar and of his father-in-law, would have been ill-advised to allude to such a scandal. But even the more persuasive instances have insufficient force as long as one is unable to prove that Philodemus in fact intended to produce a political programme in such a disguise.

X

THE 'FATHER'

I. PARENS PATRIAE

APPIAN lists the *cognomen* 'parens patriae' among the honours of 45, Dio among those of 44;[1] 45 is the more probable. The *cognomen* is first found on coins of C. Cossutius Maridianus and P. Sepullius Macer, both of 44 (pl. 17. 1–2),[2] and on three inscriptions, all belonging to the time before the Ides of March, of Brundisium, Tarentum, and Cos.[3] The circumstances which led to this honour are not recorded nor is its meaning explained. The considerable interest shown by modern scholars in the problem[4] is apt to make one forget how very little is known that can illuminate the origin and history of the term.

Its meaning is not in doubt, Dio says, when recording the same honour for Augustus, that the title 'father' first served to stress the fathers' love for their children and the childrens' respect for their fathers. Later it gave the emperors the same power over their subjects which fathers had over their children.[5] This interpretation had its

---

[1] App. *BC* 2. 106. 442; 144. 602; Dio 44. 4. 4. No date is indicated by the other evidence: Livy *Per.* 116; Nic. Dam. *v. Caes.* 80 (*FGrHist.* 90 F 130); Suet. *Caes.* 76. 1; Flor. 2. 13. 91.

[2] Sydenham 178 f.; pl. 28. 1069; Grueber 1. 549; Alföldi, *Stud. üb. Caesars Monarchie*, pls. 14. 4–6; 15. 1 (for the unconvincing view that these were posthumous issues see ibid. 45 ff.).

[3] *ILS* 71 (Degr. 407); Degr. 408 (below, p. 258. 2); L. Gasperini, 'Su alcune epigrafi di Taranto romana' (U. Cozzoli and others, *Seconda Miscellanea greca e romana*, (1968), 381 ff.: 'C. Iulio, C. [f. Cae]sare, pat[re patr.,] imperato[re, dict.] rei public[ae constit]uendae...': I owe my knowledge of this article to the courtesy of Dr. M. Torelli). This inscription would lose its significance if M. Sordi, *Epigr.* 31 (1969), 79 ff., were right in attributing it to Octavian (cf. *ILS* 76) and, therefore, in supplementing 'pat[rono]' and '[IIIviro]'. There is, however, no evidence to show that *patronus* was ever a *cognomen* or could be listed in the *cursus honorum*.

[4] Cf. Mommsen, *StR* 2. 779 f.; Skard, *Festskrift til H. Koht* (1933), 42 ff.; Berlinger, *Beitr. z. inoffiziellen Titulatur d. röm. Kaiser* (Diss. Breslau 1935), 78 ff.; v. Premerstein 166 ff. (valuable); Weber, *Princeps* 264*. 692; Bömer, *Ahnenkult u. Ahnenglaube* 63 ff.; 70 ff.; 89 ff.; id. *Ovidius, Die Fasten* 2, p. 90; Alföldi, *Mus. Helv.* 9 (1952), 204 ff.; 10 (1953), 103 ff.; 11 (1954), 133 ff. (a long and very learned discussion of Caesar's honours, but, in spite of the frequent headings, very few of the 100 or so pages really concern the problem of the *parens patriae*; see also below, pp. 202. 11; 205. 1); Classen, *Philol.* 106 (1962), 180 ff.; Dobesch, op. cit. 15; 29 ff.

[5] Dio 53. 18. 3: ἥ γε τοῦ πατρὸς ἐπωνυμία τάχα μὲν καὶ ἐξουσίαν τινὰ αὐτοῖς (sc. the emperors), ἥν ποτε οἱ πατέρες ἐπὶ τοὺς παῖδας ἔσχον, κατὰ πάντων ἡμῶν δίδωσιν, οὐ μέντοι καὶ ἐπὶ τοῦτο ἀρχὴν ἐγένετο, ἀλλ' ἔς τε τιμὴν καὶ παραίνεσιν ἵν' αὐτοί τε τοὺς ἀρχομένους ὡς καὶ παῖδας ἀγαπῶεν καὶ ἐκεῖνοί σφας ὡς καὶ πατέρας αἰδῶνται; v. Premerstein, 173. Mr. Drummond rightly draws

roots in the ageless antithesis between the good and the bad king who could be a father or a tyrant.[1] At Rome it is first found in Cicero's assessment of his own consulate.[2] It was also used, according to another passage in Dio, by Caesar when he first spoke in Rome on his victorious return in 46.[3] Later Seneca said that with the title Nero received the *patria potestas*, which, however, he used with great moderation.[4] Again, the younger Pliny said that Trajan was not a tyrant but a citizen, not a master but a father.[5]

This interpretation is clearly unexceptionable. But it does not answer the question as to the origin of the term, that is, how it could have taken root at Rome, where the institution of the annual and collegiate magistrature should have rendered it impossible. In fact there were some exceptional cases. We have already met the liberators and saviours, with the grass crown and oak wreath respectively, who were treated like fathers;[6] also Romulus, whom Ennius called father[7] because he was the founder of the whole community. We have seen how important the idea of the founder became at the time of Cicero.[8] He knew of the Greek doctrine according to which not only the real founders were called κτίσται but also the saviours and benefactors of the community, and spoke in this manner about Romulus and his apotheosis.[9] But it was Marius of whom he said about the same time, in the year of his consulate, that he deserved to be called 'pater patriae', a 'parens' of the freedom of the citizens and of the State through his victory over the enemy.[10] This is the earliest occurrence of the term, probably the result of Cicero's own reflections about the role which he, as consul,

my attention to the *patres* of the Senate (Cic. *rep.* 2. 14; Sall. *Cat.* 6. 6; Kübler, *RE* 18. 2. 2223). As a corporate body they could naturally never acquire the privileged position of a single *pater*.

[1] Cic. *rep.* 1. 64 (above, p. 180. 3); 2. 47: 'hic est enim dominus populi quem Graeci tyrannum vocant; nam regem illum volunt esse qui consulit ut parens populo'; cf., e.g., Hdt. 3. 89. 3; Xen. *Cyrop.* 8. 1. 1; Skard, l.c. 50 ff.

[2] Cic. *dom.* 94: 'me non ut crudelem tyrannum, sed ut mitissimum parentem . . . vident.' This view was not shared by Cicero's enemies, see above, p. 135.

[3] Dio 43. 17. 2: νῦν τε πολὺ μᾶλλον προθυμήσομαι μετὰ πάσης ἐπιεικείας οὐ μὰ Δι' οὐ δεσπόζειν ὑμῶν ἀλλὰ προστατεῖν, οὐδὲ τυραννεύειν, ἀλλὰ ἡγεμονεύειν. It is very likely that Caesar spoke in this manner; cf. v. Premerstein, 118. This was in fact what Cicero said about Caesar a year later, *Deiot.* 34 (above, p. 147. 8).

[4] Sen. *clem.* 1. 14. 2: 'adpellavimus patrem patriae . . . ut sciret datam sibi potestatem patriam, quae est temperantissima liberis consulens suaque post illos reponens'; v. Premerstein, 174 f.

[5] Pliny *Paneg.* 2. 3: 'nusquam ut deo, nusquam ut numini blandiamur; non enim de tyranno sed de cive, non de domino sed de parente loquimur'; 21. 4; *Paneg. lat.* 9. 15. 3.

[6] See above, pp. 149 f.; 163.   [7] Enn. *A.* 113 V.: 'o pater, o genitor, o sanguen dis oriundum.'

[8] See above, pp. 177 f.   [9] Cic. *Cat.* 3. 2; *rep.* 1. 12; 1. 64; 2. 17; above, p. 180.

[10] Cic. *Rab. perd.* 27: 'C. Marium . . . vere patrem patriae, parentem . . . vestrae libertatis atque huiusce rei publicae possumus dicere.'

ought to play in the State. What he was hoping for was soon realized. When action was taken against the Catilinarians, he considered himself a new founder and the Nones of December 63 the new birthday of Rome.[1] L. Gellius Poplicola's (*cos.* 72) proposal of an oak wreath for Cicero (which we have already discussed) followed, and the senators, of whom Cato and Q. Lutatius Catulus (*cos.* 78) are mentioned by name, acclaimed him a 'parens patriae'.[2] It is explicitly stated that Cicero was the first to be so acclaimed.[3] He often returned to the subject[4] and advised his brother Quintus later to aim at gaining a similar title in Asia.[5] His example inspired the historians. Romulus[6] and Camillus now received the title of 'parens patriae':[7] the evidence is nowhere earlier than the age of Cicero.[8] It is more important still that the new title was connected with the old tradition about the oak wreath: whoever gave this to his saviour accepted the obligation to treat him like a father.[9] But this was the first time that the wreath was proposed as a reward for a civilian.[10] If Cicero had really received it, the acclamation probably would have had the force of such an obligation, this time for all the citizens and not only for a single one. As he apparently did not, it was a passing incident without any real consequence.

There was no further holder of the title until Caesar, and it is tempting to assume that it was Cicero who proposed it,[11] in agreement, of

[1] See above, p. 189.

[2] See above, p. 165; Cic. *Pis.* 6: 'me Q. Catulus . . . frequentissimo senatu parentem patriae nominavit'; *Sest.* 121: 'me . . ., quem Q. Catulus, quem multi alii saepe in senatu patrem patriae nominarant'; Plut. *Cic.* 23. 6: καὶ προσαγορεῦσαι πατέρα πατρίδος. πρώτῳ γὰρ ἐκείνῳ δοκεῖ τοῦθ' ὑπάρξαι, Κάτωνος αὐτὸν οὕτως ἐν τῷ δήμῳ προσαγορεύσαντος.

[3] Pliny 7. 117: 'salve primus omnium parens patriae appellate'; App. *BC* 2. 7. 25: δοκεῖ τισιν ἥδε ἡ εὐφημία ἀπὸ Κικέρωνος ἀρξαμένη περιελθεῖν ἐς τῶν νῦν αὐτοκρατόρων τοὺς φαινομένους ἀξίους; Iuven. 8. 243: 'sed Roma parentem, / Roma patrem patriae Ciceronem libera dixit'; Alföldi, *Mus. Helv.* 10 (1953), 105, rejects this evidence and believes that Cicero was not the first.

[4] Cic. *Pis.* 6; *Sest.* 121 (above, n. 2); *Att.* 9. 10. 3 (49 B.C.): 'me quem non nulli conservatorem istius urbis parentemque esse dixerunt'; *Phil.* 2. 12: 'ut esset nemo, qui mihi non ut parenti gratias ageret, qui mihi non vitam suam, fortunas, liberos, rem publicam referret acceptam.'

[5] *Q.fr.* 1. 1. 31 (60/59 B.C.): 'provideas saluti, ut te parentem Asiae et dici et haberi velis.'

[6] Cic. *div.* 1. 3: 'huius urbis parens Romulus'; Livy 1. 16. 3: 'regem parentemque urbis Romanae salvere universi Romulum iubent'; 16. 6: 'parens urbis huius'.

[7] Livy 5. 49. 7; 7. 1. 10; Plut. *Cam.* 1. 1; Eutrop. 1. 20. 3; above, p. 177. 7.

[8] The title of 'new founder' or of 'a new Romulus' was created earlier: above, pp. 177 f.

[9] Polyb. 6. 39. 7; Cic. *Planc.* 72; Gell. 5. 6. 8, etc.; above, p. 163. 3.

[10] Cic. *Pis.* 6; Gell. 5. 6. 15 (above, p. 165. 7). Again, the supplications decreed on this occasion were never before decreed for a civilian, Cic. *Cat.* 3. 15; *Pis.* 6; *Phil.* 2. 13 (above, p. 63. 3); Pliny 7. 117: 'primus in toga triumphum linguaeque lauream merite et facundiae Latiarumque litterarum parens aeque (ut dictator Caesar, hostis quondam tuus, de te scripsit)'; Cic. *de cons.*, *FPL* frg. 16 M.: 'cedant arma togae, concedat laurea linguae' (or 'laudi', see Nisbet's note on Cic. *Pis.* 74; W. Allen jr., *TAPA* 87 (1956), 133); 17: 'o fortunatam natam me consule Romam!'

[11] According to Alföldi, *Mus. Helv.* 10 (1953), 109 ff., Caesar received the title for his

course, with Caesar and his friends. It is a fact that in 45 he took an active part in the deliberations of the Senate,[1] and that after the murder Brutus and Antony accused him of being responsible for much.[2] His speeches *Pro Marcello* and *Pro Ligario* show him in a most co-operative spirit and must have inspired some of the new honours.[3] We have learnt from the events of 63 that the granting of the oak-wreath and of the new title belonged together. The wreath was again for the saving not of a single citizen but of all of them; and accordingly Caesar was to be a 'father' for all. The statue on the Rostra will have been so inscribed, also the Thasian statue of which the head with the oak wreath has survived (pl. 1);[4] we have met such inscriptions from Brundisium, Tarentum, and Cos.[5] At Brundisium the words 'patri patriae' were surrounded by an oak wreath, and so were they later when a similar inscription was set up in the same place in honour of Augustus[6] (pl. 17. 4). Augustus had already been honoured with the oak wreath in 27 B.C. when it was placed over the entrance of his palace;[7] it was reproduced on coins from 23 B.C. onwards with the words 'ob civis servatos', also in an abbreviated form, in its centre.[8] This was done then in accordance with the Caesarian precedent; their corollary, the title, could not officially be inscribed as long as Augustus refused to accept it. It was put on the stone from Brundisium, which is thus datable. The two together 'p(ater) p(atriae)' and 'ob cives servatos' within the oak wreath, are found on coins of Caligula and Claudius, and later (pl. 17. 5).[9]

After Caesar's death his followers instituted a cult in the Forum and set up a statue with the inscription 'Parenti patriae'.[10] Augustus must

clemency, in contrast to Cicero who got it for his cruel suppression of the Catilinarian conspiracy. But it does not seem probable that such a comparison played any role in the considerations of the Senate. The history of the title before and after is more relevant than the single passage of Appian from the funeral oration of Antony (*BC* 2. 144. 602: ἔνθα μὲν τὸ ψήφισμα εἴποι πατέρα πατρίδος, ἐπιλέγων· τοῦτο ἐπιεικείας ἐστὶ μαρτυρία) which Alföldi, as it seems unduly, stresses: clemency was, it is true, one of the virtues of the *parens* but not the most important one.   [1] Plut. *Caes.* 57. 2; *Cic.* 40. 4.

[2] Brutus ap. Cic. *ad Brut.* 24 (1. 16). 3; Cic. *Phil.* 13. 40.

[3] See above, pp. 166 f.; 169; below, p. 220.   [4] See above, p. 167. 3.

[5] See above, p. 200. 3.

[6] The Caesarian inscription (*ILS* 71) is lost; the wreath is mentioned in *CIL* 9. 34 (= 1². 789). It can be seen around the Augustan inscription, Marzano, *Archivio storico Pugliese* 8 (1955), 25 (= *AE* 1955, 265). I owe the reference to this article to Mr. M. W. Frederiksen and the photograph to Dr. M. Torelli.

[7] *Mon. Anc.* 34. 2; Mattingly 1. 26; pl. 4. 15.   [8] Mattingly 1. 2; 7; 29 ff., etc.

[9] Caligula: Mattingly 1. 150; 152; 157; pls. 27. 24; 26; 28. 5; 8; 29. 13. Claudius: Mattingly 1. 170 ff.; 190; 198; pls. 32. 2 f.; 9; 11; 15; 18 f.; 21–3; 34. 7; 36. 1. Civil Wars: Mattingly 1. 303; pl. 51. 13. Vespasian: Mattingly 2. 82; 202; pls. 14. 1; 39. 2.

[10] Suet. *Caes.* 85 (below, p. 364. 6); cf. *ILS* 72 (below, p. 214. 6); Lucan 9. 601: 'ecce parens verus patriae (Cato), dignissimus aris, / Roma, tuis, per quem numquam iurare pudebit / et quem si steteris umquam cervice soluta, / nunc, olim, factura deum es.'

have received an offer of the same title, as the public discussion and the granting of the oak wreath show, soon after the Actian victory, and was in fact called 'father of his country' in literature, on inscriptions, and on coins (pl. 17. 3)[1] long before he accepted the title officially in 2 B.C. after long reluctance:[2] he first pretended to be no more than an ordinary citizen, which the title rendered impossible.[3] That is why Tiberius too resisted, but without giving in;[4] after him it was one of the official titles of the Roman emperors.

When Cicero was acclaimed 'pater patriae' he was not invested with a special status. If he referred to it so often, it was only to remind his fellow citizens of what he had done and therefore of what he could do again. It linked him with the great heroes of the past, Romulus, Camillus, Marius. But this link too was more lustre than substance because Cicero never again had the opportunity to act. Caesar was the first for whom the title meant more than glory. It became part of his nomenclature and was a reinterpretation of his unlimited political power: it was not tyranny but *patria potestas*.[5] It was not an entirely new start, in so far as Caesar already exercised a considerable patronage and had many political 'friends' who depended on him.[6] The consequences were far-reaching. His relation to his fellow citizens was completely changed. They all were now bound to him, like the son to his father, by *pietas*,[7] began to pray for his welfare and to swear by it, to worship his Genius as if it were their own. And conversely those who had broken this bond and were excluded from the community, the exiles, were not allowed to show themselves in his presence,[8] just as a banished son was not allowed to return to the house of his father.[9] It was the first step towards the introduction in Rome of a relationship

---

[1] Hor. *c.* 3. 24. 25; 1. 2. 50; Mattingly 1. 69 f. (*c.* 15 B.C.); *ILS* 96 (6/5 B.C.); 101; *CIL* 10. 823; v. Premerstein 169 ff.

[2] *Mon. Anc.* 35. 1; Suet. *Aug.* 58. 1 f.; Dio 55. 10. 10; *F. Praen.* 5 Febr. (Degrassi 407); Mattingly 1. 87 ff.; *ILS* 104 f.; 107; 110; 112.

[3] Mommsen, *StR* 2. 780. 3, seems to assume that for Augustus it was more a divine than a human honour.

[4] Suet. *Tib.* 26. 2.

[5] Mommsen, *StR* 2. 780, assumes that the title was just an honour without any rights, above all without the *patria potestas*. But he modifies this view in a note in which he quotes evidence for the rule that an exile was not allowed to be present where the emperor, the *pater patriae*, was (*Dig.* 48. 22. 18: 'relegatus morari non potest Romae . . . quia communis patria est, neque in ea civitate, in qua moratur princeps vel per quam transit: iis enim solis permissum est principem intueri, qui Romam ingredi possunt, quia princeps pater patriae est'); cf. Weber, *Princeps* 62*. 244.

[6] Cf., e.g., v. Premerstein 167; Alföldi, *Mus. Helv.* 9 (1952), 206 ff.

[7] See below, pp. 256 ff.   [8] *Dig.* 48. 22. 18.

[9] Livy 7. 4. 4; Cic. *Rosc. Amer.* 42; Oros. 5. 16. 8; Suet. *Aug.* 65. 1; Mommsen, *Strafr.* 23. 2; 968.

which existed in the Greek world between the ruler and his subjects.[1]
How this was done will be examined in the following sections.

2. GENIUS CAESARIS

We begin with the change concerning Caesar's Genius. Genius, the
generative power of a man, was his divine protector from birth to death.[2]
His festival was the birthday of his protégé, celebrated at home with
wine, incense, and other non-animal offerings.[3] The Genius of a benefactor could become important to others, especially to members of his
household, his freedmen, and slaves. They could call him hyperbolically
their Genius[4] as they called him their Salus and their 'life'; and they
swore by his Genius[5] instead of the great gods of oath like Iuppiter.

It is not known how and when, on the basis of the private Genius,
a Genius of the State was created. A public sacrifice was made to him
in 218 B.C. in a dangerous period of the Second Punic War,[6] a time
of many religious innovations. This Genius is isolated and unexplained;
in contrast to the private Genius he received animal sacrifice. He may
have represented a Greek god or may have been the first version of the
Genius publicus. Another Genius, the *Genius urbis Romae*,[7] was probably not
a Genius at all but the secondary name of an originally unknown, protecting spirit, comparable to the Tyche of Greek cities,[8] and served as the

---

[1] Alföldi, *Stud. üb. Caesars Monarchie* 45 ff. and *Mus. Helv.* 10 (1953), 108, suggests that
the coins with the legend 'Caesar parens patriae' (Sydenham 178 f.; above, p. 200. 2)
were issued after Caesar's death to serve Antony's political propaganda. There is nothing
to support this odd suggestion, certainly not the horseman, *desultor*, shown on one of the
coins. It is not right to say that this representation refers to the games of the Parilia of 44:
it may refer to any games held while Caesar was still alive. Nor is it right to quote evidence
for the Parilia which in fact belongs to the *ludi Victoriae Caesaris*.

[2] Censor. 3. 1: 'Genius est deus, cuius in tutela ut quisque natus est vivit. hic sive quod
ut genamur curat, sive quod una genitur nobiscum, sive etiam quod nos genitos suscipit ac
tutatur, certe a genendo Genius appellatur'; Paul. 94 M. (84 L.); Wissowa 175 ff.; Latte
103 f.

[3] Censor. 2. 2 f.; Hor. *epist.* 2. 1. 144; Tib. 2. 2. 5 ff.; Maecen. ap. Sen. *ep.* 114. 5; W.
Schmidt, *Geburtstag im Altert.* 21 ff.; id. *RE* 7. 1135 ff.; Otto, *RE* 7. 1160 f.; Wissowa 177.

[4] Plaut. *Capt.* 879: 'tuom gnatum et Genium meum'; *Curc.* 301: 'Phaedromum Genium
meum'; *Men.* 138: 'teneo dextera Genium meum'; on the related 'Salus mea' and 'mea vita'
see above, pp. 167 f.

[5] Plaut. *Capt.* 977: 'per tuom te Genium obsecro'; Ter. *Andr.* 289: 'ego per hanc te dex-
teram et Genium tuom, / per tuam fidem . . . / te obtestor'; Hor. *epist.* 1. 7. 94: 'te per Genium
dextramque deosque Penatis / obsecro et obtestor'; Tib. 4. 5. 8: 'perque tuos oculos per
Geniumque rogo'; Sen. *ep.* 12. 2: (vilicus) 'iurat per Genium meum se omnia facere';
Mommsen, *StR* 2. 809; Bömer, *Athen.* 54 (1966), 104 f.; 114 (not convincing).

[6] Livy 21. 62. 9: 'Genio maiores hostiae caesae quinque.'

[7] Serv. Dan. *Aen.* 2. 351: 'in Capitolio fuit clipeus consecratus, cui inscriptum erat "Genio
urbis Romae, sive mas, sive femina".'

[8] Cf. Ruhl–Waser, *Myth. Lex.* 5. 1332 ff.; 1361 ff. with bibliography.

model for the *Genius oppidi* or *coloniae* outside Rome.[1] The *Genius publicus*, on the other hand, is certainly relevant here: he had a festival on the Capitol on 9 October,[2] though it is not known since when. He may have been identical in concept, if not also in origin, with the *Genius populi Romani*, who had a shrine in the Forum at least by the end of the Republic[3] and first appeared on the coins of three members of the family of the Cornelii Lentuli in the first half of the first century B.C. (pl. 17. 6–8),[4] then not again until the Civil Wars of A.D. 68[5] and under Vespasian and Titus (pl. 17. 9–11);[6] on the coins of Nero he was styled as 'Genius Augusti' (pl. 17. 12).[7] It is therefore to be assumed that a Cornelius Lentulus was instrumental in establishing the cult, either Cn. Cornelius Lentulus (*cos.* 201) or a later one. This *Genius populi Romani* was the collective version of the private Genius and therefore infinitely more powerful, the Roman counterpart of the Dea Roma who was created and worshipped by the Greeks; for lack of evidence one cannot be more precise about him.

Caesar, like everyone else, had his own Genius, whose cult was his private concern. The argument that a public cult of the Genius Caesaris was created in 45 rests on the following evidence: (1) The public celebration of his birthday was decreed in 45,[8] which, however, does not imply a public offering to his Genius. (2) Dio says that an oath was performed by Caesar's 'Tyche'.[9] (3) There were cults of the Genius Augusti and of those of the later emperors which could have been the successors of the Genius Caesaris.[10] (4) There is a close analogy in the cult of the Salus Caesaris, which equally comes from the private sphere.[11]

(a) Caesar's Birthday

It was decreed in 45 that a public sacrifice should be performed on Caesar's birthday;[12] no further details are given. As far as is known, it was not done in 44 and 43. In 42 after Caesar's consecration the festival was made obligatory and defaulters were to be punished severely,

---

[1] *ILS* 5392 (Degr. 116, Nola): 'C. Catius M. f., L. Catius . . . Genio coloniae et colonorum'; Degr. 117 (Carthago Nova): 'L. Baebius . . . Genio oppidi columnam, pompam ludosque coiraverunt'; Latte 240. 4.

[2] *F. Amit.* and *F. Arv.*, Degrassi 518.   [3] Dio 47. 2. 3; 50. 8. 2.

[4] Sydenham 86 (*c.* 96–94 B.C.); 122 (*c.* 76–74 B.C.); 130 (*c.* 72 B.C.); pls. 19. 605; 21. 752; 22. 791; Gagé, *Congr. Internat. Numism. Paris 1953*, 2 (1957), 219 ff.; above, p. 42.

[5] Mattingly 1. 288 f.; 295 f.; pls. 49. 13 f.; 50. 10 f.

[6] Mattingly 2. 85; 266; pls. 14. 14 f.; 50. 10.

[7] Mattingly 1. 248; 272 f.; pls. 45. 1; 47. 3 f.   [8] Dio 44. 4. 4; 47. 18. 5.

[9] Dio 44. 6. 1; 50. 1.   [10] See below, pp. 215 f.   [11] See above, pp. 169 ff.

[12] Dio 44. 4. 4 (44 B.C.): τά τε γενέθλια αὐτοῦ δημοσίᾳ θύειν ἐψηφίσαντο. On the date of the decree see above, p. 200; below, p. 270.

which was a political move against the potential enemies of the *trium-viri*[1] and was probably ignored later. It had the form of a *supplicatio*: everybody took part in it and wore a laurel wreath.[2] It is not stated which god received the sacrifice and what kind of sacrifice it was: in the third century it was an ox and was offered to Divus Iulius.[3] The festival was always observed: it is mentioned by Horace *c*. 20 B.C.,[4] also in the calendars,[5] even in the Calendar of Dura in the third century[6] and by Polemius Silvius in the fifth.[7] But strangely enough it was not observed by the Arvals, and the temple of Divus Iulius was dedicated on a different day, 18 August 29 B.C.

There is no Roman precedent. Cicero's friend, the astrologer L. Tarutius Firmanus, calculated Romulus' horoscope:[8] this was a private affair which did not lead to an official fixing of his birthday.[9] The inspiration must have come from the East. The kings of Persia and Egypt always had public festivals on their birthdays[10] and so had the Hellenistic rulers.[11] Roman generals began to attach a greater significance to their own birthdays than they had before. Pompey, who had spent so much time in the East, celebrated his long-delayed triumph

[1] Dio 47. 18. 5: τά τε γενέσια αὐτοῦ δαφνηφοροῦντας καὶ εὐθυμουμένους πάντας ἑορτάζειν ἠνάγκασαν, νομοθετήσαντες τοὺς μὲν ἄλλους τοὺς ἀμελήσαντας αὐτῶν ἐπαράτους τῷ τε Διὶ καὶ αὐτῷ ἐκείνῳ εἶναι, τοὺς δὲ δὴ βουλευτὰς τούς τε υἱεῖς σφων πέντε καὶ εἴκοσι μυριάδας ὀφλισκάνειν; cf. Wissowa 388; below, p. 397.

[2] An annual sacrifice and procession of all citizens wearing wreaths is recorded for Lysimachus at Priene *c*. 288 B.C., *Or. gr.* 11. 19 ff., apparently on his birthday (τοῖς γενεθλίοις is a supplement); Nilsson 2. 153.

[3] *Fer. Dur.* (*YCS* 7. 146): 'ob natalem Divi Iuli Divo Iulio bovem marem.'

[4] Hor. *epist.* 1. 5. 9: 'cras nato Caesare festus / . . . dies.' Porphyrio ad loc. connects this with Caesar, Heinze with Augustus. The former is supported by 11: 'aestivam . . . noctem', which cannot point to September when Augustus was born (Manil. 4. 547: 'cum autumnales coeperunt surgere Chelae').

[5] *F. Amit.*: 'Feriae, quod eo die C. Caesar est natus'; *F. Ant. min.*: 'Divi Iulii natalis'; Degrassi 481 f.

[6] See above, n. 3.   [7] Degrassi l.c.

[8] Plut. *Rom.* 12. 5; cf. Cic. *div.* 2. 98; Solin. 1. 18; Kroll, *RE* 4A. 2408 f.

[9] I do not know on what evidence rests the assertion (Bömer, *Ovidius, Die Fasten* 2, p. 272) that his birthday coincided with that of Augustus.

[10] Plat. *I. Alcib.* 121 c: τῇ ἡμέρᾳ βασιλέως γενέθλια πᾶσα θύει καὶ ἑορτάζει ἡ Ἀσία; Hdt. 1. 133; 9. 110; Zosim. 2. 27. 1; Hellanicus, *FGrHist*. 4 F 55: στεφάνου δωρεάν, ὃν ἔπεμψεν . . . γενέθλια ἐπιτελοῦντι Πατάρμιδι, τῷ τῆς Αἰγύπτου τότε βασιλεύοντι; LXX *Gen*. 40. 20: ἡμέρα γενέσεως ἦν Φαραω καὶ ἐποίει πότον πᾶσι τοῖς παισὶν αὐτοῦ.

[11] The evidence about Alexander is not certain (Magie, *Roman Rule* 868. 51; Habicht 17); Ptolemy II (*Syll*. 463; *Or. gr.* 56. 5); Ptolemy V (*Or. gr.* 90. 46); Eumenes II (Habicht 125); Antiochus IV Epiphanes (LXX 2 *Maccab*. 6. 7); Ariarathes V (*Or. gr.* 357. 80 f.); Antiochus I of Commagene (*Or. gr.* 383. 83; 132); Herodes (Ev. Matth. 14. 4; Marc. 6. 21); cf. *Or. gr.* 2, p. 641; Schürer, *Gesch. d. jüd. Volkes* 1. 440. The evidence about Timoleon of Corinth, the liberator of Sicily about the middle of the fourth century B.C., is puzzling, Nep. *Timol.* 4. 4: 'proelia maxima natali suo die fecit omnia; quo factum est, ut eius diem natalem festum haberet universa Sicilia' (not recorded by Diod. 16. 90 or Plut. *Tim.* 39).

PLATE 17

1. Denarius of C. Cossutius Maridianus, 44 B.C. (Sydenham 178. 1069), Oxford; *obv.*: head of Caesar veiled, legend 'Caesar parens patriae'; *rev.*: legend 'C. Cossutius Maridianus, a(uro) a(rgento) a(ere) f(lando) f(eriundo)'; p. 200.

2. Denarius of P. Sepullius Macer, 44 B.C. (Sydenham 179. 1075), Paris; *obv.*: head of Caesar veiled, apex, lituus, legend 'Caesar parens patriae'; *rev.*: rider with two horses, legend 'P. Sepullius Macer'; p. 200.

3. Denarius of Augustus, 19–15 B.C. (Mattingly 1. 69. 397), Oxford; *obv.*: toga picta over tunica palmata between aquila and wreath, legend 'S.P.Q.R. Parenti Cons(ervatori) suo'; *rev.*: quadriga, in front, four miniature horses, legend 'Caesari Augusto'; p. 204.

4. Inscription from Brundisium (*AE* 1955, 265): '[Imp.] Caesari [D.] f., (in oak wreath:) Aug., pont. max., patri patriae'; p. 203.

5. Sestertius of Caligula, A.D. 39–40 (Mattingly 1. 156. 58); *obv.*: head of Caligula, legend 'C. Caesar Divi Aug. pron. Aug., p. m., tr. p. III, p. p.'; *rev.*: oak wreath, legend 'S.P.Q.R., p. p. ob cives servatos'; p. 203.

6. Denarius of P. Cornelius Lentulus, c. 95 B.C. (Sydenham 86. 604), Oxford; *obv.*: bust of Hercules with lion's skin, club and shield, legend 'Roma'; *rev.*: Roma with spear crowned by the Genius populi Romani who holds cornucopiae, legend 'Lent(ulus) Mar(celli) f.'; p. 206.

7. Denarius of Cn. Cornelius Lentulus Marcellinus, c. 75 B.C. (Sydenham 122. 752), Oxford; *obv.*: bust of Genius with sceptre, legend 'G(enius) p(opuli) R(omani)'; *rev.*: globe between rudder and sceptre, legend 'Cn. Len(tulus) q(uaestor), ex s.c.'; p. 206.

8. Denarius of P. Cornelius Lentulus, c. 75 B.C. (Sydenham 130. 791), Oxford; *obv.*: head of Hercules, legend 'q(uaestor), s.c.'; *rev.*: Genius seated with sceptre and cornucopiae, and foot on globe, crowned by Victoria, legend 'P. Lent. P. f. L. n.'; p. 206.

9. Denarius of the Civil Wars, A.D. 68 (Mattingly 1. 288. 1). Oxford; *obv.*: male bust and cornucopiae, legend 'Genio p. R.'; *rev.*: Mars helmeted with spear and shield, legend 'Marti Ultori'; p. 206.

10. Denarius of Vespasian, A.D. 69–70 (Mattingly 2. 85. 417), London; *obv.*: head of Vespasian, legend 'Imp. Caesar Vespasianus Aug.'; *rev.*: Genius with cornucopiae and patera, legend 'Genium p. R.'; p. 206.

11. As of Titus, A.D. 80–1 (Mattingly 2. 266. 210), London; *obv.*: head of Titus, legend 'Imp. T. Caes. Vesp. Aug., p. m., tr. p., cos. VIII'; *rev.*: Genius with cornucopiae sacrificing at an altar, legend 'Geni(o) p. R., S.C.'; p. 206.

12. As of Nero, A.D. 64–6 (Mattingly 1. 248. 251), Oxford; *obv.*: radiate head of Nero, legend 'Nero Claud. Caesar Aug. Ger., p. m., tr. p., imp., p. p.'; *rev.*: Genius with cornucopiae sacrificing at an altar, legend 'Genio Augusti'; p. 206.

13. Denarius of M'. Aquillius, c. 70 B.C. (Sydenham 132. 798), Oxford; *obv.*: bust of Virtus, legend 'Virtus, IIIvir'; *rev.*: M'. Aquillius (cos. 101 B.C.) raising the kneeling figure of Sicilia, legend 'M'. Aquil. M'. f. M'. n., Sicil.'; p. 231.

14. Denarius of Q. Fufius Calenus and Cordus, c. 69 B.C. (Sydenham 131. 797), Oxford; *obv.*: heads of Honos and Virtus, legend 'Ho(nos), Virt(us), Kaleni'; *rev.*: Roma with foot on globe and Italia, legend 'Ro(ma), Ital(ia), Cordi'; p. 232.

15. Denarius of P. Sepullius Macer, 44 B.C. (Sydenham 179. 1076), London; *obv.*: tetrastyle temple with globe in pediment, legend 'Clementiae Caesaris'; *rev.*: rider with two horses, legend 'P. Sepullius Macer'; p. 241.

PLATE 17

1   2   3

4

5   6

7   8   9   10

11   12   13   14   15

in 61 on his birthday, 29 September.[1] This must have impressed his contemporaries and was later imitated by Messalla in 27 B.C.[2] and by Caligula in A.D. 40.[3] Comparisons were made with kings, and it was found, for instance, that both King Attalus and Pompey died on their birthdays.[4] Moreover some Romans, it is not clear since when, began to celebrate the birthday of a friend, as Horace did Maecenas' and Silius Italicus Vergil's; Tibullus wrote a poem for the birthdays of Messalla and Cornutus, Persius for that of Macrinus.[5] But all this belonged to the private sphere, whereas Caesar's birthday was, like that of the Persian, Egyptian, and Hellenistic kings, a public festival.

Further clarification may be gathered from the history of the imperial birthdays. Augustus' birthday, 23 September, became a public festival in 30:[6] it was one of the many rewards for the Actian victory. At the same time Antony's birthday, 14 January, was declared to be an unlucky day, *dies vitiosus*,[7] which leads to the conjecture that Antony may have celebrated his birthday at Alexandria in the oriental fashion and with the intention of thus further pressing his claim to Caesar's succession. If so, the two decrees of 30 were the answer to this claim. Augustus' festival, like that of Caesar, had the form of a *supplicatio*, probably followed by a banquet, which is first mentioned for 13 B.C.;[8] for in 30 it was also decreed that libations should be offered at banquets in honour of Augustus.[9] It was further decreed that an annual sacrifice should be made on the same day to Mars, Neptune, and Apollo,[10] the gods who helped him to achieve the Actian victory. This connection with another festival was imitated later.[11] Games were added for the first time in 20 B.C., and became annual in 8 B.C.[12] The special occasion

---

[1] Pliny 37. 13; see above, p. 38.

[2] Tib. 1. 7. 1 ff.; 49 f.; 64 f.; Castiglioni, *Riv. fil.* 53 (1925), 198; for the view that the triumph took place a few days before his birthday see Hanslik, *RE* 8A. 136.

[3] Suet. *Cal.* 49. 2 (*ovatio*).

[4] Plut. *Cam.* 19. 11. Pompey probably died a day earlier (Vell. 2. 53. 3; Plut. *Pomp.* 79. 5), but some authors still supported the other view, Dio 42. 5. 5; Plut. *qu. conv.* 8. 1. 1; cf. App. *BC* 4. 113. 475 (Cassius died on his birthday).

[5] Hor. *c.* 4. 11. 17 ff.; Pliny *ep.* 3. 7. 8; Tib. 1. 7; 2. 2; Pers. 2. 1; Klingner, *Studien* 532 ff.

[6] Dio 51. 19. 2; *ILS* 112 (E.–J. 100). 15 ff.

[7] *F. Praen.*; *F. Verul.* (Degrassi 397); Dio 51. 19. 3. It was restored by Claudius, Suet. *Claud.* 11. 3. The case of Agrippina may be compared. Her birthday, 6 November, was duly recorded in the Calendars (*F. Ant. min.*) and celebrated (Henzen, *AFA* 53), before it became a forbidden day in A.D. 59, Tac. *A.* 14. 12. 1; Degrassi 529; see also below, p. 397.

[8] Dio 54. 26. 2.

[9] Dio 51. 19. 7; cf. Ov. *F.* 2. 637 f.; Hor. *c.* 4. 5. 31 f.; Petron. 60. 8.

[10] *F. Arv.* (Degrassi 512).

[11] For instance the Ara Pacis was dedicated on 30 January, the birthday of Livia, *F. Praen.*, etc. (Degrassi 404 f.); Henzen, *AFA* 51 f.

[12] Dio 54. 8. 5; 55. 6. 6.

in 20 was the birth of C. Caesar, Augustus' grandson and heir. His
birthday too was to become an annual festival with the sacrifice of an
ox,[1] the first public celebration of the birthday of an imperial prince.
Augustus' birthday was celebrated all over the empire. In the province
of Asia the beginning of the year was transferred to it *c.* 8 B.C. and the
offering was made to him;[2] this was probably also done at Mytilene,[3]
certainly at Cumae.[4] At Cumae the birthdays of the imperial princes
too were celebrated, and the recipient was Vesta.[5] At Narbo, and elsewhere, the festival lasted two days, 23 and 24 September, and the
offerings—animal sacrifice, incense, and wine—were made at the
altar of the Numen Augusti.[6] The same happened at Forum Clodii
at the altar of the Numen Augustum in A.D. 18: first animal sacrifice,
and then incense and wine; but the latter two were offered to his
Genius, also to the Genius of Tiberius on his birthday.[7] After his death
the Arvals sacrificed an ox to Iuppiter on the Capitol on the first day
and another ox to Divus Augustus at his new temple on the second day.[8]

Tiberius tried to reduce the celebrations, although he did not
eliminate them.[9] His birthday, 16 November, was recorded in the
calendars,[10] observed by the Arvals,[11] and chosen in 29 at Lapethus on
Cyprus for the dedication of his temple,[12] which may have been done
elsewhere also. But it was one of the offences committed by Seianus
that he celebrated his own birthday in public.[13] And after the death of
Seianus Tiberius refused to accept the special horse-races and banquets
which were voted for his birthday.[14]

Caligula returned to the old pomp. He celebrated the dedication of
the temple of Divus Augustus in 37 for two days with banquets, spec-
tacles, and horse-races; he had his share in this festival because the
second day, 31 August, was his own birthday.[15] In 39 he dismissed the

---

[1] Dio 54. 8. 5.

[2] *Or. gr.* 458 (E.–J. 98). 4; 23; 52; 55; U. Laffi, *Studi class. e orientali* 16 (1967), 5 ff.

[3] *Or. gr.* 456. 20 (*IGR* 4. 39).

[4] *ILS* 108: 'immolatio Caesari hostia, supplicatio.'

[5] On the birthdays of members of the imperial family see the list in Degrassi 563; A. S.
Hoey, *YCS* 7 (1940), 182 ff.; Eitrem, *Pap. Osl.* 77 (3, pp. 45 ff.; 49. 1).

[6] *ILS* 112 (E.–J. 100). 14 ff.   [7] *ILS* 154 (E.–J. 101). 10 f.

[8] Henzen, *AFA* 52.

[9] Suet. *Tib.* 26. 1: 'natalem suum plebeis incurrentem circensibus vix unius bigae adiecti-
one honorari passus est'; Dio 57. 8. 3: οὔτε ἐν τοῖς γενεθλίοις αὐτοῦ γίγνεσθαί τι παρὰ τὸ
καθεστηκὸς ἐπέτρεπεν.

[10] Degrassi 531.   [11] Henzen, *AFA* 52.   [12] *Or. gr.* 583.

[13] Dio 58. 2. 7 (A.D. 29): ἐψηφίσθη ὅπως τὰ γενέθλια αὐτοῦ δημοσίᾳ ἑορτάζηται; Mommsen,
StR 2. 813. 3.

[14] Dio 58. 12. 8.

[15] Dio 59. 7. 1 f.

consuls because they did not announce supplications for his birthday, although the races and *venationes* were held, as before, by the praetors.[1] And in 40 he long postponed his *ovatio* so that he could hold it on his birthday.[2] He was more than extravagant in the case of his dead sister Drusilla. Her birthday was celebrated in 38 in the manner of the festival of Cybele, the Megalesia, lasting two days, and her golden image was taken on a chariot of elephants to the Circus; finally a banquet was held for the senators and the knights.[3] But this whim was not repeated. It was decreed in 40 that the birthdays of Tiberius and Drusilla should be observed in the same manner as was that of Augustus.[4]

The pomp was reduced once more by Claudius. The Acts of the Arvals, however, prove that the traditional offerings were made.[5] Dio's statement that the festival of 1 August, which was Claudius' birthday, was and remained exclusively that of Mars[6] is therefore misleading. Moreover he also celebrated the birthdays of his father and mother, Drusus and Antonia, and transferred the traditional festivals of those days to other days,[7] which was the exact opposite of what was decreed about Caesar's birthday in 42 B.C. Nero's birthday, 15 December, was celebrated by the Arvals in A.D. 55 with sacrifices to the Capitoline triad, his Salus, and his Genius; in 57–60 to the same but, whereas his Genius remained, his Salus was replaced by the *Salus publica*, and Concordia was added.[8] The Arvals also sacrificed on the birthdays of various members of the imperial family, mostly to the Capitoline triad, but only until the death of Nero.[9] And yet these anniversaries must have been continued, because the Feriale Duranum records many birthdays of the Divi with the sacrifice of an ox to the Divus in question, and the birthdays of the Divae with a *supplicatio* to the Diva.[10]

The history of the imperial birthdays need not be pursued further. It is clear that it was a momentous decision in 45 and 42 to celebrate Caesar's birthday in public; it was one of the ways of showing his exceptional standing among his fellow citizens, and it was his example that was followed later. It is less clear whether, had he lived longer, he would have celebrated his festival in the same manner as his successors did theirs or would have created something different. The results of this survey, as far as the problem of Caesar's Genius is concerned, are

[1] Dio 59. 20. 1. [2] Suet. *Cal.* 49. 2. [3] Dio 59. 11. 3; 13. 8.
[4] Dio 59. 24. 7. [5] Henzen, *AFA* 53.
[6] Dio 60. 5. 3; A. S. Hoey, *YCS* 7 (1940), 124f.
[7] Dio 60. 5. 1; Suet. *Claud.* 11. 2.
[8] Henzen, *AFA* 57; above, p. 173. 4.
[9] Henzen, *AFA* 51 ff. [10] See the list in *YCS* 7. 182.

meagre. We have met the Genius of Augustus and Tiberius only once[1] and Nero's Genius in a more central position. We must return to the problem again when further evidence is available.

(b) The Oath

Various oaths, in fact too many, were created in Caesar's honour and for his protection: oaths of inviolability, of allegiance, for his welfare, for his acts, past and future.[2] It is not recorded which deity was invoked in these oaths. Dio says in a different context that an oath by Caesar's Tyche or by Caesar's Tyche and Hygieia was introduced:[3] this was no doubt a more general oath, private and public, but the special oaths too, mentioned above, may have had the same or a similar wording.

The principal god of the oath in Rome was Iuppiter, either alone (and in this case often called Dius Fidius), or together with the *Di Penates*; there were others like Hercules or Castor and Pollux.[4] A private oath could also be sworn by the Genius of an individual, especially of the *pater familias*.[5] If Dio speaks of Tyche he does so in accordance with Greek terminology: the Tyche, like the Daemon, was the divine protector of the individual and was worshipped by him privately.[6] A public cult was created for the Tyche of a king, and public as well as private oaths were sworn by her.[7] Because the corresponding Roman personal god was the Genius it has been assumed that by Tyche Dio refers not to Fortuna,[8] her usual equivalent, but to Genius—which he also does elsewhere.[9] This means the introduction of a public oath by the Genius Caesaris[10] and by the equivalent of Hygieia, the Salus Caesaris. And there must have been a further oath in his name, 'per Caesarem', as we learn from later evidence about him and his successors. It rests on

---

[1] *ILS* 154. 10 ff.; above, p. 210.

[2] Cf. App. *BC* 2. 130. 544: μῆδε Καίσαρα ὤνησαν ὅρκοι τοσοίδε καὶ ἀραί.

[3] Dio 44. 6. 1; 50. 1.   [4] Wissowa 118; 271; 279; Latte 122; 126.

[5] Plaut. *Capt.* 977, etc.; above, p. 205. 5.

[6] See above, p. 126. 7.

[7] See above, p. 127. 3. It was rightly inferred from the passages in question that this oath was performed generally (denied by Bömer, *Athen.* 54 (1966), 82 ff.): it is supported by the later oath by the Tyche of the emperors (below, p. 213. 6), and by the oath by the Daemon of the kings of Egypt (p. 127. 3).

[8] See above, p. 206.

[9] Other instances of Dio's use of Τύχη for Genius are 57. 8. 3; 58. 2. 8; 59. 4. 4; cf. the bilingual inscription from Perge: 'Genio civitatis ... Τύχη τῆς πόλεως ...' (S. Jameson, *JRS* 55 (1965), 55).

[10] Mommsen, *StR* 2. 809; accepted, e.g., by Meyer, *Caesars Monarchie* 513; L. R. Taylor 67; 151; v. Premerstein, 35; Taeger, *Charisma* 2. 68; cf. *Ath. Mitt.* 77 (1962), 310; rejected by Bömer, l.c. 79; 105.

the example of the Greek kings of Egypt[1] but also on the precedent of
Romulus, who used to be addressed with the invocation 'Equirine'.[2]

When soon after his death an altar was erected in the Forum and
oaths were sworn there, they were sworn by him, 'per Caesarem',[3]
not by his Genius; and after his consecration an oath existed for a while
'per Iovem O. M. ac Divum Iulium'.[4] Similarly there was an oath by
Augustus and later by Divus Augustus,[5] never by his Genius, although
the Greeks swore by his Tyche.[6] An attempt was made c. 13 B.C. to
swear by his Numen,[7] which was something very different, but even
this came to nothing, probably because of the resistance of Augustus.
Tiberius always refused to have an oath by his Genius,[8] but like Augustus allowed an oath by his name.[9] When Seianus tried to introduce an
oath by the Genius of both of them[10] Tiberius resisted again. Caligula made
the oath by his Genius obligatory and put to death those who refused to
swear it.[11] The absurd story that he swore by the Genius and Salus of
his horse Incitatus[12] is valuable in so far as it confirms the existence of the
oath by his Genius. Another and more reliable assertion is that he also
swore by the Numen of his sister Drusilla,[13] which recalls the similar

---

[1] Preisigke, *Sammelbuch* 5680; *Pap. Hibeh* 38; *Pap. Tebtunis* 78.

[2] Paul. Fest. 81 M. (71 L.): 'Equirine iusiurandum per Quirinum'; Diod. 37. 11 (oath
of 91 B.C.): ὄμνυμι . . . τοὺς κτίστας γεγενημένους τῆς ῾Ρώμης ἡμιθέους; Tac. *H.* 4. 58: 'te,
Iuppiter Optime Maxime . . ., te, Quirine, Romanae parens urbis, precor venerorque.'

[3] Suet. *Caes.* 85 (below, p. 364. 6).

[4] Dio 47. 18. 5 (above p. 207. 1; below, p. 392. 4).

[5] Ov. *Trist.* 2. 54: 'per te praesentem conspicuumque deum'; *P. Oxy.* 1453 (30/29 B.C.):
Καίσαρα θεόν (Wilcken, *APF* 6 (1920), 422 f.); *BGU* 543 (28/27 B.C.); *P. Tebt.* 382: Καίσαρα
Αὐτοκράτορα (Seidl, op. cit. 10); *ILS* 8781 (Gangra, 3 B.C.): . . . καὶ αὐτὸν τὸν Σεβαστόν; Wilcken,
Chrest. no. 111 (Egypt, A.D. 6): ῎Ομνυμι Καίσαρα Αὐτοκράτορα θεοῦ υἱὸν Δία ᾿Ελευθέριον Σεβα-
στόν; *JRS* 50 (1960), 75 (Cyprus, A.D. 14): τὸν ἔκγονον τῆς ᾿Αφροδίτης, Σεβαστὸν Θεὸν Καίσαρα;
ILS 190 (Aritium, A.D. 37): 'Iuppiter Optimus Maximus ac Divus Augustus ceterique omnes
di immortales'; *Syll.* 797 (Assus, A.D. 37): ῎Ομνυμεν Δία Σωτῆρα καὶ Θεὸν Καίσαρα Σεβαστόν.

[6] *BGU* 1141. 10 (Egypt 13/12 B.C.): καὶ τὴν Καίσαρος Τύχην σε ἐξορκίζω; Macrob. 2. 4. 31:
νὴ τὴν σὴν Τύχην, Σεβαστέ; cf. *UPZ* 122. 17 (157 B.C.): σὺν τοῖς θεοῖς καὶ τῇ σῇ Τύχῃ; Eitrem,
Symb. Osl. 13 (1934), 50.

[7] Hor. *epist.* 2. 1. 16: 'praesenti tibi maturos largimur honores / iurandasque tuum per
Numen ponimus aras'; cf. *c.* 4. 5. 31 ff. Mommsen, *StR* 2. 809. 4; *Ges. Schr.* 7. 180 f., quoted
this as evidence for the oath by the Genius Augusti: I prefer to think that it records the first
attempt to introduce the cult of the Numen Augusti; see above, p. 53. 13; below, p. 304. 3.

[8] Dio 57. 8. 3: οὔτ' ὀμνύναι τοῖς ἀνθρώποις τὴν ἑαυτοῦ Τύχην συνεχώρει.

[9] Dio 58. 12. 6: μήτε τοὺς ὅρκους ἐπ' ἄλλου τινὸς πλὴν τοῦ αὐτοκράτορος ποιεῖσθαι; E.-J.
117 (Egypt, A.D. 37): ὀμνύω Τιβέριον Καίσαρα, νέον Σεβαστόν.

[10] Dio 58. 2. 8 (A.D. 29): καὶ εὔχοντο ὑπὲρ ἀμφοῖν ὁμοίως καὶ ἔθυον τήν τε Τύχην αὐτῶν
ὤμνυσαν (Mommsen, *StR* 2. 810. 1).

[11] Suet. *Cal.* 27. 3: 'multos . . . condemnavit . . . quod numquam per Genium suum
deierassent'; cf. *ILS* 192 (A.D. 38): 'pro salute et pace et victoria et Genio Caesaris Augusti'.

[12] Dio 59. 14. 7: τήν τε Σωτηρίαν αὐτοῦ καὶ τὴν Τύχην ὤμνυε; cf. Suet. *Cal.* 55. 3. The 'ancestors' of Incitatus were Alexander's Bucephalas and Caesar's miraculous horse; see above,
pp. 86 f.

[13] Suet. *Cal.* 24. 2; cf. *ILS* 195: '. . . numinis honore delato'.

attempt made in honour of Augustus. As to the later emperors, it is a fact that their Genius was included in the oath. Until recently the earliest piece of evidence belonged to the reign of Domitian,[1] from which (certainly unjustified) inferences were made for the practice under Augustus.[2] The wax-tablets from Herculaneum have now provided ample evidence for Vespasian and one tablet is even Neronian. The oath was either by Iuppiter and the Genius of the emperor[3] or by the Genius alone;[4] the Neronian oath also included the Divi,[5] that is, Augustus and Claudius. The official change to the Genius of the emperor was therefore made either under Nero or earlier.

The provisional conclusion is that Dio's isolated evidence about the oath by the Genius Caesaris is to be trusted. It is supported by the evidence about Seianus, Caligula, Nero, and Vespasian, and indirectly by the evasions of Augustus and the refusal of Tiberius. It is not contradicted by the fact that after his death the oath was by Caesar or by Divus Iulius: the Genius was the protecting god only during the lifetime of the individual.[6]

(c) The Genius of the Emperor

The next question concerns the Genius of the emperor: can its origin be traced back to Caesar, and if so, what does it contribute to our knowledge of the Caesarian concept? We begin with Augustus. It will be remembered that the Genius was in the first place the private god

---

[1] *ILS* 6088. XXVI: 'iuranto . . . per Iovem et Divom Augustum et Divom Claudium et Divom Vespasianum Augustum et Divom Titum Augustum et Genium Domitiani Augusti deosque Penates'; 9059 (A.D. 94): 'iuratusque dixit per I. O. M. et Genium . . . Imperatoris Caesaris Domitiani'; Seidl, *Der Eid im römisch-ägyptischen Provinzialrecht* 11 ff.; 23 ff.

[2] Wissowa 79.

[3] Pugliese Carratelli, *Par. d. Pass.* 3 (1948), 174, no. XIX: 'scripsi iuravique per Iovem O. M. et Genium Imp. Vespasiani Caes. Aug. liberorumque eius'; similar 173 f., nos. XVII f. It is curious that the sons of Vespasian were included in the oath.

[4] Ibid. 171, no. XVI: 'scripsi et iuravi per Genium Imperatoris Aug. liberorumque eius'; 175, no. XX (= *AE* 1951, 217); 177, no. XXII; 179, no. XXIV.

[5] Arangio-Ruiz and Pugliese Carratelli, *Par. d. Pass.* 9 (1954), 64, no. LXV: 'iuravit per Iovem et numina [Divoru]m (rather than '[deoru]m') et Genium Neronis Claudi Caesaris Aug.'

[6] This remains true in spite of *ILS* 72 (Degr. 410, Aesernia): 'Genio Deivi Iuli parentis patriae, quem senatus populusque Romanus in deorum numerum rettulit.' This inscription is often quoted (see Bömer, l.c. 99. 52) but never properly explained. It is, I believe, the earliest example of those inscriptions (*Thes.L.L.* 6. 1834; W. Schwarzlose, *De titulis sepulcralibus Latinis* (Diss. Halle 1913), 34 f.; Bömer, *Ahnenkult u. Ahnenglaube* 20 f.; cf. Latte 103. 3) where the Genius refers, like the Di Manes, to a dead person, e.g. *ILS* 1795 (A.D. 39/42): 'Genio Coeti Herodiani . . .' If so, no unusual significance can be attributed to it; cf. also Arnob. 3. 41 (Varro); Ov. *F.* 2. 545: 'ille (Aeneas) patris Genio sollemnia dona ferebat' (with Bömer's note).

of the individual; and yet he was never strictly private, in so far as members of the household, freedmen and slaves, had their share in his cult.[1] This cult was naturally a limited one. It was used as the starting-point, but was widely expanded when the cult of the Genius Augusti was instituted together with that of the Lares at the *compita*, crossroads, of Rome, *c.* 12 B.C.[2] This cult was exclusively a cult of freedmen and slaves, though no longer of those of an individual household, and represented a special religious bond between them and the divine power of Augustus. This Genius received dedications,[3] but these were again from dependants like freedmen, which the Genius of anyone could receive.[4] The free citizens had no share in this cult;[5] it was not a cult of the State and was not recorded in the calendars. This Genius did not receive any offerings at the public celebration of Augustus' birthday and was not a god of the oath either. The Greeks swore by the Tyche of Augustus,[6] it is true, and meant to dedicate a temple to her (or his Genius) at Athens:[7] but this was not at Rome. This is a puzzling situation in view of what we have learnt about the Genius Caesaris. Clearly Augustus did not want a public cult and Tiberius too resisted. If their Genius had a share in the celebration of their birthdays at Forum Clodi in A.D. 18,[8] it was probably only a local arrangement which had nothing to do with the cult of the State. Seianus tried to bring about a change but in vain.[9] Caligula was equally firm at the

[1] See above, p. 205.

[2] Ov. *F.* 5. 145: 'mille Lares Geniumque ducis, qui tradidit illos, / urbs habet, et vici numina trina colunt'; *ILS* 3609 ff., etc.; Wissowa 172; Bömer, *Unters. über die Religion d. Sklaven* 1. 38 ff.; id. *Athen.* 54 (1966), 106 f.; Latte 307.

[3] *ILS* 116: 'Genio Augusti et Ti. Caesaris, Iunoni Liviae Mystes l(ibertus)'; 3218: 'Apollini Genioque Augusti Caesaris sacrum. L. Apusulenus L. l. Eros . . . d.p.s.'; *CIL* 2. 3524: 'Genio Augusti . . . L. Trebius, L. l. Menophilus'; *CIL* 10. 816: 'Mamia P. f. sacerdos public(us) Genio Aug.' (the latter two are free-born but clearly not old citizens); Genius of Tiberius: *ILS* 6080 (E.–J. 133); *CIL* 13. 941 (Aquitania): 'Iovi O. M. et Genio Ti. Augusti sacrum laniones.'

[4] Cf. *ILS* 3640: 'Genio L(ucii) nostri Felix l(ibertus)'; 3641: 'Genio M(arci) n(ostri) et Laribus duo Diadumeni liberti'; 3642 ff.; Petron. 53. 3: 'Mithridates servus in crucem actus est, quia Gai nostri Genio maledixerat'; *Thes.L.L.* 6. 1831. 67 ff.; W. F. Otto, *RE* 7. 1161.

[5] This would not be quite correct, if Dio were right in stating that a perjury committed under Tiberius involved the Genius Augusti and not, as we ought to assume, Divus Augustus (57. 9. 3: ἐγκληθέντας τινὰς ὡς καὶ ἐπιωρκηκότας τὴν Τύχην αὐτοῦ ἀπέλυσε). But Tacitus refers in the same context to the 'numen Augusti', which he uses in the more general, not in the technical, sense (*A.* 1. 73. 2: 'Rubrio crimini dabatur violatum periurio numen Augusti'; cf. 3. 66. 2: 'violatum Augusti numen').

[6] See above, p. 213.

[7] Suet. *Aug.* 60: 'reges amici atque socii . . . cuncti simul aedem Iovis Olympii Athenis . . . perficere . . . destinaverunt Genioque eius dedicare; ac saepe . . . peragranti cotidiana officia togati ac sine regio insigni more clientium praestiterunt.'

[8] *ILS* 154; above, p. 210.

[9] Dio 58. 2. 8 (above, p. 213. 7). A dedication to Tiberius' Tyche on Cos, *IGR* 4. 1096.

beginning, and even recorded on a commemorative tablet that he refused to have a public cult of his Genius.[1] Later he changed his mind, as the report about the oaths shows.[2] There is explicit evidence about Nero: it was under him that the Arvals first sacrificed to the Genius of the emperor;[3] that the legend 'Genio Augusti' first appeared on coins;[4] that an offering was made to his Genius on his birthday;[5] and that an oath by his Genius was first recorded on a document.[6] And so it went on under his successors, including Trajan.[7] Yet Pliny praised Trajan's restraint when he requested that thanksgivings should be offered to Iuppiter Capitolinus and not to his Genius:[8] the extraordinary standing of the emperor's Genius was felt even at that time.

This history of the Genius could lead, with regard to Caesar, to two different conclusions. The one would be that there was no public cult of the Genius Caesaris. The only direct piece of evidence about the oath which comes from Dio would be wrong, inspired by the practice of Dio's own time. For the birthday there would be only circumstantial evidence, for the general cult not even that. The later evidence would not supply what is missing. Augustus and Tiberius were opposed to a public cult of their Genius, who is not mentioned in connection with their birthdays. The oath was in their name, by Augustus and by Tiberius, never by their Genius. There was a cult of the Genius Augusti but not for the citizens of Rome. One would have to rely on the evidence about Caligula and Nero, which would, however, lead to the unlikely inference that Caesar, like them, wanted to rule as an autocrat.

The opposite conclusion would be that the same evidence proves that there was a cult of the Genius Caesaris. Dio's testimony should not be swept away. The oath by Caesar or by Divus Iulius is no counter-instance: the formula recorded under Nero, Vespasian, and Domitian shows that only the living emperor is represented by his Genius, the others appear as Divi. The resistance of Augustus and Tiberius does

---

[1] Dio 59. 4. 4 (A.D. 37): ψηφισθέν ποτε τῇ Τύχῃ αὐτοῦ θύεσθαι παρέμενος, ὥστε καὶ ἐς στήλην αὐτὸ τοῦτο ἐγγραφῆναι.

[2] See above, p. 210.   [3] Henzen, AFA 72.

[4] Mattingly 1. 248. At that time it was apparently thought to be extraordinary because it is not found again until Commodus (Mattingly 4. 742; 825); for later evidence see Bernhart, Handb. d. Münzkunde 177 f.

[5] See above, p. 173.   [6] See above, p. 214. 3.

[7] Cf. ILS 1824; Mitteis, Chrest. no. 203. 21 (A.D. 108): ὀμνύω θεοὺς Σεβαστοὺς καὶ τὴν Αὐτοκράτορος Καίσαρος Νερουᾶ Τραιανοῦ... Τύχην καὶ τοὺς πατρῴους θεούς; Seidl, op. cit. 12.

[8] Pliny Paneg. 52. 6: 'simili reverentia, Caesar, non apud Genium tuum bonitati tuae gratias agi, sed apud numen Iovis Optimi Maximi pateris: illi debere nos quidquid tibi debeamus'; cf. Sauter, Der röm. Kaiserkult bei Martial 42.

not render the case impossible; on the contrary it proves that there were plans, partly rejected, partly tolerated by them, which cannot have been inspired by anything else except the example of Caesar. The behaviour of Caligula is important because he often took up Caesarian ideas and cults which were avoided by Augustus and Tiberius. It is no chance that Dio's evidence about the oath by Caesar's Genius and Salus, which was suspected as anachronistic, is exactly reproduced in the tale about the oath by the Genius and Salus of Caligula's horse. This is strong support, as is the fact that Caligula, after some hesitation, insisted on the establishment of the cult of his Genius. The sacrifice to Nero's Genius and Salus on his birthday would again be no innovation but a resumption of what was done, or was about to be done, under Caesar.

The second argument is by far the stronger one. It does not eliminate evidence which seems unexceptionable and gives a satisfactory answer to the question of who was ultimately responsible for the institution of the cult of the Genius in the imperial period: not Seianus or Caligula but Caesar. If this is so, it follows that Caesar's relationship to his fellow citizens had become that of the patron to his clients (rather than that of an autocrat), which has already been apparent to us in other respects as well.[1] The startling character of Caesar's innovation can best be measured by the fact that Augustus only allowed freedmen and slaves to worship his own Genius.

3. VOWS AND OATHS

(a) Vota pro salute Caesaris

Dio mentions in a different context, for the year 44 B.C., that public vows were to be made annually for Caesar's welfare.[2] What was meant becomes clear through the obvious precedent, the *vota pro salute rei publicae*. The new consuls entering office on 1 January offered a sacrifice to Iuppiter on the Capitol in fulfilment of the vow of the past year and renewed the vow for the current year.[3] The Athenians had a similar annual sacrifice, the Eisiteria, for the Boule and the people, though it was offered by a priest and not by the archon.[4] It was now a double

---

[1] See above, p. 203.

[2] Dio 44. 6. 1: καὶ εὔχεσθαι ὑπὲρ αὐτοῦ δημοσίᾳ κατ' ἔτος ἕκαστον; 44. 50. 1: ὑπὲρ οὗ δημοσίᾳ κατ' ἔτος εὔχεσθαι ἐψηφίσαντο.

[3] Dio, frg. 102. 12 (1, p. 347 B.); 45. 17. 9; 51. 19. 7 f. (below, p. 218. 4); Livy 21. 63. 7; Ov. F. 1. 79 ff.; Tac. A. 4. 70. 1; Suet. Nero 46. 2; SHA Ael. 4. 8; Mommsen, StR 1. 616; Marquardt-Wissowa, Röm. StV. 3. 266; Himmelmann-Wildschütz, Festschr. F. Matz (1962), 116 ff.; Andreae, Festschr. U. Jantzen (1969), 9 ff.

[4] IG 2². 689. 20: ὁ ἱερεὺς ἔθυσεν τὰ εἰσιτήρια ἐπὶ τῇ σωτηρίᾳ τῆς βουλῆς καὶ τοῦ δήμου; Syll. 227. 22; Stengel, RE 5. 2149; Busolt, Griech. Staatskunde 1. 518; Deubner, Att. Feste 175.

vow *pro salute rei publicae et Caesaris*. This again must have had its analogies in the Greek tyrannies and monarchies; there is explicit evidence about Dio of Syracuse.[1] The text of the vow may have been identical to some extent with the relevant prayers of the imperial period as they are known from the Acts of the Arvals[2] and from some letters of Pliny.[3] If so, it invoked Iuppiter and promised him a sacrifice, an ox, if Caesar should live another year and if Iuppiter saved him from all dangers and preserved him in the same or a better condition. It will have been preceded by a similar prayer for the State and by the assertion that its welfare depended on Caesar's welfare.

Such vows were decreed for Octavian in 30 B.C. after the conquest of Alexandria. It is probably just an accident that Dio mentions the priests and priestesses but not the consuls.[4] It is certain that the consuls performed the sacrifice, but in addition all the priesthoods will have done the same; the Arvals in fact did it regularly.[5] The same decree was made for all the emperors after Augustus. Under Tiberius Livia was included in the vow,[6] after her death Seianus,[7] probably without the knowledge of Tiberius, who some years earlier objected to the inclusion of the princes Nero and Drusus.[8] Caligula's sisters were included[9] and later all members of the imperial family. The vows for the State

---

[1] Plut. *Dio* 13. 5: θυσία μὲν ἦν πάτριος ἐν τοῖς τυραννείοις (= palace of Syracuse)· τοῦ δὲ κήρυκος, ὥσπερ εἰώθει, κατευξαμένου διαμένειν τὴν τυραννίδα ἀσάλευτον πολλοὺς χρόνους.

[2] Henzen, *AFA* CVII: 'Iuppiter Optime Maxime, si imperator Titus ... et Caesar ... Domitianus ... vivent domusque eorum incolumis erit a.d. III Nonas Ianuarias, quae proximae ... erunt fuerint, et eum diem eosque salvos servaveris ex periculis, si qua sunt eruntve ante eum diem, eventumque bonum ... dederis, eosque in eo statu quo nunc sunt aut eo meliore servaveris, ast tu ea ita faxsis, tunc tibi nomine collegi fratrum Arvalium bubus auratis II vovemus esse futurum'; Tert. *cor.* 12: 'annua votorum nuncupatio quid videtur? ... accipe ... et verba: "tunc tibi, Iuppiter, bovem cornibus auro decoratis vovemus esse futurum".'

[3] Pliny *ep.* 10. 100: 'vota, domine, priore anno nuncupata alacres laetique persolvimus novaque rursus ... suscepimus precati deos, ut te remque publicam florentem et incolumem ea benignitate servarent, quam ... meruisti'; 10. 35; *Paneg.* 67. 3 ff.

[4] Dio 51. 19. 7: τούς τε ἱερέας καὶ τὰς ἱερείας ἐν ταῖς ὑπέρ τε τοῦ δήμου καὶ τῆς βουλῆς εὐχαῖς καὶ ὑπὲρ ἐκείνου ὁμοίως εὔχεσθαι ... ἐκέλευσαν.

[5] Henzen, *AFA* 89 ff.; cf. Ov. *Pont.* 4. 4. 29: 'templaque Tarpeiae primum tibi sedis adiri, / et fieri faciles in tua vota deos: / colla boves niveos certae praebere securi'; 4. 9. 49: 'nunc pro Caesaribus superis decernere grates, / albave opimorum colla ferire boum'; Dio 59. 3. 4: τάς τε εὐχὰς τὰς κατ᾽ ἔτος ὑπὸ τῶν ἀρχόντων καὶ ὑπὸ τῶν ἱερέων ὑπέρ τε ἑαυτοῦ καὶ ὑπὲρ τοῦ δημοσίου ποιουμένας; 75. 14. 7.

[6] Henzen, *AFA* XXXIII (A.D. 27); Kornemann, *Doppelprinzipat* 37.

[7] Dio 58. 2. 8: εὔχοντο ὑπὲρ ἀμφοῖν ὁμοίως καὶ ἔθυον.

[8] Suet. *Tib.* 54. 1: 'ut comperit ineunte anno pro eorum quoque salute publice vota suscepta, egit cum senatu non debere talia praemia tribui nisi expertis et aetate provectis'; Tac. *A.* 4. 17. 1 (A.D. 24): 'pontifices eorumque exemplo ceteri sacerdotes, cum pro incolumitate principis vota susciperent, Neronem quoque et Drusum isdem dis commendavere.'

[9] Dio 59. 9. 2 (A.D. 38): τάς τε εὐχὰς ὑπὲρ πάντων αὐτῶν ὁμοίως ἐποιήσαντο; Kornemann, op. cit. 52; v. Premerstein, 67.

were always performed on 1 January, those for the emperor were moved to another day and were fixed *c.* A.D. 38 on 3 January, where they remained during the imperial period.[1]

It had become routine to make a vow for the welfare of the emperor; it was not when it was decreed for the first time for Caesar. How did it happen? It was traditional to pray for good health or for recovery from illness, to make vows accordingly, and to fulfil them with offerings.[2] This was naturally the business of the individual, even though the offerings were made to the gods of the State. But there were situations when the health of a single man was vital for many. When M. Livius Drusus, the champion of the Italians, was taken ill in 91 B.C., public vows were made for his recovery,[3] not of course in Rome; and likewise in 50 for Pompey, whose recovery was then celebrated in all *municipia* with festive thanksgivings,[4] though again not in Rome. The system of annual and collegiate magistrates did not promote public interest in the wellbeing of an individual. But there were exceptional situations in dangerous wars and civil strife[5] when a single man of action, a dictator, was chosen: public interest then naturally concentrated on his person. Cicero wrote in his *De re publica* about the planned dictatorship of the younger Scipio, adding that the welfare of the State depended on his person.[6] He repeated it about Pompey, who was to become another dictator[7] but was then made a sole consul in 52 B.C.; and he said it again

---

[1] Plut. *Cic.* 2. 1; Lucian *Pseudolog.* 8; *IGR* 4. 915 c 9; SHA *Pert.* 6. 4; Lyd. *mens.* 4. 10; *Dig.* 50. 16. 233; Henzen, *AFA* 89 f.; Mommsen, *StR* 2. 810 f.; Marquardt, *StV* 3. 266 f.; R. O. Fink, *YCS* 7 (1940), 52 f.; J. M. Reynolds, *PBSR* 30 (1962), 33 ff.; cf. *Mullus, Festschr. f. Th. Klauser* (1964), 396.

[2] Cf. *RE* 8A. 265.

[3] *Vir. ill.* 66. 12: 'vota pro illo per Italiam publice suscepta sunt'; Münzer, *RE* 13. 879; v. Premerstein, 28; cf. the Soteria in the Greek world, Hdt. 1. 118; *Or. gr.* 4. 40 ff.; *Syll.* 391. 22 ff., etc.; Pfister, *RE* 3A. 1221 f.

[4] Cic. *Att.* 8. 16. 1: 'municipia . . . de illo aegroto vota faciebant'; 9. 5. 3; *Tusc.* 1. 86: 'coronati Neapolitani fuerunt . . . volgo ex oppidis publice gratulabantur'; Vell. 2. 48. 2: 'universa Italia vota pro salute eius primi omnium civium suscepit'; Dio 41. 6. 3; Plut. *Pomp.* 57. 1; below, p. 290. The first official vows made in Rome were for the recovery of A. Hirtius in 44 B.C., Cic. *Phil.* 7. 12; 10. 16; L. W. Daly, *TAPA* 81 (1950), 166; cf. *RE* 8A. 266 f.

[5] Cic. *leg.* 3. 9: 'quando duellum gravius, discordiae civium escunt'; *Or. Claudii, ILS* 212. I 30 f.: 'in asperioribus bellis aut in civili motu difficiliore'; Mommsen, *StR* 2. 142; 156. 2.

[6] Cic. *rep.* 6. 12: 'tu eris unus in quo nitatur civitatis salus . . . dictator rem publicam constituas oportebit'; Meyer, op. cit. 185. 1; C. Nicolet, *REL* 42 (1964), 220 ff. On Sulla as dictator 'rei publicae constituendae' see App. *BC* 1. 99. 462; Mommsen, *StR* 2. 703. 3; Nicolet, l.c. 213 ff. Mommsen, op. cit. 704, suggested that Caesar too was such a dictator; it is now proved by epigraphical evidence from Tarentum (above, p. 200. 3): L. Gasperini, l.c. 386 ff.

[7] Cic. *Q. fr.* 2. 14 (13). 5; 3. 6 (8). 4: 'rumor dictatoris iniucundus bonis . . . Pompeius plane se negat velle; antea mihi ipse non negabat'; 3. 7 (9). 3; *Att.* 4. 18. 3; Plut. *Pomp.* 54. 3; Nicolet, l.c. 217; R. G. G. Coleman, *Proc. Cambr. Phil. Soc.* 1964, 10.

about him later.[1] Caesar became *dictator rei publicae constituendae* in 49 for a short while, then annually, and in 44 for life.[2] Cicero now said about Caesar in 46[3] what he said before about Scipio and Pompey; Caesar held the same view,[4] and so probably did many others.[5] It was not Caesar's health that they were concerned with. He was a healthy man, who had endured all the hardships of his campaigns[6] and was now preparing for the Parthian expedition, which was to last for several years: all the gossip about his failing health[7] is to be judged in the light of these facts. And an occasional illness would not have justified the institution of annual vows. When Cicero spoke in 46, a plot against Caesar's life had just been discovered, which was no doubt the immediate cause of Cicero's protestations. It was the old view now applied to Caesar that became the basis of the new religious ceremony. It was an exceptional but not a divine honour: a break with tradition and the religious expression of the acceptance of Caesar's sole rule for life in the interests of the welfare of the Roman people.

(b) Sacrosanctus

Another measure, both legal and religious, to protect Caesar's life against plots was the law rendering him, like the tribunes, inviolable (*sacrosanctus*).[8] It was also decreed that he had the right to sit in the Circus on the benches (*subsellia*) of the tribunes,[9] thus demonstrating his new status in public. He won a privilege which the other magistrates did not possess: a tribune could not be arrested, offended, or harmed, and could kill an offender without trial, as could any other citizen

---

[1] Cic. *Mil.* 19; *Att.* 6. 3. 4; 8. 2. 3; above, p. 169. 4; Meyer, op. cit. 262; 268.

[2] Drumann 3. 474 f.; 507 f.; 735 ff.; Mommsen, *StR* 2. 704; above, p. 219. 6.

[3] Cic. *Marc.* 22; 25; 32; 24; 29; 33; above, p. 166.

[4] Suet. *Caes.* 86. 2: 'non tam suae quam rei publicae interesse uti salvus esset ... rem publicam, si quid sibi eveniret, neque quietam fore et aliquanto deteriore condicione civilia bella subituram.'

[5] It was often repeated in the imperial period, e.g. Henzen, *AFA* CXIV 39 (A.D. 86, Domitian): 'ex cuius incolumitate omnium salus constat'; Pliny *Paneg.* 67. 6: 'tibi salus tua invisa est, si non sit cum rei publicae salute coniuncta'; *ep.* 10. 35: 'sollemnia vota pro incolumitate tua, qua publica salus continetur, et suscepimus, domine, pariter et solvimus'; cf. Sherwin-White's note ad loc.; above, pp. 218. 2 f.

[6] Dio 44. 38. 6; Plut. *Caes.* 17.

[7] Suet. *Caes.* 45. 1; 86; Nic. Dam. *v. Caes.* 83; Dio 44. 8. 3; Plut. *Caes.* 60. 7.

[8] Dio 44. 5. 3: τά τε τοῖς δημάρχοις δεδομένα καρποῦσθαι, ὅπως, ἄν τις ἢ ἔργῳ ἢ καὶ λόγῳ αὐτὸν ὑβρίσῃ, ἱερός τε ᾖ καὶ ἐν τῷ ἄγει ἐνέχηται; 44. 49. 1: ὁ ἄσυλος; 50. 1: ὃν ἐξ ἴσου τοῖς δημάρχοις ἄσυλον ἐπεποιήκεσαν; App. *BC* 2. 144. 601: ἱερὸν καὶ ἄσυλον ... ὀνομάζοντες; Livy, *Per.* 116; Nic. Dam. 80; Mommsen, *StR* 2. 872; Hohl, *Klio* 32 (1939), 62; Strack, ibid. 363 ff.

[9] Dio 44. 4. 2: ἐν ταῖς πανηγύρεσιν ... ἐπί τε τοῦ δημαρχικοῦ βάθρου καὶ μετὰ τῶν ἀεὶ δημαρχούντων θεᾶσθαι ἔλαβε.

on his behalf.[1] The tribunician privilege was first just sworn by the *plebs*, later also guaranteed by law, the *lex Valeria-Horatia* of 449 B.C.; but the oath was preserved and with it the religious character of the act.[2] The oath was sworn in connection with a sacrifice in the name of Iuppiter Capitolinus, with the usual provision in the event of perjury. This privilege was always at the centre of political warfare, and Caesar himself justified his march on Rome in 49 with the claim that he had come to protect the rights of the tribunes Antony and Q. Cassius, who had fled to him.[3] His adversaries in turn pointed to his own offences against the tribunes L. Caecilius Metellus in 49 and C. Epidius Marullus and L. Caesetius Flavus in 44.[4]

Caesar's privilege was unprecedented. It did not mean that Caesar became a tribune—he was and remained a patrician—or that he received any of their further privileges: what was or was not decreed for him in 48 in this respect[5] is not of interest here. The initiative came from Caesar himself: so Brutus said later that the conspirators had not committed any offence against Caesar's inviolability because it was not granted him freely but extorted from the Senate after his armed entry into Rome and the murder of so many citizens.[6] The privilege provided Caesar with security and was, in contrast to that of the tribunes, not limited to one year only. The oath which was sworn for the tribunes must have been sworn for him also; but there is no explicit evidence about this. It is to be distinguished from the annual oath for his welfare which was discussed above, and from that for his acts to be considered below. The same privilege was granted to Octavian in 36,[7] although his life was not in danger, and later to all the emperors.[8]

[1] Cic. *Tull.* 47: 'legem antiquam de legibus sacratis, quae iubeat inpune occidi eum, qui tribunum pl. pulsaverit'; Livy 9. 8. 15: 'neque se ... cum sacrosancti essent, dedi hostibus violarive posse'; Dio 53. 17. 9; Mommsen, *StR* 2. 301 ff.; 879. 3.

[2] Livy 3. 55. 6: 'tribunis, ut sacrosancti viderentur ... relatis quibusdam ex magno intervallo caerimoniis renovarunt, (7) et cum religione inviolatos eos tum lege etiam fecerunt sanciendo, ut, qui tribunis plebis ... nocuisset, eius caput Iovi sacrum esset'; App. *BC* 2. 108. 453 (44 B.C., apropos the incident with Marullus): ἥ τε τῶν δημάρχων ἀρχὴ ἱερὰ καὶ ἄσυλος ἦν ἐκ νόμου καὶ ὅρκου παλαιοῦ; 2. 138. 575; Mommsen, *StR* 2. 286 f.

[3] Dion. Hal. 8. 87. 8: ὁ δὲ τῇ προφάσει ταύτῃ χρησάμενος, ὡς ἀρχὴ δήμου παναγεῖ τὸ κράτος ἀφαιρεθείσῃ παρὰ τοὺς ὅρκους τῶν προγόνων αὐτός τε σὺν δίκῃ βοηθῶν αὐτός τε σὺν τοῖς ὅπλοις ἦλθεν εἰς τὴν πόλιν καὶ τοὺς ἄνδρας ἐπὶ τὴν ἀρχὴν κατήγαγε; Mommsen, *StR* 2. 304.

[4] App. *BC* 2. 138. 575 ff.; Strack, l.c. 367.

[5] Dio 42. 20. 3; Adcock, *CAH* 9. 900 f.; Hohl, l.c. 61 ff.; Strack, ibid. 369 f.; De Visscher, *Studia et documenta historiae et iuris* 5 (1939), 103.

[6] App. *BC* 2. 138. 576: πότεροι οὖν ἐς τοὺς ἀσύλους ἡμάρτανον; ἢ Καῖσαρ μὲν ἱερὸς καὶ ἄσυλος, ὅτῳ ταῦτα οὐχ ἑκόντες, ἀλλ' ὑπ' ἀνάγκης οὐδὲ πρὶν ἐπελθεῖν αὐτὸν ἐς τὴν πατρίδα σὺν ὅπλοις καὶ τοσούσδε καὶ τοιούσδε ἀγαθοὺς πολίτας κατακανεῖν, ἐθέμεθα;

[7] *Mon. Anc.* 10. 1: 'sacrosanctus in perpetum ut essem ... , per legem sanctum est'; Dio 49. 15. 5 (who also mentions the seat on the *subsellia* of the tribunes); Mommsen, *StR* 2. 872; Strack, l.c. 363.   [8] Mommsen, *StR* 2. 879.

(c) The Oath for Caesar's Acts

A further oath was decreed in 45, probably after Caesar's return from Spain, to be sworn annually by the new magistrates, not to oppose Caesar's acts.[1] Needless to say this was against the constitution, but not without precedents. Sulla, before he left for the war against Mithridates in 87, made Cinna, the new consul and his political enemy, swear on the Capitol on entering office to maintain his measures and to show goodwill towards him, ending his oath with self-execration in the event of perjury.[2] Sulla as proconsul had no right to ask for this oath. It would have been unexceptionable in the private sphere, as shown by a second precedent, provided that it is right to connect the two cases with each other. When Caesar was still in Gaul he offered help to candidates for office on the condition that they would support his cause in Rome during his absence, and made them swear to this effect and sign a contract.[3] The oath of 45 may have been inspired by these precedents, but it was no longer a single oath like that of Cinna and his colleague, or a private oath like that of Caesar's political protégés, but an annual oath of the new magistrates. From 44 onwards it was to include his future acts also.[4] After his death it was sworn by the triumviri and by all the magistrates on the New Year's day of 42,[5] was in 29 extended to the acts of Augustus[6] and became a regular feature of the New Year ceremonies in the imperial period.[7] Caesar's acts were always included in this oath,[8] which is strange because he was

---

[1] App. BC 2. 106. 442: τὰς ἀρχὰς εὐθὺς καθισταμένας ὀμνύναι μηδενὶ τῶν ὑπὸ Καίσαρος ὁριζομένων ἀντιπράξειν (= 'se nihil contra acta Caesaris facturum': Mommsen, StR 1. 621. 7).

[2] Plut. Sulla 10. 6: Κίνναν ἀραῖς καὶ ὅρκοις καταλαβὼν εὐνοήσειν τοῖς ἑαυτοῦ πράγμασιν. (7) ὁ δὲ ἀναβὰς εἰς τὸ Καπιτώλιον, ἔχων ἐν τῇ χειρὶ λίθον, ὤμνυεν, εἶτ' ἐπαρασάμενος ἑαυτῷ μὴ φυλάττοντι τὴν πρὸς ἐκεῖνον εὔνοιαν ἐκπεσεῖν τῆς πόλεως ὥσπερ ὁ λίθος τῆς χειρός, κατέβαλε χαμάζε τὸν λίθον, οὐκ ὀλίγων παρόντων; Dio, frg. 102. 2 (1, pp. 344 f. B.): ὁ Κίννας ... οὐδὲν ὅ τι οὐ κατὰ γνώμην αὐτοῦ πράξειν, ὑπέσχετο ... (3) αὐτὸν (= Cinna) ἤδη καὶ ἑτοίμως ὥς γε καὶ ἔλεγε καὶ ὤμνυεν ἔχοντα πᾶν οἱ ὁτιοῦν ὑπουργῆσαι; Schol. Gron. Cic. Cat. p. 286 St.: 'fecit Sulla duos consules Cinnam et Octavium. iure iurando astrinxit eos, ut nullus contra acta Sullana faceret'; v. Premerstein 30; Bleicken, Jahrb. f. Num. u. Geldgesch. 13 (1963), 59; on the ceremony see Wissowa 388. 1.

[3] Suet. Caes. 23. 2: 'in magno negotio habuit ... e petitoribus non alios adiuvare aut ad honorem pati pervenire, quam qui sibi recepissent propugnaturos absentiam suam; cuius pacti non dubitavit a quibusdam ius iurandum atque etiam syngrapham exigere'; v. Premerstein 30.

[4] Dio 44. 6. 1: καὶ τὰ πραχθησόμενα αὐτῷ πάντα κύρια ἕξειν ἐνόμισαν.

[5] Dio 47. 18. 3 (below, p. 392. 2); 57. 8. 4; Mommsen, StR 1. 621. 8.

[6] Dio 51. 20. 1: τά τε πραχθέντα ὑπ' αὐτοῦ πάντα ἐν αὐτῇ τῇ τοῦ Ἰανουαρίου νουμηνίᾳ ὅρκοις ἐβεβαιώσαντο; 53. 28. 1 (below, p. 223. 3).

[7] Dio 57. 8. 5 (A.D. 15, Tiberius): ἐπὶ ταῖς τοῦ Αὐγούστου πράξεσι τούς τε ἄλλους πάντας ὥρκου καὶ αὐτὸς ὤμνυε; Tac. A. 13. 11. 1 (A.D. 54): 'cum in acta principum iurarent magistratus.'

[8] Tac. A. 16. 22. 5 (A.D. 66): 'in acta Divi Augusti et Divi Iuli non iurare.' On the omission of Divus Iulius from the oath of the imperial period see Mommsen, StR 2. 809. 3.

not counted among the emperors or the Divi, nor was an oath ever
sworn again by his name. On the other hand the oath was not sworn
for the acts of Tiberius, because he did not allow it,[1] nor for the acts
of Caligula, because they were made invalid.[2] The oath was also sworn
by the senators, it is not known since when: the first instance belongs
to the year 24 B.C.[3] It was felt, however, that the oath was against tradition and this not only by the conspirators,[4] but by Tiberius and even
by Nero, who at the beginning of his reign did not allow it and thereby
earned much praise.[5]

In sum the oath was a guarantee of legal continuity on the one hand
and an acknowledgement of Caesar's and his successors' exceptional
standing in society on the other. Its reverse was the annulment of the
acts (actorum rescissio), in the case of those emperors whose memory
was damned.[6] When the oath was extended to Caesar's future acts in
44 it enhanced his standing even more.[7] In the terms of the relevant
law about Vespasian[8] he received the right and power to do in divine
and human, public and private matters whatever seemed to him con-
ducive to the welfare and dignity of the State.

(d) The Oath of Allegiance

It is, in contrast to the other oaths, a matter of controversy whether
an oath of allegiance, a voluntary oath, was also sworn to Caesar in
44 B.C. Such an oath seems to have existed, even if in a rudimentary
form, from the earliest times, not as the rule but as the exception. The
rule was that the citizens were pledged to obedience to the magistrates
by the lex de imperio and in war by a special military oath, the sacra-
mentum: it was the submission of everyone to the legal authority.[9]
There are in addition traces of a voluntary submission of a few to a

---

[1] Tac. A. 1. 72. 2 (A.D. 15): 'neque in acta sua iurari quamquam censente senatu permisit';
Dio 57. 8. 4: . . . οὐδὲ τοῦτο τά γε πρῶτα ἐφ' ἑαυτῷ περιεῖδε γενόμενον; 59. 9. 1.

[2] Suet. Claud. 11. 3: 'Gai . . . acta omnia rescidit.' This applied to all emperors whose
memory was dishonoured, Dio 47. 18. 3; below, p. 388.

[3] Dio 53. 28. 1: ἔν τε τῇ νουμηνίᾳ ὅρκους ἡ βουλὴ βεβαιοῦσα τὰς πράξεις αὐτοῦ ἐποιήσατο;
58. 17. 2 (A.D. 32): συχνὸν ἤδη χρόνον μηκέτι κατὰ ἄνδρα τὴν βουλὴν ἐν τῇ νουμηνίᾳ ὀμνύναι,
ἀλλ' ἑνὸς . . . προομνύντος καὶ τοὺς λοιποὺς συνεπαίνειν; Mommsen, StR 2. 909. Those who did
not swear were punished, Tac. A. 4. 42. 3 (A.D. 25); 16. 22. 1 (A.D. 66).

[4] App. BC 2. 137. 572 (Brutus' speech, 44 B.C.): εἰκότως αὐτῷ δεδιότι καὶ βέβαιον ἔχοντι
τὴν τυραννίδα ἀμνηστίαν αἰτοῦντι ἔδομεν καὶ ὠμόσαμεν ὑπὲρ αὐτῆς. (573) εἰ δὲ ἡμῖν ὀμνύναι
προσέταττεν οὐ τὰ παρελθόντα μόνον οἴσειν ἐγκρατῶς, ἀλλὰ δουλεύσειν ἐς τὸ μέλλον ἑκόντας, τί
ἂν ἔπραξαν οἱ νῦν ἐπιβουλεύοντες ἡμῖν;

[5] Tac. A. 13. 11. 1.

[6] Mommsen, StR 2. 1129; Vittinghoff, Der Staatsfeind 75; below, p. 388.

[7] Mommsen, StR 2. 909.   [8] ILS 244. 17 ff. (McCrum–Woodhead, Documents 1).

[9] Mommsen, StR 1. 609; 623.

self-appointed leader in times of acute danger (*tumultus*). This was the *coniuratio*, a common oath, sworn by the leader and those who were willing to follow him to save the State.[1] This is said to have happened in 479 B.C. when the 306 Fabii went to war on their own against Veii and failed at the river Cremera;[2] and in 216 B.C. after the disaster at Cannae when the young Scipio and his company swore it and succeeded in averting the danger.[3] These two instances are legendary but the custom is certainly not.[4] A further self-appointed leader was M. Livius Drusus during the Social War, and Diodorus preserved some information about the oath which the Italians swore to him in 91 B.C.[5] They swore to have the same friends and foes as Drusus had; not to spare either their own lives or those of their children or their parents if the interests of Drusus and of their fellows so demanded; and they asked for prosperity as a reward for keeping the oath and were willing to face adversity in the event of perjury. The wording is closely related to the oath sworn later to the emperors;[6] there are differences in the strange list of gods who were invoked[7] and in the reference to Roman citizenship, which are not relevant here. It was certainly not the first oath of this kind and was not borrowed from the Greeks, who had nothing comparable. After Caesar's death many senators and knights swore such an oath to Antony at Tibur, assuring him of their *pietas* and *fides*;[8] in

---

[1] Serv. *Aen.* 8. 1: 'coniuratio . . . si esset tumultus, id est bellum Italicum vel Gallicum, in quibus ex periculi vicinitate erat timor multus. quia singulos interrogare non vacabat qui fuerat ducturus exercitum, ibat ad Capitolium . . . dicebat "qui rem publicam salvam esse vult, me sequatur", et qui convenissent, simul iurabant: et dicebatur ista militia coniuratio'; 7. 614; 2. 157; Don. Ter. *Eun.* 772; Cic. *Rab. perd.* 20; Mommsen, *Röm. Forsch.* 2. 247. 26 f.; Latte, 'Zwei Exkurse z. röm. Staatsrecht', *Nachr. Gött. Ges.* 1934, 66 (*Kl. Schr.* 347); Bleicken, *Jahrb. f. Num. u. Geldgesch.* 13 (1963), 51 ff.

[2] Serv. *Aen.* 6. 845: 'Fabii . . . trecenti sex fuerunt de una familia. qui cum coniurati cum servis et clientibus suis contra Veientes dimicarent, insidiis apud Cremeram fluvium interempti sunt'; 7. 614; Mommsen, *Röm. Forsch.* 2. 246 ff.

[3] Livy 22. 53. 10: 'ex mei animi sententia, inquit, ut ego rem publicam populi Romani non deseram, neque alium civem Romanum deserere patiar; (11) si sciens fallo, tum me, Iuppiter Optime Maxime, domum, familiam remque meam pessimo leto adficias. (12) in haec verba, M. Caecili, iures postulo ceterique qui adestis; qui non iuraverit in se hunc gladium strictum esse sciat'; Dio 15, frg. 57. 28; Meyer, *Kl. Schr.* 2. 429; v. Premerstein 51. 2. It is of no importance that the oath is here made compulsory: its wording is similar to that of the later oaths.

[4] See Mommsen, op. cit.; Latte, l.c. 66 ff.; Bleicken, l.c. 54 ff.

[5] Diod. 37. 11: Ὄμνυμι τὸν Δία τὸν Καπετώλιον . . . τὸν αὐτὸν φίλον καὶ πολέμιον ἡγήσεσθαι Δρούσῳ καὶ μήτε βίου μήτε τέκνων καὶ γονέων μηδεμιᾶς φείσεσθαι ψυχῆς, ἐὰν μὴ συμφέρῃ Δρούσῳ τε καὶ τοῖς τὸν αὐτὸν ὅρκον ὀμόσασιν . . . καὶ εὐορκοῦντι μέν μοι ἐπίκτησις εἴη τῶν ἀγαθῶν, ἐπιορκοῦντι δὲ τἀναντία; Münzer, *RE* 13. 878; v. Premerstein 27 ff.

[6] v. Premerstein 36 ff.; cf. *Athen. Mitt.* 77 (1962), 306 ff. (with bibliography).

[7] See above, p. 177. 4.

[8] App. *BC* 3. 46. 188: συνώμνυον ἑκόντες οὐκ ἐκλείψειν τὴν ἐς Ἀντώνιον εὔνοιάν τε καὶ πίστιν; 3. 58. 241; Dio. 45. 13. 5: τοὺς στρατιώτας τοὺς λοιποὺς τούς τε βουλευτὰς τοὺς σὺν αὐτοῖς ὄντας ὁρκώσας ἐς τὴν Γαλατίαν ἐξώρμησε; v. Premerstein 31; 75.

32 B.C., at the beginning of the war against Antony and Cleopatra, Italy and many provinces swore the same to Octavian,[1] and so did the remaining provinces after the war.[2] The oath became a regular feature at the accession of the emperors.[3]

One would conclude that the imperial oath must have been based on a Caesarian precedent. This has in fact been assumed,[4] but, as the evidence is not sufficiently explicit, also denied.[5] The objection rests on the assertion that the oath would have covered the same ground as the law about Caesar's inviolability, and that the evidence in question refers to this and not to an oath. There is, however, an essential difference between the two:[6] the inviolability, though it included an oath, was guaranteed by law and was therefore generally binding, whereas the allegiance was professed by a voluntary oath and was not enforceable by law. The seemingly identical evidence can easily be separated with the help of this distinction. Suetonius, by the term 'senatus consultum', refers to inviolability and by 'ius iurandum' to allegiance,[7] which was sworn, as he states in another passage, by all pledging themselves to watch over Caesar's safety.[8] Appian too stresses that this oath was sworn by all,[9] which would have been unnecessary in the case of a generally binding law: an oath for his personal welfare and his protection against conspiracy. Appian often comes back to it[10]

[1] *Mon. Anc.* 25: 'iuravit in mea verba tota Italia sponte sua, . . . iuraverunt in eadem verba provinciae Galliae, Hispaniae, Africa, Sicilia, Sardinia'; Suet. *Aug.* 17. 2; Dio 50. 6. 6; v. Premerstein 40 ff.; Berve, *Herm.* 71 (1936), 245 ff.

[2] Jos. *AJ* 17. 42; *ILS* 8781 (oath of Gangra).

[3] Dio 57. 3. 2; Tac. *A.* 1. 7. 3; Mitford, *JRS* 50 (1960), 75 ff. (oath of Cyprus to Tiberius); *ILS* 190; *Syll.* 797, etc.; v. Premerstein 40 ff.; cf. *Athen. Mitt.* 77 (1962), 306 ff.

[4] Suet. *Caes.* 84. 2; 86; App. *BC* 2. 145. 604; Nic. Dam. *v. Caes.* 80; v. Premerstein 32 ff.; Hohl, *Klio* 32 (1939), 69.

[5] Kahrstedt, *GGA* 1938. 7; Strack, *Klio* 32 (1939), 365; Kornemann, *Festschr. f. L. Wenger* 1. 289.

[6] This has not been made clear by v. Premerstein and Hohl.

[7] Suet. *Caes.* 86. 1: 'sunt qui putent confisum eum novissimo illo senatus consulto ac iure iurando etiam custodias Hispanorum . . . removisse.'

[8] Suet. *Caes.* 84. 2: 'laudationis loco consul Antonius per praeconem pronuntiavit senatus consultum, quo omnia simul ei divina atque humana decreverat, item ius iurandum, quo se cuncti pro salute unius astrinxerunt.'

[9] App. *BC* 2. 144. 601 (Antony's funeral oration): οἷς μάλιστα αὐτὸν ἐν τῷ ψηφίσματι ἐξεθείαζον, ἱερὸν καὶ ἄσυλον . . . ὀνομάζοντες; 145. 604 (Antony): ἀνεγίνωσκε τοὺς ὅρκους, ἦ μὴν φυλάξειν Καίσαρα καὶ τὸ Καίσαρος σῶμα παντὶ σθένει πάντας ἤ, εἴ τις ἐπιβουλεύσειεν, ἐξώλεις εἶναι τοὺς οὐκ ἀμύναντας αὐτῷ. Strack's assertion (l.c. 366) that 'cuncti' in Suetonius and πάντας in Appian refer only to the senators and knights, not to all citizens, is not convincing.

[10] App. *BC* 2. 124. 518; 520: ἕνεκα δὲ τοῦ μύσους καὶ ὧν Καίσαρι πάντες ὠμόσαμεν, φύλακες αὐτῷ τοῦ σώματος ἢ τιμωροὶ παθόντι τι ἔσεσθαι. εὔορκον ἦν τὸ ἄγος ἐξελαύνειν καὶ μετ' ὀλιγωτέρων καθαρῶν βιοῦν μᾶλλον ἢ πάντας ἐνόχους ὄντας ταῖς ἀραῖς; 2. 130. 544. Strack, l.c. 366, assumes that these φύλακες τοῦ σώματος were not all the citizens but the bodyguard of senators and knights decreed in 44 (Dio 44. 6. 1), which again seems an unjustified assumption.

and seems to imply that it was sworn in the name of Iuppiter and
the Di Penates, and that it included self-execration in the event of
perjury.[1] Nicolaus of Damascus says that Caesar dismissed his bodyguard because he was made sacrosanct and was assured of the affection
and the goodwill of the people.[2] Although he does not mention the oath,
there is no doubt that he refers to it with the two words 'affection' and
'goodwill', as these are typical terms of that oath.[3] Moreover, if there
was an oath for Caesar, the origins of the imperial oath are clear; if
there was not, it would have to be based on the oath for Antony; this
provoked the oath for Octavian, which in turn would have led to the
rest. But how the oath for Antony came about would remain a
mystery.

The few direct allusions to the oath, mentioned above, are not
sufficient for the reconstruction of its wording. But they help, if
the oath for Livius Drusus and the oath of Aritium, sworn at the
accession of Caligula in A.D. 37 (the only Western oath the wording
of which is known), are used for further inferences.[4] It will have invoked
Iuppiter O. M. and 'all the other gods', and included Caesar, as the
Augustan oath of Gangra included Augustus and the oath of Aritium
Divus Augustus; but it is equally possible that it invoked Iuppiter, the
Genius Caesaris, and the Di Penates.[5] It will have declared enmity to
all Caesar's enemies and readiness to take vengeance on them;[6] and
professed affection and goodwill, as mentioned in the sources and in
the oath for Drusus (though not at Aritium). Further, it will have

---

[1] App. BC 2. 145. 604 (funeral oration, see p. 225. 9, continued): ἐφ' ὅτῳ δὴ μάλιστα τὴν
φωνὴν ἐπιτείνας καὶ τὴν χεῖρα ἐς τὸ Καπιτώλιον ἀνασχών, ἐγὼ μέν, εἶπεν, ὦ Ζεῦ πάτριε καὶ
θεοί, ἕτοιμος ἀμύνειν ὡς ὤμοσα καὶ ἠρασάμην. The Di Penates, who were often connected
with Iuppiter as gods of oath (see above, p. 212), can be restored here by a slight change
in the text: ὦ Ζεῦ καὶ πάτριοι (or πατρῷοι) θεοί. There is no Iuppiter Patrius or Patrous (Ζεῦ
πατρῷε was suggested by Cobet, Mnemos. N.S. 10 (1882), 219); and the Penates are called
πάτριοι θεοί in Mon. Anc. App. 2, and πατρῷοι θεοί by Dion. Hal. 1. 57. 4; 67. 3; cf. also
Lex de piratis persequendis of 101 B.C. (Riccobono, Fontes 9 C 13, p. 128): ὀμοσάτω τὸν Δία καὶ
τοὺς θεοὺς τοὺς πατρῴους.

[2] FGrHist. 90 F 130. 80: λόγῳ τε κηλοῦντες ὡς χρεὼν εἴη ἱερὸν αὐτὸν πρὸς πάντων νομίζεσθαι
. . . καὶ ψηφίσματα περὶ τούτων γράφοντες, εἴ πως ἐκεῖνος τούτοις παραχθεὶς τῷ ὄντι πιστεύσειεν
ὑπ' αὐτῶν στέργεσθαι καὶ τοὺς δορυφόρους ἀπολύσειεν οἰόμενος τῇ πάντων εὐνοίᾳ φυλάττεσθαι.

[3] App. BC 3. 46. 188 (above, p. 224. 8); Athen. Mitt. 77 (1962), 316; v. Premerstein
32. 3.

[4] ILS 190: 'Ex mei animi sententia, ut ego iis inimicus ero, quos C. Caesari Germanico
inimicos esse cognovero, et si quis periculum ei salutique eius infert inferetque, armis bello
internicivo terra marique persequi non desinam, quoad poenas ei persolverit, neque me
neque liberos meos eius salute cariores habebo . . . si sciens fallo fefellerove, tum me liberosque
meos Iuppiter Optimus Maximus ac Divus Augustus ceterique omnes di immortales ex-
pertem patria incolumitate fortunisque omnibus faxint.'

[5] Cf. Dio 44. 6. 1: τήν τε Τύχην αὐτοῦ ὀμνύναι; 50. 1: τήν τε Τύχην ὤμνυσαν (above, p. 212).

[6] Cf. App. BC 2. 124. 520.

asserted that Caesar's welfare would be dearer to the swearer than his own or that of his children,[1] and ended with self-execration in the event of perjury.[2]

It is possible that the oath was also sworn in the provinces.[3] There is no direct evidence, but it is recommended by the practice under Augustus and his successors. There is one contemporary inscription which seems to point to the existence of this provincial oath, set up on Cos in appreciation of the *pietas* shown by the inhabitants towards Caesar.[4] If *pietas* here means an expression of allegiance supported by an oath, and if this was done elsewhere also, it would suggest that Caesar transformed the old Roman oath into an oath for his empire, which was sworn in the provinces before it was sworn at Rome.

[1] This is implied in the reference to his welfare in Dio 44. 50. 1 and in the wording of Nic. Dam. 80; cf. Suet. *Aug.* 57. 2.

[2] Cf. App. *BC* 2. 124. 520; 130. 544; 145. 604.

[3] This was suggested by v. Premerstein 35; doubted by Hohl, l.c. 69. 2 and Strack, ibid. 366. 2.

[4] Degr. 408 (below, p. 258. 2).

XI

THE STATESMAN: HIS FOUR VIRTUES

VIRTUE, a frequent theme of the philosophers, was divided into many parts, which could also be called virtues. Not all of them were equally important, and Plato had already named four which the real statesman ought to possess, σωφροσύνη, ἀνδρεία, δικαιοσύνη, ὁσιότης.[1] They were much debated and varied later, and were known at Rome at an early date. Cornificius, for instance, divided *virtus* into *prudentia, iustitia, fortitudo, modestia*; Cicero in his early writings into *prudentia, iustitia, fortitudo, temperantia*; or *clementia, iustitia, benignitas, fides, fortitudo*; or later *fortitudo, temperantia, prudentia, iustitia*.[2] He also wrote a special book *De virtutibus*, which has not survived.[3]

The Hellenistic kings often claimed that their rule met the demands of the philosophers, and historians began to attribute such virtues to the great heroes of Roman history also. For instance, *virtus* and *clementia* were ascribed to the elder Scipio,[4] who in turn advised his grandson in the *Somnium Scipionis* to exercise *iustitia* and *pietas*.[5] Cicero was probably the only consul of Rome who meant to translate political theory into practice. No other Roman had so much to say about the meaning of *virtus*;[6] and we shall see that he claimed the virtues of the statesman again and again for himself. His claim was accepted at least once. When the Senate debated the supplications to be decreed in his honour in 50 B.C., Cato testified to his four virtues: *integritas, iustitia, clementia, fides*.[7]

It was probably owing to Cicero's forensic and literary activities that the qualities of the true statesman were topical when Caesar began

[1] Plat. *Rep.* 4. 428 a; *Protag.* 349 d; *Lach.* 199 d; *Men.* 78 d; Zeno, frg. 200 A.; Chrys. *mor.* frg. 262 ff. A.; Markowski, *Eos* 37 (1936), 109 ff.; Knoche, *Magnitudo animi* 51 ff.; J. Hellegouarc'h, *Le vocabulaire latin des relations . . .* (1963), 254 ff.

[2] Cornif. *ad Her.* 3. 3; Cic. *inv.* 2. 159; *de or.* 2. 343; *fin.* 5. 67.

[3] Hieron. *in Zach.* 1. 2. p. 792 (*Patr. Lat.* 25. 1429); August. *de trin.* 14. 11. 14. There is a single fragment, Charis. 2. 208 K. (p. 270 Barw.); on the other alleged fragments see W. S. Watt, *JRS* 41 (1951), 200.

[4] Livy 21. 46. 8 (*virtus*); see also the apocryphal story about saving the life of his father, above, p. 163; *clementia*: Polyb. 15. 17. 4, etc.; below, p. 235.

[5] Cic. *rep.* 6. 16.

[6] G. Liebers, *Virtus bei Cicero*, Diss. Leipzig, 1942 (with bibliography); J. Hellegouarc'h, op. cit. 475 ff.   [7] Cic. *Att.* 7. 2. 7.

PLATE 18

Marble copy of the Clupeus Virtutis of Augustus, found at Arles, in the local Museum
(Photograph: Giraudon, Paris); p. 229.

his struggle. When he won it they became of supreme importance. There is a great deal of evidence about his single virtues, none that all four were attributed to him. But some direct Greek and indirect Roman evidence may help. At Pergamum his statues were set up εὐσεβείας ἕνεκα καὶ δικαιοσύνης[1] or πάσης ἀρετῆς ἕνεκα καὶ εὐσεβείας πρός τε τοὺς θεοὺς τήν τε πόλιν,[2] which anticipated Augustus' 'pietas erga deos patriamque'.[3] Of the indirect evidence one piece concerns Romulus, the other Augustus. The anonymous pamphlet used by Dionysius of Halicarnassus, to which reference has already been made, asserted that Romulus based his work on the four virtues of *pietas, moderatio, iustitia, virtus*.[4] They were meaningless at the time of Romulus and yet attributed to him because they were now, so we might argue, claimed for Caesar.[5] Augustus was rewarded in 27 by the Senate and the Roman people with a golden shield for, as its inscription stated, his *virtus, clementia, iustitia,* and *pietas* (pl. 18):[6] the shield, which was a frequent military decoration for bravery[7] was now transformed into a reward for the virtues of the statesman.[8] This reward cannot mean that Augustus was the first to rule in accordance with the ideals of Greek political theory: Cicero, its chief propagator, had ceased to be influential long before. But if one assumes that Augustus' reward too depends on Caesar's example, the existence of this example becomes even more credible, because it is now supported by the Greek evidence and by that about Romulus and Augustus. The following discussion will further confirm this conclusion and will borrow the Augustan terms as headings. In his time the terminological variations, which had already existed among the Greeks, were eliminated: his successors inherited his virtues unchanged.[9] The virtues will turn our attention to the cult of their personifications. This was not new. Personifications of abstract ideas had long been worshipped in Rome and among them, Clementia

---

[1] *IGR* 4. 305.

[2] *IGR* 4. 306; cf. 928 (Chios): ἀρετῆς ἕνεκεν; *IG* 7. 1835 (Thespiae): ἀρε[τῆς ἕνεκεν καὶ δικαιοσύν]ης καὶ ἀ[νδραγαθίας] (Raubitschek, *JRS* 44 (1954), 70 f.).

[3] This is the version on the shield found at Arles: below, n. 8.

[4] Dion. Hal. 2. 18. 1 f.; above, pp. 181 f.

[5] This conclusion is not valid for those who date the pamphlet in the age of Augustus or Sulla: above, p. 182. 1.

[6] *Mon. Anc.* 34. 2.   [7] See below, p. 233. 5.

[8] It was often reproduced in art: Benoit, *Rev. arch.* 6. 39 (1952), 48; Seston, *CRAI* (1954), 286 ff. (Arles); Strong, *Apotheosis and Afterlife*, pl. 7 (Rome); *CAH Plates* 4. 134 (Carthage); Mattingly 1. 59 ff. (coins); cf. Gagé, *Mél.* 49 (1932), 61 ff.

[9] Cf. M. P. Charlesworth, *The Virtues of a Roman Emperor* (1937), 10 ff.; Wickert, *RE* 22. 2232 ff.; Rogers, *Studies in the Reign of Tiberius* (1943), 35 ff.; Syme, *Tacitus* 754 ff. On artistic representations of the virtues in action see Rodenwaldt, 'Über den Stilwandel in der antoninischen Kunst', *Abh. Akad. Berlin* 1935, 3. 6 ff.

excepted, these virtues also. What was new was the connection of these deities with the statesman. This too existed before, but only in Greece, and in general never lasted long.[1] Through Caesar's example they took firm root at Rome and were very popular in the imperial period.

I. VIRTUS

Virtus was the traditional ideal of the Roman citizen, not human perfection, virtue, but manly behaviour in war[2] for which he was rewarded with military distinctions and later with a political career, the *honores*.[3] The goddess Virtus first appeared in the third century when many political and spiritual ideas received a cult. In 222 B.C., in the war against the Celts, M. Claudius Marcellus vowed a temple for Honos and Virtus at Clastidium, which was completed and dedicated by his son in 205.[4] He was a man of exceptional *virtus*, one of the great heroes of Roman history,[5] after Romulus and A. Cornelius Cossus (*cos.* 428) the third Roman to offer *spolia opima* to the gods,[6] that is, the spoils of the general of the enemy, Viridomarus, whom he had killed in battle. His *virtus* was matched by his *honores*: he had been consul five times.[7] Scipio too was a man of *virtus*. We have seen that after the victory at Zama he was called saviour and liberator;[8] but he did nothing for the goddess Virtus, perhaps because at that time her cult was closely connected with the Claudii Marcelli. But the *virtus* of the family is mentioned

---

[1] Cic. *Q.fr.* 1. 1. 31: 'tuas virtutes consecratas et in deorum numero conlocatas vides.'

[2] Cic. *Tusc.* 2. 43: 'a viris virtus nomen est mutuata'; Varr. *LL* 5. 73: 'Virtus ut Viritus a virilitate'; Sall. *Iug.* 7. 3 ff.; *Cat.* 11. 1.

[3] Cic. *rep.* 3. 40: 'vult paene virtus honorem, nec est virtutis alia merces'; *Brut.* 281: 'cum honos sit praemium virtutis'; *fam.* 10. 10. 2; Pliny *ep.* 3. 20. 5: 'audire soleo hunc ordinem comitiorum: citato nomine candidati silentium summum; dicebat ipse pro se . . . testes et laudatores dabat vel eum sub quo militaverat' (Polyb. 6. 19. 1; 6. 83. 4); Symm. *ep.* 1. 20. 1: 'maiores nostri . . . aedes Honori atque Virtuti gemella facie iunctim locarunt commenti . . . ibi esse praemia honoris, ubi sunt merita virtutis'; Kroll, *Kultur der ciceronischen Zeit* 1. 23 f.; F. Klose, *Die Bedeutung von honos u. honestus* (Diss. Breslau 1933), 27 ff.; H. Roloff, *Maiores bei Cicero* (Diss. Leipzig 1938), 10 ff.; 22 ff.; 30 ff.

[4] Livy 27. 25. 7; 29. 11. 13'; Val. Max. 1. 1. 8; Cic. *ND* 2. 61; Plut. *Marc.* 28. 2; Wissowa, *Myth. Lex.* 6. 338. A temple of Honos had been vowed in 233 in the war against the Ligures and built by Q. Fabius Maximus Verrucosus (Cic. *ND* 2. 61): it was this temple that Marcellus intended to rebuild and to dedicate to Honos and Virtus with a common *cella*, but he met the opposition of the *pontifices* (Livy 27. 25. 7 ff.).

[5] Cic. *Verr.* 2. 5. 84: 'cuius virtute captae, misericordia conservatae sunt Syracusae'; *Pis.* 58; *off.* 1. 61; Hor. *c.* 1. 12. 45.

[6] Verg. *Aen.* 6. 855 ff. (Serv. and Norden ad v. 859); Livy, *Per.* 20; Plut. *Marc.* 8. 6; on Romulus see Livy 1. 10. 5 ff. (cf. *Lex Numae*, Fest. 189 M. = 204 L.); on Cossus Livy 4. 20. 1 ff. (with Ogilvie's notes on both passages); E. Mensching, *Mus. Helv.* 24 (1967), 12 ff.; cf. also Plaut. *Amph.* 252: 'ipsusque Amphitruo regem Pterelam sua obtruncavit manu' (rewarded with a *patera*, 260 f.; 534 f.).

[7] Ascon. *Pis.* 44, p. 18 St.   [8] See above, p. 151.

on their tombstones,[1] and his grandson built a shrine or an altar for
Virtus in 133 after the conquest of Numantia.[2] A new temple of Honos
and Virtus was built by Marius, Caesar's uncle, after the victory over
the Cimbri and Teutones,[3] and games were instituted in their honour.[4]
Marius was, in contrast to his predecessors, not only a man of *virtus*, but
owed his whole career to it.[5] He was not a member of the nobility but
a *homo novus*, and yet before the end of the war against the Cimbri he had
been consul five times, in 107 and from 104 to 101 without interruption.
His adversary, Sulla, was no less distinguished and successful in war;
but he liked to stress his luck and play down his own share in his successes.[6] He made vows and dedications to Venus, Victoria, and other
gods, but not to Virtus; probably he would not further a cult favoured
by Marius.

Virtus is represented only twice on Republican coins, a helmeted
head belonging, as we know from her later representations, to an
Amazonian figure, almost identical with Minerva and Roma.[7] One
was issued by M'. Aquillius *c.* 68 B.C. to commemorate, as the reverse
shows, the bravery of his relative M'. Aquillius (*cos.* 101) in the Sicilian
Slave War (pl. 17. 13).[8] The choice of Virtus may be due to the fact
that this Aquillius was a follower of Marius: he was his colleague in the
consulate and his legate in the war against the Cimbri,[9] and may have

---

[1] *CIL* 1². 6; 10 f.; 15 (*ILS* 1; 4; 6 f. = Degr. 309; 311 f.; 316).

[2] Plut. *fort. Rom.* 5: Ἀρετῆς μέν γε παρ' αὐτοῖς ὀψὲ καὶ μετὰ πολλοὺς χρόνους ἱερὸν ἱδρύσατο
Σκιπίων ὁ Νομαντῖνος, εἶτα Μάριος τὸ Οὐιρτοῦτίς τε καὶ ᾽Ονῶρις προσαγορευόμενον. Wissowa,
Myth. Lex. 6. 337, and Latte 236. I did not accept this evidence about Scipio's shrine because
in the edition they used it was Marcellus who followed Scipio, which is chronologically
impossible. But the reading of all MSS. is Μάριος, which removes the doubts as to the existence of Scipio's shrine. A comparison with ch. 10 makes it, however, probable that the
foundation of Marcellus would have been mentioned at the beginning: it was omitted either
by Plutarch himself or by his copyists.

[3] *ILS* 59; Fest. 344 M. (468 L.); Plut. *fort. Rom.* 5; Wissowa, l.c. 339.

[4] Schol. Bob. Cic. *Sest.* 116 (p. 136 St.): 'ludos Honoris atque Virtutis, qui celebrantur in
memoriam et honorem C. Marii, a quo res bello Cimbrico feliciter gestae sunt'; 120. This
evidence would be worthless if Wissowa 150. 2 and *Myth. Lex.* 6. 339 were right in assuming
that it was caused by a misunderstanding of Cic. *Sest.* 116. But such games were also held at
Terracina (*ILS* 5051: 'ludos Honoris et Virtutis fecit') and at Ostia (*F. Ost.* A.D. 146, p. 207
Degrassi), both probably depending on the Roman model. The *ludi Victoriae* of Sulla too may
have been inspired by such Marian games.

[5] This is the theme of Sallust's version of the speech which he delivered when he became
consul in 107 (*Iug.* 85). Its substance is credible: Cato spoke similarly in *De suis virtutibus*
in 183 B.C. about the hardships of his military training (*Or. Rom. frg.* 128 ff. Malc.). That
the *homo novus* had to build his career on his *virtus* alone was an ever-recurring theme of
Cicero's speeches also.

[6] See above, p. 114.

[7] On representations of Virtus see Rodenwaldt, *Abh. Akad. Berlin* 1935. 3, 6 ff.; M. Bieber,
AJA 49 (1945), 25 ff.; Fuhrmann, *Mitt. Arch. Inst.* 2 (1949), 36. 1.

[8] Sydenham 132; pl. 23. 798.   [9] Broughton 1. 564; 577; 2. 2.

been associated with the building of the Marian temple of Virtus. The other coin issued about the same time by Q. Fufius Calenus and an otherwise unknown Cordus shows the joint heads of Honos and Virtus on the obverse and Roma and Italia clasping hands on the reverse (pl. 17. 14),[1] a clear reference to the peace after the Social War and to the new temple.

Pompey's *virtus* was often praised by Cicero. When recommending him for the war against Mithridates he quoted Sulla for the statement that it was Pompey's *virtus* that won Italy for him.[2] After that war and later Cicero never ceased to invent new superlatives for Pompey: this one man's *virtus* brought peace to the whole world; or as to *virtus*, glory, and achievements he was the leader among all races at all times.[3] Pompey's principal deities were others, Venus Victrix and Hercules Invictus; but he also combined the tradition of Marius and Sulla by dedicating shrines both to Honos and Virtus, and to Victoria and Felicitas in his new theatre in 55, and by creating for them, together with Venus Victrix, a common festival on 12 August.[4]

Caesar's *virtus* was recognized in 80, when he received the oak wreath for having saved the life of a citizen in battle.[5] Thirty-five years later he received it again for having saved the lives of all the citizens, and in addition the grass wreath, an even rarer distinction, for having liberated them.[6] A few months earlier, in 46, Cicero praised his *virtus* in the same terms as he had praised Pompey's before.[7] It was in his speech *Pro Marcello*, delivered after Caesar had granted the return of Marcellus (*cos.* 49) from exile. The ancestor of this Marcellus, who had built the first temple of Honos and Virtus, was the prototype of a man of *virtus*; and shortly before Cicero delivered his speech, Brutus wrote a book *De virtute*, in which he discussed the fate of the contemporary Marcellus, and dedicated it to Cicero;[8] Varro wrote a Logistoricus *Marcellus*, perhaps with the full title *Marcellus de virtute*,[9] clearly discussing the same theme. But now Caesar had become the man of *virtus* and

---

[1] Sydenham 131; pl. 23. 797; Mommsen, *Röm. Münzwesen* 639 f.; above, pp. 42 f.; 96.

[2] Cic. *de imp.* 30: 'testis est Italia, quam ille ipse victor L. Sulla huius virtute et subsidio confessus est liberatam.'

[3] Cic. *Cat.* 2. 11; *p. red. sen.* 5; *Balb.* 9; 13.   [4] Degrassi 493 f.; above, p. 93.

[5] Suet. *Caes.* 2; above, pp. 163 f.

[6] App. *BC* 2. 106. 441; Dio 44. 4. 5; above, pp. 148 ff.; 164 ff.

[7] Cic. *Marc.* 19: 'tantus est enim splendor in laude vera..., ut haec a Virtute donata, cetera a Fortuna commodata esse videantur' (cf. *Balb.* 9: 'in quo uno ita summa fortuna cum summa virtute certavit, ut omnium iudicio plus homini quam deae tribueretur'); 26: 'tua divina virtus' (cf. *de imp.* 36: 'est haec divina atque incredibilis virtus imperatoris').

[8] Sen. *ad Helv.* 9. 5; 8. 1; Cic. *Brut.* 250; *fin.* 1. 8; *Tusc.* 5. 1; cf. Meyer, *Caesars Monarchie* 383; Dahlmann, *Varron. Stud.* 1 (*Abh. Akad. Mainz*, 1957, No. 4), 51.

[9] Don. Ter. *Eun.* 4. 3. 7; Dahlmann, op. cit. 51 f.

seems to have planned something for the cult of Virtus. The evidence is only circumstantial. First, it was decreed in 45 that he should offer the *spolia opima* to Iuppiter Feretrius,[1] an extraordinary decree because he had not killed his adversary in battle. It was the greatest military distinction, awarded only to Romulus, Cornelius Cossus, and to the great Marcellus.[2] He was to be the fourth; it was certainly a recognition of his *virtus*. Secondly, he may have considered the building of a temple because Marius, his uncle, and Pompey, his rival, had done so. Thirdly, a plan may be inferred from the name of the Caesarian colony Itucci, called Virtus Iulia;[3] another colony, in Africa, was called Colonia Iulia Iuvenalis Honoris et Virtutis Cirta, where at least an altar was erected.[4] Here the evidence ends. It is not satisfactory, because it does not make it certain that he meant to build a temple of Virtus and does not, by itself, point the way to Augustus' 'clupeus virtutis'. It would, if it could be assumed that such a shield had been planned for Caesar. It could have been, because in origin a shield was a military reward for bravery,[5] and thus more deserved by Caesar than by Augustus. But the real support for Caesar's Virtus comes in fact from the evidence concerning his other virtues.

2. CLEMENTIA

The second virtue is far better attested; it was in fact the most important of the four. The Senate decided in 45 B.C. to build a temple to the Clementia Caesaris.[6] It is not recorded when exactly this decree

---

[1] Dio 44. 4. 3; Cic. *Deiot.* 34: 'cuius tropaeis non invidemus'(?). Syme, *HSCP* 64 (1959), 80, n. 85, suggests that the Dio passage is a 'patent anachronism': it was Augustus who made a political problem of the *spolia opima* when forbidding M. Licinius Crassus (*cos.* 30) to dedicate them although he had killed Deldo, the King of the Bastarni, in 29 (Dio 51. 24. 4; so already Dessau, *Herm.* 41 (1906), 142 ff.; v. Premerstein 253 f.). He invented the evidence about Cossus (Livy 4. 20. 1 ff.), thus implying that only the general in supreme command was entitled to make such a dedication; *contra*, Beloch, *Röm. Gesch.* 299; Latte 205. 3; E. Mensching, *Mus. Helv.* 24 (1967), 22 f. The weakest point of this theory is that it condemns the evidence of Dio, which seems unexceptionable.   [2] See above, p. 230.

[3] Pliny 3. 12; Meyer, op. cit. 486; Vittinghoff 74; Gelzer, *Caesar*, 275 f. (on the significant names of the Caesarian colonies).

[4] *ILS* 6857; Mommsen, *Ges. Schr.* 5. 474; Meyer, op. cit. 492; Vittinghoff 113 ascribes the foundation to Octavian (which would not exclude Caesarian planning); on the coins with the heads of Honos and Virtus see Grant, *From Imperium to Auctoritas*, 178 ff.; pl. 6. 15. An altar is mentioned on *CIL* 8. 6951; a triumphal arch with the statue of Virtus under Caracalla, *ILS* 2933; dedications to Honos and Virtus also at Sicca Veneria, the Nova Cirta, *ILS* 3797 f.; *CIL* 8. 15850.

[5] *ILS* 2531; 2713; P. Steiner, *BJ* 114 (1905), 11 f. Such shields were often dedicated in temples (Pliny 35. 12 f.) and inscribed, like Aeneas' shield in the temple of Apollo at Actium (*Aen.* 3. 288: 'Aeneas haec de Danais victoribus arma'), or provided with the portrait of the dedicator (Pliny 35. 13: 'origo plena virtutis, faciem reddi in scuto cuiusque, qui fuerit usus illo').   [6] App. *BC* 2. 106. 443; Dio 44. 6. 4; Plut. *Caes.* 57. 4 (below, p. 308. 9).

was passed; it was probably at the same time as those about the statues on the Rostra if it is right to argue, as will be done later, that the oak wreath has now become a symbol of *clementia*. The question where this honour belongs can therefore only be answered with the help of the term *clementia*. Its interpretation must begin with a brief history of Roman clemency, turn then to the history of the word up to Caesar and under him, and end with an explanation of the personification, which was new.

(a) The Virtue

There is nothing specifically Roman about clemency: it was a concept that had always existed everywhere.[1] It was one of the virtues ascribed by philosophers since Plato to the real statesman or the king of the ideal state; and the Hellenistic kings often tried to act accordingly. It was in the first place the kindness shown towards their fellow citizens, but then also towards the defeated enemy.[2]

The Romans did not learn it from Greek theory but in the course of long political experience. It was a traditional virtue. Cicero was once charged that he did not show the clemency of the ancestors towards an adversary.[3] Cicero himself was convinced that he possessed it, liked to refer to his *lenitas*, which he had applied to the Catilinarians,[4] and later defended himself against the charge of *crudelitas*.[5] This was the charge which was rightly levelled against Marius, Cinna, and Sulla.[6] Pompey, on the other hand, showed himself merciful towards the followers of Sertorius.[7] Secondly, clemency was demanded and often shown in the law-courts.[8] We are concerned here with a third application which became an important theme of Roman history. It was one of the two possible answers to the question of what to do with the vanquished.[9] The Romans evolved a theory of clemency probably when they

---

[1] Cic. *inv.* 2. 164: 'clementia, per quam animi . . . in odium alicuius . . . concitati comitate retinentur'; *Marc.* 8: 'animum vincere, iracundiam cohibere, victo temperare'; Sen. *clem.* 2. 3. 1: 'clementia est temperantia animi in potestate ulciscendi vel lenitas superioris adversus inferiorem in constituendis poenis'; Dahlmann, *Neue Jahrb.* 10 (1934), 18; Knoche, *Magnitudo animi* (1935), 66 f.; E. Bux, *Würzb. Jahrb.* 3 (1948), 201 ff.; below, p. 237. 1.

[2] Diod. 32. 4. 1; Polyb. 5. 10. 1.

[3] Cic. *fam.* 5. 1. 2 (62 B.C.): 'quae . . . nec ratione nec maiorum nostrorum clementia administrastis' (Harder, *Herm.* 69 (1934), 65), cf. *Rab. perd.* 13; *fam.* 13. 66. 1 (45 B.C.): 'A. Caecinam . . . non commendarem tibi, cum scirem, qua fide in tuos, qua clementia in calamitosos soleres esse . . .'

[4] Cic. *Cat.* 2. 4; 2. 27; *Sulla* 1; 92.   [5] Cic. *Cat.* 4. 11; *Sulla* 87.

[6] Plut. *Mar.* 43. 1 f.; App. *BC* 1. 70. 320 f.; below, p. 237.

[7] Cic. *Verr.* 2. 5. 153; Plut. *Pomp.* 20. 8.   [8] Cic. *Tull.* 50; *Cluent.* 105; *Sulla* 92.

[9] Livy 26. 49. 8: '. . . populi Romani . . ., qui beneficio quam metu obligare homines malit'; 30. 42. 17: 'plus paene parcendo victis quam vincendo imperium auxisse'; Norden, *Aeneis VI* 336 (ad v. 853); Fuchs, *Augustin u. d. ant. Friedensgedanke* 204. 2.

began to feel the need to justify their actions to the Greeks and others.[1]
Of the historians, Q. Fabius Pictor and P. Rutilius Rufus may have done
so already;[2] of the generals, Marcellus possibly adopted this principle
in Sicily,[3] and the elder Scipio certainly did so towards the Carthaginians.[4] Scipio claimed that clemency also served the security of Roman
rule and its extension. L. Furius Purpurio (*cos.* 196) disapproved of his
action, asserting that forgiveness had its dangers in that the vanquished
might try their luck again.[5] Titus Flamininus followed Scipio's example
at Cynoscephalae in 197 B.C.,[6] and even Cato acknowledged its usefulness
in 167 in his speech *Pro Rhodiensibus*: it helped to preserve the greatness
of Rome.[7] Clemency was a great issue again in the debate about the
fate of Carthage. Cato pleaded this time for destruction, Scipio Nasica
against it,[8] reiterating the old argument.[9] By that time the Greeks must
have known, and generally accepted, the Roman view; the earliest
evidence comes from Polybius, both directly and, through Livy, indirectly.[10] Posidonius too represented the Roman view, at least in the
only surviving fragment which deals with the pleading of Scipio
Nasica.[11] It is worth adding that in both Polybius and Posidonius the
term ἐπιείκεια began to prevail.

It is surprising to observe that there was no corresponding Latin term
for a long time to come. *Clementia* is not an old word: it is first found
in Terence—in Plautus only the adjective *clemens*—never in Naevius,
Ennius, Lucilius, nor in the fragments of early scenic poetry, history,
or oratory.[12] And it never became an exclusive term at Rome: the

---

[1] Gelzer, *Kl. Schr.* 3. 54.

[2] Gelzer, *Kl. Schr.* 3. 89 f.; Strasburger, *JRS* 55 (1965), 40 f.

[3] Cic. *Verr.* 2. 2. 4: 'M. Marcellus, cuius in Sicilia virtutem hostes, misericordiam victi,
fidem ceteri Siculi perspexerunt.'

[4] Polyb. 15. 17. 4: πρᾴως . . . καὶ μεγαλοψύχως; 10. 3. 1; Livy 33. 12. 7: 'Romanos praeter
vetustissimum morem victis parcendi praecipuum clementiae documentum dedisse pace
Hannibali et Carthaginiensibus data'; Gelzer, *Kl. Schr.* 2. 56.

[5] Livy 31. 31. 16; Gelzer 2. 58.

[6] Polyb. 18. 37. 7; *Syll.* 593; Gelzer, *Kl. Schr.* 3. 90. 144; Walbank, *JRS* 55 (1965), 9.

[7] Cato ap. Gell. 6. 3. 47: 'ignoscentias utiles esse rebus humanis docet . . . si ignoscatur,
conservatum iri ostendit populi Romani magnitudinem'; 52: 'nunc clementiae, nunc
mansuetudinis maiorum . . . commonefacit'; Sall. *Cat.* 51. 5; Gelzer, *Kl. Schr.* 2. 54.

[8] Cf. Gelzer 2. 39 ff.

[9] Posid., *FGrHist.* 87 F 112. 5: σῳζομένης μὲν τῆς Καρχηδόνος ὁ ἀπὸ ταύτης φόβος ἠνάγκαζεν
ὁμονοεῖν τοὺς Ῥωμαίους καὶ τῶν ὑποτεταγμένων ἐπιεικῶς καὶ ἐνδόξως ἄρχειν, ὧν οὐδὲν κάλλιον
ἐστι πρὸς ἡγεμονίας διαμονήν τε καὶ αὔξησιν; Gelzer 2. 47 f.; 51; Klingner, *Herm.* 63 (1928),
181 f.; H. Fuchs, *HSCP* 63 (1958), 367; 379 ff.; W. Hoffmann, *Hist.* 9 (1960), 309 ff.

[10] Polyb. 15. 17. 4; 18. 37. 7; 21. 4. 10; Diod. 32. 2; Gelzer 2. 64 f.; Klingner, l.c.; Strasburger, l.c. 46.

[11] See above, n. 9; he found the Celtiberians too ἐπιεικεῖς καὶ φιλάνθρωποι, F 117; Strasburger 47.

[12] *Thes.L.L.* 3. 1334 (Ter. *Ad.* 861; Cato, above, n. 7?).

concept could also be described by other nouns, 'misericordia', 'mansuetudo', 'lenitas', 'comitas', and the like, with the related adjectives
or with verbs like 'parcere' and 'ignoscere'.¹ When the Greek theory
about the virtues of the true statesman first appeared at Rome in rhetorical works, the concept was listed there under various names: Cornificius
called it 'modestia', and Cicero 'temperantia' or 'clementia'.² It is
political clemency that matters here. It is not known what Roman
historians like Rutilius Rufus called it, because their writings have not
survived. The word *clementia*, applied to Roman rule, is first found
in Cicero's *Verrines*, 70 B.C.,³ but it sounds as if it had been so used
before. A few years later, in 66, Cicero used other terms, 'humanitas'
and 'mansuetudo', when he recommended Pompey as the ideal general.⁴
Pompey in fact exercised clemency in 66 towards Tigranes and in 63
towards the Jews.⁵

We have now reached the age of Caesar and Cicero, and notice with
surprise that *clementia* was a rare word; so the suspicion arises that
it was intentionally avoided in Roman politics. This suspicion is confirmed by an examination of the writings of Caesar and Cicero. The
word is found twice in the *Bellum Gallicum* but in indirect speech, the
Gauls appealing to Caesar's clemency;⁶ never in the *Bellum Civile*.
Cicero used it twice in the early *Verrines* about Roman rule abroad,⁷
from the point of view of Roman politics an innocent usage; three times
in his speeches of the fifties in a legal context,⁸ which is equally irrelevant
here. He suddenly adopted the word with the beginning of the Civil
War. His letters now referred to Caesar's clemency again and again.
His three Caesarian speeches, of 46 and 45, used the word thirteen
times, more often than all other speeches put together; the balance is
even more disproportionate if one deducts the four passages of the
Philippics from the other side, as they belong in this respect to the Caesarian period. So do his philosophical writings, which have a few examples,

---

¹ Cf. the valuable list of related Greek and Roman terms in H. Fuchs, *Basler Zeitschr. f. Gesch.* 42 (1943), 43. 19.

² Cornif. *ad Her.* 3. 3; Cic. *inv.* 2. 159; *de or.* 2. 343; above, p. 228.

³ Cic. *Verr.* 2. 5. 115: 'illam clementiam mansuetudinemque nostri imperii in tantam crudelitatem inhumanitatemque esse conversam'; cf. *Q. fr.* 1. 1. 25 (60/59 B.C.): 'toto . . . imperio . . . omnia plena clementiae, mansuetudinis, humanitatis'; *Sex. Rosc.* 154.

⁴ Cic. *de imp.* 42.

⁵ Val. Max. 5. 1. 9; Plut. *Pomp.* 28. 4; Diod. 40. 2; Gelzer 2. 151.

⁶ Caes. *BG* 2. 14. 5: 'petere . . . Bellovacos . . ., ut sua clementia ac mansuetudine in eos utatur'; 2. 31. 4: 'pro sua clementia ac mansuetudine'; cf. 2. 28. 3 (*misericordia*); 8. 44. 1 (*lenitas*); 8. 3. 5 (*clementia*); 21. 2 (*clementia* and *humanitas*); above, p. 166. 1.

⁷ Cic. *Verr.* 2. 5. 115; so also *Q. fr.* 1. 1. 25.

⁸ Cic. *Tull.* 50; *Cluent.* 105; *Sulla* 92; cf. *fam.* 5. 1. 2 (above, p. 234. 3). It would be interesting to know what Cato meant when, in 50, he praised Cicero's *clementia, Att.* 7. 2. 7.

and Caesar's continuators, which have five. Clearly Caesar's appearance on the scene created a break with tradition and demanded a new term.

(b) Caesar's Clemency

The innovator then was Cicero, but the first move came from Caesar.[1] And it came almost at the beginning of the Civil War, immediately after the capitulation of the Pompeians at Corfinium (21 February 49). He said that he wanted to regain the goodwill of everybody and to make his victory lasting by showing mildness (misericordia) and generosity (liberalitas), in contrast to others, especially Sulla, who by their cruelty could not escape hatred.[2] These words applied equally to Pompey, whose vindictiveness was stressed even by his friends: he wanted to be another Sulla, another man of proscriptions.[3] Caesar repeated his pledge when he arrived at Rome,[4] then at Spain,[5] and on the battlefield of Pharsalus: as soon as the battle turned in his favour, he instructed his soldiers to spare all Roman citizens and let the Pompeians know that this would be done.[6] He spoke to those who surrendered of his mildness (lenitas) and saw to it that no harm was done to them.[7] He later wrote to his friends that the greatest pleasure the victory brought for him was to save the lives of the citizens who had been fighting against him.[8] The correspondence he captured among Pompey's possessions (and later among those of Scipio) he burnt unread so that

[1] Cf. Dahlmann, Neue Jahrb. 10 (1934), 18 ff.; Wickert, Klio 30 (1937), 234 ff.; id. RE 22. 2237 (bibliography); Fuchs, l.c. 38 ff.; M. Treu, Mus. Helv. 5 (1948), 197 ff.; Rambaud, L'art de la déformation historique dans les Commentaires de César, 1966 (1952), 283 ff.; Winkler, RAC 3. 207 ff. (bibliography); M. Fuhrmann, Gymn. 70 (1963), 507 ff.; Cicero, pro Marc. ed. Ruch (1965), 10 ff.; R. Combès, Imperator (1966), 369 ff.

[2] Caes. ap. Cic. Att. 9. 7C. 1 (c. 3 March): 'temptemus hoc modo . . . omnium voluntates recuperare et diuturna victoria uti, quoniam reliqui crudelitate odium effugere non potuerunt neque victoriam diutius tenere, praeter unum L. Sullam, quem imitaturus non sum. haec nova sit ratio vincendi, ut misericordia et liberalitate nos muniamus'; Wickert, Klio 30 (1937), 238; Syme, Rom. Rev. 159; M. Treu, Mus. Helv. 5 (1948), 197 ff.

[3] Cic. Att. 8. 16. 2; 9. 7. 3: 'Gnaeus noster Sullani regni similitudinem concupivit'; 9. 10. 6: 'sullaturit . . . et proscripturit iam diu'; 10. 7. 1; 8. 11. 2; Caes. BC 1. 76. 5; Treu, l.c. 201 f.

[4] Dio 41. 15. 4; 16. 4.

[5] Caes. BC 1. 72. 3: 'movebatur etiam misericordia civium, quos interficiendos videbat; quibus salvis . . . rem optinere malebat'; 1. 74. 7: 'magnumque fructum suae pristinae lenitatis omnium iudicio Caesar ferebat'; 1. 84. 5; Dio 41. 23. 1; App. BC 2. 43. 174.

[6] App. BC 2. 74. 309 f.; 80. 336; Suet. Caes. 75. 2; Vell. 2. 52. 6; Flor. 2. 13. 50; Cic. Deiot. 34.

[7] Caes. BC 3. 98. 2: 'ubi . . . passisque palmis proiecti ad terram flentes ab eo salutem petiverunt, consolatus consurgere iussit et pauca apud eos de lenitate sua locutus, quo minore essent timore, omnes conservavit.'

[8] Plut. Caes. 48. 4: τοῖς δὲ φίλοις εἰς Ῥώμην ἔγραφεν, ὅτι τῆς νίκης ἀπολαύοι τοῦτο μέγιστον καὶ ἥδιστον, τὸ σῴζειν τινὰς ἀεὶ τῶν πεπολεμηκότων πολιτῶν αὐτῷ.

nobody should be prosecuted for his past allegiance.[1] Before the battle of Thapsus Caesar distributed pamphlets among Scipio's soldiers offering them pardon and rewards if they surrendered.[2]

The news about the release of the prisoners at Corfinium caused great surprise in Rome, and people who had left Rome began to return.[3] Cicero, who had been wondering what kind of tyrant Caesar was going to be, benevolent like Pisistratus or an evil one like Phalaris,[4] now referred for the first time to the *clementia*, though insidious *clementia*, of this Pisistratus.[5] But when he wrote to Caesar a few days later he praised it ('clementia Corfiniensis').[6] The fact could not be denied, but it could be argued, as was done by Curio, that it proved, not that Caesar was not cruel but that he wanted to please the people.[7] When Caesar went to Asia after the victory at Pharsalus, he treated the Greek cities which had been siding with Pompey similarly.[8] Cicero came to the conclusion that Caesar's clemency was to be had everywhere, and in fact it was exercised again in Africa and Spain.[9]

We have seen Caesar in action and quoted four passages with *clementia* from Cicero's correspondence; three more can be added from Caesar's continuators but none from Caesar himself. The conclusion is that it was now an accepted political term in Rome, and that Cicero was its initiator. But it may be doubted if all this could have had any further consequence by itself. A new situation was created, it seems, after the triumph of 46, and it was due again to Cicero. He delivered three speeches in front of Caesar in 46 and 45, pleading for Marcellus, Ligarius, and King Deiotarus. It will be recalled that we found the word *clementia* thirteen times in these speeches; there are also other words: 'misericordia', 'aequitas', 'humanitas', 'magnitudo animi', 'liberalitas', and the verb 'ignoscere'.[10] Again, there is the noun 'salus'[11]

[1] Dio 41. 63. 5; 43. 13. 2; Sen. *de ira* 2. 23. 4; Pliny 7. 94. Pompey did the same before him with Sertorius' correspondence, Plut. *Pomp.* 20. 8.   [2] Dio 43. 5. 2.

[3] Cic. *Att.* 9. 1. 2; 9. 8. 1; Plut. *Caes.* 34. 9.   [4] Cic. *Att.* 7. 20. 2 (5 Febr.).

[5] Cic. *Att.* 8. 16. 2 (7 March); cf. 8. 9a. 2 (25 Febr.): 'metuo ne omnis haec clementia ad Cinnanam illam crudelitatem conligatur.'

[6] Cic. *Att.* 9. 16. 1 (26 March); Caesar's reply, ibid. 2: 'recte auguraris de me . . . nihil a me abesse longius crudelitate.'

[7] Cic. *Att.* 10. 4. 8 (15 April).   [8] App. *BC* 2. 89. 373.

[9] Cic. *fam.* 15. 15. 2 (July 47): 'eandem clementiam experta esset Africa, quam cognovit Asia, quam etiam Achaia'; *B. Afr.* 86. 2: 'Vergilium appellavit invitavitque ad deditionem suamque lenitatem et clementiam commemoravit'; 88. 6: 'se in C. Caesaris clementia magnam spem habere'; 92. 4: 'rumore . . . perlato de eius lenitate clementiaque . . . equites Zamam perveniunt ad Caesarem ab eoque sunt metu periculoque liberati.'

[10] *Clementia* is the most frequent; it is interesting to note that 'ignoscere' is not found in *Marc.*, but occurs eight times in *Lig.* and twice in *Deiot.* (12; 30). On the speech *Pro Ligario* see Walser, *Hist.* 8 (1959), 93 f.; Kumaniecki, *Herm.* 95 (1967), 455 f.

[11] Cic. *Marc.* 22; 25; **32** f. (cf. 24; 29); *Lig.* 28; 31; **36**; 38 (cf. 34); *Deiot.* 40.

and the verb 'conservare'.[1] There is no need to quote the evidence in full: the praise is often extravagant, the expression hyperbolic. But all this left its mark, especially passages where Cicero spoke of the divine nature of clemency or of the man who, by saving the lives of others, comes near to divinity.[2] Further, he demanded literary praise and *monumenta* of this clemency, and asserted in the latest speech that many such *monumenta* existed.[3] One literary work is known. A. Caecina, the author of an invective against Caesar, received pardon and wrote in gratitude a book *Querelae*, drafts of which he submitted to Cicero.[4] There must have been many others: exiles were allowed to return in ever-increasing numbers, to get back their property and to receive offices.[5]

Clemency, in origin the virtue of the Roman State and its generals and exercised towards the defeated enemy, was now the virtue of an individual and exercised towards his fellow citizens. It was against Republican tradition, and that is why it had so difficult a start, why Caesar cannot have had a direct share in its creation, and why a single innovator, Cicero, has to be assumed. But Cicero could not have done it alone; he must have been supported by his friends and many senators. One of these must have been the anonymous pamphleteer used by Dionysius of Halicarnassus, who, as we have already seen, ascribed to Romulus the four virtues of the true statesman,[6] among them *moderatio*, which is nothing else but Caesar's clemency.

Caesar's example left an indelible mark behind. This would not have been possible if there had been not generosity but just political calculation and cheap propaganda.[7] After the murder Brutus said that he would show clemency towards his adversaries, for which he was criticized by Cicero.[8] The *triumviri* declared in 43, at the time of the

---

[1] Cic. *Marc.* 12; 15; 17; 20 f.; 34; *Lig.* 1; 19; 33; 38 (cf. 7); not in *Deiot.*

[2] Cic. *Marc.* 1: 'inauditamque clementiam'; 8: 'non ego eum cum summis viris comparo, sed simillimum deo iudico'; 26: 'rerum tuarum inmortalium, C. Caesar, hic exitus futurus fuit . . ., vide quaeso ne tua divina virtus admirationis plus sit habitura quam gloriae'; 27: 'tuus animus . . . semper inmortalitatis amore flagravit'; *Lig.* 38: 'homines enim ad deos nulla re propius accedunt quam salutem hominibus dando.'

[3] Cic. *Lig.* 6: 'o clementiam admirabilem atque omnium laude, praedicatione, litteris monumentisque decorandam!' *Deiot.* 40: 'multa sunt monimenta clementiae tuae.'

[4] Suet. *Caes.* 75. 5; Cic. *fam.* 6. 6. 8 (Sept. 46): 'in Caesare haec sunt: mitis clemensque natura, qualis exprimitur praeclaro illo libro Querelarum tuarum'; 6. 7.

[5] Suet. *Caes.* 75; Dio 43. 49. 1; 43. 43. 50; Cic. *fam.* 11. 28. 2; Treu, l.c. 216. 99.

[6] Dion. Hal. 2. 18. 1 f.; above, pp. 181 f.

[7] After the murder Cicero forgot all his praise and spoke, as he did at the beginning (above, p. 238. 5), of deception, *Phil.* 2. 116: 'adversarios clementiae specie devinxerat.' Nor is the modern verdict unanimous: Meyer, op. cit. 339, Treu (political weapon); Dahlmann, Wickert, Syme, *Tacitus* 414 (also generosity); Rambaud (vindictiveness).

[8] Cic. *ad Brut.* 5 (2. 5). 5 (April 43): 'video te lenitate delectari . . . sed aliis rebus, aliis

proscriptions, that they would imitate neither the cruelty of Marius and Sulla nor the clemency of Caesar.[1] But they changed their minds. Cicero praised Lepidus for the clemency which he showed towards Sex. Pompeius, and wanted him rewarded with an equestrian statue on the Rostra.[2] Octavian wrote to the Senate in 42 on his way home from Philippi that he would act with the same clemency as had his father.[3] *Clementia* was one of the four virtues for which he was rewarded in 27 with the golden shield.[4] He was also rewarded with two laurel trees at the door of his house and an oak wreath above it. The oak wreath, with the inscription 'ob civis servatos' between two laurel branches or surrounding the shield with the same inscription, is frequent on Augustan coins.[5] The oak wreath, since Caesar the symbol of the *parens patriae*, apparently again refers to *clementia*.[6] It was one of the principal virtues of the emperors, endlessly referred to; Seneca wrote a book *De clementia* for the use of Nero.[7]

The *monumenta* demanded by Cicero for Caesar[8] included the temple to the Clementia Caesaris, which will be discussed presently, and some statues, including the statue wearing the oak wreath on the Rostra.[9] He explicitly says that the latter was in fact a reward for Caesar's clemency.[10] It is confirmed by what Seneca and Pliny say about the meaning of the oak wreath.[11] Seneca adds that no decoration of the imperial palace was more worthy and beautiful than the wreath with the inscription 'ob cives servatos'.

temporibus locus esse solet debetque clementiae'; 8 (1. 2a). 2: 'vehementer a te, Brute, dissentio nec clementiae tuae concedo, sed salutaris severitas vincit inanem speciem clementiae; quod si clementes esse volumus, numquam deerunt bella civilia'; 23 (1. 15). 10.

[1] Dio 47. 13. 3.

[2] Cic. *Phil.* 5. 39 f.; *fam.* 10. 35 (Lepidus writes of saving the citizens and of 'misericordia nostra'); App. *BC* 3. 84. 345.

[3] Dio 48. 3. 6: ὁ Καῖσαρ . . . ἐπέστειλε τῇ γερουσίᾳ . . . προσυπισχνούμενος πάντα καὶ πρᾴως καὶ φιλανθρώπως κατὰ τὸν πατέρα ποιήσειν.

[4] *Mon. Anc.* 34. 2.

[5] Mattingly 1. 2; 7; 29 ff.; 59; 63; 67; K. Kraft, *Mainzer Zeitschr.* 46/7 (1951/2), 31 ff.

[6] Mommsen, *Res gestae* 153: 'virtus aperte respondet lauris, clementia coronae civicae'; on the oak wreath of the *parens patriae* see above, pp. 202 f.

[7] Knoche, op. cit. 82 ff.; M. Fuhrmann, *Gymn.* 70 (1963), 481 ff.

[8] Cic. *Lig.* 6; *Deiot.* 40 (above, pp. 167. 1 f.; 239. 3).

[9] See above, p. 163.

[10] Cic. *Deiot.* 34: 'quem . . . non modo non tyrannum sed etiam clementissimum in victoria ducem vidimus . . . de statua quis queritur, una praesertim, cum tam multas videat? . . . si locus adfert invidiam, nullus locus est ad statuam quidem Rostris clarior.'

[11] Sen. *clem.* 1. 26. 5: 'nullum ornamentum principis fastigio dignius pulchriusque est quam illa corona ob cives servatos'; Pliny 16. 7: 'civicae coronae, militum virtutis insigne clarissimum iam pridem vero, et clementiae imperatorum.'

(c) Clementia Caesaris

The principal monument of Caesar's clemency was to be the temple of the Clementia Caesaris.[1] Whether Cicero wanted and planned it or not, all he said about the divine nature of clemency and of the statesman who exercised it logically led to this decree of the Senate: a common temple of Caesar and the new personification, with their statues in the act of clasping hands. In the following year, 44 B.C., P. Sepullius Macer issued a coin showing a tetrastyle temple with the legend 'Clementia Caesaris' (pl. 17. 15),[2] the temple which was to be built; and there may have been many others outside Rome. No trace of them is left, as there is no trace of dedications either.[3] Augustus, who had inherited Caesar's virtue, did not build her a temple. Tiberius issued a coin in A.D. 22/3 with the legend 'Clementiae' (pl. 19. 1–2),[4] and the Senate erected an altar to her in 28.[5] It was, as so often, Caligula who returned to the Caesarian conception. An annual festival was instituted in 39 in honour of the Clementia of Caligula: his golden image, an *imago clipeata*, was carried in procession to the Capitol and his virtues, including no doubt his clemency, praised; a cow was then sacrificed at the altar of Clementia.[6] It is possible that this ritual derived from what was planned for Caesar. In 66 the Arvals included Clementia in a sacrifice made in honour of Nero on the occasion of a thanksgiving.[7] The personification, a seated figure holding a sceptre and branch, first appears on a coin of Vitellius in 69 (pl. 19. 3),[8] and for the second

[1] App. *BC* 2. 106. 443 (45 B.C.); Dio 44. 6. 4 (44 B.C.); Plut. *Caes.* 57. 4; see below, p. 308. 7–9. [2] Sydenham 179; pl. 28. 1076.

[3] There are not, even later, any inscriptions dedicated to Clementia.

[4] Mattingly 1. 132; pl. 24. 4: a bust of Tiberius surrounded by a laurel wreath on a shield. If this represents an *imago clipeata*, it may imply that the ritual performed in honour of Caligula (see above) had already existed in the time of Tiberius. A similar representation but without the wreath and with the legend 'Moderationi' ibid.; pl. 24. 5; cf. Suet. *Caes.* 75. 1; Tac. *A.* 3. 56. 1; Sutherland, *JRS* 28 (1938), 129 ff.; pls. 12 f.; id. *Coinage in Roman Imperial Policy* (1951), 97 f.; 193 f.; Pöschl, *Grundwerte* 59 ff.; Rogers, *Studies in the Reign of Tiberius* (1943), 38 ff.; 60 ff.; dated in A.D. 34–7 by M. Grant, *Rom. Ann. Issues* (1951), 47 ff. (for Tiberius' 'vicennium': not convincing).

[5] Tac. *A.* 4. 74. 3: 'aram Clementiae, aram Amicitiae effigiesque circum Caesaris ac Seiani censuere'; Sutherland, l.c. 139 f.; Rogers, op. cit. 49 ff.

[6] It is attempted in the text above to harmonize the following two passages: Dio 59. 16. 10: τῇ Φιλανθρωπίᾳ αὐτοῦ βουθυτεῖν κατ' ἔτος ἔν τε ἐκείνῃ τῇ ἡμέρᾳ ἐν ᾗ ταῦτα ἀνεγνώκει καὶ ἐν ταῖς τῷ Παλατίῳ προσηκούσαις, εἰκόνος τε αὐτοῦ χρυσῆς ἐς τὸ Καπιτώλιον ἀναγομένης καὶ ὕμνων ἐπ' αὐτῇ διὰ τῶν εὐγενεστάτων παίδων ᾀδομένων ἐψηφίσαντο; Suet. *Cal.* 16. 4: 'decretus est ei clipeus aureus, quem quotannis certo die collegia sacerdotum in Capitolium ferrent, senatu prosequente nobilibusque pueris ac puellis carmine modulato laudes virtutum eius canentibus'; cf. Wickert, *RE* 22. 2241.

[7] Henzen, *AFA* LXXXI f.; 85: 'in Capitolio ob supplicationes a senatu decretas Iovi . . . Iunoni . . . Minervae . . . Felicitati vaccam, Clementiae vaccam.'

[8] Mattingly 1. 384; pl. 61. 14 f.; cf. Tac. *H.* 1. 75: 'Vitellius victor clementiae gloriam tulit.'

time, but now as a standing figure, on many coins of Hadrian (pl. 19. 4).[1] But such statues must have existed long before, under Caesar, Augustus, and some of his successors.

The further circumstances of the planning of the cult remain obscure.[2] The assertion that she was to share her temple and even her priest with Caesar will be discussed later.[3] There was no related personification and no related cult either in Greece or at Rome, with one exception, the altars of Eleos at Athens,[4] at Epidaurus,[5] and perhaps also elsewhere. But this was a male figure—if a figure ever existed. Thus there were no precedents. Nor is it known what was to be the precise function of the temple. One might infer from the name of the goddess that it was to provide some help to those in distress, the protection of an asylum. The Altar of Mercy at Athens afforded this protection[6] but no temple or altar at Rome,[7] although people often took refuge in temples.[8] This suggestion may be supported by the fact that Caesar himself was interested in this privilege at that time: in the East he granted or renewed the right of asylum to some temples;[9] further,

---

[1] Mattingly 3. 449; 458, etc.; pls. 84. 8 f.; 86. 1 f.; Strack, op. cit. 2. 95 f.; 123; cf. SHA *Hadr.* 5. 5: 'tantum autem statim clementiae studium habuit, ut ... neminem laederet.' This Clementia was modelled on Iustitia (Strack 2. 50; 96): Caesar's Clementia must have been different because the cult of Iustitia was not created before A.D. 13 (Wissowa 333). For Clementia on coins of later emperors see W. Köhler, *Personifikation abstrakter Begriffe auf röm. Münzen* (1910), 63 ff.; Bernhart, *Handb. d. Münzkunde* 86; 153.

[2] It could be assumed that Caesar himself meant to create the cult immediately after the outbreak of the Civil War in 49, if S. E. Cesano, *Rend. Pont. Accad.* 23/4 (1947/9), 125 f., Alföldi, *Mus. Helv.* 10 (1953), 110; pls. 3. 1; 3. 3, and K. Kraft, *Jahrb. f. Numism.* 3/4 (1952/3), 25 f., were right in identifying with Clementia the female head (named until now, without justification, Venus or Pietas, Sydenham 167; pl. 27. 1008; 1010) wearing an oak wreath on Caesar's coins of *c.* 49. It is at first sight an attractive suggestion because it would provide a further reason for Caesar's clemency becoming so topical at that time, and because the oak wreath was in the end connected with clemency. If this were acceptable, it would have to be admitted that the history of the oak wreath would become more difficult and the above argument to a great extent impossible. But the identification cannot be accepted for two further reasons. First, the reverse of those coins shows a Gallic trophy and a captive seated in front of it, a representation which does not go well with clemency. Secondly, Clementia does not wear an oak wreath when she does appear, that is, on the coins of Vitellius, Hadrian, and the later emperors. Again, on the coin of Tiberius (above, p. 241. 4) with the legend 'Clementiae', his bust is surrounded with a laurel wreath.

[3] See below, p. 309.

[4] Paus. 1. 17. 1; Kaibel, *Epigr.* 792; Stat. *Theb.* 12. 481 ff.; Waser, *RE* 5. 2320 f. The Latin translation is either 'Misericordia' (Sen. *contr.* 10. 5. 10; Quintil. 5. 11. 38; Serv. *Ecl.* 6. 3; *Aen.* 3. 607; Apul. 11. 15. 1) or 'Clementia' (Stat. l.c.).

[5] *Syll.* 1149.   [6] Waser, l.c.

[7] Mommsen, *Strafr.* 458 f.; Wissowa 474. 3 (on the exception at the temple of Ceres, Varro ap. Non. 44 M.); Bömer, *Ovidius, Die Fasten* 2, p. 173; contra, Van Berchem, *Mus. Helv.* 17 (1960), 29 ff.

[8] Cato as tribune of 62 found refuge in the temple of Castor (Plut. *Cat. min.* 28. 3), Bibulus as consul of 59 in the temple of Iuppiter Stator (App. *BC* 2. 11. 40), the murderers of Caesar in that of Iuppiter Capitolinus (Dio 44. 21. 2; App. *BC* 2. 120. 503).

[9] See below, p. 395.

one of the last decrees before Caesar's death was that nobody should be harmed who took refuge with him;[1] and finally, the first temple at Rome to possess the official right of an asylum was the temple of Divus Iulius.[2] Even his statues were granted it. That is probably why there was then no need to build a temple for the Clementia Caesaris.

3. IUSTITIA

One would not perhaps postulate *iustitia* as one of Caesar's four virtues if it were not found on the golden shield of Augustus. It is true that δικαιοσύνη was the most constant of the four Greek virtues, and that accordingly *iustitia* appears in all Roman lists, in Cornificius, Cicero, and Dionysius of Halicarnassus.[3] It is also true that 'iustitia', with 'ius', 'iustus', and 'iurare', belongs to the earliest Latin vocabulary,[4] often used by Cicero, more in his philosophical writings, especially in *De re publica* and *De legibus*, than in his speeches, and that Caesar, unlike Sallust, does not avoid it. But this usage was to some extent due to Greek influence: the old term was *fides*.[5] The definitions, even if they connect it with *fides*, *aequitas*, and *pietas*, are more Greek than Roman and do not state more than the obvious.[6] It is also relevant that the personification was not an old goddess.[7] One aspect of *iustitia*, however, had very ancient roots, and together with Greek δικαιοσύνη probably made the term *iustitia* prevail: its function in international relations, especially in war.

The *bellum iustum* was never an aggressive war but one waged in self-defence, in defence of treaties, for the protection of the citizens and of their property;[8] it had to be declared by a special priest, the fetial,

---

[1] App. *BC* 2. 144. 602; cf. the related privileges of the *flamen Dialis* and the Vestals, Gell. 10. 15. 8; 10; Serv. *Aen.* 2. 57; 3. 608; Plut. *Numa* 10. 6; Wissowa 507.

[2] Dio 47. 19. 2 (below, p. 395. 6).   [3] See above, p. 228.

[4] It is mere chance that 'iustitia' is first found in Terence (*Heaut.* 646), because there is 'iniustitia' in Plaut. *Merc.* 47, who often uses 'iniuria' (also as a playful personification, *Mil.* 436).   [5] Heinze, *Vom Geist d. Römertums* 57; Pöschl, *Grundwerte* 81.

[6] Cic. *inv.* 2. 160: 'iustitia est habitus animi communi utilitate conservata suam cuique tribuens dignitatem'; *rep.* 3. 24: 'iustitia autem praecipit parcere omnibus, consulere generi hominum, suum cuique reddere, sacra publica aliena non tangere'; *off.* 1. 20; 23: 'fundamentum . . . est iustitiae fides'; 64: (aequitas) 'est iustitiae maxime propria'; *part. or.* 78: 'iustitia . . . erga deis religio, erga parentes pietas . . . nominatur'; *ND* 1. 4; 1. 116 (Pease ad loc.); *fin.* 5. 65; U. v. Lübtow, *Zeitschr. Sav. Stift.* 66 (1948), 458 ff.; Wickert, *RE* 22. 2248 ff.; H. Dieter, *Eirene* 7 (1968), 33 ff.

[7] Wissowa 333; Latte 300. 4.

[8] Cic. *leg.* 3. 9: 'duella iusta iuste gerunto'; *rep.* 3. 34; *off.* 1. 35; Livy 30. 16. 9: 'omnes gentes sciant populum Romanum et suscipere iuste bella et finire'; 45. 22. 5; A. Heuss, *Die völkerrechtl. Grundlagen der röm. Aussenpolitik* (1933), 18 ff.; Dahlmann, *Varron. Stud.* 1 (1957), 48; Drexler, *Rhein. Mus.* 102 (1959), 97 ff.; R. Combès, *Imperator* 358 ff.

in a solemn form, stressing the justice of the Roman cause.[1] The war was often called 'iustum et pium',[2] which may have implied, or sought, divine approval for it. The opposite was *iniustum bellum*, an arbitrary war without a cause and against the treaties.[3] This was generally the war undertaken by the enemies of Rome, who then had to suffer for it. When a Roman general happened to be guilty, the Senate repaired the damage caused by him.[4]

The Roman belief in their just wars was stressed by Roman historians, perhaps already by Fabius Pictor,[5] in order to meet Greek criticism. Their claim was accepted by Polybius,[6] Panaetius, and Posidonius,[7] and led to the concept of the *iustum imperium* of the Romans.[8] This was a philosophical concept and depended ultimately on the discussion of justice in Plato's *Republic*. That is why *iustitia* became one of the four virtues and why Cicero devoted to it the third book of his *State*,[9] where he set out to prove that the ideal of δικαιοσύνη had become a reality in the Roman State.

The next step was to attribute the gift of justice, which was formerly a collective virtue of the Roman State, to the true statesman. The elder Scipio admonishes his grandson in the *Somnium Scipionis* to cultivate *iustitia* and *pietas*,[10] thus resuming a theme of the preceding books, which listed justice among the virtues of the 'rector civitatis'.[11]

---

[1] Cic. *off.* 1. 36: 'belli quidem aequitas sanctissime fetiali populi Romani iure praescripta est. ex quo intellegi potest nullum bellum esse iustum, nisi quod aut rebus repetitis geratur aut denuntiatum ante sit et indictum'; *rep.* 2. 31; 3. 35; Livy 1. 32. 6 f.; Non. 284 M. (= Varr. *vita p. R.* frg. 121 Riposati); Wissowa 550 ff.; Heuss, op. cit. 20 f.; Gelzer, *Kl. Schr.* 2. 319. 34; 3. 91; Hanell, *Entretiens* 4 (1956), 159 f.

[2] Cic. *inv.* 2. 70; Livy 3. 25. 3; 9. 8. 6; 33. 29. 8; 42. 23. 6; 42. 47. 8; Ulrich, *Pietas* 22 f.; Latte 40; Gabba, *Entretiens* 13 (1967), 140 (Naevius).

[3] Cic. *rep.* 3. 35: 'illa iniusta bella sunt, quae sunt sine causa suscepta. nam extra quam ulciscendi aut propulsandorum hostium causa bellum geri iustum nullum potest'; Livy 8. 39. 10; *Mon. Anc.* 26. 3; Suet. *Aug.* 21. 2; Heuss, op. cit. 19; 21; Gelzer 3. 61.

[4] Livy 43. 4. 13: 'nuntiarent senatum Abderitis iniustum bellum inlatum conquirique omnes, qui in servitute sint, et restitui in libertatem aecum censere'; 9. 8. 6; Cic. *off.* 3. 109; below, p. 245. 3; Heuss, op. cit. 23.

[5] Gelzer, *Kl. Schr.* 3. 56.   [6] Polyb. 36. 2. 3; Diod. 32. 5 (Polyb.).

[7] *FGrHist.* 87 F 59.

[8] Livy 22. 13. 11 (217 B.C.): 'nec tamen is terror . . . fide socios dimovit, videlicet quia iusto et moderato regebantur imperio'; Sall. *Cat.* 52. 21: 'domi industria, foris iustum imperium'; Capelle, *Klio* 25 (1932), 97; Pöschl, *Grundwerte* 81 ff.

[9] Pöschl, *Röm. Staat u. griech. Staatsdenken bei Cicero* (1936), 127 ff.; Klingner, *Römische Geisteswelt*[4] 663 ff.

[10] Cic. *rep.* 6. 16. The two virtues were connected already by Plato, *Euthyphr.* 12 e, and often later, see Diod. 12. 20. 3; Clem. Alex. *Strom.* 6. 15. 125. 5; Pease ad Cic. *ND* 1. 116; Posidonius found both of them in the Roman State (above, n. 7).

[11] Cic. *rep.* 3. 27: 'vir . . . summa iustitia, singulari fide'; 5. 2: 'sapiens sit et iustus et temperans et eloquens'; 5. 5; 2. 43: 'ut unius perpetua potestate et iustitia omnique sapientia regatur salus . . . civium'; *off.* 2. 43; *Planc.* 33: 'Q. Scaevolam, virum omnibus ingenio, iustitia, integritate praestantem.'

It is possible that it was in fact consciously stressed in the age of the Scipios. So it could be said that Marius committed an offence against *fides* and *iustitia* by his attack on Metellus, his commander, in 108 B.C., when he tried to secure the consulship for the following year.[1] This was justice in political warfare; it was also required in the law-courts,[2] and of course in international relations. In 55 Cato proposed in the Senate that Caesar should be handed over to the Germans for punishment because of his wanton attack, *iniustum bellum*, upon them, so as to avert divine punishment for this sacrilege from all the Romans.[3] There is no doubt that Cato meant what he said and was probably inspired by Cicero's similar attack on Piso, Caesar's father-in-law, two months earlier.[4]

Caesar's conquest of Gaul was a just cause.[5] He stressed it on various occasions in his fight against Ariovistus[6] and at his crossing of the Rhine,[7] he let the Gauls refer to his own justice[8] and praised the same virtue among friendly leaders and tribes.[9] There is nothing remarkable in this: it was traditional Roman behaviour. When he arrived at Rome in March 49 after the outbreak of the Civil War, he spoke in the Senate about the *iniuria* of his adversaries and about his intention to win by *iustitia* and *aequitas*.[10] More than traditional behaviour, this was another version of his political programme and closely related to his claim of clemency. It did not make him a disciple of the philosophers

---

[1] Cic. *off.* 3. 79: (Marius) 'a fide iustitiaque discessit.'

[2] Cic. *Cluent.* 42: 'ut aut iuste pieque accusaret.'

[3] Suet. *Caes.* 24. 3: 'nec ... belli occasione ... iniusti ... abstinuit, ... adeo ut ... nonnulli dedendum eum hostibus censuerint'; Plut. *Caes.* 22. 4: Τανύσιος δὲ λέγει (*HRR* 2. 50) Κάτωνα τῆς βουλῆς ἐπὶ τῇ νίκῃ ψηφιζομένης ἑορτὰς καὶ θυσίας, ἀποφήνασθαι γνώμην, ὡς ἐκδοτέον ἐστὶ τὸν Καίσαρα τοῖς βαρβάροις, ἀφοσιουμένους τὸ παρασπόνδημα ὑπὲρ τῆς πόλεως, καὶ τὴν ἀρὰν εἰς τὸν αἴτιον τρέποντας; Plut. *Cat. min.* 51 f.; *Crass.* 37. 3; App. *Celt.* 18. Caesar's version of the campaign: *BG* 4. 11–15 (supplications for 20 days, 4. 38. 5); Meyer, *Caesars Monarchie* 172; Strasburger, *Hist. Zeitschr.* 175 (1953), 239 (= *Caesar im Urteil seiner Zeitgenossen* (1967), 24 f.; 74 f.); Balsdon, *Greece and Rome* 26 (1957), 21 f.; Gelzer, *Caesar* 118 f.; *Kl. Schr.* 3. 318; 324; id. *Festgabe f. P. Kirn* (1961), 46 ff.; Heuss, op. cit. 24; cf. Octavian's Pannonian expedition represented (by Antony?) as an *iniustum bellum*, Dio 49. 36. 1; above, p. 244. 4.

[4] Cic. *Pis.* 84 f.

[5] Caes. *BG* 1. 45. 3: 'populi Romani iustissimum esse in Gallia imperium'; Gelzer, *Kl. Schr.* 2. 8.

[6] Caes. *BG* 1. 43. 6: 'docebat etiam, quam veteres quamque iustae causae necessitudinis ipsis cum Haeduis intercederent'; Dio 38. 45. 1: ὅτι μὲν δικαιότατα ἂν αὐτῷ πολεμήσαιμεν, οὐδένα ἀμφισβητήσειν οἴομαι; Gelzer, ibid.

[7] Caes. *BG* 4. 16. 1; 3.

[8] Caes. *BG* 5. 41. 8: 'sperare se pro eius iustitia quae petierint impetraturos.'

[9] Caes. *BG* 1. 19. 2: 'Diviciaci fratris ... egregiam fidem, iustitiam, temperantiam cognoverat'; 6. 24. 3: 'quae gens ... summam habet iustitiae et bellicae laudis opinionem.'

[10] Caes. *BC* 1. 32. 2: 'coacto senatu iniurias inimicorum commemorat ... (9) se vero ... iustitia et aequitate velle superare'; cf. 1. 5. 5: 'exspectabatque ... responsa, si qua hominum aequitate res ad otium deduci posset'; 1. 35. 3: 'discernere utra pars iustiorem habeat causam.'

or even of Cicero, but it opened the way to an interpretation of his actions with the help of contemporary theory. According to the anonymous pamphlet the four virtues of Romulus included *iustitia*, which prevented the citizens from doing injury to one another and led to concord; and Romulus made laws which served this aim.[1] About the same time, in 46, Cicero praised Caesar's *iustitia* and *lenitas* and said that they would have a lasting effect.[2] He thus alluded to Caesar's promises made at the beginning of the Civil War[3] and acknowledged that he had succeeded. But he wanted more: the law-courts should be reconstituted, loyalty restored, decay stemmed with the help of severe laws.[4] There is no doubt Caesar meant to do this and would then have become a man of *iustitia*. And what would have been his reward: a cult, comparable to that of the Clementia Caesaris? This question could be answered in the affirmative, if it could be shown that at the time of these legislative plans Iustitia was also propagated as a goddess for the first time in Rome. She had already appeared as a personification in Catullus[5] in connection with the old tale about the lawlessness of the Iron Age, often told from Hesiod to Aratus, when Nemesis or, in the later version, Dike left the earth.[6] If in Vergil she is again leaving the earth[7] but also returning to it,[8] it is possible to assume that before Vergil a poet of the Civil War had given her this dual role, ascribing her return to the rule of Caesar. The theme is also found in Horace's *Carmen saeculare*,[9] in a context which recalls the programme of justice sketched in Cicero's *Pro Marcello*, but this time as something that had been achieved. The poetical symbolism which Horace uses elevates it above the sphere of everyday life: the return of

---

[1] Dion. Hal. 2. 18. 1: τὴν σωφροσύνην τε καὶ δικαιοσύνην, δι' ἃς ἧττον ἀλλήλους βλάπτοντες μᾶλλον ὁμονοοῦσι . . . (2) ἔγνω διότι νόμοι σπουδαῖοι καὶ καλῶν ζῆλος ἐπιτηδευμάτων εὐσεβῆ καὶ σώφρονα καὶ τὰ δίκαια ἀσκοῦσαν καὶ τὰ πολέμια ἀγαθὴν ἐξεργάζονται πόλιν; see above, pp. 181 f.

[2] Cic. *Marc.* 12: 'at haec tua iustitia et lenitas floresceret cotidie magis . . . et ceteros quidem omnes victores bellorum civilium iam ante aequitate et misericordia viceras'; 32: 'sed iam omnis fracta dissensio est armis, extincta aequitate victoris'; Val. Max. 9. 15. 5: 'a Sullana violentia Caesariana aequitas rem publicam reduxit.'

[3] See above, p. 245. 10.

[4] Cic. *Marc.* 23: 'constituenda iudicia, revocanda fides, . . . omnia quae dilapsa iam diffluxerunt, severis legibus vincienda sunt'; Gelzer, *Caesar* 260 f.

[5] Catull. 64. 398: 'Iustitiamque omnes cupida de mente fugarunt, / perfudere manus fraterno sanguine fratres.'

[6] Hes. *Erg.* 174 ff.; Arat. 129 ff.

[7] Verg. *Georg.* 2. 473: 'extrema per illos / Iustitia excedens terris vestigia fecit'; Ov. *F.* 1. 249; cf. Arat. 100; 133; 470.

[8] Verg. *Ecl.* 4. 6: 'iam redit et Virgo, redeunt Saturnia regna'; *Aen.* 1. 292: 'cana Fides et Vesta, Remo cum fratre Quirinus / iura dabunt'.

[9] Hor. *c. s.* 57: 'iam Fides et Pax et Honos Pudorque / priscus et neglecta redire Virtus / audet'; Vell. 2. 126. 2: 'revocata in forum fides . . . sepultaeque ac situ obsitae iustitia, aequitas, industria civitati redditae'; Fraenkel, *Horace* 376 f.

Fides and Pax, of Honos and Virtus to earth indicates the beginning of the new Golden Age. The complementary theme about Caesar's reward for having brought about the return of Iustitia may also have existed, but we can again quote only Augustan evidence, Horace's ode about the man of justice who, like the Greek heroes, would achieve immortality.[1] Romulus was among these, whose justice removed the curse for Laomedon's perjury from the descendants of Troy;[2] and Augustus would one day join their company.[3] The ode intentionally concentrates on a single virtue: in fact Hercules, the Dioscuri, and Liber pater excelled more in other fields, and even Romulus was not only a lawgiver. And that is why it is possible to date this theme too back to the age of Caesar: we have seen that Romulus' justice was probably invented for the benefit of Caesar. The view that perjury, caused by breach of contract, brought on the people a curse which had to be purged, was much older.[4] There was no perjury in Caesar's case because he had crossed the Rubicon in order to fight for justice and equity.[5]

This is all that can be said about Caesar's Iustitia. She now ceased to be the personification borrowed from Hesiod and Aratus and became a Roman goddess.[6] She did not yet possess a cult, and Caesar did not create one. Nor did Augustus until A.D. 13; and it may have been created even later.[7] She seldom appeared in inscriptions;[8] on coins only in the time of Tiberius (pl. 19. 5–6),[9] Vespasian,[10] Nerva,[11] and especially of Hadrian and later (pl. 19. 7–8).[12] But the virtue was

---

[1] Hor. *c.* 3. 3. 1: 'Iustum et tenacem propositi virum / non civium ardor prava iubentium / . . . / mente quatit solida'; 9: 'hac arte Pollux et vagus Hercules / enisus arcis attigit igneas'; Heinze, *Vom Geist des Römertums* 228 f.; Fraenkel, *Horace* 269.

[2] Hor. *c.* 3. 3. 33: 'illum ego lucidas / inire sedes, discere nectaris / sucos et adscribi quietis / ordinibus patiar deorum'; Verg. *Georg.* 1. 501: 'satis iam pridem sanguine nostro / Laomedonteae luimus periuria Troiae.'

[3] Hor. *c.* 3. 3. 11: 'quos inter Augustus recumbens / purpureo bibet ore nectar.'

[4] See above, p. 244. 4.; 245. 3. [5] Caes. *BC* 1. 32. 2; 8.

[6] It is not clear where Hor. *c.* 1. 24. 6 ('cui Pudor et Iustitiae soror / incorrupta Fides nudaque Veritas / quando ullum inveniet parem!') should be placed.

[7] Ov. *Pont.* 2. 1. 33 f.; 3. 6. 23 ff.; *Fast. Praen.* 8 Jan.: 'signum Iustitiae Augustae . . . Ti. Caesar dedicavit Planco et Silio consulibus' (Degrassi 392 f. suggests that there was only a statue, dedicated by Tiberius in A.D. 13). It is represented on his coins with sceptre and branch, Mattingly 1. 124 ff.; pl. 22. 20–23. 9: her identity is proved by the legend on the coins of Nerva (below, n. 11); cf. Strack, op. cit. 1. 52. 128; Grant, *Aspects* 80; id. *Rom. Ann. Issues* 38 ff.

[8] *ILS* 3790a; 5525a (Iustitia Augusta); 2924 ('Iovis et Iustitiae' in an apparently Etruscan context; cf. Paul. 105 M. = 93 L.: 'Ioviste compositum a Iove et iuste') ; more in *Diz. epigr.* 4. 315. On altars of Δικαιοσύνη in the East see L. Robert, *Mél. Dussaud* 2. 731 ff.; id. *Documents de l'Asie Mineure Méridionale* (1966), 25 ff.

[9] Mattingly 1. 124 ff.; 131; cf. *ILS* 159: 'principi optumo ac iustissimo'; Syme, *Tacitus* 755. [10] Mattingly 2. 75 (?). [11] Mattingly 3. 2; 6; 8; 16.

[12] Mattingly 3. 238; 240; 249; 305; 311; 456 f.; 462 f.; 471; 483; Strack, op. cit. 2. 50; 123; 126; Bernhart, *Handb. d. Münzkunde* 191; H. Lange, *Zeitschr. Sav. Stift.* 52 (1932), 298 ff.;

claimed for Caesar, and Augustus inherited the claim:[1] that is how *iustitia* appeared among his virtues on the golden shield. Horace wrote the ode in his third book to celebrate this event and to point to its implications.

4. PIETAS

(a) The Virtue and the Goddess

Pietas is a term which at first sight does not seem relevant here.[2] Caesar uses it only once in his writings, in the sense of the tribal loyalty of the Gauls, and 'impius' in another context of those who commit offences against the gods;[3] this does not indicate great interest in the concept. A closer examination of the origin and history of the term will change this verdict. *Pietas* comes from *pius*, and both belong to the early Latin vocabulary, as they often appear in Plautus. In its original sense 'pium est', like 'fas est', indicates what can be done without committing a religious offence;[4] 'pium et iustum bellum' is a war in accordance with divine and human law.[5] The definition, Greek in origin, that *pietas* is to do justice to the gods[6] is right in so far as it presents 'iustitia' and 'pietas' as related terms; by implying the worship of the gods, however, it reflects later developments. Another definition which contrasts 'religio' and 'pietas', the former being concerned with the cult of the gods, the latter with the right attitude towards one's parents and homeland,[7] is wrong: already in Plautus

---

Wickert, *RE* 22. 2250 ff.; Dikaiosyne on coins of the Greek provinces, Waser, *RE* 5. 564 f.; Head, *HN* 506; 577; 677; 683; 863; Vogt, *Die alexandrinischen Münzen* 2. 8 ff. (beginning with Nero).

[1] Dio 50. 24. 1 (31 B.C., Actium): τὰ πλεῖστα καὶ μέγιστα τῶν πολεμικῶν . . . τοῖς τά τε δικαιότερα καὶ τὰ εὐσεβέστερα καὶ φρονοῦσι καὶ πράττουσι κατορθούμενα; 52. 18. 3 (29 B.C.): ὅτι μὲν ὀρθῶς καὶ δικαίως πάντα ταῦτ' ἐποίησας, οὐδεὶς ἀγνοεῖ; Ov. *Met.* 15. 832: 'pace data terris animum ad civilia vertet / iura suum legesque feret iustissimus auctor'; *Trist.* 4. 4. 12: 'principe tam iusto'.

[2] The evidence is collected by Pease ad Verg. *Aen.* 4. 393 and ad Cic. *ND* 1. 3; 1. 115 f.; cf. Val. Max. 5. 4–6 ('De pietate erga parentes et fratres et patriam'); Wissowa, *Myth. Lex.* 3. 2499 ff.; Tromp, *De Romanorum piaculis* (1921), 4 ff.; Ulrich, *Pietas* (1930), 4 ff.; Liegle, *Zeitschr. f. Num.* 42 (1935), 71 ff.; C. Koch, *RE* 20. 1221 ff.; Knoche, *Festschr. f. Snell* (1956), 89 ff.; Latte 39 f.; 238 f.; H. Fugier, *Recherches sur l'expression du sacré dans la langue latine* (1963), 371 ff.

[3] Caes. *BG* 5. 27. 7: 'quibus quoniam pro pietate satisfecerit, habere nunc se rationem officii pro beneficiis Caesaris'; 6. 13. 7: 'hi numero impiorum ac sceleratorum habentur.'

[4] Latte 39 f., quoting Volscan 'pihom estu' (Vetter 222).

[5] See above, p. 244. 2.

[6] Cic. *ND* 1. 116: 'est enim pietas iustitia adversum deos'; for the Greek evidence see Pease ad loc., e.g. Sext. Emp. *adv. Phys.* 1. 124: ἡ ὁσιότης δικαιοσύνη τις οὖσα πρὸς θεούς.

[7] Cic. *inv.* 2. 66; 2. 161.

pietas is concerned with both spheres.[1] It can also lead to reciprocity: there is evidence for the *pietas* of parents towards their children and of the community towards its citizens;[2] but not of the gods towards men; and yet divine favour may have been called so once, as in Oscan a god too can be called 'pius'.[3]

Naevius uses *pietas* in relation to the gods,[4] but Ennius' *pius Anchises* may equally be a man loyal to his parents.[5] In Plautus there is ample evidence for both spheres. As a civic virtue we first meet it in Polybius, who says that the attachment of the Romans to their gods, their δεισιδαιμονία, had great advantages, in so far as they kept their oaths and observed their treaties.[6] This correctly reflects the concept of the 'iustum et pium bellum'. The praetor M. Valerius maintained in a letter to Teos in 193 B.C. that their *pietas* earned the benevolence of the gods for the Romans:[7] the expression is Greek and traditional for such occasions,[8] but the Roman concept with its reciprocity may be concealed behind it. This was part of the defence of Roman imperialism by the early Roman historians:[9] it was not only *iustitia* but also *pietas* that helped them to win mastery of the world, and not, as their Greek critics asserted, mere chance and the whim of Tyche.[10] Polybius accepted the Roman view, and Posidonius' praise of Roman justice and piety too[11] is best understood in this sense. The next step was to

---

[1] Plaut. *Rud.* 25: 'nihil ei (Iovi) acceptumst a periuris supplici; / facilius si qui pius est a dis supplicans, / quam qui scelestust, inveniet veniam sibi'; 11; 29; *Tri.* 281: 'patrem tuom si percoles per pietatem'; *Asin.* 509: 'hocine est pietatem colere, matris imperium minuere?' *Poen.* 1137.

[2] Cornif. 2. 19: 'natura ius est quod cognationis aut pietatis causa observatur: quo iure parentes a liberis et a parentibus liberi coluntur'; Plaut. *Poen.* 1137; 1277; Cic. *fam.* 14. 1. 3: 'mihi fructum videbor percepisse et vestrae pietatis et meae'; *Phil.* 14. 29: 'est autem fidei pietatisque nostrae declarare fortissimis militibus, quam memores simus quamque grati'; 14. 35: 'populi Romani pietatem'; Knoche, l.c. 90. 5; Latte 40. 3.

[3] Vetter 218. 10: 'regenai peai cerre iovia'; 147 B 15: 'diuvei piihiui regaturei' (Iovi Pio 'Irrigatori'); Schwyzer, *Rhein. Mus.* 84 (1935), 177 f.; Knoche, l.c. 91. 1 (who also quotes Iuppiter's 'pietas antiqua', Verg. *Aen.* 5. 688); Latte 40. 3; Devoto, *Studi Etr.* 35 (1967), 193.

[4] Naev. 10 Str. (12 M. = 49 Mariotti): 'senex fretus pietate deum adlocutus . . . Neptunum.'

[5] Enn. *A.* 30 V.: 'pium . . . Anchisen'; Latte 40. 3 assumes that this indicates Anchises' piety towards his children.

[6] Polyb. 6. 56. 7; 14; 24. 13. 3; cf. Diod. 28. 3.

[7] *Syll.* 601. 13: . . . τῆς πρὸς τοὺς θεοὺς εὐσεβείας; cf. the letter of the consul C. Livius and the senate to Delphi, 189 B.C., *Syll.* 611. 22, promising help: διὰ τὸ πάτριον ἡμῖν εἶναι τοὺς θεοὺς σέβεσθαί τε καὶ τιμᾶν τοὺς ὄντας πάντων αἰτίους τῶν ἀγαθῶν. Scipio Africanus was honoured on Delos in 188 B.C. with a laurel wreath for his *virtus* and *pietas*, *Syll.* 617. 16: ἀρετῆς ἕνεκεν καὶ εὐσεβείας τῆς περὶ τὸ ἱερόν; cf. Vogt, *Vom Reichsgedanken d. Römer* (1942), 140 f.; Gelzer, *Kl. Schr.* 2. 17. 60.   [8] Cf., e.g., *Syll.* 372. 18; 615. 5.   [9] See above, p. 235.

[10] Dion. Hal. 1. 4. 2: οὐ δι' εὐσέβειαν δὲ καὶ δικαιοσύνην καὶ τὴν ἄλλην ἀρετὴν ἐπὶ τὴν ἁπάντων ἡγεμονίαν σὺν χρόνῳ παρελθούσης, ἀλλὰ δι' αὐτοματισμόν τινα καὶ Τύχην ἄδικον κτλ.

[11] *FGrHist.* 87 F 59.

ascribe all the success to divine favour, which the Romans gained by their piety.[1] This view was often held in the first century, by Cicero, Varro, Horace, Livy.[2]

As a personification, Pietas is first found in Plautus, representing the due attitude of children towards their parents.[3] Her first temple was vowed in 191 in the battle at Thermopylae against Antiochus III by M'. Acilius Glabrio (cos. 191) and dedicated ten years later by his son.[4] The fact that the vow was made in the battle suggests that she was to be the goddess of the civic piety towards the gods which the Romans propagated in the East about that time. She could have been the goddess of filial piety if, as has been suggested,[5] the son had saved his father in the battle, an action which was ascribed to the elder Scipio probably about that time.[6] A story of filial piety was later connected with the temple;[7] this would not prove anything even if the story were less irrelevant than it is. There was another temple in the Circus Flaminius, which must have existed before 91 B.C.;[8] there is no evidence about its origin or its character.

In the first century Cicero had much to say about *pietas* towards the gods in the sense of the Greek εὐσέβεια,[9] but also towards parents and the homeland.[10] It was this aspect of *pietas* that had received greater attention in Roman life. M. Herennius issued a coin *c.* 107 B.C. with a female head and the legend 'Pietas' on the obverse and a man carrying another on his shoulder on the reverse (pl. 19. 9).[11] The

[1] Diod. 28. 3.

[2] Cic. *har. resp.* 19: 'pietate ac religione . . . omnis gentis nationesque superavimus'; Varr. *Ant. rer. div.* 1, frg. 36 Ag. (Tert. *Apol.* 25; cf. Min. Fel. 25. 1); Hor. *c.* 3. 6. 5: 'dis te minorem quod geris, imperas'; Livy 44. 1. 11: 'favere enim pietati fideique deos, per quae populus Romanus ad tantum fastigii venerit'; 6. 41. 8.

[3] Plaut. *Asin.* 506: 'ubi piem Pietatem'; *Curc.* 639: 'o Pietas mea'; cf. *Bacch.* 1176: 'sine, mea pietas, te exorem.'

[4] Livy 40. 34. 4; *Fast. Ant. Mai.* 13 Nov. (Degrassi 530); cf. Koch, *RE* 20. 1224.

[5] Wissowa 331; *contra*, Latte 239. 1.

[6] See above, p. 163.

[7] Pliny 7. 121; Val. Max. 5. 4. 7; Wissowa 331.

[8] Obs. 54 (91 B.C.); Cic. *div.* 1. 98; *F. Amit.* 1 Dec. (Degrassi 533). For the identity of the two temples: Castagnoli, *Gnom.* 33 (1961), 607; Coarelli, *Bull. comun.* 80 (1965/7), 40 f.; *contra*, Degrassi 533.

[9] Cic. *dom.* 107: 'nec est ulla erga deos pietas sine honesta de numine eorum ac mente opinione'; *leg.* 2. 19: 'ad divos adeunto caste, pietatem adhibento, opes amovento'; 2. 15; 2. 25 f.; *Cluent.* 194; *off.* 2. 11.

[10] Cic. *Planc.* 80: 'quid est pietas nisi voluntas grata in parentes'; *har. resp.* 43; *p. red. Quir.* 6; *Sest.* 7; *Phil.* 2. 99, etc., esp. in his correspondence; *rep.* 6. 16: 'iustitiam cole et pietatem, quae cum magna in parentibus et propinquis, tum in patria maxima est'; *Phil.* 13. 46: 'Caesar, singulari pietate adulescens, . . . intellegit maximam pietatem conservatione patriae contineri'; 14. 29 (above, p. 249. 2); 14. 35.

[11] Sydenham 77; pl. 19. 567 (dated by Grueber *c.* 91 B.C.); cf. Mommsen, *Röm. Münzwesen* 566. 315; Wissowa ,*Myth. Lex.* 3. 2501 f.; Liegle, *Zeitschr. f. Num.* 42 (1935), 76 f.

moneyer, probably the consul of 93 and of Sicilian origin,[1] reproduced a local tradition of Catana. Once two youths, Amphinomus and Anapias, saved their parents from the lava after an eruption of Mount Aetna by carrying them on their shoulders.[2] They had become the symbols of filial piety,[3] had their monument in Catana, and were also represented on local coins (pl. 19. 10).[4] Why Herennius chose one of the brothers with the father and Pietas (this is her earliest representation) for his coins is not known: his possible Sicilian origin explains the choice, but not the particular occasion. At any rate, this was an instance of filial piety. The next instance was that of Q. Caecilius Metellus Pius (*cos.* 80), whose coins issued *c.* 81 B.C. show the head of Pietas again without legend (pl. 19. 11),[5] but the identification is certain because a stork, her symbol,[6] is added. He received the *cognomen* 'Pius' when he succeeded in persuading the Senate to recall his father from exile;[7] and this is clearly what was commemorated by the coins.

The third coin with the head of Pietas, identified by the legend, was issued by Decimus Iunius Brutus Albinus at the beginning of the Civil War, 49/48 B.C. (pl. 19. 12);[8] the reverse shows two hands clasping a caduceus, symbols of concord and peace respectively. These were the political concepts frustrated by the outbreak of the Civil War; Brutus now propagated them, and he was a partisan of Caesar. So we must turn to Caesar. One might argue that Caesar's *pietas* could only be that of the statesman. He was bound by tradition to do for the gods what was due to them. In addition he was the *pontifex maximus* and dictator with unlimited power, the right man to reform religion. We have already surveyed various proposals made in this direction, by Cicero in his works *De re publica* and *De legibus*; by the anonymous author used by Dionysius of Halicarnassus, who ascribed such reforms to Romulus; and by Varro in his *Antiquitates rerum divinarum.*[9] There is no doubt that Caesar was aware of the problem and intended to act. He began with the reform of the calendar,[10] which was a great achievement. He built

[1] Münzer, *RE* 8. 664, no. 10.
[2] Lycurg. *Leocr.* 95; *Aetna* 625 ff.; Val. Max. 5. 4 Ext. 4, etc.
[3] Paus. 10. 28. 4: τοῖς καλουμένοις εὐσεβέσιν; Kaibel, *Epigr.* 887: Εὐσεβέων κλυτὸν ἄστυ.
[4] Hill, *Coins of Ancient Sicily* 205 f.; pl. 14. 16; Head, *HN* 134.
[5] Sydenham 122; pl. 21. 750; Wissowa, l.c. 2502; Liegle, l.c. 77.
[6] Publ. Syr. 7 f. R.: 'Ciconia . . . pietaticultrix'; Babr. *fab.* 13. 7: πτηνῶν πελαργὸς εὐσεβέστατον ζῴων; Steier, *RE* 4A. 71.
[7] Cic. *p. red. sen.* 37, etc.; Münzer, *RE* 3. 1221; cf. Eusebes, title of some Hellenistic rulers (Willrich, *RE* 6. 1364 f.).
[8] Sydenham 158; pl. 26. 942; Liegle, l.c. 78; cf. Münzer, *RE* Suppl. 5. 371.
[9] See above, pp. 180 ff.
[10] Suet. *Caes.* 40 (46 B.C.); see above, p. 197.

PLATE 19

1. Dupondius of Tiberius, A.D. 22–3 (Mattingly 1. 132. 85), London; *obv.*: head of Tiberius, legend 'Ti. Caesar Divi Aug. f. August., imp. VIII'; *rev.*: bust of Tiberius surrounded by laurel wreath on shield within a thick circle of petals, legend 'Clementiae, S.C.'; p. 241.

2. Dupondius of Tiberius, A.D. 22–3 (Mattingly 1. 132. 90), Vienna; *obv.*: as on the preceding; *rev.*: as above, but laurel wreath outside the petals, legend 'Moderationi, S.C.'; p. 241.

3. Aureus of Vitellius, A.D. 69 (Mattingly 1. 384. 79), London; *obv.*: head of Vitellius, legend 'A. Vitellius Imp. Germanicus'; *rev.*: Clementia seated with sceptre and branch, legend 'Clementia Imp. German.'; p. 241.

4. Sestertius of Hadrian, A.D. 119–38 (Mattingly 3. 449. 1382), London; *obv.*: bust of Hadrian, legend 'Hadrianus Augustus'; *rev.*: Clementia with sceptre and patera, legend 'Clementia Aug(usta) ,cos. III, p. p., S.C.'; p. 242.

5. Aureus of Tiberius, c. A.D. 16–21 (Mattingly 1. 124. 30), Oxford; *obv.*: head of Tiberius, legend 'Ti. Caesar Divi Aug. f. Augustus'; *rev.*: seated Iustitia(?) with sceptre and branch, legend 'pontif. maxim.'; p. 247.

6. Dupondius of Tiberius, A.D. 22–3 (Mattingly 1. 131. 79), Oxford; *obv.*: legend 'S.C, Ti. Caesar Divi Aug. f. Aug., p. m., tr. pot. XXIIII'; *rev.*: bust of Livia as Iustitia, legend 'Iustitia'; p. 247.

7. Denarius of Nerva, A.D. 96 (Mattingly 3. 2. 13), London; *obv.*: head of Nerva, legend 'Imp. Nerva Caes. Aug., p. m., tr. p., cos. II, p. p.'; *rev.*: Iustitia seated with sceptre and branch, legend 'Iustitia August.'; p. 247.

8. Denarius of Hadrian, A.D. 117 (Mattingly 3. 238. 12), London; *obv.*: bust of Hadrian, legend 'Imp. Caes. Traian. Hadrian. Opt. Aug. Ger. Dac.'; *rev.*: Iustitia seated with sceptre and patera, legend 'Iustitia, Parthic. Divi Traian. Aug. f., p. m., tr. p., cos., p. p.'; p. 247.

9. Denarius of M. Herennius, c. 107 B.C. (Sydenham 77. 567), Oxford; *obv.*: head of Pietas, legend 'Pietas'; *rev.*: youth carrying his father, legend

'M. Herenni(us)'; p. 250.

10. Bronze of Catana (*BMC Sicily* 52), London; *obv.*: horned head, legend Ἀδανός; *rev.*: Amphinomus and Anapias carry their parents, legend Καταναίων; p. 252.

11. Denarius of Q. Caecilius Metellus Pius, c. 81 B.C. (Sydenham 122. 750), Oxford; *obv.*: head of Pietas and stork; *rev.*: elephant, legend 'Q.C.M.P. I(mperator)'; p. 251.

12. Denarius of D. Postumius Albinus, 48 B.C. (Sydenham 158. 942), Oxford; *obv.*: head of Pietas, legend 'Pietas'; *rev.*: clasped hands with caduceus, legend 'Albinus Bruti f.'; p. 251.

13. Denarius of Caesar 47 B.C. (Sydenham 168. 1013), Oxford; *obv.*: bust of Venus; *rev.*: Aeneas with Anchises and the Palladium, legend 'Caesar'; p. 253.

14. Denarius of Sex. Pompeius, 45 B.C. (Sydenham 174. 1042), Paris; *obv.*: head of Pompey, legend 'Sex. Magn. imp., Sal(pensa)'; *rev.*: Pietas with sceptre and branch, legend 'Pietas'; p. 254.

15. Denarius of Sex. Pompeius, 45 B.C. (Sydenham 174. 1043), London; *obv.*: head of Pompey, legend 'Sex. Magnus Sal(pensa) imp.'; *rev.*: Pietas with sceptre and branch, legend 'Pietas'; p. 254.

16. Sestertius of Galba, A.D. 68 (Mattingly 1. 358 n.), Paris; *obv.*: bust of Galba, legend 'Ser. Sulpi. Galba Imp. Caesar Aug., tr. p.'; *rev.*: Pietas at altar on which relief with Aeneas, Anchises, and Ascanius, legend 'Pietas Augusti, S.C.'; p. 253.

17. Aureus of Antony, 41 B.C. (Sydenham 190. 1171), London; *obv.*: head of Antony with lituus, legend 'M. Antonius imp. IIIvir r(ei) p(ublicae) c(onstituendae)'; *rev.*: Pietas with censer and cornucopiae on which two storks, legend 'Pietas cos.'; p. 255.

18. Denarius of Antony, 41 B.C. (Sydenham 190. 1172), Paris; *obv.* and *rev.*: the same; p. 255.

PLATE 19

temples and planned more; and he also planned to reorganize the priesthoods.[1]

(b) Pius Aeneas

This was the *pietas* of the statesman; but *pietas* had another, and no less important, side. Resuming the survey of the coins, we must omit two issues showing a female head, identified with Pietas without justification:[2] the legend and her symbol, the stork, are missing. But another coin is certainly relevant here. It was issued by Caesar himself in 47 with a female head (without legend) on the obverse, and Aeneas with the Palladium and carrying Anchises on the reverse (pl. 19. 13).[3] It has been assumed that the coin relates to the mythical descent of the Iulii from Aeneas and ultimately from Venus, who is thought to be represented on the obverse.[4] This is clearly the most obvious interpretation. But recalling the Sicilian youth and his father on the coin of M. Herennius, one could suggest instead that Caesar's coin too refers to *pietas*. Aeneas had long been a famous example of such piety in Greek literature,[5] and was represented as such in art on numberless occasions, in Greece and in Italy as well.[6] Caesar was the first to reproduce this group on a Roman coin, on the coin in question, and he did so in order to illustrate his own *pietas*. It is possible that he even dedicated the same group on a relief to Pietas. This conjecture is based on a coin of Galba with Pietas standing at an altar, which is decorated with Aeneas carrying Anchises and leading Ascanius, and with the legend 'Pietas Augusti' (pl. 19. 16).[7] It is possible but not certain; it is equally possible that the coin of Galba shows a later altar, for example the Ara Pietatis Augustae vowed by Tiberius in 22 and dedicated by Claudius in 43.[8] But even if Caesar

---

[1] See above, p. 32.

[2] Sydenham 167; 168; 169; pl. 27. 1008; 1010; 1017; Grueber pl. 49. 16; Cesano, *Rend. Pont. Acc.* 23/24 (1947/50), 126; pl. 1. 7; above, p. 242. 2.

[3] Sydenham 168; pl. 27. 1013; Cesano, l.c. 122 f.; pl. 1. 2.   [4] Cf. Grueber 2. 469. 1.

[5] The evidence begins with Stesichorus as recorded on the *Tabula Iliaca* (*PLG* 3. 212); Timaeus (?) ap. Diod. 7. 4 (Geffcken, *Timaios* 147): ἐφαίνετο γὰρ ὁ ἀνὴρ ἐν τοῖς μεγίστοις κινδύνοις πλείστην φροντίδα πεποιημένος τῆς τε πρὸς γονεῖς ὁσιότητος καὶ τῆς πρὸς θεοὺς εὐσεβείας; Lycophr. 1270: καὶ παρ' ἐχθροῖς εὐσεβέστατος κριθείς; [Xen.] *Cyneg.* 1. 15: Αἰνείας δὲ σώσας μὲν τοὺς πατρῴους καὶ μητρῴους θεούς, σώσας δὲ καὶ αὐτὸν τὸν πατέρα, δόξαν εὐσεβείας ἐξηνέγκατο; Apollod. *Epit.* 5. 21; Heinze, *Virgils epische Technik* 29.

[6] M. Schmidt, *Troika* (1917), 71 ff.; Bömer, *Rom u. Troja* (1951), 15 ff.; V. Spinazzola, *Pompei alla luce degli scavi nuovi*, 1 (1953), 150 ff., 623; Alföldi, *Die trojan. Urahnen d. Römer* (1957), 14 ff.; Schauenburg, *Gymn.* 67 (1960), 176 ff.; 76 (1969), 42 ff.; H. Kenner, *Österr. Jahresh.* 46 (1961/3), 45 ff.; G. Siebert, *BCH* 90 (1966), 493 f.; W. Fuchs, *AJA* 72 (1968), 384 f.; pl. 131 f.

[7] Mattingly 1. 358 n.; Liegle, l.c. 60 ff.; Kraay, *The Aes Coinage of Galba* (1956), pl. 32 P. 196; another coin of Galba shows a man crowning the emperor and the legend 'Senatus Pietati Augusti' (Mattingly 1. 359; pl. 59. 3).   [8] See below, p. 255.

did not set up such an altar, the new interpretation of his coin receives fresh support from this evidence.

Aeneas had exercised the virtue of *pietas* as it was due to both gods and parents: he saved the gods of his ancestors and his father from the ruins of Troy. In adopting Aeneas as the symbol of his own piety, Caesar did not create anything fundamentally new. We have seen that Aeneas was closely connected with Roman origins; that he had had a place in poetry since Naevius and Ennius, and in historiography; and that there are strong traces of an early tradition all over Latium. But we must add again that the Trojan legend was also cultivated by the family of the Iulii; that they worshipped the son of Aeneas as the founder of the family, and particularly Venus, the mother of Aeneas.[1] It is therefore possible to suggest that in spite of all the earlier tradition, literary and religious, the Trojan legend would not have become popular and prominent without the intervention of Caesar. It was he who built a temple for Venus as Genetrix,[2] and who made Aeneas, his ancestor, a national hero and a symbol of piety: without his initiative Vergil could not have created his epic about *pius Aeneas*.[3]

Caesar's plans must have been more comprehensive than can be assessed on the basis of the available evidence This may be inferred from the reaction against them, if it is right to explain later events in this sense. Sex. Pompeius reproduced Pietas (identified by the legend) on his coins of 45/44 B.C. (pl. 19. 14–15), called himself 'Pius',[4] and in the battle of Munda, 17 March 45, the password of the Pompeians was 'Pietas':[5] it was *pietas* towards their father, Pompey, which also meant taking vengeance for his death. At the same time it will have been their own version of *pietas* in contrast to that propagated by Caesar. After Caesar's murder Octavian, having become his heir, was bound by the duty of piety to take vengeance on the murderers. In 43 the moneyer L. Livineius Regulus issued an *aureus* with Octavian's head on the obverse and Aeneas with Anchises on the reverse:[6] this time the latter did not refer to Octavian's *pietas* but to his heroic ancestry. For Livineius Regulus also issued *aurei* for the other two *triumviri*, Antony

---

[1] See above, pp. 15 ff.   [2] See above, pp. 80 ff.

[3] Verg. *Aen.* 1. 10: 'insignem pietate virum'; 1. 378: 'sum pius Aeneas, raptos qui ex hoste Penatis / classe veho mecum'; 1. 544: 'quo iustior alter / nec pietate fuit nec bello maior et armis' (= three of the four virtues); 6. 403: 'pietate insignis et armis'. Knoche, l.c. 90, suggests that 'pius Aeneas' was created by Vergil.

[4] Sydenham 174; pl. 27. 1042 f.; Wissowa, *Myth. Lex.* 3. 2502 f.; Liegle, l.c. 79 f.; Grant, *From Imperium to Auctoritas* 22; Alföldi, *Studien* 30. 7; Syme, *Hist.* 7 (1958), 174 f.; Buttrey, *Num. Chron.* 6. 20 (1960), 83 ff.   [5] App. *BC* 2. 104. 430.

[6] Sydenham 182; pl. 28. 1104a; cf. Münzer, *RE* 13. 808 f.

and Lepidus, showing the hero Anton and the Vestal Aemilia respectively.[1] But Octavian did not forget his duty. It was probably after
the battle of Philippi (23 October 42) that he founded the colony
Pietas Iulia, Pola,[2] his duty of piety having been fulfilled by the
punishment of the conspirators. The claim to piety was taken up by
the other side as well. In 43 M. Oppius (*aed.* 37) carried his old, proscribed father on his shoulders out of Rome unmolested to safety, and
his achievement was then promptly compared with that of Aeneas.[3]
Antony issued coins as *triumvir* in 41 with the figure of Pietas, identified
by the legend and her symbol, the stork (pl. 19. 17–18).[4] That was
the time of conflict among the *triumviri* and of the Perusine War, and
the coins indicate that Antony now considered himself the heir and
Octavian one of the adversaries. His brother, L. Antonius, took the
cognomen 'Pietas' about the same time, either, as Dio asserts, in order
to show his devotion to his brother,[5] or in order to support his brother's
claim. Finally, Sex. Pompeius again issued coins *c.* 42–38 B.C. with the
head of his father, styling himself 'Pius' on the obverse, and with
Neptune standing between those two brothers from Catana with their
parents on their shoulders on the reverse (pl. 20. 1):[6] a clear polemic
against the Caesarian concept.

But Octavian won in the end, and Aeneas became a national hero.
On the golden shield of 27 B.C. *pietas* was listed as the fourth of his
virtues:[7] he had proved by his vengeance on the conspirators, this time
including Sex. Pompeius and Antony, and by his religious reforms that
he was a man of *pietas*. There may have been dedications and altars
to the goddess: there certainly were some in Pietas Iulia. She is not
found on coins of Augustus, but for the first time under Tiberius,[8]

[1] Sydenham 182; pl. 28. 1103; 1105.
[2] Pliny 3. 129. The date 42/41 was suggested by Degrassi, *Scritti* 2. 915 ff.; id. *Il confine nord-orientale dell'Italia Romana* (1954), 61 ff.; the time after the treaty of Brundisium, Oct. 40, by Polaschek, *RE* 21. 1219; *c.* 33 B.C. by Kornemann, *RE* 4. 526. An even later date, after the victory at Actium but before 27 B.C., does not seem impossible.
[3] App. *BC* 4. 41. 172; Münzer, *RE* 18.1. 739.
[4] Sydenham 190; Grueber, pl. 104. 2; 6–8; Wissowa, *Myth. Lex.* 3. 2502 f.; Liegle, l.c. 80 f.; Syme, *Rom. Rev.* 157; id. *Sallust* 256.
[5] Dio 48. 5. 4. In the same year L. Trebellius (*tr. pl.* 47) called himself 'Fides', Cic. *Phil.* 6. 11; 13. 26; Munzer, *RE* 6A. 2263.
[6] Sydenham 210; Grueber, pl. 120. 5; 7 f.; cf. Liegle, *Transact. Int. Numism. Congr.* (London, 1936), 211 ff.
[7] *Mon. Anc.* 34. 2.
[8] Mattingly 1. 133 (A.D. 22/3); also on coins of Macedonia (*Grant, Aspects of the Principate of Tiberius* 13; 113 f.; pl. 4. 10, with the legend 'Pietas Augusta') and in Spain (Vives, *La Moneda Hispánica* 4. 80. 37; pl. 50. 3, with the legend 'Pietatis Augustae C.C.A.', and a hexastyle temple on the rev.); cf. Mattingly 1, p. cxxxvi; Grant, *Rom. Ann. Issues* 35 ff.; Wissowa, l.c. 2503; Koch, *RE* 20. 1227.

who also vowed an altar for Pietas Augusta;[1] then only under Caligula[2] and Galba,[3] but frequently from the second century onwards (pl. 20. 2–4).[4]

(c) Pietas towards Caesar

Caesar also propagated another form of *pietas*, due to him from his fellow citizens and from the subject peoples of his empire. He did not create it but gave it clear substance and permanence. It had its roots in the relationship of the client, Roman or foreign, an individual or a community, to the patron, for which in origin *fides* was the term, not *pietas*.[5] There are numerous dedications,[6] public and private, expressing gratitude for benevolence and help, but again *pietas* does not appear in such a context until the Social War, 90 B.C.: in that year Minatius Magius was rewarded with Roman citizenship for his loyalty (*pietas*) to the Romans.[7] One could say that *pietas* stands here for *fides*, which would render this case insignificant. But others followed; the first was Cicero. When he returned from exile in 57 he expressed his gratitude to his supporters in warm, often extravagant language.[8] In the following years he described his attitude to his main helpers, Lentulus and Milo, consul and tribune of 57 respectively, as one of *pietas*,[9] but to these alone, not to anyone else. This was then a new form of relationship, which apparently transferred to a stranger[10] to whom one owed one's life or something as valuable as life the affection and reverence due to one's father. In the following troublesome years *pietas* to a political leader

---

[1] *ILS* 202; Tac. *A.* 3. 64. 3; cf. *ILS* 3785. It is an unjustified conjecture that some reliefs now in the Villa Medici at Rome belonged to this altar; see also above, p. 253. 7. An altar at Mylasa, Caria, dedicated to the Εὐσέβεια of Claudius, *CIG* 2697; L. Robert, *Ant. Class.* 35 (1966), 418. 1.

[2] Mattingly 1. 153; 156 f.; pl. 28. 6; 29. 14 (the rev. shows the temple of Divus Augustus, with Aeneas, Anchises, and Ascanius on the *fastigium*).

[3] Mattingly 1. 358 n.; 359; pl. 59. 3; see above, p. 253.

[4] Wissowa, l.c. 2503 ff.; Bernhart, op. cit. 209 ff.; Strack, op. cit. 1. 75 f.; 2. 51 ff.; 169 ff.; Koch, *RE* 20. 1228 ff.; cf. the column dedicated in A.D. 98/99: 'Pietati Imp. Caesaris . . . Traiani . . .'(*ILS* 283).

[5] Gelzer, *Kl. Schr.* 1. 68 ff.; 89 ff.; Heinze, *Vom Geist d. Römertums* 39 ff.

[6] *ILS* 8766 ff.; Degr. 174–81; cf. Degrassi, *Scritti* 1. 415 ff.

[7] Vell. 2. 16. 3: 'cuius illi pietati plenam populus Romanus gratiam rettulit ipsum viritim civitate donando' (2: 'tantam hoc bello Romanis fidem praestitit').

[8] Cf. his two speeches *post reditum*.

[9] Cic. *fam.* 1. 1. 1 (56 B.C.): 'pietate erga te'; 1. 8. 2 (55 B.C.): 'me pietas utilitasque cogit'; 1. 9. 1 (54 B.C.): 'intellexi te perspicere meam in te pietatem. quid enim dicam benevolentiam, cum illud ipsum gravissimum et sanctissimum nomen pietatis levius mihi meritis erga me tuis esse videatur?' 1. 9. 23; 2. 6. 3 (53 B.C.): 'in Milonis consulatu . . . me non officii solum fructum sed etiam pietatis laudem debere quaerere'; 2. 6. 5; *Mil.* 100: 'tibi, T. Anni, nullum a me amoris, nullum studii nullum pietatis officium defuit'; see below, pp. 292 f.

[10] Publ. Syr. *sent.* 44 R.: 'patri pietatem, amicis praestabis fidem.'

became a reality. Caesar created such bonds in Gaul, first in Gallia Cisalpina from 59 onwards,[1] later elsewhere too. Ambiorix owed loyalty to him for his benefactions,[2] and so did the city of Massilia, which, however, could not join him at the beginning of the Civil War because it was similarly bound to Pompey.[3] On his march through Italy in 49 the *municipia* received him like a god,[4] and many of them will have attached themselves formally to him: dedications to Caesar as the patron of the *municipium* have been found at Bovianum in Samnium, Alba Fucens, and Vibo Valentia.[5] In relation to fellow citizens the term *pietas* first appears in a letter written by Balbus to Cicero on Caesar's behalf in March 49, in which he agrees that Cicero's *fides* and *pietas* towards Caesar should exclude the possibility of Cicero turning against him.[6] Balbus, himself bound by *fides* and *pietas* to Pompey and Lentulus, asserts that he could not turn against them for the same reason.[7] Another follower of Caesar, T. Labienus, in fact deserted his cause and joined Pompey, to whom he, as a Picene, was bound by loyalty.[8]

During the Civil War and later Caesar must have cultivated this type of political patronage systematically. Lepidus seems to have been one of these friends,[9] Asinius Pollio another (he later said that he had been bound to Caesar by *fides* and *pietas*[10]), and L. Munatius Plancus a third.[11] Plancus wanted, after the murder, to join the cause of the Senate under Cicero's leadership and wrote to the latter about his *pietas* towards him, and to express his gratitude for his help.[12] Caesar extended this relationship to the provinces also, where he took over the long-standing patronage of Pompey. After the victory at Pharsalus he praised

---

[1] See below, pp. 300; 407.   [2] Caes. *BG* 5. 27. 7 (above, p. 248. 3).

[3] Caes. *BC* 1. 35. 5: 'paribus eorum beneficiis parem se quoque voluntatem tribuere debere et neutrum eorum contra alterum iuvare'; Gelzer, *Kl. Schr.* 1. 72; 90; v. Premerstein, 39.

[4] Cic. *Att.* 8. 16. 1 (below, p. 300. 6).

[5] *ILS* 70 (Degr. 406); De Visscher, *Ant. Class.* 33 (1964), 98 ff. (*AE* 1964, 7); *AE* 1967, 107 (46 B.C.).

[6] Cic. *Att.* 9. 7B. 1: 'de te et tua fide et pietate idem . . ., mi Cicero, sentio quod tu, non posse tuam famam et officium sustinere, ut contra eum arma feras a quo tantum beneficium te accepisse praedices.' Was this bond created by frequent political help or even by the loan which was not yet paid back (Gelzer, *Caesar* 125; 152. 286)? In 55 Cicero still spoke of his bond of *pietas* with Pompey, *fam.* 1. 8. 2; J. Klass, *Cicero u. Caesar* 108 f. (believes that in fact it was an expression of his dependence on Caesar).

[7] Cic. *Att.* 9. 7B. 2: 'meumque officium, fidem, pietatem iis praesto'; Cic. *pro Balbo* (he owed his citizenship to Pompey); Syme, *CQ* 32 (1938), 42; Gelzer, *Caesar* 186.

[8] Syme, *JRS* 28 (1938), 119; 123; 125.

[9] He was called by Antony 'piissimus homo' (Cic. *Phil.* 13. 43).

[10] Cic. *fam.* 10. 31. 3 (March 43): 'Caesarem vero, quod me in tanta fortuna modo cognitum vetustissimorum familiarium loco habuit, dilexi summa cum pietate et fide.'

[11] Cic. *fam.* 10. 24. 5.

[12] Cic. *fam.* 10. 23. 7 (June 43): 'opto, ut mihi liceat iam praesenti pietate meorum officiorum tua beneficia tibi facere iucundiora'; on his relation to Cicero see Hanslik, *RE* 16. 546.

the princes and the peoples who had loyally supported Pompey and reproached Pharnaces who had not.[1] The Roman citizens resident on Cos
set up a statue of the personification of the island in 45 or 44 in recognition of the natives' *pietas* towards Caesar.[2] What was done there must
have been done elsewhere also.[3] The new *cognomen* 'parens patriae'
must have lent a particular significance to this bond of political
pietas.[4]

Augustus followed. M. Valerius Messalla Corvinus (*cos.* 31), who
was at first on the side of the conspirators, was proscribed in 43 and
surrendered to Antony after the battle at Philippi, embraced the cause
of Octavian after 40 and was then described as a model of a pious
man.[5] This was not an empty phrase: it is stated that even his son,
Messalinus, the consul of 3 B.C., was bound by *pietas* to the emperor.[6]
But Augustus saw to it that it was not limited to individual cases:[7] in
the imperial period it was the common attitude to the ruler in Rome
and abroad.[8] The Cypriots included a vow of *pietas* towards Tiberius
and the *domus Augusta* in their oath of allegiance of A.D. 14.[9] Two Apronii,
father and son, set up Tiberius' statue at the temple of Venus Erycina
in Sicily in A.D. 20 as a sign of their *pietas*,[10] and reference is made to
Piso's, Seianus', and the Senate's *pietas* towards him.[11] Cyzicus was
similarly bound to Caligula and the *domus Augusta*,[12] and when Nero
proclaimed the freedom of the Greeks at Corinth in A.D. 67 he also

---

[1] Dio 41. 62. 4; 63. 1 ff.; 42. 47. 4.

[2] Degr. 408: 'Cives Romani qui Coi negotiantur Civitatem Coam pietatis in C. Iulium
Caesarem pontificem maximum, patrem patriae deumque et benevolentiae erga se caussa'
('deum' is an uncertain supplement); cf. Degrassi, *Scritti* 535 ff. (ascribed to Claudius by
Raubitschek, *JRS* 44 (1954), 75. 25).

[3] In the Greek world it took the place of the τιμαὶ ἰσόθεοι (Diod. 20. 102. 2) due to the
rulers and benefactors; for the evidence see Habicht, op. cit. 172. 20; 196. Caesar too was
often honoured as σωτήρ, εὐεργέτης, πάτρων, see Raubitschek, *JRS* 44 (1954), 65 ff.; Robert,
Hellenica 10. 257 ff.; P. Herrmann, *Ath. Mitt.* 75 (1960), 100 f.; above, p. 166. 2.

[4] See above, pp. 200 ff.

[5] Vell. 2. 71. 1: 'Corvinus Messalla . . . servari beneficio Caesaris maluit . . . nec . . .
maius exemplum hominis grati ac pii, quam Corvinus in Caesarem fuit' (not quite correct,
see Hanslik, *RE* 8A. 137 ff.).

[6] Ov. *Pont.* 2. 2. 21: 'quaeque tua est pietas in totum nomen Iuli.'

[7] Suet. *Aug.* 66. 2: 'laudavit quidem pietatem tanto opere pro se indignantium' (the
senators who had accused Cornelius Gallus).

[8] Cf. Dessau, *Herm.* 46 (1911), 623. 1; Ulrich, *Pietas* 40; Syme, *Tacitus* 415.

[9] *Ath. Mitt.* 77 (1962), 306, l. 13: σεβάσεσθαι Τιβέριον Καίσαρα . . . σὺν τῷ ἅπαντι αὐτοῦ οἴκῳ;
316.

[10] *ILS* 939. 21 (*CLE* 1525): 'Caesaris effigiem posuit par cura duorum: / certavit pietas,
summa in utroque fuit.'

[11] Tac. *A.* 3. 16. 5 (A.D. 20): 'cum fide adversum te, neque alia in matrem tuam pietate';
3. 51. 2 (A.D. 21): 'Tiberius . . . cum extolleret pietatem quamvis modicas principis iniurias
acriter ulciscentium'; 4. 40. 1 (A.D. 25): 'laudata pietate Seiani'.

[12] *Syll.* 798. 24 (A.D. 37): τὸ δὲ ψήφισμα εἶναι περί τ' εὐσεβείας τῆς εἰς τὸν Σεβαστόν; 799. 4
(A.D. 38): τῆς εἰς τὸν Σεβαστὸν εὐσεβείας; 10: τὴν πρὸς τὸν Σεβαστὸν οἶκον . . . εὐσέβειαν.

referred to their *pietas*.[1] At Acraephium in Boeotia an altar of Nero was set up and his and Messalina's statues were placed as σύνναοι θεοί in the temple of Apollo as symbols of *pietas* towards the *domus Augusta*.[2] He will have been honoured similarly in many other places in Greece. Under Claudius Vitellius' father was honoured after his death with a statue at the Rostra with the inscription: 'Pietatis immobilis erga principem',[3] the same honour with which Cos was rewarded under Caesar. Another dignitary of Claudius, (M. Antonius) Pallas, was even rewarded with the insignia of a praetor, money, and a sepulchral inscription which commemorated this fact: 'huic senatus ob fidem pietatemque erga patronos ornamenta praetoria decrevit et sestertium centiens quinquagiens, cuius honore contentus fuit.'[4] Domitian once referred to the *pietas* of the Senate,[5] Trajan to that of Pliny who wanted to set up a statue of the emperor.[6] Pliny in turn spoke of it as a common attitude all over the empire,[7] and mentioned in particular Iulius Largus, who left money for the execution of public works or the institution of games in honour of Trajan.[8] The conclusion is that it was not Augustus who created the bond of loyalty between the ruler and his subjects but Caesar. He saw right from the beginning where his actions would lead him and conceived the relationship which was then systematically furthered by Augustus and his successors.

[1] *Syll.* 814. 1 (*ILS* 8794): τῆς εἰς με εὐνοίας τε καὶ εὐσεβείας.

[2] Ibid. 54: ἵνα ... καὶ ἡ ἡμετέρα πόλις φαίνηται πᾶσαν τειμὴν καὶ εὐσέβειαν ἐκπεπληρωκυῖα εἰς τὸν τοῦ κυρίου Σεβαστοῦ Νέρωνος οἶκον.

[3] Suet. *Vit.* 3. 1; Syme, *Tacitus* 415.

[4] Pliny *ep.* 7. 29. 2; 8. 6. 1 (with Sherwin-White's notes); cf. Tac. *A.* 12. 52. 2.

[5] Suet. *Dom.* 11. 3: 'permittite, patres conscripti, a pietate vestra impetrari.'

[6] Pliny *ep.* 10. 9: 'statuam poni mihi a te ... patior, ne impedisse cursum erga me pietatis tuae videar.'

[7] Pliny *ep.* 10. 52: 'provincialibus certatim pietate iurantibus'; 10. 100: 'novaque (vota) rursus certante commilitonum et provincialium pietate suscepimus'; *Paneg.* 75. 3: 'ut orbis terrarum pietatis nostrae adhiberetur testis'; Syme, *Tacitus* 325. 10.

[8] Pliny *ep.* 10. 75. 1: 'Iulius ... Largus ... dispensationem quandam mihi erga te pietatis suae ministeriumque mandavit. (2) rogavit enim testamento ... utrum opera facienda, quae honori tuo consecrarentur, putarem, an instituendos quinquennales agonas, qui Traiani appellarentur.'

XII

THE STATESMAN: HIS ACHIEVEMENTS

CAESAR's political achievements are relevant here only in so far as they have a religious background. They were freedom, security, and concord at home, victory and peace abroad. Some of these topics have been anticipated under the headings Libertas, Salus, Victoria; two remain: Concordia and Pax.

1. CONCORDIA NOVA

Concordia as a political concept and as a goddess had had a long history in Rome[1] when the Senate decreed in 44 B.C. a temple for Concordia Nova in Caesar's honour because he had restored peace.[2] It created another link between Caesar and the great hero of early Rome, Camillus,[3] who restored the *concordia ordinum* in 367 B.C. by admitting the plebeians to the consulate, built the first temple of Concordia and added a fourth day to the three days of the *ludi Romani*.[4] She received temples again at critical stages of Roman history, during the Samnite and Punic Wars,[5] because fear of the enemy often drove the Romans to concord;[6] and again at the time of the Gracchan revolt

[1] The term is already found in Plautus and was no doubt used much earlier, nor first under the influence of the Greek ὁμόνοια; cf. *Thes.L.L.* 4. 83 ff.; Strasburger, *Concordia ordinum* (1931), 1 ff.; 71 ff.; Skard, *Zwei religiöse Begriffe, Euergetes-Concordia* (1932), 70 ff.; Momigliano, *CQ* 36 (1942), 111 ff. (= *Secondo Contributo* 89 ff.); Pease ad Cic. *ND* 2. 61; Nicolet, *REL* 38 (1960), 260 f.; P. Jal, *REL* 39 (1961), 218 ff.; M. Amit, *Iura* 13 (1962), 133 ff.; J.-Cl. Richard, *Mél.* 75 (1963), 307 ff.

[2] Dio 44. 4. 5 (below, p. 265. 1).   [3] See above, pp. 71 ff.

[4] Livy 6. 42. 12: 'ita ab diutina ira tandem in concordiam redactis ordinibus cum ... senatus censeret ... ut ludi maximi fierent et dies unus ad triduum adiceretur'; Plut. *Cam.* 42. 4: ὑποσχόμενος ναὸν Ὁμονοίας ἱδρύσειν τῆς ταραχῆς κατάστασης ... (6) τῇ δ᾽ ὑστεραίᾳ συνελθόντες ἐψηφίσαντο τῆς μὲν Ὁμονοίας ἱερόν, ὥσπερ ηὔξατο Κάμιλλος, εἰς τὴν ἀγορὰν ... ταῖς δὲ καλουμέναις Λατίναις (wrong: Latte 145. 1) μίαν ἡμέραν προσθέντας ἑορτάζειν τέτταρας, παραυτίκα δὲ θύειν καὶ στεφανηφορεῖν Ῥωμαίους ἅπαντας; Ov. *F.* 1. 639 ff. The tradition ascribing the first temple to Camillus is accepted by Mommsen, *Ges Schr.* 4. 152; Wissowa 328; De Sanctis, *Storia dei Romani* 4. 2. 298. 781; M. Guarducci, *Rend. Pont. Acc.* 34 (1961/2), 102; Richard, l.c. 307 f.; rejected by Hirschfeld, *Kl. Schr.* 285 f.; Skard, op. cit. 102; W. Hoffmann, *Rom u. die griech. Welt* 89; Momigliano, l.c. 115 ff.; Latte 237. 8 and Degrassi 399 are undecided.

[5] A temple was built by Cn. Flavius in 304 (Livy 9. 46. 6; 14; Pliny 33. 19), another on the Capitol by L. Manlius in 216 (Livy 22. 33. 7 f.; 23. 21. 7); a statue was set up by Q. Marcius Philippus in 164 (Cic. *dom.* 130 f.; 136 f.); cf. Wissowa 328 f.; Momigliano, l.c. 115 f.; Skard, op. cit. 102 ff.

[6] Livy 2. 39. 7: 'externus timor maximum concordiae vinculum'; cf. Scipio Nasica's

when internal order was threatened.[1] The concept too, developed further, came near to the Greek ideal of ὁμόνοια when exemplified by Menenius Agrippa's parable of the limbs and the body[2] or when defined by Cicero with the help of musical harmony.[3] The *concordia ordinum* never ceased to be a problem; and a new problem of the concord of the powerful arose. It was then said that once Romulus and Titus Tatius ruled in concord,[4] and that Numa established a sacrifice to Mars to make the concord between Romans and Sabines secure;[5] and finally, that in the new millennium Romulus would rule again together with his brother Remus,[6] that is, instead of killing him. Cicero pledged at the beginning of his consulate in 63 B.C. that he would be a defender of *otium* and *concordia*[7] and often returned to the theme. And he saw to it that he ruled in concord with his fellow consul.[8]

The theme was never so topical as during Caesar's rise to power. The first 'triumvirate' was founded in 60 B.C. under the auspices of Concordia. A year or two earlier Paullus Aemilius Lepidus issued a coin with the head of Concordia (pl. 20. 5),[9] which is the first coin showing her. The triumviri may have followed with a statue. She appeared for the second time on coins of 55 B.C. (pl. 20. 6),[10] that is, after the triumvirate was renewed. She appeared for the third time on coins of 42, after the second triumvirate was founded (pl. 20. 7),[11] and for the fourth in 40, when the pact between Octavian and Antony

---

argument against the destruction of Carthage, Posid., *FGrHist.* 87 F 112 (p. 298); above, p. 235; Cic. *har. resp.* 61: 'hunc statum . . . nulla alia re nisi concordia retinere possumus'; App. *BC* 4. 14. 56; Oros. 5. 8. 1; Tac. *H.* 5. 12; Gelzer, *Kl. Schr.* 2. 47; Skard, op. cit. 77; Earl, *The Political Thought of Sallust* 41 ff.; Strasburger, *JRS* 55 (1965), 49; M. Amit, l.c. 136 ff.

[1] The temple built or rebuilt by L. Opimius in 121 (Plut. *C. Gracch.* 17; App. *BC* 1. 26. 120; August. *CD* 3. 25; cf. Dion. Hal. 2. 11. 2 (below, p. 264. 9)).

[2] Livy 2. 32. 8 ff.; Skard, op. cit. 88 ff.; Momigliano, l.c. 117 f.

[3] Cic. *rep.* 2. 69.

[4] Livy 40. 46. 10; Plut. *Rom.* 23. 2.

[5] Fest. 372 M. (510 L.): 'tunc (in the spring) rem divinam instituerit Marti Numa Pompilius pacis concordiae obtinendae gratia inter Sabinos Romanosque' (puzzling); cf. Schwegler, *Röm. Gesch.* 1. 492. 18; Preller, *Röm. Myth.* 1. 364. 2.

[6] Verg. *Aen.* 1. 292: 'Remo cum fratre Quirinus / iura dabunt'; see above, p. 196.

[7] Cic. *leg. agr.* 3. 4: 'otii et concordiae patronum me in hunc annum . . . professus sim'; *Cat.* 2. 19; 4. 15, etc.; Strasburger, op. cit. 39 ff.

[8] Cic. *leg. agr.* 2. 103: 'quod ego et concordia, quam mihi constitui cum conlega, . . . providi'; cf. *Phil.* 13. 2: 'Cinna si concordiam cum Octavio confirmare coluisset (87 B.C.), hominum in re publica sanitas remanere potuisset'; Plut. *Sulla* 6. 9 (concord between Sulla and his colleague Metellus in 80 B.C.).

[9] Sydenham 154 f.; pl. 25. 926; J. R. Hamilton, *Num. Chron.* 6. 15 (1955), 224 f.; Richard, l.c. 318 f.; M. Amit, l.c. 142 f.; for the date see M. H. Crawford, *Roman Republican Coin Hoards* (1969), table XIII.

[10] Coins of P. Fonteius Capito (Sydenham 149; pl. 25. 901) and of L. Vinicius (ibid., pl. 26. 930a); Hamilton, l.c. 224; Richard 323 f.; M. Amit, l.c. 141 f.

[11] Coins of Mussidius Longus, Sydenham 181; Grueber, pl. 56. 17.

PLATE 20

1. Denarius of Sex. Pompeius, 40 B.C. (Sydenham 210. 1344), Oxford; *obv.*: head of Pompey between jug and lituus, legend 'Mag(nus) Pius imp. iter(um)'; *rev.*: Neptune with his foot on prow stands between Anapias and Amphinomus who carry their parents, legend 'praef(ectus) clas(sis) et orae marit(imae) ex s.c.'; p. 255.

2. Dupondius of Tiberius, A.D. 22–3 (Mattingly 1. 133. 98), Oxford; *obv.*: legend 'S.C., Drusus Caesar Ti. Augusti f. tr. pot. iter(um)'; *rev.*: bust of Livia as Pietas, legend 'Pietas'; pp. 255 f.

3. Sestertius of Caligula, A.D. 39–40 (Mattingly 1. 156, 58†), Oxford; *obv.*: Pietas seated with patera, legend 'Pietas, C. Caesar Divi Aug. pron. Aug., p. m., tr. p. III, p. p.'; *rev.*: Caligula sacrifices in front of the temple of Divus Augustus, legend 'Divo Aug(usto). S.C.'; p. 256.

4. Sestertius of Galba, A.D. 68 (Mattingly 1. 359. 260 §), Oxford; *obv.*: head of Galba, legend 'Ser. Sulpi. Galba Imp. Caesar Aug., p. m., tr. p.'; *rev.*: Senatus with branch crowns Galba who holds Victoria and branch, legend 'Senatus Pietati Augusti, S.C.'; p. 256.

5. Denarius of Paullus Aemilius Lepidus, c. 62 B.C. (Sydenham 154. 926), Oxford; *obv.*: head of Concordia, legend 'Paullus Lepidus, Concordia'; *rev.*: trophy between Perseus, his two sons and L. Aemilius Paullus, legend 'ter (sc. imperator?), Paullus'; p. 261.

6. Denarius of P. Fonteius Capito, c. 55 (Sydenham 149. 901), Oxford; *obv.*: head of Concordia, legend 'P. Fonteius Capito IIIvir, Concordia'; *rev.*: a building, legend 'T. Didi(us) imp., Vil(la) pub(lica)'; p. 261.

7. Denarius of L. Mussidius Longus, 42 B.C. (Sydenham 181. 1092), London; *obv.*: head of Concordia, legend 'Concordia'; *rev.*: clasped hands with caduceus, legend 'L. Mussidius Longus'; p. 261.

8. Aureus of C. Vibius Varus, 42 B.C. (Sydenham 186. 1142), London; *obv.*: head of Octavian, legend 'C. Caesar IIIvir r(ei) p(ublicae) c(onstituendae)'; *rev.*: clasped hands, legend 'C. Veibius Vaarus'; p. 263.

9. Quinarius of Antony and Octavian, 39 B.C. (Sydenham 192. 1195), London; *obv.*: head of Concordia, legend 'IIIvir r.p.c.'; *rev.*: clasped hands with caduceus, legend 'M. Anton., C. Caesar'; p. 263.

10. Denarius of C. Vibius Pansa and D. Postumius Albinus, 48 B.C. (Sydenham 158. 944), Oxford; *obv.*: mask of Pan, legend 'C. Pansa'; *rev.*: clasped hands with caduceus, legend 'Albinus Bruti f.'; p. 264.

11. Quinarius of L. Aemilius Buca, 44 B.C. (Sydenham 177. 1065), London; *obv.*: head of Pax, legend 'Paxs'; *rev.*: clasped hands, legend 'L. Aemilius Buca IIIIvir'; p. 265.

12. Denarius of C. Annius Luscus and L. Fabius Hispaniensis, c. 81 B.C. (Sydenham 121. 748), Oxford; *obv.*: bust of Pax(?) with caduceus and scales, legend 'C. Anni(us) T. f. T. n. pro cos. ex s.c.'; *rev.*: Victoria with palm in quadriga, legend 'q(uaestor), L. Fabi(us) L. f. Hisp(aniensis)'; p. 267.

13. Denarius of Q. Sicinius, 49 B.C. (Sydenham 157. 938), Oxford; *obv.*: head of Fortuna, legend 'Fort(una) p. R.'; *rev.*: palm, caduceus, wreath, legend 'Q. Sicinius IIIvir'; p. 268.

14. Bronze of Pax Iulia (Lusitania), age of Augustus (Vives, *La moneda hispánica* 4. 124), London; *obv.*: head of Augustus; *rev.*: seated Pax with caduceus and cornucopiae, legend 'Pax Iul.'; p. 269.

15. Denarius of L. Flaminius Chilo, 43 B.C. (Sydenham 180. 1089), Oxford; *obv.*: head of Caesar; *rev.*: Pax with sceptre and caduceus, legend 'L. Flaminius IIIIvir'; p. 269.

16. Denarius of Octavian, 42 B.C. (Sydenham 206. 1322), London; *obv.*: head of Octavian, legend 'Caesar IIIvir r.p.c.'; *rev.*: sella curulis with a wreath, inscribed 'Caesar dic(tator) per(petuo)'; p. 272.

17. Aureus of Titus, A.D. 80 (Mattingly 2. 233. 64), London; *obv.*: head of Titus, legend 'Imp. Titus Caes. Vespasian. Aug., p. m.'; *rev.*: sella curulis with a wreath, legend 'tr. p. IX, imp. XV, cos. VIII, p. p.'; p. 272.

18. Denarius of Domitian, A.D. 81 (Mattingly 2. 302. 18), London; *obv.*: head of Domitian, legend 'Imp. Caes. Domitianus Aug., p. m.'; *rev.*: sella curulis with a wreath, legend 'tr. p., cos. VII des(ignatus) VIII, p. p.'; p. 272.

19. Aes of Octavian, c. 38 B.C. (Sydenham 208. 1335), Oxford; *obv.*: head of Octavian, legend 'Caesar Divi f.'; *rev.*: head of Caesar with metal wreath, legend 'Divos Iulius'; p. 272.

PLATE 20

1

2

3

4

5

6

7

8

9

10

11

12

13

14

15

16

17

18

19

was made at Brundisium (pl. 20. 8–9).[1] And this time there is explicit
evidence about statues set up in her honour.[2] That is why it is probable
that the first 'triumvirate' too was celebrated with such statues.

Caesar began his consulate of 59 with a speech about concord with
his fellow consul Bibulus,[3] thus following Cicero's example in 63, and
there is no doubt that at first he tried to act in this spirit. The consulate
ended in discord, and so did the triumvirate when the guarantor of
concord, Iulia, Caesar's daughter and Pompey's wife, died in 54 B.C.[4]
In his writings Caesar never uses the words 'concordia' or 'discordia'
('concordia' is found once in the *Bellum Hispaniense*),[5] but rather 'con-
sensus' and 'dissensio' and the verbs 'consentire' and 'dissentire'. What
he says is neither new nor remarkable. He speaks or makes the Gauls
speak of the advantages of consent and of the dangers of dissent;[6] he
repeats commonplaces, that greed leads to discord,[7] and that the whole
world could not resist a united people.[8] But he applies the theme
here to the Gauls under Vercingetorix's leadership, not to the Roman
empire. He calls the Civil War a 'civilis dissensio':[9] that is all.

At the outbreak of the Civil War Cicero intervened and tried in vain
to bring Pompey back to concord, reminding him of the dangers to the
state.[10] Nigidius Figulus too seems to have intervened. His views can
be recovered from his *Tonitruale*, a divinatory calendar, which inter-
prets the thunder occurring through the year and which often predicts

---

[1] Coins of Antony and Octavian, Sydenham 192; Grueber, pl. 113. 17 f.; cf. the coins of
C. Vibius Varus with the heads of the *triumviri* on the obv. and joined hands on the rev.,
Sydenham 186; pl. 28. 1142; Grueber 1. 587 f.

[2] *ILS* 3784; Syme, *CQ* 31 (1937), 41. 1.

[3] App. *BC* 2. 10. 34: λόγους ἐν τῇ βουλῇ περὶ ὁμονοίας διέθετο πρὸς Βύβλον; cf. Dio 38. 1. 1 f.;
Gelzer, *Caesar* 64.

[4] Vell. 2. 47. 2: 'inter Cn. Pompeium et C. Caesarem concordiae pignus, Iulia, uxor
Magni, decessit'; Val. Max. 4. 6. 4: 'totius terrarum orbis ... tranquillitas tot civilium
bellorum truculentissimo furore perturbata non esset, si Caesaris et Pompei concordia communis sanguinis vinculo constricta mansisset'; Pohlenz, *Epitymbion H. Swoboda* (1927), 204.

[5] *B. Hisp.* 42. 5: 'neque in otio concordiam neque in bello virtutem ullo tempore retinere
potuistis.'

[6] Caes. *BG* 5. 31. 2: 'facilem esse rem ... simodo unum omnes sentiant ac probent; contra
in dissensione nullam se salutem perspicere'; 7. 29. 6; 33. 1: 'Caesar ... non ignorans,
quanta ex dissensionibus incommoda oriri consuessent ... (34. 1) cohortatus Haeduos, ut
controversiarum ac dissensionis obliviscerentur'; cf. above, p. 260. 6.

[7] Caes. *BG* 6. 22. 3: 'nequa oriatur pecuniae cupiditas, qua ex re factiones dissensionesque
nascuntur'; cf. Cic. *fin.* 1. 44; *off.* 2. 78; 'Sall.' *ep. ad Caes.* 1. 7. 3.

[8] Caes. *BG* 7. 29. 6: 'Galliae ... consensu ne orbis quidem terrarum possit obsistere';
cf. Cornif. 4. 44: 'quod si concordiam retinebimus, imperii magnitudinem solis ortu atque
occasu metiemur'; above, p. 139. 1.   [9] Caes. *BC* 1. 67. 3; 3. 1. 3; 3. 88. 2.

[10] Cic. *Att.* 7. 3. 5 (Dec. 50): 'Pompeium separatim ad concordiam hortabor; sic enim
sentio maximo in periculo rem publicam esse'; 7. 4. 2: 'Pompeium vidi ... de re publica
autem ita mecum locutus est quasi non dubium bellum haberemus: nihil ad spem concordiae.'

peace and concord or civil war.[1] After Pompey left and Caesar approached Rome, Cicero tried again, writing this time to Caesar.[2] He also played with the idea of writing an essay on concord to influence the two antagonists, for he borrowed Demetrius Magnes' book Περὶ ὁμονοίας from Atticus.[3] Caesar gratefully acknowledged his letter and encouraged him in his efforts;[4] Balbus too wrote to him on Caesar's behalf, asking him to carry on with his work of reconciliation.[5] On arrival in Rome Caesar spoke of peace and concord and proposed to send messengers to Pompey to restore them.[6] There must have been at first serious hopes, for coins of the year, issued by Caesar's followers, reproduced two clasped hands, the symbol of concord (pl. 20. 10).[7] But all in vain; Cicero's efforts led to nothing, and he returned Demetrius' book to Atticus.[8]

The theme became topical again after the victory of Pharsalus. But it was no longer the same theme: it did not concern a powerful colleague or the warring factions of the people, but Caesar's own contribution to concord. The anonymous pamphleteer used by Dionysius of Halicarnassus said that Romulus was the founder of concord in Rome, which had lasted 630 years up to the time of C. Gracchus and ended in bloodshed,[9] implying that Caesar, the new Romulus, should bring it back. The first *Epistula ad Caesarem senem* too advised Caesar to restore peace and concord.[10] Caesar himself must have been active because he founded or planned colonies with the name Concordia Iulia,[11] no doubt with

---

[1] Lyd. *ost.* 76. 13 W.: εὐετηρίαν μεθ' ὁμονοίας δηλοῖ; 78. 16: ὁμονοήσει ὁ δῆμος πρὸς εἰρήνην; 69. 3: πόλεμον ἐμφύλιον ἀπειλεῖ; so also 77. 10; 27; 80. 13; 84. 16; 26; Kroll, *RE* 17. 208 f.; cf. *PBSR* 19 (1951), 140.

[2] Cic. *Att.* 8. 2. 1 (Febr. 49): 'ad Caesarem unas Capua litteras dedi ... cum maxima laude Pompei; id enim illa sententia postulabat qua illum ad concordiam hortabar.'

[3] Cic. *Att.* 8. 11. 7 (27 Febr. 49).

[4] Cic. *Att.* 9. 11A. 1 (March 49, to Caesar): 'de "gratia" et de "ope" quid significares mecum ipse quaerebam, spe tamen deducebar ad eam cogitationem, ut te ... de otio, de pace, de concordia civium agi velle arbitrarer ... (3) et ad tuam fidem et ad rem publicam pertinet me et pacis et utriusque vestrum amicum et ad vestram et ad civium concordiam per te quam accommodatissimum conservari.'

[5] Cic. *Att.* 8. 15A. 1 (March 49): 'obsecro te, Cicero, suscipe curam ..., ut Caesarem et Pompeium perfidia hominum distractos rursus in pristinam concordiam reducas'; 9. 7B. 1: 'ab Caesare epistulam accepi cuius exemplum tibi misi; ex qua perspicere poteris quam cupiat concordiam et Pompeium reconciliare'; *Phil.* 2. 24.   [6] Dio 41. 15. 4; 16. 4.

[7] Coins of Decimus Brutus and C. Vibius Pansa, 49 B.C., Sydenham 158; pl. 26. 942; 944; Richard, l.c. 326.

[8] Cic. *Att.* 9. 2. 2 (17 March 49); cf. Gelzer, *Caesar* 175. 394; 183. 22.

[9] Dion. Hal. 2. 11. 2: οὕτω δὲ ἄρα βέβαιος ἦν ἡ Ῥωμαίων ὁμόνοια τὴν ἀρχὴν ἐκ τῶν ὑπὸ Ῥωμύλου κατασκευασθέντων λαβοῦσα ἐθῶν, ὥστε οὐδέποτε δι' αἵματος καὶ φόνου τοῦ κατ' ἀλλήλων ἐχώρησαν ἐντὸς ἑξακοσίων καὶ τριάκοντα ἐτῶν; Skard, op. cit. 97.

[10] 'Sall.' *ep. ad Caes.* 1. 5. 3; 1. 6. 5; Skard, op. cit. 99; Richard, l.c. 341.

[11] Nertobrigae (Pliny 3. 14), Apamea (Pliny 5. 149), Carthage, Hadrumetum; cf. *Thes.L.L. Onom.* 2. 558; Vittinghoff 82; 88.

a temple and image of the goddess. It was one of the last decrees made in his honour in 44 that a temple of Concordia Nova be built and a festival created because he had restored peace.[1] A contemporary coin shows the head of Pax on the obverse and the clasped hands holding the caduceus, symbols of concord and peace, on the reverse (pl. 20. 11).[2] The two concepts were often joined together before and later, which is not surprising and will require some further comment.[3] The temple was never built—Caesar was dead a few weeks later.

How is this temple to be understood? It was to belong to Concordia Nova, a goddess with a most unusual epithet,[4] which raises the question of who the old one was. The obvious answer is, the Concordia of Camillus: Caesar was to be the new Camillus. Clearly he cannot have followed the example of the founders of the other temples, of Cn. Flavius, Q. Marcius Philippus, C. Cassius, L. Opimius. This answer can be supported by the following facts. The *ludi Romani*, held in honour of Iuppiter Capitolinus, used to last three days in the fourth century; when Camillus built his temple of Concordia a fourth day was added.[5] Now it is recorded that in 44 Antony, the consul, requested that a fifth day should be added in Caesar's honour.[6] As no change had been made at the *ludi Romani* from the time of Camillus until then, the conclusion seems unavoidable that Antony made his request in connection with the decree about the temple of Concordia Nova. It is not recorded whether Camillus was especially honoured at those games; even if he was, the practice did not last. But the additional day of 44 was to be celebrated annually in Caesar's honour after Iuppiter had been honoured on the preceding four days. It never was, because Caesar was murdered. The Concordia Nova made Caesar a hero like Camillus; but unlike Camillus he was also to be rewarded with honours due only to the gods,[7] with a share in the *ludi Romani*. It was extraordinary, but not without Greek analogies. The Samians turned their Heraia into Lysandreia

---

[1] Dio 44. 4. 5: νεών τε ʿΟμονοίας Καινῆς, ὡς καὶ διʼ αὐτοῦ εἰρηνοῦντες, οἰκοδομῆσαι καὶ πανήγυριν αὐτῇ ἐτησίαν ἄγειν ἔγνωσαν.

[2] Coin of L. Aemilius Buca, Sydenham 177; Grueber, pl. 54. 13; Richard, l.c. 327.

[3] See below, pp. 267 f..

[4] 'Novus Liber Pater', the name of Antony (Vell. 2. 82. 4), cannot be compared because it is a translation of Νέος Διόνυσος. Caesar spoke at the beginning of the Civil War of his 'nova ratio vincendi' which meant clemency, not destruction, for the vanquished (Cic. *Att.* 9. 7c. 1). In Greek νέος is frequent for gods and men, Nock, *JHS* 48 (1928), 35 and *HTR* 41 (1948), 213 (Νεωτέρα).

[5] Livy 6. 42. 12; Plut. *Cam.* 42. 6 (above, p. 260. 4); Mommsen, *Röm. Forsch.* 2. 48; 53; Wissowa 453. 6.

[6] Cic. *Phil.* 2. 110: 'nescis heri quartum in Circo diem ludorum Romanorum fuisse? te autem ipsum ad populum tulisse, ut quintus praeterea dies Caesari tribueretur?'

[7] See below, p. 316.

in honour of Lysander, the Athenians their Dionysia into Demetria in honour of Demetrius Poliorcetes.[1] A day was added in honour of Seleucus I to the festival of Athena at Ilium in 281 and in honour of Eumenes II to the festival of the Panionion by the Ionian κοινόν in 167.[2]

The great topicality of concord after Caesar's death cannot be understood without his initiative and example. At the first meeting of the Senate on 17 March Antony delivered an impressive speech about it, acknowledging Dolabella as his colleague, which he had refused to do before.[3] Cicero too spoke of concord when recommending the compromise of an amnesty on the one hand and confirmation of Caesar's acts on the other.[4] Finally, the conspirators too pledged themselves to it[5] and when they descended from the Capitol the people forced the consuls to clasp hands with them,[6] which was the traditional sign of concord. Later Cicero referred to it frequently in his *Philippic Orations*, more often than in any of his other speeches. Concord was the symbol of the second triumvirate, of the reconciliation between Antony and Octavian in 40[7] and of their attempted reconciliation in 35.[8] When the temple of Concordia was restored under Augustus a bronze caduceus, the symbol of peace, was let into the step which led to the *cella*.[9] He set up a statue of Concordia in 11 B.C. together with those of Ianus, Salus, and Pax,[10] and in turn received dedications together with Concordia and Pax in the provinces.[11] She was now also called Concordia Augusta and could represent the concord in the imperial family. When Tiberius repaired her old temple in A.D. 11 he inscribed it with his and his dead brother Drusus' names.[12] Livia built her another shrine in the Porticus Liviae in 7 B.C., demonstrating her concord with her son Tiberius.[13] Concordia thus became one of the principal concepts which distinguished the emperors during their rule.[14]

[1] Plut. *Lys.* 18. 6; Philochor., *FGrHist.* 328 F 166; Plut. *Dem.* 12. 2; Nock, *HSCP* 41 (1930), 60; above, p. 154.

[2] *Or. gr.* 212 (L. Robert, *Ét. anat.* 181); 763. 51 (Welles, *Royal Corresp.* 52. 51); Habicht 82 f.; 149.

[3] Cic. *Phil.* 1. 31: 'quae fuit oratio de concordia! quanto metu, quanta sollicitudine civitas tum a te liberata est, cum collegam tuum . . . illo primum die conlegam tibi esse voluisti.'

[4] Cic. *Phil.* 1. 23; 13. 10; Dio 44. 33.

[5] Dio 44. 34. 3.   [6] App. *BC* 2. 142. 594; cf. Drumann 1. 70.

[7] See above, pp. 261; 263.

[8] Dio 49. 18. 6: (Octavian) εἰκόνας ἐν τῷ Ὁμονοείῳ ἔστησε (of himself and Antony?).

[9] Hülsen, *Das Forum Romanum* 87; cf. *JRS* 50 (1960), 49.

[10] Ov. *F.* 3. 881; Dio 54. 35. 2.

[11] *ILS* 3786; v. Premerstein 126; cf. *JRS* 50 (1960), 49. 64.

[12] Dio 55. 8. 2; 56. 25. 1; Suet. *Tib.* 20; M. Guarducci, *Rend. Pont. Accad.* 34 (1961/2), 102 ff.; Pekáry, *Röm. Mitt.* 73/4 (1966/7), 105 ff.

[13] Ov. *F.* 6. 637; 1. 649; cf. *ILS* 3785; Wissowa 328. 5.

[14] Wissowa 329; on Concordia on coins of the imperial period see M. Amit, l.c. 145–69.

2. PAX

We have seen that all the work for concord was at the same time work for peace, and that the project to build a temple for Concordia was justified by reference to peace. There had been no cult of Pax in Rome, and there is no direct evidence to prove that Caesar wanted to create one. But the indirect evidence is so strong as to make us assume that the cult of Pax was inspired by Caesar and did not begin with the Ara Pacis Augustae.

Pax, a root-noun of the verb *pacisci*, did not originally mean peace but a pact which ended a war and led to submission, friendship, or alliance.[1] It began to mean peace at an early date—it is so found in Plautus already[2]—and could be represented symbolically by a caduceus,[3] the attribute of the Greek Eirene. Eirene in turn had it from the heralds, who carried it, the symbol of Hermes, when they were sent out for parleys about peace.[4] It was for foreign countries that the term was coined; but in the course of time they ceased to be equals of Rome, and *pax* was no longer a pact among equals but a submission to Rome, just as *pacare* began to refer to conquest. The Romans argued that submission meant protection and security,[5] and there were some Greek philosophers who accepted their argument.[6] It was not an idyllic peace but the peace of Roman imperialism. It was in the age of Sulla that *pax* was first used of the citizens of Rome at the end of the Civil War. Sulla must have made some propaganda about his peace: attacks of adversaries prove it,[7] as do coins showing the caduceus.[8] The caduceus is attached on one coin to a female bust (pl. 20. 12):[9] if she is the personified Pax, this was her first appearance in Rome.

Caesar often had to deal with requests for peace in Gaul. This was peace for foreigners, who threw themselves at his feet, offered surrender, and to whom he then granted *pax* with *amicitia*.[10] When it came to the

---

[1] *JRS* 50 (1960), 45.   [2] Plaut. *Amph.* 1127; *Curc.* 270, etc.

[3] Gell. 10. 27. 3; *JRS* 50. 45. 13.

[4] Thuc. 1. 53; Diod. 5. 75. 1; Paul. Fest. 47 M. (41 L.); Serv. *Aen.* 4. 242; Livy 8. 206.

[5] Cic. *Q.fr.* 1. 1. 34; *prov. cons.* 31; Tac. *A.* 13. 56. 1; *H.* 4. 74; H. Fuchs, *Augustin u. der ant. Friedensgedanke* 197; 202.

[6] Panaetius: Cic. *rep.* 3. 36; Capelle, *Klio* 25. 94 f.; Pohlenz, *RE* 18/2. 437; Posidonius: *FGrHist.* 87 F 8; Strab. 3. 3. 8. p. 156; Capelle, l.c. 103.

[7] Sall. *hist.* 1. frg. 55. 24 (p. 26 Maur.): 'specie concordiae et pacis, quae sceleri et parricidio suo nomina indidit'; Lucan 2. 171: 'omnia Sullanae lustrasse cadavera pacis.'

[8] Sydenham 118; 121; 131; 133.   [9] Sydenham 121; pl. 21. 748.

[10] Caes. *BG* 1. 27. 1: 'Helvetii ... legatos de deditione ad eum miserunt. qui cum eum in itinere convenissent seque ad pedes proiecissent suppliciterque locuti flentes pacem petissent'; 2. 13. 3: 'item ... pueri mulieresque ex muro passis manibus suo more pacem ab Romanis petiverunt'; 4. 18. 3: 'pacem atque amicitiam petentibus liberaliter respondet'; 7. 66. 4; 7. 78. 2.

Civil War the situation was different: one citizen could not surrender to another.[1] Caesar made great efforts right from the beginning. He engaged the help of Cicero,[2] who then wrote to Pompey,[3] but he also exchanged letters with Pompey.[4] Peace among citizens depended on concord, and Cicero concentrated on this. His essay *De concordia*, which he planned but never wrote,[5] would have dealt with the problem of peace in great detail.[6] The caduceus appeared on coins issued on both sides (pl. 19. 12; 20. 13).[7] Caesar tried again later in Epirus by sending a letter to Pompey.[8] It was of no avail; to a later attempt Labienus replied that peace could be had if Caesar's head was handed over to them.[9] Another time Caesar approached Metellus Scipio and made it clear to him what an agreement might mean.[10] Scipio was not chosen without due consideration: he must have been a key-figure, not only politically. He was the chief character in Varro's Logistoricus *Pius aut de pace*,[11] which was certainly not a philosophical or semi-philosophical essay

[1] On this unusual situation see Caes. *BC* 3. 19. 2: 'liceretne civibus ad cives de pace duos legatos mittere, quod etiam fugitivis ab saltu Pyrenaeo praedonibusque licuisset, praesertim cum id agerent, ne cives cum civibus armis decertarent?'

[2] Cic. *Att.* 7. 21. 3 (8 Febr. 49): 'ipse me Caesar ad pacem hortatur.'

[3] Cic. *Att.* 8. 11D. 6 (27 Febr. 49, to Pompey): 'mea quae semper fuerit sententia primum de pace vel iniqua condicione retinenda, ... meminisse te arbitror ... (7) ... suscepto bello, cum pacis condiciones ad te adferri a teque ad ea honorifice et large responderi viderem, duxi meam rationem', etc.

[4] Caes. *BC* 1. 24. 4: 'reducitur ad eum deprensus ex itinere N. Magius Cremona, praefectus fabrum Cn. Pompei. (5) quem Caesar ad eum remittit cum mandatis'; 26. 2: 'haec Caesar ita administrabat, ut condiciones pacis dimittendas non existimaret; ac tametsi magnopere admirabatur Magium, quem ad Pompeium cum mandatis miserat, ad se non remitti'; Cic. *Att.* 9. 13. 8 (24 March 49): 'Pompeius N. Magium de pace misit et tamen oppugnatur'; 9. 13A. 1 (22/3 March, Caesar): 'misit ad me N. Magium de pace. quae visa sunt respondi'; Dio 41. 12. 2; Gelzer, *Caesar* 186. 48.

[5] See above, p. 264.

[6] Cf. Cic. *Att.* 9. 11A. 1 (19/20 March 49, to Caesar): 'spe tamen deducebar ad eam cogitationem, ut te ... de otio, de pace, de concordia civium agi velle arbitrarer. ... (2) quod si ita est et si qua de Pompeio nostro tuendo et tibi ac rei publicae reconciliando cura te attingit, magis idoneum quam ego sum ad eam causam profecto reperies neminem, qui et illi semper et senatui ... pacis auctor fui.'

[7] The Pompeian Q. Sicinius issued a coin with the head of the *Fortuna populi Romani* on the obv., a caduceus and palm branch on the rev. (Sydenham 157; Grueber, pl. 49. 10; J.-Cl. Richard, *Mél.* 75 (1963), 322); on Caesar's side, Decimus Brutus another, with the head of Pietas on the obv., clasped hands holding the caduceus on the rev. (Sydenham 158; pl. 26. 942; Richard, l.c. 326).

[8] Caes. *BC* 3. 10. 7 (above, p. 117. 3).

[9] Caes. *BC* 3. 19. 8: 'tum Labienus: "desinite ergo de conpositione loqui; nam nobis nisi Caesaris capite relato pax esse nulla potest".'

[10] Caes. *BC* 3. 57. 4: 'quod si fecisset, quietem Italiae, pacem provinciarum, salutem imperii uni omnes acceptam relaturos.' This sounds like a political programme and is highly valued by Gelzer, *Caesar* 199. 117; 213. 191; 305; *Kl. Schr.* 2. 301; *contra*, Strasburger, *Hist. Zeitschr.* 175 (1953), 256 (*Caesar im Urteil seiner Zeitgenossen* 49); cf. Weber, *Princeps* 233*. 658.

[11] Gell. 17. 18; Fuchs, op. cit. 93 ff.; Dahlmann, *Varron. Stud.* 1. 45 f.; Gelzer, *Caesar* 213. 190; cf. *JRS* 50. 46; Richard, l.c. 334. 1.

(as Cicero's would have been—had it been written) but of an antiquarian character. He seems to have thought that Scipio would be the proper person to restore peace because of his knowledge of fetial law and the like, and gave him all the details necessary for peace-making.[1] Caesar's and Varro's approaches led to nothing.[2] Scipio carried on the war after Pharsalus, referred to the old prophecy about the invincibility of the Scipiones in Africa,[3] and issued a coin with Victoria holding the caduceus (pl. 9. 8 f.) :[4] he hoped to achieve peace only by victory, and ultimately committed suicide.

Those who remained in Rome, like Cicero, hoped for peace after the victories at Pharsalus, the Nile, and Zela,[5] and hopes rose again after Caesar's triumph. Caesar must have responded in the end. A coin of L. Aemilius Buca issued before Caesar's death shows a female head with the legend 'Paxs' on the obverse and clasped hands on the reverse (pl. 20. 11) :[6] this then was to be the new goddess. Caesar founded a colony in Lusitania, Pax Iulia,[7] the modern Beja; another colony in Gallia Narbonensis was called Colonia Pacensis or Forum Iulium Pacatum,[8] the modern Fréjus. They must have had at least an altar of the new goddess: a coin of Pax Iulia shows a seated Pax with the caduceus on the reverse (pl. 20. 14).[9] Caesar may have made his plan of a cult known when the building of the temple of the Concordia Nova was decreed.[10] He had embarked on this plan in Spain and Gaul, perhaps also in Africa. At Rome he will have postponed it until the end of the Parthian campaign. After the murder there were still long echoes of this propaganda. Antony praised him in his funeral oration as a peace-maker;[11] Cicero used the word *pax* in his *Philippics* more often than in all his other speeches put together. Pax appeared on coins of 43 and later (pl. 20. 15).[12] Augustus never lost sight of her and created her cult at the Ara Pacis Augustae in 13 B.C.

---

[1] Varro's *Antiquitates rerum humanarum* also contained a book 'de bello et pace': Gell. 1. 25. 1.

[2] Cf. Caes. *BC* 3. 90. 1 : '... quanto studio pacem petisset.'

[3] Suet. *Caes.* 59; see above, p. 98. 3.

[4] Sydenham 175; pl. 28. 1050; Richard, l.c. 322 f.

[5] Cic. *Att.* 11. 16. 1 (5 June 47) : '... neque si qui ex Asia veniunt quicquam auditum esse dicunt de pace'; 11. 19. 1 : 'est autem unum quod mihi sit optandum, si quid agi de pace possit'; *fam.* 15. 15. 1 (Aug. 47, to Cassius) : 'etsi uterque nostrum spe pacis et odio civilis sanguinis abesse a belli necessaria pertinacia voluit...'

[6] Sydenham 177; Grueber, pl. 54. 13; *JRS* 50. 46; pl. 5. 5 f.; Richard, l.c. 327.

[7] *ILS* 6899; Ptolem. *Geogr.* 2. 5. 4; *Itin. Anton.* pp. 204–6 P.–P.

[8] Pliny 3. 35; *ILS* 6984. [9] *JRS* 50. 46; pl. 5. 7.

[10] It was decreed because peace was achieved by Caesar: Dio 44. 4. 5 (above, p. 265.1).

[11] Dio 44. 49. 2. [12] Sydenham 180 f.; 183; 192; 207.

XIII

KINGSHIP AND DIVINITY

THE honours decreed before Caesar's death went far beyond earlier decrees. He was granted the dress of the kings and triumphators for all functions; the privilege of riding in a chariot and sitting on a golden throne; his statue and his attributes were to be carried in the procession of the gods and placed on the couch of the gods in the Circus; his throne and golden crown were to be exhibited in the theatres; his house received a pediment, temples were decreed, a *flamen* appointed, and he was to be called Iuppiter Iulius. He was granted an extraordinary *ovatio*, treated like a king, and was even offered a diadem. This is a startling list, mainly due to Dio and Appian.[1] Dio records it for 44 but does not explicitly ascribe all the honours to that year,[2] which would be wrong: the time before the Ides of March was much too short for so many decrees. In earlier years Caesar was mostly absent from Rome and did not always know or approve of all that was decreed.[3] This time he was in Rome and certainly knew in advance what the Senate was offering. He was not present at the meetings because, so it is asserted, he did not want to influence the senators.[4] This may be true. But it will be argued that the principal items fit into a grand scheme which cannot have been planned by anyone else except Caesar himself. The honours of the preceding years grew out of the political situation created first by the victory over Pompey and then by the establishment of Caesar's sole rule. Now the political situation had changed again: it was the time of the preparations for the Parthian expedition and of the expectation of Caesar's departure and long absence from Rome.

I. THE REGAL ATTRIBUTES

We begin with what at first sight appears to be a perpetuation of the triumphal privileges. It will be recalled that in 45 Caesar was granted

---

[1] Dio 44. 4–6; App. *BC* 2. 106. 440 ff. (45 B.C.).

[2] Dio 44. 4. 1: ἐγένετο δὲ τὰ δοθέντα αὐτῷ . . . τοσάδε καὶ τοιάδε· καθ' ἓν γάρ, εἰ καὶ μὴ πάντα ἅμα μήτε ἐσηνέχθη μήτε ἐκυρώθη, λελέξεται; for 45 Hohl, *Klio* 34 (1942), 113 f.; Gelzer, *Caesar* 293; for 45 and 44 Drumann 3. 593 f.; 598 ff.; for 44 Meyer, *Caesars Monarchie* 513 ff.

[3] See above, pp. 40; 61; 133.

[4] Dio 44. 8. 2: ἀπόντος γὰρ αὐτοῦ τὰ τοιαῦτα, τοῦ μὴ δοκεῖν ἀναγκαστοὶ ἀλλ' ἐθελονταὶ αὐτὰ ποιεῖν, ἐχρημάτιζον.

the triumphal dress for all games[1] and for the sacrifices,[2] and was entitled to wear the laurel wreath always and everywhere; the golden crown at first probably in the Circus only. It was decreed earlier in that year that his ivory statue should be kept in the Capitoline temple and, wearing the triumphal dress, be carried in the procession of the gods in the *pompa circensis*;[3] this ceremony rested on the precedent of Scipio Africanus[4] and was apparently performed only during Caesar's absence. Examining the relevant decree of 44 we notice a certain change in the terminology. The dress was still called occasionally, as in 45, 'triumphal dress',[5] but more often just 'purple'[6] and twice even 'regal dress'.[7] This distinction is important. The regal dress was always purple[8] and so was the early triumphal dress until the third century B.C. when it was replaced by the embroidered dress, the *toga picta*.[9] If the archaic dress was adopted in 44, it may have appeared as another triumphal dress but was in fact the regal dress.[10]

---

[1] Dio 43. 43. 1: τήν τε στολὴν τὴν ἐπινίκιον ἐν πάσαις ταῖς πανηγύρεσι κατὰ δόγμα ἐνεδύετο καὶ τῷ στεφάνῳ τῷ δαφνίνῳ ἀεὶ καὶ πανταχοῦ ὁμοίως ἐκοσμεῖτο; Suet. *Caes.* 45. 2: 'ius laureae coronae perpetuo gestandae'; Mommsen, *StR* 1. 428. 1.

[2] App. *BC* 2. 106. 442: καὶ θύειν μὲν αὐτὸν αἰεὶ θριαμβικῶς ἠμφιεσμένον; cf. Dio 60. 6. 9 (Claudius); Mommsen, *StR* 1. 414. 4.

[3] Dio 43. 45. 2: ἀνδριάντα αὐτοῦ ἐλεφάντινον . . . ἐν ταῖς ἱπποδρομίαις μετὰ τῶν θείων ἀγαλμάτων πέμπεσθαι ἔγνωσαν. [4] Livy 38. 56. 13 (above, p. 36. 1); Val. Max. 4. 1. 6.

[5] Plut. *Caes.* 61. 4: καθήμενος ἐπὶ τῶν Ἐμβόλων ἐπὶ δίφρου χρυσοῦ, θριαμβικῷ κόσμῳ κεκοσμημένος.

[6] Cic. *Phil.* 2. 85: 'sedebat in Rostris . . . amictus toga purpurea in sella aurea, coronatus'; *div.* 1. 119: 'qui cum immolaret illo die, quo primum in sella aurea sedit et cum purpurea veste processit'; Pliny 11. 186: 'quo die primum veste purpurea processit atque in sella aurea sedit'; Val. Max. 1. 6. 13: 'eo die quo purpurea veste velatus aurea in sella consedisti'; Nic. Dam. *v. Caes.* (*FGrHist.* 90 F 130) 71: καθημένῳ δὲ Καίσαρι ἐπὶ τῶν Ἐμβόλων λεγομένων ἐπὶ χρυσοῦ θρόνου καὶ ἱμάτιον ἀλουργὲς ἀμπεχομένῳ.

[7] Dio 44. 6. 1: δίφρος τέ οἱ ἐπίχρυσος καὶ στολὴ ᾗ ποτε οἱ βασιλῆς ἐκέχρηντο . . . ἐδόθη; 44. 11. 2: ἐπὶ τοῦ Βήματος τῇ τε ἐσθῆτι τῇ βασιλικῇ κεκοσμημένος καὶ τῷ στεφάνῳ τῷ διαχρύσῳ λαμπρυνόμενος ἐς τὸν δίφρον τὸν κεχρυσωμένον ἐκαθίζετο; cf. 46. 17. 5: τῇ τε σκευῇ τῇ τῶν βασιλέων χρῆσθαι. Mommsen, *StR* 1. 416. 2, assumes that Dio, misled by reports with different wording, recounts the same event twice, in 44. 4. 2 (below, p. 273. 8) and 44. 6. 1 (above); accepted by Hohl, *Klio* 32 (1939), 71. 2. But they must be two different decrees: one about the right to a chariot and about the privilege in the Circus, the other about the golden throne; for the former the (alleged) triumphal dress is granted, for the latter the regal one.

[8] Dion. Hal. 2. 34. 2 (Romulus): ἐσθῆτα μὲν ἠμφιεσμένος ἀλουργῆ, δάφνῃ δὲ κατεστεμμένος τὰς κόμας.

[9] Fest. 209 M. (228 L.): 'Picta quae nunc toga dicitur purpurea ante vocitata est, eaque erat sine pictura. eius rei argumentum est pictura in aede Vertumni et Consi, quarum in altera M. Fulvius Flaccus (*cos.* 264 B.C.), in altera T. Papirius Cursor (*cos.* 293 and 272) triumphantes ita picti sunt.' The cloak among the royal insignia sent by the Romans to foreign kings is described as the purple toga (Livy 27. 4. 8; 31. 11. 12; App. *Pun.* 32. 137), or *toga picta* (Livy 30. 15. 11), or just triumphal dress (Dion. Hal. 5. 35. 1); Mommsen, *StR* 1. 410. 2; 3. 592. 3.

[10] For the regal dress Alföldi, *Röm. Mitt.* 50 (1935), 30; id. *Mus. Helv.* 8 (1951), 210 and *Studien* 21; K. Kraft, *Jahrb. f. Num. u. Geldgesch.* 3/4 (1952/3), 35; for the triumphal dress D. Felber, op. cit. 224 f.; 275.

The same variation may be observed with regard to the golden crown. Caesar was granted it in 45 for the Circus,[1] in 44 also for other occasions: it is known that he wore it at the Lupercalia.[2] As we shall see later, a crown was also to be exhibited in the Circus on the golden throne during his absence.[3] These were in fact two different crowns. The second was decorated with gems[4] like that which Pompey was entitled to wear;[5] and numismatic evidence shows that it also had a ribbon, again like that of Pompey (pl. 20. 16). It is found on coins of Faustus Sulla referring to Pompey[6] and on some of Octavian referring to Caesar;[7] later also on coins of Titus and Domitian (pl. 20. 17–18).[8] The ribbon had the function of holding together the branches of the laurel or oak of which the wreath was formed. It was not needed for a wreath made of metal, and yet quite naturally an imitation of the ribbon in metal was often added.[9] The other crown which Caesar wears on coins, and must also have worn at the Lupercalia, is without ribbon and was therefore a different one, though equally of metal, that is, of gold (pl. 20. 19):[10] it was the crown of the Etruscan and Roman kings.[11] Here again one may conclude that first the republican triumphal tradition was continued and Pompey's triumphal crown was copied, but that then it was made a regal attribute.

Caesar further received in 44 a golden throne for the Curia, for the platform of the magistrates, and for other official functions—he used it on the Rostra at the Lupercalia—but not for the theatre where he was to sit on the *subsellia* of the tribunes.[12] Wherever he sat it was on a raised

---

[1] This is implied by Dio 43. 43. 1 (above, p. 271. 1) and by the precedents of Aemilius Paullus and Pompey.

[2] Dio 44. 11. 2; Cic. *Phil.* 2. 85; Pliny 11. 186; above, p. 271. 6; below, p. 331.

[3] See below, pp. 281 f.

[4] Dio 44. 6. 3: τὸν στέφανον τὸν διάλιθον καὶ διάχρυσον.

[5] Dio 37. 21. 4; Vell. 2. 40. 4 (above, p. 108. 6); the gems can be seen on the coins (n. 6).

[6] Sydenham 146; pl. 24. 882 (upside down); above, p. 39.

[7] Sydenham 206; Grueber, pl. 104. 12; Alföldi, *Röm. Mitt.* 50 (1935), pl. 14. 10; id. *Herm.* 86 (1958), 482 f.; pl. 3. 1–3.

[8] Mattingly 2. 233 f.; 302; pl. 45. 16–18; 59. 13.

[9] Steiner, *BJ* 114 (1905), 35, fig. 23; 18, fig. 13; pls. 1. 4 f.; 2. 3.

[10] Sydenham 207 f.; Grueber, pl. 105. 8–10. This was first observed by Kraft, l.c. 10 ff., who compared it with representations of the golden crown in Greek and Etruscan art (ibid., pl. 2): a valuable observation (accepted, e.g., by Gelzer, *Caesar* 293. 208; Carson, *Gnom.* 28 (1956), 184; Felber, op. cit. 274), even though Kraft overstated his case (above, n. 9). Felber, op. cit. 274 ff., nevertheless argues that it represented the triumphal crown.

[11] Cf. Dion. Hal. 2. 34. 2; 3. 62. 1; Mommsen, *StR* 1. 427. 2; Kraft, l.c. 17 f.

[12] Dio 44. 4. 2; 6. 1 (above, p. 271. 7 and below, p. 273. 8); Suet. *Caes.* 76. 1: 'sedem auream in Curia et pro tribunali'; Cic. *Phil.* 2. 85; *div.* 1. 119; Pliny 11. 186; Val. Max. 1. 6. 13; Nic. Dam. *v. Caes.* 71; App. *BC* 2. 106. 442; Plut. *Caes.* 61. 4 (above, p. 271. 5).

seat to express his higher status.[1] As can be seen on coins, the throne was identical in shape with the *sella curulis*[2] but was made of gilded metal instead of ivory. Golden thrones were used by kings everywhere in the East as well as in Greece, also by the Hellenistic,[3] Etruscan,[4] and probably Roman kings. But whenever the Romans wanted to honour foreign kings they presented them with the insignia of kingship together with the *sella curulis*, but not with the golden throne,[5] which may have been repugnant to them. Foreigners, on the other hand, always honoured Roman generals with a golden throne.[6] Caesar's throne was thus without republican precedent[7] and against tradition: it is clear that it again was to be a regal privilege.

Next the chariot, first mentioned among the honours of 44: he was now granted it even for Rome, and the triumphal dress with it.[8] The following facts may be relevant. It was a privilege of the kings to ride in it[9] and this survived in the name of the chair of the magistrates, the *sella curulis*.[10] In the republican period chariots were forbidden inside the city, in contrast to the litter and sedan-chair which were in general use. There were some exceptions.[11] L. Caecilius Metellus (*cos.* 251 and 247) was entitled to drive in a chariot to the meetings of the Senate, apparently

[1] Suet. *Caes.* 76. 1: 'suggestum in orchestra'; Flor. 2. 13. 91: 'suggestus in Curia', cf. Dio 45. 7. 3; 59. 26. 3; Suet. *Claud.* 21. 1; Mommsen, *StR* 3. 939. 5; Alföldi, *Röm. Mitt.* 50 (1935), 22 f.; 42; Hug, *RE* 4A. 663.

[2] Mommsen, *StR* 1. 439 f.; cf. the coin of Octavian issued in 42 with a chair inscribed Caesar dic(tator) per(petuo)' and a wreath placed upon it on the rev.: Sydenham 206; Grueber, pl. 104. 12; Alföldi, *Röm. Mitt.* 50 (1935), 135; pl. 14. 10; id. *Stud. über Caesars Monarchie* 22 and *Herm.* 86 (1958), 482 f.; pl. 3. 1–3. Did the legs of the chair end at the top in doves, the symbol of Venus (Mommsen 1. 439. 5), or in eagles (Alföldi, l.c. 482. 6)?

[3] Herter, *Rhein. Mus.* 74 (1925), 164 ff.; Schramm, *Herrschaftszeichen u. Staatssymbolik* 1. 316 ff.; 3. 1095 ff.

[4] Prop. 4. 10. 27: 'heu Veii veteres! et vos tum regna fuistis, / et vestro posita est aurea sella foro.'

[5] Dion. Hal. 5. 35. 1; Livy 27. 4. 8; 30. 15. 11; 31. 11; 12; App. *Pun.* 32. 137.

[6] Plut. *Pomp.* 36. 10 (the Iberi to Pompey): κλίνην καὶ τράπεζαν καὶ θρόνον, ἅπαντα χρυσᾶ; Dio 51. 6. 5 (to Octavian, 30 B.C.): ἡ Κλεοπάτρα σκῆπτρόν τέ τι χρυσοῦν καὶ στέφανον χρυσοῦν τόν τε δίφρον τὸν βασιλικόν . . . ἔπεμψεν. In 36 the Parthian king Phraates sat on a golden chair while negotiating with Antony's envoys (Dio 49. 27. 4), so also in 34 Cleopatra in Alexandria during Antony's triumph (Dio 49. 40. 3), and Antony himself began to do the same (Dio 50. 5. 3).

[7] Mommsen, *StR* 1. 439, calls it a triumphal chair, but there is no evidence for such a chair (Alföldi, *Röm. Mitt.* 50. 41): or is the term 'sella curulis' and what is quoted in n. 10 relevant?

[8] Dio 44. 4. 2: τὰ μὲν γὰρ πρῶτα φέρεσθαί τε αὐτὸν ἀεὶ καὶ ἐν αὐτῇ τῇ πόλει τὴν στολὴν τὴν ἐπινίκιον ἐνδεδυκότα, καὶ καθέζεσθαι ἐπὶ τοῦ ἀρχικοῦ δίφρου πανταχῇ πλὴν ἐν ταῖς πανηγύρεσιν ἐψηφίσαντο· τότε γὰρ ἐπί τε τοῦ δημαρχικοῦ βάθρου καὶ μετὰ τῶν ἀεὶ δημαρχούντων θεᾶσθαι ἔλαβε.

[9] See above, p. 54.

[10] Mommsen, *StR* 1. 395 f.; on the Greek (Aesch. *Ag.* 1054: τόνδ' ἁμαξήρη θρόνον) and Oriental analogies see Alföldi, *Nouv. Clio* 1/2 (1950), 342 ff. and *Studies in Honor of A. M. Friend* (1955), 33.   [11] Mommsen, *StR* 1. 393 ff.

in recognition of some heroic achievement in the First Punic War, and not, as is recorded, because he was blinded while saving the Palladium from the burning temple of Vesta,[1] a story inspired by the derivation of Caecilius from *caecus*. Other men too will have been granted this privilege for their achievements; it was always granted for the triumph. Further, priests were entitled to chariots for certain ritual acts:[2] this was clearly another survival from the regal period, protected by religious conservatism against the legal prohibition. There was also the magistrate in charge of the *ludi Romani* and *ludi Apollinares*, when he drove from the Capitol to the Circus in the *pompa circensis*.[3] His privilege derived from that of the principal exception, the triumphator, provided it is right to assume that originally the games were part of the triumph.[4] But in general the prohibition remained the rule. Caesar himself restated it and its exceptions in his *lex Iulia municipalis*,[5] although it was about that time, 44 B.C., that he was granted the use of the chariot inside Rome. He probably never had the opportunity of using it. But the honour survived and in 19 B.C. was granted to Augustus, who, however, refused to accept it.[6] Needless to say, the permanent use of the chariot and of the triumphal dress again represented a regal privilege.

A further privilege is mentioned by Dio, our only source, among the honours of 44 but it may have been decreed already in 45.[7] What he says has been understood in two ways. Either the Senate called Caesar 'parens patriae' and authorized the engraving of his head on coins;[8] or else they called him 'parens patriae' and it was this title that was engraved.[9] The question then is whether Caesar was granted the right of portraiture. Zonaras understood Dio in this sense,[10] and there is some comparative evidence for such engraving.[11] It is further

---

[1] Pliny 7. 141. [2] Livy 1. 21. 4; Tac. *A.* 12. 42. 3.

[3] Dion. Hal. 5. 57. 5; Livy 45. 1. 6 f.; Mommsen, *StR* 1. 413. 2; 394. 4.

[4] Mommsen, *Röm. Forsch.* 2. 42 ff.

[5] *ILS* 6085. 56 ff. (Bruns 18 = Riccobono 13); Kornemann, *RE* 16. 611 f.

[6] *Chron. Min.* 2, p. 135 Mms.: 'Caesari ex provinciis redeunti currus cum corona aurea decretus est, quo ascendere noluit.' The chariot and the triumphal garb are represented on contemporary coins, Mattingly 1. 69 f.; pl. 8. 20; 9. 1–3; above, p. 57. 6. Mommsen, *Res gestae* 151 and *StR* 1. 395. 1, suggests (wrongly, as it seems) that none of this refers to the right to a chariot but to the triumph which was decreed but not held.

[7] Dio 44. 4. 4: πρός τε τούτοις τοιούτοις οὖσι πατέρα τε αὐτὸν τῆς πατρίδος ἐπωνόμασαν καὶ ἐς τὰ νομίσματα ἐνεχάραξαν; on the problem of dating see above, pp. 200; 270.

[8] Eckhel, op. cit. 6. 7; Mommsen, *Röm. Münzwesen* 658. 558; 739 f.

[9] This view has now been revived by Grant, *From Imperium to Auctoritas* 15 f.; Felber, *Caesars Streben nach der Königswürde* 218 f.

[10] Zonar. 10. 12: πατέρα τε αὐτὸν τῆς πατρίδος ἐπονομάζεσθαι, καὶ ἐς τὸ νόμισμα ἐγχαράττεσθαι.

[11] Aristot. frg. 528 R.: ἐν νομίσματι αὐτὸν (Βάττον) ἐχάραξαν . . ., ὥστε καὶ ἐν τῷ νομίσματι . . . Ἄμμωνα . . . ἐγκεχαράχθαι; Lucian. *Alex.* 58: νόμισμα καινὸν κόψαι ἐγκεχαραγμένον τῇ μὲν τοῦ Γλύκωνος (sc. εἰκόνι?).

a fact that hitherto no portrait of a living person had been shown on coins and that Caesar's portrait was shown by all the moneyers of 44.[1] Two of these added the title 'parens patriae' in the legend;[2] but this title also appeared, as we have seen, on inscriptions.[3] It must therefore have been the right of portraiture that the Senate decreed. It was another radical break with the past but had its analogies in the Hellenistic kingdoms and was thus a further monarchic privilege. We shall see presently that it was begun in the Greek provinces about the time of the victory of Pharsalus;[4] now it was also introduced in Rome. After the murder Brutus, though not Cassius, followed Caesar's example, but only in the Greek East;[5] so too Octavian in Rome as early as 43[6] and the *triumviri* in and outside Rome.[7] Later the privilege was reserved for the emperors and their families. In sum, it was again a privilege first granted to Caesar. It is important to add that his head reappeared on coins after the consecration; but it had changed its function: it was now a divine portrait.[8]

Finally, a piece of evidence which at first sight fits well into this context must be eliminated. Towards the end of 45 (rather than in early 44) Caesar sat at the temple of Venus Genetrix when the Senate, led by the consuls and all the other magistrates, came to inform him of the honours just decreed. What is said to have scandalized the senators was that Caesar remained seated in their presence.[9] The following facts are relevant: it was the privilege of the magistrates and of senators to conduct official business seated; a citizen rose when a magistrate came, as did a minor magistrate in the presence of a higher-ranking one; again, men of special merits were honoured by rising at their appearance.[10] There is not a single piece of evidence to show that Caesar here committed an offence against tradition or that, as modern scholars maintain,[11] he wanted to demonstrate his new monarchic status. What is quoted in this respect, including the case of the tribune

---

[1] Sydenham 176–9; above, p. 99.
[2] See above, p. 200. [3] See above, p. 200. 3.
[4] See below, pp. 297; 299. [5] Sydenham 202. 1295; 203. 1297; 1301.
[6] Sydenham 206. 1321; see below, pp. 394 f.
[7] Sydenham 182 ff.; 205 ff.
[8] See below, p. 395.
[9] Suet. *Caes.* 78. 1; Livy, *Per.* 116; Dio 44. 8. 2 ff.; Plut. *Caes.* 60. 4 ff.; App. *BC* 2. 107. 445 f.; Nic. Dam. 22. 78 f.; Eutrop. 6. 25. Appian and Plutarch are certainly wrong in asserting that the incident took place at the Rostra, and Nicolaus in attributing the incident to 44.
[10] Mommsen, *StR* 1. 397 f.; Hug, *RE* IA. 2065 f.; Kroll, *Kultur d. ciceron. Zeit* 2. 64; Alföldi, *Röm. Mitt.* 49 (1934), 42 f.
[11] Drumann 3. 601; Meyer, *Caesars Monarchie* 518 f.; Gelzer, *Caesar* 294.

L. Pontius Aquila, is irrelevant.[1] As dictator he was superior to the consuls and could therefore remain seated in their presence; and the senatorial privilege only meant that they were not obliged either to rise in the presence of a magistrate. As to the alleged demonstration of his monarchic status, we have met other and really significant actions and decrees to this effect. At the Lupercalia of 44 when he was officially approached by his fellow consul Antony he remained seated again, and nobody was scandalized on this account.[2]

The probability is that the incident was transformed into a scandal long after it had taken place; its theme was suggested by the encounter with L. Pontius Aquila which had annoyed Caesar. Another incident which occurred within a few weeks may show how quickly such myths could be created and obscure the facts. The consul Q. Fabius Maximus died on 31 December 45 and C. Caninius Rebilus was made consul for the rest of that day. Ancient and modern writers condemn Caesar for this 'cynical' contempt of republican institutions.[3] But here again Caesar was not guilty. In 40 an aedile and in 33 a praetor were created for a few hours when the holders of the offices died on the last day of their tenure.[4] At the end of 43 all the praetors were sent to the provinces and were replaced for five days; in 40 the consuls and praetors were so replaced for other reasons for the last few days.[5] There was no public outcry on these occasions. Clearly the replacement was a constitutional necessity[6] which Caesar scrupulously observed.

2. THE DOMUS PUBLICA AND ITS PEDIMENT

The chapter in Dio which refers to the new temple of Libertas and to Caesar's title 'Liberator'[7] ends after a long digression about the *praenomen* 'Imperator' with a further honour decreed by the Senate at that time: to build a house for him so that he might live in State property.[8]

---

[1] Augustus greeted the senators as they sat in the Curia (Suet. *Aug.* 53. 3); Tiberius stood in the presence of the consuls (Suet. *Tib.* 31. 2). Aquila did not rise when Caesar passed in his triumph of 45 (Suet. *Caes.* 78. 2): as a tribune he was probably not bound by the general rule and at any rate could not be prosecuted.   [2] See below, p. 331.

[3] Cic. *fam.* 7. 30. 1 f.; Dio 43. 46. 2 ff.; Plut. *Caes.* 58. 2 f.; Suet. *Caes.* 76. 2, etc.; Meyer 459 f.; Gelzer 288. An exception is Adcock, *CAH* 9. 733. When Nero refused to create, and later Vitellius did create, such a one-day consul, reference was made to the Caesarian precedent, Suet. *Nero* 15. 2; Tac. *H.* 3. 37. The initiator was apparently Cicero who had already commented about Vatinius' brief consulate in 47 in such extravagant terms, Macrob. 2. 3. 5; cf. Dio 42. 55. 4; Meyer 381. 2.

[4] Dio 48. 32. 3; 49. 43. 7.   [5] Dio 47. 15. 3; 48. 32. 1.
[6] Cf. Suet. *Cal.* 17. 1.   [7] See above, p. 133.
[8] Dio 43. 44. 6: καὶ οἰκίαν ὥστε ἐν τῷ δημοσίῳ οἰκεῖν.

There is no other evidence about this honour. It is possible to infer from the context that this was another reward for his fight for freedom; but this inference must find some support in the history of this privilege to become more convincing. After that it must be explained why it is treated here in the context of kingship and not in the chapter about the Liberator.

Caesar had first lived in the Subura, but when he became *pontifex maximus* in 63 he moved to the *domus publica* on the Sacra Via[1] near the Regia, which was his office. He had this privilege of an official residence in common with the *flamines* and the *rex sacrorum*.[2] It has therefore been assumed that Dio was the victim of a confusion when he spoke of the decree of another *domus publica* for Caesar.[3] A later decree of this kind will prove that Dio's record is correct. But if this is so, the question arises: why was a second public building to be erected for Caesar?

Augustan evidence shows that this question is justified. Augustus first lived in the house of the orator C. Licinius Calvus near the Forum and then in the house of Hortensius on the Palatine.[4] In 36 he intended to build a house on the Palatine on his private property; but, prompted by a prodigy, he gave it up for the temple of Apollo. And that is why —so it is stated—the Senate decided to build him a house on State property.[5] This wish to compensate him does not seem to be a proper

---

[1] Suet. *Caes.* 46: 'habitavit primo in Subura modicis aedibus, post autem pontificatum maximum in Sacra via domo publica'; Pliny 19. 23: 'Caesar dictator totum forum Romanum intexit viamque Sacram ab domo sua.' It could also be called Regia as in Serv. Dan. *Aen.* 8. 363 ('domus enim, in qua pontifex habitat, Regia dicitur, quod in ea rex sacrificulus habitasse consuesset')—a false explanation, because the *rex sacrificulus* lived elsewhere (Wissowa 502. 7)—just as the Atrium Vestae could be so called (Ov. *F.* 6. 263: 'hic locus exiguus, qui sustinet Atria Vestae / tunc erat intonsi Regia magna Numae'; Livy 26. 27. 3; 27. 11. 16: 'atrium regium'). This is how Cic. *Att.* 10. 3a (7 April 49): 'visum te aiunt in Regia', is to be understood: Atticus called upon Caesar in the *domus publica*. It is certain that the *domus publica* and the Regia were two different buildings; see Rosenberg, *RE* 1A. 465 f.; Platner–Ashby 58; 440; Nash, op. cit. 1. 362 f.; 2. 264 ff.

[2] Paul. 89 M. (79 L.): 'Flaminiae aedes domus flaminis Dialis'; 106 M. (94 L.); Gell. 10. 15. 7; Serv. Dan. *Aen.* 2. 57: 'flaminia autem domus flaminis dicitur sicut Regia regis domus'; 8. 363; Dio 54. 24. 2; Livy 5. 40. 8: 'aedibus flaminis Quirinalis'; Fest. 293 M. (372 L.): 'Sacram viam . . . a Regia ad domum regis sacrificuli'; Wissowa 502. 7. It was not called, like the *flaminia* or *regia domus*, 'pontificia' or 'pontificalis domus' but 'domus publica', an unexpected expression: the *aedes publicae* (*Thes.L.L.* 1. 909. 10 ff.; 912. 48 ff.; Mommsen, *StR* 2. 47 ff.; 435 ff.; 461 f.) or the *Villa publica* (Varr. *RR* 3. 2; Livy 4. 22. 7, etc.; Sydenham 149; Platner–Ashby s.v.) may be compared; see also below, p. 278.

[3] Drumann 3. 599. 6.

[4] Suet. *Aug.* 72. 1.

[5] Dio 49. 15. 5: τότε δὲ οἰκίαν τε αὐτῷ ἐκ τοῦ δημοσίου δοθῆναι ἔγνωσαν· τὸν γὰρ τόπον ὃν ἐν τῷ Παλατίῳ, ὥστ' οἰκοδομῆσαί τινα, ἐώνητο, ἐδημοσίωσε καὶ τῷ Ἀπόλλωνι ἱέρωσεν, ἐπειδὴ κεραυνὸς ἐς αὐτὸν ἐγκατέσκηψε. τὴν δὲ οἰκίαν αὐτῷ ἐψηφίσαντο. The other evidence does not contain the information about the building at public expense, Suet. *Aug.* 29. 3: 'templum Apollinis in ea parte Palatinae domus excitavit, quam fulmine ictam desiderari a deo haruspices

justification for the decree. Nor would the offer of the office of *pontifex maximus*, which was made about the same time, explain it. Not only because he refused to accept the offer then and later, in fact as long as Lepidus, the disgraced holder of the office, was alive,[1] but also because, had he accepted it, he too could have lived in the *domus publica* on the Sacra Via. The house on the Palatine was subsequently built next to the temple of Apollo but it was not public property. In 12 B.C., when Augustus was elected *pontifex maximus*, he did not move to the *domus publica* but presented it to the Vestals and made part of his own house public, so that he did not commit an offence against the requirements of his new office.[2] In A.D. 3 when his house, which had been destroyed by fire, was rebuilt with public and private help he made his whole house public property.[3] Later Nerva even inscribed 'aedes publicae' on his palace.[4] The existence of the Caesarian decree is thus supported by its successor made in honour of Augustus. The problem of the second *domus publica*, inherent though not mentioned in the Caesarian decree, is solved by an examination of the case of Augustus: Caesar like Augustus preferred a public palace to a public residence. But there is still no explanation of how it was possible for a second house to be built for Caesar.

We have seen that Caesar was often supposed to have followed the example of the heroes of the past, among them L. Brutus;[5] here the precedent seems to be another legendary hero of the first year of the Republic, P. Valerius Poplicola.[6] Two versions of his story are relevant here. According to the one he began to build a house on the Velia where the kings Ancus Marcius, Tullus Hostilius, and Tarquinius Priscus had had their houses, but demolished it because he wanted to avoid the suspicion that he was aiming at kingship. He rebuilt it instead at the foot of the Velia on ground given by the people in accordance

---

pronuntiarant'; Vell. 2. 81. 3: 'Caesar . . . contractas emptionibus complures domos per procuratores, quo laxior fieret ipsius, publicis se usibus destinare professus est, templumque Apollinis . . . facturum promisit, quod ab eo singulari extructum munificentia est.'

[1] Dio 49. 15. 3.

[2] Dio 54. 27. 3: οὔτ' οἰκίαν τινὰ δημοσίαν ἔλαβεν, ἀλλὰ μέρος τι τῆς ἑαυτοῦ, ὅτι τὸν ἀρχιερέων ἐν κοινῷ πάντως οἰκεῖν ἐχρῆν, ἐδημοσίωσεν. τὴν μέντοι τοῦ βασιλέως τῶν ἱερῶν (he means the *domus publica*, although it never was the residence of the *rex sacrificulus*: Wissowa 502. 7) ταῖς ἀειπαρθένοις ἔδωκεν, ἐπειδὴ ὁμότοιχος ταῖς οἰκήσεσιν αὐτῶν ἦν.

[3] Dio 55. 12. 5: ὁ δὲ Αὔγουστος τὴν οἰκίαν οἰκοδομήσας ἐδημοσίωσε πᾶσαν, εἴτε δὴ διὰ τὴν συντέλειαν τὴν παρὰ τοῦ δήμου οἱ γενομένην, εἴτε καὶ ὅτι ἀρχιερέως ἦν, ἵν' ἐν τοῖς ἰδίοις ἅμα καὶ ἐν τοῖς κοινοῖς οἰκοίη; Suet. *Aug.* 57. 2.

[4] Pliny *Paneg.* 47. 4: 'parens tuus hanc ante vos principes arcem "publicarum aedium" nomine inscripserat.'

[5] See above, pp. 145 ff.; 153 ff.

[6] Schwegler, *Röm. Gesch.* 2. 48 ff.; Volkmann, *RE* 8A. 180 ff.

with a law proposed by him.[1] The other version is that the house was built for his services, on public property and at public expense.[2] Such a house was built later for his brother M. Valerius (*cos.* 505) on the Palatine for his victories over the Sabines,[3] perhaps also for another brother, M'. Valerius Maximus (*dict.* 494), for his reconciliation of the patricians and the plebeians,[4] and even for a fourth Valerius, the Sicilian Myttones, who during the Second Punic War came over to the Romans and became a Roman citizen under the name of M. Valerius Mottones.[5] This version was clearly made up by Valerius Antias but not wholly invented by him: the connection of the Valerii with the Velia and the house on the Palatine were facts, and moreover part of the evidence seems to be independent of Valerius Antias.[6]

Both versions were known in the time of Caesar and both suited his case; but the first was more topical. Poplicola was rewarded with a house because he was a man of liberty and did not want to become or even to appear a tyrant. Accordingly, one might assume that the new house was to be a further reward for Caesar the liberator; the existing *domus publica* was not a reward but an official residence.

This then is the answer to our question; but it is not yet the whole story. There was another man who lived in such a *domus publica*, Antiochus IV, when he spent fourteen years (189–175) as a hostage in Rome.[7] It was not because he was a man of liberty or for any other merits; in his case it was a royal privilege.[8] Consequently, we must assume that the kings of Rome too had it before him. And this turns our attention again to the *pontifex maximus*. He inherited the royal house, the Regia, from the kings, used it as his office but did not live there,

---

[1] Cic. *rep.* 2. 53: 'aedis suas detulit sub Veliam, posteaquam, quod in excelsiore loco Veliae coepisset aedificare eo ipso ubi rex Tullus habitaverat, suspicionem populi sensit moveri'; Plut. *Popl.* 10. 3 ff.; 6: ἐδέχοντο γὰρ οἱ φίλοι τὸν Οὐαλέριον, ἄχρι οὗ τόπον ἔδωκεν ὁ δῆμος αὐτῷ καὶ κατεσκεύασεν οἰκίαν ἐκείνης μετριωτέραν; Livy 2. 7. 6 ff.; Val. Max. 4. 1. 1; Dion. Hal. 5. 19. 1 f.; *vir. ill.* 15. 2 f.; Serv. *Aen.* 4. 410.

[2] Cic. *har. resp.* 16: 'P. Valerio pro maximis in rem publicam beneficiis data domus est in Velia publice'; Ascon. *Pis.* 52, p. 19 St.: 'Iulius Hyginus dicit in libro priore de viris claris (frg. 2 P.) P. Valerio Volesi filio Publicolae aedium publice locum sub Veliis, ubi nunc aedis Victoriae est, populum ex lege quam ipse tulerat concessisse'; Pliny 36. 112.

[3] Dion. Hal. 5. 39. 4; Ascon. *Pis.* 52, pp. 18 f. St. (Varro); Pliny 36. 112; Plut. *Popl.* 20. 2; Volkmann, *RE* 7A. 2308 f.

[4] Ascon. *Pis.* 52, p. 18 St. (Val. Ant. frg. 17 P.); Hirschfeld, *Kl. Schr.* 819; *contra*, Volkmann, *RE* 7A. 2309 (modified (?) ibid. 8A. 119 f.).

[5] Ascon. *Pis.* 52, p. 19 St. (Varro *de vita p. R.* 3, frg. 96 Rip.); Ehrenberg, *RE* 16. 1429; Volkmann, *RE* 8A. 171.

[6] Cf. Münzer, *Beitr. z. Quellenkritik d. Naturgesch. d. Plinius* 169 f.

[7] Ascon. *Pis.* 52, p. 19 St.: 'tradunt et Antiochi regis filio obsidi domum publice aedificatam inter quos Atticus in Annali (frg. 6 P.): quae postea dicitur Lucili poetae fuisse.'

[8] Cf. Livy 42. 6. 9; Wilcken, *RE* 1. 2470.

which would have made him a pretender, but in a house nearby. That was, it may be suggested, why the royal privilege of a public dwelling was given to this house. The same applies to Poplicola. He gave up his plan to live on the Velia where some of the kings had lived and was therefore rewarded with what was due to kings. The other version of the story was created because it was not right to be in possession of royal privileges: it was for their achievements that the house was granted to the heroes of the Valerii. In the case of the *pontifex maximus* this origin of the privilege had no practical significance for the normal holder of the office. The conclusion then is that Caesar the liberator was rewarded with a privilege which was in origin due to the kings.

The Senate also decreed that a pediment should be placed on his house.[1] This was not necessarily part of the same decree. The house was never built but the pediment was erected, one may assume provisionally, on the *domus publica*. It was the subject of Calpurnia's dream the night before the Ides of March.[2] Needless to say, this was an even more extraordinary privilege. The explanation that it was for the ornament and dignity of his house[3] is not satisfactory. No human dwelling had it at that time: it belonged to the temples of the gods[4] and on the stage to the palace of the kings.[5] Here Augustus did not follow Caesar's example; his palace had no pediment:[6] a coin of L. Caninius Gallus, issued in 12 B.C. (pl. 21. 1),[7] and the Sorrento base[8] reproduce the doors of the palace with the *corona civica* over them but without a pediment. On the other hand, Seneca records that the imperial palace had a pediment, decorated with the *corona civica*,[9] and Suetonius that a *corona*

---

[1] Cic. *Phil.* 2. 110: 'fastigium'; Suet. *Caes.* 81. 3: 'fastigium domus'; Flor. 2. 13. 91: 'fastigium in domo'; see also the following note; Eitrem, *Symb. Osl.* 11 (1932), 32.

[2] Obs. 67: 'Calpurnia uxor somniavit fastigium domus, quod s.c. erat adiectum, ruisse'; Plut. *Caes.* 63. 9: ἦν γάρ τι τῇ Καίσαρος οἰκίᾳ προσκείμενον οἷον ἐπὶ κόσμῳ καὶ σεμνότητι τῆς βουλῆς ψηφισαμένης ἀκρωτήριον, ὡς Λίβιος ἱστορεῖ. τοῦτ' ὄναρ ἡ Καλπουρνία θεασαμένη καταρρηγνύμενον ἔδοξε ποτνιᾶσθαι καὶ δακρύειν; below, p. 346.

[3] Plut. *Caes.* 63. 9: ... οἷον ἐπὶ κόσμῳ καὶ σεμνότητι ...

[4] Cic. *de or.* 3. 180: '... Capitolium ... nullam sine fastigio dignitatem habiturum fuisse videatur'; cf. Aristoph. *Av.* 1109: εἶτα πρὸς τούτοισιν ὥσπερ ἐν ἱεροῖς οἰκήσετε / τὰς γὰρ ὑμῶν οἰκίας ἐρέψομεν πρὸς αἰετόν (= fastigium). On its further significance cf. P. Hommel, 'Giebel u. Himmel', *Istanb. Mitt.* 7 (1957), 11 ff. (not convincing).

[5] Vitr. 5. 6. 9: '(scaenae) tragicae deformantur columnis et fastigiis et signis reliquisque regalibus rebus'; Alföldi, *Studies in Honor of A. M. Friend* (1955), 35.

[6] It does not follow from Ovid's hyperbolical lines, *Trist.* 3. 1. 33: 'video fulgentibus armis / conspicuos postes tectaque digna deo. / "et Iovis haec" dixi "domus est?" quod ut esse putarem, / augurium menti querna corona dabat.'

[7] Mattingly 1. 26; pl. 4. 15.　　　　　　　　[8] Rizzo, *Bull. Comun.* 60 (1933), 79 f.; pl. 4.

[9] Sen. *clem.* 1. 26. 5: 'nullum ornamentum principis fastigio dignius pulchriusque est quam illa corona ob cives servatos.'

navalis was added to it by Claudius.[1] The pediment therefore must have been added either by Caligula or by Claudius. Caligula is clearly the more probable choice.

What was the pediment to indicate, the dwelling of a king or of a god? We found it on the palace of the kings on the stage, which was not necessarily a borrowing from Greek plays. For probably the Regia too had it,[2] which is more important, provided it was not because the Regia was consecrated as a shrine where certain sacrifices were performed;[3] for then the Regia would indicate a god. This alternative would be supported by the fact that about that time Caesar was also granted a *tensa* and a *pulvinar*, both with pediments.[4] But one would have to admit that these had it by necessity because they belonged to the apparatus of the gods; if they were borrowed for Caesar, this fact did not necessarily make him a god. The later evidence does not lead to a clear decision either. Augustus avoided the pediment because he did not want to appear in Rome as a king or a god. For Caligula it was no doubt a symbol of divinity, but for the later emperors it was certainly not. We must therefore decide Caesar's case on its own merits. The *domus publica* with its pediment now resembled even more the Regia, and it is tempting to assume that this was intended. Had the new house, or rather palace, been built, it would have been done in the same manner and could have become the real successor of the Regia of king Numa. This consideration then favours the alternative of the king, which would be in accordance with the fact that Caesar's first task at that time was to establish the monarchy. But we cannot exclude the possibility that it was for him a divine symbol: we shall see presently that his divinity too was propagated. Thus, with probability on the side of a regal interpretation, the case must remain open.

3. THE DIVINE ATTRIBUTES

A decree, issued after 26 January and before 9 February 44 B.C. and designating Caesar *dictator perpetuo*,[5] granted him a golden chair for the

---

[1] Suet. *Claud.* 17. 3: 'inter hostilia spolia navalem coronam fastigio Palatinae domus iuxta civicam fixit.'

[2] Plut. *Numa* 14. 1; Ov. *F.* 6. 263 f.; Serv. *Aen.* 8. 363; Platner–Ashby s.v.; for the reconstructions see Degrassi, *Scritti* 239 ff.; F. E. Brown, *Mem. Amer. Acad.* 12 (1935), 67 ff.

[3] Fest. 278 M. (346 L.); Dio 48. 42. 6; Wissowa 502. 4.

[4] See below, p. 284; Alföldi, *Röm. Mitt.* 50 (1935), 132; id. *Ant. Class.* 8 (1939), 349; A. L. Abaecherli, *Boll. Assoc. Intern. Studi Medit.* 6 (1935/6), 1 ff.; pl. 6.

[5] The date of the decree is suggested by Octavian's coin quoted above, p. 273. 2: it shows the wreath on the chair which bears the inscription 'Caesar dic(tator) per(petuo)'. Caesar was still *dictator quartum* on 26 January 44 (*F. Triumph.*: '... dict(ator) IIII ovans...

theatre as well, not for his personal use but for his golden crown to be placed on it;[1] and a special carriage which should take his symbols to the Circus where they were to be placed on the couch of the gods. It will be seen that this decree is neither a duplication of the earlier one nor a supplement to it, but something new.

It was not an improvisation nor a fanciful idea of the Senate to place an empty chair in the theatre, but part of a symbolism which had ancient roots everywhere.[2] Such chairs were set up in honour of the gods in the East and in Greece, and were also used for the banquets of the gods, the *theoxenia*.[3] They were further used in honour of dead rulers. Alexander's golden throne, with his diadem and sceptre on it, was set up by Eumenes in 318 B.C. when he held consultations with his advisers:[4] Alexander's symbolic presence vouched for the legality and the right spirit of the deliberations. Ptolemy I's golden throne with a wreath on it was carried in the procession at a festival in Alexandria *c.* 270 B.C.[5]

In Rome too the gods had their thrones,[6] which were carried in procession and used sometimes at their banquets, the *sellisternia*,[7] though more often couches were used, the *lectisternia*.[8] The thrones were also taken to the theatre and exhibited there with their symbols placed upon them, such as thunderbolt, helmet, wreath, etc.[9] There is no evidence for a chair set up in honour of a dead or absent ruler or magistrate, with one exception. It is recorded that whenever Romulus was acting in an official capacity and therefore seated on his chair, another *sella curulis* was set up next to him for the dead Remus with the sceptre, crown, and other regal insignia placed on it to indicate their common rule.[10]

ex monte Albano VII K. Febr.'), *dictator quartum* and *dictator designatus in perpetuum* on 9 February (Jos. *AJ* 14. 211 : δικτάτωρ τὸ τέταρτον ὕπατός τε τὸ πέμπτον, δικτάτωρ ἀποδεδειγμένος διὰ βίου), but *dictator perpetuo* already on 15 Febr. (Cic. *Phil.* 2. 87: 'adscribi iussit in Fastis ad Lupercalia C. Caesari dictatori perpetuo M. Antonium consulem populi iussu regnum detulisse: Caesarem uti noluisse'); Gelzer, *Caesar* 296. 229.

[1] Dio 44. 6. 3: ἔς τε τὰ θέατρα τόν τε δίφρον αὐτοῦ τὸν ἐπίχρυσον καὶ τὸν στέφανον τὸν διάλιθον καὶ διάχρυσον ἐξ ἴσου τοῖς τῶν θεῶν ἐσκομίζεσθαι κἀν ταῖς ἱπποδρομίαις ὄχον ἐσάγεσθαι ἐψηφίσαντο. On Flor. 2. 13. 91 see below, p. 382.

[2] *JRS* 47 (1957), 147 (with bibliography); add Herter, *Wien. Stud.* 79 (1966), 556 ff.

[3] Porph. *v. Pyth.* 17; *Or. Sib.* 8. 48 f.; cf. *JRS* 47. 147. 27.

[4] Diod. 18. 61. 1; Polyaen. 4. 8. 2; cf. Ephipp., *FGrHist.* 126 F 4; Theocr. 17. 18 f.; Herter, l.c. 564 f.

[5] Kallixeinos, *FGrHist.* 627 F 2. 34 = Athen. 5. 202 ab.

[6] Suet. *Aug.* 70. 1: 'fugit et auratos Iuppiter ipse thronos'; Cumont, *Rel. or.* 53, fig. 3.

[7] Fest. 298 M. (386 L.); Tert. *spect.* 7; *ad nat.* 1. 10 (p. 77. 21 R.–W.); Wissowa, *RE* 12. 1115; L. R. Taylor, *CP* 30 (1935), 122 ff.

[8] Wissowa, *RE* 12. 1108 ff.   [9] Dio 44. 6. 3; for the symbols see *JRS* 47. 148.

[10] Serv. *Aen.* 1. 276: 'sella curulis cum sceptro et corona et ceteris regni insignibus semper iuxta sancientem aliquid Romulum ponebatur, ut pariter imperare viderentur'; cf. Mommsen, *Ges. Schr.* 4. 19. 1; *StR* 2. 745. 2.

This may be real or fictitious evidence about an original double kingship. But the symbolism is certainly not invented; another version of it appears in the record about Caligula's chair which was set up in the Capitoline temple and received homage from the senators during his absence.[1]

Caesar's chair was apparently not intended to have so general a function; it was to be exhibited only in the theatres. There were other chairs there for the gods with their symbols. Caesar's symbol was the golden crown—not the regal one, which was plain and which he was entitled to wear—decorated with precious gems like the triumphal crown;[2] its description as 'Caesar's Iuppiter-crown'[3] is illuminating. The chair was never exhibited while Caesar was alive. After his death Octavian tried twice to exhibit it in 44, but was prevented from doing so by Antony;[4] he succeeded later and exhibited it on many occasions.[5] He never claimed such a chair for himself and did not grant it to anyone either except in the form of a memorial chair, commonly set up at tombs and elsewhere in honour of the dead.[6] This was originally limited to the private sphere. But when Marcellus died in 23 a *sella curulis* with a golden wreath on it was set up in the theatre, placed between the chairs of the aediles;[7] it was a combination of Caesar's chair with those of 'Remus' and Caligula. The golden wreath represented Marcellus as it had Caesar before; but his place between the aediles was to indicate that he was, together with them, in charge of the games, just as the chairs of Remus and Caligula represented their office. Such a chair, but with an oak wreath on it, was set up later in honour of the dead Germanicus and Drusus in the theatres at the *ludi Augustales*;[8] it was not for their political status but for their priestly office as *flamines Augustales*. Seianus returned to the Caesarian tradition: a golden chair was set up for him and another for Tiberius in the theatres in A.D. 30 while both were alive and Tiberius at least absent.[9] Numismatic evidence suggests that similar

---

[1] Dio 59. 24. 4 (A.D. 40): ἐς τὸ Καπιτώλιον ἀθρόοι οἱ βουλευταὶ ἀναβάντες τάς τε θυσίας ἔθυσαν καὶ τὸν τοῦ Γαΐου δίφρον τὸν ἐν τῷ ναῷ κείμενον προσεκύνησαν; cf. Plin. *Paneg.* 52. 1 (of Domitian): 'media inter deos sedes auro staret aut ebore augustioribusque aris et grandioribus victimis invocaretur.' [2] See above, pp. 271 f.

[3] Mommsen, *StR* 1. 427. 3. This note seems to have been overlooked by later writers.

[4] In May: Cic. *Att.* 15. 3. 2 (22 May); App. *BC* 3. 28. 105 f.; Plut. *Ant.* 16. 5; in July: Dio 45. 6. 5; App. *BC* 3. 28. 107; below, p. 368.

[5] See the coin quoted above, p. 273. 2; Dio 50. 10. 2 (31 B.C.); 56. 29. 1.

[6] *JRS* 47. 153 (with bibliography).

[7] Dio 53. 30. 6: καὶ οἱ καὶ εἰκόνα χρυσῆν καὶ στέφανον χρυσοῦν δίφρον τε ἀρχικὸν ἔς τε τὸ θέατρον ἐν τῇ τῶν Ῥωμαίων πανηγύρει ἐσφέρεσθαι καὶ ἐς τὸ μέσον τῶν ἀρχόντων τῶν τελούντων αὐτὰ τίθεσθαι ἐκέλευσε.

[8] Tac. *A.* 2. 83. 2; *Tab. Heb.* 50 ff. (E.-J. 94a); *CIL* 6. 31200 c 13; *JRS* 47. 146 ff.

[9] Dio 58. 4. 4: δίφρους τε ἐπιχρύσους ἐς τὰ θέατρα ἀμφοῖν ἐσέφερον . . . καὶ τέλος καὶ ταῖς εἰκόσιν αὐτοῦ ὥσπερ καὶ ταῖς τοῦ Τιβερίου ἔθυον.

arrangements were made under Titus and Domitian (pl. 20. 17–18),[1] perhaps also under the Antonines.[2] Commodus' chair was covered with the lion skin and the club, representing him as the Roman Hercules, whether he was present or not.[3] In A.D. 193 it was decreed that golden chairs should be placed in the theatres in honour of the dead Pertinax.[4] All this evidence rests ultimately on Caesar's precedent; but it is by no means homogeneous and is, as will be seen eventually, not all equally valuable for the interpretation of the Caesarian honour.

The Senate made different arrangements, as always, for the Circus. They are nowhere fully described but must be reconstructed with the help of odd scraps of evidence. Dio mentions a carriage,[5] Cicero a *pulvinar*,[6] Suetonius a *tensa* and *ferculum*.[7] These terms belong to the ritual of a *lectisternium*, which is sufficiently known and is to be described first.[8] Couches, *pulvinaria*, at which offerings were made were set up at the temples for certain functions such as supplications. These couches were at first primitive wooden structures, later permanent and more artistic. The expression 'ad omnia pulvinaria' suggests that most of the temples possessed them: Iuppiter's is mentioned once,[9] and so is Sol's on the Quirinal, which was decorated with a relief representing Helios on his chariot in the company of Phosphorus and Hesperus.[10] The symbols of the gods were placed on the couches at the festivals in question, originally just branches formed into some sort of wreath and held together by ribbons, later busts of the gods.[11] Such *lectisternia* were also held in the Circus, where the images and symbols were taken and placed on another set of *pulvinaria*; these were again probably improvised until they were replaced by a permanent construction, the Pulvinar.[12] This procession

---

[1] Mattingly 2. 233 f.; 298 f.; 302; Alföldi, *Röm. Mitt.* 50. 137, figs. 4; 6; L. R. Taylor, *CP* 30 (1935), 130.   [2] Mattingly 4. 64; 491; 654; cf. Dio 71. 31. 2.

[3] Dio 72. 17. 4.   [4] Dio 74. 4. 1.

[5] Dio 44. 6. 3: κἂν ταῖς ἱπποδρομίαις ὄχον ἐσάγεσθαι ἐψηφίσαντο.

[6] Cic. *Phil.* 2. 110: 'quem is honorem maiorem consecutus erat, quam ut haberet pulvinar, simulacrum . . . ?'   [7] Suet. *Caes.* 76. 1: 'tensam et ferculum circensi pompa.'

[8] Wissowa, *RE* 12. 1108 ff.; A. K. Lake (Michels), *Quantulacumque, Studies pres. to K. Lake* (1937), 244 ff.; Hug, *RE* 23. 1977 f.; Latte 242 ff.

[9] Dio 59. 9. 3: Μαχάων τις δοῦλος ἐπί τε τὴν κλίνην τοῦ Διὸς τοῦ Καπιτωλίου ἐπανέβη; cf. Wissowa, *RE* 12. 1110.   [10] Quintil. 1. 7. 12; cf. *RE* 8A. 1714 f.

[11] Paul. 346 M. (473 L.): 'struppi vocabantur in pulvinaribus fasciculi de verbenis facti, qui pro deorum capitibus ponebantur'; 64 M. (56 L.): 'capita deorum appellabantur fasciculi facti ex verbenis'; Fest. 313 M. (410 L.); Livy 40. 59. 7 (179 B.C.): 'deorum capita, quae in lectis erant, averterunt se'; Obs. 7 (179 B.C.): 'in lectisternio Iovis terrae motu deorum capita se converterunt'; Latte 244. 1; Herter, l.c. 562.

[12] It was rebuilt by Augustus, *Mon. Anc.* 19. 1: '. . . Pulvinar ad Circum Maximum . . . feci'; Suet. *Aug.* 45. 1: 'ipse circenses ex amicorum fere libertorumque cenaculis spectabat, interdum ex Pulvinari'; *ILS* 7496: '. . . pomarius de Circo Maximo ante Pulvinar'; 7287; Suet. *Claud.* 4. 3. The seats of the imperial family were apparently attached to this construction; cf. Weber, *Princeps* 217* ff.

of the images and symbols, the *exuviae*, was the *pompa circensis*[1] which had become, under Greek influence, a splendid spectacle. At the festival of Zeus Sosipolis at Magnesia, for instance, the images of the twelve gods wore beautiful dresses and were taken to specially decorated couches at the altar of the Twelve Gods.[2]

Caesar had his place in this procession in 45 already when his ivory statue was carried on a hand-barrow, *ferculum*, following the precedent of Scipio.[3] It was first carried in April at the Parilia in the company of Romulus-Quirinus and then in July at the *ludi Victoriae Caesaris* in that of Victoria.[4] But in 44 it was placed for the first time on a special carriage, ὄχος, as Dio calls it;[5] by ὄχος he always means a *tensa*[6] and the *tensa* is in fact mentioned by Suetonius among Caesar's new privileges. It was made of ivory and silver and was drawn by four horses, and selected youths were in charge of it.[7] Its traditional function was to take the symbols, *exuviae*, of the gods at the games to the Pulvinar in the Circus.[8] It was not for all the gods, as only the *tensae* of the Capitoline deities are known from literary evidence and from coins (pl. 21. 2–4);[9] the symbols of the other deities were carried on barrows, *fercula*. It was then the special privilege of the Capitoline triad that was now granted to Caesar. The *tensa* will have contained his ivory statue in triumphal dress and perhaps his golden wreath. In the Circus they were exhibited at the *pulvinar* of the Capitoline deities. The images of the other deities too were exhibited, but apparently not at the same place. This privilege gains in significance, if it is assumed that it was decreed at the same time that a special day in honour of Caesar should be added to the four days of the *ludi Romani*, 19 September. The four days were in honour of

[1] Mommsen, *Röm. Forsch.* 2. 45 f.; Wissowa, *Religion* 127; 452.

[2] *Syll.* 589. 41 ff.; Wissowa, *RE* 12. 1113; Eitrem, *Symb. Osl.* 10. 193. 36; cf. also the festival in honour of the imperial family at Gytheum, E.–J. 102.

[3] Livy 38. 56. 13; above, p. 36. 2.   [4] See above, pp. 111; 185.

[5] Dio 44. 6. 3 (above, p. 284. 5).

[6] This was observed by Mommsen, *Röm. Forsch.* 2. 505. 17 (the ἅρμα, however, in Dio 43. 45. 2 must be, again, this *tensa* and has nothing to do with the chariot set up on the Capitol in 46, Dio 43. 14. 6 (above, pp. 54 ff.): see above, pp. 41. 6; 185).

[7] Val. Max. 1. 1. 16; Cic. *Verr.* 2. 1. 154 (and Ps.-Ascon., p. 255 St.); 5. 186; *har. resp.* 23; Plut. *Coriol.* 25. 6; see also the following note.

[8] Fest. 364 M. (500 L.): 'tensam ait vocari Sinnius Capito vehiculum, quo exuviae deorum ludicris circensibus in Circum ad Pulvinar vehuntur. fuit et ex ebore, ut apud Titinium in Barbato, et ex argento'; Serv. *Aen.* 1. 17: 'thensam . . ., qua deorum simulacra portantur'; C. Koch, *RE* 5A. 533 (with full evidence and bibliography); A. L. Abaecherli, *Boll. Assoc. Intern. Studi Medit.* 6 (1935/6), 7 ff.; *tensa* of the Capitoline triad on a relief: A. Sorrentino, *BC* 38 (1910), 49; pl. 5.

[9] Coins of L. Rubrius Dossenus, 87/86 B.C., show the *tensae* of Iuppiter, Iuno, and Minerva respectively (Sydenham 109; pl. 21. 705–7), and Dio mentions those of Iuppiter and Minerva (47. 40. 4; 50. 8. 2; 66. 1); *ILS* 6282 (Minerva); Val. Max. 1. 1. 16 (Iuppiter); Suet. *Vesp.* 5. 7 (Iuppiter).

Iuppiter; on this fifth day Caesar would no doubt have received special homage at his *pulvinar* in the Circus.[1]

The golden throne in the theatre with the golden crown on it, and the *tensa* and *pulvinar* with the ivory statue in the Circus differ in appearance but agree in their significance: they were divine honours. No triumphator and no king could have received them. It was said that Scipio was granted the ivory statue: even if he was, it disappeared again; and if it was to initiate a cult of Scipio, this did not last either. Both the empty throne and the ivory statue were to indicate, as divine symbols always did, a spiritual but not a physical presence. The ivory statue was first used in 45 when Caesar was still in Spain. Similarly these startling divine honours only make sense if they were planned for Caesar's absence in Parthia: he was not to see them. While he was fighting in the East, his rule in Rome was to be strengthened by religious means; his divinity was to be established gradually.

[1] Cic. *Phil.* 2. 110 (above, p. 265. 6). In the Caesarian Colonia Genetiva Iulia a fourth day of games in honour of Venus was added to the three of Iuppiter, Iuno, and Minerva, *ILS* 6087, § 71.

XIV

IUPPITER IULIUS

THE last move was to build temples and altars for Caesar and to create a priest. Appian mentions many temples, among them a temple common to Caesar and his Clementia, in which they were to be represented in the act of clasping hands.[1] Plutarch mentions only the temple of Clementia.[2] The most important information comes from Dio: the Senate called Caesar Iuppiter Iulius, decreed a temple to be built for him and his Clementia, and appointed Antony as their priest like some *flamen Dialis*.[3] It will be seen that Dio conflated two pieces of evidence into one: one was concerned with the temple of the Clementia Caesaris, the other with him alone as Iuppiter Iulius and with his own priest, comparable to the *flamen Dialis*. Of these three items the first about Iuppiter Iulius is not found anywhere else, but is strongly supported by the relevant evidence about Caligula;[4] the second about Antony as his *flamen* is confirmed by Cicero,[5] a contemporary source; the third about the analogy of the *flamen Dialis* has now become clear in its full significance through the discovery of the Tabula Hebana. The first is the crucial point: it raises the question of divine honours in general and of the meaning of the identification with Iuppiter in particular.[6]

I. HEROES AND GODS

It was an old Greek belief that great achievements on earth deserved divine honours, and that is why the mythical heroes, Heracles, the

---

[1] App. *BC* 2. 106. 443 (below, p. 308. 7).   [2] Plut. *Caes.* 57. 4 (below, p. 308. 9).
[3] Dio 44. 6. 4 (below, p. 305. 10; cf. [Sen.] *Oct.* 500 f. (above, p. 188. 8).
[4] Caligula was called Iuppiter (Dio 59. 26. 5; 8; 28. 8; 30. 1a); Optimus Maximus (Suet. *Cal.* 22. 1; cf. Cic. *rep.* 1. 50; 3. 23; R. Frei-Stolba, *Mus. Helv.* 26 (1969), 28); Iuppiter Latiaris (Suet. *Cal.* 22. 2; Dio 59. 28. 3); Olympius (Suet. ibid.; Dio 59. 28. 3); cf. Philo *leg. ad Gai.* 43. 346 (Zeus Epiphanes Neos Gaios in Jerusalem); 29. 188; Jos. *AJ* 19. 1. 4; 19. 2. 11; Eitrem, *Symb. Osl.* 10 (1932), 54 f.
[5] Cic. *Phil.* 2. 110 (below, p. 306. 1).
[6] This is, not surprisingly, the most controversial piece of evidence concerning Caesar's divine honours, see, e.g., Meyer, *Caesars Monarchie* 513 ff.; L. R. Taylor 68 f.; Adcock, *CAH* 9. 719; Strack, *Probleme d. august. Erneuerung* 25 ff. (*contra*, W. Steidle, *Sueton u. die ant. Biographie* (1951), 60 ff.); Vogt, *Studies pres. to D. M. Robinson* 2. 1138 ff. L. R. Taylor 68 ff. suggests that there was not to be a Iuppiter Iulius but only a Divus Iulius: the error was committed by Dio (accepted by Carcopino, *Les étapes de l'impérialisme romain* 147; Vogt, l.c. 1145). Dio's evidence is accepted by Steidle, op. cit. 62; Lambrechts, *Ant. Class.* 23 (1954), 130 f.; Taeger, *Charisma* 2. 70 f.

Dioscuri, Dionysus, became gods after their death.[1] But their divine
features could already be recognized while they were on earth. Homer
said that Hector was like a god among men[2] and others followed,[3] even
Aristotle.[4] This was more often than not a hyperbolical expression without any consequence. But there were exceptions. Lysander was the
first to receive divine honours, after his victory at Aegospotami in 405
B.C.[5] Isocrates said that the conquest of Persia would be the achievement of demigods[6] and that Philip would become a god if he succeeded.[7]
There was a great deal of exaggeration, *Graeca adulatio*,[8] and there was
criticism.[9] At the beginning of the fourth century B.C. King Agesilaus
of Sparta was said to have doubted that the Thasians could make him
a god as they could not become gods themselves;[10] and in Comedy
reference was made to the mortality of the 'humani Ioves' who then
could no longer support the cause of their protégés.[11] The theme was
taken up by the philosophers. The Stoics, like Aristotle, accepted the old
lore about the apotheosis of the heroes, the Epicureans did not.[12] But
the cult of the heroes was a fact, and their case became even stronger
when the Hellenistic kings joined their company.

Alexander and his successors received cults, temples, and altars during
their lifetime and after their death from the State as well as in many
cities.[13] The Roman generals followed. Marcellus had an old cult at

---

[1] Aristot. *EN* 7. 1. 2 (1145a23): ἐξ ἀνθρώπων γίνονται θεοὶ δι' ἀρετῆς ὑπερβολήν; Isocr.
Phil. 132 (Heracles): ὃν ὁ γεννήσας διὰ τὴν ἀρετὴν εἰς θεοὺς ἀνήγαγε; Cic. *leg.* 2. 19; *Tusc.*
1. 28; *ND* 2. 62 (with Pease's notes); Nilsson 2. 145 ff.; Charlesworth, *HTR* 28 (1935),
8 ff.; Nock, *HTR* 37 (1944), 141 ff.; Habicht 17 ff.; 140 ff.

[2] Hom. *Il.* 24. 258 (Priam speaks): Ἕκτορά θ' ὃς θεὸς ἔσκε μετ' ἀνδράσιν, οὐδὲ ἐῴκει / ἀνδρός
γε θνητοῦ παῖς ἔμμεναι, ἀλλὰ θεοῖο.

[3] Theogn. 339: χοὕτως ἂν δοκέοιμι μετ' ἀνθρώπων θεὸς εἶναι; Antiphan. 209. 5 K.; Ter.
Ad. 535: 'facio te apud illum deum' (with praise).

[4] Arist. *Pol.* 3. 8. 1 (1284a3): εἰ δέ τίς ἐστιν εἰς τοσοῦτον διαφέρων κατ' ἀρετῆς ὑπερβολήν . . .
ὥσπερ γὰρ θεὸν ἐν ἀνθρώποις εἰκὸς εἶναι τὸν τοιοῦτον; *EN* 7. 1. 3 (1145a27): ἐπεὶ δὲ σπάνιον
καὶ τὸ θεῖον ἄνδρα εἶναι, καθάπερ οἱ Λάκωνες εἰώθασι προσαγορεύειν, οἳ ὅταν ἀγασθῶσι σφόδρα
του, σεῖος ἀνήρ φασιν.

[5] Plut. *Lys.* 18. 5; above, pp. 265 f.; Brasidas was so honoured after his death, Thuc. 5.
11; Charlesworth, l.c. 11 f.

[6] Isocr. *Phil.* 137: δόξαντας ἡμιθέους εἶναι διὰ τὴν στρατείαν τὴν ἐπ' ἐκείνους; cf. 145: ἰσόθεον
. . . δόξαν; Balsdon, *Hist.* 1 (1950), 366.

[7] Isocr. *ep.* 3. 5: οὐδὲν γὰρ ἔσται λοιπὸν ἔτι πλὴν θεὸν γενέσθαι; Taeger, *Herm.* 72 (1937),
356.   [8] Tac. *A.* 6. 18; Curt. 8. 5. 7 f.

[9] Pind. *Isthm.* 5. 14; *Ol.* 5. 56; below, p. 301. 8; cf. also the punishment of Salmoneus,
below, p. 301. 4.

[10] Plut. *Apophth. Lac. Ages.* 25; Charlesworth, l.c. 12; Habicht 179 ff. (against accepting the
evidence); 213 ff. (criticism of further alleged instances).   [11] Plaut. *Cas.* 333 ff.

[12] Cf. e.g. Cic. *ND* 1. 38: 'Persaeus, . . . Zenonis auditor, eos esse habitos deos a quibus
aliqua magna utilitas ad vitae cultum esset inventa . . . (Epicurean reply) quo quid absurdius
quam . . . homines iam morte deletos reponere in deos, quorum omnis cultus esset futurus in
luctu.'

[13] Bickerman, *Institutions des Séleucides* 236 ff.; Habicht, op. cit. 17 ff.; 140 ff.; Nilsson 2. 145 ff.

Syracuse,[1] T. Flamininus at Chalcis, Corinth, Argos, and Gytheum,[2] M'. Aquillius, pro-consul of 128, at Pergamum,[3] Q. Mucius Scaevola, pro-consul of 97, in the province of Asia.[4] Divine honours, including temples, were decreed for Cicero in Asia twice, in 60 and 50, but he refused to have them.[5]

It is not necessary to go into further detail—this is a vast subject— because only one or two points are relevant here. The festivals in honour of rulers and generals were inspired by the processions of the gods and had become more and more frequent after the fabulous Indian 'triumph' of Alexander.[6] The arrival (παρουσία or ἐπιφάνεια or ἐπιδημία)[7] of a king or of a victorious general at home and abroad was often treated like the epiphany of a god. Demetrius Poliorcetes was given a cult at Athens on the spot where he descended from his chariot on his arrival in 304 B.C. He was called, like a god, 'Kataibates' and received an altar and sacrifices.[8] Mithridates of Pontus was acclaimed a god and Soter after his victory over the Romans in 88, and the inhabitants of the cities went out to meet him—a frequent honour called an ἀπάντησις.[9] In the West Ti. Sempronius Gracchus (cos. 215) was so received by the inhabitants of Beneventum after his victory over the Carthaginians in 214, and meals were offered to his soldiers in front of the houses.[10] Cn. Domitius Ahenobarbus (cos. 122), after his victory over the Allobroges

---

[1] Cic. Verr. 2. 51: 'Syracusis Marcellia . . . quem illi diem festum cum recentibus beneficiis C. Marcelli debitum reddebant.'

[2] Plut. Flamin. 16. 7; E.-J. 102. 11; Hirschfeld, Kl. Schr. 475; Nilsson 2. 178; Latte 312; Daux, BCH 88 (1964), 575; Bousquet, ibid. 607 f.

[3] IGR 4. 293. 24; Magie, Roman Rule in Asia Minor 158.

[4] Dittenberger–Purgold, Inschr. v. Olympia 327 (mentioning the games, the Μουκίεια).

[5] Cic. Q.fr. 1. 1. 26 (60 B.C.): 'cum ad templum monumentumque nostrum civitates pecunias decrevissent . . ., id . . . accipiendum non putavi'; Att. 5. 21. 7 (above, p. 55. 5).

[6] Diod. 17. 106; Curt. 9. 10. 24 ff.; Plut. Alex. 67.

[7] Cf. Deissmann, Licht vom Osten⁴ 314 ff.; Dibelius, An die Thessalonicher³ 15 (on 1. 2. 20); Pfister, RE Suppl. 4. 277 ff.; W. Bauer, Wörterb. z. N.T., s.v. παρουσία; Alföldi, Röm. Mitt. 49 (1954), 88 f.; E. Pax, Epiphaneia, 1955 (Nock, Gnom. 29 (1957), 229 f.) and RAC 5. 832 ff. (with bibliography); L. Robert, Essays in Honor of C. B. Welles (1966), 186.

[8] Plut. Dem. 10. 5; de Alex. fort. 2. 5. 338 a; Clem. Alex. Protr. 4. 54. 6; K. Scott, AJP 49 (1928), 164 f.; Nilsson 2. 184; Habicht 48 ff.; L. Robert, REA 65 (1963), 314 f. In origin the sacrifice was in honour of a god, Καταιβάτης, Ἐπι- or Ἀποβατήριος (Jessen, RE 6. 28; Adler, RE 10. 2461 f.). Alexander set up altars to Zeus Apobaterios when crossing from Europe to Asia, Arr. Anab. 1. 11. 7. See also p. 296 f.

[9] Diod. 37. 26; Posid., FGrHist. 87 F 36 (p. 246. 4 ff.); cf. Athenion's reception at Athens, 88 B.C., with sacrifice ἐπὶ τῇ Ἀθηνιῶνος παρουσίᾳ (Posid., FGrHist. 87 F 36, pp. 244 f.; 245. 8). On ἀπάντησις see Wilcken, Chrest. 1. 2, no. 1, col. 2. 22 ff. (FGrHist. 160); Or. gr. 382. 33 ff.; Polyb. 16. 25. 5 ff., etc.; E. Peterson, Zeitschr. f. syst. Theol. 7 (1930), 683 ff. (I owe the reference to this article with its valuable collection of the evidence to Prof. E. Dinkler); above, pp. 62. 3; 71. 5; below, pp. 290. 2; 299. 12; 300. 6.

[10] Livy 24. 16. 14 ff.; above, p. 135 f; cf. the meals at the triumph of Cincinnatus in 458 (Livy 3. 29. 5) and at the lectisternia of 399 (Livy 5. 13. 7); see also below, pp. 77 f.

and Arverni in 121, rode through Gallia Narbonensis on the back of
an elephant, accompanied by his soldiers in a kind of triumphal procession.[1] When Pompey was entrusted with the command against the
pirates in 67 he succeeded in avoiding a tumultuous reception at Rome;[2]
at Athens he was received soon afterwards with divine honours.[3] When
in the summer of 50 he was taken ill at Naples, vows were made for his
recovery at Naples and Puteoli, and were celebrated accordingly.[4]
After his recovery and on his way back to Rome, he was met by the
inhabitants of the cities, who wore wreaths, carried torches, accompanied him in a procession, and so on.[5] The celebration of the Adventus
of the Roman emperors had its roots in this kind of festival in East and
West.[6]

We shall find such cults and ideas at Rome too, and conclude that
they were not in the first place due to Greek influence. But the Greek
influence was strong from an early date. Sulla accepted the plea of the
inhabitants of Oropus that their local hero Amphiaraus was a god,
and granted them privileges accordingly. But the Roman tax-farmers,
who were financially interested in the issue, contested this decision,
declaring in the manner of the Epicureans that those who had been
men could not be immortal. The consuls of 73, their advisers and the
Senate decided against them and confirmed Sulla's verdict.[7] But Cicero,
who was one of those advisers, quoted the view of the tax-farmers later
with approval.[8] Cicero in fact often changed sides. In 63 he declared,
in accordance with the Stoic doctrine, that Romulus had become a
god 'ob virtutem';[9] he applied this doctrine ten years later in his *De
re publica* to statesmen in general[10] and in 46 to Caesar.[11] But after
Caesar's death he returned to the Epicurean argument that a dead man

---

[1] Suet. *Nero* 2. 1. If this story is true, Domitius did it because he wanted to represent the
victorious hero in accordance with a certain Greek symbolism (which was later very influential at Rome), and not because the elephants had a share in the battle and victory
(Flor. 1. 37. 5; Oros. 5. 13. 2); see also above, pp. 77 f.

[2] Plut. *Pomp.* 26. 1. But after his quick successes in the West people went out to meet him
(27. 2).

[3] Plut. *Pomp.* 27. 3.   [4] Cic. *Tusc.* 1. 86; Dio 41. 6. 3; above, p. 219. 4.

[5] Plut. *Pomp.* 57. 1; Meyer, *Caesars Monarchie* 268; Miltner, *RE* 21. 2173; cf. Cicero's
exaggerated account of his own return from exile in a continuous 'triumphal' procession
from Brundisium to Rome, Cic. *Pis.* 51 f.; *dom.* 75.

[6] See above, p. 289. 7; Kantorowicz, *Selected Studies* (1965), 43 ff.; T. Hölscher, *Victoria
Romana* (1967), 50 ff.; G. Koeppel, 'Profectio u. Adventus', *BJ* 169 (1969), 130–94.

[7] *Syll.* 747; Mommsen, *Ges. Schr.* 5. 495 ff.

[8] Cic. *ND* 3. 49: 'nostri quidem publicani, cum essent agri in Boeotia deorum inmortalium excepti lege censoria, negabant immortales esse ullos, qui aliquando homines fuis-
sent'; above, p. 288. 12.   [9] Cic. *Cat.* 3. 2 (above, p. 180. 1).

[10] Cic. *rep.* 1. 12; 64; 2. 17; 6. 13 (above, p. 180. 3).

[11] Cic. *Marc.* 8; 26 ff.; *Lig.* 38 (above, p. 239. 2).

cannot be a god.[1] We have seen that he refused to accept divine honours in Asia;[2] but in 45 he wanted to build a shrine for his daughter Tullia, who had just died, to achieve her apotheosis.[3]

One must also consider an old and genuine Roman tradition. It began with the cult of the dead.[4] Cicero's 'law' requiring divine honours for the dead[5] was in accordance with an old custom. Sons performed rites at the grave of their father as they did at the temples of the gods; and they called the deceased a god at the cremation at the moment when they found the first bone.[6] The *Divi parentum* had their collective festival annually at the Parentalia,[7] the individual dead on the anniversary of their birth.[8] The collective cult was naturally the lasting one (pl. 21. 7). The *Di Manes* were all the dead of the community, and it was only towards the end of the Republic that dedications were made to the *Di Manes* of a single person,[9] which was illogical but unavoidable, because the singular 'Deus Manes' did not exist.[10]

The *Divi parentum* and the *Di Manes* represented one aspect of the divine nature of the past members of the family: as dead they were given what was due to the dead. Another aspect of it was represented

[1] Cic. *Phil.* 1. 13: 'an me censetis ... decreturum fuisse, ut parentalia cum supplicationibus miscerentur ... ut decernerentur supplicationes mortuo? ... adduci tamen non possem, ut quemquam mortuum coniungerem cum deorum immortalium religione, ut cuius sepulchrum usquam extet ubi parentetur, ei publice supplicetur'; cf. Pliny 7. 188: 'et Manes colendo deumque faciendo qui iam etiam homo esse desierit.'

[2] See above, pp. 55; 289.

[3] Cic. *Att.* 12. 36. 1: 'fanum fieri volo ... sepulchri similitudinem effugere ... studeo, quam ut maxime adsequar ἀποθέωσιν'; 12. 1; 37. 2; 37a; 18. 1; 41. 4; 43. 3; *Consol.* frg. 11 M. (Lact. 1. 15. 16); *RE* 8A. 924; Charlesworth, *HTR* 28 (1935), 23; Boyancé, *REA* 46 (1944), 179; Shackleton Bailey, *Cicero's Letters* 5. 404 ff.

[4] See for the following F. Bömer, *Ahnenkult u. Ahnenglaube im alten Rom*, 1943 (with bibliography); Wagenvoort, *Studies* 290 ff.

[5] Cic. *leg.* 2. 22: 'Deorum Manium iura sancta sunto. ⟨bo⟩nos (?) leto datos divos habento'; Catull. 64. 404: 'inpia non veritast divos scelerare parentes'; *ILS* 1078: 'Dis genitoribus...'; Bömer, op. cit. 1 ff.; 6 f.; 26 f.

[6] Plut. *QR* 14: ἐπὶ τῶν τάφων, ὥς φησι Βάρρων (*Ant. rer. div.* 15, frg. 9b Ag.), περιστρέφονται καθάπερ θεῶν ἱερὰ τιμῶντες τὰ τῶν πατέρων μνήματα. καὶ καύσαντες τοὺς γονεῖς, ὅταν ὀστέῳ πρῶτον ἐντύχωσι, θεὸν γεγονέναι τὸν τεθνηκότα λέγουσι; Aug. *CD* 8. 26: 'Varro dicit (ibid., frg. 9a) omnes ... mortuos (existimari) Manes deos et probat per ea sacra, quae omnibus fere mortuis exhibentur, ubi et ludos commemorat funebres, tamquam hoc sit maximum divinitatis indicium, quod non soleant ludi nisi numinibus celebrari.'

[7] Wissowa 232 ff.; Latte 98.

[8] *RE* 8A. 923 f.; W. Schmidt, *Geburtstag im Altertum* 44; Bömer, op. cit. 31 f.

[9] *ILS* 880; 8393. 79 (*laud. Turiae*, cf. Durry's note); Wissowa 239; Bömer, op. cit. 52; Latte 99. 4. There is probably an even earlier reference to such individual Manes in Cic. *Pis.* 16 (suggested by Nisbet ad loc.).

[10] *Gramm. Lat.* 5. 195. 38: 'numero singulari nemo dicit hic manis aut hic manes'; Apul. *de deo Socr.* 15 (p. 153); Latte 99. 3 (*contra*, *JRS* 51 (1961), 212). The plural is also used on an inscription of Antiochus I of Commagene, l. 154: πατρός τε δαίμοσι and 8: περὶ πατρῴων δαιμόνων (F. K. Dörner, *Arsameia am Nymphaios* (1963), 42; 50; 74; H. Dörrie, *Der Königskult des Antiochos v. Kommagene* (1964), 177 f.); Lucian. *Peregr.* 36: δαίμονες μητρῷοι καὶ πατρῷοι.

by the ancestral cult. The *Lares* were all the ancestors together,[1] and the single *Lar familiaris*[2] may have been in origin the founder of the family. The founders of the community were treated accordingly. Lar Aeneas was the ancestor of all Aeneadae and had a cult near Lavinium; as god he was also called Aeneas Indiges, or Iuppiter Indiges, or Indiges pater.[3] Romulus as founder of Rome received a cult as soon as the legend was universally accepted, and was identified with Quirinus, one of the three principal gods of Rome.[4] This cult will have existed long before it was justified in the Greek manner as a reward for achievements on earth.[5] We have seen that Iulus, the founder of the Gens Iulia, was worshipped by his descendants and identified with Vediovis.[6] Other families will have had similar cults together with, or in addition to, the cult of their *Lar familiaris*[7] or special *Lares*.[8]

Divine honours for the living followed, due more to Greek influence than to the Roman past. In Plautus a parasite calls his patron 'Iuppiter terrestris', a 'saviour' asserts that he is Iuppiter, and another demands that he should receive an altar and sacrifice as a god.[9] This was not just loose talk: Lucretius called Epicurus a god,[10] and likewise Cicero

[1] Paul. 121 M. (108 L.): 'Lares... animae putabantur esse hominum redactae in numerum deorum'; Arnob. 3. 41: 'Varro (*Ant. rer. div.* 15, frg. 8 Ag.) ... (Lares) heroas pronuntiat appellari... et functorum animas'; *JRS* 50 (1960), 116 (with bibliography).

[2] Cato *agr.* 143. 2; Plaut. *Aulul.* 384 ff. The *Lar familiaris* could be replaced by *noster Lar* (Plaut. *Aulul.* 385; *Tri.* 39) and by *familiai Lar pater* (Plaut. *Merc.* 834).

[3] See above, p. 10; Anchises, like Aeneas, was already honoured in the Greek world. His tomb was located in many places (Wörner, *Myth. Lex.* 1. 339; Pfister, *Reliquienkult* 158. 582) and he had a common cult with Aphrodite in Arcadia and on Mount Eryx in Sicily (Paus. 8. 12. 8 f.; Verg. *Aen.* 5. 759 ff.; annual sacrifice at his tomb on Mount Ida: Eustath. *Il.* 12. 98). But it was in the Roman sense that his son Aeneas treated him as a god (Verg. *Aen.* 5. 47: 'divinique ossa parentis'), offered him libations (Verg. *Aen.* 7. 133: 'nunc pateras libate Iovi precibusque vocate / Anchisen genitorem et vina reponite mensis') and built him, Pater Indiges, a *heroon* at the river Numicus (Dion. Hal. 1. 64. 5, generally attributed to Aeneas Indiges: above, p. 10. 6); cf. Bömer, *Ahnenkult u. Ahnenglaube* 13 ff.; 60 f.

[4] See above, pp. 176 f.   [5] See above, pp. 179 f.   [6] See above, p. 10.

[7] For a different view see Latte 98: '(Divi parentum) nirgends finden wir eine Spur, dass etwa der Archeget der Familie aus ihnen herausgehoben wäre und als solcher besondere Ehren genösse. Wo wir von einem Sonderkult eines einzelnen Geschlechts in Rom hören, gilt er auch sonst bekannten Göttern und nicht einem mythischen Ahnherrn des Geschlechts.'

[8] Cf., e.g., the Lares Hostilii of the old Gens Hostilia, Paul. 102 M. (90 L.); W. F. Otto, *Arch. Lat. Lex.* 15 (1906), 120; Wissowa 169. 8; above, p. 11. 8.

[9] Plaut. *Pers.* 99: 'o mi Iuppiter terrestris' ([Eur.] *Rhes.* 355: σύ μοι Ζεὺς ὁ φαναῖος); *Asin.* 712: 'si quidem mihi statuam et aram statuis / atque ut deo mi hic immolas bovem: nam ego tibi Salus sum'; *Pseud.* 326: 'accerse hostias, / victumas, lanios, ut ego huic sacruficem summo Iovi; / nam hic mihi nunc est multo potior Iuppiter quam Iuppiter', etc. (cf. 265 ff.); *Capt.* 863: 'ego nunc tibi sum summus Iuppiter, / idem ego sum Salus, Fortuna, Lux, Laetitia, Gaudium'; *Cas.* 331 ff. (criticism of 'humani Ioves' who may die at any time); 406; Fraenkel, *Plautinisches im Plautus* 97; 115; cf. Caecilius Stat. Com. 265 R.: 'homo homini deus est, si suum officium sciat'; 36 R.: 'nam nobis equidem deus repertus est Iovis'; above, pp. 167 f.

[10] Lucr. 5. 8: 'deus ille fuit, deus.'

Lentulus, who had helped him to return from exile.[1] It was a passing mood for Cicero but not for Lucretius. And yet even here the background was essentially Roman. There was the old bond between the saviour and benefactor and his protégé, the patron and his client, the *pater familias* and his household, which was governed by a sense of *pietas* like that between father and son.[2] If it came to worship, this was granted to the Genius of the person and not to the person himself.[3] There are, however, a few cases where the Romans went beyond this limit, and it is difficult to decide whether they did it independently or under Greek influence. It was a reward of statesmen for their great achievements, and the cult, private or public, was created during their lifetime or after their death.

The earliest is the god Minucius, with an altar or shrine or both, who gave his name to the *Minucia porta* of unknown location.[4] It has been assumed that he was the god of the Gens Minucia,[5] to be compared with the goddess Ancharia of the Ancharii, Venilia of the Venilii, perhaps Egeria of the Egerii, and the like.[6] This is clearly a serious possibility even though one would expect a goddess, not a god. Another assumption, however, is not—namely, that this god was no other than Hercules[7] or Triptolemos.[8] But it is more probable that he was a person of history, L. Minucius Augurinus (*cos.* 458), who as the *praefectus annonae* of 439 was honoured with a statue mounted on a column at the Porta Trigemina because he provided the people with cheap grain.[9] His fame

---

[1] Cic. *p. red. sen.* 8: 'parens ac deus nostrae vitae, fortunae, memoriae, nominis'; *p. red. Quir.* 11; 18; 25; *Sest.* 144; Nock, *JHS* 48 (1928), 31. 51; Alföldi, *Mus. Helv.* 11 (1954), 146 ff.; above, p. 256.   [2] See above, pp. 256 ff.   [3] See above, pp. 214 ff.

[4] Paul. 122 M. (109 L.): 'Minucia porta Romae est dicta ab ara Minuci, quem deum putabant'; 147 M. (131 L.): 'Minucia porta appellata est eo, quod proxima esset sacello Minucii.'

[5] Otto, *Rhein. Mus.* 64 (1909), 449; Wissowa, 245. 4; Marbach, *RE* 15. 1939.

[6] Otto, l.c. 449 ff.; Wissowa 33. 3; Latte 58.

[7] Pais, *Storia critica di Roma* 2. 194 ff.; accepted by Bayet, *Les origines de l'Hercule romain* 289 f.; *contra*, Wissowa 245. 4; Welin, (see n. 9) 167 (who assumes that the column was a funeral monument); cf. also Gagé, *Mél.* 78 (1966), 79 ff. (not convincing).

[8] H. Lyngby, *Eran.* 59 (1961), 148 ff.; 61 (1963), 55 ff.; *Opuscula Romana* 6 (1968), 93 f. (Triptolemos no longer mentioned).

[9] Pliny 18. 15: 'qua de causa statua ei extra portam Trigeminam a populo stipe conlata statuta est'; 34. 21: (columna) 'item L. Minucio praefecto annonae extra portam Trigeminam unciaria stipe conlata'; Dion. Hal 12. 4. 6: Μηνυκίῳ στάσιν ἀνδριάντος ἐψηφίσατο ἡ βουλή; Livy 4. 16. 2: 'L. Minucius bove aurato extra portam Trigeminam est donatus' ('wrong': Mommsen, *Röm. Forsch.* 2. 203. 109; Ogilvie ad loc.; accepted by Gagé, l.c. 113); cf. Münzer, *RE* 15. 1953 f.; Momigliano, *Stud. Hist. Doc. Iur.* 2 (1936), 374 ff. (= *Quarto Contributo* 331 ff.); Vessberg, *Stud. z. Kunstgesch. d. röm. Rep.* 19 f.; Welin, *Stud. z. Topographie d. Forum Romanum* 156 ff. (Romanelli, *Gnom.* 26 (1954), 263); Lyngby, l.c. 136 ff.; Becatti, *La Colonna Coclida* 34 ff. The *portae Minucia* and *Trigemina* were therefore either identical or close together, see Platner–Ashby 133; 409 f.; 418; Lyngby, *Opuscula Romana* 6 (1968), 75 ff. (with report on excavations at the Porta Trigemina).

was kept alive in the family. The moneyers C. and Ti. Minucius Augurinus reproduced the column with his statue on their coins *c.* 135 (pl. 21. 5–6).[1] It was also said that two early ancestors, P. and M. Minucius, the consuls of 492 and 491, had already relieved a famine in Rome;[2] and later the Porticus Minucia, built by M. Minucius Rufus (*cos.* 110), served as the seat of the distribution of grain.[3] Minucius' reward was not exceptional, even if the statue on the column cannot have been of an early date:[4] for the same service statues were set up for M. Seius, aedile of 74, on the Capitol and the Palatine,[5] though it is not recorded that divine honours were attached to them. But we shall see that the statue and altar of Minucius was not an isolated phenomenon: the Gracchi and Marius Gratidianus also received statues and offerings for a while,[6] Caesar even a column and altar in the Forum after his death.[7]

There is good evidence to suggest that the elder Scipio too had a cult.[8] In Ennius he himself predicts his own immortality,[9] and Cicero[10] and Horace[11] mention it as a fact, so that it cannot be ascribed to Ennius' poetical fancy. One is therefore bound to assume the existence of a

---

[1] Sydenham 54; 60; pl. 18. 463; 494; Münzer, *RE* 15. 1945; 1947.

[2] Livy 2. 34. 3; 7; Münzer, *RE* 15. 1945 f.

[3] Vell. 2. 8. 3; Kroll, *RE* 15. 1936 f.; Platner–Ashby 424 f.; Castagnoli, *Il Campo Marzio* (*Mem. Linc.* 8. 1. 4, 1947), 175 ff.; Coarelli, *Bull. Comun.* 80 (1965/7), 46 ff.

[4] Statues on columns were frequent in Greece (Welin, op. cit. 151 ff.); at Rome there was the column of C. Maenius (*cos.* 338) for his victory at Antium (Pliny 34. 20; Livy 8. 13. 9 (?); Platner–Ashby 131 f.; Welin 131 ff.), of C. Duillius (*cos.* 260) (Pliny 34. 20; Platner–Ashby 134), etc. After the victory at Pydna, 168 B.C., L. Aemilius Paullus placed his own statues on columns built by Perseus, Polyb. 30. 10. 2; cf. Mommsen, *StR* 3. 1184 f.; Welin 155 f.; Strack, *Unters. z. röm. Reichsprägung* 1. 137. 542.

[5] Pliny 18. 16: '⟨M.⟩ Seius in aedilitate assibus populo frumentum praestitit, quam ob causam et ei statuae in Capitolio ac Palatio dicatae sunt, ipse supremo die populi umeris portatus in rogum est'; Münzer, *RE* 2A. 1121. This evidence seems to decide the problem of the goddess Seia, allegedly the goddess of the seed (Pliny 18. 8; Aug. *CD* 4. 8 = Varr. *Ant. rer. div.* 14, frg. 70a Ag.; Macrob. 1. 16. 8; accepted by Wissowa 201; Latte 51, also in *RE* 2A. 1112; Le Bonniec, *Le culte de Cérès* 186 ff.): she was probably, as suggested by Otto l.c. 454 f., the goddess of the Gens Seia; cf. Ehlers, *RE* 7A. 1612 f. (Tutilina, goddess of the Tutilii). Seia had a statue mounted on a column in the Circus (Pliny 18. 8; Tert. *spect.* 8).

[6] See below, p. 295.   [7] See below, pp. 365 f.

[8] Cf. Elter, *Donarem pateras* 40. 28 ff.; *contra*, Classen, *Philol.* 106 (1962), 180; cf. above, pp. 19. 4; 36; 185; 286; below, p. 302.

[9] Lact. *div. inst.* 1. 18. 11: 'aput Ennium sic loquitur Africanus (*V.* 23 V.): "si fas endo plagas caelestum ascendere cuiquam est, / mi soli caeli maxima porta patet".'

[10] Lact. ibid. 13: 'est vero, inquit (Cicero), Africane: nam et Herculi eadem ista porta patuit' (= Cic. *rep.* frg. inc. 6 Zgl.). Lactantius seems to allude to this passage of Cicero, not quite correctly, in 1. 9. 1: 'Hercules qui ob virtutem clarissimus et quasi Africanus inter deos habetur.'

[11] Hor. *c.* 4. 8. 14: 'spiritus et vita rédit bonis / post mortem ducibus, non celeres fugae / reiectaeque retrorsum Hannibalis minae / . . . / eius qui domita nomen ab Africa / lucratus rediit.' Even if these verses are spurious (C. Becker, *Herm.* 87 (1959), 212 ff.), the evidence they contain is valuable; cf. also Sil. Ital. 13. 635: 'nec in caelum dubites te attollere factis.'

public cult however short-lived it may have been. But the private cult certainly survived in the family, and that is perhaps why Cornelia, the mother of the Gracchi, also expected to be honoured after her death as a *deus parens*.[1] It is possible that the Claudii Marcelli had a cult of M. Marcellus (*cos.* 166, 155, 152) who died in 148 B.C.;[2] further evidence is lacking. We are better informed about Ti. and C. Gracchus. The place where they died was considered sacred, statues were set up for them everywhere, offerings were made, even daily by some people, and they were treated like gods.[3] This was clearly a spontaneous cult of benefactors; but it did not last long. Marius received libations together with the gods in every house after his victory over the Cimbri at Vercellae in 101 B.C.,[4] something often done before in Greece[5] and later also in Rome;[6] but again it was no more than a passing honour. Marius Gratidianus (*pr.* 85) received statues and libations in all *vici* of Rome because of his suppression of the debased currency.[7] It was the Lares who were worshipped at the *vici*; honouring Marius in the same manner is significant and must rest on an old tradition completely lost to us: the cult of Augustus too was connected with the altars of the Lares at the *vici* in 12 B.C.[8] Cn. Domitius Ahenobarbus (*cos.* 122) held a 'triumph'

---

[1] *Ep. Corneliae*, Nep. frg. 15 (*HRR* 2. p. 39. 20 P.): 'ubi mortua ero, parentabis mihi et invocabis deum parentem.' This is a difficult and much discussed passage (see the bibliography in Bömer, op. cit. 101 ff.). Latte 98. 2 believes that this *deus parens* was a late version of the *Divi parentum*; so also Classen, *Gymn.* 70 (1963), 324. Her statue was set up later in public, which was an exceptional privilege, Pliny 34. 31; Plut. *C. Gracch.* 25 (4). 4; *ILS* 68; Mommsen, *StR* 1. 448. 2.

[2] Cic. *Pis.* 44: 'M. Marcellus ... summa virtute pietate gloria militari periit in mari; qui tamen ob virtutem gloria et laude vivit'; Münzer, *RE* 3. 2758 f. (cf. Plaut. *Capt.* 690: 'qui per virtutem periit, at non interit'). A cult of his grandfather, Prop. 3. 18. 33 ('qua Siculae victor telluris Claudius et qua / Caesar ab humana cessit in astra via').

[3] Plut. *C. Gracch.* 39 (18). 3: εἰκόνας τε γὰρ αὐτῶν ἀναδείξαντες ἐν φανερῷ προυτίθεντο, καὶ τοὺς τόπους ἐν οἷς ἐφονεύθησαν ἀφιερώσαντες ἀπήρχοντο μὲν ὧν ὧραι φέρουσι πάντων, ἔθυον δὲ καὶ καθ' ἡμέραν πολλοὶ καὶ προσέπιπτον ὥσπερ θεῶν ἱεροῖς ἐπιφοιτῶντες; Classen, l.c. 324.

[4] Val. Max. 8. 15. 7: 'nemo fuit, qui non illi tamquam dis immortalibus apud sacra mensae suae libaverit'; Plut. *Mar.* 27. 9: μετὰ παίδων καὶ γυναικῶν ἔκαστοι κατ' οἶκον ἅμα τοῖς θεοῖς καὶ Μαρίῳ δείπνου καὶ λοιβῆς ἀπήρχοντο; Weynand, *RE* Suppl. 6. 1396; Fraenkel, *Horace* 447; Alföldi, *Mus. Helv.* 11 (1954), 155; Classen, l.c. 327 f. Libations to Fabius Maximus by the army of M. Minucius Rufus, 217 B.C. (above, pp. 149 f.), Sil. Ital. 7. 749 f.

[5] Plut. *Dio* 27 ff.; Diod. 16. 10 ff.; 20. 6 (Dio at Syracuse, 357 B.C.); Curt. 5. 1. 20 (Alexander at Babylon); Iustin. 24. 3. 4 (Ptolemaeus Ceraunus at Cassandrea); *P. Oxy.* 27, no. 2465 (Arsinoe at Alexandria); *FGrHist.* 160 § 4 =Wilcken, *Chrest.* no. 1, col. 2. 21 (Ptolemy III Euergetes at Seleucia); Habicht 234; L. Robert, *Essays in Honor of C. B. Welles* (1966), 186 ff.

[6] Libations for Augustus from 30, Dio 51. 19. 7; Hor. *c.* 4. 5. 29 ff.; Fraenkel, op. cit. 447.

[7] Cic. *off.* 3. 80: 'omnibus vicis statuae, ad eas tus, cerei'; Sen. *de ira* 3. 18. 1: 'cui vicatim populus statuas posuerat, cui ture ac vino supplicabat'; Pliny 33. 132; 34. 27; Münzer, *RE* 14. 1827; Alföldi, l.c. 156; Classen, l.c. 326; Latte 313; M. H. Crawford, *Proc. Cambr. Philol. Soc.* N.S. 14 (1968), 1 ff.

[8] See above, p. 215.

in Gaul, T. Albucius (*pr. c.* 105) another in Sardinia, but the latter was reproached for it by the Senate.[1] Q. Caecilius Metellus Pius (*cos.* 80) was received by the Roman citizens of Spain in 74 with unusual honours after he put down an uprising in Lusitania: he wore the *toga picta* of the triumphators, supplications were offered as if he had been a god, banquets and games were held.[2] This was clearly an improvisation, made up of elements of the triumphal celebration and of Greek ritual discussed earlier in connection with the epiphany of a god, king, or general; it was certainly not invented for the occasion. There were some other cases testifying to such popular sentiment where Greek and Roman elements were thus combined.[3]

2. CAESAR

The Greeks treated Caesar as they had treated their kings and other Roman generals before him. He was not a newcomer in the East. We have seen that his family had an early relationship with Ilium and was honoured accordingly;[4] in Delos a statue of his father stood in the temple of Apollo,[5] and he himself had an early statue in the temple of Nike at Tralles.[6] After the victory at Pharsalus his statues were set up everywhere.[7] What matters here is that in some cities, Ephesus, Mytilene, Carthaea in Keos, Demetrias in Thessaly, he was styled a god on the inscriptions.[8] That of Ephesus reveals the full significance of this honour: there the province of Asia called him θεὸς ἐπιφανής.[9] This was an old epithet, given in origin to gods and kings whose power had become 'manifest' to their worshippers.[10] It seems probable that this old-established epithet was not automatically transferred to Caesar but served

---

[1] See above, pp. 77 f.; Cic. *prov. cons.* 15; *Pis.* 92.

[2] Sall. *hist.* 2. 70 M.: 'venienti ture quasi deo supplicabatur. toga picta plerumque amiculo erat accumbenti'; Val. Max. 9. 1. 5: 'in Hispania adventus suos ab hospitibus aris et ture excipi patiebatur'; Münzer, *RE* 3. 1223; L. R. Taylor 56; Schulten, *Sertorius* 128.

[3] Cf., e.g., Jos. *BJ* 7. 73 (Vespasian); *CIL* 13. 1370 (dedicated to the *adventus* of Tiberius in Gaul: Heurgon, *Ant. Class.* 17 (1948), 323 ff.).

[4] *ILS* 8770; *IGR* 4. 195; 197; above, p. 97.   [5] *Inscr. de Délos* 1701.

[6] Caes. *BC* 3. 105. 6; above, p. 17.

[7] Raubitschek, *JRS* 44 (1954), 65 ff.; Magie, op. cit. 405 f.

[8] *Syll.* 760; *IG* 12. 5. 165b; 557 (above, p. 166. 3); 12. 2. 35 (*IGR* 4. 33); L. R. Taylor 267 f.; Magie 1261. 9; Raubitschek, l.c. 66. At Thessalonica he was styled θεός on coins issued after his death (below, p. 404. 2): they may have called him so while he was still alive.

[9] *Syll.* 760: αἱ πόλεις αἱ ἐν τῇ Ἀσίᾳ . . . Γάϊον Ἰούλιον . . . Καίσαρα . . . τὸν ἀπὸ Ἄρεως καὶ Ἀφροδείτης θεὸν ἐπιφανῆ καὶ κοινὸν τοῦ ἀνθρωπίνου βίου σωτῆρα; above, pp. 84; 129; 166; 183; below, p. 403.

[10] Cf. Pfister, *RE* Suppl. 4. 301; 306 ff.; Nock, *JHS* 48 (1928), 40 f.; Larsen, *CP* 51 (1956), 155 f.; above, p. 289.

to indicate that his victorious appearance, ἐπιφάνεια, in the province created a belief in his manifest divinity. His lieutenant Cn. Domitius Calvinus was called a god at Zela,[1] and another, P. Servilius Isauricus, must have received a cult at Ephesus because he still had a priest there in the second century A.D.[2] It is clear that they were so honoured because they represented Caesar; their honours were of no consequence, but those of Caesar remained. Nicaea was the first Greek city to issue coins with Caesar's portrait, under C. Vibius Pansa in 48/7 B.C. (pl. 21. 8);[3] it is relevant to add that it had already issued coins with Roma seated on shields and holding Victoria under C. Papirius Carbo in 61–59 B.C. (pl. 21. 9),[4] and that it was the first city in Bithynia to receive Augustus' permission in 29 to build a provincial shrine of the Dea Roma and Divus Iulius for the use of resident Roman citizens;[5] for the Greeks this cult must have existed earlier.

Caesar did not remain a passive recipient of these honours, but also took the initiative. When he landed at Alexandria in 48 he was received with divine honours as Caesar Epibaterios:[6] we have seen that such honours were offered to a god, e.g. Zeus Kataibates, at his epiphany, but also to Demetrius Kataibates on his arrival at Athens in 304 B.C.[7] At Alexandria Caesar began to build the first Caesareum,[8] which was the new name for a type of basilica[9] and was later used for his cult. Back in Asia he laid the foundations of another Caesareum in 47 at Antioch-on-the-Orontes with statues of the Dea Roma and himself.[10] There were no doubt many other shrines of this kind, and some of the later Augustea may have been built first for Caesar.[11] Greek cities and Roman colonies followed his lead with more modest temples or even altars. His colonies

[1] IGR 3. 108.

[2] Ephesos 3, no. 60 (J. Keil, Österr. Jahresh. 18 (1915), Beibl. 281); Magie 416 f.; 1270 f.; Nilsson 2. 179; Münzer, Adelsp. 356; L. Robert, Hell. 6. 40 ff.

[3] BMC Pontus 153; pl. 31. 13; Curtius, Röm. Mitt. 45 (1932), 231, fig. 15; Vessberg, op. cit. 142; pl. 8. 1; Johansen, Anal. Rom. Inst. Dan. 4 (1967), fig. 1.

[4] BMC Pontus 152; pl. 31. 11; Head, HN 516; cf. 497; above, p. 96.

[5] Dio 51. 20. 6.

[6] Philo leg. ad Gai. 22. 151: τὸ λεγόμενον Σεβαστεῖον, 'Επιβατηρίου Καίσαρος νεώς. Trajan was called Zeus Embaterios at Hermione, IG 4. 701, and there were games, Epibateria, in Hadrian's honour at Erythrae, IGR 4. 1542; Pfister, RE Suppl. 4. 303; Cook, Zeus 2. 1180. 4; Nock, HSCP 41 (1930), 22. 3.

[7] See above, p. 289. 8.

[8] Malal. 217. 12: τὸ Καισάριον ἔκτισεν ὁ αὐτὸς 'Ιούλιος ὁ Καῖσαρ ἐν Ἀλεξανδρίᾳ τῇ μεγάλῃ; Pliny 36. 69: 'et alii duo (obelisks) sunt Alexandreae ad portum in Caesaris templo'; Dio 51. 15. 5; cf. A. Schenk v. Stauffenberg, Die röm. Kaisergesch. b. Malalas 3; 118 f.; Nock, JRS 47 (1957), 119. 36; Th. Hastrup, Anal. Rom. Inst. Dan. 2 (1962), 54 f.

[9] Cf. E. Sjöqvist, Opusc. Rom. 1 (1954), 86 ff.; J. B. Ward Perkins, PBSR 26 (1958), 175 ff.

[10] Malal. 216. 19; 287. 3; Schenk v. Stauffenberg, op. cit. 3; 54; 474 ff.; Sjöqvist, l.c. 92 ff.; G. Downey, AJA 41 (1937), 197; id. A History of Antioch in Syria (1961), 154 f.

[11] For a list of the Caesarea see Ward Perkins, l.c. 177 f.

PLATE 21

1. Aureus of L. Caninius Gallus, 12(?) B.C. (Mattingly 1. 26. 126), London; *obv.*: head of Augustus, legend 'Augustus Divi f.'; *rev.*: a door between two laurel-branches, a wreath above it, legend 'ob c(ivis) s(ervatos), L. Caninius Gallus'; p. 280.

2. Denarius of L. Rubrius Dossenus, c. 87 B.C. (Sydenham 109. 705), Oxford; *obv.*: head of Iuppiter with sceptre, legend 'Dossen.'; *rev.*: tensa decorated with thunderbolt, above, Victoria with wreath, legend 'L. Rubri(us)'; p. 285.

3. Denarius of L. Rubrius Dossenus, c. 87 B.C. (Sydenham 109. 706), Oxford; *obv.*: head of Iuno with sceptre, legend 'Dos.'; *rev.*: tensa decorated with eagle on thunderbolt, above, Victoria, legend L. Rubri(us)'; p. 285.

4. Denarius of L. Rubrius Dossenus, c. 87 B.C. (Sydenham 109. 707), Oxford; *obv.*: bust of helmeted Minerva with aegis, legend 'Dos.'; *rev.*: tensa decorated with eagle on thunderbolt, above, Victoria in biga, legend 'L. Rubri(us)'; p. 285.

5. Denarius of C. Minucius Augurinus, c. 135 B.C. (Sydenham 54. 463), Oxford; *obv.*: helmeted female head, legend 'Roma'; *rev.*: Ionic column surmounted by statue, between corn-ears and two men, one holding a dish, the other a lituus, legend, 'C. Aug.'; p. 294.

6. Denarius of Ti. Minucius Augurinus, c. 134 B.C. (Sydenham 60. 494), Oxford; *obv.*: helmeted female head,; *rev.*: Ionic column surmounted by statue, between corn-ears, and two men, one holding a dish, the other a lituus, legend 'Roma, Ti. Minuci C. f. Augurini'; p. 294.

7. Altar in the Museo Archeologico, Aquileia (photo: Museo) inscribed 'Deum Parentum'; p. 291.

8. Bronze of Nicaea, 48/47 B.C. (*BMC Pontus* 153), London; *obv.*: head of Caesar, legend Νικαιέων; *rev.*: Victoria with wreath and palm, legend ἐπὶ Γαίου Οὐιβίου Πάνσα, γλσ (= 235 = 47 B.C.); p. 297.

9. Bronze of Nicaea, 61–59 B.C. (*BMC Pontus* 152), London; *obv.*: head of Dionysus, legend Νικαιέων; *rev.*: Roma seated on shields with Nike and sceptre, legend ἐπὶ Γαίου Παπιρίου Καρβῶνος, 'Ρώμη; p. 297.

10. Bronze of Parium or Lampsacus, after 44 B.C. (?) (Grant *FITA* 246) Munich; *obv.*: head of Caesar, legend 'C(olonia) G. I(ulia) L(?)'; *rev.*: priest ploughing with oxen, legend 'Q. Lucreti(o) L. Pontio II vir, M. Turio leg.'; p. 299.

11. Bronze of Apamea(?), 27 B.C. (Grant, *FITA* 255), London; *obv.*: head of Augustus, legend 'Augustus Div. f., cos. VII, imp. .... C. Ruf.'; *rev.*: head of Caesar, legend 'Divos Iulius, C. Cassius C. f. II vir C(oloniae) I(uliae) C(oncordiae) f(aciendum) c(uravit)'; p. 299.

12. Bronze of Alexandria, Troas (?), 44 B.C. (?) (Grant, *FITA* 244), Oxford; *obv.*: head of Caesar, legend 'Princeps felix (?)'; *rev.*: Athena holding Nike, legend 'Colonia Iulia, II vir' and two monograms 'Ale(x).' and 'PE' or 'EP'; p. 299.

13. The same, Berlin.

14. Bronze of Sinope, 38 B.C. (Grant, *FITA* 253. 3. 1), Oxford; *obv.*: head of Caesar, legend 'C(olonia) F(elix) I(ulia) ..., an. VIII'; *rev.*: clasped hands with cornucopiae, legend 'ex d(ecreto) d(ecurionum)'; p. 299.

15. Bronze of Corinth, c. 45 B.C. (Grant, *FITA* 266), Vienna(?); *obv.*: head of Caesar, legend 'Caesar'; *rev.*: statue in hexastyle temple, legend '(C)or.'; p. 299.

16. Bronze of Corinth, c. 45? (38?) B.C. (*BMC Corinth* 58), London; *obv.*: head of Caesar, legend 'Laus Iuli(a) Corint(hus)'; *rev.*: Bellerophon mounted on Pegasus, legend '(L.) Certo Aefrico C. Iulio IIvir.'; p. 299.

17. Bronze of Corinth, Tiberian period (*BMC Corinth* 63 f.), Oxford; *obv.*: radiate head of Augustus, legend 'L. Arrio Pere[grino] IIvir(o)'; *rev.*: hexastyle temple inscribed 'Gent(i) Iuli(ae)', legend 'L. Furio Lab[eone IIvir(o)], Cor.'; p. 299.

PLATE 21

1

2

3

4

5

6

7

8

9

10

11

12

13

14

15

16

17

in the Troas, Alexandria, Lampsacus, and Parium, issued coins with his head and had local priests for his cult (pl. 21. 10; 12 f.).[1] Coins with his head were also found at Apamea (Myrlea) and Sinope (pl. 20. 11; 14).[2] Some of this evidence is of post-Caesarian date but put together it strongly suggests a Caesarian origin. This is certain for Corinth, the Colonia Laus Iulia since 46,[3] where probably P. Vatinius (*cos.* 47) was acting on Caesar's behalf.[4] Although it can no longer be maintained that Caesar is called on one coin 'Creator', 'founder',[5] at least one of its coins was issued with his head while he was still alive (pl. 21. 15–16);[6] on the reverse there is a hexastyle temple with a statue which may be his statue in any temple or in his own temple, real or projected. After his consecration in 42 there were dedications to the new god.[7] There was later a hexastyle temple of the Gens Iulia under Tiberius (pl. 21. 17),[8] a local *flamen* of Divus Iulius,[9] and the tribes of the colony were named after members of his family, Aurelia, Calpurnia, Atia.[10]

The West did not treat Caesar in the same manner, but there too exceptional honours began to abound. He was welcomed in some places just as Marius, Metellus, and Pompey before him.[11] When he arrived in Gallia Cisalpina from Gaul in 51 at the end of his provincial administration people decorated their houses and went out with their children to meet him, sacrifices were offered, banquets were held.[12] There had

[1] Grant, *From Imperium to Auctoritas* 244 ff.; pl. 8. 5 f.; Kraft, *Jahrb. f. Num. u. Geldgesch.* 3/4 (1952/3), 10; pl. 1. 7 f. A coin of Parium, issued *c.* 29 B.C. (*BMC Mysia* 103, no. 84; Grant 249), bears the legend 'P. Vibio sac(erdote) Caes(aris)'. The Caesarian foundation is accepted by Vittinghoff for Lampsacus (88. 1), doubted for Parium (130. 7), rejected for Alexandria (130. 8). See below, p. 405. 5.

[2] Apamea, Colonia Iulia Concordia, Grant, op. cit. 255 f.; 278. 3; pl. 8. 15 (the *cognomen* 'Concordia' does not necessarily suggest a post-Caesarian foundation); Kraft, l.c. 10; pl. 1. 4. Sinope, Colonia Felix Iulia since 46, issued a coin in 38 with the head of Caesar, Milne, *Num. Chron.* (1935), 194; cf. Grant, op. cit. 253; Magie 1267. 33; Vittinghoff 89. 4; Kraft, l.c. 9; pl. 1. 6. Another coin, A. S. Robertson, *Rom. Imp. Coins in the Hunterian Coin Cabinet* 1. 58, no. 299; pl. 9. 299, tentatively attributed by Grant, op. cit. 69 f., to Apamea, is according to Dr. Kraay a forgery.

[3] Grant, op. cit. 266; Vittinghoff 86; Lenschau, *RE* Suppl. 4. 1033.

[4] This is an inference from the existence of a *tribus Vatinia* at Corinth, J. H. Kent, *Corinth* 8. 3: *Latin Inscr.* (1966), no. 222.

[5] *BMC Corinth* 92; pl. 23. 10; Grant, op. cit. 266; for the correct reading, 'Cn. Publicio M. Ant. Orest.', see Sutherland, *Num. Chron.* 1947, 87 f.

[6] Grant, op. cit. pl. 8. 19 (the temple is a reproduction of the temple of Vesta from the coin of Q. Cassius, *c.* 57 B.C., Sydenham 152; pl. 25. 917). A further coin with Caesar's head and the legend 'Laus Iuli. Corint.' (*BMC Corinth* 58; pl. 15. 2; K. M. Edwards, *Corinth* 6: *Coins* (1933), 16, no. 16; Vessberg, op. cit. pl. 6. 9) may have been issued during Caesar's lifetime.

[7] Kent, op. cit. no. 50: 'Divo Iulio Caesari sacrum'.

[8] Grant, *Aspects of the Principate of Tiberius* 15; 92 ff.; pl. 5. 4; 7; cf. A. B. West, *Corinth* 8. 2: *Lat. Inscr.* (1931), 16, no. 17; *Syll.* 790; below, p. 405. 7.   [9] See below, p. 405.

[10] A. B. West, op. cit. no. 68 (Calpurnia); 97 (Aurelia); 86 (Atia); cf. J. H. Kent, op. cit. p. 23; above, p. 160.

[11] See above, p. 293.   [12] [Caes.] *BG* 8. 51. 1; above, p. 289. 9.

been a strong bond between Caesar and the inhabitants since his first consulate in 59, when he granted citizenship to many colonists,[1] and later, when he granted it to those who had served in his legions.[2] Many of these citizens will have received the gentilician name 'Iulius'; we know of one who even bore the significant *praenomen* 'Kaeso'.[3] Caesarea were also built at Mutina and Ateste at least,[4] and Caesar's cult with a personal *flamen* was instituted in more cities than elsewhere.[5]

In 49 after the outbreak of the Civil War, he was received in the *municipia* of Italy like a god.[6] Pompey had just departed, and Caesar's arrival brought security instead of the expected terror. This was in the first moments of excitement and will not have lasted long. But there were also private persons who were in Caesar's debt and began to call him a god.[7] And it will be remembered that in 46, albeit for a short while, even in Rome there was an inscription on an official statue to the effect that he was a demigod.[8] In the following year he was called Deus Invictus on a statue which was set up in the temple of Quirinus and was to remain there.[9] The other divine or quasi-divine honours followed, and finally came the name of Iuppiter Iulius. This then did not arise all of a sudden; but it was more extraordinary than the rest and therefore requires explanation and justification to counter suspicion and prejudice.

3. IUPPITER AND THE KINGS

Again the origins are Greek. Homer spoke about the supreme power of Zeus among the gods and the need to have one ruler in one land.[10] He derived the kings' power from Zeus, as did Hesiod after

---

[1] Suet. *Caes.* 28. 3 (rogatio Vatinia); 80. 2; Strab. 5. 213; App. *BC* 2. 28. 98; Gelzer, *Caesar* 86.

[2] Caes. *BG* 1. 10. 3; Suet. *Caes.* 24. 2; Dio 41. 36. 3 (49 B.C.).

[3] Callegari, *NSc* 1933, 137 (Ateste); see below, p. 333. 4.

[4] *CIL* 11. 948; 5. 2533.   [5] See below, p. 407.

[6] Cic. *Att.* 8. 16. 1 (March 49): 'municipia vero deum ... (2) ... quas fieri censes ἀπαντήσεις ex oppidis, quos honores?' (Gelzer, *Caesar* 185. 39). 'Deum' is, however, the reading of a single MS. (accepted by C. F. W. Müller and Shackleton Bailey, *Towards a Text of Cicero 'ad Atticum'* (1960), 40); the majority of the MSS. have 'ad eum' (accepted by Sjögren); 'ad-⟨ulantur⟩ eum' is suggested by Watt, *Mnem.* 4. 16 (1963), 398 f.; cf. above, p. 289. 9.

[7] *CIL* 1². 1611 (*ILS* 6343 = Degr. 630, Nola): 'M. Salvio Q. f. Venusto decurioni beneficio dei Caesaris'; 6. 14211 (*CLE* 964, of Calpurnia): '... patrona / magnifici coniunx Caesaris illa dei'; Boyancé, *REL* 33 (1955), 113.

[8] See above, p. 53.   [9] See above, pp. 186 f.

[10] e.g. *Il.* 2. 669: ὅς τε θεοῖσι καὶ ἀνθρώποισιν ἀνάσσει; 2. 204: οὐκ ἀγαθὸν πολυκοιρανίη· εἷς κοίρανος ἔστω, / εἷς βασιλεύς; Nilsson, *Opuscula* 2. 871 ff.; Béranger, op. cit. 240; O. Murray, *JRS* 55 (1965), 178.

him.[1] Political theory often described the power of Zeus in the universe in terms of an all-powerful king[2] and on the other hand ascribed all the qualities of Zeus to the king of an ideal state.[3] But political practice was at first hostile and did not accept the comparison. Salmoneus was the mythical example of the impious man who claimed to be Zeus, usurped his chariot, brandished his thunderbolt, and demanded sacrifice; he was punished for his presumption.[4] Political enemies, as we learn from Comedy, accused Pericles of wanting to be another imitator of Zeus.[5] The Persians believed, so the Greeks asserted wrongly, that their king was Zeus,[6] and that is why the tyrants of Syracuse and their imitators, wanting to represent Zeus on earth, dressed like the Persian kings. And so did a lesser mortal, the Syracusan physician Menecrates, who also called himself Zeus.[7] There were constant warnings against such impudence[8] but there was on the other hand the belief that great men had a divine nature.[9] Such divine benefactors are frequent in Comedy,[10] and we have already met them in Plautus claiming to be Iuppiter and demanding altars and sacrifices for themselves.[11]

There is no need to inquire here into the origins of ruler cult. It is enough to state the fact that when kings reappeared in the Greek world they were soon connected with the sphere of Zeus. Alexander was said to have been a son of Zeus, as powerful on earth as Zeus was on Olympus,[12] and was painted by Apelles with a thunderbolt.[13]

[1] e.g. *Il.* 2. 196: . . . διοτρεφέων βασιλήων, | τιμὴ δ' ἐκ Διός ἐστι, φιλεῖ δέ ἑ μητίετα Ζεύς; Hes. *Theog.* 96.

[2] Plat. *Phil.* 30 d; *Epist.* 2. 312 e; Isocr. 3 (*Nicocl.*). 26; Aristot. *de mundo* 6. 398b. Zeus Basileus is relatively late: Wilamowitz, *Glaube d. Hell.* 1. 140. 1.

[3] Aristot. *Pol.* 3. 13. 7 (1284b25); 3. 17. 2 (1288a15).

[4] Apollod. 1. 89; Verg. *Aen.* 6. 585 ff. with Servius; Hygin. *fab.* 61; Robert, *Heldensage* 2. 202 f.

[5] Aristoph. *Acharn.* 530: ἐντεῦθεν ὀργῇ Περικλέης οὐλύμπιος | ἤστραπτ', ἐβρόντα, ξυνεκύκα τὴν Ἑλλάδα; Plut. *Per.* 8. 3 f.; 13. 10 (Cratinus); Cic. *Or.* 29; Quint. 2. 16. 19.

[6] Hdt. 7. 56: τί δὴ ἀνδρὶ εἰδόμενος Πέρσῃ καὶ οὔνομα ἀντὶ Διὸς Ξέρξην θέμενος ἀνάστατον τὴν Ἑλλάδα θέλεις ποιῆσαι; 7. 220 (oracle): Ζηνὸς γὰρ ἔχει μένος (but 7. 203: οὐ γὰρ θεὸν εἶναι τὸν ἐπιόντα ἐπὶ τὴν Ἑλλάδα ἀλλ' ἄνθρωπον, εἶναι δὲ θνητόν); Gorg. frg. 5a D.–K. (Ps.-Longin. 3. 2): Ξέρξης ὁ τῶν Περσῶν Ζεύς; Aesch. *Pers.* 157 (Atossa): θεοῦ μὲν εὐνάτειρα Περσῶν, θεοῦ δὲ καὶ μήτηρ ἔφυς; Curt. 8. 5. 11: 'Persas . . . reges suos inter deos colere'; Gow, *JHS* 48 (1928), 134 f.; Wilcken, *Sitz. Ber. Berlin* 1938, 303; H. J. Rose ad Aesch. *Pers.* 157; Nilsson 2. 136.

[7] See above, p. 73.

[8] Pind. *Isthm.* 5. 14: μὴ μάτευε Ζεὺς γενέσθαι; *Ol.* 5. 56; Weinreich, *Menekrates* 83.

[9] See above, p. 287 f.

[10] Eupol. *Dem.* frg. 117 K.: οἱ στρατηγοί . . . οἷς ὡσπερεὶ θεοῖσιν ηὐχόμεσθα· καὶ γὰρ ἦσαν.

[11] Plaut. *Capt.* 863; *Cas.* 333 ff.; *Pers.* 99; *Asin.* 712; above, pp. 167 f.; 288.

[12] Plut. *Alex.* 33. 1 (Callisthenes); Diod. 17. 51. 1 ff.; Arrian. 33. 2; Curt. 4. 7. 25, etc.; Plut. *de Alex. fort.* 1. 9: Ἀλέξανδρος ἐγὼ Διὸς μὲν υἱός; *Anth. Pal.* 16. 120. 4: γᾶν ὑπ' ἐμοὶ τίθεμαι, Ζεῦ, σὺ δ' Ὄλυμπον ἔχε; Tarn, *Alexander the Great* 2. 350 ff.; Balsdon, *Hist.* 1 (1950), 384.

[13] Pliny 35. 92; Plut. *Alex.* 4. 3.

Seleucus I was called Zeus Nicator,[1] and there was a Seleucus Keraunos and a Ptolemy Keraunos. Callimachus, quoting the line from Hesiod, spoke with regard to Ptolemy II Philadelphus of the divine qualities of kings who were established by Zeus.[2]

One would not expect to find a similar development at Rome at an early date. Its kings were rulers of a small city-state and could not possibly have claimed a superhuman standing. In the Republic the annual change of power and its sharing within that year could not favour a comparison with Iuppiter either. And yet the triumphator wore the dress of Iuppiter, the *toga picta* and *tunica palmata*, and painted his face red, just like the statue of Iuppiter in the Capitoline temple.[3] That is to say, on the day of his triumph he represented Iuppiter; but just for one day. We have seen that even this was probably an innovation ascribed to Camillus.[4] When Greek historiography became influential in Rome the life of Scipio Africanus was refashioned in the pattern of Alexander's life. He too was now of divine descent, a son of Iuppiter, and was in all his activities inspired by Iuppiter, whose temple on the Capitol he regularly visited for inspiration.[5] His wax image was kept in the *cella* of the temple and taken thence to the funeral processions of the Cornelii.[6] It is probable that his statue too was kept in that *cella* and, wearing triumphal dress, was carried in the procession of the gods in the *pompa circensis*.[7] A dictator was even more suited for such a role: Sulla's dictatorial power was compared with that of Iuppiter in agreement with a famous Homeric passage[8] which had long been influential at Rome too.[9] Sulla did not go any further but resigned: he clearly did not want to become another Iuppiter. The theme must have been very much alive at Rome at that time, though not in a complimentary sense. It could be applied to those who were accused of aiming at kingship and tyranny. It was so applied to Cicero, who was not entirely innocent. In his poem *De consulatu* he was

---

[1] *Or. gr.* 245. 10; Stähelin, *RE* 2A. 1233; cf. the Zeus Seleukios in Lydia, Nock, *JHS* 48 (1928), 41 f.; *SEG* 15. 183; L. Robert, *Hell.* 6 (1948), 24 f. and *REG* 64 (1951), 133 f.; P. M. Fraser, *CR* 63 (1949), 92 ff.

[2] Call. *hymn.* 1. 77 ff.; cf. Theocr. 17. 1 ff.   [3] See above, p. 67.

[4] See above, pp. 73 f.   [5] See above, p. 19. 4; cf. p. 294.

[6] Val. Max. 8. 15. 1; App. *Iber.* 23. 89; Mommsen, *Röm. Forsch.* 2. 503. 164.

[7] See above, pp. 36; 185.

[8] Cic. *Rosc. Amer.* 131: 'si Iuppiter Optimus Maximus, cuius nutu et arbitrio caelum terra mariaque reguntur . . ., quid miramur . . . L. Sullam, cum solus rem publicam regeret orbemque terrarum gubernaret imperiique maiestatem, quam armis receperat, legibus confirmaret, aliqua animadvertere non potuisse?' Hom. *Il.* 1. 528: ἦ καὶ κυανέῃσιν ἐπ' ὀφρύσι νεῦσε Κρονίων· / ἀμβρόσιαι δ' ἄρα χαῖται ἐπερρώσαντο ἄνακτος / κρατὸς ἀπ' ἀθανάτοιο, μέγαν δ' ἐλέλιξεν Ὄλυμπον; cf. 2. 350; 8. 175; 246.

[9] Enn. *Sc.* 380 V.; Catull. 64. 204; Varr. *LL* 7. 85; Fest. 173 M. (178 L.), etc.

both extravagant and indiscreet, and said among other things that Iuppiter had invited him to the council of the gods,[1] a distinction which had not hitherto been granted to any mortal except Heracles, Dionysus, Alexander, Romulus, and the like. Cicero was carried away by his poetical fancy without bothering much about its implications. But Clodius said it was the talk of the town that Cicero used to call himself Iuppiter and claim that Minerva was his sister.[2] It is not impossible that something similar stood also in the poem. But it is more probable that Clodius and his friends maliciously distorted what Cicero said at the time of the Catilinarian conspiracy and later.[3] He liked to refer to Iuppiter's help in his speeches[4] and worshipped especially Minerva Custos, whose image he took from his house and dedicated on the Capitol when he left for his exile.[5] Cicero's case is valuable only in so far as it is a further instance of an arbitrary identification with Iuppiter; it is for the rest insignificant, because he never again had an opportunity to wield power in Rome.

Caesar's identification with Iuppiter depended then both on Greek doctrine and example, and on some Roman tradition, real or legendary. He too, though not a son of Iuppiter, was of divine descent and had the virtues of the ideal ruler, as demanded by Greek philosophers. His statue too was placed in the *cella* of Iuppiter, was carried, wearing Iuppiter's triumphal garb, in the procession of the gods in the *pompa circensis* on a special carriage, *tensa*, which only the Capitoline deities possessed, and was placed in the Circus next to the *pulvinar* of the Capitoline deities. In the theatre his golden crown was to be exhibited on a golden throne apparently in the same manner as the crown of Iuppiter. The *ludi Romani*, which were held in honour of Iuppiter, received an additional day in honour of Caesar. When at the Lupercalia of 44 he was offered the diadem, he sent it to Iuppiter because, so he said, Iuppiter alone was a king in Rome;[6] the parallelism is, even in

---

[1] Ps.-Sall. *in Cic.* 2. 3: 'se Cicero dicit in concilio deorum immortalium fuisse'; 4. 7; Quintil. 11. 1. 24: 'Iovem illum a quo in concilium deorum advocatur'; W. Allen jr., *TAPA* 87 (1956), 134 f.

[2] Cic. *dom.* 92: 'inducis etiam sermonem urbanum . . . me dicere solere esse me Iovem, eundemque dictitare Minervam esse sororem meam.'

[3] An interesting case of distortion: Cic. *p. red. sen.* 39: 'me . . . Italia cuncta paene suis umeris reportarit' (from exile); Ps.-Sall. *in Cic.* 4. 7: 'Italia exulem humeris suis reportavit.' But Cicero may have been partly responsible for this distortion, see Macrob. 2. 3. 5; he even asserted that Clodius too wanted to bring him back on his shoulders, *dom.* 40.

[4] e.g. Cic. *Cat.* 3. 22: 'ille, ille Iuppiter restitit . . . ille cunctam urbem, ille vos omnis salvos esse voluit. dis ego immortalibus ducibus hanc mentem . . . suscepi', etc.; 2. 29.

[5] Cic. *dom.* 144; *leg.* 2. 42; *fam.* 12. 25. 1; Dio. 38. 17. 5; 45. 17. 3; Plut. *Cic.* 31. 6.

[6] Dio 44. 11. 3: ἀπεκρίνατο μὲν ὅτι Ζεὺς μόνος τῶν Ῥωμαίων βασιλεὺς εἴη καὶ τὸ διάδημα αὐτῷ ἐς τὸ Καπιτώλιον ἔπεμψεν; below, p. 339.

this negative form, obvious. The night before he was murdered he dreamt that he was raised above the clouds and grasped the hand of Iuppiter.[1] And the people wanted to cremate and bury him in the temple of Iuppiter Capitolinus.[2]

Caesar was murdered, but the theme of a Iuppiter on earth was not dead: it became topical again as soon as Augustus' rule was firmly secured. He too was compared with the heroes who were granted immortality because of their achievements on earth, Hercules, Castor and Pollux, Liber pater, Romulus—though not with Caesar. Augustus would join them, or in contrast to them, as Horace said later, he would become a god while still on earth.[3] Horace hesitated about the identification with Iuppiter and tried to play it down. Once he spoke of the belief, long established, that Iuppiter rules in the heavens, and turned to the new belief that Augustus would rule as a god on earth after the conquest of Britain and Persia.[4] But a year or two later he presented the theme in a different form. Iuppiter rules in the heavens, Augustus on earth as before, but he does so under the protection of Iuppiter, whose supremacy he acknowledges.[5] One is tempted to find here some polemics against exaggerated views. It was about that time that the Greeks identified Augustus with Zeus again and again. He was Zeus Aineiades,[6] Zeus Sebastos Kronides,[7] Zeus Eleutherios in Egypt,[8] Zeus Patroos in Asia,[9] Olympius at Athens[10] and in Asia,[11] Iuppiter Augustus at Cyrene[12] and in Dalmatia,[13] and so on.[14] At Rome itself Ovid had no

---

[1] Suet. *Caes.* 81. 3 (below, p. 346. 7); Dio 44. 17. 1 : ἐν γὰρ τῇ νυκτὶ ἐν ᾗ ἐσφάγη ... ὁ Καῖσαρ ἐπί τε τῶν νεφῶν μετέωρος αἰωρεῖσθαι καὶ τῆς τοῦ Διὸς χειρὸς ἅπτεσθαι(ἔδοξε); below, p. 357.

[2] App. *BC* 2. 148. 615; Dio 44. 50. 2; Suet. *Caes.* 84. 3 (below, p. 355. 6).

[3] Hor. *c.* 3. 3. 9: 'hac arte Pollux et vagus Hercules / enisus arcis attigit igneas, / quos inter Augustus recumbens / purpureo bibet ore nectar'; 4. 5. 31 : 'alteris / te mensis adhibet deum; / te multa prece, te prosequitur mero / defuso pateris, et Laribus tuum / miscet numen, uti Graecia Castoris / et magni memor Herculis'; *epist.* 2. 1. 5: 'Romulus et Liber pater et cum Castore Pollux, / post ingentia facta deorum in templa recepti ... (15) praesenti tibi maturos largimur honores / iurandasque tuum per numen ponimus aras'; above, pp. 53. 13; 213. 7.   [4] Hor. *c.* 3. 5. 1; cf. Sen. *clem.* 1. 1. 2.

[5] Hor. *c.* 1. 12. 49; 'gentis humanae pater atque custos, / orte Saturno, tibi cura magni / Caesaris fatis data : tu secundo / Caesare regnes ... (56) te minor latum reget aequus orbem; / tu gravi curru quaties Olympum.'

[6] *Anth. Pal.* 9. 307; cf. 9. 297.   [7] Page, *Greek Lit. Pap.* 113. 13 (p. 470).

[8] *IGR* 1. 1295 (Kaibel, *Epigr.* 978); 1117; 1163 (*Or. gr.* 659); 1206; 1322; *P. Oslo.* 26; Wilcken, *Chrest.* no. 111; E.-J. 117.

[9] E.-J. 98a; *IGR* 4. 1410; 1608; 522 (*Or. gr.* 479).

[10] Suet. *Aug.* 60; Mattingly 1. 108; pl. 16. 10 f.

[11] *IGR* 4. 11; 72; 76; 95; *IG* 12, Suppl. 42; 59 (Mytilene); P. Herrmann, *Ath. Mitt.* 75 (1960), 101 f. (Samos); Jos. *BJ* 1. 217. 414 (Caesarea Philippi); gr. Kruse, *RE* 18. 256.

[12] The temple of Zeus was re-dedicated 'Iovi Augusto': Goodchild–Reynolds, *PBSR* 26 (1958), 30 ff.

[13] *ILS* 3088 : 'Iovi Augusto Appuleia M. f. Quinta suo et L. Turpili Brocchi Liciniani filii nomine t(est.) p(on.) i(uss.).'   [14] He was also Uranios, Epuranios, Polieus.

inhibitions:[1] Augustus is a god on earth.[2] He often compares Augustus' rule with that of Iuppiter,[3] but more often Augustus is for him just Iuppiter.[4] His palace is Iuppiter's house,[5] his marriage with Livia is identical with that of Iuppiter and Iuno,[6] and he inflicts punishment with Iuppiter's lightning.[7] Other poets, Propertius and Manilius, did the same[8] and, considering the epigraphical evidence, these cases cannot be dismissed as sheer flattery.

Caesar's idea was brought to life again against the wishes of Augustus and perhaps of the leading personalities of his age. It was a necessary revival, as it answered the question as to the religious position of the monarch in a monarchy. It does not prove that this was exactly what Caesar meant by his divine aspirations, but it does prove that the solitary and disputed evidence of Dio is unexceptionable. It does not follow that Caesar was to become a Iuppiter Iulius at Rome overnight. What was said above about the divine honours at the Circus and the theatre must be repeated again: Caesar was going to Parthia and was to be absent for some years to come. It was for this period and after that Caesar was to be a Iuppiter on earth, just as was planned for Augustus twenty years later:[9]

> Caelo tonantem credidimus Iovem
> regnare; praesens Divus habebitur
> Augustus adiectis Britannis
> imperio gravibusque Persis.

4. CAESAR'S FLAMEN

Dio further says that Antony was appointed Caesar's first priest, a *flamen*.[10] This evidence cannot be rejected on the grounds that Dio was

---

[1] K. Scott, *TAPA* 61 (1930), 43 ff.; M. M. Ward, *Studi e materiali* 9 (1933), 203 ff.

[2] Ov. *F.* 3. 421: 'ignibus aeternis aeterni numina praesunt / Caesaris'; *Pont.* 1. 1. 63: 'ut mihi di faveant, quibus est manifestior ipse'; 1. 4. 55.

[3] Ov. *Met.* 15. 858: 'Iuppiter arces / temperat aetherias et mundi regna triformis, / terra sub Augusto est; pater est et rector uterque'; 2. 130; *Trist.* 2. 215; *Pont.* 1. 2. 101.

[4] *Trist.* 5. 2. 46: 'si fas est homini cum Iove posse loqui.'

[5] *Trist.* 3. 1. 33: 'video ... / ... tectaque digna deo ... (38) et magni verum est hanc Iovis esse domum'; *Pont.* 3. 1. 135: 'domus Augusti Capitoli more colenda'.

[6] *F.* 1. 650: 'sola (Iuno) toro magni digna reperta Iovis'; *Pont.* 3. 1. 117.

[7] *Trist.* 1. 1. 81; 2. 143; 179; 3. 5. 7; 4. 5. 5; 4. 8. 45; *Pont.* 1. 7. 49; 3. 6. 17.

[8] Manil. 1. 799: 'descendit caelo caelumque replebit, / quod reget, Augustus, socio per signa Tonante, / cernet et in coetu divum magnumque Quirinum'; 1. 916 (at Actium): 'rector Olympi'.

[9] Hor. *c.* 3. 5. 1 ff.

[10] Dio 44. 6. 4: καὶ τέλος Δία τε αὐτὸν ἄντικρυς Ἰούλιον προσηγόρευσαν, καὶ ναὸν αὐτῷ τῇ τ᾽ Ἐπιεικείᾳ αὐτοῦ τεμενισθῆναι ἔγνωσαν, ἱερέα σφίσι τὸν Ἀντώνιον ὥσπερ τινὰ Διάλιον προχειρισάμενοι.

a late writer: the fact is also recorded by Cicero.[1] First a word about the priesthood is needed. The *flamines* were the personal priests of many early deities, altogether fifteen in the republican period: three *flamines maiores* (*Dialis, Martialis, Quirinalis*) and twelve *flamines minores*, some of whom were in charge of more or less obsolete cults.[2] The *flamines maiores* were not elected or co-opted as were the other priests, but were chosen out of three candidates (nominated probably by the pontifical college) by the *pontifex maximus* by means of the ancient ritual of 'picking' (*captio*), also used for the Vestals.[3] They had to be patricians, born of parents married by the rite of the *confarreatio*, and to be married by the same rite.[4] The *captio* was only part of the ritual; the new *flamen* could not officiate as long as he was not inaugurated. This was done by an *augur* in the presence of the *pontifex maximus* and the whole community, the *comitia calata*.[5]

We learn from these rules that Antony could not have been chosen as the fourth of the *flamines maiores* without the active participation of Caesar, who as the *pontifex maximus* had to 'pick' him. We are therefore bound to ask two questions: why did he want a *flamen*, and why did he choose Antony? The first question can be answered by reference to the *flamen Quirinalis* and *flamen Dialis*. Plutarch records that in origin there were only two *flamines*, the *Dialis* and *Martialis*, and that it was Numa who created the third, the *Quirinalis*, in honour of Romulus-Quirinus.[6] It is therefore possible that here, as so often, Caesar had the example of Romulus in mind: if Romulus had the third *flamen*, he should have the fourth. But that served him only as a precedent. His real model was the *flamen Dialis*. We shall see presently how he used this model for far-reaching innovations. As to the choice of Antony, the answer is simpler. He could not choose C. Octavius, if he wanted to make him his heir. Antony had been an *augur* since 50 and was now the

---

[1] Cic. *Phil.* 2. 110: 'est ergo flamen, ut Iovi, ut Marti, ut Quirino, sic Divo Iulio M. Antonius.'

[2] Wissowa 504 ff. A *flamen Dialis* is also found at Lavinium (*ILS* 5004; *CIL* 14. 4176), Lanuvium (*ILS* 6196), Tibur (*ILS* 1158), and Mutina (*CIL* 11. 856); a *flamen Martialis* at Lavinium (*ILS* 5004), Lanuvium (*ILS* 6200), Aricia (*ILS* 6193) and Pompeii (*ILS* 6364); there is no evidence for a *flamen Quirinalis* outside Rome; Wissowa, *Herm.* 50 (1915), 22; 29.

[3] Gell. 1. 12. 15; Livy 27. 8. 5; Tac. *A.* 4. 16. 2; Mommsen, *StR* 2. 25; 34 f.; Wissowa 510; *RE* 3. 1509; Latte 402.

[4] Tac. *A.* 4. 16. 2; Paul. 151 M. (137 L.); Gai. 1. 112; Serv. Dan. *Aen.* 4. 103; 374; Cic. *dom.* 38; Wissowa 506.

[5] Gell. 15. 27. 1; Mommsen, *StR* 2. 34; Wissowa 490; Latte 403.

[6] Plut. *Numa* 7. 9: τοῖς οὖσιν ἱερεῦσι Διὸς καὶ Ἄρεως τρίτον Ῥωμύλου προσκατέστησεν, ὃν Φλάμινα Κυρινάλιον ὠνόμασεν. According to Livy 1. 20. 2 and *vir. ill.* 3. 1 Numa created all three *flamines*; cf. also Dion. Hal. 2. 63. 2.

magister of the newly created *luperci Iulii.*[1] He had held no political office from 47 to 44 when he became consul with Caesar. The answer then is that Caesar trusted Antony more than any other of his followers in the last months of his life. We shall observe later that without this trust Antony could not have been the chief actor at the Lupercalia of 44. But they had to overcome difficulties. Antony was a plebeian and married to a plebeian, hardly by the rite of the *confarreatio.* Caesar made him a patrician,[2] as he made his great-nephew C. Octavius too,[3] and as he was entitled to do through the *lex Cassia* of 45.[4] The condition about the marriage of the parents must have been waived in Antony's case. He was not inaugurated during Caesar's lifetime. In September 44 Cicero maliciously asked him, or rather pretended to ask him, why he did not see to his inauguration.[5] In fact, although Caesar was consecrated as Divus Iulius in 42, Antony was inaugurated only after the peace of Brundisium in October 40 at the request of Octavian.[6] At that time Fulvia was dead and his new wife, Octavia, was, like her brother, a new patrician, whom he will have married by the rite of the *confarreatio.*

Dio says that Caesar's priest was to be like some *flamen Dialis*[7]—a brief and obscure statement. The *flamen Dialis* was the most important and influential of the *flamines maiores*, but his life was regulated by a great number of archaic and cumbersome rules. There is no need to enumerate them here;[8] what is important is to stress that he was compensated for his restrictions with exceptional privileges. He alone of all the priests had the political rights of a magistrate: he was entitled to a *sella curulis*, had a seat in the Senate and a lictor, and always wore the *toga praetexta.*[9]

The wording of Dio should have led to the conclusion long ago that these privileges, without the restrictions, were also granted to Caesar's *flamen.* This conclusion has now become obvious and certain through the discovery of the Tabula Hebana. This has nothing to do with Caesar but with the posthumous honours of Germanicus. It prescribes that

---

[1] Dio 45. 30. 2; cf. 44. 6. 2; Cic. *Phil.* 2. 85. Antony may have been particularly suitable for the priesthood because through his mother Iulia he was related to Caesar: see below, p. 308.　　　[2] This has been suggested by Mommsen, *Röm. Forsch.* 1. 39. 66.

[3] Suet. *Aug.* 2. 1; Dio 45. 2. 7; cf. 46. 22. 3 (Cicero).

[4] Tac. *A.* 11. 25. 3; Dio 43. 47. 3; Suet. *Caes.* 41. 1; Mommsen, *StR* 2. 1101; 3. 33; Kübler, *RE* 18.2. 2230.

[5] Cic. *Phil.* 2. 110: 'quid igitur cessas? cur non inauguraris? sume diem, vide qui te inauguret.' The speech was written for 19 September but not delivered.

[6] Plut. *Ant.* 33. 1; below, p. 399.　　　[7] Dio 44. 6. 4 (above, p. 305. 10).

[8] Gell. 10. 15; Wissowa 506 f.; Latte 402 f.; W. Pötscher, *Mnem.* 4. 21 (1968), 215 ff.

[9] Livy 1. 20. 2; 27. 8. 8; Paul. 93 M. (82 L.); Plut. *QR* 113; Mommsen, *StR* 1. 390 f.; 403.

sellae curules with oak wreaths upon them should be placed in the theatres at the *ludi Augustales* in honour of Germanicus because he had been the *flamen Augustalis*.[1] This clause makes sense only if one assumes that Germanicus, as the first *flamen* of Divus Augustus, was entitled to a *sella curulis* as a symbol of his office while he was alive, in the theatres as well as at any other public functions. This, however, leads to the inference that the *flamen Augustalis* was modelled on the *flamen Dialis* and possessed all his political privileges;[2] and to the further inference that the *flamen Dialis* was only the ultimate model, because the direct model must have been the *flamen Divi Iulii*. If so, Caesar created a unique priesthood: his *flamen* had all the political privileges of the *flamen* of Iuppiter but was not hampered by the restrictions of the latter. From this we may deduce far-reaching plans. What these plans may have been will become clear when the organization of his cult in East and West after his death and consecration is described. What matters here is to add that according to the original plan Antony was to be his *flamen* during his lifetime. Two further holders of the priesthood in Rome are known, Sex. Appuleius, Augustus' brother-in-law,[3] and D. Iunius Silanus Torquatus,[4] who was also related to the imperial family. Many more *flamines* of his provincial cult are known;[5] they too were generally distinguished citizens.

5. THE TEMPLES

The temples are mentioned by Suetonius, Appian, and Dio but not by Cicero, the only contemporary author: the sceptic may refer to him in support of his negative attitude. Suetonius does not give details,[6] Appian speaks of many temples, one of which Caesar would have to share with his Clementia,[7] Dio of one temple only, common to Iuppiter Iulius and his Clementia,[8] Plutarch of the temple of Clementia only.[9]

---

[1] E.-J. 94a. 50: 'utique ludis Augustalibus cum subsellia sodalium ponentur in theatris, sellae curules Germanici Caesaris inter ea ponantur cum querceis coronis in honorem eius sacerdoti'; Tac. *A.* 2. 83. 2.

[2] *JRS* 47 (1957), 150 f.   [3] *ILS* 8963.

[4] *IG* 2–3. 4180; Mommsen, *Ges. Schr.* 8. 198 f.; *Herm.* 38 (1903), 127. 1; Hohl, *RE* 10. 1104; M. W. H. Lewis, *The Official Priests of Rome under the Julio-Claudians* (1955), 38.

[5] See below, pp. 405 ff.

[6] Suet. *Caes.* 76. 1: 'templa, aras, simulacra iuxta deos, pulvinar, flaminem.'

[7] App. *BC* 2. 106. 443: καὶ νεὼς ἐψηφίσαντο πολλοὺς αὐτῷ γενέσθαι καθάπερ θεῷ καὶ κοινὸν αὐτοῦ καὶ 'Επιεικείας ἀλλήλους δεξιουμένων.

[8] Dio 44. 6. 4 (above, p. 305. 10).

[9] Plut. *Caes.* 57. 4: καὶ τό γε τῆς 'Επιεικείας ἱερὸν οὐκ ἀπὸ τρόπου δοκοῦσι χαριστήριον ἐπὶ τῇ πρᾳότητι ψηφίσασθαι.

The alternatives then are: Caesar was to have many temples, or only one in common with Clementia, or none.

The temple of Clementia is well documented—there is also numismatic evidence (pl. 25. 1):[1] it cannot be denied that it was decreed, although it is certain that it was never built.[2] If it was to be a common temple, Caesar would have been a σύνναος θεός there, as he was already in the temple of Quirinus, and was probably to be in the temple of Salus and in many other temples in and outside Rome.[3] Caesar's own temples are not so well documented, as Dio seems to contradict Suetonius and Appian. But Dio's evidence cannot be correct as it stands. First, a *flamen* cannot belong to two gods: the later common *flamen* of Augustus and Roma[4] was developed from the *flamen* of Augustus. Secondly, a goddess may have her own *flamen* but not one whose standing could be compared only with that of the most important of the three *flamines maiores*,[5] that of Iuppiter. Thirdly, Caesar's new name, Iuppiter Iulius, would have become meaningless in his secondary role of a σύνναος θεός. In other words, Dio must have compressed two pieces of evidence into one: one would have been that Caesar was to become Iuppiter Iulius with his own temple and own *flamen*, the other that he was also to share a temple with his Clementia. One is tempted to go a step further and to interpret these two pieces of evidence in accordance with Augustus' religious policy;[6] that is, that the personal temples were to be built only outside Rome and the temple of Clementia Caesaris in Rome. This interpretation, however, is rendered impossible because it fails to account for the supreme importance of the new *flamen*.

What followed confirms the decree and its interpretation. An altar was set up where the pyre had stood in 44; Caesar was consecrated in 42 as Divus Iulius, though not as Iuppiter Iulius; the cult was organized in East and West after 40; the temple at Rome was begun in 36 and dedicated in 29. There were many temples in the provinces, in the first place the Caesarea, partly begun by Caesar himself, then independent temples, no doubt more than we are able to trace, and finally some temples in common with the Dea Roma. His *flamen* became the chief

---

[1] Sydenham 179; pl. 28. 1076: a tetrastyle temple with a globe in the pediment, and the legend 'Clementiae Caesaris'.

[2] E. Meyer, op. cit. 514, doubted it. There is no trace of a later temple either; see above, pp. 241 f.

[3] App. *BC* 2. 106. 440: καὶ ἀναθημάτων ἐν πᾶσιν ἱεροῖς καὶ δημοσίοις χωρίοις ἀνὰ φυλὴν ἑκάστην καὶ ἐν ἔθνεσιν ἅπασι . . . σχήματά τε ἐπεγράφετο ταῖς εἰκόσι ποικίλα; Dio 44. 4. 4: ἐν ταῖς πόλεσι τοῖς τε ναοῖς τοῖς ἐν τῇ Ῥώμῃ πᾶσιν ἀνδριάντα τινὰ αὐτοῦ εἶναι ἐκέλευσαν.

[4] e.g. *CIL* 12. 983. There was already a *flamen* of Roma and Caesar at Arelate (below, p. 408).

[5] See Wissowa 504.

[6] Suet. *Aug.* 52; Dio 51. 20. 7.

priest of the provinces.[1] The provincial cult was firmly secured owing
to extensive organizational work under Augustus; but the initiative
was due to Caesar, not Augustus.[2]

6. THE *LUDI QUINQUENNALES*

Dio records that the honours of 44 also included the institution of a
pentaeteric festival, as for a hero.[3] These are Greek terms and imply
that games were to be held every four years as was appropriate to
Caesar's superhuman status. The Romans will have called them, as
they called similar festivals later, 'ludi quinquennales'. Other evidence
is found in Appian: it was decreed in 45 that the priests and priestesses
should perform public prayers for him every four years,[4] clearly 'vota
quinquennalia pro salute Caesaris'. It seems obvious that Dio and
Appian refer to two aspects of the same festival. And yet, if Dio is right
in classifying the games as an honour due to a hero, they were intended
to be lasting, whereas the vows for Caesar's welfare could only be made
during his lifetime. Nevertheless, these vows too were extraordinary,
in so far as the Roman State had not hitherto been concerned with the
welfare of an individual.[5] As there is no other direct evidence, no clear
decision can be made. We must therefore turn for clarification to possible precedents, games which followed his example and Roman and
Greek analogies.

There were originally no periodic festivals in Rome. The *lustra* were
at first not held at regular intervals,[6] and the *ludi saeculares* were not
created until 249 B.C.[7] It was probably under the influence of the Greek
olympiads that a *lustrum* began to denote a period of four years.[8] A
census was held at its end, a sacrifice offered, and a new sacrifice vowed
for the end of the next *lustrum*, should Rome find itself in a better condition and be more powerful by then.[9] This sacrifice and vow were the
source of later institutions but also of a certain confusion. Owing to
the ambiguity of the term *quinquennium*, a census could also be held
every five years; and as time passed the confusion increased.[10]

---

[1] See below, pp. 401 ff.   [2] See below, p. 413.

[3] Dio 44. 6. 2: καὶ πενταετηρίδα οἱ ὡς ἥρωι . . . ἀνέθεσαν.

[4] App. *BC* 2. 106. 442: ἱερέας δὲ καὶ ἱερείας ἀνὰ πενταετὲς εὐχὰς δημοσίας ὑπὲρ αὐτοῦ τίθεσθαι.

[5] See above, p. 219.

[6] Mommsen, *Röm. Chronol.* 162 ff.; *StR* 2. 342 ff.; Leuze, *Zur Gesch. d. röm. Censur* 1 ff.

[7] Censor. 17. 8; 10; Livy, *Per.* 49; Nilsson, *RE* 1A. 1704; above, p. 193.

[8] Mommsen, *StR* 2. 343.

[9] Val. Max. 4. 1. 10; Suet. *Aug.* 97. 1; Varro *RR* 2. 1. 10; Dion. Hal. 4. 22. 1; Serv. *Aen.*
8. 183; Wissowa 142; Latte 119.

[10] Mommsen, op. cit.; Leuze, op. cit. 42 ff.; Howard, *CQ* n.s. 8 (1958), 1 ff. (elementary).

Two odd quinquennial festivals are known, the *ieiunium Cereris*, a fast instituted in 191 B.C., which later became annual,[1] and a puzzling sacrifice on behalf of the college of *pontifices*.[2] They seem to have followed the pattern of the *lustra* but it is not known why. There were, further, the *quinquennalia vota* which were repeatedly made during the Second Punic War, promising sacrifice and presents to the gods and the institution of special *ludi magni*, provided that the State remained in the same condition at the end of the next *quinquennium*.[3] Here again the term 'quinquennium' was ambiguous, as it could mean a period of four years, 'in quintum annum', but, on the basis of a five-year period, it also inspired the *decennalia vota* which were made at least twice during the Second Punic War and once more in 172 B.C.[4] Such *ludi magni*, which have only the name in common with those held annually in September,[5] were also vowed without any time limit at the beginning of a war or after a defeat or in any other emergency.[6] In contrast to the *lustra*, the quinquennial vows and games of the Second Punic War were discontinued when the danger passed; another difference is that no games were held at the end of a *lustrum*. These then are the possible Roman precedents; how far they were the real precedents for the Caesarian festival cannot be decided without an examination of the other evidence.

A second means of clarification is suggested by the festivals which were created on the Caesarian model. They were decreed for Augustus in 30 in connection with the honours for the Actian victory and held for the first time in 28. Dio mentions both the decree and its first execution. In the earlier passage he describes it in the same words as he did the Caesarian festival,[7] omitting, however, the point that it was an honour

---

[1] Livy 36. 37. 4; *F. Amit.* 4 Oct.; Wissowa 301; Le Bonniec, *Le culte de Cérès* 446 ff.; Latte 50. 1; Degrassi 517.

[2] Paul. 57 M. (50 L.) s.v. 'caviares hostiae'; Wissowa 516. 5; Latte 390. 7.

[3] Livy 22. 10. 2; 27. 33. 8; 30. 2. 8; 30. 27. 11 f.; 31. 9. 9 f.; Wissowa 382 f.; Mommsen, *StR* 2. 346. 2; Leuze, op. cit. 91 f.

[4] Livy 21. 62. 10; 42. 28. 8; Eckhel, *Doctrina numorum* 8. 473 ff.; Wissowa 382 f.

[5] Wissowa 452 f.; Degrassi 506 f.

[6] Livy 22. 9. 9; Suet. *Aug.* 23. 2 ('clades Variana').

[7] Dio 51. 19. 2: καὶ πανήγυρίν οἱ πεντετηρίδα ἄγεσθαι ... ἔγνωσαν; see above, p. 310. 3. Dio also mentions prayers of the priests and priestesses for Augustus' welfare (ibid. 7: τούς τε ἱερέας καὶ τὰς ἱερείας ἐν ταῖς ὑπέρ τε τοῦ δήμου καὶ τῆς βουλῆς εὐχαῖς καὶ ὑπὲρ ἐκείνου ὁμοίως εὔχεσθαι ... ἐκέλευσαν) which closely resembles Appian's version of the Caesarian festival (above, p. 310. 4). But Dio does not say that it was a quinquennial act, and Appian on the other hand does not include the people and the Senate in those prayers. Consequently, in spite of the similarities, these words in Dio must refer to something else, to the annual vow *pro salute populi Romani* and the inclusion of Augustus in this vow in 30 B.C. (above, p. 218).

fitting for a hero. In the later passage he adds that the games were given in turn by each of the four great priestly *collegia*.[1] Augustus mentions the pentaeteric festival in the same terms as does Dio in the second passage, with the further detail that in addition to the priesthoods the consuls also took their turn in organizing the games.[2] He also adds that these games were held in consequence of vows for his welfare, and that they were to be held only as long as he was alive.[3] They were regularly repeated and ceased in fact after his death;[4] they were never decreed for his successors, perhaps because of the resistance of Tiberius. But the Neronia, created in 60, were equally pentaeteric and held for the welfare of Nero, though they were completely Greek for the rest;[5] and so was the *agon Capitolinus* of Domitian in 86, although it was held in honour of Iuppiter.[6]

There is no other precedent for the Augustan festival than the Caesarian one, a strange precedent because it was decreed but never executed. Consequently, the latter too was to consist of vows and games in fulfilment of these vows; in other words, Dio and Appian in fact described the two parts of the same festival. But there are also differences, though these existed only at Rome: the games did not imply divine honours for Augustus and ceased after his death. The question, therefore, as to the origin and function of the Caesarian festival is not

---

[1] Dio 53. 1. 4: τὴν πανήγυριν τὴν ἐπὶ τῇ νίκῃ τῇ πρὸς τῷ Ἀκτίῳ γενομένῃ ψηφισθεῖσαν ἤγαγε μετὰ τοῦ Ἀγρίππου . . . (5) καὶ αὕτη μὲν διὰ πέντε ἀεὶ ἐτῶν μέχρι τοῦ ἐγίγνετο, ταῖς τέσσαρσιν ἱερωσύναις ἐκ περιτροπῆς μέλουσα, λέγω δὲ τούς τε ποντίφικας καὶ τοὺς οἰωνιστὰς τούς τε ἑπτὰ καὶ τοὺς πεντεκαίδεκα ἄνδρας καλουμένους.

[2] *Mon. Anc.* 9. 1: 'vota p[ro salute mea susc]ipi per consules et sacerdotes quinto quoque anno decrevit senatus. ex iis votis saepe fecerunt vivo me ludos aliquotiens sacerdotum quattuor amplissima collegia, aliquotiens consules.' The supplement 'pro salute' is not the accepted one and will be justified in the Additional Note on p. 317.

[3] The words 'vivo me' (see the preceding note) mean just this and nothing else. Kornemann (*Klio* 3 (1903), 84 and *Mausoleum u. Tatenbericht* 47) and K. Scott (*CP* 27 (1932), 284) suggest instead that these two words reveal a contrast with Caesar: such games were also decreed for Caesar but held only long after his death when his temple was dedicated in 29 B.C (Dio 51. 22. 4). But clearly the latter games were those which usually followed the dedication of temples. There is no reason why one should connect them with those decreed in 44, which were to be pentaeteric games.

[4] Suet. *Aug.* 44. 3; Pliny 7. 158; Dio 54. 19. 8 confuses it with a quinquennial celebration of Augustus' *imperium* (p. 313) and so does Latte 314.

[5] Dio 61. 21. 1: ὑπὲρ δὲ δὴ τῆς σωτηρίας τῆς τε διαμονῆς τοῦ κράτους αὐτοῦ . . . ἀγῶνα πενταετηρικὸν κατεστήσατο, Νερώνεια αὐτὸν ὀνομάσας; Suet. *Nero* 12. 3; Tac. *A.* 14. 20. 1; 16. 4. 1; Mattingly 1. 250 ff.; Wissowa 465; Friedländer, *Sittengesch.* 2. 147; Hartke, *RE* 17. 42 ff.; Bolton, *CQ* 42 (1948), 81 ff.; MacDowall, *CQ* 52 (1958), 192 ff. (coins). Nero's *quinquennium* (Aurel. Vict. *Caes.* 5. 2; *Epit. de Caes.* 5. 2; Lepper, *JRS* 47 (1957), 95 ff.; O. Murray, *Hist.* 14 (1965), 41 ff.) would be relevant, if it could be shown that the story dates from Nero's reign.

[6] Suet. *Dom.* 4. 4: 'instituit et quinquennale certamen Capitolino Iovi . . .'; Censor. 18. 15; Stat. *Silv.* 3. 5. 92; 4. 2. 62: 'saepe coronatis iteres quinquennia lustris'; Leuze, op. cit. 80; Wissowa 465; Friedländer, op. cit. 2. 148; cf. Dio 60. 6. 2 on Claudius.

yet solved, as the precedents do not offer more than possibilities, which are insufficient without further confirmation.

A third means of clarification may be found with the help of an analogy, the quinquennial period of office, also created on the model of the *lustra* and lasting again for four or five years. Caesar received Gaul as his province in 59 for a *quinquennium*,[1] which was renewed in 55[2] when the same number of years was also granted to Pompey and Crassus for their own provincial administration.[3] Caesar thus held Gaul for two *quinquennia* but not, as Cicero asserts, for ten years.[4] When he received the dictatorship for ten years in 46[5] the model may have been his apparent, though not real, stay in Gaul. In 44, when he became dictator for life, the consulship was decreed to him for ten years—which, however, he did not accept.[6] The second triumvirate was limited to five years, and was renewed for another five, this time really five.[7] Augustus received his *imperium* in 27 for ten years, renewed twice for five years and twice for ten years;[8] after him Tiberius twice for ten years.[9] Other quinquennial periods of office too were created on this pattern[10] but are of no consequence here: they were no more than convenient periods for the tenure of an office. But there remain some relevant cases. Whenever Augustus'[11] and Tiberius'[12] ten-year periods ended a festival was held; and

[1] Vell. 2. 44. 5: 'tum Caesari decretae in quinquennium Galliae'; Meyer, *Caesars Monarchie* 159; Gelzer, *Kl. Schr.* 2. 217.

[2] Suet. *Caes.* 24. 1: 'perfecitque ... ut in quinquennium sibi imperium prorogaretur'; Cic. *Phil.* 2. 24; Vell. 2. 46. 2; App. *BC* 2. 18. 65.

[3] Dio 39. 3. 2 (lex Trebonia).

[4] Cic. *Att.* 7. 7. 6 (Dec. 51): 'annorum enim decem imperium'; 7. 9. 4: 'tenuisti provinciam per annos decem.'

[5] Dio 43. 14. 4: αὐτὸν ... δικτάτορα ἐς δέκα (ἔτη) ἐφεξῆς εἵλοντο; v. Premerstein 164.

[6] App. *BC* 2. 106. 442: καὶ δικτάτωρ ἐς τὸν ἑαυτοῦ βίον ᾑρέθη καὶ ὕπατος ἐς δέκα ἔτη; 107. 447: τὰς δὲ ἄλλας τιμὰς χωρὶς τῆς δεκαετοῦς ὑπατείας προσέμενος.

[7] *Mon. Anc.* 7. 1; Dio 46. 55. 3; 48. 54. 6; App. *BC* 4. 7. 27; 5. 95. 398; F. Colot. (Degrassi, *Inscr. Ital.* 13. 1. 274).

[8] Dio 53. 13. 1; 16. 2; 54. 12. 4 (18 B.C.); 56. 28. 1 (A.D. 13); cf. v. Premerstein 121, who, however, is wrong in suggesting (ibid. 117 ff.) that Augustus possessed a special office, the *cura et tutela rei publicae*: *contra*, e.g. Béranger, *Recherches sur l'aspect idéologique du principat* 203 ff.

[9] Dio 57. 24. 1 (A.D. 24); 58. 24. 1 (A.D. 34); below, n. 12.

[10] Agrippa was granted the *tribunicia potestas* for five years in 18 B.C. and this was then extended for another five (Dio. 54. 12. 4; 54. 28. 1; Suet. *Aug.* 27. 5; *Pap. Colon.* 4701, ed. L. Koenen, *Zeitschr. f. Pap. u. Epigr.* 5 (1970), 226; Mommsen, *StR* 2. 1160; Kornemann, *Doppelprinzipat* 14 ff.; v. Premerstein 121; L. Koenen, l.c. 232 f.); Tiberius held it later three times for five years (Dio 55. 9. 4; 55. 13. 2; 56. 28. 1; cf. *Ath. Mitt.* 77 (1962), 321. 81). Municipal officers were often appointed for a quinquennial period, *praetor quinquennalis*, *aedilis quinquennalis* (= *aed. lustralis* at Tusculum), etc., see Dessau, *ILS* 3, p. 698.

[11] Dio 53. 16. 3 (27 B.C.): διὰ τοῦτο καὶ οἱ μετὰ ταῦτα αὐτοκράτορες ... ὅμως διὰ τῶν δέκα ἀεὶ ἐτῶν ἑώρτασαν ὡς καὶ τὴν ἡγεμονίαν αὖθις τότε ἀνανεούμενοι· καὶ τοῦτο καὶ νῦν γίγνεται.

[12] Dio 57. 24. 1 (A.D. 24): ἡ μέντοι πανήγυρις ἡ δεκαετηρὶς ἐποιήθη; 58. 24. 1 (A.D. 34): τὴν δεκετηρίδα τὴν δευτέραν ἑώρτασαν.

what this festival meant we learn from a related institution of the later imperial period, the *decennalia vota*.[1] Vows were made at the beginning of the
period and a festival was held at its end just as at the *lustra* and at the
Augustan *ludi quinquennales*. Needless to say, no festival marked Caesar's
provincial administration in Gaul but one may have been planned for the
intended periods of his dictatorship. The inspiration of the *lustra* is obvious
but the relationship to the quinquennial games is not clear at all.
Augustus' quinquennial games were held in 28, 24, 20, 16, 12 and so
on,[2] whereas the decennial festivals were held in different years. One
was certainly held in 27,[3] and others were due at least in 18 B.C. and
A.D. 13, for which years there is an explicit record about the renewal of
the office.[4] On the other hand, Tiberius held decennial festivals in A.D. 24
and 34 but quinquennial games never. If this institution represents an
analogy it is also a duplication, at least in the age of Augustus. It does
not lead to further conclusions with regard to the Caesarian festival.

The fourth means of clarification is provided by the Greek analogies.
Two of the four great games, the Olympia and Pythia, were pentaeteric
and inspired local festivals in honour of local gods,[5] including the
great Panathenaea, and later others in honour of rulers. Ptolemy II
instituted such a pentaeteric festival for his father at Alexandria
c. 280 B.C.,[6] the city of Ilium for Seleucus I,[7] Sardes for Eumenes II
c. 167 B.C.[8] This practice was continued under Roman rule. The cult
of the Dea Roma was created in the Confederacies, Koina, and had
existed in individual cities from the beginning of the second century B.C.,
first in the Lycian Koinon and in the cities of Smyrna, Antiochia-on-
Maeander, Caunus, Cibyra, Alabanda, Rhodes, with altars, temples,
priests, and games.[9] There is evidence for pentaeteric games in honour
of the Dea Roma in the Lycian Koinon,[10] and in the cities of Caunus
(in association with the principal goddess, Leto),[11] of Rhodes,[12] of Lagina
(together with Hecate Soteira),[13] of Oropus (together with the local

---

[1] Eckhel, *Doctrina numorum* 8. 473 ff.; Wissowa 382 f.; Mattingly, *Proc. Brit. Acad.* 1955,
155 ff.; P. Veyne, *REL* 38 (1960), 306 ff.　　　　[2] See above, p. 312. 1 f.
[3] Dio 53. 16. 3.　　　　　　　　[4] Dio 54. 12. 4; 56. 28. 1; above, p. 313. 8.
[5] Reisch, *RE* 1. 844; Stengel, *Griech. Kultusaltert.* 254; Ziehen, *RE* 19. 537 ff.; Wissowa
465; Friedländer, op. cit. 2. 145 ff.
[6] *Syll.* 390; Kallixeinos, *FGrHist.* 627 F 2 (Athen. 5. 197 D); a personification of Penteteris
was carried in the procession (§ 27).
[7] *Or. gr.* 212. 10; L. Robert, *Études anatol.* 172 ff.; Habicht 82.
[8] *Or. gr.* 305. 8.　　　　[9] See below, pp. 403 ff.　　　[10] *Or. gr.* 556 (*IGR* 3. 563).
[11] *SEG* 12. 466 (second cent. B.C.): . . . ἐν τοῖς τιθεμένοις ὑπὸ τοῦ δήμου Λητοῖ καὶ ʻΡώμῃ
πενταετηρικοῖς ἀγῶσιν . . . ; her place was given later to Caesar or Augustus, Pugliese Carratelli, *Annuario* 30/32 (1955), 292, no. 66a. 9 (first cent. A.D.?): ἐν Καύνῳ Λητῷα Καισάρεια . . .
καὶ τᾷ δεύτερον πενταετηρίδι κτλ.; L. Robert, *Arch. Eph.* 1966, 114 ff.
[12] *Syll.* 724. 7 (second cent. B.C.).　　　　　　　[13] *Or. gr.* 441. 131 (age of Sulla).

hero, Amphiaraus).[1] The cults of Roman generals followed, beginning with those of Marcellus and T. Flamininus.[2] Games are recorded for T. Flamininus, M. Annius (*quaestor* 119?), Sulla, Lucullus, Antony;[3] pentaeteric games only for Q. Mucius Scaevola (*cos.* 95), instituted by the province of Asia *c.* 98 B.C. in connection with the old-established Soteria.[4] There will have been others.

There is at first sight no evidence for Caesar, so that we must turn to the post-Caesarian evidence. The victory at Actium seems to have led to the first move. There had long been the Actia held annually in honour of the Actian Apollo;[5] Augustus now transformed them into pentaeteric games and added them to the four great games.[6] Actiads were introduced and counted on the model of the olympiads,[7] just as a new era was begun in many places dating from the Actian victory, 2 September 31 B.C.[8] At Rome, as we have seen, the pentaeteric games in honour of Augustus were decreed about the same time in 30, and were first held in 28.[9] Such games were soon founded all over the empire; according to Suetonius almost every city had them.[10] They

[1] *Syll.* 287. 12; 747. 47 (73 B.C.); 1064; Stengel, op. cit. 254; L. Moretti, *Iscrizioni agonistiche greche* (1953), 118; 145.

[2] Cic. *Verr.* 2. 2. 114; 154 (Syracuse, after 212 B.C.); Plut. *Flamin.* 16. 5 (after 195 B.C.); E.-J. 102. 11 f. (Gytheum); Daux, *BCH* 88 (1964), 575 (Argos: Titieia).

[3] Games for Annius at Leta, Macedonia, *Syll.* 700. 37 ff.; the Συλλεῖα and Κορνήλια at Athens (*IG* 2². 1039. 57; Meritt, *Hesp.* 17 (1948), 44, no. 35d; Raubitschek, *Studies . . . in Honor of A. C. Johnson* (1951), 49 ff.); the Λευκόλλεια in cities of Asia *c.* 73 B.C. (Plut. *Luc.* 23. 2; App. *Mithr.* 76. 330); the Ἀντωνιῆα τὰ Παναθηναϊκὰ Ἀντωνίου θεοῦ Νέου Διονύσου at Athens (*IG* 2². 1043. 22); cf. Nilsson 2. 178 f.; Bömer, *RE* 21. 1896; Classen, *Gymn.* 70 (1963), 337 f.

[4] *Or. gr.* 438 (*IGR* 4. 188): τῶν Σωτηρίων καὶ Μουκιείων; 437; 439; Cic. *Verr.* 2. 2. 51: 'Mucia'; Ps.-Ascon. *div.* p. 202 St.: 'hic est Mucius in cuius honorem Asiani diem festum Mucia nominaverunt'; p. 262 St.; Pfister, *RE* 3A. 1229; Magie, *Roman Rule* 1064 f.

[5] Strab. 7. 325; *IG* 9.1². 583; Reisch, *RE* 1. 1213 f.; Gagé, *Mél.* 53 (1936), 93 f.; Habicht, *Herm.* 85 (1957), 102 ff.; Th. Ch. Sarikakis, *Arch. Eph.* 1965, 145 ff.

[6] Dio 51. 1. 2 (31 B.C.): ἀγῶνά τέ τινα . . . πεντετηρικὸν ἱερόν . . . κατέδειξεν, Ἄκτια αὐτὸν προσαγορεύσας; Suet. *Aug.* 28. 2; Strab. 7. 325; Gagé, l.c. 92 ff.; Moretti, op. cit. 205 ff.; Larsen, *Representative Government* 111. For epigraphical evidence of the Actian games, also of those held under this name elsewhere, see Friedländer, op. cit. 2. 145 f.; Moretti, op. cit. 275 (Index, s.v.); Latte 303. 2.

[7] Jos. *BJ* 1. 20. 4, 398; *BCH* 1 (1877), 294.   [8] Magie, op. cit. 1289. 37.

[9] See above, p. 311. There is of course some connection between these and the Actian games. But if these *ludi quinquennales* were inspired in the first place by the Caesarian precedent, Dio cannot be right in asserting that they commemorated the Actian victory (53. 1. 4: τὴν πανήγυριν τὴν ἐπὶ τῇ νίκῃ τῇ πρὸς τῷ Ἀκτίῳ γενομένῃ ψηφισθεῖσαν . . .) He may be confusing them with the annual festival held on 2 September for this purpose (Degrassi 505; forbidden by Caligula: Dio 59. 20. 1; Suet. *Cal.* 23. 1). The much quoted Leningrad Cameo with the impossible inscription 'vot(a) pub(lica) Oct(avius) Caes(ar) Aug(ustus) ter(ra) mar(i)q(ue)' (Maximova, *Rev. arch.* 30 (1929), 64 ff.; Gagé, l.c. 72, fig. 2) must be a forgery.—Tac. *A.* 15. 23. 3 (A.D. 63, birth of Nero's daughter): 'certamen ad exemplar Actiacae religionis decretum', is puzzling: beginning of a new era?

[10] Suet. *Aug.* 59: 'provinciarum pleraeque super templa et aras ludos quoque quinquennales paene oppidatim constituerunt'; Aur. Vict. 1. 6.

were certainly pentaeteric at Naples, Mytilene, Caesarea Augusta,[1] and probably in many, if not all, other places;[2] at Pergamum they were celebrated 'pro salute et victoria' of Augustus.[3] They were often connected with the games held in honour of the Dea Roma, the Romaia, no doubt in all those cities where she had a joint cult with Augustus.[4] But in contrast to the games at Rome they were continued after the death of Augustus.

These games of the provinces must have been preceded by Caesarian games, just as the Augustan games at Rome depended on the games planned before in honour of Caesar. The discussion of his cult which will follow later[5] will provide a great deal of further circumstantial evidence for such games and an inscription from Ephesus will be treated as direct evidence, as it leads to the conclusion that the games were in fact instituted by Antony soon after Caesar's death. They will have been called *ludi Caesaris* or *Caesarea*: this name is suggested by the earlier Marcellia, Mucia, Λουκούλλεια, also by those *Caesarea* which were held later in honour of Augustus but perhaps already existed in some places before his time; and there was in Rome the further analogy of the *ludi Augustales* or *Augustalia*.[6]

Returning to Caesar's *ludi quinquennales*, we have to decide which of the relevant festivals should be considered the real precedent. The choice is in fact not difficult. If, as Dio says, they represent a divine honour,[7] which we found confirmed in the provinces, then they can only have been inspired by the Greek games, held in honour of rulers, alive or dead, and of the Dea Roma. The Roman precedents, the vows of the *lustra* and the *ludi magni* of an emergency, must be excluded because they were never instituted in the interest of an individual but were for the welfare of the whole Roman people. It was in a similar emergency that Caesar's dictatorial power was created, and if a celebration was planned for each term this too is to be excluded, because it would clearly have been inspired by those precedents. The same applies to what followed Caesar's example, Augustus' and Tiberius' imperial power, the *decennia* of which are known to have ended with celebrations.

---

[1] Naples: Strab. 5. 246; Dio 55. 10. 9; 56. 29. 2; Vell. 2. 123. 1; Suet. *Aug.* 98. 5 (Pfister, *RE* IA. 1062); Mytilene: *Or. gr.* 456. 7; Caesarea Augusta: Jos. *AJ* 16. 137 f.; *BJ* 1. 415.

[2] On the controversy see Magie, op. cit. 1296 (with bibliography); Moretti, op. cit. 154.

[3] *IGR* 4. 316; *AE* 1904, 224. 13.

[4] See the collection in Moretti, op. cit.

[5] See below, pp. 402 ff.

[6] Tac. *A.* 1. 15. 3; E.-J. 94a. 50; *Mon. Anc.* 11; Dio 54. 10. 3; 34. 2.

[7] Dio 44. 6. 2 (above, p. 310. 3).

They have vows and festivals in common with the *ludi quinquennales*, but differ from them in so far as they are concerned with the welfare of the emperor and not with his divinity. The *ludi quinquennales* make sense only in the context of divine honours, with priests and temples at Rome as well as in the provinces.

ADDITIONAL NOTE

(to p. 312, note 2)

Mon. Anc. 9. 1 appeared above, p. 312 n. 2, in the following form: 'vota p[ro salute mea susc]ipi per consules et sacerdotes quinto quoque anno decrevit senatus.' Mommsen's almost universally accepted supplement was 'p[ro valetudine . . .]', of which Weber, *Princeps* 174*. 613, claims to have recovered '[vale]tudin[e]' from very uncertain traces. The supplement 'salute' is commended: (1) by the difference between 'salus' and 'valetudo', 'welfare' and 'health' (*RE* 8A. 264 ff.); (2) by the Greek version εὐχὰς ὑπὲρ τῆς ἐμῆς σωτηρίας ἀναλαμβάνειν, instead of ὑγιείας, which would be required for 'valetudo'; (3) by the coin of L. Mescinius Rufus, issued in 16 B.C., (that is, in a year when *ludi quinquennales* were held), with the legend: 'I(ovi) O(ptimo) M(aximo) S(enatus) P(opulus)q(ue) R(omanus) v(otum) s(olvit) pr(o) s(alute) Imp(eratoris) Cae(saris) quod per eu(m) r(es) p(ublica) in amp(liore) atq(ue) tran(quilliore) s(tatu) e(st)' (Mattingly 1. 17 f.; pl. 3. 14); (4) by the reference to it in the *Acta ludorum saecularium* of 17 B.C., *CIL* 6. 877 a 4: '[pro ludis,] quos pro salute Caesaris fecerunt'; (5) by Pliny 7. 158 (A.D. 9): 'ludis pro salute Divi Augusti votivis'; (6) by the relationship between the *vota pro salute rei publicae* and those for Caesar and Augustus, discussed above, pp. 217 f.; cf. also Latte 314. 2 (for the supplement 'salute').

XV

THE INVESTITURE

THREE attempts were made in 44 to make Caesar a king: in January after his return from the Feriae Latinae, in February at the Lupercalia, and in March with the help of a Sibylline Oracle.[1] The evidence is substantial and clear and yet not generally accepted. It is agreed that in fact Caesar had monarchic power but it is argued that it was unwise to call it kingship: the name of a king meant tyranny for the Romans. It is therefore often suggested that Caesar had no share and no knowledge of these plans, which he rejected. They were made either by his friends, who were over-zealous, or by his enemies, who wanted to destroy him. The villain of the piece is usually Mark Antony.

It is true that it was a dangerous game. We have reviewed the old republican tradition, beginning with the feat of L. Brutus and the punishment of the pretenders. We have also seen that, in the year before, Caesar himself was anxious to be celebrated as another liberator in various forms, and that nevertheless he was often accused of aiming at kingship. Cicero, for instance, called him a tyrant at the beginning of the Civil War and repeated the charge, though not without contradictions, right to the end.[2] On the other hand, this severe condemnation of kingship was modified for the sake of the heroic past and of political theory. The kings of Rome, with the exception of the last Tarquinius, were praised by the historians for their achievements,[3] and Caesar himself proclaimed in his youth with pride that his father was descended on his mother's side from the Marcii Reges.[4] Cicero too intro-

[1] Meyer, *Caesars Monarchie* 508 ff.; Adcock, *CAH* 9. 718 ff.; Gelzer, *Caesar* 295 ff.; Carcopino, *Les étapes de l'impérialisme romain* 154 ff.; Alföldi, *Studien über Caesars Monarchie* 19 ff.; K. Kraft, 'Der goldene Kranz Caesars u. die Entlarvung des "Tyrannen" ', *Jahrb. f. Num. u. Geldgesch.* 3/4 (1952/3), 39 ff. (with bibliogr. on p. 39. 186; 40. 187); D. Felber, 'Caesars Streben nach der Königswürde' (in Altheim's *Untersuch. z. röm. Gesch.* 1 (1961), 259 ff.; G. Dobesch, *Caesars Apotheose zu Lebzeiten u. sein Ringen um den Königstitel* (1966), 104 ff.; M. Liberanome, *Riv. fil.* 96 (1968), 407 ff.

[2] Cic. *Att.* 7. 20. 2 (Febr. 49) : 'ad fugam hortatur . . . turpitudo coniungendi cum tyranno'; 13. 37. 2 (Aug. 45) : 'nisi viderem scire regem me animi nihil habere'; *Att.* 14. 14. 2; 15. 20. 2; *Phil.* 2. 114: 'hi . . . in regnantem impetum fecerunt'; *off.* 3. 83: 'qui rex populi Romani dominusque omnium gentium esse concupiverit idque perfecerit.'

[3] Cf. Schwegler, *Röm. Gesch.* 1. 516 ff.

[4] Suet. *Caes.* 6. 1 : 'maternum genus ab regibus ortum . . . nam ab Anco Marcio sunt Marcii Reges . . . est ergo in genere et sanctitas regum, qui plurimum inter homines pollent . . .'

duced another type of king, the just ruler of the ideal state, as was demanded by Greek political theory.[1] What was Caesar to be: a new Romulus, or a tyrant, or the king of Cicero's *De re publica*, or something of his own creation—or did he really leave the initiative to his friends or enemies?

I. THE DIADEMED STATUES

Two pieces of evidence are connected and confused. One is that sometime in January 44 Caesar's statues on the Rostra were decorated with diadems. The tribunes C. Epidius Marullus and L. Caesetius Flavus removed them and sent the guilty man to prison.[2] The other is that Caesar, returning from the Alban Mount where he had celebrated the Feriae Latinae and entering Rome on 26 January in the form of a solemn *ovatio*, was acclaimed king by the people, and that it was on this occasion that the statues were decorated with a diadem.[3] Caesar replied that his name was Caesar, not Rex.[4] The two tribunes punished the man who was the first to acclaim him. The people now acclaimed the tribunes as 'Bruti' (liberators),[5] but Caesar retorted that they were 'bruti' (stupid).[6] Caesar was angry but did nothing. On the second occasion he took action, and the tribunes lost their office.[7] It is possible that the decoration came first and the acclamation second, and that the tribunes intervened on both occasions. It is equally possible that acclamation and decoration took place on the same day, during the

---

[1] Cic. *rep.* 1. 50; *fin.* 3. 75; Béranger, *REL* 13 (1935), 91 ff.; R. Klein, *Königtum u. Königszeit bei Cicero* (Diss. Erlangen 1962); Michelfeit, *Philol.* 108 (1964), 262 ff.

[2] Dio 44. 9. 2: τὴν εἰκόνα αὐτοῦ τὴν ἐπὶ τοῦ Βήματος ἑστῶσαν διαδήματι λάθρᾳ ἀνέδησαν. (3) καὶ αὐτὸ Γαΐου τε Ἐπιδίου Μαρύλλου καὶ Λουκίου Καισητίου Φλάουου δημάρχων καθελόντων ἰσχυρῶς ἐχαλέπηνε; App. *BC* 2. 108. 449: εἰκόνα δ' αὐτοῦ τις τῶν ὑπερεθιζόντων τὸ λογοποίημα τῆς βασιλείας ἐστεφάνωσε δάφναις, ἀναπεπλεγμένης ταινίας λευκῆς· καὶ αὐτὸν οἱ δήμαρχοι . . . ἀνευρόντες ἐς τὴν φυλακὴν ἐσέβαλον.

[3] Suet. *Caes.* 79. 1: 'cum in (?) sacrificio Latinarum revertente eo inter inmodicas ac novas populi acclamationes quidam e turba statuae eius coronam lauream candida fascia praeligata inposuisset et tribuni plebis Epidius Marullus Caesetiusque Flavus coronae fasciam detrahi hominemque duci in vincula iussissent . . .'

[4] Dio 44. 10. 1: ὡς μέντοι μετὰ τοῦτο ἐσιππεύοντα αὐτὸν ἀπὸ τοῦ Ἀλβανοῦ βασιλέα αὖθίς τινες ὠνόμασαν καὶ αὐτὸς μὲν οὐκ ἔφη βασιλεὺς ἀλλὰ Καῖσαρ καλεῖσθαι; App. *BC* 2. 108. 450: ἑτέρων δ' αὐτὸν ἀμφὶ τὰς πύλας ἰόντα ποθὲν βασιλέα προσειπόντων καὶ τοῦ δήμου στενάξαντος, εὐμηχάνως εἶπε τοῖς ἀσπασαμένοις· "οὐκ εἰμὶ Βασιλεύς, ἀλλὰ Καῖσαρ"; Suet. *Caes.* 79. 2: 'plebei regem se salutanti Caesarem se non regem esse responderit . . .'; Plut. *Caes.* 61. 8: ὤφθησαν δ' ἀνδριάντες αὐτοῦ διαδήμασιν ἀναδεδεμένοι βασιλικοῖς, καὶ τῶν δημάρχων δύο . . . ἐπελθόντες ἀπέσπασαν, καὶ τοὺς ἀσπασαμένους βασιλέα τὸν Καίσαρα πρώτους ἐξευρόντες ἀπῆγον εἰς τὸ δεσμωτήριον.

[5] Postum. Albin. frg. 2 P.; Livy 1. 56. 8; above, p. 146. 7.

[6] Plut. *Caes.* 61. 9 f. Soon after the murder Cicero made use of this double meaning in order to distinguish between Brutus and some other conspirators, *Att.* 14. 14. 2.

[7] Val. Max. 5. 7. 2; Meyer, op. cit. 527.

ovatio. The suspicion of a duplication, however, cannot be excluded, especially as the diademed statues were on the Rostra, which was to be the scene of the presentation of the diadem to Caesar in person. A choice is not possible except with the help of further analysis.

The decoration of statues was not new. The two statues in question wore an oak wreath and a grass wreath respectively.[1] This was a special distinction, but a diadem meant more than that. A statue of Ap. Claudius Caecus, set up at Forum Clodi *c.* 312 B.C., had a diadem and will have to be discussed later.[2] This was not at Rome; but at Rome itself the statues of the kings on the Capitol were diademed, at least for the previous two hundred years or so.[3] The kings of the Greek East always wore a diadem, and the Romans knew what it implied; much more will be said about it later.[4] Here the question is to be raised: who was responsible for it? Certainly not the man who was caught and sent to prison. It was not an isolated and meaningless action but was inspired by someone who was behind the further relevant moves. The monarchy was planned, and the reaction of the public tested.

The return from the Feriae Latinae either followed this or took place at the same time. If it followed, the *ovatio* for the return must have been decreed about the time when this experiment with the diadem was made—which will prove to be important. If it was done at the same time, the *ovatio* with its acclamation and the diadem must have served the same purpose in two different ways.

2. THE FERIAE LATINAE

The Feriae Latinae were the annual festival of the Latin League at the temple of Iuppiter Latiaris on the Alban Mount.[5] It dated from the time when Alba Longa was the principal city of Latium. All member cities sent their magistrates but Alba was in charge of the festival. It was probably after the destruction of Alba that Rome took over the organization.[6] It was now a responsibility of the consuls, who announced after entering office when the festival would be held—it was not on a fixed date but was to be held before they left for the

---

[1] See above, pp. 148 ff.; 163 ff.   [2] Suet. *Tib.* 2. 2; see below, p. 334.

[3] Iuven. 8. 259 f.: 'diadema Quirini'; Numa and Ancus Marcius on coins: Sydenham 172; 111; 149; cf. H. W. Ritter, *Diadem u. Königsherrschaft* (1965), 13. 2; above, pp. 145; 176. 8.   [4] See below, pp. 334 ff.

[5] *Fast. Fer. Lat.* (Degrassi, *Inscr. Ital.* 13. 1. 143 ff.); Varr. *LL* 6. 25: Dion. Hal. 4. 49. 2, etc.; Mommsen, *Röm. Forsch.* 2. 97 ff.; Chr. Werner, *De feriis Latinis* (Diss. Leipzig 1888); Samter, *RE* 6. 2213 ff.; Wissowa 40; 124 f.; Latte 144 ff.; Alföldi, *Early Rome and the Latins* 29 ff.

[6] Dion. Hal. 4. 49. 3: τὴν ἡγεμονίαν τῶν ἱερῶν ἔχουσι Ῥωμαῖοι.

provinces.[1] All the magistrates had to be present, and a *praefectus urbi* was appointed for the time of their absence from Rome.[2]

The Feriae Latinae had some unusual features under Caesar, which in view of the Alban origin of his family is not surprising. He held the festival three times, in 59, 49, and 44. There is no record about 59, the year of his first consulate; he could not take part in the festival in 48, 46, and 45 during his second, third, and fourth consulates, because he was absent.[3] He held one in December 49 as dictator before he departed for the war against Pompey.[4] There are three possible explanations for his holding it at so unusual a time: because the consuls of the year omitted it or because they committed a ritual error or because it was a special occasion. An omission used to lead to catastrophe. C. Flaminius perished at Lake Trasimene in 217, and Hirtius and Pansa died in 43;[5] in 257, during the First Punic War, a 'dictator Latinarum feriarum caussa', Q. Ogulnius Gallus (*cos.* 269), was appointed to repair such an omission.[6] It is true that the consuls of 49, C. Claudius Marcellus and L. Cornelius Lentulus, left Rome in great haste with Pompey in January, and it has been assumed that they therefore omitted the festival.[7] But the festival was in fact held,[8] and Caesar was not appointed dictator specially for it but 'dictator rei publicae constituendae', for a great deal of necessary legislative work.[9] The second possibility would be a repetition because of a portent or ritual error. It is recorded that, against the rules, no *praefectus urbi* was chosen;[10] also that the flame which was lit to indicate the end of the Feriae split into two parts and blazed on the two peaks of the Mount like the pyre of the two warring Theban brothers, Eteocles and

---

[1] Livy 21. 63. 8; 22. 1. 6; 44. 19. 4.

[2] Strab. 5. 229; Dion. Hal. 8. 87. 6; Dio 41. 14. 4; *ILS* 186; 1051; 1171 f., etc.; Mommsen, *StR* 1. 666 f.; for a complete list of the recorded *feriae* see Werner, op. cit. 57–63.

[3] The Fasti explicitly mention Augustus' absence for the years 26 and 25 (Degrassi, op. cit. 151); the record for Caesar's consulates has not survived.

[4] Caes. *BC* 3. 2. 1: 'his rebus et feriis Latinis comitiisque omnibus perficiendis XI dies tribuit dictaturaque se abdicat et ab urbe proficiscitur'; Lucan. 5. 400 ff.: 'nec non Iliacae numen quod praesidet Albae, / haud meritum Latio sollemnia sacra subacto, / vidit flammifera confectas nocte Latinas.'

[5] Livy 21. 63. 8; Dio 46. 33. 4.

[6] *Fast. cons. Capit.* (Degrassi, op. cit. 43); Münzer, *RE* 17. 2066; on such special dictatorships see Mommsen, *StR* 2. 156. 7.

[7] Drumann 3. 426; Gelzer, *Caesar* 203.

[8] Dio 41. 14. 4; Lucan. 1. 550 ff.

[9] Caes. *BC* 3. 1. 1; Dio 41. 36. 3; Gelzer 202 f.; L. Gasperini, l.c. (above, p. 200. 3) 386 ff.

[10] Dio 41. 14. 4 (list of portents): καὶ πολίαρχος οὐδεὶς ἐς τὰς ἀνοχάς, ὥσπερ εἴθιστο, ᾑρέθη, ἀλλ' οἱ στρατηγοὶ πάντα τὰ ἐπιβάλλοντα αὐτῷ, ὥς γέ τισι δοκεῖ, διῴκησαν· ἕτεροι γὰρ ἐν τῷ ὑστέρῳ ἔτει φασὶν αὐτοὺς τοῦτο ποιῆσαι. The same is recorded for 36 B.C., Dio 49. 16. 2.

Polynices—an evil portent.[1] The festival had been repeated in 396, in the time of Camillus, because it was not correctly announced;[2] in 176 because the magistrate of Lanuvium omitted a prayer;[3] in 56 because of an unspecified ritual error.[4] In 49 the portent and the omission of the appointment of the *praefectus urbi* would have been reported to the Senate, the advice of the pontifical college and of its head, Caesar, sought, and the decision taken that the dictator Caesar should repeat the Feriae.[5] This is a real possibility, as part of the political and religious struggle, provided that the irregularities were not invented at a later date by a Caesarian poet or historian. The third possibility is that Caesar's Feriae had nothing to do with the earlier one but were decreed for him as a special honour. In 449, the consuls L. Valerius Potitus and M. Horatius Barbatus held them three times[6] for reasons which are not known; in 396 Camillus as dictator held them for the second time after the conquest of Veii, clearly as an additional celebration of his victory.[7] In 168 special Feriae lasting three days were held in honour of the praetor L. Anicius Gallus (*cos.* 160) for his victories in Illyria,[8] although he also held a triumph in the following year. A similar repetition was planned in 9 B.C. for Drusus because of his successes in Germany, but he died before it could be held.[9] If this was the case, the Senate empowered Caesar to hold his special Feriae because of his successes against the Pompeians in Italy and Spain or because of the conquest of Gaul. The proper precedent will have been that of Camillus, whether a fact or a legend, although it is not impossible that the legend was created after Caesar. This alternative is clearly preferable to the other two.

Nothing is known about the details. It is possible that Caesar chose to resign his dictatorship not at Rome but on the Alban Mount, as

---

[1] Lucan. 1. 550: 'et ostendens confectas flamma Latinas / scinditur in partes geminoque cacumine surgit / Thebanos imitata rogos'; cf. Lyd. *ost.* p. 103. 15 W. (*PBSR* 19 (1951), 140).

[2] Livy 5. 17. 2; 19. 1; Plut. *Cam.* 4. 6; Werner, op. cit. 58. 5.   [3] Livy 41. 16. 1; 5.

[4] Cic. *Q.fr.* 2. 4. 2; 5. 2; Dio 39. 30. 4.

[5] For the procedure see Livy 41. 16. 2.

[6] *Fast. Fer. Lat.* (Degrassi, op. cit. 147).

[7] Degrassi, op. cit. 147: 'Tribunis militaribus pro consulibus Latinae fuerunt pr. Non .... M. Furio L. f. Sp. n. Camillo dictatore iterum Latinae fuerunt pr. K. Nov.'; Mommsen, *Röm. Forsch.* 2. 109; Werner 58. 5; Degrassi, op. cit. 156.

[8] Livy 45. 3. 2: 'ob eas res gestas ductu auspicioque L. Anici praetoris senatus in triduom supplicationes decrevit. iterum Latinae edictae a consule sunt in ante diem quartum et tertium et pridie Idus Novembres'; cf. 44. 19. 4; 22. 16; Mommsen, *Röm. Forsch.* 2. 106; Latte 145.

[9] Dio 55. 2. 5: καί γε αἱ ἀνοχαὶ δεύτερον τὴν χάριν αὐτοῦ, πρὸς τὸ τὰ νικητήρια ἐν ἐκείναις αὐτὸν ἑορτάσαι, γενήσεσθαι ἔμελλον.

Augustus resigned his consulate there in 23 B.C.[1] It is also tempting to attribute a further special feature to these Feriae. It is a fact that the prescribed victim was a bull.[2] It is recorded in another context that Caesar was about to sacrifice a bull to Fortuna before his departure for the war against Pompey but that it escaped and swam through a lake, thus portending that Caesar would win if he crossed the sea.[3] We have already examined this evidence and found that the bull was not the proper sacrificial animal for a female deity, and that the escape of the victim was normally of evil significance.[4] But we have also found that such a bull had escaped once before from the Mount and was caught on the spot where Bovillae was founded later;[5] this story is relevant because Bovillae was the home of the Gens Iulia. It is in this context important to stress the point that it was from the Alban Mount that the bull of Bovillae escaped, because it leads to the conjecture that Caesar's bull too, and what it portended, was originally connected with the sacrifice on the Alban Mount in December 49. If so, it was used again for another version of the story when the idea of the Fortuna Caesaris began to be propagated. The question as to fact or fiction need not detain us, because the bull became henceforth the animal symbol of Caesar's legions.[6]

It is to be assumed that Caesar took an interest in the Feriae in the following years. Nothing is known about 48, the year of Pharsalus. In 47 his great-nephew C. Octavius became the *praefectus urbi* at the age of sixteen[7] immediately after he had taken the *toga virilis* and had been elected *pontifex*. Nothing is known of 46, and in 45 the Feriae lasted three days with a new *praefectus urbi* for every day, which was unusual.[8]

In 44 Caesar was both consul and dictator, held the festival, and returned from the Alban Mount in an official *ovatio* on 26 January.[9] No further direct evidence has survived; and yet the festival may receive an unexpected significance if considered in the light of Caesar's aspirations, and in connection with the Alban tradition and the place of the Iulii in it. At first Alba was in charge of the festival, represented by

---

[1] Dio 53. 32. 3; *Fast. Fer. Lat.* (Degrassi, op. cit. 151): 'Imp. Caes. consulatum abdicavit. iterum Latinae fuerunt . . . K. Nov. . . .' (clearly in Augustus' honour but the reasons are not known).

[2] Dion. Hal. 4. 49. 3; Arnob. 2. 68.   [3] Dio 41. 39. 2.   [4] See above, p. 118.

[5] Schol. Pers. 6. 55; Non. 122 M. (s.v. Hillas); above, pp. 6 ff.

[6] See above, pp. 118 ff.   [7] Nic. Dam. *v. Caes.* 5. 13 (*FGrHist.* 90 F 127).

[8] Dio 43. 48. 4.

[9] Suet. *Caes.* 79. 1: 'in (?) sacrificio Latinarum revertente eo'; Dio 44. 4. 3: μετά τε τὰς ἀνοχὰς τὰς Λατίνας ἐπὶ κέλητος ἐς τὴν πόλιν ἐκ τοῦ Ἀλβανοῦ ἐσελαύνειν ἔδοσαν; 10. 1: ἐσιππεύοντα αὐτὸν ἀπὸ τοῦ Ἀλβανοῦ; *Fast. Triumph.*: '. . . ovans . . . ex monte Albano VII K. Febr.'

the king,[1] later by his successor, the dictator,[2] who could also be called 'king'.[3] The dictator still had a special function at the festival in Roman times, when Alba and the League had long ceased to have any political significance, and he was, like all other priests of the Latin cities, one of the public priests of Rome and a Roman citizen.[4] The Iulii were, through Aeneas and Iulus, descendants of the kings of Alba, and had a hereditary priesthood at neighbouring Bovillae.[5] It is recorded that in 45 Caesar began to wear the red boots of the Alban kings,[6] which was clearly a demonstration of his descent. But he could not have done it without the authorization of the Senate, and the Senate in turn could only have done it by appointing him dictator of Alba.[7] He was thus entitled to wear all that the dictators inherited from the kings, including the boots. This was, then, in preparation for the Feriae of 44. Caesar now appeared there as the consul and dictator of Rome and as the dictator, who was also 'king', of Alba. This position was relevant for the acclamation on his return.

Here was another manifestation of Caesar's attachment to the traditions of his family, although one might feel that this archaic and parochial role was inconsistent with his world-wide aspirations. And yet it is possible to argue that that role was an important means of achieving his aims. If he wanted to be a king, he had to dress up as a king, and

[1] Strab. 5. 3. 4, p. 231: (Albans and Romans) βασιλευόμενοι δ' ἑκάτεροι χωρὶς ἐτύγχανον; Livy 1. 22. 7: 'nuntiate . . . regi vestro'; 1. 23. 7: 'regem nostrum Cluilium'; 1. 24. 2: 'cum trigeminis agunt reges.'

[2] Plut. Rom. 27. 1: ἐπεὶ δὲ τοῦ πάππου Νομήτορος ἐν Ἄλβῃ τελευτήσαντος αὐτῷ βασιλεύειν προσῆκον, εἰς μέσον ἔθηκε τὴν πολιτείαν δημαγωγῶν καὶ κατ' ἐνιαυτὸν ἀπεδείκνυεν ἄρχοντα τοῖς Ἀλβανοῖς; Licin. Macer, frg. 10 P. (Dion. Hal. 5. 74. 4): . . . παρ' Ἀλβανῶν οἴεται τὸν δικτάτορα 'Ρωμαίους εἰληφέναι τούτους λέγων πρώτους μετὰ τὸν Ἀμολίου καὶ Νεμέτορος θάνατον ἐκλιπούσης τῆς βασιλικῆς συγγενείας ἐνιαυσίους ἄρχοντας ἀποδεῖξαι τὴν αὐτὴν ἔχοντας ἐξουσίαν τοῖς βασιλεῦσι, καλεῖν δ' αὐτοὺς δικτάτορας; Dion. Hal. 3. 23. 3: Μέττιος Φουφέττιος . . . τρίτον ἔτος ἐπὶ τῆς αὐτοκράτορος ἀρχῆς διέμενε Τύλλου κελεύσαντος; 3. 28. 6; 3. 7. 3; Mommsen, StR 2. 171; Rosenberg, Staat d. alt. Italiker 79; contra, H. Rudolph, Stadt u. Staat im röm. Italien 9 f.; P. Catalano, Linee del sistema sovranazionale romano 1 (1965), 212; criticism of Rudolph by E. Manni, Per la storia dei municipii (1947), 96 ff.

[3] Livy 1. 23. 4: 'in his castris Cluilius, Albanus rex, moritur'; Mommsen, StR 2. 171. 3.

[4] ILS 4955 (Rome): 'L. Fonteius Flavianus . . . pontifex, dictator Albanus'; 9507 (Ostia, A.D. 249): 'P. Flavio . . . Prisco . . . pontifici et dictatori Albano'; cf. Wissowa, Herm. 50 (1915), 2 ff.   [5] See above, pp. 7; 29.

[6] Dio 43. 43. 2 (45 B.C.): τῇ ὑποδέσει . . . ἐνίοτε καὶ ὑψηλῇ καὶ ἐρυθροχρόῳ κατὰ τοὺς βασιλέας τοὺς ἐν τῇ Ἄλβῃ ποτὲ γενομένους, ὡς καὶ προσήκων σφίσι διὰ τὸν Ἰουλον, ἐχρῆτο; Fest. 142 M. (128 L.): 'mulleos genus calceorum aiunt esse; quibus reges Albanorum primi, deinde patricii sunt usi'; Mommsen, StR 3. 888 f.; Wilcken, 'Zur Entwicklung der röm. Diktatur', Abh. Akad. Berl. (1940), No. 1. 20; Alföldi, Der frühröm. Reiteradel 54 ff.—It is also ascribed to Romulus, Dio 1, frg. 6. 1 (1, p. 10 B.): πεδίλοις ἐκεχρῆτο ἐρυθροῖς.

[7] This seems to be the conclusion of Mommsen in the neglected note, StR 2. 171. 3: 'Wenn ferner von dem Dictator Caesar gesagt wird, dass er den Schuh der albanischen Könige anlegte . . ., so ist dabei gewiss nicht an Theater- oder Malerherkommen zu denken, sondern an den Mulleus des priesterlichen Dictators von Alba.'

the Alban kingship was both legitimate and innocuous. Alexander readily accepted the Persian costume after the conquest of Persia;[1] no reference is made to high boots, probably because he had them already as the king of Macedon.[2] Demetrius Poliorcetes wore not only the red cloak, *causia*, and diadem, but also special red boots with golden embroidery.[3] If Caesar, as will be argued later, was planning to appear as a king in the East, he had to dress accordingly. And the regal costume of Alba was one of the means of achieving this aim.[4]

A further step may be made in the same direction. Suetonius records in a different context that Caesar used to wear a long-sleeved tunic.[5] That was an oriental custom: the traditional Greek and Roman tunic was without sleeves.[6] It was considered effeminate, a sign of luxury and depravity,[7] and was usually ascribed to a political adversary, as by Cicero to Verres, Catilina, Clodius, and Antony.[8] Suetonius' information, therefore, must come from an anti-Caesarian source. Nevertheless, the substance of the story may be true and only the interpretation wrong. As we have seen, Alexander too put on the 'barbarian' dress when he reached Persia.[9] It is also relevant that the fancy-dress of Caligula is described[10] in almost the same terms as Curtius uses about the Persian costume.[11] There is no more that can be said here. But the story about the tunic well supports our conclusions about the boots and will gain further significance in connection with the diadem.[12] Whether Caesar wore the tunic or planned to wear it in the East naturally cannot be decided: but even the plan must have caused a great stir.

[1] Curt. 3. 3. 17 ff.; 6. 6. 1 ff.: Diod. 17. 77. 5; cf. Xen. *Cyrop.* 8. 3. 13.

[2] E. Neuffer, *Das Kostüm Alexanders d. Gr.* (Diss. Giessen 1929), 7; 10 f.; 31 ff.; cf. Bieber, *RE* 11. 1520 ff.; Alföldi, *Studies in Honor of A. M. Friend* (1955), 50 f.

[3] Duris, *FGrHist.* 76 F 14 (Athen. 12. 535 F); Plut. *Dem.* 41. 4.

[4] Caesar's example was followed by Caligula (Suet. *Cal.* 52: 'modo in crepidis vel coturnis, modo in speculatoria caliga, nonnumquam socco muliebri'; Sen. *const. sap.* 18. 4), perhaps also by Nero (Dio 63. 22. 4).

[5] Suet. *Caes.* 45. 3: 'etiam cultu notabilem ferunt: usum enim lato clavo ad manus fimbriato...'; Dio 43. 43. 2 mentions only his loose girdle (also in Suet. and Macrob. 2. 3. 9) but in the context of the boots.

[6] Blümner, *Privatleben d. Römer* 207; Alföldi, *Studies in Honor of A. M. Friend* (1955), 41 ff. (valuable, with bibliography).

[7] It was, however, used in Eleusis (Athen. 1. 21 C) and especially for the representation of Dionysus (Bieber, *Arch. Jahrb.* 32 (1917), 21 ff.).

[8] Cic. *Verr.* 2. 5. 31; *Cat.* 2. 22: 'manicatis et talaribus tunicis'; *in Clod.* frg. 22; 24 Sch. (p. 448); *Phil.* 11. 26; cf. Gell. 6. 12. 1 ff. (the younger Scipio about P. Sulpicius Galus: 'chirodota tunica'); Verg. *Aen.* 9. 614 ff. (Numanus about the Trojans); Sen. *ep.* 33. 2.

[9] Plut. *Alex.* 45. 1: εἰς τὴν Παρθικὴν ἀναζεύξας καὶ σχολάζων, πρῶτον ἐνεδύσατο τὴν βαρβαρικὴν στολήν.

[10] Suet. *Cal.* 52: 'saepe depictas gemmatasque indutus paenulas, manuleatus et armillatus in publicum processit.' On Caligula as imitator of Caesar see above, p. 191. 5.

[11] Curt. 3. 3. 13: 'illi aureos torques, illi vestem auro distinctam habebant manicatasque tunicas gemmis etiam adornatas.'   [12] See below, pp. 338 ff.

3. THE *OVATIO*

The Senate decreed, probably at the time when the arrangements were made for the Feriae Latinae, that Caesar should hold an *ovatio* on his return[1]—an extraordinary decree. An *ovatio*[2] was held whenever the conditions of a triumph were not fulfilled, e.g. when victory was won although war was not declared, or when the war came to an end without bloodshed.[3] The general entered Rome on foot or horseback, not in a chariot, and came at the head of the procession, and not at the end of it. He wore not the triumphal dress but the *trabea* or the *toga praetexta*, not the laurel and the golden wreaths but a myrtle wreath only; he wore special shoes, and did not have the sceptre. The army did not take part, only the Senate. And there were only flute-players, instead of the trumpeters.[4]

Caesar's *ovatio* was an innovation. There was no war and no victory, not even a 'mild' victory.[5] And yet it was an official *ovatio ex Monte Albano*: it was recorded in the Fasti.[6] It had happened once before that a general held an *ovatio* after having been on the Alban Mount, but that case was different. In 211 B.C. after the conquest of Syracuse Marcellus was not granted a triumph—it would have been his third—but only an *ovatio*. He therefore held his triumph, as he was entitled to do, on the Alban Mount and returned from there to Rome on the following day to hold his *ovatio*.[7] One could not call this a precedent.

Caesar's *ovatio* was an innovation in another respect too. The *ovatio* was always distinguished from the triumph, notably in the Fasti; it was the lesser honour and was often called the minor triumph,[8] and by the Greeks the πεζὸς θρίαμβος,[9] because it was performed on foot, not in a chariot. This fact is sufficiently reflected in the Roman usage: Livy, for instance, often uses the expression 'ovans inire',[10] others use the verbs 'incedere' and 'praecedere'.[11] On the other hand, Dio always

[1] Dio 44. 4. 3: μετά τε τὰς ἀνοχὰς τὰς Λατίνας ἐπὶ κέλητος ἐς τὴν πόλιν ἐκ τοῦ Ἀλβανοῦ ἐσελαύνειν ἔδοσαν; 10. 1: ἐσιππεύοντα αὐτὸν ἀπὸ τοῦ Ἀλβανοῦ.

[2] G. Rohde, *RE* 18.1. 1890 ff.   [3] Gell. 5. 6. 21; Paul. 195 M. (213 L.).

[4] Dion. Hal. 5. 47. 3; Plut. *Marc.* 22. 2; *Suet.* p. 283 Reiff.

[5] e.g. Pliny 15. 125 (P. Postumius Tubertus, 503 B.C.): 'primus omnium ovans ingressus urbem est, quoniam rem leniter sine cruore gesserat, myrto Veneris Victricis coronatus incessit.'

[6] *F. Triumph.* (Degrassi, op. cit. p. 87; 567): 'C. Iulius C. f. C. n. Caesar VI, dictator IIII, ovans a. DCCIX ex monte Albano VII K. Febr.' ('VI' because of the fourfold triumph of 46 and the Spanish one of 45).

[7] Livy 26. 21. 6: 'pridie quam urbem iniret in monte Albano triumphavit; inde ovans multam prae se praedam in urbem intulit.'

[8] Pliny 15. 19; Serv. *Aen.* 4. 543; Dion. Hal. 8. 67. 10; G. Rohde, l.c. 1890.

[9] Dion. Hal. 5. 47. 3; 8. 67. 10; 9. 36. 3; 9. 71. 4; Plut. *Crass.* 11. 11; *Marc.* 22. 2; see also below, p. 327. 4.   [10] Livy 26. 21. 4; 31. 20. 4; 39. 29. 5.

[11] *Suet.* p. 283 Reiff.; Pliny 15. 125.

speaks of riding into Rome on horseback,[1] even when other authors
record an entry on foot. The tradition must have been confused, and
the antiquarians tried to deal with the confusion. Some of them argued
that the *ovatio* was always performed on horseback, which is demonstrably wrong, and Sabinus Masurius, the lawyer of the Julio-Claudian
age, that it was held on foot, which is equally wrong when thus expressed.[2]
It may be suggested that the confusion was caused by an innovation of
Caesar: until then the *ovantes* went on foot, but he wanted to ride into
Rome on horseback and was allowed to do so, as is to be conjectured,
by a decree of the Senate. What appears to be a precedent must have
been created under the influence of his example. Livy records about the
double triumph *de Poenis et Hasdrubale* of the consuls of 207 B.C., M.
Livius Salinator and C. Claudius Nero, that the Senate decreed a triumph
for Livius and an entry on horseback for Nero.[3] But he contradicts
himself because he also refers to an entry on foot, which was probably
what happened; the other version must have been due to a post-
Caesarian, and not very successful rewriting of the event. Another con-
tradiction is found in the evidence about Augustus' two ovations in 40
and 36. According to Dio he rode into Rome on horseback, but Augustus
himself speaks of an entry on foot.[4] It is possible that the wording πεζὸν
ἐθριάμβευσα could here refer to an entry on horseback and that Augustus
was therefore the first to follow Caesar's example; but it is more probable
that he refused to do so and returned to the ancient ritual.

Caesar's *ovatio* was an extraordinary feat for a further reason. He was
dictator at that time, and dictators were forbidden by an ancient law
to ride a horse;[5] the *magister equitum* was entitled to do this, and that
is why they always appointed one. If they wanted to do it themselves,
and the circumstances of war required it, they had to ask for special

---

[1] Dio 44. 4. 3; 48. 31. 3; 49. 15. 1; 54. 8. 3; 54. 33. 5; 55. 2. 4; below, n. 4.

[2] Gell. 5. 6. 27: 'dissensisse veteres scriptores accipio. partim enim scripserunt, qui ovaret,
introire solitum equo vehentem; set Sabinus Masurius pedibus ingredi ovantis dicit sequenti-
bus eos non militibus, sed universo senatu.'

[3] Livy 28. 9. 10: 'convenit, ... ut M. Livium quadrigis urbem ineuntem milites
sequerentur, C. Claudius equo sine militibus inveheretur ... (15) iret alter consul sublimis
curru multiiugis ... equis: uno equo per urbem verum triumphum vehi, Neronemque,
etiamsi pedes incedat, ... gloria memorabilem fore'; *Per.* 28; Val. Max. 4. 1. 9; *vir.
ill.* 48. 5; Rohde 1894.

[4] Dio 48. 31. 3: ἐπί τε ἵππων ... ἐσαγαγόντες; 49. 15. 1: ἐφ' ἵππου ἐσελάσαι; *Mon. Anc.* 4. 1:
δὶς πεζὸν ἐθριάμβευσα καὶ τρὶς ἐφ' ἅρματος; cf. Euseb. ad annum Abr. 1896: Αὔγουστος πεζὸν
ἐθριάμβευσε θρίαμβον = Syncell. 305 D (1, p. 578. 18 Dd.); Mommsen, *Res gestae* 10;
Weber, *Princeps* 109*. 452.

[5] Plut. *Fab. Max.* 4. 2: οὐ γὰρ ἐξῆν, ἀλλ' ἀπηγόρευτο κατὰ δή τινα νόμον παλαιόν, εἴτε τῆς
ἀλκῆς τὸ πλεῖστον ἐν τῷ πεζῷ τιθεμένων καὶ διὰ τοῦτο τὸν στρατηγὸν οἰομένων δεῖν παραμένειν
τῇ φάλαγγι καὶ μὴ προλείπειν, εἴθ' ὅτι τυραννικὸν εἰς ἅπαντα τἆλλα καὶ μέγα τὸ τῆς ἀρχῆς κράτος
ἐστίν, ἔν γε τούτῳ βουλομένων τὸν δικτάτορα τοῦ δήμου φαίνεσθαι δεόμενον; Zonar. 7. 13 (Dio

permission from the people or the Senate. Two certain cases are recorded, both during the Second Punic War, Q. Fabius Maximus, dictator of 217 B.C., and M. Iunius Pera (*cos.* 230), dictator of 216 B.C.;[1] and two legendary cases, L. Quinctius Cincinnatus of 458 and M. Valerius Corvus (*cos.* 348) of 342.[2] When the Senate granted Caesar the extraordinary *ovatio*, because no victory was won and because he was to hold it on horseback, they must also have granted him as dictator the special permission to ride a horse. There were the precedents, it is true, but those were justified by the necessities of war; here there was no war. And his *magister equitum*, Lepidus, was no doubt present. Moreover, many dictators held triumphs before Caesar, but none an *ovatio*.

It is most unlikely that Caesar followed the normal rules of an *ovatio*[3] even in other ways. He should have worn a *trabea* and the myrtle, but he probably wore the triumphal cloak and the laurel wreath to which he was entitled for all functions since 45 B.C.[4] For the laurel wreath there was a precedent. In 71 B.C. a triumph was decreed for Pompey but only an *ovatio* for Crassus for his victory over the slaves and Spartacus. Crassus was upset, and the Senate granted him the laurel instead of the myrtle for his *ovatio*.[5] The precedent may have been welcome to Caesar and the Senate, but they were hardly influenced by it.

It is further unlikely that he wore the special shoes prescribed for an *ovatio*:[6] he will have continued to wear, as during the Feriae Latinae,

---

1, p. 42 B.); Mommsen, *StR* 2. 159; Leifer, *Studien z. ant. Ämterwesen* 117 f.; Alföldi, *Der frühröm. Reiteradel* 18; id. *Festschr. K. Schefold* (1967), 43; Momigliano, *JRS* 56 (1966), 17; 21.

[1] Plut. *Fab. Max.* 4. 1: ἀποδειχθεὶς δικτάτωρ Φάβιος . . . πρῶτον μὲν ᾐτήσατο τὴν σύγκλητον ἵππῳ χρῆσθαι παρὰ τὰς στρατείας; Livy 23. 14. 2: 'dictator M. Iunius Pera rebus divinis perfectis latoque, ut solet, ad populum, ut equom ascendere liceret . . .' Mr. Drummond infers from this that the dispensation was quite usual and assumes that Caesar will have received it long before 44 B.C.: a very attractive suggestion. But then the question arises whether it was a general dispensation or had to be renewed whenever there was a need for it; and if it was a general dispensation, whether it could be extended to an *ovatio*, a non-warlike activity.

[2] Dion. Hal. 10. 24. 2: ἵππους τ' αὐτῷ . . . προσῆγον καὶ πελέκεις ἅμα ταῖς ῥάβδοις εἰκοσιτέτ-ταρας παρέστησαν ἐσθῆτά τε ἁλουργῆ καὶ τἆλλα παράσημα οἷς πρότερον ἡ τῶν βασιλέων ἐκεκόσμητο ἀρχὴ προσήνεγκαν; Livy 3. 28. 1: 'dictator . . . equo circumvectus'; 7. 41. 3: 'dictator equo citato ad urbem revectus' (not a dictator: 7. 42. 3; Volkmann, *RE* 7A. 2417).

[3] See above, p. 326. 5; Rohde l.c. 1898.

[4] Dio 43. 43. 1; Suet. *Caes.* 45. 2; above, pp. 270 f. He might also have worn his new, long-sleeved tunic (above, p. 325).

[5] Gell. 5. 6. 23: 'murteam coronam M. Crassus, cum bello fugitivorum confecto ovans rediret, insolenter aspernatus est senatusque consultum faciundum per gratiam curavit, ut lauro, non murto, coronaretur'; Cic. *Pis.* 58: 'Crasse, . . . quid est quod . . . coronam illam lauream tibi tanto opere decerni volueris a senatu?' Pliny 15. 125. His example may have inspired a later member of his family at the time of Claudius' triumph over Britain in A.D. 43, Suet. *Claud.* 17. 3: 'secuti et triumphalia ornamenta eodem bello adepti, sed ceteri pedibus et in praetexta, M. Crassus Frugi (*cos.* A.D. 27) equo phalerato et in veste palmata, quod eum honorem iteraverat'; Groag, *RE* 13. 343. [6] Plut. *Marc.* 22. 2.

the red boots of the Alban kings. He may have had the flute-players instead of the trumpeters in his procession, but whom else? There was no army, no booty, and no prisoners to exhibit. His Spanish bodyguard certainly followed him, then his lictors, at least 72 of them, the magistrates and the senators, that is, all those who were bound to be present at the Feriae Latinae. His fellow consul, Antony, and his *magister equitum*, Lepidus, were thus in his company but not on horseback; Antony had an opportunity to ride on horseback later in his own artificial *ovatio* of 40 B.C. after the peace of Brundisium.

Caesar went to the Capitol to perform the prescribed sacrifice, and it was on the way that he was acclaimed king and that, according to one version of the story, his statues were crowned with a diadem. The acclamation could have had two meanings: 'king of Alba', which he was through his sacred dictatorship and which was probably apparent in his dress, and 'king of Rome'. The first, some sort of a 'rex sacrorum', was harmless, as it did not imply any exceptional power; the second was not. But even if the first was meant, it was only to prepare for the second. Caesar evaded the issue with a joke; but the tribunes were right in assuming that in fact the people meant the king of Rome. They intervened and sent the originator of the acclamation to prison.

This kind of *ovatio* had never been held before but was imitated later.[1] Octavian's entry into Rome at the end of the Perusine War in 41 B.C., in the triumphal dress and with a laurel wreath, does not belong here: it was neither a triumph nor an *ovatio* and was not recorded in the Fasti.[2] It was no doubt due to the fact that L. Antonius, his adversary, whom he defeated, had held a triumph in the same year. In the following year, 40, however, Octavian and Antony held an *ovatio* to celebrate the peace of Brundisium; it was official and recorded in the Fasti, although again there was no war and no enemy.[3] Next, in A.D. 21 an *ovatio e Campania* was decreed for Tiberius after a rebellion in Gaul was suppressed by C. Silius.[4] Tiberius refused to hold it, with the argument

---

[1] Cf. Alföldi, *Röm. Mitt.* 49 (1934), 93.

[2] Dio 48. 16. 1 : τὸν Καίσαρα ἔν τε στολῇ ἐπινικίῳ ἐς τὸ ἄστυ ἐσεκόμισαν καὶ δαφνίνῳ στεφάνῳ ἐτίμησαν, ὥσθ᾿ ὁσάκις οἱ τὰ νικητήρια πέμψαντες εἰώθεσαν αὐτῷ χρῆσθαι, καὶ ἐκεῖνόν οἱ κοσμεῖσθαι.

[3] Dio 48. 31. 3 : ἐπί τε ἵππων αὐτοὺς ὥσπερ ἐν ἐπινικίοις τισὶν ἐσαγαγόντες καὶ τῇ νικητηρίᾳ στολῇ ἐξ ἴσου τοῖς πέμψασιν αὐτὰ κοσμήσαντες; F. *Triumph.* (Degrassi, op. cit., p. 87): 'Imp. Caesar Divi f. (C. f.) IIIvir rei publicae constituendae ovans... quod pacem cum M. Antonio fecit; M. Antonius . . . IIIvir rei publicae constituendae ovans . . . quod pacem cum Imp. Caesare fecit.'

[4] Tac. *A.* 3. 47. 4: 'Dolabella Cornelius (*cos.* A.D.10) . . . censuit ut ovans e Campania urbem introiret. (5) igitur secutae Caesaris litterae, quibus se non tam vacuum gloria

that he had had no share in that campaign, and that his absence in the vicinity of Rome and his return from there did not deserve this kind of celebration. A similar *ovatio* without war and victory was decreed for Caligula in 39, but he too rejected it.[1] The conclusion is that these artificial festivals were based on Caesar's precedent in 44; the resistance against them shows how artificial it was. Otherwise, they do not help us further as they do not produce an answer to the question why this strange *ovatio* was held at all.

We must return to the theme of the solemn processions, resembling the processions of gods, held in the Greek world on the return of a king or general after victory or at the first appearance, epiphany, of a new king or god.[2] Alexander, Demetrius Poliorcetes, and later Mithridates were so received; but also Caesar after the victory at Pharsalus in Egypt and Asia.[3] Similar festivals were held in the West also, for instance in honour of Caesar on his arrival in Gallia Cisalpina in 51 B.C.[4] They were not 'triumphal' celebrations, and yet they had their influence on the later more elaborate triumphal processions. It is clear that Caesar's *ovatio* belongs in this context. But if it was not the celebration of a victory, it must have had another function, and one is then bound to think of an 'epiphany', of a kind, however, where a horse instead of a chariot was used. That this form too existed is proved by Jesus' entry into Jerusalem on horseback as the 'king of the Jews', his subsequent decoration with the purple cloak and the crown of thorns instead of the diadem.[5] It is further proved by the parody of this investiture performed in A.D. 38 at Alexandria. Carabas, an idiot, was called 'king' and dressed up, but with a rug instead of the purple, with a diadem of papyrus instead of the real one, and so on;[6] the horse, however, is not recorded in his case. If these analogies are valid, the conclusion is that the *ovatio* of 44 was to represent the *adventus* of the king; the acclamation was a necessary part of the action and so was the decoration

---

praedicabat, ut post ferocissimas gentes perdomitas, tot receptos in iuventa aut spretos triumphos, iam senior peregrinationis suburbanae inane praemium peteret.'

[1] Dio 59. 16. 11: τά τε ἐπινίκια τὰ σμικρότερα ὡς καὶ πολεμίους τινὰς νενικηκότι πέμψαι αὐτῷ ἔδωκαν . . . (17. 1) Γάϊος δὲ ἐκείνης μὲν τῆς πομπῆς οὐδὲν προετίμησεν (οὐδὲ γὰρ οὐδὲ μέγα τι ἐνόμιζεν εἶναι ἵππῳ δι' ἠπείρου διελάσαι).

[2] Cf. Pfister, *RE* Suppl. 4. 306 ff.; Nilsson 2. 183 ff.; above, p. 289.

[3] See above, pp. 296 f.   [4] [Caes.] *BG* 8. 51. 1 (above, pp. 299 f.).

[5] Mark 11. 7 ff.; 15: 16 ff.; Matt. 21. 7 ff.; 27. 27 ff.; Luke 19. 30 ff.; John 12. 12 ff.; 19. 2 ff. (3 Kings 1. 33 ff.; 41 ff.; Zachar. 9. 9). On πῶλος = young horse (not ass) see W. Bauer, *Journ. Bibl. Lit.* 72 (1953), 220 ff. (= *Aufsätze* (1967), 109 ff.); O. Michel, *New Test. Stud.* 6 (1959/60), 81 f.; cf. also Wiesner, *Arch. Anz.* 84 (1969), 543 f.

[6] Philo *in Flacc.* 6. 36 ff. Both cases were further influenced by Eastern festivals, at which the investiture of a mock king was celebrated, see *Mullus, Festschr. Th. Klauser* (1964), 391 ff.

of the statues with the diadem. As this conclusion partly rests on analogies and not on an explicit proof it still needs further confirmation. At any rate, Caesar made a joke of it, and the tribunes intervened. But the investiture was attempted again in another form little more than two weeks later.

4. THE LUPERCALIA

The colourful incident at the Lupercalia, 15 February 44, is one of the most discussed events in Caesar's life.[1] He watched the festival from the Rostra, seated for the first time on his golden throne and wearing his new purple cloak and his golden crown. Antony, his fellow consul, ran up to the throne, addressed Caesar as king and placed the diadem on his head. The people lamented, but rejoiced when Caesar rejected it. Antony kneeled down, implored Caesar to accept it, and placed it again on his head. The people were grieved, but applauded again when Caesar refused for the second time and sent the diadem to the Capitoline temple. Caesar then recorded in the Fasti that Antony had by order of the people offered the kingship to Caesar, the *dictator perpetuus*, who, however, did not want to make use of it. This is the record of Cicero,[2] with some modifications and additions from Livy, Suetonius, Appian, and Dio.[3] The more extensive and more colourful narrative

[1] Drumann 3. 612 f.; Meyer, op. cit. 527 f.; Hohl, *Klio* 34 (1942), 92 ff. (the most detailed discussion; criticized by Kraft, l. c. 92 ff.); Carcopino, op. cit. 157 ff.; Alföldi, *Studien über Caesars Monarchie* 23 ff.; Carson, *Greece and Rome* 26 (1957), 50 f.; Balsdon, *Hist.* 7 (1958), 83 f.; Dobesch, op. cit. 113 ff.

[2] Cic. *Phil.* 2. 85: 'sedebat in Rostris conlega tuus amictus toga purpurea in sella aurea coronatus. escendis, accedis ad sellam,—ita eras lupercus, ut te consulem esse meminisse deberes—diadema ostendis. gemitus toto Foro . . . tu diadema inponebas cum plangore populi, ille cum plausu reiciebat . . . (86) supplex te ad pedes abiciebas . . . (87) at etiam adscribi iussit in fastis ad Lupercalia C. Caesari dictatori perpetuo M. Antonium consulem populi iussu regnum detulisse: Caesarem uti noluisse.'

[3] Livy, *Per.* 116: 'a M. Antonio cos., collega suo, inter lupercos currente diadema capiti suo inpositum in sella ('cella ⟨Iovis⟩' suggested by Hohl, l.c. 104; could it be the chair placed there for Antony?) reposuit'; Suet. *Caes.* 79. 2: 'Lupercalibus pro Rostris a consule Antonio admotum saepius capiti suo diadema reppulerit atque in Capitolium Iovi Optimo Maximo miserit'; Dio 44. 11. 2: ἐπειδὴ γὰρ ἐν τῇ τῶν Λυκαίων γυμνοπαιδίᾳ ἔς τε τὴν ἀγορὰν ἐσῆλθε καὶ ἐπὶ τοῦ Βήματος τῇ τε ἐσθῆτι τῇ βασιλικῇ κεκοσμημένος καὶ τῷ στεφάνῳ τῷ διαχρύσῳ λαμπρυνόμενος ἐς τὸν δίφρον τὸν κεχρυσωμένον ἐκαθίζετο, καὶ αὐτὸν ὁ Ἀντώνιος βασιλέα τε μετὰ τῶν συνιερέων προσηγόρευσε καὶ διαδήματι ἀνέδησεν, εἰπὼν ὅτι "τοῦτό σοι ὁ δῆμος δι᾽ ἐμοῦ δίδωσιν", (3) ἀπεκρίνατο μὲν ὅτι "Ζεὺς μόνος τῶν Ῥωμαίων βασιλεὺς εἴη", καὶ τὸ διάδημα αὐτῷ ἐς τὸ Καπιτώλιον ἔπεμψεν, οὐ μέντοι καὶ ὀργὴν ἔσχεν, ἀλλὰ καὶ ἐς τὰ ὑπομνήματα ἐγγραφῆναι ἐποίησεν ὅτι τὴν βασιλείαν παρὰ τοῦ δήμου διὰ τοῦ ὑπάτου διδομένην οἱ οὐκ ἐδέξατο; App. *BC* 2. 109. 456: οὐ μὴν αἴ γε περὶ τῆς βασιλείας πεῖραι κατεπαύοντο οὐδ᾽ ὥς, ἀλλὰ θεώμενον αὐτὸν ἐν ἀγορᾷ τὰ Λουπερκάλια ἐπὶ θρόνου χρυσέου, πρὸ τῶν Ἐμβόλων, Ἀντώνιος ὑπατεύων σὺν αὐτῷ Καίσαρι . . . ἐπὶ τὰ Ἔμβολα ἀναδραμὼν ἐστεφάνωσε διαδήματι. (457) κρότου δὲ πρὸς τὴν ὄψιν παρ᾽ ὀλίγων γενομένου καὶ στόνου παρὰ πᾶν πλειόνων, ὁ Καῖσαρ ἀπέρριψε τὸ διάδημα, καὶ ὁ Ἀντώνιος αὖθις ἐπέθηκε, καὶ ὁ Καῖσαρ αὖθις ἀπερρίπτει κτλ.

of Nicolaus of Damascus, which has rightly been criticized, is ignored here.[1]

(a) The Festival

The first question concerns the festival, the Lupercalia. Was it a special function, suitable for such king-making, or was it just the first occasion that chance offered? It was a festival of the pastoral community dating from the time when how to keep the wolves away from the herds was still a problem.[2] The running of the young men around the community was designed to serve this purpose and was still preserved in the ritual of the festival; it was also concerned with purification and with the promotion of fertility, human and animal. There is no need to go into detail: it is obvious that a solemn coronation does not fit well into such a festival. Nevertheless, it has been asserted that it was also the New Year's festival of the regal period and because of this was intentionally chosen by Caesar for his initiation as the new Romulus and king of Rome.[3] No evidence, no discussion, and no proof was produced, and yet the assertion was often repeated. In the end it was elaborated with the help of some conjectures which are neither plausible nor relevant.[4]

The festival was adapted in another respect for the special occasion, through the creation of a new sodality, the *luperci Iulii* or *Iuliani*, with their own organization and revenue.[5] Hitherto two sodalities had been in charge of the festival, the *luperci Quinctiales* and the *luperci Fabiani*.[6] The addition of the third seems to have been justified with the argument that the Iulii had a relevant peculiarity in common with the other two

---

[1] *FGrHist*. 90 F 130. 71–5; criticized by Jacoby ad l.; Hohl, l.c. 95 ff., but accepted by Carcopino, op. cit. 158. 2.

[2] Wissowa 209 f.; Latte 84 f.; K. H. Welwei, *Hist*. 16 (1967), 65 ff. (with bibliography); add Gruber, *Glotta* 39 (1961), 274 f.: *lupercus* = '*lupo-sequos*', *qui lupum sequitur* (not convincing).

[3] Alföldi, *Mus. Helv*. 8 (1951), 211; id., *Der frühröm. Reiteradel* 91. 210; id., *Early Rome and the Latins* 45. 4; 254; Burkert, *Hist*. 11 (1962), 357; Dobesch, op. cit. 127. 222; 128. 224.

[4] G. Binder, *Die Aussetzung des Königskindes, Kyros und Romulus* (1964), 96 ff.; see the excellent criticism by K. W. Welwei, 46 ff. (with references also to the related studies of U. Bianchi and R. F. Rossi); O. Murray, *CR* 81 (1967), 331.

[5] Dio 44. 6. 2: ἱεροποιούς τε ἐς τὰς τοῦ Πανὸς γυμνοπαιδίας, τρίτην τινὰ ἑταιρίαν ἦν Ἰουλίαν ὠνόμασαν . . . ἀνέθεσαν; Suet. *Caes*. 76. 1. Aelius Tubero, frg. 3 P. (Dion. Hal. 1. 80. 2) records that the *luperci* already ran in three groups at the time of Romulus. This was clearly part of the Caesarian argument (Burkert, l.c. 372. 78) which strangely survived although the *luperci Iulii* were abolished in 43 B.C., cf. Cic. *ad Caes. Iun.* 2, frg. 19 (Watt): 'cum constaret Caesarem lupercis id vectigal dedisse'; Cic. *Phil*. 7. 1: 'de lupercis tribunus plebi refert'; 13. 31: 'vectigalia Iuliana lupercis ademistis.'

[6] Fabii and Quintilii: Ov. *F*. 2. 377 f.; *Or. g. R*. 22. 1; Paul. 87 M. (78 L.: Quintiliani; cf. Fest. 257 M. = 308 L.); Quinctialis: *ILS* 1923; Wissowa 559.

families. The *praenomen* 'Kaeso' was at first used only by the Fabii and Quinctii, precisely, so it has been suggested, because of their ritual duty of striking with the goat-skin, *februis caedere*, at the festival.[1] This suggestion remains convincing even if later the *praenomen* was used by other families also. Now the *cognomen* 'Caesar' was in origin another *praenomen*[2] and was explained in many ways. One explanation was again based on the verb 'caedere', though in a different sense, for cutting the walls of the abdomen for the 'Caesarian' birth.[3] It was then possibly argued that the name 'Caesar' of the Iulii was identical with the 'Kaeso' of the two families,[4] and that therefore the Iulii too were entitled to such a sodality. The old sodalities were no longer limited to members of the families; nor were the *luperci Iulii*, as can be seen from the choice of their *magister*, Mark Antony.[5] It was at the end of the ritual course and still in the dress of a *lupercus*, that is, wearing only a goatskin round his loins, that Antony ran up to Caesar and offered him the diadem. But of course one must not overestimate this aspect of the events. It is a fact that Caesar became personally associated with other Roman institutions as well; it is enough to recall the *mensis Iulius* and the *tribus Iulia*.[6]

(b) The Diadem

The diadem, a head-band, usually white, was together with the tiara and the purple cloak the principal attribute of the Persian kings.[7] It was first adopted in the Greek world by Dionysius I, the tyrant of Syracuse,[8] but his example remained for some time without any consequence. It was through Alexander that it became a symbol of royalty among the Greeks. After the conquest of Persia he claimed the succession of the Persian kings for himself and *c.* 330 B.C. adopted the Persian

---

[1] Mommsen, *Röm. Forsch.* I. 17; *Röm. Gesch.* I. 52 n.; accepted by Wissowa 559. 2; rejected by W. F. Otto, *RE* 6. 2063; Latte 85. 1.

[2] *Auct. de praen.* 3.

[3] Pliny 7. 47: 'primusque Caesarum a caeso matris utero dictus, qua de causa et Caesones appellati'; *Auct. de praen.* 6; Non. 556 f. M.; Serv. *Aen.* 1. 286; 10. 316; Alföldi, *Hist. Aug.-Colloquium 1966/67* (1968), 9 ff.; above, p. 12.

[4] A republican inscription from Ateste, *CIL* I². 2806 (Callegari, *NSc.* 1933, 137), mentions a 'K(aeso) Iulius'.

[5] Dio 45. 30. 2: τὰ γὰρ Λυκαῖα ἦν, καὶ ἐπὶ τοῦ ἑταιρικοῦ τοῦ Ἰουλίου ἐτέτακτο; 46. 5. 1; Cic. *Phil.* 2. 85; Plut. *Ant.* 12. 2.

[6] See above, pp. 152 ff.; 158 ff.

[7] H. W. Ritter, *Diadem u. Königsherrschaft*, 1965 (with bibliography); *Thes.L.L.* 5. 1. 945; Mau, *RE* 5. 303 f.; Alföldi, *Röm. Mitt.* 50 (1935), 145 ff.; H. Brandenburg, *Studien zur Mitra* (1966), 154 ff.

[8] Livy 24. 5. 4 (below, p. 334. 6). Berve, *Die Tyrannis bei den Griechen* (1967), 653, suggests that the diadem was wrongly ascribed to Dionysius and that he wore only a golden wreath, Duris, *FGrHist.* 76 F 14 (not convincing).

dress, including the diadem.[1] After his death there was no successor for a while. It was Antigonus and his son Demetrius Poliorcetes who first wore it after their victory at Salamis in 306 B.C.; their rivals, Ptolemy and Seleucus, followed suit, and it was then generally adopted by their successors.[2]

At Rome it was probably not before the second century B.C. that the kings were represented with a diadem;[3] but it must have been known long before. Not at the time of the traditional pretenders, Sp. Cassius, Sp. Maelius, and M. Manlius:[4] the diadem is not mentioned in their stories, which incidentally supports their historicity. The first piece of evidence concerns Appius Claudius Caecus, the censor of 312 B.C.: he tried to conquer Italy with the help of his clients, and set up his diademed statue at Forum Appi, the town he founded on the Via Appia, also built by him.[5] If this is true, he could have done it under Sicilian influence —it was much too early for the successors of Alexander. There the initiative of Dionysius I[6] at first remained without any imitators; and Agathocles explicitly refused to wear the diadem. But Hieronymus wore it during the Second Punic War, and so did the kings of the slave revolts of the second century, Eunus and Athenion,[7] and T. Vettius, the Roman knight and leader of another slave revolt in southern Italy in 104 B.C.[8] This series of 'pretenders' points to the existence of an early Sicilian tradition which must have been known to Ap. Claudius. He may have adopted the diadem in order to express the Roman claim to Sicily by it, or else because of a mere extravagance, and even this only outside Rome. At any rate his later political career does not suggest that he seriously wanted to be a pretender.

[1] Iustin. 12. 3. 8: 'post haec Alexander habitum regum Persarum et diadema insolitum antea regibus Macedonicis . . . adsumit'; Diod. 17. 77. 5; Curt. 6. 6. 4; Ritter 31 ff.

[2] Plut. *Demetr.* 17. 3 ff.; Diod. 20. 53 ff., etc.; Ritter 79 ff.; below, pp. 337 f.

[3] See above, p. 320.

[4] See above, p. 134.

[5] Suet. *Tib.* 2. 2: 'Claudius †Drusus† statua sibi diademata ad Appi Forum posita Italiam per clientelas occupare temptavit.' The identification was convincingly made by Mommsen, *Röm. Forsch.* 1. 308; cf. Hirschfeld, *Kl. Schr.* 795 f.

[6] Livy 24. 5. 4 (215 B.C., Hieronymus): 'conspexere purpuram ac diadema ac satellites armatos quadrigisque etiam alborum equorum interdum ex regia procedentem more Dionysi tyranni'; Berve, *König Hieron II* (1959), 88 f.

[7] Posid., *FGrHist.* 87 F 108. 14 (136 B.C.): αἱρεῖται βασιλεὺς ὁ Εὔνους . . . (16) περιθέμενος δὲ διάδημα καὶ πάντα τὰ ἄλλα τὰ περὶ αὐτὸν βασιλικῶς διακοσμήσας; Flor. 2. 7. 6: 'regisque . . . decoratus insignibus'; Diod. 36. 5. 2 (Athenion, 104 B.C.): ὑπὸ δὲ τούτων αἱρεθεὶς βασιλεὺς καὶ διάδημα περιθέμενος; Flor. 2. 7. 10: 'veste purpurea argenteoque baculo et regium in morem fronte redimita'.

[8] Diod. 36. 2. 4: ἀναλαβὼν διάδημα καὶ περιβόλαιον πορφυροῦν καὶ ῥαβδούχους καὶ τὰ ἄλλα σύσσημα τῆς ἀρχῆς, καὶ βασιλέα ἑαυτὸν συνεργίᾳ τῶν δούλων ἀναδείξας: H. Gundel, *RE* 8A. 1850.

It was Ti. Gracchus who was accused of being a pretender in 133 B.C. His enemies alleged that with his agrarian reform he aimed at kingship. After a clash with them he escaped to the Capitol and pointed to his forehead with his fingers in order to show that his life was in danger: he could not make himself understood otherwise because of the noise. His enemies interpreted this gesture as a request to have the diadem placed on his head, and Scipio Nasica killed him for it, as anyone was entitled to kill a tyrant.[1] The 'confirmation' followed. Q. Pompeius (*cos.* 141) reported in the Senate that in fact Gracchus had a diadem and a purple cloak in his house. They had belonged to King Attalus and were brought by Eudemus from Pergamum to Rome.[2] It was a senseless accusation but, true or false, it was believed and it stuck: C. Gracchus was still bound to refer to this 'purple and diadem' in a speech in defence of his brother.[3] But Gracchus was neither forgotten nor forgiven.

The next pretender was Pompey. It was alleged that he had Alexander's purple cloak in his possession and even wore it in his triumph of 61 B.C. instead of the prescribed *toga picta*.[4] In the following year M. Favonius (*pr.* 49) accused him of wearing the diadem and wanting to be a king: it was only a white bandage on his leg to cover an ulcer.[5] This was not just a bad and dangerous joke. Pompey was at the height of his power and popularity, and his adversaries watched him carefully. And a bandage had been once before an omen of future kingship. Alexander hit the forehead of Lysimachus by chance with the spike of his spear and in order to stop the bleeding he placed his diadem on the wound; and Lysimachus became a king later.[6] Pompey knew well what a diadem was; he had met many kings on his Eastern campaigns in the preceding years and had placed the diadem on the heads of some of them.[7] But the charge against him was not repeated again. There were others who were accused of aiming at kingship, Cicero and later Caesar, but the diadem was left out of the political game until the early days of 44 B.C.

Before returning to Caesar, we must survey the later history of the

---

[1] Plut. *Ti. Gracch.* 19. 2; Flor. 3. 14. 7; *vir. ill.* 64. 6; Diod. 34. 33. 6; Cic. *Lael.* 41; Sall. *Iug.* 31. 7; Cic. *Mil.* 8.   [2] Plut. *Ti. Gracch.* 14. 1 ff.; Meyer, *Kl. Schr.* 1. 408. 1; Ritter 161.

[3] C. Gracch. frg. 62 (*ORF* p. 197 Malc.): 'purpura et diadema' (wrongly ascribed to the tragedian Gracchus by Ribbeck, *TRF* p. 266).

[4] App. *Mithr.* 117. 577 (above, p. 38. 8).

[5] Val. Max. 6. 2. 7: 'cui candida fascia crus alligatum habenti Favonius "non refert, inquit, qua in parte sit corporis diadema", exigui panni cavillatione regias ei vires exprobrans'; Amm. Marc. 17. 11. 4: 'quodque aliquandiu tegendi ulceris causa deformis fasciola candida crus colligatum gestabat . . . ut novarum rerum cupidum adserebant; nihil interesse . . ., quam partem corporis redimiret regiae maiestatis insigni'; for the date see Cic. *Att.* 2. 3. 1; Münzer, *RE* 6. 2074.   [6] Iustin. 15. 3. 13 f.   [7] See below, pp. 337 f.

diadem. Antony wore the purple cloak and the diadem in Egypt[1] and gave another to his son, Ptolemy Philadelphus, when he made him king of Phoenicia, Syria, and Cilicia.[2] But this was his oriental aberration, or rather a necessity if he wanted to be a successor of the kings of Egypt. Nobody could accuse Augustus or Tiberius of wanting a diadem; Augustus built his monarchy on other foundations. Caligula was suspected, certainly for good reasons, of wishing to wear it:[3] if he did he followed Caesar's precedent here again closely. Titus too was suspected, but without justification, of planning to create a kingship for himself in the East, because he wore the diadem at a sacrifice at Alexandria: but this he did because it was part of the ritual.[4] He was and remained loyal to his father. It was Aurelian who first wore the diadem at Rome and made it a regular attribute of the Roman emperors.[5]

(c) The Coronation

There was no ceremonial coronation in Persia. The new king put the tiara and diadem on his head himself and took his seat on the throne.[6] There were exceptions, whenever the succession was contested. Thus when Xerxes became king, Ariamenes, his brother, first performed the ritual of the προσκύνησις, that is, he prostrated himself before him, then placed the diadem on his head and seated him on the throne.[7] Alexander did it himself in the regular manner;[8] that was what made him the king of Asia,[9] and there was no other form of legitimation of

[1] Flor. 2. 21. 3: 'purpurea vestis ingentibus obstricta gemmis; ⟨nec⟩ diadema deerat, ut regina rex et ipse frueretur; Ritter 150 f.

[2] Plut. Ant. 54. 8: Πτολεμαῖον δὲ κρηπῖσι καὶ χλαμύδι καὶ καυσίᾳ διαδηματοφόρῳ κεκοσμημένον; Ritter 150 f. On the other hand, it is not certain that Agrippa wore a diadem on his Eastern campaigns, although he is so represented on a gem, see Delbrück, Antike 8 (1932), 10. fig. 8; Alföldi, Röm. Mitt. 50 (1935), 147; Hanslik, RE 9A. 1252.

[3] Suet. Cal. 22. 1: 'nec multum afuit quin statim diadema sumeret speciemque principatus in regni formam converteret'; Aur. Vict. Caes. 3. 13: 'dominum dici atque insigne regni nectere capiti tentaverat'; Epit. de Caes. 3. 8: 'Caligula ... primus diademate imposito dominum se iussit appellari.'   [4] Suet. Tit. 5. 3.

[5] Epit. de Caes. 35. 5: 'Aurelianus ... primus apud Romanos diadema capiti innexuit'; Alföldi, Röm. Mitt. 50 (1935), 148 f.   [6] Ritter 27 f.

[7] Plut. reg. et imp. apophth. Xerxes 1. 173 C: ἀποδειχθέντος δὲ τοῦ Ξέρξου βασιλέως ὁ μὲν Ἀριαμένης εὐθὺς προσεκύνησε καὶ τὸ διάδημα περιέθηκεν, ὁ δὲ Ξέρξης ἐκείνῳ τὴν δευτέραν μεθ' ἑαυτὸν ἔδωκε τάξιν; de frat. amore 18. 488 f: Ἀριαμένης δ' εὐθὺς ἀναπηδήσας, προσεκύνησε τὸν ἀδελφὸν καὶ λαβόμενος τῆς δεξιᾶς εἰς τὸν θρόνον ἐκάθισε τὸν βασίλειον; Ritter 20; 27. 1; cf. on Cyrus, Nic. Dam., FGrHist. 90 F 66. 45: Κῦρος εἰς τὴν σκηνὴν παρελθὼν καθίζει εἰς τὸν τοῦ Ἀστυάγου θρόνον καὶ τὸ σκῆπτρον αὐτοῦ λαμβάνει. ἐπευφήμησαν δὲ Πέρσαι, καὶ Οἰβάρας αὐτῷ τὴν κίδαριν ἐπιτίθησιν; Ritter 29.

[8] Diod. 17. 77. 5: τό τε Περσικὸν διάδημα περιέθετο καὶ τὸν διάλευκον ἐνεδύσατο χιτῶνα; 17. 116. 3; Curt. 6. 6. 4: 'diadema ... capiti circumdedit vestemque Persicam sumpsit.' He also seated himself on the throne, Diod. 17. 66. 3: καθίσαντος γὰρ αὐτοῦ ἐπὶ τὸν βασιλικὸν θρόνον; Curt. 5. 2. 13: 'consedit deinde in regia sella'; Ritter 49 ff. (with further evidence and discussion); H. Montgomery, Op. Ath. 9 (1969), 1 ff.   [9] Ritter 85.

his kingship; the acclamation by his army was not part of it. Antigonus and Demetrius, on the other hand, were first acclaimed kings by the assembly of the army in 306, and the 'coronation' was performed by Antigonus' friends; Antigonus sent the diadem to Demetrius and called him 'king' in a letter.[1] thereafter acclamation and coronation became the rule under the Diadochs:[2] Antigonus Doson (229–221 B.C.) threw his purple and diadem down at a revolt and refused for a while to assume the kingship again, though ordered by the people.[3] In Parthia it was the privilege of the Surenas, the second in command, to put the diadem on the head of the new ruler.[4]

Roman rule naturally brought a change. The possession of the diadem depended on the Roman generals and later on the emperors. Those who used to receive the obeisance of their subjects now prostrated themselves before the Romans and laid their diadem at their feet, as did King Perseus in 167 B.C. before the praetor Cn. Octavius. But he did not get his diadem back: it was carried in the triumph of Aemilius Paullus.[5] Pompey had to deal with the task more than once. In 66 B.C. King Tigranes of Armenia lay before him as a suppliant without a diadem, but Pompey returned it to him.[6] In 63 he did not allow King Hyrcanus of Judaea to wear it[7] and installed Ariobarzanes II as king of Cappadocia.[8] Caesar seems to have restored Deiotarus of Galatia to his kingship in 47,[9] perhaps also others. In the course of time a certain

---

[1] Plut. *Demetr.* 17. 6 (Aristodemos): ἐκτείνας τὴν δεξιὰν ἀνεβόησε μεγάλῃ τῇ φωνῇ· "χαῖρε, βασιλεῦ Ἀντίγονε,⌐νικῶμεν Πτολεμαῖον ναυμαχίᾳ"... (18. 1) ἐκ τούτου πρῶτον ἀνεφώνησε τὸ πλῆθος Ἀντίγονον καὶ Δημήτριον βασιλέας. Ἀντίγονον μὲν οὖν εὐθὺς ἀνέδησαν οἱ φίλοι, Δημητρίῳ δ' ὁ πατὴρ ἔπεμψε διάδημα καὶ γράφων ἐπιστολὴν βασιλέα προσεῖπεν; Diod. 20. 53. 2, etc.; Ritter 79 ff.

[2] Diod. 20. 53. 3 f.

[3] Iustin. 28. 3. 12: 'proiectoque in vulgus diademate ac purpura dare haec eos alteri iubet... (16) cum populus... reciperet eum regnum iuberet, tam diu recusavit, quoad seditionis auctores supplicio traderentur'; Ritter 156 f.

[4] Plut. *Crass.* 21. 8: ἐκέκτητο βασιλεῖ γινομένῳ Πάρθων ἐπιτιθέναι τὸ διάδημα πρῶτος; Tac. *A.* 6. 42. 6 (A.D. 36): 'multis coram et adprobantibus Surena patrio more Tiridaten insigni regio evinxit.'

[5] Livy 45. 19. 16: 'diadema ... ad pedes victoris hostis prostratus posuerit'; Plut. *Aem. Paul.* 33. 5; Ritter 157.

[6] Val. Max. 5. 1. 9: 'in conspectu suo diutius iacere supplicem passus non est, sed... diadema, quod abiecerat, capiti reponere iussit.'

[7] Jos. *AJ* 20. 244: διάδημα δὲ φορεῖν ἐκώλυσεν.

[8] Val. Max. 5. 7, *Ext.* 2: 'Ariobarzanes... Cn. Pompei... cum tribunal conscendisset invitatusque ab eo in curuli sella sedisset, postquam filium in cornu scribae humiliorem fortuna sua locum obtinentem conspexisset, ... protinus sella descendit et diadema in caput eius transtulit hortarique coepit ut eo transiret, unde ipse surrexerat... (refusal and Pompey's intervention) filium... et regem appellavit et diadema sumere iussit et in curuli sella considere coegit.'

[9] *B. Alex.* 67. 1: 'Deiotarus... depositis regiis insignibus... supplex ad Caesarem venit ... (68. 1)... Caesar... regium vestitum ei restituit.'

ritual emerged, or rather the old one was adapted to the new conditions. Pompey sat on his *sella curulis* on a *tribunal*, called Ariobarzanes king, asked him to take the diadem and to take his seat on a *sella curulis*, which clearly represented the royal throne.[1] Caligula did this with Herodes Agrippa I of Judaea at Rome in A.D. 37,[2] and so did Nero in 66 when Tiridates of Armenia came. Tiridates had already performed the ritual of submission in Corbulo's camp two years earlier. He went to the *tribunal*, made obeisance to Nero's image which stood there on a *sella curulis*, and surrendered his diadem.[3] Later, at Rome, Nero, wearing the triumphal dress, sat on his *sella curulis* on the Rostra; Tiridates came, knelt down before him, was raised and kissed by Nero, who then placed the diadem on his head.[4] In A.D. 116 Trajan sat on a platform at Ctesiphon, surrounded by Romans and Parthians, who were probably there for the ritual acclamation; Trajan made Parthamaspates king of Parthia and placed the diadem on his head.[5]

(d) Caesar's Diadem

The Lupercalia provided the opportunity for the second, or if one counts the diademed statues separately, for the third attempt to make Caesar a king. It can only be explained as a pre-arranged staging, and with the help of Eastern analogies. Distrust of foreign analogies, often justified, is out of place here, because the diadem itself was of foreign origin. And the assumption of deliberate staging best explains why Caesar wore his new purple cloak and golden crown and sat on his golden throne when he received the offer of the diadem. Watching the festival would not be a sufficient explanation. There were, of course, special seats in the Circus for the races,[6] also at the Rostra for the gladiatorial games, granted as a privilege;[7] this may explain the fact but not the

[1] Val. Max. 5. 7, Ext. 2 (above, p. 337. 8).

[2] Jos. *AJ* 18. 237: τὸ διάδημα περιτίθησιν τῇ κεφαλῇ καὶ βασιλέα καθίστησιν αὐτὸν τῆς Φιλίππου τετραρχίας.

[3] Tac. *A.* 15. 29. 5: 'medio tribunal sedem curulem et sedes effigiem Neronis sustinebat. (6) ad quam progressus Tiridates, caesis ex more victimis, sublatum capiti diadema imagini subiecit'; Dio 62. 23. 3; K. H. Ziegler, *Die Beziehungen zwischen Rom u. dem Partherreich* (1964), 72 ff.

[4] Suet. *Nero* 13. 1: 'curuli residens apud Rostra triumphantis habitu ... (2) et primo per devexum pulpitum subeuntem admisit ad genua, adlevatumque dextra exosculatus est, dein precanti tiara deducta diadema inposuit'; Dio 62 (63). 5. 4; Cumont, *Riv. fil.* 61 (1933), 145 ff.

[5] Dio 68. 30. 2: συνεκάλεσεν ... πάντας μὲν τοὺς Ῥωμαίους, πάντας δὲ τοὺς Πάρθους ... καὶ ἐπὶ βῆμα ὑψηλὸν ἀναβάς ... Παρθαμασπάτην τοῖς Πάρθοις βασιλέα ἀπέδειξε, τὸ διάδημα αὐτῷ ἐπιθείς.

[6] *ILS* 50; Livy 2. 31. 3; Fest. 344 M. (464 L.); Mommsen, *StR* 1. 452; Kübler, *RE* 2A. 1313 f.   [7] Cic. *Phil.* 9. 16; Pliny 34. 24.

pomp. The explanation is, then, to be based on the evidence presented in the preceding sections.

Caesar sat on the Rostra, as Pompey and Trajan sat on a high platform and Nero on the same Rostra at Rome for the investiture of a king. He sat on the throne and wore the purple as the other kings did. He wore the golden crown as the Persian kings wore the tiara and the Macedonians the *causia*: the diadem used to be added to these.[1] Antony, the consul and thus the second in command, ran up to him, probably on a sloping platform, as Tiridates did to Nero.[2] He called him 'king'[3] because this was the first item of the ritual. He then knelt down before him, not to implore him because of his refusal[4] but in order to perform the act of προσκύνησις. Next he referred to the will of the people which corresponds to the acclamation by the assembly of the army, and finally placed the diadem on Caesar's head, for which we have met instances from Xerxes to Nero and Trajan. It is certainly true that Antony tried it more than once; it might be forcing the analogies too far if one referred to the refusal and insistence in the cases of Antigonus Doson and Ariobarzanes.[5]

The offer of the diadem can be understood in two ways. One is that Caesar should become king of Rome. That is how the people understood it and why they showed their displeasure, and how Caesar reacted when he sent the diadem to Iuppiter as the only king in Rome.[6] The

[1] Ritter 6 ff.; 55 ff.

[2] Suet. *Nero* 13. 2 (above, p. 338. 4).

[3] Dio 44. 11. 2: αὐτὸν ὁ Ἀντώνιος βασιλέα τε μετὰ τῶν συνιερέων προσηγόρευσε.

[4] Needless to say, kneeling itself was not a foreign import. It was often done, e.g., when asking the gods for help; it was also a sign of submission by the defeated enemy (above, p. 46.1 f.), and it was used in the ritual of the *supplicatio* (Livy 3. 7. 7; Tac. *H.* 1. 63; above, p. 62). Caesar was said to have knelt on the steps of the Capitol in his triumph of 46 B.C. (Dio 43. 21. 2; above, p. 77). When Augustus was offered the dictatorship in 22 B.C., he implored the people on his knees not to insist (Suet. *Aug.* 52: 'dictaturam magna vi offerente populos genu nixus . . . deprecatus est'): he was thus asking for mercy because as a dictator he would have become an outlaw.

[5] One could also compare the refusal of power which was later so frequent, e.g. *Mon. Anc.* 5. 1; 6. 1, etc.; Béranger, *Recherches sur l'aspect idéologique du principat* 137 ff.; Fuhrmann, *Mitt. Arch. Inst.* 2 (1949), 41 ff., suggested that the relief from the Via Cassia (above, pp. 45 ff.) is an artistic representation of the scene at the Lupercalia. His view rests on the assumption that the kneeling woman holds a diadem, which however she does not. Moreover, it is improbable that the scene should have found its artistic representation in the last four weeks of Caesar's life; after his death nobody wanted to be reminded of it.

[6] Iuppiter was apparently called Rex in the regal period: Iuno always remained Regina, and Romulus still offered his sacrifice to Iuppiter Rex (Dion. Hal. 2. 5. 1: εὔχετο Διί τε Βασιλεῖ); cf. Cic. *rep.* 3. 23: 'tyranni . . . se Iovis Optimi nomine malunt reges vocari'; Livy 3. 39. 4: 'nec nominis (of rex) homines tum pertaesum esse, quippe quo Iovem appellari fas sit'; frequent later in poetry, e.g. Verg. *Aen.* 10. 112: 'rex Iuppiter omnibus idem'; Mommsen, *StR* 2 15. 2. Alföldi, *Studien* 3 ff.; 25, believes that one issue of the *denarius* of M. Mettius (Sydenham 177; pl. 28. 1057; above, p. 99. 8) shows the diadem hung on a nail in the

other interpretation is based on the fact that the diadem was a foreign symbol. It then referred to a kingship outside Rome. It will be seen presently that such a kingship was in many people's minds, perhaps even of those who would not have put up with a king of Rome. And that is why a final attempt was to be made.

5. THE SIBYLLINE ORACLE

L. Aurelius Cotta (*cos.* 65), one of the *quindecimviri*, intended to report to the Senate on the Ides of March that, according to the *libri Sibyllini*, Parthia could be conquered only by a king, and that therefore Caesar should be called 'king'.[1] This is not necessarily an oracle invented for the occasion. There were many oracles in circulation which were concerned with the empires and the mastery of the world.[2] The Persian empire always had a great attraction for the Greeks, and there was, for instance, the belief that whoever ruled over Persia deserved divine honours.[3] The Romans transferred this special interest to Parthia, especially after the débâcle of Crassus. The oracle will have depended on such views and could easily have been adapted to Caesar's claim to a kingship. It was not to be just a decoration but the solution of a serious problem: Caesar's long stay in the East during his Parthian campaign would have been made easier if he had been there not as a dictator or a general but as king of all Eastern territories.[4] It will be recalled that Alexander took the diadem after the conquest of Persia,

temple, not the usual *lituus*, behind Caesar's head: *contra*, e.g., Kraay, *Num. Chron.* 6. 14 (1954), 18 f.; Carson, *Gnom.* 28 (1956), 182 and *Greece and Rome* 26 (1957), 49; Felber, op. cit. 212 ff.; Dobesch, op. cit. 32. 52; M. H. Crawford, *Anc. Numismatics* (*A Survey of Num. Research* [*1960–5*], 1, ed. by O. Mørkholm, 1967), 160 (with references to further articles by Alföldi).

[1] Suet. *Caes.* 79. 3: 'proximo autem senatu Lucium Cottam quindecimvirum sententiam dicturum, ut, quoniam fatalibus libris contineretur Parthos nisi a rege non posse vinci, Caesar rex appellaretur'; Cic. *div.* 2. 110: 'Sibyllae versus . . . quorum interpres nuper falsa quadam hominum fama dicturus in senatu putabatur eum, quem re vera regem habebamus, appellandum quoque esse regem'; App. *BC* 2. 110. 460: λόγος ἄλλος ἐφοίτα Σιβύλλειον εἶναι προαγόρευμα μὴ πρὶν ὑπακούσεσθαι Ῥωμαίοις Παρθυαίους, εἰ μὴ βασιλεὺς αὐτοῖς ἐπιστρατεύσειε; Dio 44. 15. 3: λόγου γάρ τινος . . . διελθόντος ὡς τῶν ἱερέων τῶν πεντεκαίδεκα καλουμένων διαθροούντων ὅτι ἡ Σίβυλλα εἰρηκυῖα εἴη μήποτ' ἂν τοὺς Πάρθους ἄλλως πως πλὴν ὑπὸ βασιλέως ἁλῶναι, καὶ μελλόντων διὰ τοῦτο αὐτῶν τὴν ἐπίκλησιν ταύτην τῷ Καίσαρι δοθῆναι ἐσηγήσεσθαι; Meyer, op. cit. 529; Carcopino, op. cit. 170; Alföldi, *Studien* 37 ff.; Kraft, l.c. 56; Balsdon, *Hist.* 7 (1958), 85; Felber, op. cit. 254.

[2] Cf. H. Fuchs, *Der geistige Widerstand gegen Rom* 62 ff.

[3] Isocr. *ep.* 3. 5; Hor. *c.* 3. 5. 2 ff.; above, p. 288. 6 f. and p. 305.

[4] App. *BC* 2. 110. 461: καί τινες ἀπὸ τοῦδε ἐτόλμων λέγειν ὅτι χρὴ Ῥωμαίων μὲν αὐτόν, ὥσπερ ἦν, δικτάτορα καὶ αὐτοκράτορα καλεῖν καὶ ὅσα ἄλλα ἐστὶν αὐτοῖς ἀντὶ βασιλείας ὀνόματα, τῶν δὲ ἐθνῶν, ὅσα Ῥωμαίοις ὑπήκοα, ἄντικρυς ἀνειπεῖν βασιλέα. ὁ δὲ καὶ τόδε παρῃτεῖτο; Plut. *Caes.* 64. 3: προθύμους εἶναι ψηφίζεσθαι πάντας, ὅπως τῶν ἐκτὸς Ἰταλίας ἐπαρχιῶν βασιλεὺς ἀναγορεύοιτο καὶ φοροίη διάδημα τὴν ἄλλην ἐπιὼν γῆν τε καὶ θάλασσαν.

and that the Diadochs did not use it except when they were in possession of parts of the former Persian empire. Caesar wanted to make his conquest with the diadem on his head. This explains the stubborn insistence on the kingship after the two refusals in the preceding weeks. It was to be tried again on the Ides of March; but that meeting of the Senate ended with the murder of the 'pretender'. Augustus faced the same problem later and found its solution in the *imperium proconsulare maius* for the provinces, which was less glamorous, and politically less ambitious, but safer.

XVI

THE IDES OF MARCH

I. THE PRODIGIES

IT was not for the first time that Caesar was warned by portents of coming disaster.[1] We have mentioned the Greek inscription found in Capys' tomb which reflected the resentment at Capua created by Caesar's agrarian law of 59 B.C. and was certainly produced long before 44 B.C.[2] Nigidius Figulus, the great diviner and a follower of Pompey who died in exile in 45, seems to have predicted the death of the tyrant again and again.[3] In 49 when Caesar sacrificed before his departure against Pompey the victim escaped, which was an evil sign: we have seen how Caesar turned it into a favourable one.[4] It escaped again in 46 when he was about to sail to Africa against Scipio and Cato: in spite of the warning of the *haruspex maximus* (certainly not Spurinna) he did not delay his departure,[5] and on arrival he interpreted another ominous incident as a sign of the coming victory.[6] In 45, when fighting against the last Pompeians in Spain and sacrificing, perhaps before the battle at Munda, he found that the heart of the victim was missing;[7] this belonged to the *pestifera auspicia*,[8] but he contested the validity of the portent in his endeavour to encourage his soldiers. The modern critic is often unwilling to deal with this type of evidence. But it is a fact that heavenly signs were constantly sought in daily life, private and public, and what we have quoted so far rests on good contemporary tradition.

The tradition about the prodigies of 44 is perhaps even better. Cicero recorded some of them a few weeks after the murder.[9] The almost

---

[1] Suet. *Caes.* 81; Obs. 67; Nic. Dam. 84 ff. (*FGrHist.* 90 F 130); App. *BC* 2. 116. 488 f.; Plut. *Caes.* 63; Dio 44. 17 f.; Drumann 3. 651; Theander, *Studi in onore di A. Calderini e R. Paribeni* 1 (1956), 143 ff.

[2] Suet. *Caes.* 81. 1; above, p. 179.

[3] Lyd. *ost.* p. 71. 15 W.: ἐκ διχονοίας τοῦ πολιτεύματος τύραννος ἀναστήσεται, καὶ αὐτὸς μὲν ἀπολεῖται, ζημίαις δὲ ἀφορήτοις οἱ δυνατοὶ ὑποστήσονται; p. 71. 18: ὁ κακὸς δυνάστης βουλῇ θεοῦ πεσεῖται; Kroll, *RE* 17. 208; cf. *PBSR* 19 (1951), 140.

[4] Dio 41. 39. 2; above, p. 118.

[5] Cic. *div.* 2. 52; Suet. *Caes.* 59; Münzer, *RE* 3A. 1888; above, pp. 98, 118.

[6] Suet. *Caes.* 59; above, p. 22.

[7] App. *BC* 2. 116. 488; Polyaen. 8. 23. 33; Suet. *Caes.* 77. On the dangerous situation at Munda and Caesar's prayer see above, p. 27.

[8] Paul. 244 M. (287 L.).   [9] Cic. *div.* 1. 119; below, p. 344.11.

complete list in Suetonius is equally valuable,[1] because in his biography of Caesar he quotes authors of the Caesarian age only,[2] which leads to the probable, though not certain, conclusion that he did not use any later source either. In the relevant chapter the only author he mentions by name is Cornelius Balbus, Caesar's friend and biographer. Strabo and Livy, quoted by Plutarch,[3] and Nicolaus of Damascus too were contemporaries, although they began to write later. In fact the growth, variation, and dramatization of these prodigies would not have been possible without extensive contemporary literary activities.[4] Of the historians Asinius Pollio, whom Suetonius, Plutarch, and Appian quote for earlier events,[5] will have been one of the principal sources. Socrates of Rhodes wrote about the 'Civil War',[6] Potamon of Mytilene wrote in praise of both Caesar and Brutus,[7] Empylus of Rhodes in praise of Brutus alone.[8] L. Calpurnius Bibulus and P. Volumnius, who fought on the side of Brutus, wrote later about the campaign in prose,[9] and on the other side Anser and Boethus of Tarsus wrote epic poems about Antony.[10] There will have been others and many of them will have begun conveniently with the murder and what preceded it.

These are just names for us; but even if we knew more about them, their evidence certainly could not equal Cicero's. Before turning to him we must deal first with Balbus and an anonymous piece of evidence in Suetonius, because they refer to earlier incidents. Suetonius relates the story of Capys, it is true, in our context, but he does not expressly state that it really happened about the Ides of March: we have connected it with earlier events.[11] The incident which immediately follows in Suetonius (and may again depend on Balbus or Asinius Pollio)[12] took place 'proximis diebus', which must refer at least to the beginning of the conspiracy. This leads us back to the events of 49, to the secret crossing of the Rubicon. It was a suitable subject for legendary elaboration, in which portents were bound to get their place. Of these we have already met Caesar's dream which promised him mastery of the world.[13]

---

[1] Suet. *Caes.* 81; below, pp. 344. 3; 345. 1; 346. 1; 5; 7.

[2] Observed by Haupt, *Opuscula* 1. 72; not considered in subsequent studies.

[3] Plut. *Caes.* 63. 3 (*FGrHist.* 91 F 19); 63. 9.

[4] H. Peter, *Die geschichtliche Litteratur* 1. 169 ff.

[5] Suet. *Caes.* 30. 4; 55. 4; 56. 4; Plut. *Pomp.* 72. 4; App. *BC* 2. 82. 346 (*HRR* 2, p. 68 P.); cf. Hor. *c.* 2. 1; Tac. *A.* 4. 34. 6.

[6] *FGrHist.* 192 (Athen. 4. 29. 147 E).   [7] *FGrHist.* 147 (Suid.).

[8] *FGrHist.* 191 (Plut. *Brut.* 2. 4).   [9] Plut. *Brut.* 13. 3; 23. 6; 48. 2 (*HRR* 2, pp. 51 f. P.).

[10] *FGrHist.* 194 (Strab. 14. 674); Serv. *Ecl.* 9. 36.

[11] Suet. *Caes.* 81. 1; Serv. Dan. *Aen.* 2. 35; above, p. 179.

[12] Asinius Pollio was present at the crossing of the Rubicon, Plut. *Caes.* 32. 7; Meyer, *Caesars Monarchie* 293. 1; 609; 614. 3.   [13] Plut. *Caes.* 32. 9; above, p. 22.

As it was a move from the province into Italy proper, auspices and sacrifice must have taken place.[1] A divine guide appeared suddenly and sounded a trumpet for the crossing.[2] This will have been the moment for Caesar to make his vow for a successful crossing: he vowed and later dedicated a herd of horses to the river and released them. They lived then in freedom without any surveillance. That was in 49; now before the murder they did not take food and wept copiously.[3] This story has traditional elements. Gods used to own sacred herds, quadrupeds, birds, fishes;[4] Helios, for instance, cattle and sheep,[5] Hera cows at Argos and Croton;[6] and at Rome there were Iuno's geese on the Capitol.[7] Further, horses were supposed to have foresight and were often used for divination.[8] Achilles' horses knew of Patroclus' death and wept;[9] in the *Aeneid* Pallas' horse too wept.[10] It is therefore credible that there were such sacred horses at the Rubicon and understandable that some foreboding of the coming disaster was ascribed to them. Thus literary reminiscences helped to create this portent, probably at the time when records of the events were being made.

Cicero inserted the relevant evidence in his work *De divinatione* a few weeks after the murder.[11] He began with the Lupercalia of 15 February. The bull which Caesar sacrificed had no heart; the *haruspex* Spurinna therefore warned him that his plans and his life were in danger. On the following day the 'head', that is, a lobe on the liver of the victim,[12] was missing: this was no longer a warning but the announcement of the coming disaster. This is clearly the nucleus of the later versions of the story. It is important to stress the point that for

---

[1] Fest. 245 M. (284 L.): 'Peremne dicitur auspicari, qui amnem, aut aquam, quae ex sacro oritur, auspicato transit'; 250 M. (296 L.); Cic. *div.* 2. 77 (with Pease's note); *ND* 2. 9.

[2] Suet. *Caes.* 32.

[3] Suet. *Caes.* 81. 2: 'proximis diebus equorum greges, quos in traiciendo Rubiconi flumini consecrarat ac vagos et sine custode dimiserat, comperit pertinacissime pabulo abstinere ubertimque flere.'

[4] Eustath. *Od.* 12. 131 (2, p. 18).

[5] Hom. *Od.* 12. 127 ff.; Hdt. 2. 92; *h. Hom. Apoll.* 412.

[6] Hypothes. Pind. *Nem.* 3 (3, p. 3 Dr.); Livy 24. 3. 6; cf. Cic. *div.* 1. 48.

[7] Livy 5. 47. 4; Diod. 14. 116. 6; Plut. *fort. Rom.* 12; Wissowa 190. 10.

[8] Pliny 8. 157: 'praesagiunt pugnam et amissos lugent dominos: lacrimas interdum desiderio fundunt'; Isid. 12. 1. 44; Solin. 45. 13; Serv. Dan. *Aen.* 3. 537; Tac. *Germ.* 10. 2.

[9] Hom. *Il.* 17. 426 ff.; cf. 19. 404 ff.

[10] Verg. *Aen.* 11. 89 f.; on mourning animals see Theocr. 1. 71 ff.; Verg. *Ecl.* 5. 24 ff.

[11] Cic. *div.* 1. 119: 'cum immolaret illo die quo primum in sella aurea sedit et cum purpurea veste processit, in extis bovis opimi cor non fuit . . . qua †ille rei novitate perculsus, cum Spurinna diceret timendum esse ne et consilium et vita deficeret; earum enim rerum utramque a corde proficisci. postero die caput in iecore non fuit. quae quidem illi portendebantur a dis immortalibus, ut videret interitum, non ut caveret . . .'; Val. Max. 1. 6. 13; Pliny 11. 186 (both depend on Cicero); Hohl, *Klio* 34 (1942), 110 ff.

[12] Cf. Thulin, *Etr. Disc.* 2. 31 and *RE* 7. 2451.

Cicero these prodigies occurred in February; he has nothing to say about the Ides of March. Moreover, the first portent concerning Caesar's plan must have been known some time before the murder: that plan was clearly the offering of the diadem. Caesar refused it, so the contemporary argument will have run, precisely because Spurinna had warned him. If so, the portent was created or reshaped with the help of popular speculation about Caesar's unexpected behaviour at the Lupercalia. The portent of the following day, on the other hand, must have been produced after the murder. It does not make sense on that day, for which nothing particular is recorded. And yet this second portent, in fact a variation of the earlier one, made the catastrophe unavoidable.

Suetonius, who depends on a historian rather than on Cicero, mentions the warning of Spurinna in the form that the danger would come by the Ides of March.[1] That is to say, his source too dates the portent earlier; but it already connects it with the murder. Instead of the second portent he produces the idea of a critical period. Valerius Maximus (that is, probably, Livy) is much clearer about this idea:[2] those thirty days represented the predetermined time, the *dies fatales*, any of which could bring the disaster. This line of thought was not invented for the situation. There was a related term, the *fatalis annus*, which could bring ruin on Rome,[3] and once a *fatalis dies* had brought the deluge.[4] But generally *fatalis dies* meant the day of death,[5] and that is its meaning here too.[6] Nor was the time-limit of thirty days invented, but borrowed from a very different usage: in the law-courts the same period ended with another type of *fatalis dies* on which an appeal was heard.[7]

Whoever created this close relationship between the portent of the Lupercalia and the Ides of March will also have created the altercation between Caesar and Spurinna on the Ides of March and the new

---

[1] Suet. *Caes.* 81. 2: 'et immolantem haruspex Spurinna monuit, caveret periculum, quod non ultra Martias Idus proferretur.'

[2] Val. Max. 8. 11. 2: (Spurinna) 'praedixerat C. Caesari ut proximos xxx dies quasi fatales caveret, quorum ultimus erat Idus Martiae ...'; Meyer, *Caesars Monarchie* 526. 2; Wilcken, 'Zur Entwicklung der röm. Diktatur', *Abh. Akad. Berlin* (1940), 1. 24. 4; Hohl, l.c. 112; on 30-day periods see Düll, *Festschr. f. Koschaker* 1. 27 ff.

[3] Cic. *Cat.* 4. 9 (the tenth and twentieth year after disastrous events).

[4] Sen. *NQ* 3. 27. 1.

[5] Tac. *dial.* 13. 9 (with Gudeman's note); *Thes.L.L.* 6. 333 f.; Schulze, *Kl. Schr.* 138 ff.; 'fatalis hora': Suet. *Nero* 49. 2; Lucan. 9. 87.

[6] Cf. Cic. *Phil.* 13. 33: 'Caesaris mortem ulcisci volebant, quam omnes fatalem fuisse arbitrabantur.'

[7] *Cod. Iust.* 7. 62. 32. 1; 7. 63. 2. 1; *Thes.L.L.* 6. 334. 41 ff.; cf. Cic. *Vatin.* 33.

unsuccessful offerings.[1] This is the version of Suetonius and his source and can, with slight variations, easily be recognized in the narratives of Appian, Plutarch, and Dio. Caesar certainly made the usual offerings on the Ides of March when he left his house and before he entered the Senate;[2] if they had really been of evil significance Cicero would have mentioned them. He knew only of the signs of the Lupercalia and the day after.

Suetonius, as before, proceeds chronologically. The day before the Ides a bird, called *regaliolus*, flew into the Curia Pompei, where the Senate was to meet, and was there torn to pieces by other birds.[3] It was another portent, produced this time, as so often, by birds, and its message was obvious: a 'regal' bird was destroyed. In the night Calpurnia dreamt that the pediment of the house, the regal symbol which had been added recently, collapsed,[4] and that Caesar was stabbed to death. This was a telling dream and was supplemented by another evil sign, the opening of the door of her bedroom.[5] This was a frequent prodigy but generally connected with temples;[6] its special function here is not quite clear. Caesar's dream was complementary to that of Calpurnia: he saw himself flying above the clouds and clasping the hand of Iuppiter.[7] This sign indicated a favourable outcome and cannot have been added to the others before Caesar's consecration in 42 B.C.

2. THE FUNERAL

The drama of the murder need not detain us.[8] But it is worth mentioning that it was due to those who wrote it up and mixed facts and

---

[1] Suet. *Caes.* 81. 4: 'dein pluribus hostiis caesis, cum litare non posset, introiit curiam spreta religione Spurinnamque irridens et ut falsum arguens, quod sine ulla sua noxa Idus Martiae adessent: quanquam is venisse quidem eas diceret, sed non praeterisse.' This then became the standard version, Dio 44. 18. 4; Plut. *Caes.* 63. 6. According to Val. Max. 8. 11. 2 (Livy?) the meeting took place in the house of Cn. Domitius Calvinus, not at the Curia, which would not be impossible, if the thrust and riposte were really facts of history. Spurinna, though a *haruspex*, was a respected citizen (Münzer, *RE* 3A. 1888), also a friend of Cicero (*fam.* 9. 24. 2).

[2] App. *BC.* 2. 117. 488: ἔθος δ' ἐστὶ τοῖς ἄρχουσιν εἰς τὴν βουλὴν ἐσιοῦσιν οἰωνίζεσθαι; Gell. 14. 7. 9; Dio 56. 31. 3; Mommsen, *StR* 3. 935. 2.

[3] Suet. *Caes.* 81. 3. It is not recorded by anyone else.

[4] Suet. *Caes.* 81. 3; Plut. *Caes.* 63. 9 (who quotes Livy); Obs. 67 (above, p. 280. 1 f. Dio 44. 17. 3 (on the following morning Caesar's statue collapsed in the vestibule, 44. 18. 2).

[5] Suet. *Caes.* 81. 3: 'ac subito cubiculi fores sponte patuerunt'; Obs. 67; Plut. *Caes.* 63. 8; Dio 44. 17. 2.   [6] Cf. Weinreich, *Genethliakon W. Schmid* (1929), 257 ff.; 263.

[7] Suet. *Caes.* 81. 3: 'ipse sibi visus est per quietem interdum supra nubes volitare, alias cum Iove dextram iungere'; Dio 44. 17. 1; below, p. 157; cf. Suet. *Cal.* 57.3: 'pridie quam periret, somniavit consistere se in caelo iuxta solium Iovis impulsumque ab eo dextri pedis pollice et in terras praecipitatum.'

[8] Suet. *Caes.* 82; App. *BC* 2. 117. 491 ff.; Dio 44. 19; Plut. *Caes.* 66, etc.; Drumann 3. 654 ff.; Gelzer, *Caesar* 304 f.

fiction that it became a real drama. Some writers suggested, wrongly, that there had been a conspiracy in 66 B.C. to murder the consuls of 65, and it was alleged by Tanusius Geminus, the elder C. Scribonius Curio (*cos.* 76), and M. Actorius Naso that Caesar was involved in it and was even to give the agreed sign for the attack, that is, to let his toga fall from his shoulder.[1] In 44 the sign for the attack is said to have been almost the same:[2] L. Tillius Cimber (*pr.* 45?) gave it by pulling the toga from Caesar's shoulders.[3] It is clear that one of the two versions was made up on the model of the other, either by the conspirators of 44, which is not likely, or by later writers. The model must be the sign of 65 (although it was never given) because this particular item comes from Curio who had died in 53 B.C. There is no doubt that facts and fiction were similarly mixed in the other parts of the description of the murder.

After the murder one of the conspirators fixed the liberty-cap on the end of a spear:[4] this is probable because liberty much exercised the minds of all before and after.[5] But then everybody, friend and foe, fled from the Curia and left the corpse alone; it was then taken home by three slaves.[6] The last item is certainly true, but the rest recalls an important precedent to which we shall have to return, the death of Romulus.[7] People taking part at an assembly fled when a storm broke out, an eclipse of the sun and other celestial phenomena occurred, and Romulus disappeared.[8] According to the other version the senators who murdered him left the Curia in haste, each taking a part of Romulus' body, which was then buried.[9] Caesar's ascension was said to have taken place there and then: this will be discussed together with the other relevant evidence.[10]

The conspirators held that it was right to kill the tyrant[11] and accordingly intended to prevent his funeral. The corpse was to be left

---

[1] Suet. *Caes.* 9. 2; *HRR* 2, pp. 49 f.; 45 P.; *ORF* 86, p. 302 Malc.; Meyer, op. cit. 18; Strasburger, op. cit. 107; Gelzer, 35; E. S. Gruen, *CP* 64 (1969), 20 ff.

[2] Observed by Münzer, *RE* 4A. 2231.

[3] Dio 44. 19. 4; Plut. *Caes.* 66. 6; Suet. *Caes.* 82. 1 and App. *BC* 2. 117. 491 are less clear.

[4] App. *BC* 2. 119. 499 (above, p. 147. 9).   [5] See above, pp. 133 ff.; 142.

[6] Suet. *Caes.* 82. 3; App. *BC* 2. 118. 498; Nic. Dam. 97 (*FGrHist.* 90 F 130).

[7] See below, p. 357.

[8] Livy 1. 16. 1; Dion. Hal. 1. 56. 2; Ov. *F.* 2. 491 ff.; Plut. *Rom.* 27. 4.

[9] Cic. *rep.* 2. 20; Val. Max. 5. 3. 1; Dion. Hal. 1. 56. 3 f.; Plut. *Rom.* 27. 6; App. *BC* 2. 114. 476 (Caesar's murderers chose the Curia because of the example of Romulus' murderers).   [10] See below, pp. 358 f.

[11] 'Iure caesus' (Suet. *Caes.* 76. 1; Cic. *Phil.* 13. 2); the expression is already found in the XII Tables, 8. 12 (Macrob. 1. 4. 19) and had also been applied to the murder of Ti. Gracchus, Cic. *Mil.* 8; *off.* 2. 43; Vell. 2. 4. 4; Flor. 3. 14. 7; cf. Sen. *NQ* 1. 16. 1; Tac. *A.* 14. 43. 5; Steidle, *Sueton u. die ant. Biographie* (1951), 60. 3; Astin, *CQ* 54 (1960), 135 ff.

unburied, perhaps, as often, exhibited, and then thrown into the Tiber.[1] This plan was frustrated by Caesar's followers, particularly Antony, at the meeting of the Senate on 17 March,[2] which not only granted a funeral but even a public funeral at the request of L. Calpurnius Piso (cos. 58), Caesar's father-in-law.[3]

A public funeral used to be held at public expense by the magistrates instead of the family, the aediles lifted the restrictions concerning public expenses, the quaestors hired the undertakers, and a free burial place was granted to the dead man and his descendants; the details were decreed by the Senate.[4] It had often been held before for foreign dignitaries; for Roman citizens it was a novelty, first granted to Sulla, although men like Valerius Poplicola, Agrippa Menenius, and Siccius Dentatus were said to have been so honoured.[5] Valerius Poplicola and Agrippa Menenius were buried at public expense because of their poverty. Sulla was not poor. The Senate granted it to him at the request of the consul Q. Lutatius Catulus, who was supported by Pompey against the opposition of his fellow consul M. Aemilius Lepidus and his friends.[6] They asked for it probably because Sulla left instructions to this effect; but what made Sulla want it remains a puzzle. The influence of the

---

[1] Suet. Caes. 82. 4: 'fuerat animus coniuratis corpus occisi in Tiberim trahere'; App. BC 2. 134. 559 (Antony's speech in the Senate): τὸ δὲ σῶμα τοῦ Καίσαρος συρόμενον καὶ αἰκιζόμενον καὶ ἄταφον ῥιπτούμενον (καὶ γὰρ ταῦτα ἐκ τῶν νόμων τοῖς τυράννοις ἐπιτέτακται) περιόψεσθαι νομίζετε τοὺς ἐστρατευμένους αὐτῷ; 2. 128. 535 (below, p. 389. 3); Dio 44. 35. 1; Plut. Brut. 20. 1; on this kind of punishment see Suet. Tib. 75. 1; Vesp. 19. 2; Tac. A. 6. 19. 5; Dio 58. 1. 3; 11. 5; 15. 3; 60. 35. 4; Mommsen, Strafr. 988 f.; Münzer, Herm. 47 (1912), 173; Vittinghoff, Der Staatsfeind 43 f.; below, p. 389.

[2] Plut. Brut. 20. 1: τῶν περὶ τὸν Ἀντώνιον ἀξιούντων τάς τε διαθήκας ἀναγνωσθῆναι καὶ τοῦ σώματος ἐκφορὰν γενέσθαι μὴ κεκρυμμένην μηδ' ἄτιμον; contra, e.g., Cic. Att. 14. 10. 1 (19 Apr. 44): 'meministine te clamare causam perisse, si funere elatus esset?' In spite of this disagreement they were all pledged to concord, above, p. 266.

[3] App. BC 2. 135. 566; 136. 569; Lact. div. inst. 1. 15. 30 is misleading (Münzer, RE 3. 1389; 10. 470).

[4] The locus classicus is Cic. Phil. 9. 16: 'cumque antea senatus auctoritatem suam in virorum fortium funeribus ornamentisque ostenderit, placere eum quam amplissume supremo suo die efferri. (17) et cum Ser. Sulpicius ... ita de re publica meritus sit, ut iis ornamentis decorari debeat, senatum censere atque e re publica existimare aediles curules edictum, quod de funeribus habeant, Ser. Sulpici ... funeri remittere; utique locum sepulchro in campo Esquilino C. Pansa consul seu quo in loco videbitur pedes triginta quoquo versus adsignet, quo Ser. Sulpicius inferatur: quod sepulchrum ipsius, liberorum posterorumque eius esset, uti quod optimo iure publice sepulchrum datum esset.' The decree for Caesar will have had a similar wording, omitting however the last part, because a burial-place had already been granted to his daughter in 54 B.C. (see below, p. 350. 1). On public funerals see Marquardt–Mau, Privatalt. 1. 350; Mau, RE 2. 331; Hug, RE Suppl. 3. 530 f.; Dessau, ILS 3, p. 944.

[5] Livy 2. 16. 7; 3. 43. 7; Dion. Hal. 6. 96. 3, etc.; Mommsen, StR 3. 1188. 2.

[6] App. BC 1. 105. 493: τῶν μὲν ἄγειν ἀξιούντων τὸ σῶμα διὰ τῆς Ἰταλίας ἐπὶ πομπῇ καὶ ἐς τὴν Ῥώμην ἐν ἀγορᾷ προτιθέναι καὶ ταφῆς δημοσίας ἀξιοῦν; Plut. Sulla 38. 2; Gran. Licin. 36, p. 33 Fl.: 'in campo Romae sepultus est amplissimo funere elatus magna populi frequentia'; Livy, Per. 90; Drumann 2. 423 f.; Eitrem, Beitr. z. griech. Rel. 3. 69. 1.

funeral processions of the Greek kings and nobles was strongly felt at Rome,[1] and similar splendour was exhibited by many Roman families, so much so that legislation was introduced, also by Sulla, to limit such luxury.[2]

Sulla's funeral was intended to surpass all its predecessors. His body was brought on a richly decorated couch from Puteoli to Rome. At Rome, if the traditional order was kept, the funeral was led by trumpeters, dancers, and mimes; the *imagines* followed, that is, actors wearing the ancestral masks and preceded by lictors.[3] Then came, as in the triumphal procession, the exhibits. These were carried on 210 rather than 6,000 barrows and included, so it is alleged, 2,000 golden crowns contributed by legions, cities, and friends.[4] They also included the spices given by the matrons; there was so much of these that statues of Sulla and of a lictor were carved of the wood of a frankincense- and a cinnamon-tree and carried on a special barrow, a strange feature of the procession to which we shall have to return.[5] The usual torchbearers will have preceded Sulla's magnificent funeral couch, which was followed by priests and priestesses, the magistrates and the senators.[6] Then came the knights, the people, and Sulla's legionaries.[7] The corpse was exhibited in the Forum and the most eloquent orator of the age delivered the funeral oration from the Rostra.[8] Thence the senators carried the bier to the funeral pyre on the Campus Martius. The cremation followed, and the knights and soldiers ran round the fire.[9] The remains were buried in a tomb on the Campus Martius given by the Senate.[10] The matrons mourned for a whole year, as was normally done for a father.[11]

Sulla's public funeral remained unique until Caesar,[12] although a

[1] On Greek funerals see Eitrem, op. cit. 3. 62 ff.; Bömer, *RE* 21. 1884 f.

[2] Cic. *leg.* 2. 60 f.; Plut. *Sulla* 35. 3; Mommsen, *StR* 2. 510. 1; Marquardt–Mau, op. cit. 1. 345 f.

[3] Marquardt–Mau, op. cit. 1. 351 f.; on the *imagines* see, e.g., Polyb. 6. 53. 6 ff.; Bömer, *Ahnenkult* 104 ff.

[4] App. *BC* 1. 106. 496; Plut. *Sulla* 38. 3; Serv. *Aen.* 6. 861.

[5] Plut. *Sulla* 38. 3: λέγεται δὲ τοσοῦτο πλῆθος ἀρωμάτων ἐπενεγκεῖν αὐτῷ τὰς γυναῖκας, ὥστ'... πλασθῆναι μὲν εἴδωλον εὐμέγεθες αὐτοῦ Σύλλα, πλασθῆναι δὲ καὶ ῥαβδοῦχον ἔκ τε λιβανωτοῦ πολυτελοῦς καὶ κινναμώμου; Marquardt–Mau 1. 348. 1; below, pp. 360 f.

[6] App. *BC* 1. 106. 497. [7] Ibid. 498. [8] Ibid. 500.

[9] Ibid. 500: καὶ τὸ πῦρ οἵ τε ἱππεῖς καὶ ἡ στρατιὰ περιέδραμον.

[10] Livy, *Per.* 90: 'honosque ei a senatu habitus est, ut in campo Martio sepeliretur'; Plut. *Lucull.* 43. 3.

[11] Gran. Licin. 36, p. 33 Fl.: 'matronaeque eum toto anno luxerunt'; cf. Livy 2. 7. 4; 2. 16. 7.

[12] The next should have been Pompey, Lucan. 8. 729: 'non pretiosa petit cumulato ture sepulchra / Pompeius ... (732) ut Romana suum gestent pia colla parentem, / praeferat ut veteres feralis pompa triumphos, / ut resonent tristi cantu fora, totus ut ignes / proiectis maerens exercitus ambiat armis.'

burial place on the Campus Martius had already been granted to others too, to Lucullus (*cos.* 74) in 56 and to Iulia, Caesar's daughter and Pompey's wife, in 54; she was, however, buried there before permission was granted.[1] Thus the puzzle of this new institution reappears. Caesar made his last testament in 45[2] probably in expectation of the Parthian campaign. Like that of Augustus[3] it contained instructions about his funeral; we know a single item, viz. that Atia, his niece, was to organize it.[4] But the probability is that it also contained the request for a public funeral because Piso, his father-in-law, having produced the testament at the meeting of the Senate on 17 March, requested it after Antony had frustrated the plans of the conspirators. In granting it the Senate will have decided all the details[5] in co-operation with Piso and no doubt in agreement with Caesar's instructions.

The funeral took place probably on 20 March.[6] The preparations included the setting up of a shrine on the Rostra and of the funeral pyre on the Campus Martius next to the tomb of Iulia. The heralds who announced the funeral directed the public to come and bring their gifts by all routes possible to the Campus Martius, that is, not to join the funeral cortège:[7] the precedent of Sulla clearly showed that it would have been an endless procession. The cortège proper began at the house, the *domus publica* at the Regia, with the usual participants, musicians, dancers, *mimi*, and *imagines*, followed by the exhibits. Torch-bearers and freedmen whom Caesar had just set free by testament preceded the couch,[8] on which normally the corpse was lying or reclining; this time it was hidden inside and represented outside by an image in wax.[9] The couch—which was of ivory with coverlets of gold and purple—was carried by the magistrates and ex-magistrates[10] and not as at a private funeral by members of the family. These followed with the rest of the dignitaries and the people. When the Forum was reached gladiatorial contests were held.[11] At the Rostra the ivory couch was placed in the

---

[1] Plut. *Lucull.* 43. 3; Livy, *Per.* 106; Dio 39. 64; Plut. *Pomp.* 53. 5 f.; cf. Marquardt–Mau 1. 360. 12.   [2] Suet. *Caes.* 83. 1.   [3] Dio 56. 33. 1.

[4] Nic. Dam. 17. 48 (*FGrHist.* 90 F 130): ἐπισκήψειε δὲ καὶ Ἀτίᾳ ... τῆς ἑαυτοῦ ταφῆς ἐπιμεληθῆναι; Schmitthenner, *Oktavian u. das Testament Caesars* 35 f.

[5] See the formula in Cic. *Phil.* 9. 16 (above, p. 348. 4); App. *BC* 3. 34. 136: τό τε σῶμα τεθάφθαι βασιλικῶς.

[6] Cf. Drumann–Groebe 1. 73 (funeral); 407 ff. (events after the murder); 417 (date of the funeral).   [7] Suet. *Caes.* 84. 1.

[8] This is an inference from the general rule (Livy 38. 55. 2; App. *Mithr.* 2; Schol. Pers. 3. 105 f.; *Cod. Iust.* 7. 6. 5 (below, p. 361. 2)) and from the fact that it was Caesar's freedmen who took his ashes to his burial-place, Dio 44. 51. 1 (below, p. 355. 10).

[9] See below, p. 360.   [10] Suet. *Caes.* 84. 3.

[11] Suet. *Caes.* 84. 2: 'inter ludos cantata sunt quaedam ad miserationem et invidiam caedis eius accommodata'; Pliny 15. 78: 'gladiatorio munere Divi Iuli, quod novissime pugnavit in

gilded shrine which had been made on the model of the temple of
Venus Genetrix and erected there, and Caesar's robe was hung on a pole
which was somehow attached to the shrine.[1] This is an extraordinary
feature of the funeral, recorded only by Suetonius—the robe with the
pole is found in a different form in Appian[2]—and will require serious
attention.[3] The funeral oration was delivered by the consul Antony,
which was an innovation, but was often repeated later;[4] usually a member of the family spoke, though at Sulla's funeral, as we have seen, the
best orator of the age.[5]

The contents of the oration are inevitably controversial.[6] Cicero, the
contemporary, who was not present, knew of it,[7] probably even read
it in a published form in April[8] and often referred to it.[9] He quoted
the expressions 'very great man' and 'most distinguished citizen', also
the theme that clemency caused Caesar's downfall, and he was convinced that it was Antony's speech that inflamed the populace.[10] According to Suetonius, Antony spoke just a few words, after he had
made a herald recite the honours decreed for Caesar and the oath sworn

foro.' It is probable that a dirge was sung during these contests and not only after the funeral
oration, but it is very unlikely that the verses from Pacuvius and Atilius were also recited,
as Suetonius asserts; they belong to the laments after the oration, where Appian in fact quotes
the verse from Pacuvius, BC 2. 146. 611; see below, p. 353.

[1] Suet. Caes. 84. 1 (below, p. 360. 2); App. BC 2. 143. 598: Πείσωνος τὸ σῶμα φέροντος ἐς
τὴν ἀγορὰν . . . μετὰ βοῆς καὶ πομπῆς δαψιλοῦς ἐπὶ τὰ Ἔμβολα προυτέθη.

[2] App. BC 2. 146. 610 (below, p. 353. 4).

[3] See below, p. 353.

[4] App. BC 2. 143. 599: ὁ Ἀντώνιος . . . ᾑρημένος εἰπεῖν τὸν ἐπιτάφιον; Cic. Phil. 2. 90:
'funeri tyranni, si illud funus fuit, sceleratissime praefuisti'; cf. Quintil. 3. 7. 2: 'et funebres
laudationes . . . ex senatus consulto magistratibus saepe mandantur.'

[5] See above, p. 349.

[6] Suet. Caes. 84. 2; App. BC 2. 144 f., 600–6; Dio 44. 36–49; Plut. Ant. 14. 6; F. Vollmer,
'Laudationum funebrium Romanorum historia', Jahrb. f. Phil. Suppl. 18 (1891), 456; 483;
Drumann–Groebe 1. 417 ff.

[7] Cic. Att. 14. 10. 1 (19 Apr.): 'at ille etiam in foro combustus laudatusque miserabiliter.'

[8] Cic. Att. 14. 11. 1 (21 Apr.): 'cum contionem lego de "tanto viro", de "clarissimo civi",
ferre nequeo.' The attribution of this contio to Antony is denied by Vollmer, l.c. 468; Drumann–
Groebe 1. 418; Shackleton Bailey ad loc.; Groebe's argument, however, that contio cannot
mean a funeral oration, is wrong: see Cic. de or. 2. 341; leg. 2. 62; Quintil. 11. 3. 153; Thes.L.L.
4. 733.

[9] Cic. Att. 14. 22. 1 (14 May): 'clarissimum virum interfectum, totam rem publicam illius
interitu perturbatam, irrita fore quae ille egisset simul ac desisteremus timere, clementiam
illi malo fuisse, qua si usus non esset, nihil ei tale accidere potuisse'; 15. 20. 2 (20 June):
'ego quo die audivi illum tyrannum in contione clarissimum virum appellari subdiffidere
coepi.'

[10] Cic. Phil. 2. 91 (19 Sept.): 'tua illa pulchra laudatio, tua miseratio, tua cohortatio;
tu, tu, inquam, illas faces incendisti, et eas quibus semustilatus ille est'; cf. 2. 5: 'quod si
esset beneficium, numquam qui illum interfecerunt a quo erant conservati . . . tantam essent
gloriam consecuti' (polemical reference to the verse of Pacuvius, below, p. 353. 7); 116:
'maioribus habes beneficiis obligatos, quam ille quosdam habuit ex iis, a quibus est inter-
fectus.'

for his safety.[1] What we have learnt from Cicero shows that Suetonius is here much too reticent. This impression is confirmed by the other evidence, which also describes the proper course of events, as Suetonius does not. There is an elaborate oration in Appian and a very much longer one in Dio. We shall discuss only that in Appian, as it proves to be the closest to the historical events and is in agreement with Cicero's brief allusions. His source, direct or indirect, was no doubt Asinius Pollio.[2] In Appian too, as in Suetonius, the decrees were recited, but by Antony himself, who added comments to each of them; he too mentions the oath which was to vouch for Caesar's safety. This made Antony turn to Iuppiter and state that he was ready to avenge him; but seeing the effect of these words he withdrew what he had said and ended with the hope that the danger of civil war would be avoided.[3] This is certainly not all he said. A funeral oration usually began with the person of the deceased: his ancestry, past members of the family, his career, and his achievements.[4] All this is found in Dio but also in Appian, though only in the laments which follow. Appian clearly shortened his report in order to avoid repetition.

Members of the family used to wail over the deceased during the whole funeral. In addition there was a professional wailing-woman, the praefica, who performed a song, the nenia, to the accompaniment of a flute, praising and lamenting the dead man.[5] When it concerned a distinguished man this song was not left to one woman.[6] The Greeks had choruses who used to take up the song of one of the mourners.[7] At Augustus' funeral the sons and daughters of leading citizens sang the nenia;[8] and in the imperial period such choruses stood at the Rostra and sang hymns in praise of the dead.[9] The valuable description of the

[1] Suet. Caes. 84. 2: 'laudationis loco consul Antonius per praeconem pronuntiavit senatus consultum, quo omnia simul ei divina atque humana decreverat, item ius iurandum, quo se cuncti pro salute unius astrinxerant; quibus perpauca a se verba addidit'; accepted by M. E. Deutsch, 'Antony's Funeral Speech', Univ. Calif. Publ. Class. Phil. 9. 5 (1928), 127 ff.

[2] Cf. Schwartz, RE 2. 226; 229 f. (critical comment on Appian's narrative); Meyer, op. cit. 608; 613 ff.; J. André, La vie et l'œuvre d'Asinius Pollion (1949), 41 ff.

[3] App. BC 2. 144 f., 600–6.

[4] See Vollmer, l.c. 480 ff.; Münzer, Adelsp. 263. 1.

[5] Fest. 161 M. (154 L.); Non. 145 M.; Kroll, RE 16. 2390 ff.; J. L. Heller, TAPA 70 (1939), 357 ff.; 74 (1943), 215 ff.; Latte 101. 3.

[6] Cic. leg. 2. 62: 'honoratorum virorum laudes in contione memorentur, easque etiam cantus ad tibicinem prosequatur, cui nomen neniae, quo vocabulo etiam apud Graecos cantus lugubres nominantur.'

[7] It began with the lament for Patroclus and Hector in the Iliad, 18. 351 ff.; 24. 719 ff.; Nilsson, Opuscula 1. 75 ff.; E. Reiner, Die rituelle Totenklage der Griechen (1938), 8 ff.

[8] Suet. Aug. 100. 2: 'canentibus neniam principum liberis utriusque sexus.'

[9] Herodian. 4. 2. 5: ἐπὶ μὲν θατέρου μέρους (of the Rostra) τῶν εὐγενεστάτων καὶ εὐπατριδῶν χορὸς ἔστηκε παίδων, ἐν δὲ τῷ ἀντικειμένῳ γυναικῶν τῶν ἐν ἀξιώσει εἶναι δοκουσῶν· ᾄδουσι δὲ

nenia by Cicero gives the impression that by his time it had long been refashioned in the pattern of the Greek wailing songs; the evidence about Augustus and the imperial period confirms this impression. But even so what Appian reports about Caesar's funeral is unique and surprising.[1] Antony ended his funeral oration with the request that the traditional hymn and lament should now conduct Caesar to the blessed.[2] He then intoned his hymn on Caesar, who had become a god, recited his achievements, mourned his cruel fate, and wept; he did all this in a theatrical fashion.[3] He then uncovered Caesar's body, lifted his robe, torn and red with blood, with a spear.[4] The audience, seeing this, mourned with him like the chorus in a play. They then formed two choruses and began to chant the *nenia* in the 'traditional manner' to the accompaniment of a flute, reciting his achievements and fate again.[5] One of them impersonated Caesar[6] and recalled what he had done for each of his murderers and gave expression to his amazement with a verse from Pacuvius' tragedy *Armorum iudicium*: 'have I saved them that they might murder me?', and with another verse from Atilius' translation of Sophocles' *Electra*, which was similar.[7] Someone then raised an image of Caesar made of wax above the bier and turning it round by a mechanical device showed all the wounds.[8] This sight inflamed the people even more and drove them to action.

ἑκάτεροι ὕμνους τε καὶ παιᾶνας ἐς τὸν τετελευτηκότα, σεμνῷ μέλει καὶ θρηνώδει ἐρρυθμισμένους; Dio 74. 4. 5.

[1] It was noticed by Kroll, l.c. 2392, who rightly assumed Greek influence.

[2] App. *BC* 2. 145. 606: προπέμπωμεν οὖν τὸν ἱερὸν τόνδε ἐπὶ τοὺς εὐδαίμονας, τὸν νενομισμένον ὕμνον αὐτῷ καὶ θρῆνον ἐπᾴδοντες.

[3] App. *BC* 2. 146. 607: πρῶτα μὲν ὡς θεὸν οὐράνιον ὕμνει καὶ ἐς πίστιν θεοῦ γενέσεως τὰς χεῖρας ἀνέτεινεν, ἐπιλέγων ὁμοῦ σὺν δρόμῳ φωνῆς πολέμους αὐτοῦ καὶ μάχας καὶ νίκας ... (609) πολλά τε ἄλλα ἐπιθειάσας τὴν φωνὴν ἐς τὸ θρηνῶδες ἐκ τοῦ λαμπροτέρου μετεποίει καὶ ὡς φίλον ἄδικα παθόντα ὠδύρετο καὶ ἔκλαιε κτλ.

[4] App. *BC* 2. 146. 610: εὐφορώτατα δὲ ἐς τὸ πάθος ἐκφερόμενος τὸ σῶμα τοῦ Καίσαρος ἐγύμνου καὶ τὴν ἐσθῆτα ἐπὶ κοντοῦ φερομένην ἀνέσειε, λελακισμένην ὑπὸ τῶν πληγῶν καὶ πεφυρμένην αἵματι αὐτοκράτορος. [5] App. *BC* 2. 146. 610 f. (κατὰ πάτριον ἔθος).

[6] An actor similarly impersonated Vespasian, Suet. *Vesp.* 19. 2; cf. Nilsson, *Opuscula* 1. 109.

[7] App. *BC* 2. 146. 611: ὡς δ' ἐπὶ τοῖς λόγοις ἕτεροι θρῆνοι μετὰ ᾠδῆς κατὰ πάτριον ἔθος ὑπὸ χορῶν ἐς αὐτὸν ᾔδοντο καὶ τὰ ἔργα αὖθις αὐτοῦ καὶ τὸ πάθος κατέλεγον καί που τῶν θρήνων αὐτὸς ὁ Καῖσαρ ἐδόκει λέγειν, ὅσους εὖ ποιήσειε τῶν ἐχθρῶν ἐξ ὀνόματος καὶ περὶ τῶν σφαγέων αὐτῶν ἐπέλεγεν ὥσπερ ἐν θαύματι· "ἐμὲ δὲ καὶ τούσδε περισῶσαι τοὺς κτενοῦντάς με"; Suet. *Caes.* 84. 2: 'cantata sunt quaedam ad miserationem et invidiam caedis eius accommodata, ex Pacuvi Armorum iudicio (frg. XV, 40 R.): "men servasse, ut essent qui me perderent?", et ex Electra Acili ad similem sententiam'; cf. Cic. *Phil.* 2. 5, above, p. 351. 20. In Pacuvius' tragedy (cf. Aeschylus' Ὅπλων κρίσις and Accius' *Armorum iudicium*) these are Aias' words; after his suicide it was forbidden to bury him (frg. 16 R.; Soph. *Ai.* 1049; Hor. *sat.* 2. 3. 187; Helm, *RE* 18. 1. 2163): this theme too will have provided suitable verses for the Caesarian lament. On Atilius' *Electra* see Cic. *fin.* 1. 2. 5.

[8] App. *BC* 2. 147. 612: ἀνέσχε τις ὑπὲρ τὸ λέχος ἀνδρείκελον αὐτοῦ Καίσαρος ἐκ κηροῦ πεποιημένον· τὸ μὲν γὰρ σῶμα, ὡς ὕπτιον ἐπὶ λέχους, οὐχ ἑωρᾶτο. τὸ δὲ ἀνδρείκελον ἐκ μηχανῆς ἐπεστρέφετο πάντῃ κτλ.

A a

What should one think of this narrative? It was certainly not invented by Appian or Asinius Pollio. One is inclined to object to the repetitions. And there was more than one repetition if, as is probable, the funeral oration already contained the same story. But this also happened in the Greek laments, the θρῆνοι: one intoned the song and the others took it up; it was natural that the laments for the dead were repetitive.[1] Again, one might object that Antony acted like the leader of a chorus. But it was equally exceptional that he delivered the funeral oration. The Senate which charged him with the one task will have charged him with the other. It is a more serious point that Antony first exhibited the robe and then someone else the wax image, both having the same function. We cannot choose between the two items. The robe on the top of the spear corresponds to the robe on the pole in Suetonius' record;[2] and the wax image was an important feature of such funerals, though, as we shall presently see, it had a different function.[3] The difficulty would be resolved if Appian's record rested not only on the facts of history as told by Asinius Pollio but also on a Praetexta called *Iulius Caesar*. There is no evidence about such a play, but it is not impossible that it existed, considering that there was a Praetexta by Curiatius Maternus about Cato.[4]

However critical one may be of this narrative,[5] it is clear that it contains a great deal of reliable information. If so, the conclusion is inevitable that the programme was not made up in the great haste and confusion of those four days but was planned by Caesar long before and was only modified at the last moment to take account of the murder. It was to be a funeral as there never was before, like that of Sulla but with a new fusion of Greek and Roman elements, and, above all, including divine honours. Whether Plutarch was right or wrong in asserting that

---

[1] Cic. *leg.* 2. 62 (above, p. 352. 6); Tac. *A.* 3. 5. 6; Dio 74. 4. 5; 5. 1 (Pertinax).

[2] It was, like the wax image, a symbol of the dead Caesar (according to G. Ch. Picard, *Les trophées romains* (1957), 226 f., it represented his Genius; *contra*, Brendel, *Gnom.* 36 (1964), 504). In 48 the Alexandrians hung Caesar's cloak similarly on a trophy in the belief that he had perished (Dio 42. 40. 5; App. *BC* 2. 90. 377; *contra*, Suet. *Caes.* 64; cf. Gelzer, *Caesar* 231. 282). It is also relevant, though in a different sense, that the wax images of Augustus and Pertinax were dressed in the triumphal garb at their funerals (Dio 56. 34. 1; 74. 4. 3), and that Trajan was represented by his image in his posthumous Parthian triumph in A.D. 117 (SHA *Hadr.* 6. 3; J.-C. Richard, *REL* 44 (1966), 358).

[3] See below, pp. 360 f.

[4] Tac. *dial.* 2. 1; cf. Teuffel–Kroll 2. 296 (under Vespasian).

[5] It is, e.g., unlikely that Antony uncovered the body (App. *BC* 2. 146. 610; Dio 44. 35. 4; Plut. *Caes.* 68. 1; *contra*, App. *BC* 2. 147. 612): as a priest—he was an *augur*—he was not allowed to see it, Tac. *A.* 1. 62. 3; Dio 54. 28. 4; 54. 35. 4; 56. 31. 3; 60. 13. 3; Serv. *Aen.* 3. 64; 6. 176; Sen. *consol. Marc.* 15. 3; *ILS* 6964. 7; Wissowa 507. 4; Weber, *Princeps* 40 ff.; 47* f.

these honours were decreed by the Senate after the murder, we shall see presently that some of the new features of the funeral cannot be explained otherwise.[1]

What followed was not in accordance with the plan—this is expressly stated.[2] The plan was that the bier should be carried from the Rostra, presumably by the magistrates and ex-magistrates again,[3] to the Campus Martius where the funeral pyre had been prepared next to the tomb of his daughter Iulia, which had been made a burial-place for the Iulii and was now to contain Caesar's ashes as well.[4] Instead of this the people, inflamed, began to improvise, though not in a senseless manner. They took up the bier and carried it on their shoulders—this was an honour which the people used to grant spontaneously to deserving men[5]—up to the Capitol with the intention of cremating and burying Caesar in the *cella* of Iuppiter so as to place him among the gods.[6] This was a novelty but must have rested on competent advice. Those involved were convinced that Caesar was now a god because of the relevant decrees made before his death and probably also because they understood the preceding funeral rites in this sense. They will have remembered that Caesar was somehow to be connected with Iuppiter:[7] they were now going to make him a participant in the cult of the Capitoline temple. They were, however, not allowed by the priests to do this, so they took the corpse back to the Forum, improvised a pyre, and cremated it there.[8] Soldiers and civilians, men and women, went round the pyre and threw into it gifts such as arms, robes, and jewels.[9] In the end Caesar's freedmen collected the ashes and buried them in the Iulian monument as had been planned.[10]

[1] Plut. *Caes.* 67. 8: ἡ δὲ σύγκλητος . . . Καίσαρα μὲν ὡς θεὸν τιμᾶν ἐψηφίσατο.

[2] Tac. *A.* 1. 8. 6: 'populumque edicto monuit (Tiberius) ne, ut quondam nimiis studiis funus Divi Iulii turbassent, ita Augustum in foro potius quam in Campo Martis sede destinata cremari vellent.'   [3] See above, p. 350; cf. Suet. *Aug.* 100. 3: 'senatorum umeris delatus'.

[4] See above, p. 350.

[5] Pliny 18. 16: 'Seius . . . supremo die populi umeris portatus in rogum est'; above, p. 294; Plut. *Num.* 22. 1; *Aem. Paul.* 39. 8; Lucan 8. 732 (Plat. *leg.* 12. 947c; Plut. *Timol.* 39. 2).

[6] Suet. *Caes.* 84. 3: 'quem cum pars in Capitolini Iovis cella cremare pars in curia Pompei destinaret'; App. *BC* 2. 148. 615: ὁ δὲ δῆμος ἐπὶ τὸ λέχος τοῦ Καίσαρος ἐπανελθὼν ἔφερον αὐτὸ ἐς τὸ Καπιτώλιον ὡς εὐαγὲς θάψαι τε ἐν ἱερῷ καὶ μετὰ θεῶν θέσθαι; Dio 44. 50. 2.

[7] See above, p. 303 and below, p. 357.

[8] Suet. *Caes.* 84. 3; App. *BC* 2. 148. 616; Cic. *Phil.* 2. 91; *Att.* 14. 10. 1.

[9] Suet. *Caes.* 84. 4: 'deinde tibicines et scaenici artifices vestem, quam ex triumphorum instrumento ad praesentem usum induerant, detractam sibi atque discissam iniecere flammae et veteranorum militum legionarii arma sua, quibus exculti funus celebrabant; matronae etiam pleraeque ornamenta sua, quae gerebant, et liberorum bullas atque praetextas'; App. *BC* 2. 148. 616 (wreaths and *dona militaria*); see above, p. 349 (Sulla); Dio 56. 42. 2 (Augustus).

[10] Dio 44. 51. 1: τὰ γὰρ ὀστᾶ αὐτοῦ οἱ ἐξελεύθεροι προανείλοντο καὶ ἐς τὸ πατρῷον μνημεῖον κατέθεντο; Drumann–Groebe 1. 421; Hirschfeld, *Kl. Schr.* 451; Platner–Ashby 542; Weber, *Princeps* 81*. 363.

3. THE ASCENSION

The last decrees of 45 and 44 were intended to create a cult for Caesar; and the rites of the funeral will have been designed accordingly. So there must have been a plan. What it was can to some extent be reconstructed with the help of some Caesarian evidence, of precedents, Greek and Roman, and of what was done later for Augustus and his successors, assuming that it was based on the ritual created for Caesar.

This does not mean that it was a new departure. Divine honours were always granted to the dead individually, who were then called *Di Manes* or *Di parentum*, and to the ancestors collectively, the *Lares*. Moreover, a special cult could be created for a distinguished ancestor.[1] All this belonged to the private sphere. But there were public and lasting cults of the founders, Aeneas and Latinus outside Rome and Romulus-Quirinus in Rome.[2] And there was the example of the Greek heroes, Dionysus, the Dioscuri, Heracles, and of the kings, Alexander and his successors; no doubt also of Scipio Africanus.[3]

The dead man or his 'soul' had first to be removed to the abode of the gods: that was his ascension, an ageless theme in the Orient and Greece.[4] There were various forms of this disappearance: a cloud, a storm, an eagle or another winged creature, or a chariot could be the means of this translation.[5] But it could also be achieved by drowning. It was said that Alexander wanted to jump into the Euphrates[6] and that Aeneas in fact disappeared in the river Numicus;[7] and there were others.[8] The Romans adopted most of these forms for their own heroes but were influenced by none so much as that described in the case of Heracles.[9] Heracles mounted the pyre on Mount Oeta, but the fire was quenched by rain and amid storms and thunder Heracles went to heaven.[10]

---

[1] See above, pp. 291 ff.

[2] See above, p. 292; less certain is the evidence about King Saturnus (Macrob. 1. 7. 24) and King Aventinus (August. *CD* 18. 21; Serv. *Aen.* 7. 657).

[3] Enn. *V.* 23 V.: 'si fas endo plagas caelestum ascendere cuiquam est, / mi soli caeli maxima porta patet' (Lact. *div. inst.* 1. 18. 11; 13); Hor. *c.* 4. 8. 14 ff.; above, pp. 294 f.

[4] Dieterich, *Mithrasliturgie* 181 ff.; Brendel, *Studies in Honor of F. W. Shipley* (1942), 75 ff.; Mühl, *Rhein. Mus.* 101 (1958), 107 ff.; G. Strecker, *RAC* 5. 461 ff.; see also the following note.

[5] Rohde, *Psyche* 2. 375 f.; Pease, *HSCP* 53 (1942), 10 ff.; cf. *PBSR* 19 (1951), 144. 103.

[6] Arr. *Anab.* 7. 27. 3; Pease, l.c. 20 f.

[7] Dion. Hal. 1. 64 f.; Serv. Dan. *Aen.* 1. 259; *Or. g. R.* 14. 3 f. (Anchises at Anchialos: Procop. *B. Goth.* 4. 22. 31); above, p. 292. 3; Pease, l.c. 10. 78; 14. 109.

[8] Greg. Naz. *or.* 5. 14 (*PG* 35. 681) on Julian's attempt; cf. Straub, *Gymn.* 69 (1962), 314 (on Julian's consecration: Eutrop. 10. 16. 2; Liban. *or.* 18. 304; Eunap. frg. 1; 23; 26; Straub 316 f.; 321 f.).—Suet. *vir. ill.* 28 (p. 124 Reiff.) on Epidius; for further evidence see Pease, l.c. 10. 78; A. Hermann, *RAC* 6. 370 ff. (with bibliography).

[9] Pease, l.c. 31; Mühl, l.c. 120 ff.

[10] Soph. *Philoct.* 726 f.; Diod. 4. 38. 4; Apollod. 2. 160; Paul. 100 M. (89 L.); Ov. *Met*

PLATE 22

2. Marble altar in the Vatican Museum: ascension of the new god in a quadriga with winged horses, witnessed by a man on l. and a woman with two youths on r.; above, an eagle between the chariot of Sol and the half-figure of Caelus (Photograph: German Archaeological Institute, Rome); p. 359.

1. Attic red-figured pelike in the Glyptothek, Munich: Heracles taken by Athena in a quadriga to Olympus; below, his armour is burning on the pyre (Photograph: Kohlroser, Munich); p. 357.

On vases we see a chariot of Heracles over the pyre or on its way to Olympus (pl. 22. 1).[1] In the Roman apotheosis too there is the storm, but not for quenching the fire.[2] Quenching was not needed, since the Romans adopted the doctrine that through burning the body the 'soul' was released and taken to heaven.[3] At Rome also there is the pyre and the new deity over it, flying or driven on a chariot; and the chariot too without the pyre.[4] On the stage the ascension will have been performed by a mechanical device. Such a device was used at Rome about 186 B.C. in the cult of Bacchus whenever the illusion was to be created that someone was being removed by the gods to heaven.[5]

To return to Caesar. Suetonius records that Caesar dreamt the night before the murder that he was flying over the clouds and then clasping the hand of Iuppiter.[6] 'Flying over the clouds' can mean that it was a cloud that removed him from earth. It was an old belief that a cloud could make someone invisible and even remove him from a dangerous spot in a battle.[7] It could do more: together with other celestial phenomena, such as a tempest or solar eclipse, it could make someone vanish, Ganymede for instance[8] or, what matters here, Romulus.[9] Romulus disappeared in a tempest during an assembly of the people at the *Caprae palus* on the Campus Martius.[10] It is true that according to Ennius, our earliest authority, it was Mars, his father, who carried him to heaven on his chariot,[11] but the two versions do not exclude one another and in fact Ovid combines the two.[12]

9. 250 f.; 270 f.; Nilsson, *Opuscula* 1. 348 ff. On Heracles' imitators, Peregrinus (Lucian. *Peregr.* 33 ff.) and others, see Pack, *AJP* 67 (1946), 334 ff.

[1] Furtwängler, *Myth. Lex.* 1. 2238 ff.; 2250 f.; Mingazzini, *Mon. Linc.* 6. 1. 6 (1925); Cook, *Zeus* 3. 512 ff.; G. Richter, *AJA* 45 (1941), 370 f.; Beazley, *Etr. Vase Painting* 103 ff.; H. Metzger, *Les représentations dans la céramique attique* (1951), 210 ff.

[2] The motif was still used but in a different sense. Sulla was lucky even in his death because a storm began only after the cremation (Plut. *Sulla* 38. 4 ff.); heavy rain, an evil omen, poured down at Britannicus' funeral, Tac. *A.* 13. 17. 2; Dio 61. 7. 4.

[3] Pind. frg. 131b Sn. (= Plut. *Rom.* 28. 8; Rohde, *Psyche* 2. 373. 1; Cumont, *Lux Perpetua* 17; 78; 143 ff.; 180 ff.); cf. Cic. *rep.* 3. 40; 6. 24; Ov. *Met.* 15. 844 f.; *F.* 3. 701 f. (below, p. 359. 2).

[4] See below, pp. 358; 362.   [5] Livy 39. 13. 13; Rohde, *Psyche* 2. 374. 3.

[6] Suet. *Caes.* 81. 3 (above, p. 346. 7); Dio 44. 17. 1 (above, p. 304. 1).

[7] Hom. *Il.* 3. 381; 11. 751; 20. 321; cf. the vanishing into thin air, Verg. *Aen.* 4. 278 (with Pease's note), and the disappearance of Oedipus, Soph. *Oed. Col.* 1649 ff.

[8] *Hymn. Hom. Ven.* 202 ff.; Brendel, l.c. 87 f.; more often he is carried by an eagle.

[9] Pease, l.c. 15 f.; Bömer, *Ahnenkult* 68 ff.

[10] Livy 1. 16; Ov. *F.* 2. 491 ff.; Dion. Hal. 1. 56. 2; Plut. *Rom.* 27. 6 ff.; *RE* 17. 857 ff.; Latte 128; Burkert, *Hist.* 11 (1962), 362; 368 f.

[11] Enn. *A.* 65 V.: 'unus erit quem tu tolles in caerula caeli / templa'; 115 ff.; Serv. Dan˙ *Aen.* 6. 777; Ov. *Met.* 14. 820; *F.* 2. 496: 'patriis astra petebat equis'; Hor. *c.* 3. 3. 16: 'Martis equis Acheronta fugit'; *JRS* 50 (1960), 118; Classen, *Philol.* 106 (1962), 179; Richard, *Mél.* 78 (1966), 76.

[12] Ov. *F.* 2. 491 ff.

Caesar's dream was followed by the dreams of others, which may help us to understand it better. Octavius saw Augustus dressed like Iuppiter and riding on a chariot with twelve white horses;[1] Alexander Severus' father dreamt the night before his son was born that he himself was being carried to heaven by Victoria;[2] and shortly before his death Septimius Severus dreamt that he was being taken to heaven by four eagles and a chariot led by a winged figure.[3] These three dreams are clearly variations of the Caesarian dream. The first will have portended Augustus' ascension in its original form; as we have it, it represents him as a god who rules on earth, the terrestrial Iuppiter. The second dream too must have had an earlier version: for only the ascension of Alexander Severus makes sense, not that of his father; his flight on the back of Victoria is acceptable as it can be supported with the cases of Sabina and of Faustina I.[4] The vision of Septimius Severus, on the other hand, is in its proper setting because it announces his death and his apotheosis. But it has become a threefold ascension, by eagles, a chariot, and a winged figure. The eagle is often found in this context[5] and the four eagles clearly correspond to the four horses of the chariot. This abundance of 'transport' is not exceptional: it is found elsewhere too. The conclusion is that Caesar's dream may incorporate two stories, either separately or combined. It could have been the cloud alone, or the chariot, or both, which removed him from earth: the precedent of Romulus would provide support for all these versions, and so would some Caesarian evidence which will be discussed presently. The second half of Caesar's dream can mean two things: he clasped Iuppiter's hand either as a sign of greeting on his arrival in heaven, or because he was to share the Capitoline temple with him, as was apparently planned by the people.[6] An illuminating analogy may be recalled: it was decreed in 45 that his statue should be set up in the proposed temple of the Clementia Caesaris in the act of clasping hands with Clementia.[7]

There are three further versions of Caesar's ascension. According to Ovid it was either Venus, his ancestress, who removed his 'soul' from

---

[1] Suet. *Aug.* 94. 6 (above, p. 69. 2).

[2] SHA *Alex. Sev.* 14. 2; *RE* 8A. 2539; Straub, *Heidnische Geschichtsapologetik* (1963), 146; 148.

[3] SHA *Sev.* 22. 1.

[4] Relief in the Palazzo dei Conservatori, Rome: Stuart-Jones, *Catal.* pl. 105; Schrade, *Vortr. Bibl. Warburg 1928–1929*, pl. 3. 5; D. Strong, *Rom. Imp. Sculpt.* pl. 78; Brendel, l.c. 81 f.; Nash 1. 86.—Faustina on coins: Mattingly 4. 230; pl. 34. 8; Strack, op. cit. 3. 88 f.; pl. 18. 1234.

[5] Cumont, *Ét. syr.* 35 ff.   [6] See above, p. 355.

[7] App. *BC* 2. 106. 443: above, p. 308. 7)

the Curia Pompeia,[1] or Vesta, whose priest he was, as *pontifex maximus*.[2] Both versions imply a chariot as the means of transport, and, what is important to note, before the funeral, as in the case of Romulus but not in that of Heracles. The third version is found on one of the four reliefs of an altar in the Vatican Museum (pl. 22. 2):[3] a man is mounting a chariot with four winged horses to go up to heaven, with an eagle over his head. It is far from certain that it is Caesar who is represented here; but even if it is not, the relief proves the existence of an early version of an ascension by a chariot and an eagle: the altar was set up after 12 B.C. probably while C. and L. Caesar were still alive and at any rate long before the death of Augustus.[4] It is possible that this version also presupposes the funeral: the chariot could have departed from the pyre. It is a fact that Augustus' and his successors' ascensions are connected with the funeral and thus clearly follow the pattern of Heracles. It does not really matter that it is an eagle, not a chariot, that carries Augustus to heaven.[5] The example of Romulus could not have helped here because in his case there was no corpse and no funeral.

It is possible, even probable, that Caesar's funeral would be seen to be the model for that of Augustus right to the end, had it been held on the Campus Martius as was planned. But the cremation was improvised in the Forum after it was forbidden on the Capitol,[6] and the evidence does not disclose any specific ritual features. And yet, as we shall see presently, a cult was begun immediately after the funeral. We must therefore review the procedure again to see whether it was carried out in such a way that it could lead to the creation of a cult.

[1] Ov. *Met.* 15. 843: 'media cum sede senatus / constitit alma Venus nulli cernenda suique / Caesaris eripuit membris neque in aera solvi / passa recentem animam caelestibus intulit astris.' Ovid seems to combine two versions here, ascension to the abode of the gods and to the stars. For such placing among the stars see Theocr. 17. 48 (Berenice); Callim. frg. 228 Pf. (Arsinoe); Pfeiffer, *Kallimachosstudien* 6; see also the comet, below, pp. 370 ff.

[2] Ov. *F.* 3. 701: 'ipsa virum rapui simulacraque nuda reliqui. / quae cecidit ferro, Caesaris umbra fuit.'

[3] Helbig 1[4]. 198 ff., no. 255 (E. Simon); *CAH Plates* 4. 130a; Mrs. Strong, *Apotheosis*, pl. 7; Ryberg 56; pl. 14. 28a; Cumont, op. cit. 98 f.; Zanker, *Röm. Mitt.* 76 (1969), 205 ff.

[4] The *terminus post quem* of the altar is 12 B.C. because Augustus is called 'pontifex maximus' on its inscription (*ILS* 83). The ascension is attended by a male and female adult and two youths, that is, Augustus, Livia (or Iulia), and the princes C. and L. Caesar. This would fit just one person, Agrippa, who died in 12; but he was not consecrated (although a comet appeared after his death, Dio 54. 29. 8; M. Reinhold, *Marcus Agrippa* 128. 23), and the representations on the other three reliefs of the altar are against his presence on the fourth. They are in favour of Caesar; but the chronological difficulty remains unsolved.

[5] Dio 56. 42. 3; considered an anachronism by Vittinghoff, *Der Staatsfeind* 106 ff.; Strack, op. cit. 3. 88. 255. This relief, the cameo in Paris with the ascension of 'Germanicus' (Schrade, l.c., pl. 5. 8; Alföldi, *Röm. Mitt.* 50, pl. 20. 1), and above all the numerous Greek examples (Cumont, *Ét. syr.* 35 ff.) prove that it was not; cf. also Suet. *Aug.* 97. 1.

[6] See above, p. 355.

The funeral oration listing Caesar's achievements and honours must have referred to the relevant decrees of the last months. The laments of Antony and of the 'chorus' certainly did more: they mentioned his divine ancestry and his new divinity.[1] There was also the 'Venus'-shrine on the Rostra, in which the couch with the body was placed, an exceptional feature of the funeral.[2] The interpretation must begin with the couch. The dead man used to be placed on it in his house and lamented by members of the family; he was then carried in procession, on a chariot in Greece, by bearers at Rome. These two scenes are often shown, especially on early Dipylon vases (pl. 23. 1);[3] at Rome we have both depicted. A marble relief from the tomb of the Haterii shows the scene in the house (pl. 23. 2):[4] the dead woman is lying on the couch surrounded by torches, mourners, and flute-players. A relief from Amiternum shows the procession (pl. 23. 3):[5] the dead man reclining on the couch is carried by eight bearers and is preceded by musicians and followed by the mourners. The couch is surmounted by a baldachin which is embroidered with the crescent moon and stars. Such baldachins are also found at the back of Greek couches, where they merely serve as decoration: here the motif of the stars may allude to a belief in an afterlife.[6] Caesar's couch will have been similar, though it was of gold and ivory and in other respects too more sumptuous; but there was a fundamental difference. His body could not be seen as it was hidden underneath in a coffin; on the couch there was his wax image instead.[7] How is this to be understood? Tacitus refers to an old custom of placing an effigy on the couch;[8] but it is not clear how old the custom really was. Such an image was always used whenever a body was not available: it was then a *funus imaginarium*.[9] But as we have seen at Sulla's funeral,

[1] See above, p. 352.

[2] Suet. *Caes.* 84. 1: 'pro Rostris aurata aedes ad simulacrum templi Veneris Genetricis collocata; intraque lectus eburneus auro ac purpura stratus et ad caput tropaeum cum veste, in qua fuerat occisus.'

[3] Zschietzschmann, *Ath. Mitt.* 53 (1928), 17 ff.; Boardman, *BSA* 50 (1955), 51 ff.; E. Hinrichs, 'Totenkultbilder d. att. Frühzeit', *Annales Univ. Saraviensis* 4 (1955), 129 ff.; J. N. V. Coldstream, *Greek Geometric Pottery* (1968), 29 ff.; pls. 6 ff. (with bibliography).

[4] Helbig, *Führer* I⁴. 776 ff., no. 1075 (E. Simon); Blümner, *Röm. Privataltert.* 486; D. Strong, op. cit., pl. 66. It is also found in Etruria, Rumpf, *Katalog der etr. Skulpturen* (Berlin), 19 f.; pl. 16; E. Paribeni, *Studi Etr.* 12 (1938), 68 ff.; G. Camporeale, *Röm. Mitt.* 66 (1959), 31 ff.

[5] Blümner, op. cit. 492; Mrs. Strong, op. cit., pl. 23; Ryberg 36. 76; pl. 9. 19b; Cumont, *Symb. fun.* 239; pl. 19; L. Franchi, *Studi miscellanei* 10, 1963/4 (1966), 23 ff.

[6] Mrs. Strong, op. cit. 176; Cumont, op. cit. 239.

[7] App. *BC* 2. 147. 612 (above, p. 353. 8).

[8] Tac. *A.* 3. 5. 6: 'ubi illa veterum instituta, propositam toro effigiem ...?'

[9] Serv. *Aen.* 6. 327; Lact. Plac. Stat. *Theb.* 8. 341; SHA *Pert.* 15. 1; *ILS* 7212; Weber, *Princeps* 77*. 342; Vittinghoff, *Der Staatsfeind* 112. 527; Hohl, *Klio* 31 (1938), 174. 3; Cumont, *Lux Perpetua* 24.

PLATE 23

1

2

3

(For description see overleaf)

1. Detail of a Dipylon vase, National Museum, Athens: laying out of the dead, and members of the family mourning (Photograph: Hirmer Fotoarchiv, Munich); p. 360.

2. Marble relief from the tomb of the Haterii, Vatican (formerly Lateran) Museum, Rome: a dead woman on the funerary couch; behind, two mourners, a man putting up garlands, and torches; on the sides, candelabra; below, a flute-player, four mourners between two censers, three women (Photograph: German Archaeological Institute, Rome); p. 360.

3. Marble relief from Amiternum in the Museum of L'Aquila: the dead on a couch is carried by eight bearers who are preceded by musicians and two wailing women, and followed by the mourners (Photograph: Alinari); p. 360.

his image carved in wood was carried on a special bier:[1] this is certainly
relevant evidence. Later a wax image was a constant feature of imperial
funerals. It was accompanied by freedmen, whose task was to fan it[2]—
an obscure rite.[3] The wax image is explicitly recorded for Augustus
and Pertinax, also that Augustus' body was hidden below in a coffin.[4]
This practice led to the mistaken theory that in the second century
a double funeral was instituted: the emperors were first cremated *in
corpore*, then *in effigie*.[5] No source explains why the image was used; at
the *funus imaginarium* it had the function of representing the missing
corpse. One might say accordingly that it also represented the dead
man whenever, as at Caesar's funeral, the corpse could not be shown.
If so, its function was to represent Caesar and not his wounds, nor was
it provided with a mechanical device so that it could be turned round.[6]

Now to the shrine in which the couch with the body and the image
was placed. It was made on the model of the temple of Venus Genetrix
—that is all that is said about it. We learn more through Pertinax's
funeral, the only occasion when such a shrine is mentioned again.
Pertinax's shrine was without walls but surrounded by columns made
of gold and ivory;[7] which temple it represented is not stated. The
conclusion is obvious: the *lectus* of all emperors, or at least of those
who were to be consecrated, beginning with Augustus, were placed in
such a shrine. Our next task is to find the precedents on which Caesar's
shrine rested and what it signified.

---

[1] Plut. *Sulla* 38. 3 (above, p. 349. 5).

[2] *Cod. Iust.* 7. 6. 5: 'domini funus pileati antecedunt vel in ipso lectulo stantes (cf. the
wall-painting in Kertch, below, p. 362, and the relief of the Haterii, pl. 23. 2) cadaver ventilare
videntur'. At the funeral of Pertinax a youth did it with peacock feathers, his alleged task
being to keep the flies away (Dio 74. 4. 3); on the freedmen see above, p. 350. 8.

[3] It will have depended on the old ceremonial of the kings of Egypt, Babylonia, and
Persia, who used to be accompanied by fan-bearers (Mau, *RE* 6. 1959 ff.; Leclercq, *Dict.
d'Arch. Chrét.* 5. 1610 ff.; L. Curtius, *Arch. Jahrb.* 43 (1928), 288; Chapouthier, *REA* 46 (1944),
209 ff.; Diez–Klauser–Pannold, *RAC* 7. 217 ff.), rather than on the widespread use of the
fan in Greece and Rome which had been adopted from the same source (Eur. *Or.* 1426 ff.
[Chapouthier, l.c.]; Dion. Hal. 7. 9. 4; Plaut. *Trin.* 251; Ter. *Eun.* 595; Prop. 2. 24. 11):
Augustus, for instance, used to be fanned during the hot summer nights(Suet. *Aug.* 82. 1; cf.
H. Stern, *Le Calendrier de 354*, 261 f.). The old Oriental ceremonial reappeared in the Church
(*Constit. apost.* 8. 12. 3; Klauser, l.c.) and at the Court of Byzantium (Const. Porphyrog. *de
caerim.* 2. 12 : p. 553 R.), which would not have been possible had it not been preserved in those
funeral processions. If so, there it may have served to stress the divinity of the dead ruler.

[4] Dio 56. 34. 1; 74. 4. 3 (Pertinax's body had been buried two months earlier).

[5] Bickermann, *ARW* 27 (1929), 1 ff.; *contra*, Weber, op. cit. 78*. 342; Vittinghoff, op. cit.
108 ff.; Hohl, l.c. 169 ff.   [6] App. *BC* 2. 147. 612 (above, p. 353.8).

[7] Dio 74. 4. 2: ἐν τῇ ἀγορᾷ τῇ Ῥωμαίᾳ βῆμα ξύλινον ἐν χρῷ τοῦ λιθίνου κατεσκευάσθη, καὶ
ἐπ' αὐτοῦ οἴκημα ἄτοιχον περίστυλον, ἔκ τε ἐλέφαντος καὶ χρυσοῦ πεποικιλμένον, ἐτέθη, καὶ ἐν
αὐτῷ κλίνη ὁμοία, (3) κεφαλὰς πέριξ θηρίων χερσαίων τε καὶ θαλασσίων ἔχουσα, ἐκομίσθη
στρώμασι πορφυροῖς καὶ διαχρύσοις κεκοσμημένη, καὶ ἐς αὐτὴν εἴδωλόν τι τοῦ Περτίνακος
κήρινον, σκευῇ ἐπινικίῳ εὐθετημένον, ἀνετέθη κτλ.

What we need is a baldachin composed of columns and a roof; and this was in fact an old and frequent construction in Greece and the ancient East for gods and kings.[1] For gods there is evidence, for instance, in Elis,[2] Magnesia,[3] and elsewhere, especially for Heracles;[4] for kings it could still be seen on the stage in later periods.[5] It is also found at Rome with the images of Apollo and Diana,[6] or Mars (pl. 25. 2),[7] or their symbols and votive offerings;[8] later for emperors, Domitian,[9] Antoninus Pius (pl. 25. 3 f.),[10] and others; later still the throne of the living emperor was placed under a baldachin in the imperial palace.[11] Such a baldachin could be improvised for a festival to receive the images of the gods, as was done at Magnesia;[12] and it could be placed on a chariot with gods travelling in it,[13] for instance Zeus (pl. 25. 5.)[14] or Dionysus (pl. 24. 1).[15]

Such a shrine was also used in the cult of the dead[16] and for their transport, and this is what really matters here. Alexander's funeral chariot, as described by Diodorus, carried such a shrine (pl. 24. 2).[17] The coffin was covered with red cloth, was surrounded with columns and had a domed roof above; on the four corners of the roof there were Nikai carrying trophies. Such chariots will have been built for his successors too. A related and yet in some respects different arrangement is found on a wall-painting of the imperial period at Kertch (pl. 24. 3).[18] The dead man is carried on a bier, not on a chariot, and there are two attendants, one at each end of the *lectus*.[19] There is a baldachin over them, consisting

[1] Alföldi, *Röm. Mitt.* 50 (1935), 127 f.; Cüppers, *BJ* 163 (1963), 33 ff.

[2] Paus. 6. 24. 9.   [3] *Syll.* 589. 8; 43.

[4] Frickenhaus, *Ath. Mitt.* 36 (1911), 121 ff.; O. Walter, *Ath. Mitt.* 62 (1937), 41 ff.

[5] Vitruv. 5. 6. 9: 'deformantur columnis et fastigiis et signis reliquisque regalibus rebus'; Alföldi, l.c. 132.

[6] Pliny 36. 36; Platner–Ashby 42.   [7] Mattingly 1. 58; pl. 5. 20.

[8] Mattingly 1. 66; 114; pls. 8. 2 ff.; 17. 12.

[9] Mattingly 2. 343; Alföldi, l.c., pl. 14. 1.

[10] Mattingly 4. 135; pl. 19. 7; Alföldi 129; pl. 14. 2–4; Strack, op. cit. 3. 160; pls. 3. 335; 15. 1191.

[11] Corrip. *laud. Iust.* 3. 194 ff.; Alföldi, l.c. 127 f.

[12] *Syll.* 589. 8; 43; Weinreich, *Myth. Lex.* 6. 792 f.; 838.   [13] Cüppers, l.c. 45 ff.

[14] S. Smith, *Brit. Mus. Quart.* 13 (1939), 17; pl. 9d; Cüppers 49; pl. 11. 1 (chariot with elephants).

[15] Deubner, *Att. Feste* 104; 115; pls. 11. 4; 13. 3; Rumpf, *BJ* 161 (1961), 210 f.

[16] Paus. 2. 7. 2 (Sicyon); cf. Müller (n. 17), 49. 2; often found on vases from Southern Italy, Sichtermann, *Griech. Vasen in Unteritalien* (1966), pls. 112–15; 120; 125; 129; Hommel, *Studien zu den röm. Figurengiebeln* (1954), 105 ff. (list of funeral monuments, tombstones, sarcophagi).

[17] Diod. 18. 26; K. F. Müller, *Der Leichenwagen Alexanders d. Gr.* (1905), 25 ff. (with a reconstruction); cf. Kallixeinos, *FGrHist.* 627 F 2. 34 = Athen. 5. 202 A (Alexander's golden image, with Athena and Nike on either side of him, on a chariot with elephants in a procession, 271/270 B.C.: a shrine?).

[18] Müller, op. cit. 48, fig. 7; Rostovtzeff, *Anc. Decorative Wall-painting in South. Russia*, pl. 88. 1; Reinach, *Rép. de peintures* 244. 1.   [19] See above, p. 361. 2.

PLATE 24

1

2

4

3

(For description see overleaf)

1. Oinochoe in the Metropolitan Museum, New York: Dionysus with thyrsus and cantharus on his throne under a baldachin which is covered with ivy-leaves and erected on a chariot (From: M. Bieber, *Hesp.* Suppl. 8, pl. 5); p. 362.

2. Reconstruction of the funeral chariot of Alexander: the coffin is surrounded with columns which hold a domed roof, on the corners Nikai with trophies (From K. F. Müller, *Der Leichenwagen Alexanders d. Gr.*); p. 362.

3. Wallpainting in Kertch: the dead on a couch with attendants standing at its ends; the couch is surmounted by a domed roof resting on four columns and is placed on a bier which is carried by eight bearers; it is preceded by four flute-players and followed by eight mourners (From Rostovtzeff, *Ant. Decor. Wallpainting in South. Russia*, pl. 88. 1); p. 362.

4. Diptych of Antoninus Pius (?) in the British Museum; for the description see p. 363 (Photograph: British Museum).

of four columns and a domed roof. Musicians march in front, mourners follow at the back. On a diptych in the British Museum three scenes are combined (pl. 24. 3).[1] The emperor, probably Antoninus Pius, with his chariot, is on the top of a funeral pyre and has two eagles at his side. Above he is carried to heaven by two winged youths. On the right a quadriga with elephants carries an open shrine formed by four columns and a roof with a pediment; inside the shrine there is the image of the emperor, seated on a throne, wearing a toga and holding a sceptre, no doubt the deified emperor. (pl. 25. 6–7.)[2]

The conclusion is that Caesar's open shrine with a pediment on the Rostra had its Greek antecedents not only in the shrines of the gods but also in the funeral chariot of Alexander. It will be recalled that in 45 in accordance with a decree of the Senate a pediment was built on his house,[3] which thus became a royal palace or even a temple; also that temples were to be built for him.[4] Placing the coffin and the wax image over it in that shrine, then, was another indication of his divinity; that it was a shrine of Venus meant that he was, at least provisionally, to be worshipped in her temple; in fact Octavian set up his statue there later.[5] This shrine became, as the cases of Augustus and, even more, Pertinax show, a substantial feature of the consecration. If it was not created in the days after the Ides, it must have been planned long before and referred to in Caesar's testament. At any rate, it was so understood, and that is one of the reasons why immediately after the funeral a cult was instituted.

---

[1] H. Graeven, *Röm. Mitt.* 28 (1913), 271 ff. (Constantius Chlorus); Delbrück, *Die Consulardiptychen* (1929), no. 59 (Ant. Pius); K. Wessel, *Arch. Jahrb.* 63/4 (1948/9), 141 (Julian); Rumpf, *BJ* 155/6 (1955/6), 127 ff. (Ant. Pius); Mrs. Strong, op. cit. 227 f.; pl. 31; Cumont, *Ét. syr.* 101; Schrade, *Vortr. Bibl. Warb. 1928–1929*, pl. 3. 6; Straub, *Gymn.* 69 (1962), 322 f.; pl. 1a.

[2] Cf. a coin of Marcus Aurelius with Antoninus Pius (Mattingly 4. 528; pl. 72. 5; Graeven, l.c. pl. 8. 7) and of Commodus with Marcus Aurelius seated in the shrine on the *quadriga* (Mattingly 4. 763; pl. 101. 9). A coin of Titus shows the empty shrine of Divus Vespasianus on a *quadriga* with horses, Mattingly 2. 243 f.; pl. 47. 2 f.

[3] See above, p. 280.   [4] See above, pp. 308 f.

[5] Dio 45. 7. 1: χαλκοῦν αὐτὸν ἐς τὸ Ἀφροδίσιον, ἀστέρα ὑπὲρ τῆς κεφαλῆς ἔχοντα, ἔστησεν; see below, p. 393.

XVII

THE NEW GOD

I. THE ALTAR

AFTER the funeral the people improvised a cult where the pyre had stood.[1] It is difficult to ascertain the facts, because at first sight the evidence appears to be conflicting. Cicero speaks of a funeral monument and a column set up by the people and destroyed by the consul Dolabella at the end of April 44.[2] In May Brutus and Cassius called it an altar, when complaining in a letter to Antony that Caesar's veterans intended to re-erect it.[3] According to Dio too it was an altar at which the people proposed to sacrifice to Caesar as to a god; but it was destroyed by the 'consuls'.[4] Appian ascribes the erection of the altar to Amatius (Pseudo-Marius); after his execution in April the people demanded that in his place the consuls should dedicate it and be the first to sacrifice there.[5] Suetonius speaks of a twenty-foot-high column which the people set up and inscribed 'Parenti patriae'; there they sacrificed, made vows, and settled disputes by an oath in the name of Caesar for a long time.[6] The problem then is first of nomenclature: how are the terms, 'funeral monument', 'column', and 'altar', to be understood? Secondly, how could it have been used if it was destroyed before it was dedicated?[7]

---

[1] Drumann 1. 77 f.; 94 f.; Alföldi, *Studien* 70 ff.

[2] Cic. *Phil.* 1. 5: 'idemque (the people) bustum in foro facerent, qui illam insepultam sepulturam effecerant . . . eversio illius execratae columnae'; *Att.* 14. 15. 1: 'o mirificum Dolabellam meum! . . . columnam tollere, locum illum sternendum locare!' *Phil.* 2. 107: 'illud, quod venerari solebas, bustum in foro evertit'; 1. 30; *Att.* 14. 16. 2; *fam.* 9. 14. 1; 12. 1. 1; Lact. *div. inst.* 1. 15. 30.

[3] Cic. *fam.* 11. 2. 2: 'putesne nos tutos fore in tanta frequentia militum veteranorum, quos etiam de reponenda ara cogitare audimus?'

[4] Dio 44. 51. 1: βωμὸν δέ τινα ἐν τῷ τῆς πυρᾶς χωρίῳ ἱδρυσάμενοι . . . θύειν τε ἐπ᾽ αὐτῷ καὶ κατάρχεσθαι τῷ Καίσαρι ὡς καὶ θεῷ ἐπεχείρουν. (2) οἱ οὖν ὕπατοι ἐκεῖνόν τε ἀνέτρεψαν, καί τινας ἀγανακτήσαντας ἐπὶ τούτῳ ἐκόλασαν.

[5] App. *BC* 2. 148. 616: ἔνθα βωμὸς πρῶτος ἐτέθη; 3. 2. 3: Ἀμάτιος ἦν ὁ Ψευδομάριος . . . γιγνόμενος οὖν κατὰ τήνδε τνὴ ὑπόκρισιν συγγενὴς τῷ Καίσαρι, . . . βωμὸν ἐπῳκοδόμει τῇ πυρᾷ; 3. 3. 7: τὰς ἀρχὰς ἐκέλευον ἀντὶ Ἀματίου τὸν βωμὸν ἐκθεοῦν καὶ θύειν ἐπ᾽ αὐτοῦ Καίσαρι πρώτους(?).

[6] Suet. *Caes.* 85: 'postea solidam columnam prope viginti pedum lapidis Numidici in foro statuit (sc. plebs) inscripsitque "Parenti patriae". apud eam longo tempore sacrificare, vota suscipere, controversias quasdam interposito per Caesarem iure iurando distrahere persevera-vit.'

[7] The difficulties are stated by Casaubon (ad Suet. *Caes.* 85), and Mommsen, *Ges. Schr.*

The course of events was probably as follows. It was Amatius who acted first. He had long pretended to be a grandson of Marius and thus a relation of Caesar, but was banished by him. After the murder he returned, acquired a large following, and pledged to avenge Caesar.[1] It is therefore credible that he in fact built the altar but did not live to complete it. It was never used, because two weeks later Dolabella demolished it. This was at the time when Caesar's statues were removed from their pedestals and broken up, to the great annoyance of his followers.[2] The column which was in use 'for a long time' must have been erected after that; if so, the veterans really achieved what they demanded in May. Octavian, who was already in Rome, will have set it up and provided it with the inscription.[3] It cannot have been Antony, because he set up another statue with another inscription and in another place, the Rostra, in September.[4] Moreover, Octavian swore at the altar in November, when he joined Antony's adversaries at an assembly of the people:[5] he would not have done this at an altar built by Antony.

The column could have been with or without a statue: the word 'columna' is often used when a statue is also meant.[6] Such statues were set up in Greece and Rome in the first place for the gods but also for distinguished men.[7] In the latter case they did not mean superhuman honours but, as Pliny says, setting someone above other mortals;[8] they commemorated exceptional merit.[9] There were such columns with statues for C. Maenius, C. Duilius, L. Aemilius Paullus, M. Seius.[10] These were no doubt the precedents followed when Caesar's column was set up; but it was certainly to be more than a memorial.

A column could also be a funeral monument, and Cicero was right in so calling it.[11] But again if it had been no more than that it would

---

4. 182, seems to have found a solution for them. What follows is an attempt to say what he may have had in mind; for a different interpretation see Alföldi, *Studien* 70 ff.

[1] Drumann 1. 77 f.; Münzer, *RE* 14. 1815 ff.; Alföldi, op. cit. 73 ff.

[2] App. *BC* 3. 3. 8 f.; cf. Vittinghoff, *Der Staatsfeind* 13 f.

[3] Cic. *Phil.* 2. 107 (above, p. 364. 2) suggests either that there was no column in September or that there was a different one with which Antony was not connected. The second alternative is chosen above in the text.   [4] Cic. *fam.* 12. 3. 1 (below, p. 385. 6).

[5] Cic. *Att.* 16. 15. 3: 'at quae contio (of Nov.)! nam est missa mihi. iurat "ita sibi parentis honores consequi liceat" et simul dextram intendit ad statuam.' This statue must have been that on the column because the assembly took place nearby at the temple of Castor; cf. App. *BC* 3. 41. 168 f.; Dio 45. 12. 4 f.; Drumann 1. 158.

[6] *Thes.L.L.* 3. 1739 f.

[7] Cf. Welin, *Stud. z. Topographie d. Forum Romanum* 151 ff.

[8] Pliny 34. 27: 'columnarum ratio erat attolli super ceteros mortales, quod et arcus significant novicio invento'; 34. 20.

[9] Enn. *V.* 1 V. (Scipio): 'quantam statuam faciet populus Romanus, / quantam columnam quae res tuas gestas loquatur.'   [10] See above, p. 294.

[11] Cic. *Phil.* 1. 5 (above, p. 364. 2); Welin, op. cit. 167; 171.

have been set up at his tomb on the Campus Martius and not on the site of the pyre. In so far as it was a funeral monument it was the task of the family to take the initiative, and this was in fact done by Pseudo-Marius and later probably by Octavian. There is an important analogy in the column of Minucius,[1] in itself no different from the columns for other distinguished men but which, combined with the *Minucius deus* and his altar,[2] will have represented a family-cult of the Minucii. The analogy is close as far as column, statue, altar, and cult are concerned; and, as far as is known, they were not at the tomb either. The difference is, and it is a substantial one, that Caesar's cult was not restricted to members of his family. In this respect the analogy of the Gracchi is closer. The place where they died was sacred, statues were set up for them and offerings were made to them as to gods.[3] It is not known whether the statues stood on columns; if they did, they again would have represented a combination of a funeral monument with a memorial of distinguished men. It was an unofficial cult and did not last. Catilina received offerings from his followers at his tomb.[4] His case is relevant here only in so far as his ephemeral cult was not limited to members of his family. Thus the funeral monument was to be the first site of the cult which, though officially decreed, the magistrates were reluctant to establish. According to Suetonius it existed for a long time: how long? We have seen that Octavian performed a solemn vow and oath there in November 44.[5] The probability then is that it still existed in the following year and was replaced after Caesar's consecration by an official altar which survived even after the temple was built.[6]

The altar, column, and statue represented then the unofficial beginning of the new cult. What is not yet clear is why the new god was named here 'Parens patriae', which was rather a title of the living, and why the transactions and oaths at the altar are specially mentioned. An answer to these questions can be offered with the help of Lucan. Praising Cato on his African campaign he calls him the real 'parens patriae', worthy of altars at Rome, of oaths by his name, and of being consecrated a god, as he would be sooner or later.[7] Lucan clearly

---

[1] Pliny 18. 15; 34. 21, etc.; above, p. 293. 9.
[2] Paul. 122; 147 M. (109; 131 L.); above, p. 293. 4.
[3] Plut. *C. Gracch.* 18. 3; cf. v. Premerstein, 89.
[4] Cic. *Flacc.* 95; L. R. Taylor, 56.
[5] Cic. *Att.* 16. 15. 3 (above, p. 365. 5).
[6] See below, p. 400.
[7] Lucan. 9. 601: 'ecce parens verus patriae, dignissimus aris, / Roma, tuis, per quem numquam iurare pudebit / et quem, si steteris umquam cervice soluta, / nunc, olim, factura deum es.'

alludes here in a hostile manner to the events of 44 which we are discussing. We learn what is not so apparent in the other evidence, that the inscription and the oath were in fact a necessary part of the scheme. We must therefore recall the events of 45 when Caesar received the *cognomen* 'Parens patriae' and the oath by his Genius and Salus was established, and conclude that at that time this was instituted for all kinds of transactions for which formerly only Iuppiter and the other gods of oath were invoked.[1] The murder will have put an end to this practice and created a hiatus. The continuity was now restored at the altar which presumably replaced an earlier one demolished in the weeks after the murder and was made clear by the inscription. Even if it does not seem to be an integral part of the new cult, it was at that time a necessary, and perhaps the most urgent, part of it. The oath by Caesar's Genius and Salus was no longer possible and that by Divus Iulius could not be sworn before his consecration in 42 B.C.[2]

2. ANTONY AND OCTAVIAN

The struggle between Caesar's enemies and followers was continued in the religious field as well. We have seen that the one side destroyed Caesar's statues and even his altar, while the other paid the honours due to him as if nothing had happened. When the festival of the Parilia was held on 21 April the attendance was not what it should have been.[3] This was because the year before a new feature had been added in Caesar's honour, games in the Circus.[4] But those taking part at the festival saw to it that the games were held. As had been decreed they also wore wreaths in Caesar's honour and carried his ivory statue in the procession of the gods. But when this statue arrived in the Circus they took off their wreaths as a sign of mourning and lamented Caesar's fate.[5] It is not clear who was the driving spirit behind this open defiance of the new order. Octavian, the heir, had not arrived and Antony was trying to please everybody.

A few days later Octavian arrived. One of his first moves was to fulfil the requirement of another decree which prescribed that Caesar's

---

[1] See above, pp. 171; 212.   [2] See below, p. 392.

[3] Dio 45. 6. 4: τὴν πανήγυριν (of Venus) . . . ἐν ὀλιγωρίᾳ, ὥσπερ που καὶ τὴν τῶν Παριλίων ἱπποδρομίαν, ἐποιοῦντο.

[4] See above, pp. 173; 185.

[5] Cic. *Att.* 14. 14. 1 (29/30 Apr. 44) : 'coronatus Quintus noster Parilibus! solusne? . . . scire cupio qui fuerint alii; quamquam satis scio nisi improbum neminem'; 14. 19. 3 (8 May 44) : 'de coronatis . . . rescripsit se coronam habuisse honoris Caesaris causa, posuisse luctus gratia.' The paraphrase above is based on Reid's brilliant interpretation of this passage (ap. Tyrrell–Purser ad loc.) ; cf. above, p. 185.

golden throne with his golden crown placed upon it should be taken to the theatres and set up there among the thrones of the gods.[1] It is not clear which games were involved. It cannot have been the *ludi Ceriales* of 12–19 April[2] or those of the Parilia, because on 22 April Octavian was still outside Rome, at Puteoli in the company of Cicero.[3] It cannot have been the *ludi Martiales* of 12 May either,[4] because these were created later.[5] At any rate, Octavian attempted to include the throne in the procession but was prevented from doing so by Antony, the consul.[6] This is not surprising. Although Antony was the leading Caesarian, Octavian was for him a rival, not an ally. Soon after the murder he had arranged Lepidus' election as *pontifex maximus* in haste and in an irregular manner,[7] in order to prevent Octavian from getting that office, although this had been the wish of Caesar.[8] Octavian made another move about the middle of May. It concerned the *ludi Victoriae Caesaris* which were due in July. Caesar had made the necessary financial provisions when he created them in 46 and founded a college which was to arrange them. In 44 the college was reluctant to act, since this Caesarian festival too had become unpopular. Octavian now decided to give the games personally and at his own expense;[9] also to combine them with solemn funeral games dedicated to the memory of Caesar.[10] We have seen that such games, gladiatorial contests, had often been held before in honour of distinguished men,[11] also by Caesar in memory of his father[12] and later of his daughter Iulia.[13] They were in fact a solemn and more spectacular repetition of the contests which used to take place at funerals.[14] He held those for Iulia together with the *ludi Veneris Genetricis* in 46,[15] and Octavian clearly followed his example when he now planned to

---

[1] Dio 44. 6. 3; Flor. 2. 13. 91; above, p. 282. 1; below p. 382. 12.

[2] Mommsen, *Ges. Schr.* 4. 181; Drumann 1. 89; T. Rice Holmes, *The Architect of the Roman Empire* 1. 191; L. R. Taylor, 87. 15.

[3] Cic. *Att.* 13. 12. 2.   [4] Alföldi, *Studien* 77.

[5] Ov. *F.* 5. 597; *F. Maff.*; Degrassi 457.

[6] App. *BC* 3. 28. 105 f.; Cic. *Att.* 15. 3. 2 (22 May 44): 'de sella Caesaris bene tribuni'.

[7] Dio 44. 53. 6 f.; App. *BC* 2. 132. 552; Livy, *Per.* 117; Vell. 2. 63. 1; Cic. *Phil.* 5. 40 f.; 13. 7; 15; *Att.* 16. 5. 4; 11. 8; Sydenham 206; pl. 30. 1323; cf. 189; pl. 29. 1161; Drumann 1. 11.

[8] See above, p. 33.

[9] Suet. *Aug.* 10. 1: 'ludos autem Victoriae Caesaris non audentibus facere quibus optigerat id munus ipse edidit'; Obs. 68: 'ludis Veneris Genetricis, quos pro collegio fecit'; Pliny 2. 93; Dio 45. 6. 4 (above, p. 367. 3); Nic. Dam. *v. Caes.* 28. 108 (*FGrHist.* 90 F 130).

[10] Serv. *Aen.* 8. 681: 'dum sacrificaretur Veneri Genetrici et ludi funebres Caesari exhiberentur'; 1. 287; 6. 790; *Ecl.* 9. 47.

[11] See above, p. 89.   [12] Dio 37. 8. 1; Pliny 33. 53.

[13] Suet. *Caes.* 26. 2; Dio 43. 22. 3; Plut. *Caes.* 55. 4; App. *BC* 2. 102. 423.

[14] Cic. *Mil.* 86; Caesar's funeral: Suet. *Caes.* 84. 2; Pliny 15. 78 (above, p. 350. 11).

[15] See above, p. 89.

combine the two types again. He announced his plans in a speech about
18 May and engaged the help of friends like C. Matius, M. Curtius
Postumus (*pr.* 47 or 46), and P. Hostilius Saserna (*tr. pl.* 44).[1] Cicero was
angry and expressed his displeasure to Matius, who was a friend of his.[2]
Matius defended himself with the claim that it was a private affair
which did not concern the State; that he owed it to the memory and
distinction of his dead friend, and moreover, that he could not refuse his
help when the young Caesar requested it.[3] The defence was one of
loyalty, which Cicero later accepted.[4] It was also a well-founded defence:
the terms 'munus' and 'procuratores' which occur in the argument
normally referred to gladiatorial contests,[5] and show that the help of
these friends was principally requested for the private *ludi funebres*.

Meanwhile, Antony and the conspirators were concerned with the
official *ludi Apollinares* which were due earlier.[6] Antony, as consul, announced that they would be held 'Nonis Iuliis'.[7] It was at Antony's
request that the Senate had decreed at the beginning of the year that the
month Quintilis should be renamed Iulius;[8] but it was felt to be a provocation that instead of ignoring it he now used the new name for the first
time officially. The offence was the greater because Brutus as the *praetor
urbanus* was in charge of the games. As he was in Campania they had to
be prepared and held in his name by his colleague C. Antonius. They
were a great success—much money had been spent on them[9]— aroused
great sympathy for Brutus and Cassius, and the spectators demanded
their recall.[10] Octavian's games therefore acquired the additional task
of counteracting these dangerous political demonstrations. Caesar's
birthday could not be used for this purpose. It was due about that time
(12 July) and would have been a public festival according to a decree
of 45;[11] but it is most unlikely that it was celebrated in the midst of such

[1] Cic. *Att.* 15. 2. 3 (19 May): 'de Octavi contione idem sentio quod tu, ludorumque eius apparatus et Matius ac Postumus mihi procuratores non placent; Saserna conlega dignus.'

[2] Cf. Münzer, *RE* 14. 2209; Heuss, *Hist.* 5 (1956), 59; 69; 11 (1962), 118; Combès, *REL* 36 (1958), 176 ff.; Kytzler, *Hist.* 9 (1960), 107.

[3] Cic. *fam.* 11. 28. 6: 'at ludos . . . curavi. at id ad privatum officium, non ad statum rei publicae pertinet; quod tamen munus et hominis amicissimi memoriae atque honoribus praestare etiam mortui debui, et optimae spei adulescenti ac dignissimo Caesare petenti negare non potui.'

[4] Cic. *fam.* 11. 27. 7 (end of July): 'alia quae defendam a te pie fieri et humane, ut de curatione ludorum . . .'

[5] Mommsen, *StR* 2. 951. 4.   [6] 6–13 July; Degrassi 477 f.

[7] Cic. *Att.* 16. 1. 1; 16. 4. 1 (above, p. 157. 1).

[8] Dio 44. 5. 2; Macrob. 1. 12. 34 (above, p. 257. 1).

[9] Cic. *Att.* 15. 18. 2; 26. 1; 16. 2. 3; 5. 1; *Phil.* 1. 36; App. *BC* 3. 24. 90; Plut. *Brut.* 21. 3; Dio 47. 20. 2.

[10] Cic. *Phil.* 2. 31: 'ludi Apollinares incredibili M. Bruti honore celebrati.'

[11] Dio 44. 4. 4; above, p. 206.

B b

great excitement. The *ludi Victoriae Caesaris* were due a week later.
Octavian again proposed to carry Caesar's golden throne and crown to
the theatre, but was again prevented from doing so by Antony.[1] Octavian overcame this defeat too with the help of an unexpected event, the
appearance of a comet during his games, and the interpretation of what
it portended.

3. *CAESARIS ASTRUM*

The portents which followed the murder were numerous but not so
significant as those which had preceded it: an eclipse of the sun or pale
light all through the year, earthquakes, thunderbolts, storms damaging
statues, temples, and trees, and inundations.[2] Such portents were often
reported in times of trouble. Whether they were so reported in 44 too is
not certain; the list may have been made up later. But one of them, the
comet, did in fact occur[3] and received an unusual and far-reaching
interpretation.[4]

We begin again with Suetonius, because he uses authors of the
Caesarian age.[5] The comet shone on seven nights at the games and was
believed to be Caesar's soul and to prove that he had been received into
heaven; that is why a star was placed on the head of his statue. His
divinity, which had been officially decreed, was now accepted by the
people. According to this account, then, it was the comet that created
the general belief. About the same time as Suetonius' source, that
is, a year or two after the event, Vergil made a brief mention of the
comet, calling it 'Caesaris astrum':[6] the farmer should expect abundance
in the fields and in the vineyards from it rather than from the rise of
the old stars. These lines add a new feature to the story, the belief in
the beginning of a new *saeculum*. We have seen that this had long been

---

[1] App. *BC* 3. 28. 107; Dio 45. 6. 5.

[2] Verg. *Georg.* 1. 466 ff.; Ov. *Met.* 15. 783 ff.; Plut. *Caes.* 69. 4; *vir. ill.* 78. 10. The pale
light of the sun, however, was an unusual portent and part of an important theme: below,
pp. 382 f.

[3] Obs. 68 (mentions it twice, once for itself and then among the other portents).

[4] Cf. Mommsen, *Ges. Schr.* 4. 180 ff.; Wagenvoort, *Studies* 12 ff.; G. Pesce, *Hist.* 7 (1933),
402 ff.; K. Scott, *CP* 36 (1941), 257 ff.; Bömer, *BJ* 152 (1952), 27 ff.; Schilling, *La religion
romaine de Vénus* 319 ff.; I. Hahn, *Acta Antiqua* 16 (1968), 239 ff.

[5] Suet. *Caes.* 88: 'in deorum numerum relatus est, non ore modo decernentium, sed et
persuasione volgi. si quidem ludis, quos primos consecrato ei heres Augustus edebat, stella
crinita per septem continuos dies fulsit exoriens circa undecimam horam, creditumque est
animam esse Caesaris in caelum recepti; et hac de causa simulacro eius in vertice additur
stella.'

[6] Verg. *Ecl.* 9. 47: 'quid antiquos signorum suspicis ortus? / ecce Dionaei processit Caesaris
astrum, / astrum quo segetes gauderent frugibus et quo / duceret apricis in collibus uva
colorem.'

expected and that it was also Vulcanius' interpretation of the comet.[1]
It was to be the new golden age under the rule of the new god. Augustus
modified this view later by asserting that the comet portended his own
rise and his era.[2] But in his Memoirs, quoted by Pliny and Servius,
he adopted the other interpretation and propagated it,[3] and it was he
who placed the star over Caesar's statues; he also engraved it on his
helmet.[4] Dio does not add anything new except that he also refers to other
interpretations of the comet.[5] Finally there is the evidence of contemporary coins,[6] the most valuable of all. It will be discussed later after
an examination of the relevant doctrines concerning comets and stars.

The accepted interpretation was unusual. Comets had been observed at
Rome often before and were always considered to be of evil significance.[7]
In the recent past they had announced the Catilinarian conspiracy,[8] the
Civil War between Caesar and Pompey,[9] now another Civil War between the *triumviri* and the conspirators,[10] later also as in the Orient the
change or the death of a ruler.[11] The only favourable interpretation
known is about the comet that rose at the birth of Mithridates and again
at his accession,[12] and it will have been his example that Augustus
followed when he spoke about his own star.[13] These exceptions were
due to the application of a doctrine about the stars to the comets.

There was an old oriental belief in the divinity of the stars, which
was adopted by, among others, the Pythagoreans and inspired them to

---

[1] See above, p. 195.

[2] Pliny 2. 94; Serv. Dan. *Ecl.* 9. 46; cf. Avienus ap. Serv. Dan. *Aen.* 10. 272; Campestris
ap. Lyd. *ost.* 15. Vergil cannot have meant Augustus (as Horace did later, below, p. 383)
because 'Dionaeus' can refer only to Caesar, the descendant of Venus. It is true that in Hor.
c.s. 50 'clarus Anchisae Venerisque sanguis' is Augustus: but this poem was written much later.

[3] Pliny 2. 94; Serv. *Aen.* 8. 681: 'quod sidus Caesaris putatum est Augusto persuadente';
Serv. Dan. *Ecl.* 9. 46: 'ipse animam patris sui esse voluit.'

[4] Serv. *Aen.* 8. 681; cf. the Christian monogram or star on Constantine's helmet, Euseb.
v. Const. 1. 31. 4; *h.e.* 9. 9; Prudent. *c. Symm.* 1. 489; Alföldi, *JRS* 22 (1932), 10 f.; pl. 4. 14 ff.
— A star on the helmet of a Hellenistic ruler (?), Richter, *Engraved Gems of the Greeks and
Etruscans* (1968), no. 672: decoration?

[5] Dio 45. 7. 1 : ἐπεί... αὐτὸ κομήτην τέ τινων καλούντων καὶ προσημαίνειν οἷά που εἴωθε λεγόντων
οἱ πολλοὶ τοῦτο μὲν οὐκ ἐπίστευον, τῷ δὲ δὴ Καίσαρι αὐτὸ ὡς καὶ ἀπηθανατισμένῳ καὶ ἐς τὸν
τῶν ἄστρων ἀριθμὸν ἐγκατειλεγμένῳ ἀνετίθεσαν, θαρσήσας χαλκοῦν αὐτὸν ἐς τὸ Ἀφροδίσιον,
ἀστέρα ὑπὲρ τῆς κεφαλῆς ἔχοντα, ἔστησεν. He mentions the comet again among the evil signs
of 43 B.C., 47.17. 4.

[6] Cf. Pesce, *Hist.* 7 (1933), 404 ff.; K. Scott, *CP* 36 (1941), 257 ff.; D. Felber, op. cit. 247 ff.

[7] Manil. 1. 892 ff.; Pliny 2. 89 ff.; Sen. *NQ* 7; Serv. Dan. *Aen.* 10. 272; Lyd. *ost.* 11 ff.;
Wülker, *Die geschichtl. Entwicklung d. Prodigienwesens b. d. Römern* (Diss. Leipzig 1903), 10 f.
(with a list); W. Gundel, *De stellarum appellatione et religione Romana* (1907), 141 ff.; Pease
ad Cic. *div.* 1. 18.   [8] Cic. *de cons.* (*FPL*) 11. 15 Mor.   [9] Pliny 2. 92; Lucan. 1. 528 f.

[10] Calp. Sic. *Ecl.* 1. 82; Plut. *Caes.* 69. 3; Gundel, op. cit. 144.

[11] Lucan. 1. 529; Stat. *Theb.* 1. 708; Sil. Ital. 8. 637; R. S. Rogers, *TAPA* 84 (1953),
237 ff. (on the Neronian comets, Tac. *A.* 14. 22; 15. 47, etc.).

[12] Iustin. 37. 2. 1 f.   [13] Pliny 2. 94.

create the doctrine of the immortality of the soul and its descent from, and ascent to, the stars at the times of birth and death respectively.[1] The frequent metaphor that a distinguished man was a brilliant star[2] ultimately rested on such beliefs. The astronomers went even further in giving individuality to the stars. They first subjected the planets to the control of the principal gods and later identified them: the 'stella Veneris', for instance, became Venus.[3] Like their oriental predecessors they also discovered mythical figures in the starred heaven: the Gemini were no other than the Dioscuri, who were then often represented with a star over their heads.[4] Other mythical figures followed, especially those whose ascension was known, for example Erigone:[5] this placing among the stars, καταστερισμός, became a favourite topic of astronomers and poets. The philosophers in turn examined the problems of the divinity of the stars and of the astral immortality of distinguished men; the Stoics among them accepted the doctrine,[6] but the Epicureans did not.[7] Their controversy was known at Rome, where the Stoic view seems to have prevailed.[8] It is particularly relevant here that the Epicurean Philodemus, a friend of Piso, Caesar's father-in-law, attacked the Stoic view in 44 and seems to have opposed Caesar's deification on this ground.[9]

---

[1] Aristoph. *Pax* 832; Plat. *Tim.* 42 b; *CCAG* 9. 1, pp. 106 f.; P. Capelle, *De luna stellis lacteo orbe animarum sedibus* (Diss. Halle 1917), 25; Cumont, *Symb. fun.* 116. 4 and *Lux Perpetua* 172; Nilsson, *Opuscula* 3. 255.

[2] Hom. *Il.* 6. 401; Aristoph. *Av.* 1709 ff.; Eur. *Hipp.* 1121; *Anth. Pal.* 7. 669 f.; *Or. gr.* 194. 19; Hor. *c.* 1. 12. 47 (Augustus); Kaibel, *Epigr.* 978. 3 (Augustus); Lucan. 10. 89 f. (Caesar); Plut. *Marc.* 30. 8; Kleinknecht, *ARW* 34 (1937), 294 ff.; F. J. Dölger, *Ant. u. Christ.* 6 (1940/50), 31 f.; R. Hutmacher, *Das Ehrendekret f. den Strategen Kallimachos* (1965), 53 f. It was a frequent metaphor in the imperial period, see Eitrem, *Symb. Osl.* 11 (1932), 19. 1; F. Sauter, *Der röm. Kaiserkult bei Martial u. Statius* 137 ff.; Straub, *Heidnische Geschichtsapologetik* 171. 136.—Cf. also Plut. *Pomp.* 14. 4 (Pompey the rising Sun).

[3] Cic. *ND* 2. 52 f.; Pease ad l.; Cumont, *Ant. Class.* 4 (1935), 5 ff.

[4] Eratosth. *Catast.* 10, pp. 86 f. Rob.; Ov. *F.* 5. 699 ff. (with Bömer's note); Robert, *Heldensage* 2. 322 f.; Chapouthier, *Les Dioscures au service d'une déesse*, passim; pls. 9. 99; 10. 60 bis; 11; 14 f.; for further instances see Nilsson, op. cit. 3. 251 ff.

[5] Hygin. *Astron.* 2. 4 (p. 36. 17 f. B.); *fab.* 130; Serv. Dan. *Georg.* 1. 33; Merkelbach, *Miscellanea . . . in memoria di A. Rostagni* (1963), 511.

[6] Cic. *ND* 2. 39; 42 f. (with Pease's notes); cf. Hipparch. ap. Pliny 2. 95; Gundel, op. cit. 128; Nilsson, *Opuscula* 3. 31 ff.

[7] Epicur. frg. 342 Us.; Philippson, *Herm.* 53 (1918), 359 ff.; G. Freymuth, *Zur Lehre von den Götterbildern in der epikur. Philosophie* (1953), 13 ff.

[8] Varr. *Ant. rer. div.* 1, frg. 25a Ag. (Comm. Lucan. 9. 6): 'Stoici virorum fortium animas existimant in modum siderum vagari in aere et esse sic immortales'; frg. 25b (Comm. Lucan. 9. 9): 'Pythagoras dixit animas in stellas converti virorum fortium.'—Cf. also Verg. *Georg.* 4. 225 ff. (the bees return to the stars after death). It is a different doctrine that places the abode of the heroes in the lunar sphere: that is where Pompey's soul arrives, Lucan 9. 1 ff.; Cumont, *Lux Perpetua* 177.

[9] Philod. περὶ θεῶν 3, col. 8. 37 ff.; col. 10. 2 ff. (Diels, *Abh. Akad. Berl.* 1916, no. 6. 27 ff.); Philippson, l.c. 384; Nisbet, *Cicero, In L. Calpurnium Pisonem* (1961), p. 185.

The claim that the comet was Caesar's star, though illogical, is understandable. Its sudden appearance could better confirm the belief in the emergence of a new god than the traditional doctrine. Those who spread the claim apparently did not bother about the consequences of the equally sudden disappearance of the comet; or about the fact that it could not be identified in the sky like any other star. Its identification was not attempted either, except later in Egypt, at a point in the sky, however, which was not visible at Rome.[1] In contrast, when some ten years later Vergil spoke about Augustus' ultimate return to heaven he wanted to assign a section of the zodiac to him;[2] and Hadrian claimed to recognize the star of Antinous (who had just died) in the sky.[3] Nevertheless, Caesar's καταστερισμός was never given up: it stood side by side with the other versions of his deification. Ovid described how Caesar changed during his ascension: he began to fly, his hair became fiery, and then he found his place among the stars.[4] From there, so Propertius reported, he watched the battle of Actium.[5] The star was placed on his statues, on Augustus' helmet, and on the forehead of later aspirants to immortality. One gains the impression that the rise of the comet had been a welcome incident, but that the symbolism of the stars would have exerted its influence even without it. That symbolism had had a long history before Caesar.

This history need not be treated here in great detail. We can at once eliminate the frequent artistic representations where the stars had long lost their meaning and were used singly or in greater number merely for decoration. What matters here is that they often indicated the starred heaven; five or seven stars, the planets;[6] a star, often with seven rays,[7] the sun, and when combined with a crescent, the sun and moon, which pair was also the symbol of astral immortality and of eternity.[8]

---

[1] Pliny 2. 178: 'non cernit ... Italia ... quem sub Divo Augusto cognominavere Caesaris thronon, insignes ibi stellas'; Böker, *RE* Suppl. 8. 918 ff. (with bibliography), is not convincing.

[2] Verg. *Georg.* 1. 32 ff. According to Germanic. *Arat.* 558, at his death it was Capricorn that took Augustus up to heaven.

[3] Dio 69. 11. 4; cf. SHA *Pert.* 14. 3 (stars seen the day before Pertinax died).

[4] Ov. *Met.* 15. 843 ff.

[5] Prop. 4. 6. 59: 'at pater Idalio miratur Caesar ab astro: / "sum deus: est nostri sanguinis ista fides."'

[6] Cumont, *Symb. fun.* 93; 241 f.; Schauenburg, *Ant. Kunst* 5 (1962), 51 ff.

[7] Procl. *Tim.* 11 e (1, p. 34 D.): ὁ Ἑπτάκτις (Ἥλιος); Iulian. *or.* 8 (5). 172 d; Psell. *Scr. min.* 1. 262. 19; 446. 26; Bouché–Leclercq, *L'astrologie grecque* 81. 3; Cumont, *Syria* (1928), 103; pl. 38. 2; *Symb. fun.* pls. 21; 22 bis; A. Roes, *Syria* 26 (1949), 117 ff.

[8] Cumont, op. cit. 79. 5; 94; 208. 1.—The particularly brilliant star of Sirius which was often represented (Cook, *Zeus* 2. 630, fig. 535; Boll, *Sternglaube*, pl. 20, fig. 40; Roeder, *Myth. Lex.* 4. 1279, fig. 2; Chapouthier, op. cit. 258, fig. 42) need not be considered here.

PLATE 25

1. Denarius of P. Sepullius Macer, 44 B.C. (Sydenham 179. 1076), London; *obv.*: tetrastyle temple with globe in pediment, legend 'Clementiae Caesaris'; *rev.*: youth on horseback with a second horse, palm and wreath, legend 'P. Sepullius Macer'; p. 309.

2. Aureus of Augustus, 18–17 B.C. (Mattingly 1. 58. 315), London; *obv.*: head of Augustus, legend 'Augustus'; *rev.*: Mars in circular domed shrine with aquila and standard, legend 'Martis Ultoris'; p. 362.

3. Aureus of Domitian, A.D. 95 (Mattingly 2. 343. 229), London; *obv.*: head of Domitian, legend 'Imp. Caes. Domit. Aug. Ger. cos. XVII, cens(or) per(petuus), p. p.'; *rev.*: shrine with seated figure, Victoria r. and l.; p. 362.

4. Denarius of Antoninus Pius, A.D. 157–8 (Mattingly 4. 135. 915), London; *obv.*: head of Antoninus, legend 'Antoninus Aug. Pius, p. p., tr. p. XXI'; *rev.*: shrine of four columns and an arch above them, inside a statue on a base, legend 'cos. IIII'; p. 362.

5. Gem from Iraq in the British Museum, second cent. B.C. (S. Smith, *Brit. Mus. Quart.* 13, 17; photo: Brit. Mus.): Zeus with sceptre and thunderbolt seated in a shrine of four columns which is placed on a chariot of elephants; p. 362.

6. Sestertius of Marcus Aurelius, A.D. 161 (Mattingly 4. 528. 891), London; *obv.*: head of Antoninus Pius, legend 'Divus Antoninus'; *rev.*: Antoninus Pius with sceptre seated inside a shrine with four columns, set on a chariot of four elephants, legend 'S.C.'; p. 363.

7. Sestertius of Commodus, A.D. 180 (Mattingly 4. 763. 397), London; *obv.*: head of Marcus Aurelius, legend 'Divus M. Antoninus Pius'; *rev.*: Marcus Aurelius with sceptre(?) seated inside a shrine with four columns, set on a chariot of four elephants, legend 'Consecratio, S.C.'; p. 363.

8. Copper coin of Cyprus, Ptolemaic period (*BMC Cyprus*, p. lxxxi), Paris; *obv.*: head of Zeus; *rev.*: Zeus standing with corn-ear and sceptre, a star above his head; p. 375.

9. Copper coin of Salamis, fourth cent. B.C. (*BMC Cyprus*, p. cvii), Berlin; *obv.*: head of Aphrodite, *rev.*: star; p. 375.

10. Denarius of M. Furius Philus, c. 119 B.C. (Sydenham 67. 529), Oxford; *obv.*: head of Ianus, legend 'M. Fouri L. f.'; *rev.*: helmeted Roma with sceptre and a star over her head is crowning a trophy, legend 'Phili, Roma'; p. 376.

11. Denarius of Cn. Cornelius Blasio, c. 110 B.C. (Sydenham 75. 561), London; *obv.*: helmeted head of Mars with a star overhead, on l. caduceus (symbol), legend 'Cn. Blasio Cn. f.'; *rev.*: Iuppiter between Iuno and Minerva, legend 'Roma'; p. 376.

12. Denarius of Q. Pomponius Musa, c. 65 B.C. (Sydenham 136. 823), Oxford; *obv.*: laureate head of Apollo, behind, star; *rev.*: Urania touching globe placed on tripod with her wand, legend 'Q. Pomponi(us) Musa'; p. 376.

13. Denarius of L. Cornelius Lentulus and C. Claudius Marcellus, 49 B.C. (Sydenham 171. 1030), Oxford; *obv.*: head of Apollo (?), legend 'L. Lent. C. Marc. cos.'; *rev.*: Iuppiter with eagle and thunderbolt at an altar, l. a star, legend 'q(uaestor)'; p. 376.

14. Denarius of M. Calpurnius Piso Frugi, c. 60 B.C. (Sydenham 136. 825), Oxford; *obv.*: terminal bust of a god, r. cup, l. wreath, behind head, star; *rev.*: patera, knife, legend 'M. Piso M. f. Frugi' all in laurel-wreath; p. 376.

15. Aes of C. Clovius, 45 B.C. (Sydenham 170. 1026), London; *obv.*: bust of Victoria, behind head, star, legend 'Caesar dic. ter.'; *rev.*: Minerva carrying trophy, shield and spears, at her feet, serpent, legend 'C. Clovi(us) praef(ectus)'; p. 376.

16. Denarius of Caesar, 46 B.C. (Sydenham 168. 1015), London; *obv.*: bust of Venus with Cupid, lituus and sceptre, star in her hair; *rev.*: trophy with spears, shields, prisoners, legend 'Caesar'; p. 377.

17. Gem in Berlin, imperial period (Furtwängler, *Geschn. Steine* no. 2589; cast: Staatl. Museen, Berlin): emperor (?) between (?) the Dioscuri standing on crescent surrounded by the seven planets; p. 375.

18. Sestertius of L. Aemilius Buca, 44 B.C. (Sydenham 178. 1066), London; *obv.*: head of Diana surmounted by crescent; *rev.*: star, legend 'L. Aemilius Buca'; p. 377.

19. Bronze of Syria (?), c. 20 B.C. (Grant, *FITA* 125), Paris; *obv.*: head of Augustus; *rev.*: star, legend 'Ρήγλος'; p. 377.

20. Denarius of P. Sepullius Macer, 44 B.C. (Sydenham 178. 1071), Oxford; *obv.*: head of Caesar, behind, star, legend 'Caesar imp.'; *rev.*: Venus with Victoria and sceptre resting on star, legend 'P. Sepullius Macer'; p. 377.

21. Tetradrachm of Tigranes, c. 83–69 B.C. (*BMC Syria* 104 f.), Oxford; *obv.*: head of Tigranes wearing Armenian tiara with star; *rev.*: Tyche of Antioch with river-god at her feet, legend Βασιλέως Τιγράνου; p. 375.

PLATE 25

1 2 3

4

5

6 7

8 9 10 11

12 13 14 15 16

17

18 19 20 21

The association of a star with the traditional gods naturally depends on such representations. The most frequent was that of the Dioscuri[1] who had been identified with the sign of the Gemini; there is some evidence for Zeus (pl. 25. 8),[2] more for Aphrodite alone (pl. 25. 9),[3] or with Phosphorus and Hesperus.[4]

A new development began when the first mortal, Alexander, was connected with them. His head on a plastic vase from Amisus in Pontus is surmounted by a crescent, with the larger star of the sun above it and two smaller stars on its right and left (pl. 27. 1).[5] The painting of Apelles, then, which according to our literary record[6] placed Alexander between the Dioscuri, the symbol of the two hemispheres in such a context,[7] may be equally relevant here. It will have set him, as may be inferred from an imitation of the imperial period, on a crescent surrounded by the seven stars of the planets (pl. 25. 17),[8] all indicating Alexander's ascent to the heavenly bodies. On coins from Syria a star is placed over the head of Antiochus IV Epiphanes (pl. 28. 1) or on the tiara of Tigranes (pl. 25. 21),[9] probably indicating the same symbolism in an abbreviated form. The deification of other Hellenistic rulers too will have been expressed in the same manner. The result of this survey so far is that the stars can represent first the starred heaven or just the planets or the sun and moon alone; secondly the traditional gods, especially Aphrodite and the Dioscuri; and thirdly the deified rulers. A new category is found in Egypt. There the priests of Helios wore a diadem with a star of seven rays in its centre;[10] others a wreath with such a star

---

[1] Chapouthier, op. cit. (above, p. 372. 4).

[2] Cook, *Zeus* 2. 982, fig. 882 (*BMC Galatia* 274; pl. 33. 4); 1. 741, fig. 542 (*BMC Cyprus*, p. lxxxi); 747, fig. 545.

[3] *BMC Cyprus*, p. lxxxviii; pl. 22. 8 (Paphos, 4th. cent. B.C.): *obv.* Aphrodite, *rev.* dove and star; p. cvii; pl. 24. 16 (Salamis): *obv.* head of Aphrodite, *rev.* star; cf. Cook, *Zeus* 1. 574, fig. 443a.

[4] Chapouthier, op. cit. 277, fig. 50 (altar in the Louvre).

[5] Cumont, *Symb. fun.* 208; pl. 16. 1. The same arrangement is found on some gravestones (Cumont, op. cit. 229) and on a stele from Thasos (F. Salviat, *Rev. arch.* 1966, 33 ff.).

[6] Pliny 35. 93 (above, p. 66. 6).   [7] Cumont, op. cit. 64 ff.

[8] Gem of the imperial period in Berlin, Furtwängler, *Geschnittene Steine*, no. 2589; Chapouthier, op. cit. 324, no. 67; Cumont, op. cit. 93, fig. 12; 242 f.; cf. *RE* 8A. 2526; 2540.

[9] *BMC Syria* 34; 104 f.; pls. 11. 1; 27. 9 ff.; Head, *HN* 762; 772 f. A gem (Richter, *Engraved Gems of the Greeks and Etruscans* (1968), 682) shows two stars over two wreathed heads; even if these should be Hellenistic rulers the influence of representations of the Dioscuri is obvious.

[10] On sculptured heads: P. Graindor, *Bustes et statues—portraits d'Égypte rom.* (1937), 56, no. 15; 88, no. 37; 91, no. 40; pls. 15; 31; 33b; in the Museo Barracco at Rome, Helbig, *Führer* 2⁴. 619 f. (H. v. Heintze); Curtius, *Röm. Mitt.* 55 (1940), 220 ff.; fig. 1; ai Berlin, *Amtl. Ber.* 53 (1932), 40. On a painted portrait from Egypt, Parlasca, *Mumienporträts* (1966), 85 ff.; pl. 23. 2.—Cf. Malal., p. 299. 20 B. (p. 67 v. Stauff.): (Aurelian) ἐφόρει διάδημα ἔχον ἀστέρα; *Epit. de Caes.* 35. 5; Alföldi, *Röm. Mitt.* 50 (1935), 149.

(pl. 26. 1–3),[1] no doubt members of a religious community dedicated to the cult of Helios. It will have been their distinctive mark, comparable to the tattoos which were more widespread.[2] The Jews often wore the sign of a cross on their foreheads,[3] the worshippers of Dionysus the symbol of the ivy on some part of their bodies,[4] those of the Dea Syria the initials of the deity,[5] and those of Mithras another sign.[6]

In the Roman world, where the evidence at first rests on coin-issues only, we find a greater variety. One type, the most frequent one, can be excluded at once: the appearance of the star on the *denarii*, whenever it was merely a symbol of that denomination. But then we find a star over, or beside, the head of Roma,[7] Mars,[8] Apollo,[9] Iuppiter,[10] 'Terminus',[11] Victoria (pl. 25. 10–15);[12] its function is not clear. They are all gods, though without any apparent relationship to astral religion. Some help can be found when one turns to Venus. The star of Aphrodite had a special position among the planets because of her brilliance already in ancient Babylonia, then in Greece and the Hellenistic East.[13] That is probably why the Aphrodite of Cyprus and the related Dea Caelestis of Carthage were provided with a star.[14] If a coin of Cyprus portrays a star alone,[15] it is no doubt Aphrodite's star. The same conclusion

---

[1] Parlasca, op. cit., pls. 23. 3 f.; 41. 4.

[2] Cf. Hepding, *Attis* 163. 2; Deissmann, *Bibelstudien* 265 ff.; Tondriau, *Aegyptus* 30 (1950), 57 ff.; Dinkler, *Signum Crucis* (1967), 15 ff.; H. v. Heintze, *Röm. Mitt.* 64 (1957), 81 ff.

[3] LXX Levit. 19. 28; Ezech. 9. 4 ff.; Epist. ad Gal. 6. 17; other signs: Apocal. 13. 16 f.; 14. 9 ff; 16. 9; 19. 20; 20. 4; Dinkler, op. cit.

[4] LXX 3 Maccab. 2. 29; *Et. Magn.* s.v. Γάλλος; Cumont, *La stèle du danseur d'Antibes* (1942), 31 ff.; figs. 16; 18.

[5] Lucian *dea Syr.* 59; Wilcken, *Festgabe f. Deissmann* (1927), 7 ff.

[6] Tert. *de praescr. haeret.* 40; Cumont, *Die Mysterien d. Mithra*[3] 144; cf. Lyd. *ost.* 4. 53, p. 110. 16 W. (Apollo).

[7] Coin of M. Fourius Philus, *c.* 110 B.C., Sydenham 67; Grueber, pl. 94. 5.

[8] Coin of Cn. Cornelius Blasio, *c.* 110 (Crawford), Sydenham 75; pl. 19. 561E. The helmeted head is generally ascribed to Scipio Africanus, recently also by M. L. Vollenweider, *Mus. Helv.* 15 (1958), 38 f.; pl. 4. 2–5; *contra*, E. S. G. Robinson, *Essays presented to H. Mattingly* 42 f.; Scullard, *Roman Politics* 255. If it were really Scipio, it would provide the first instance of a star over the head of a mortal.

[9] Coin of A. Postumius Albinus, *c.* 92, Sydenham 87 f.; Grueber pl. 96. 12 f.: the star is behind the head of 'Apollo'; of L. Valerius Acisculus, *c.* 45, Sydenham 166; pl. 27. 998A; 1000: the star is over the head of 'Apollo Soranus'.

[10] Coin of L. Cornelius Lentulus and C. Claudius Marcellus, the Pompeian consuls of 49, with the star at the side of Iuppiter, Sydenham 171; pl. 27. 1030.

[11] Coin of M. Calpurnius Piso, 68–66 B.C., with the star behind the head of the alleged Terminus, Sydenham 136; pl. 23. 825.

[12] Coin of C. Clovius, 45, with the head of Victoria and the star behind it, Sydenham 170; Grueber, pl. 53. 18.

[13] Cumont, *Ant. Class.* 4 (1935), 5 ff. (with bibliography).

[14] A star is at her side on a relief in the Museo Capitolino showing the pediment of her temple, M. Guarducci, *BC* 72 (1946/8), pl. 1; Hommel, op. cit. 50 f.; pl. 10; also on coins of the imperial period, Cook, *Zeus* 2. 68. 2.   [15] See above, p. 375. 3.

PLATE 26

1. Basalt head from Egypt in the Museo Barracco, Rome: priest of Helios wearing a headband with a star in the centre (Photograph: Alinari); pp. 375 f.
2. Painted portrait from Egypt in the National Gallery, London: a priest of Helios wearing a metal band with a star of seven rays in the centre (Photograph: National Gallery, London); pp. 375 f.   3. Painted portrait from Egypt in the National Gallery, London: a member of a cult-association wearing a laurel wreath with a star in front (Photograph: National Gallery, London); pp. 375 f.

must then be drawn for the similar star on the *sestertius* of L. Aemilius Buca[1] and on later coins of Syria (pl. 25. 18–19).[2] At Rome the initiative belonged to Caesar. In 48 he issued coins showing Venus, with a star as an ornament in her hair, and Cupid on the obverse, and a trophy on the reverse: a reference to the victory in Gaul and the help of Venus (pl. 25. 16).[3] About the same time as Aemilius Buca, that is, shortly before Caesar's death, P. Sepullius Macer represented Venus with her spear resting on a star (pl. 25. 20);[4] this in turn is to be connected with an Augustan coin of the East with Venus and a shield behind her decorated with a star (pl. 13. 15).[5] This star is no longer just the bright star so much admired and even worshipped in the East: at Rome it had been incorporated in the Trojan legend. According to Varro it was the star of Venus that led Aeneas on his way from Troy to Italy and disappeared only after his landing at the *ager Laurens*.[6] One may assume that it was this star of the divine ancestress that was represented on some of the puzzling coins mentioned above, especially those of the Caesarian age, that is, on the coins of L. Valerius Acisculus over the head of the alleged Apollo Soranus and almost certainly on those of C. Clovius behind the head of Victoria.

The star next appears behind Caesar's head on the obverse of those coins of Sepullius Macer which show Venus with sceptre and star on the reverse. The star is in the same place as on Clovius' Victoria-coins. There are three possibilities. First, this star could again be the star of Venus and refer to Caesar's divine descent and to the Trojan legend.[7] Secondly, it could represent him as a god in accordance with the decree of early 44;[8] and thirdly, as the same but after the appearance of the comet, which is the more or less generally accepted interpretation.[9] But however attractive this is the probability is against it. There is nothing on the coins to suggest that they were posthumous issues: the star could, but, as we have seen, need not, indicate something of this kind. This view

[1] Sydenham 178; Grueber, pl. 54. 14.

[2] Coin of Regulus, *obv.* head of Augustus, *rev.* star, Grant, op. cit. 125; pl. 4. 20.

[3] Sydenham 168. 1015; Grueber, pl. 101. 9; see above, pp. 43; 61. 6; 86.

[4] Sydenham 178; Grueber, pl. 54. 15 ff.; Alföldi, *Studien*, pls. 6–10.

[5] Mattingly 1. 98; pl. 14. 16 f.; for stars on shields in general see Crous, *Röm. Mitt.* 48 (1933), 101.

[6] Serv. *Aen.* 1. 382: 'Varro in secundo divinarum dicit "ex quo de Troia est egressus Aeneas, Veneris eum per diem cotidie stellam vidisse, donec ad agrum Laurentem veniret, in quo eam non vidit ulterius: qua re terras cognovit esse fatales"'; 2. 801.

[7] This is the view of Liegle, *Arch. Jahrb.* 56 (1941), 95 f.; Grueber 1. 545. 2; 547. 2 is undecided.

[8] See the preceding note. For a far-reaching version of this view see Alföldi, *Studien* 35; *contra*, Felber, op. cit. 247 ff.

[9] See above, p. 371. 6.

would, moreover, imply that they were issued in those turbulent months by an official moneyer to serve Octavian's propaganda, which was certainly opposed by the consul Antony. The choice then is between the star of Venus and that of the divine ruler. We have seen that Alexander and Antiochus IV had already been so represented; at Rome Caesar would be the first mortal with his own star. Even if one decides for the alternative of Venus' star, one has to add that soon afterwards that star in fact became Caesar's star. Nevertheless, the distinction is important. Caesar adopted the star of his ancestress while he was still alive. But he certainly knew that the star was also the symbol of the divine or deified ruler, and that was why he adopted it. The comet then only served as a welcome confirmation of the existing symbol, made it acceptable to the populace, and prompted Octavian to action.

The star (over a prow) is already Caesar's on coins issued by Antony and Cn. Domitius Ahenobarbus in 40 B.C. in celebration of their reconciliation,[1] then on two coins of Octavian issued in Africa[2] and Gaul (Lugdunum) (pl. 28. 2–5)[3] with the same prow to commemorate naval victories, the latter showing Caesar's head with or without the star over it on the obverse. This was some years after Caesar's consecration when Octavian and Antony still acted in concord.[4] On coins issued by Agrippa in 38 B.C., that is, somewhat earlier than the last two, the star appears for the first time in front of Caesar's forehead instead of above or behind the head (pl. 28. 6),[5] obviously representing a statue on which the star was engraved, fixed, or embossed on his forehead, for which procedure we shall meet later instances presently. The next issue was by Octavian in 36 with the projected temple in Rome and the star in its pediment (pl. 28. 7).[6] We come to the battle of Actium, where according to Vergil and Propertius the star appeared;[7] it is very likely that more was said about it in contemporary poetry. The next piece of evidence would belong to 25 B.C., if it were right to say that Horace by 'Iulium sidus' meant Caesar's star;[8] in fact he uses 'sidus' here in

---

[1] Sydenham 191; pl. 29. 1178; App. BC 5. 55 f., 232 ff.; K. Scott, CP 36 (1941), 262.

[2] Grant, op. cit. 50 f.; pl. 2. 12 (obv.: head with the legend 'Divos Iulius'); Kraft, l.c. 10; pl. 1. 2.

[3] Grant, op. cit. 207; pl. 7. 22 f.; cf. Mattingly 2. 38 f.; pl. 6. 11 f. (Vespasian).

[4] See below, pp. 398 f.

[5] Sydenham 207; Grueber, pl. 105. 8; Kraft, l.c. 78; pl. 3. 9 f.; on gems apparently not copied from this coin, Pesce, l.c. 405, no. 1 (genuine?); Furtwängler, Ant. Gemmen, pl. 47. 34 (Pesce, ibid. no. 5).

[6] Sydenham 208; Grueber, pl. 122. 4 f.; below, p. 399.

[7] Verg. Aen. 8. 681: 'patriumque aperitur vertice sidus'; Prop. 4. 6. 59 (above, p. 373. 5).

[8] Hor. c. 1. 12. 46: 'micat inter omnis / Iulium sidus velut inter ignis / luna minores.' This passage is quoted in all comments on the comet.

PLATE 27

I

2

3

(For description see overleaf)

a metaphorical sense of Augustus,[1] the brilliant star of the age. This does not exclude an intentional allusion to the comet, but it could have been only in the sense favoured by Augustus, namely that it was his own star.[2]

In 17 B.C., the year of the saecular games, a comet appeared again[3] and the moneyer M. Sanquinius reproduced it on his coins over the head of Caesar, with the legend 'Divus Iulius'; a provincial mint omitted the head and filled the reverse with an enlarged comet and the legend (pl. 28. 8–9).[4] This was the first time that the comet took the place of the star on such coins.[5] It can only mean a revised version of the prophecy of Vulcanius:[6] in 44 as well as in 17 the comet announced the beginning of a new *saeculum*. What Caesar should have initiated had now become a reality under Augustus and was celebrated in that year. Next L. Lentulus issued a coin, the date of which is controversial, with Augustus placing the star over the head of Caesar (pl. 28. 10).[7] This issue leads us back to the events of 44, when statues of this kind were set up.[8] It is important to note that the type of figure seen on the coin is found on the later reliefs from Ravenna and Carthage (pl. 27. 2–3).[9] On the former it stands in the company of Mars and Venus and has a hole in the forehead where the metallic star, now lost, was fitted in; on the latter the star—which has seven rays—is embossed on the forehead.[10] Neither relief represents Caesar but a Julio-Claudian prince as a new god. When Augustus died Tiberius issued coins with a star over Augustus' head (pl. 28. 11–12);[11] but there is no evidence that such statues were ever set up. Valerius Maximus calls

---

[1] See Heinze ad loc.; Fraenkel, *Horace* 296; Nisbet in his forthcoming commentary; above, p. 372. 2.   [2] See above, p. 371.   [3] Obs. 71; Dio 54. 19. 7 quotes it for 16 B.C.

[4] Mattingly 1. 13; 59; 63; pls. 2. 19 f.; 3. 1; 6. 6–8; 7. 9. Do the two stars on an *aureus* of M. Durmius, 18 B.C., in front of the head of Honos and behind it (Mattingly 1. 10; pl. 2. 8 = our pl. 29. 4) represent Caesar and Augustus as the 'heroes' of the *ludi saeculares*? On Honos and the games see Heinze on Hor. *c. s.* 56; two stars on coins of Caligula, below, p. 364. 6.

[5] Pesce, l.c. 410 f.; fig. 1, publishes a marble relief in the Museum of Velletri, found in 'Anzio', with Caesar's head, the comet, and the strange inscription 'Divus Caesar Augustus' in front of it: it is clearly a forgery. In fact the comet is found only once more, on a column of the temple of Augustus at Arelate, below, p. 408. Another forgery, a lamp with Caesar's head in the University of Mississippi, is revealed again by the wording of its inscription, 'Imp. Iulius Caesar': H. G. Buchholz, *Arch. Jahrb.* 76 (1961), 173 ff.   [6] See above, p. 195.

[7] Mattingly 1. 26; pl. 4. 14; above, p. 102.   [8] See above, p. 371.

[9] *CAH Plates* 4. 136b; 160a. It is also found on the cuirass from Cherchel, Durry, *Musée de Cherchel*, Supplement (1924), 100 f.; pls. 11 f.; Vermeule, *Berytus* 13 (1959/60), 55; pl. 15. 45. There, as on the coin, Caesar (or an emperor) holds Victoria in his right hand.

[10] It can be seen only on the reproductions by Curtius, *Mitt. Arch. Inst.* 1 (1948), 81; pl. 30 and by Hafner, *Röm. Mitt.* 62 (1955), 170; pl. 63. 1; 3; cf. also Zanker, *Forum Augustum* (1969), 33 nn. 109 and 111 (returns to the view that Caesar is represented on both reliefs).

[11] Mattingly 1. 124; 141; pls. 22. 18 f.; 26. 3.

PLATE 28

1. Tetradrachm of Antiochus IV Epiphanes, c. 175-164 B.C. (*BMC Syria* 34), London; *obv.*: diademed head of Antiochus with star overhead; *rev.*: Apollo on omphalos, legend Βασιλέως Ἀντιόχου θεοῦ, *14*; p. 375.

2. Aureus of Antony and Cn. Domitius Ahenobarbus (Sydenham 191. 1178), London; *obv.*: head of Antony, legend 'Ant. imp., IIIvir r.p.c.'; *rev.*: prow with star, legend 'Cn. Domit. Ahenobarbus imp.'; p. 378.

3. Bronze coin from Lugdunum, c. 37 B.C. (Grant, *FITA* 207), London; *obv.*: heads of Caesar and Octavian, legend 'Divi Iuli, Imp. Caesar Divi f.'; *rev.*: prow with mast and globe with a star superimposed, legend 'Copia' (sc. Colonia Copia = Lugd.); p. 378.

4. The same, Berlin, but *obv.* star over Caesar's head, part of legend cut off; *rev.* no globe, legend no longer legible.

5. Bronze coin from Africa, c. 37 B.C. (Grant, *FITA* 50 f.), Copenhagen; *obv.*: head of Caesar, legend 'Divos Iulius'; *rev.*: prow with star over it, legend 'Caes[ar] dictator perp.'; p. 378.

6. Aureus of Agrippa, 38 B.C. (Sydenham 207. 1329), London; *obv.*: head of Caesar with star at forehead, legend 'Imp. Divi Iuli f. ter. (?) III vir r.p.c.'; *rev.*: legend 'M. Agrippa cos. desig.'; p. 378.

7. Denarius of Octavian, 36 B.C. (Sydenham 208. 1338), Oxford; *obv.*: head of Octavian, legend 'Imp. Caesar Divi f., IIIvir iter(um) r.p.c.'; *rev.*: tetrastyle temple with Caesar's statue holding a lituus, on pediment star, frieze inscribed 'Divo Iul.', on l. altar, legend 'cos. iter(um) et ter(tium) desig(natus)'; p. 378.

8. Denarius of M. Sanquinius, 17 B.C. (Mattingly 1. 13. 71), Oxford; *obv.*: head of Augustus, legend 'Augustus Divi f.'; *rev.*: head of Caesar, above, a comet, legend 'M. Sanquinius IIIvir'; p. 379.

9. Denarius of Augustus, c. 17 B.C. (Mattingly 1. 59. 323), Oxford; *obv.*: head of Augustus, legend 'Caesar Augustus'; *rev.*: comet, legend 'Divus Iulius'; p. 379.

10. Denarius of L. Lentulus, 12 B.C. (?) (Mattingly 1. 26. 124), Paris; *obv.*: head of Augustus, legend 'Augustus'; *rev.*: Augustus with shield inscribed 'c(lupeus) v(irtutis)' is placing a star over the head of Caesar who holds Victoria and sceptre, legend 'L. Lentulus flamen Martialis'; p. 379.

11. Aureus of Tiberius, A.D. 14-15 (Mattingly 1. 124. 28), London; *obv.*: head of Tiberius, legend 'Ti. Caesar Divi Aug. f. Augustus'; *rev.*: head of Augustus, above, star, legend 'Divos August(us) Divi f.'; p. 379.

12. As of Tiberius, c. A.D. 15-16 (Mattingly 1. 141. 151), Oxford; *obv.*: radiate head of Augustus with star over it and thunderbolt on l., legend 'Divus Augustus Pater'; *rev.*: seated female figure with sceptre and patera, legend 'S.C.'; p. 379.

13. Quinarius of M'. Cordius Rufus, 46 B.C. (Sydenham 163. 979), London; *obv.*: radiate head of Sol, legend 'M'. Cordius'; *rev.*: eagle, legend 'Rufus'; p. 382.

14. Denarius of L. Valerius Acisculus, 45 B.C. (Sydenham 166. 1002), Oxford; *obv.*: radiate head of Sol, legend 'L. Valerius'; *rev.*: Diana in biga with a crescent over her head, legend 'L. Valerius'; p. 382.

15. Dupondius of Tiberius, c. A.D. 15-16 (Mattingly 1. 140. 142), London; *obv.*: radiate head of Augustus, legend 'Divus Augustus Pater'; *rev.*: round temple, legend 'S.C.'; p. 384.

16. Sestertius of Tiberius, A.D. 22-3 (Mattingly 1. 130. 74), Oxford; *obv.*: legend 'S.C., Ti. Caesar Divi Aug. f. August, p. m., tr. pot. XXIIII'; *rev.*: Augustus, radiate, seated with sceptre and branch, in front of him an altar, legend 'Divus Augustus Pater'; p. 384.

PLATE 28

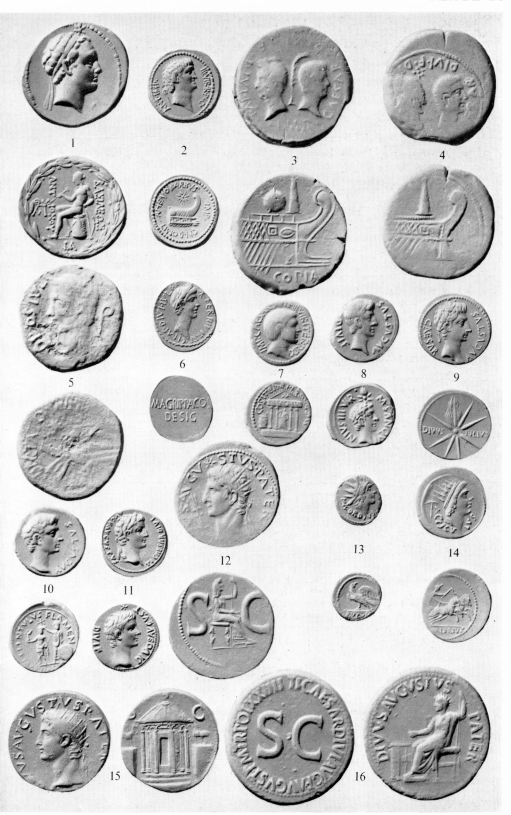

1   2   3   4
5   6   7   8   9
10   11   12   13   14
15   16

him a star when mentioning him together with Caesar.[1] Caligula was
called 'Sidus' when he entered Rome as the new emperor,[2] and so later
was Claudius by Seneca.[3] Nero's head with a star over it is seen on a
cameo at Cologne (pl. 29. 11):[4] the star has now become a regular
symbol of deification (pl. 29. 3–5).[5]

The fitting of the star over Caesar's head or on his forehead recalls
not only Alexander and his successors but also the priests and worshippers of Helios in Egypt with the star on their diadem and wreath
respectively.[6] But the analogy is not complete. Caesar was not a priest
nor a worshipper but a god; he wore the star whereas Helios did not, and
the Romans in turn did not wear it, unlike the worshippers of Helios.
But the analogy is useful in another respect. We have seen that the
star could indicate astral immortality, the divinity of the Hellenistic
rulers, Caesar's divine ancestress, and his own divinity. But astral symbolism, once adopted, had further consequences. The ruler on earth,
who had long been associated with the ruler in heaven, Zeus or Iuppiter, was now also connected with the king of the stars, Helios. It
was due to the solar theology of the Hellenistic age that the supremacy
of Helios was thus accepted;[7] and those who wrote about kingship
compared the king of the ideal State with him as well as with Zeus.[8]
Demetrius of Phaleron was called ἡλιόμορφος in 307 and Antigonus I
ʼλίου παῖς καὶ θεός.[9] Demetrius Poliorcetes was then celebrated at
Athens as Helios,[10] and later Hellenistic rulers were provided with the

[1] Val. Max. 1 *praef.* (of Tiberius): 'tua (divinitas) . . . paterno avitoque sideri par videtur,
quorum eximio fulgore multum caerimoniis nostris inclitae claritatis accessit'; 2. 1. 10:
'caeli clarissima pars, divi fulserunt Caesares.' Caesar alone: 3. 2. 19: 'siderum clarum
decus (cf. Hor. *c.s.* 2: 'lucidum caeli decus'), Divum Iulium'; 6. 9. 15: 'C. autem Caesar
. . . clarissimum mundi sidus.'

[2] Suet. *Cal.* 13. It is less likely that this Sidus was like Plato's Ἀστήρ (*Anth. Pal.* 7. 669 f.;
translated by Apul. *Apol.* 10 'mi sidus') just a term of endearment; cf. 'ocellus': Plaut.*Asin.*
664; Catull. 31. 2; 50. 19; see below, p. 384. 7–9.

[3] Sen. *cons. ad Pol.* 13. 1: 'sidus hoc, quod praecipitato in profundum et demerso in tenebras
orbi refulsit, semper luceat!'

[4] Möbius, *Arch. Anz.* 1948/9, 111 ff. and *Schweiz. Münzbl.* 16 (1966), 115 ff.—A star
over the head of a boy, that is, a Julio-Claudian prince, on a glass medallion: Drexel, *Ant.
Plastik W. Amelung* . . . (1927), 69 f.; fig. 8; *Germania Romana* 5², pl. 36. 3; also over the head
of another boy, not a prince, on a relief from Albano Laziale, Galieti, *Röm. Mitt.* 58 (1943),
70 ff.; pl. 3; Cumont, *Lux Perpetua*, 184; pl. 2.

[5] A restored *aureus* of Trajan (Mattingly 3. 143; pl. 24. 4) shows 'Divus Vespasianus'
on the *obv.*, a large star with eight rays and, above it, busts of Iuppiter (?) and Mercury on
the *rev.* (pl. 29. 5): a unique and puzzling representation.   [6] See above, p. 375.

[7] Cumont, 'La théologie solaire du paganisme romain', *Mémoires Acad. Inscr.* 12 (1909),
447 ff.; Nilsson 2. 510 ff.; id. *Opusc.* 2. 492 ff.

[8] Ecphant. ap. Stob. 4. 7. 64 (4, pp. 272 f. W.–H.); Goodenough, *YCS* 1 (1928), 75 ff.

[9] Duris, *FGrHist.* 76 F 10; Plut. *Is. et Os.* 24; *reg. et imp. apophth.* Ant. 7.

[10] Duris, *FGrHist.* 76 F 13: σεμνόν τι φαίνεθ', οἱ φίλοι πάντες κύκλῳ, ἐν μέσοισι δ' αὐτός, / ὅμοιον
ὥσπερ οἱ φίλοι μὲν ἀστέρες, / ῞Ηλιος δ' ἐκεῖνος. Homer as the second Helios, *Anth. Pal.* 7. 6. 2.

radiate crown,[1] the symbol of Helios.[2] By that time their model, Alexander, must also have been so represented.[3] All this was known at Rome, where Sol had an old cult and also possessed the radiate crown.[4] When the younger Scipio died in 129 B.C. it was said that the second Sun was extinguished;[5] in 43 Brutus was called the Sol of Asia.[6] We have seen that the chariot with white horses, an attribute of both Iuppiter and Helios, was given to Aeneas and Latinus, to Latinus also the radiate crown.[7]

In the age of Caesar, Sol with his radiate crown is found on coins of M'. Cordius Rufus, c. 46,[8] and of L. Valerius Acisculus, c. 45 (pl. 28. 13–14),[9] that is, about the time when Caesar held his triumph in a chariot with white horses.[10] It was soon afterwards that it was decreed that his golden crown should be carried to the theatres.[11] Florus calls it a radiate crown[12] in contrast to the other authors; that they were right we learn from the precedent of Pompey and from coins which show a jewelled crown. And yet the evidence of Florus cannot be dismissed: he certainly did not confuse the symbolism of his own age with that of Caesar's.[13] He rather referred, in the wrong place, to another decree which will have honoured Caesar with the radiate crown also. Lucan knew of such a crown,[14] and Caligula was said to have worn it,[15] which, by implication, confirms the existence of the Caesarian decree. And one of the portents reported after Caesar's death was that the Sun had

---

[1] Alföldi, *Röm. Mitt.* 50 (1935), 141, fig. 18; H. St. J. Hart, *Journ. Theol. Stud.* N.S. 3 (1952), 66 ff.; pl. 1 (with the suggestion that Jesus' crown of thorns, John 19. 2–5, was an imitation of the radiate crown); A. Krug, *Arch. Anz.* 84 (1969), 189 ff. (Mithridates VI).

[2] Cf. Alföldi, l.c. 139 ff.

[3] Alexander with the radiate crown: Helbig, *Führer* 2⁴, no. 1423; Gebauer, *Ath. Mitt.* 63/4 (1938/9), 83, G 33 (pl. 4. 13); 42; 87, K 16; cf. [Liban.] *descr.* 27. 4 (8, p. 534 F.); Plut. *de Alex. fort.* 1. 2. 8 (330 D); E. Neuffer, *Das Kostüm Alexanders des Grossen* (1929), 17; 48 ff.

[4] Sydenham 9; pl. 14. 97 (c. 222–187 B.C.); cf. 74; Grueber, pl. 95. 11; Mattingly 1. 7 f.; pl. 1. 20; 2. 2.

[5] Cic. *ND* 2. 14: 'Tuditano et Aquilio consulibus ... P. Africanus, Sol alter, extinctus est.' This praise lost its original significance when it was connected with the frequent phenomenon of two suns (parhelion), an evil portent; see also Cic. *div.* 1. 97 (with Pease's note).

[6] Hor. *sat.* 1. 7. 24: 'Solem Asiae Brutum adpellat stellasque salubris / adpellat comites'; see above, p. 381. 10; cf. Kaibel, *Epigr.* 906 (L. Robert, *Hellenica* 4. 15): Leontius a second Helios of Illyria; Kantorowicz, *Selected Studies* (1965), 327 ff. (two Suns in Byzantium, Christ and the Emperor).   [7] See above, p. 68.   [8] Sydenham 163; Grueber, pl. 51. 16.

[9] Sydenham 166; Grueber, pl. 53. 8; he also issued a coin with a star over the head of the alleged Apollo, above, p. 376. 9.   [10] See above, pp. 68 ff.   [11] See above, pp. 281 f.

[12] Flor. 2. 13. 91: 'in theatro distincta radiis corona.'

[13] Thus Mommsen, *StR* 1. 427. 3; 428. 6; *contra*, Eckhel, *Doctr. num.* 6. 270; Alföldi, *Röm. Mitt.* 50 (1935), 142.

[14] Lucan. 7. 457: 'bella pares superis facient civilia divos, / fulminibus manes radiisque ornabit et astris / inque deum templis iurabit Roma per umbras.'

[15] Philo, *leg. ad Gai.* 13. 95 (Caligula dressing up as Apollo): στεφάνοις μὲν ἀκτινοειδέσι τὴν κεφαλὴν ἀναδούμενος; cf. SHA *Gall.* 16. 4: 'radiatus saepe processit.'

a pale light all through the year, so that the people feared eternal night.[1] It will be remembered that this pale light was also observed after Scipio's death when with him the second Sun was extinguished.[2] The darkness at the death of Jesus was caused by an eclipse of the Sun;[3] his resurrection was the rise of a new Sun,[4] and he then wore a radiate crown which could be one of twelve rays.[5]

After Caesar's death Sol is found on the coins of L. Mussidius Longus *c.* 42,[6] of P. Clodius *c.* 41,[7] and of Antony 38/7.[8] They need not be relevant to the Caesarian symbolism[9] and yet they vouch for its continuity. We are on safer ground again with regard to Augustus. His father dreamt that, wearing a radiate crown, he was riding on a chariot with twelve white horses, though he wore the dress, and carried the attributes, of Iuppiter;[10] or simply that it was the Sun that rose from Atia's womb.[11] Horace called him the 'Iulium sidus' in 25,[12] proposed to acclaim him at his triumph on his return from Gaul in 16 'the brilliant Sun',[13] and spoke a year or two later of lack of light which only Augustus could bring back to Rome,[14] and of his brilliance that no star had matched before or would match again.[15] He was called 'the star of Greece' in

---

[1] Obs. 68: 'soles tres fulserunt . . . et postea in unum circulum sole redacto multis mensibus languida lux fuit'; Verg. *Georg.* 1. 466: 'ille etiam exstincto miseratus Caesare Romam, / cum caput obscura nitidum ferrugine texit / impiaque aeternam timuerunt saecula noctem'; Plut. *Caes.* 69. 4 f.; Pliny 2. 98; *vir. ill.* 78. 10; Usener, *Kl. Schr.* 4. 307 f.

[2] See above, p. 382. 5; cf. Suid. s.v. Καρνεάδης: . . . φασὶ δὲ τελευτήσαντος αὐτοῦ τὴν σελήνην ἐκλιπεῖν καὶ τὸν ἥλιον ἀμυδρὸν γενέσθαι (Diog. Laert. 4. 64).

[3] Luke 23. 44: σκότος ἐγένετο ἐφ' ὅλην τὴν γῆν ἕως ὥρας ἐνάτης τοῦ ἡλίου ἐκλιπόντος; Matt. 27. 45; Mark 15. 33; Dölger, *Sol Salutis*[2] 336 ff.

[4] Firmic. *err.* 24. 2: 'ante praefinitum tempus praecipitat diem mundi rotata vertigo, et sol non completo diurnarum horarum spatio properato cursu vergit in noctem . . . (4) ecce post triduum lucidior a solito dies oritur, et reddita soli praeteriti luminis gratia omnipotens deus Christus splendidioribus solis radiis adornatur'; Dölger, op. cit. 372 f. and *Ant. u. Christ.* 6 (1940/50), 16 f.

[5] Zeno of Verona 2. 9. 2 (*Patr. Lat.* 11. 417, fourth cent. A.D.): 'hic Sol noster . . . quem duodecim radiorum, id est apostolorum duodecim, corona circumdat'; Dölger, l.c. 1; 36 ff. (with further evidence); above, p. 69; Apocal. Joh. 12. 1 (Regina Caeli wearing a crown decorated with twelve stars); Mart. Cap. 1. 75 (Iuno); Boll, *Aus der Offenbarung Joh.* 99; Norden, *Die Geburt des Kindes* 159.

[6] Sydenham 181; Grueber, pl. 57. 4 f.   [7] Sydenham 183; Grueber, pl. 58. 2 ff.

[8] Sydenham 193; Grueber, pl. 114. 6.

[9] P. Clodius, reproducing the crescent and the planets on the rev., will have had oriental ideas in mind; also Antony who called his son 'Helios' about that time (Dio 50. 25. 4; Plut. *Ant.* 36. 5).   [10] Suet. *Aug.* 94. 6 (above, p. 69. 2).

[11] Dio 45. 1. 3.   [12] See above, pp. 378 f.

[13] Hor. *c.* 4. 2. 46: ' "o Sol / pulcher, o laudande" canam recepto / Caesare felix.'

[14] Hor. *c.* 4. 5. 5: 'lucem redde tuae, dux bone, patriae: / instar veris enim voltus ubi tuus / adfulsit populo, gratior it dies / et soles melius nitent'; Heinze ad loc.; Cic. *dom.* 75; Fraenkel, *Horace* 442. For a bold generalization see Pliny 27. 3: '(dei) Romanos velut alteram lucem dedisse rebus humanis videntur.'

[15] Hor. *epist.* 2. 1. 17: 'nil oriturum alias, nil ortum tale fatentes' (l. 13 refers to Hercules' 'fulgor', in l. 14 'extinctus' to his death).

Egypt in 7 B.C.,[1] but on the whole little was done officially to promote this symbolism while he was alive. After his death Tiberius issued coins with Augustus' radiate head,[2] also with the star over it (pl. 28. 15–16; 29. 1),[3] which points to sculptures of this kind; on a cameo at Vienna Livia-Cybele holds a radiate bust of Augustus (pl. 29. 2).[4] Manilius praises Tiberius as the source of light in the world,[5] and Caligula issued coins with the radiate heads of both Augustus (pl. 29. 3) and Tiberius.[6] Caligula was called 'Sidus' in the West,[7] 'Neos Helios' in the East,[8] and may have worn the radiate crown among the many divine attributes which he was said to have appropriated.[9] Claudius issued coins with such a head of Augustus,[10] Nero with his own head (pl. 29. 6–8).[11] Nero was acclaimed 'the New Sun' in East and West[12] and was so represented in the Circus.[13] In the age of the Flavians and later, solar symbolism had become part of the imperial cult.[14] The conclusion is that all this began under Caesar and for Caesar; also that it was unavoidable because of the growing popularity of belief in the stars. The belief in astral immortality too spread all over the Roman empire: the return to the stars became a favourite topic of epitaphs in poetry and prose and was often represented in art.[15]

[1] *IGR* I. 1295 (Kaibel 978): . . . ἄστρῳ ἁπάσας / Ἑλλάδος ὃς Σωτὴρ Ζεὺς ἀνέτειλε μέγας.

[2] Mattingly I. 140 ff.; pls. 25. 10 ff.; 26. 1 f.; also, with the full, seated figure (A.D. 22/3), 129; pl. 23. 17.

[3] Mattingly I. 141; pl. 26. 3; 5.

[4] Furtwängler, *Ant. Gemmen* 3. 318; Eichler–Kris, *Die Kameen im Kunsthist. Mus.* 57; pl. 5; Delbrück, *Ant. Porträts*, op. cit., on other cameos with the radiate head of Augustus see Furtwängler, op. cit. 317.

[5] Manil. 4. 765: (Rhodus) 'tumque domus vere Solis, cui tota sacrata est, / cum caperet lumen magni sub Caesare mundi' (Housman ad loc.).

[6] Mattingly I. 146; pl. 27. 1–4; 8 (the former with two stars: Augustus and Tiberius; cf. Mattingly I, p. cxiv; Vittinghoff, *Der Staatsfeind* 87. 382?); 160; 162 f.; pls. 28. 2; 30. 7 (Augustus).

[7] See above, p. 381. 2; on the emperor as 'sidus' see Sauter, *Der röm. Kaiserkult bei Martial u. Statius* 137 ff.

[8] *Syll.* 798 (*IGR* 4. 145); Malal. 10, p. 243(?); Eitrem, *Symb. Osl.* 11 (1932), 19; Aalders, *Mnem.* 4. 13 (1960), 242 f.

[9] See above, p. 382. 15; he also created a new military decoration, the *corona exploratoria*, ornamented with the figures of the Sun, Moon, and stars, Suet. *Cal.* 45. 1.

[10] Mattingly I. 195; pl. 37. 7.

[11] Mattingly I. 266 ff.; pl. 47. 1; on the cameo in Cologne (above, p. 381) Agrippina is placing the star over his head.

[12] *Carm. Einsidl.* I. 27 (*Anth. Lat.* 725 R.): 'seu caeli mens illa fuit seu solis imago' (Pfligersdorfer, *Herm.* 87 (1959), 370); *Anth. Pal.* 9. 178; *Syll.* 814; *IGR* 3. 345; Riewald, op. cit. 314 f.; Nilsson 2. 518.

[13] Dio 63. 6. 2; cf. 61. 2. 1; Tac. *A.* 15. 74. 1.

[14] Cf. Menand., *Rhet. Gr.* 3. 378. 10 Sp. (of the ruler): ἥκεις . . . ἄνωθεν λαμπρός, ὥσπερ ἡλίου φαιδρά τις ἀκτὶς ἄνωθεν ἡμῖν ὀφθεῖσα.

[15] e.g. *CLE* 1109; 1433. 4; more in Capelle, op. cit. (above, p. 372. 1), 34 ff.; R. Lattimore, *Themes in Greek and Roman Epitaphs* 30 ff.; Cumont, *Symbolisme funéraire*, passim.

XVIII

THE CULT

THE popular interpretation of the comet was not accepted immediately, perhaps not even by Octavian. He may have attached the star to the head of Caesar's statue a few weeks later; but it was completely ignored. It had no role in the subsequent debates of the Senate about Caesar's divinity, and there is not a word about it in Cicero's *Philippic Orations*. Nor is there any numismatic evidence, at least in the opinion of those who believe that the coins showing a star were issued while Caesar was still alive.[1] The earliest information belongs to Suetonius' Caesarian source and to Vergil, both writing probably after Caesar's consecration in 42.[2] Philodemus' testimony, if it is testimony, belongs, it is true, to 44; but it concerns the popular belief which he is fighting against, not its official acceptance.

Antony chose other means of promoting Caesar's deification. It will be recalled that it was he who persuaded the Senate to confirm Caesar's acts after the Ides of March and later produced the *lex Antonia de actis Caesaris confirmandis*.[3] Accordingly, he took the initiative in putting parts of the earlier legislation into effect: the *mensis Iulius* was accepted, sacrifices were held on the anniversaries of Caesar's victories, and supplications were decreed for him.[4] He was selective, and Cicero reminded him of this in his *Second Philippic Oration*: a *pulvinar, simulacrum, fastigium* too had been decreed; also that Antony was to be the *flamen* of Divus Iulius. He should not delay his inauguration. Again, that day, 19 September, should have been the additional day of the *ludi Romani* decreed in Caesar's honour at the request of Antony: so he ought to be holding those games.[5] It is clear that Antony intended to proceed gradually; but he had to fight on two fronts, against Caesar's enemies and against Octavian. He alleged that it was he whom Caesar had adopted by testament, and set up a statue on the Rostra with the inscription 'Parenti optime merito' in September,[6] apparently after Octavian had restored

---

[1] See above, pp. 377 f.   [2] See above, p. 370.

[3] Cic. *Att.* 16. 16C. 11; *Phil.* 2. 100; 5. 10; Drumann–Groebe 1. 415 f.; 422 ff.; v. Premerstein, *Zeitschr. Sav. St.* 43 (1922), 129 ff.; 135 ff.; Gelzer, *Caesar* 75. 74; 268. 70.

[4] Dio 45. 7. 2; Cic. *Phil.* 1. 13 (above, pp. 107. 9; 157. 2; 291. 1; cf. pp. 111; 152).

[5] Cic. *Phil.* 2. 110; above, pp. 265. 6; 280. 1; 284. 6; 306. 1; 307. 5.

[6] Cic. *Phil.* 2. 71: 'testamento, ut dicebas ipse, filius'; Nic. Dam. (*FGrHist.* 90 F 130)

the altar and the other statue.[1] Octavian in turn had the support of
the veterans, who resented Antony's opposition to the exhibition of
Caesar's throne,[2] and also of many loyal followers of Caesar. He made
that strange oath at Caesar's statue in their presence in November,
that he would aim at the same honours Caesar had achieved.[3] The
rivalry led meanwhile to hostility; the Mutinensian War ensued, in
which Octavian fought on the side of the new consuls against Antony.
Octavian became consul in August 43, his adoption was confirmed by
a *lex curiata*, and he consequently undertook to avenge his father's death.
The *lex Pedia* was created for this purpose, the conspirators were condemned to exile in their absence, and their property was confiscated.[4]
But no progress could be made while the rivalry lasted; it ended, for
a time, on 27 November when the triumvirate of Antony, Octavian,
and Lepidus was created.

I. THE CONSECRATION

The consecration was decreed on or about 1 January 42.[5] No further
information has survived; and yet it is possible to reconstruct the procedure followed by the Senate. *Consecratio* was in the first place a religious act, in which something or somebody was made *sacrum*, that is,
the property of a deity.[6] Later it also meant the creation of a cult,
and it is this meaning that matters here.[7] New cults had often been
started in this manner: when gods were transferred to Rome from
cities in Latium and elsewhere; when Greek gods were introduced;[8]
when new gods were created, for instance by the deification of human
virtues[9] or of heroes.[10] The decision was made by the Senate,[11] as in

---

21. 74; Meyer, *Caesars Monarchie* 380. 1.—Cic. *fam.* 12. 3. 1 (early October): 'in statua
quam posuit in Rostris inscripsit "Parenti optime merito", ut non modo sicarii sed iam
etiam parricidae iudicemini.'   [1] See above, pp. 364 f.

[2] Nic. Dam. *v. Caes.* 28. 108: εἰσιόντα γε μὴν αὐτὸν εἰς τὸ θέατρον ἐκρότει ὁ δῆμος εὖ μάλα
καὶ οἱ πατρικοὶ στρατιῶται ἠχθημένοι διότι τὰς πατρῴους ἀνανεούμενος τιμὰς διεκωλύθη.

[3] Cic. *Att.* 16. 15. 3 (above, p. 365. 5); cf. Nic. Dam. 18. 53.

[4] *Mon. Anc.* 2; Vell. 2. 69. 5, etc.; Weber, *Princeps* 148* ff.

[5] App. *BC* 2. 148. 616: νῦν δ' ἐστὶ νεὼς αὐτοῦ Καίσαρος θείων τιμῶν ἀξιουμένου. (617) ὁ γάρ
τοι θεὸς αὐτῷ παῖς 'Οκτάουιος . . . τὸν πατέρα τιμῶν ἰσοθέων ἠξίωσεν; Dio 47. 18. 3 ff.

[6] Fest. 321 M. (424 L.), etc.; Wissowa, *RE* 4. 896 ff.

[7] Mommsen, *StR* 3. 1049 ff.; Wissowa, *RE* 4. 901.

[8] Cic. *ND* 2. 62: 'nostri maiores auguste sancteque Liberum cum Cerere et Libera con-
secraverunt.'

[9] Cic. *leg.* 2. 28: 'Mens, Pietas, Virtus, Fides consecrantur humanae, quarum omnium
Romae dedicata publice templa sunt'; cf. *ND* 3. 51: 'Tempestates ... populi Romani
ritibus consecratae sunt.'

[10] Cic. *leg.* 2. 27: 'quod autem ex hominum genere consecratos, sicut Herculem et ceteros,
coli lex iubet, indicat omnium quidem animos inmortalis esse, sed fortium bonorumque
divinos.'   [11] Tert. *Apol.* 13. 3: 'status dei cuiusque in senatus aestimatione pendebat.'

Greece by the individual cities.[1] It mostly depended on the merit of the gods concerned and even more on that of the heroes. What the philosophers had said about the founders, benefactors, and conquerors had long been adopted by the authorities: heroes like Hercules, Castor and Pollux, Liber pater, and Romulus did not go to the Underworld after their death but ascended to heaven.[2] The Roman emperors joined the list of these heroes, and in their case we learn something about the procedure which led up to the decree of consecration.[3]

It was based on the ageless lore about the Judgement of the Dead,[4] which was often described from Pindar and Plato[5] onwards. It was said that the dead were tried by the judges of the Underworld, Minos, Rhadamanthys, or Aeacus, and were accordingly rewarded or punished. The doctrine was well known at Rome[6] and was there exposed, not surprisingly, to the influence of the Roman criminal law. It is enough to mention the Necyia in Vergil's *Aeneid*[7] and Seneca's *Apocolocyntosis*, the former for the judgement in general, the latter for its application to the emperors. In Seneca the outlines of the procedure can easily be detected.[8] On Claudius' arrival in heaven Iuppiter holds a meeting of the gods, presiding like a consul in the Senate. He first calls upon Ianus pater, the other consul, to speak, and he then proposes that Claudius should not be made a god. Diespiter, a *consul designatus*, follows; he speaks in his favour and submits the wording of his proposal to this effect. Finally, Divus Augustus speaks against Claudius, mentioning by name all the relations whom he had murdered and referring to his numberless other victims. Accordingly, he puts his own proposal forward, suggesting severe punishment and expulsion from heaven. The gods vote for this proposal in the manner of Roman senators, by going over to the side of the mover, *per discessionem*, and Mercury takes Claudius to the Underworld. The trial is resumed there at the *tribunal* of Aeacus, Pompeius Pedo prosecuting and presenting the charge-sheet

---

[1] Habicht, 160 ff. [2] See above, p. 356.

[3] Mommsen, *StR* 2. 756; 817 f.; 886; 1134; 3. 1049; Wissowa 342 ff. and *RE* 4. 901 f.; Bickermann, *ARW* 27 (1929), 1 ff.; Vittinghoff, *Der Staatsfeind* 75 ff.; Koep, *RAC* 3. 284 ff.

[4] The consecration was first so interpreted by Mommsen, *StR* 2. 1133 f.; but already Drumann 1. 66 had called the meeting of the Senate after the Ides of March a 'Totengericht' (1834).

[5] Aesch. *Suppl.* 220; Pind. *Ol.* 2. 62 ff.; Plat. *Gorg.* 523 e (with Dodds' note), etc.; Rohde, *Psyche* 1. 301 ff.; 2. 208 f.; Dieterich, *Nekyia* 109 ff.; L. Ruhl, *De mortuorum iudicio* (1903); Norden, *Aeneis VI*, 34 ff.; Wilamowitz, *Pindaros* 248 ff. and *Glaube d. Hell.* 2. 182 ff.; E. Wüst, *RE* 23. 1449 ff.; Nilsson 1. 693; 823 f.

[6] Plaut. *Capt.* 998 f.; Cic. *Tusc.* 1. 6; Prop. 4. 11. 18; the post-Vergilian evidence is collected by Ruhl, op. cit. 49 ff.

[7] Verg. *Aen.* 6. 426 ff.; 566 ff.; Norden, op. cit. 245 f.; 274.

[8] Sen. *Apocol.* 9–11; 14.

with a list of the murders. After refusing to listen to P. Petronius who tries to be the defence counsel, Aeacus condemns Claudius on this account. The punishment is then considered and decided.

A great deal of this narrative is irrelevant here: what is burlesque or fanciful or due to imitation of Greek models. But it is clear that the substance correctly reproduces the Roman trial with its alternatives: *consecratio* or *damnatio memoriae*. What is done in Seneca by Iuppiter and the gods or Aeacus was the task of the consuls and the Senate. They were the judges who heard the plea for the dead, considered various proposals, and then made their choice. When the corpse of Augustus arrived at Rome at the beginning of September A.D. 14 the first meeting of the Senate was devoted exclusively to his case.[1] Tiberius spoke for him, but he was also made to plead for himself through a recital of his testament, of his *Res gestae*, and of his other writings.[2] The consultation of the senators followed[3] with the result that his plea was accepted, which clearly means that his acts were declared valid; and this led to the decree of a public funeral. Its details were due again to a corporate decision; individual senators made various suggestions, not all of which were accepted.[4] After the funeral another meeting of the Senate took place and passed the decrees about the consecration and cult with all the necessary details.[5] In contrast, Caligula was condemned. His corpse would not have been buried at all if friends and relations had not done it in secret.[6] His acts were rescinded by Claudius[7] and his images destroyed.[8] Hadrian's case is interesting and particularly relevant here, as both alternatives were pleaded: the Senate wanted to declare him a public enemy, but Antoninus Pius spoke in his favour and succeeded in achieving his consecration.[9] In the course of time some details were changed, but the principal points remained constant.[10]

Considering the case of Caesar, one soon realizes that such a Judge-

[1] Tac. *A.* 1. 8. 1: 'nihil primo senatus die agi passus est nisi de supremis Augusti.'

[2] Tac. *A.* 1. 8. 1; Suet. *Aug.* 101. 1; 4; Dio 56. 33. 1; Weber, *Princeps* 44 ff.

[3] Tac. *A.* 1. 8. 4: 'tum consultatum de honoribus.'

[4] Ibid. 1. 8. 4 ff.; Suet. *Aug.* 100. 2 f.; Dio 56. 34; 42; Weber, op. cit. 75 f.

[5] Tac. *A.* 1. 10. 8: 'sepultura more perfecta templum et caelestes religiones decernuntur'; *F. Amit.* 17 Sept. (Degrassi 510): '... Divo Augusto honores caelestes a senatu decreti'; Vell. 2. 124. 3; Tac. *A.* 12. 69. 4; Mommsen, *StR* 2. 886. 2; Vittinghoff, op. cit. (above, p. 387. 3) 81 f.; Weber, op. cit. 87 ff.

[6] Suet. *Cal.* 59. Galba's corpse was left unburied and was mutilated by the mob, Tac. *H.* 1. 49.

[7] Suet. *Claud.* 11. 3; Dio 60. 4. 1; on *rescissio actorum* see Mommsen, *StR* 2. 1129.

[8] Dio 60. 4. 5 f.; cf. Mommsen, *StR* 2. 1135; v. Premerstein 87 f.; 97 f.; Vittinghoff, op. cit. 102.

[9] Dio 69. 2. 5; 23. 3; 70. 1. 2 f.; Vittinghoff, op. cit. 87 f.

[10] For further details see Vittinghoff, op. cit. 81 ff.

ment of the Dead was held at the meeting of the Senate on 17 March 44.[1] The chief conspirators were absent, but their friends demanded that Caesar should be declared a tyrant, a funeral therefore be denied him, and his corpse be thrown into the Tiber; further, that his acts should be annulled and, as may be inferred from later events, that his statues be destroyed. Antony on the other hand provided the defence. The day before, he got hold of Caesar's testament and the written record of his official activities.[2] He did not read these in the Senate but concentrated on the alternatives of the 'trial':[3] if Caesar was a properly elected ruler, his acts would remain valid; if he was a usurper, they would not, and he should be punished as the others demanded. He then insisted on the importance and usefulness of many of his acts, and they were then confirmed. This in turn implied that Caesar had not been a tyrant and was therefore entitled to a funeral, which was granted at the request of Piso, no doubt with all or most of the details which we have already considered. One might add that the 'trial' was continued, unofficially, after the meeting of the Senate. Antony provided the proper defence, which was impossible in the Senate, first with the help of Caesar's testament, which was read to the people, next in his funeral oration, when he recited Caesar's achievements and honours, making use of all the documents in his possession. Caesar's partisans then instituted a cult by setting up an altar; his adversaries removed his statues and destroyed them; they also destroyed the altar, which was, however, re-erected by Octavian.

It follows that the meeting of the Senate on 1 January 42 was dedicated to the second part of the 'trial'. The funeral having been held long before, celestial honours were to be decreed. This time it was no doubt Octavian who pleaded Caesar's case, and there was, of course, no opposition. He will have recited Caesar's achievements and requested the confirmation of Caesar's acts again. Whether he referred to the portent of the comet to prove Caesar's divinity is not clear; the portent of the ascension was a constituent part of Augustus' and his successors' apotheoses, as it was said to have been before for Romulus.[4] The conclusion is that the procedure of the 'judgement' of dead emperors

---

[1] What follows here is the re-interpretation of the evidence discussed above (pp. 347 f.; 351 f.), in the sense of a 'trial'.

[2] App. BC 2. 125. 524; Plut. Ant. 15. 2; v. Premerstein, Zeitschr. Sav. St. 43 (1922), 130 f.

[3] App. BC 2. 128. 535: ἄρχοντος μὲν αὐτοῦ καὶ αἱρετοῦ προστάτου γενομένου τὰ πεπραγμένα καὶ δεδογμένα πάντα κύρια μενεῖ, δόξαντος δ' ἐπὶ βίᾳ τυραννῆσαι τό τε σῶμα ἄταφον τῆς πατρίδος ὑπερορίζεται καὶ τὰ πεπραγμένα πάντα ἀκυροῦται.

[4] Vir. ill. 2. 13; Suet. Aug. 100. 4; Dio 56. 42. 3; 46. 2; 59. 11. 4 (Drusilla); Iustin. Apol. 1. 21. 3; Bickermann, l.c. 8 ff.

was created not after the death of Augustus but in those stormy days
after the Ides of March. It was not entirely new. The condemnation
of the tyrants, the confiscation of their property, the condemnation of
their memory, the refusal of a funeral, were part of the old criminal
law.[1] On the positive side there must have been some sort of a 'trial'
before Sulla's public funeral was decreed; it was debated in the
Senate and the opposition to it had to be overcome.[2] There may have
been more; but evidence is lacking.

The statement that Caesar was made a god by the Senate and the
Roman people[3] can only mean that the decree of the Senate was submitted to the *comitia* for confirmation. For Augustus and his successors
only the Senate is mentioned, but it is implied once that the people used
to be consulted.[4] The same divergence can be observed in the history
of the act of consecration in general. Whenever a new god, a piece of
ground, an altar or a temple was to be consecrated, the decree of the
Senate used to be sufficient;[5] but reference is often made to the people's
consent, and according to the *lex Papiria* it was required.[6] It is therefore
possible that, considering the overwhelming evidence about the sole
role of the Senate,[7] the consent of the *comitia* was not often sought at
the consecration of the emperors; but for Caesar it was.[8]

The act of consecration will have consisted of a solemn invocation of the
new god and of the creation of the statutes of the cult, the *lex templi*. The
former was probably by acclamation. Marcus Aurelius was so acclaimed
a 'propitious god',[9] and Livy gives further details with regard to
Romulus: the people greeted him as a god who was descended from a god,
and as king and father of Rome, and asked him in their prayer to be
always propitious and willing to preserve his descendants.[10] This wording

---

[1] See above, p. 348. 1 f.   [2] See above, p. 348.

[3] *ILS* 72 (Aesernia): 'Genio Deivi Iuli parentis patriae, quem senatus populusque Romanus
in deorum numerum rettulit.'

[4] SHA *M. Ant. Phil.* 18. 3: 'senatus populusque non divisis locis sed in una sede propitium
deum dixit'; Aur. Vict. 16. 15: 'denique, qui seiuncti in aliis, patres ac vulgus soli omnia
decrevere, templa columnas sacerdotes'; *Epit. de Caes.* 16. 14: 'et quod de Romulo aegre
creditum est, omnes pari consensu praesumpserunt Marcum caelo receptum esse. ob cuius
honorem templa columnae multaque alia decreta sunt.'

[5] Mommsen, *StR* 2. 619; 3. 339 f.; Wissowa 406.

[6] Cic. *dom.* 127; Mommsen, *StR* 3. 1050. 1; Münzer, *RE* 18. 2. 1012.

[7] Mommsen, *StR* 2. 886.   [8] Mommsen, *StR* 2. 756; 3. 1050. 3; 1257. 4 is undecided.

[9] SHA *M. Ant. Phil.* 18. 3 (above, n. 4); cf. Jos. *AJ* 19. 345 (King Herodes Agrippa
I in the theatre of Caesarea, A.D. 44): ἄλλος ἄλλοθεν φωνὰς ἀνεβόων, θεὸν προσαγορεύοντες
εὐμενής τε εἴης ἐπιλέγοντες; Acts 12. 22; Schürer, *Gesch. d. jüd. Volkes* 1. 563; Meyer, *Ursprung
u. Anfänge d. Christ.* 3. 167; Lösch, *Deitas Jesu u. ant. Apotheose* (1933), 10 ff.; cf. also *RE* 23. 824 f.

[10] Livy 1. 16. 3: 'deinde a paucis initio facto deum deo natum, regem parentemque urbis
Romanae salvere universi Romulum iubent; pacem precibus exposcunt, uti volens propitius
suam semper sospitet progeniem.'

is part of the old ritual vocabulary[1] and will have been so applied to Caesar in 42 before Livy came to record it for Romulus. In fact Valerius Maximus, whose warm devotion to Caesar is for the time of Tiberius both exceptional and puzzling, invokes Divus Iulius with a similar prayer at the beginning of his work.[2] As to the statutes, a number of related instances are known;[3] it will be enough to mention the Ara Numinis Augusti at Narbo[4] and the temple of Mars Ultor at Rome.[5] There is no such direct evidence for Caesar; but our sources record quite a few facts which must ultimately have formed part of those statutes. Our next task is their reconstruction and interpretation.

2. LEX TEMPLI

The most important source is a long chapter in Dio.[6] He does not, however, mention the principal item, the name of the new god. There was a rule, real or fictitious, that the name had to be changed:[7] Aeneas became Iuppiter Indiges, Latinus Iuppiter Latiaris, Romulus Quirinus. The names given to Caesar during his life time, ἡμίθεος, Deus Invictus, Iuppiter Iulius,[8] were no longer valid. The new name, Divus Iulius, was not coined by the Senate in 42; it was already mentioned by Cicero in September 44[9] and was therefore either decreed by the Senate early in 44 or was suggested in Caesar's testament. In either case it still required confirmation by the Senate, which was given in 42. 'Divus' was in origin nothing but another form of 'deus'; the two forms were used indiscriminately.[10] Varro tried to find a difference[11] and succeeded in finding one which is demonstrably wrong. It will have been Caesar, another linguistic expert, who, inspired by the Varronian

---

[1] See Ogilvie ad loc.; Wagenvoort, *Studies* 294; on 'propitius' see also *RE* 23. 822 ff.

[2] Val. Max. 1. 6. 13: 'tuas aras tuaque sanctissima templa, Dive Iuli, veneratus oro, ut propitio ac faventi numine tantorum casus virorum sub tui exempli praesidio ac tutela delitescere patiaris'; cf. R. E. Wolverton, *Laudatores temporis acti, Studies in Memory of W. E. Caldwell* (1964), 84 f.

[3] *ILS* 4906–16; Wissowa 6. 3; 473.   [4] *ILS* 112 (E.–J. 100).

[5] Dio 55. 10. 2 ff.   [6] Dio 47. 18. 3 ff.

[7] Lact. *div. inst.* 1. 21. 22: 'solent enim mortuis consecratis nomina immutari, credo ne quis eos putet homines fuisse. (23) nam et Romulus post mortem Quirinus factus est et Leda Nemesis et Circe Marica . . .'

[8] See above, pp. 53; 186; 303.   [9] Cic. *Phil.* 2. 110 (above, p. 306. 1).

[10] *Thes.L.L.* 5. 1649; 1655; W. Schwering, *Indogerm. Forsch.* 34 (1914/15), 1 ff.; Walde–Hofmann 1. 345 f.

[11] Serv. Dan. *Aen.* 12. 139: 'Varro ad Ciceronem tertio (*LL*, frg. 2, p. 3 G.–Sch.): ita respondeant cur dicant deos, cum de omnibus antiqui dixerint divos'; Serv. *Aen.* 5. 45: 'Varro et Ateius . . . dicentes divos perpetuos, deos qui propter sui consecrationem timentur, ut sint dii manes'; 12. 139: 'quod Graece δέος, Latine timor vocatur, inde deus dictus est, quod omnis religio sit timoris.'

speculations, created a real distinction which was to be lasting: 'Divus' was from now on a god who had previously been a man.[1]

Dio begins with the oath sworn by the *triumviri* and everybody else on 1 January 42 to respect Caesar's acts.[2] This oath had already been decreed in 45,[3] and its renewal was a logical consequence of the confirmation of Caesar's acts after the Ides of March. It was probably sworn in the name of Iuppiter and Divus Iulius[4] and was repeated by all magistrates annually. It inspired the regular oath for the acts of the ruling and past emperors, with the exception of those who were dishonoured, but including Caesar.[5] This is strange because Caesar was not officially included among the Divi of the imperial period nor was an oath sworn again in his name.[6]

The *lex* provided for a priest of the new god. This is not mentioned by Dio here but earlier among the last decrees of 44; there was to be a *flamen* of Divus Iulius, and Antony was chosen for this post.[7] The choice was made, as always in the case of the *flamines*, by the *pontifex maximus*,[8] that is, by Caesar himself. It was also decreed that he was to have the same privileges as the *flamen Dialis* possessed. This exceptional standing of the new *flamen* has already been explained, and will have to be stressed again in connection with the institution of the cult in the provinces.[9] Doubtless in 42 the same statute was renewed and Antony will have been picked again as *flamen* by the *pontifex maximus*, this time Lepidus. That special standing of the *flamen* will have been set out in the *lex templi*, in the same manner as can still be seen in the *lex Narbonensis* with regard to the provincial *flamen*.[10] Antony was not inaugurated as *flamen* until 40,[11] but he soon began to organize the cult in the East and to create priesthoods of the same kind.[12]

As to the temple, neither Aeneas nor Latinus possessed one at Rome; but Romulus did. It was the *aedes Romuli* or *casa Romuli* on the Palatine, mentioned as early as the third century B.C. in the document of the

---

[1] Serv. *Aen.* 5. 45: 'quamquam sit discretio, ut deos perpetuos dicamus, divos ex hominibus factos, quasi qui diem obierint: unde divos etiam imperatores vocamus'; 12. 139; Mommsen, *StR* 2. 756. 1; Schwering, l.c. 20 f.

[2] Dio 47. 18. 3: ἔν τε γὰρ τῇ πρώτῃ τοῦ ἔτους ἡμέρᾳ αὐτοί τε ὤμοσαν καὶ τοὺς ἄλλους ὥρκωσαν βέβαια νομιεῖν πάντα τὰ ὑπ' ἐκείνου γενόμενα.

[3] App. *BC* 2. 106. 442; Dio 44. 6. 1; above, p. 222.

[4] This is an inference from the formula of execration in the same chapter, 47. 18. 5: τοὺς ἀμελήσαντας αὐτῶν ἐπαράτους τῷ τε Διὶ καὶ αὐτῷ ἐκείνῳ εἶναι; above, pp. 207. 1; 213.

[5] Tac. *A.* 16. 22. 5 (above, p. 222. 8).   [6] Mommsen, *StR* 2. 809. 3.

[7] Dio 44. 6. 4; Cic. *Phil.* 2. 110.   [8] See above, p. 306.

[9] See above, pp. 307 f., and below, pp. 404; 709.

[10] *ILS* 6964 (McCrum–Woodhead 128); below, p. 409.

[11] Plut. *Ant.* 33. 1.   [12] See below, pp. 401 ff.

Argei.[1] It did not cease to function even after the cult of Romulus was transferred to the temple of Quirinus.[2] The temple was to be built in the Forum on the spot where Caesar had been cremated;[3] it will be recalled that an altar already existed there.[4] This was again a renewal of an earlier decree, which had provided for temples at Rome and everywhere in Italy.[5] It seems certain that nothing had been done about it before at Rome; and another plan to build a temple of the Clementia Caesaris, which Caesar would have shared with the new goddess,[6] was dropped. The same or a related clause will have stipulated that statues should be set up in and outside Rome. They were to be different from the earlier statues which had stood on the Capitol, the Rostra, and other public sites, and were destroyed after the Ides of March. Octavian had already taken the initiative after the appearance of the comet by erecting statues fitted with a star, one in the Forum, another in the temple of Venus, and some more elsewhere.[7] The new statues were given a special function, which was probably outlined in the mysterious *lex Rufrena*; we shall come back to this point presently.[8] The bases of such statues have been found at Ocriculum, Picenum (near Interamnia), Minturnae.[9] Another statue, which was kept in Caesar's temple or in that of Venus, was to be carried in the *pompa circensis* in the company of Venus.[10] This clause recalls the earlier occasions when Caesar's image was carried in the company of Romulus-Quirinus and then in that of Victoria, that is, of the deity of the festival.[11] It was a logical change that Caesar should now receive a constant place in the procession in the company of his divine ancestress. A further clause prescribed that his image should not be carried in the funeral processions of his relations:[12]

---

[1] Varro *LL* 5. 54; Dion. Hal. 1. 79. 11; Koch, *Religio* 31; Richard, *Mél.* 78 (1966), 74; not accepted by Classen, *Philol.* 106 (1962), 175.

[2] Dio 48. 43. 4 (38 B.C.).

[3] Dio 47. 18. 4: καὶ ἡρῷόν οἱ ἔν τε τῇ ἀγορᾷ καὶ ἐν τῷ τόπῳ ἐν ᾧ ἐκέκαυτο προκατεβάλοντο; App. *BC* 2. 148. 616 f. (above, pp. 364. 5; 386. 5).

[4] See above, pp. 364 ff.   [5] Suet. *Caes* 76. 1; App. *BC* 2. 106. 443.

[6] Dio 44. 6. 4; App. l.c.; above, pp. 308 f.

[7] Pliny 2. 94; Dio 45. 7. 1 (above, p. 371. 5); Suet. *Caes.* 88 (above, p. 370. 5); Serv. Dan. *Aen.* 8. 681; *Ecl.* 9. 46 (above, p. 41. 6).

[8] See below, p. 397.

[9] *ILS* 73: 'Divo Iulio iussu populi Romani statutum est lege Rufrena'; 73a; J. Johnson, *RE* Suppl. 7. 478; 487; Degrassi, *Scritti* 3. 102 ff.

[10] Dio 47. 18. 4: καί τι καὶ ἄγαλμα αὐτοῦ ἐν ταῖς ἱπποδρομίαις μεθ' ἑτέρου Ἀφροδισίου ἔπεμπον. This image may have been kept in the temple of Venus until the new temple was completed: later a golden image of Augustus was provisionally kept in the temple of Mars Ultor, Dio 56. 46. 4; cf. *JRS* 47 (1957), 146.

[11] See above, pp. 111; 185.

[12] Dio 47. 19. 2: ἀπεῖπον μὲν μηδεμίαν εἰκόνα αὐτοῦ, καθάπερ θεοῦ τινος ὡς ἀληθῶς ὄντος, ἐν ταῖς τῶν συγγενῶν αὐτοῦ ἐκφοραῖς πέμπεσθαι.

if he was a god he could not share the company of the dead ancestors. This rule was in fact observed at Augustus' funeral.[1]

A related privilege was the representation on coins. The moneyers of 44 had already adopted that, and it was, as we have seen, a radical innovation.[2] The murder created a new situation. It is a fact that in January 43 the Senate discussed matters of coinage,[3] and a probable conjecture that it decided against the practice of 44. At any rate, the moneyers who can safely be attributed to 43 did not show Caesar's head.[4] It reappeared on the coins of 42 and later, which must, then, have been the result of a relevant decree at the time of the consecration. This sequence of events can be true only if two problematic issues are satisfactorily explained, a *denarius* of L. Flaminius Chilo and an *aureus* of Octavian. Flaminius Chilo has not yet got a safe place in the chronology of the moneyers: he has been attributed to 44, 43, and 42.[5] His *denarius* shows Caesar's head on the obverse and Pax with caduceus on the reverse (pl. 29. 9).[6] It was, of course, the head that led to the dating in 44; but it had to be assumed that he was then the fifth moneyer that year and that one of the four had to be replaced in the course of it. Pax on the reverse seemed to support this contention, because it could be connected with the head of Pax on the *quinarius* of L. Aemilius Buca.[7] Moreover, a Flaminius (Chilo) was active in 44 as a candidate for the tribunate and perished in the proscriptions of 43.[8] The second dating, in 43, is possible in so far as a place among the moneyers is available. But the representation of Caesar's head would isolate him from his colleagues and could not be further supported except by the *aureus* of Octavian; so this date must remain for the moment open. The attribution to 42 in turn could be justified in the same manner as that to 44: there would again have been a supernumerary moneyer. It could be supported by the fact that Flaminius, like the moneyers of 42 and in contrast to those of 44, shows Caesar's head without legend; the caduceus too can be found on the coins of 42, though not the figure of Pax.[9]

The other problematic issue is the *aureus* of Octavian (pl. 29. 10).[10]

---

[1] Dio 56. 34. 2.   [2] See above, p. 274.   [3] Cic. *Phil.* 7. 1.

[4] P. Accoleius Lariscolus and Petillius Capitolinus, Sydenham 187; for the dating see Crawford, op. cit., table XV.

[5] Mommsen, *Röm. Münzwesen* 658. 558 (44); Grueber, Alföldi (n. 6), and Crawford (43); Sydenham (42); even 45 has been proposed, see Münzer, *RE* 6. 2503.

[6] Sydenham 180. 1089; pl. 28. 1089; Alföldi, *Nederl. Kunsthist. Jaarb. 5 (Festschr. A. W. Byvanck)*, 1954, 163; pl. 3. 4–8; 4. 1–4.

[7] Sydenham 177. 1065; above, p. 269.

[8] App. *BC* 3. 31. 120; 4. 27. 117; Münzer, l.c.; Broughton 2. 325 and Suppl. 25.

[9] L. Mussidius Longus and L. Livineius Regulus, Sydenham 181. 1092; 183. 1106; above, p. 43. 9.   [10] Sydenham 206. 1321; pl. 30. 1321.

It shows the head of Octavian on the obverse, that of Caesar on the reverse. As Octavian is styled *consul, pontifex,* and *augur,* the coin must have been issued between August 43, when he became consul, and November 43, when he became a *triumvir.*[1] And yet it is attributed to 40 with the argument that the term 'consul' is only commemorative of his having held that office.[2] This is not a convincing contention and is further weakened by the fact that on this coin Octavian is not styled *triumvir* as he often was about 40. The attribution to 43 is therefore to be preferred, which leads to an important conclusion. Immediately after entering office as consul, Octavian took the initiative and restored Caesar's image to the coins; he will have produced a decree of the Senate to this effect. The decree of 42, the existence of which we had to assume above, was, then, only sanctioning his action of a few months earlier; this time, however, he had the support of Antony and Lepidus. The *aureus* is important also for the case of Flaminius Chilo. He could have been, after all, one of the moneyers of 43, the only one who followed Octavian's lead in representing Caesar on his coins. Similar issues followed later at Rome as well as in the provinces,[3] all ultimately depending on Octavian's initiative. It was no longer, as in 44, a privilege of the ruler but an honour for the new god. The star was added to it only on a coin of Agrippa in 38 and on a provincial issue which followed his example.[4] In the imperial period it became a symbol of the consecrated rulers and of those for whom divinity was claimed.[5]

Further, the right of asylum was granted to the temple. Whoever sought refuge there could not be driven or dragged away.[6] This was new at Rome;[7] but it was suggested above that it had already been planned by Caesar for the temple of the Clementia Caesaris.[8] It was also prepared by one of the last decrees before his death, which provided that nobody should be harmed who took refuge with him.[9] The right of

---

[1] Crawford 3 and table XVII.   [2] Thus Grueber 2. 404. 2 and Sydenham.

[3] See below, pp. 399; 404; 407 ff.

[4] Sydenham 207. 1329; above, p. 378; on the provincial issue (Gaul) see below, p. 408.

[5] See above, p. 381.

[6] Dio 47. 19. 2: ἀπηγόρευσαν δὲ μηδένα ἐς τὸ ἡρῷον αὐτοῦ καταφυγόντα ἐπ' ἀδείᾳ μήτε ἀνδρηλατεῖσθαι μήτε συλᾶσθαι; App. *BC* 2. 144. 602; v. Premerstein 35.

[7] On the alleged asylum of Romulus see Schwegler, *Röm. Gesch.* 1. 464 ff.; Latte, *Gnom.* 26 (1954), 19; on Greek influence at the temple of Feronia at Terracina (Serv. *Aen.* 8. 564) see Latte 190.

[8] See above, p. 272. The right of asylum may be the answer to the question as to why Caesar's *flamen* had the oak wreath as a symbol of his office (as is to be inferred from the fact that the *flamen Augustalis* had it, Tac. *A.* 2. 83. 2; *Tab. Heb.* [E.–J. 94a] 51; *JRS* 47 (1957), 152): he inherited it from Caesar, the *pater patriae,* as saviour of the citizens (above, pp. 202 f.), to indicate that he was now the protector of those in distress.

[9] App. *BC* 2. 144. 602.

PLATE 29

1. As of Tiberius, c. A.D. 15–16 (Mattingly I. 141. 151), Oxford; obv.: radiate head of Augustus with star over it and thunderbolt on l., legend 'Divus Augustus Pater'; rev.: seated female figure with sceptre and patera, legend 'S.C.'; p. 384.

2. Cameo in the Kunsthistorisches Museum, Vienna (Eichler–Kris, Die Kameen im Kunsthist. Mus. 57): Livia as Cybele, with mural crown, tympanum, corn-ears, and poppy, holds a radiate bust of Augustus; p. 384.

3. Aureus of Caligula, A.D. 37–8 (Mattingly I. 146. 2), Oxford; obv.: head of Caligula, legend 'C. Caesar Aug. Germ., p. m., tr. pot., cos.'; rev.: radiate head of Augustus between two stars; pp. 381; 384.

4. Aureus of M. Durmius, 18 B.C. (Mattingly I. 10. 51), London; obv.: head of Honos between two stars, legend 'M. Durmius III vir Honori'; rev.: legend 'Augusto ob c(ivis) s(ervatos)' in oak-wreath; p. 379. 4.

5. Restored aureus of Trajan, A.D. 107 (?) (Mattingly 3. 143. 702), London; obv.: head of Vespasian, legend 'Divus Vespasianus'; rev.: heads of Mercury (with caduceus) and Iuppiter(?) over a large star, legend 'Imp. Caes. Traian. Aug. Ger. Dac., p. p., rest(ituit)'; p. 381. 5.

6. Dupondius of Claudius, A.D. 41–2 (Mattingly I. 195. 224), Oxford; obv.: radiate head of Augustus, legend 'Divus Augustus, S.C.'; rev.: Livia seated with torch and corn-ears, legend 'Diva Augusta'; p. 384.

7. Dupondius of Nero, A.D. 64–6 (Mattingly I. 240. 210), Paris; obv.: radiate head of Nero, legend 'Nero Claud. Caesar Aug. Ger., p. m., tr. p., imp., p. p.'; rev.: helmeted Roma, seated on a cuirass with foot on helmet, holds Victoria and sword, legend 'Roma, S.C.'; p. 384.

8. Dupondius of Nero, A.D. 64–6 (Mattingly I. 239. 202), Oxford; obv.: radiate head of Nero r. (not l.), legend 'Imp. Nero Claud. Caesar Aug. Ger., p. m., tr. p., p. p.'; rev.: temple of Ianus, legend 'Pace p. R. ubiq. parta Ianum clusit, S.C.'; p. 384.

9. Denarius of L. Flaminius Chilo, 43 B.C. (Sydenham 180. 1089), Oxford; obv.: head of Caesar; rev.: Pax with sceptre and caduceus, legend 'L. Flaminius IIII vir'; p. 394.

10. Aureus of Octavian, 43 B.C. (Sydenham 206. 1321), Oxford; obv.: head of Octavian, legend 'C. Caesar cos. pont(ifex) aug(ur)'; rev.: head of Caesar, legend 'C. Caesar dict. perp., pont. max.'; p. 394.

11. Cameo in the Diözesanmuseum, Cologne (Möbius, Arch. Anz. 1948–9 112 ff.; photo: Professor T. Dohrn, Cologne): Nero-Iuppiter with aegis, sceptre, eagle, and a star over his head is crowned by a goddess who holds a cornucopiae; pp. 382; 384.

12. Bronze of Philippi, c. 2 B.C. (?) (Grant, FITA 275), London; obv.: head of Augustus, legend 'Col(onia) Aug(usta) Iul(ia) Phil(ippi) iussu Aug(usti)'; rev.: Augustus and Caesar on a cippus, in front of them an altar, legend 'Aug. Divi f. Divo Iul(io)'; pp. 401 f.

13. Denarius of Augustus, issued at Ephesus, 19–18 B.C. (Mattingly I. 114. 705), Oxford; obv.: head of Augustus, legend 'imp. IX, tr. po. V'; rev.: hexastyle temple inscribed 'Rom(ae) et August(o)', legend 'Com(mune) Asiae'; p. 403.

PLATE 29

asylum existed at many Greek temples, also at the temples and statues of the Hellenistic monarchs.[1] Caesar himself had settled the problems of asylum at the temple of Aphrodite at Aphrodisias in Caria and at that of Apollo at Didyma,[2] his lieutenant P. Servilius Isauricus at Hierocaesarea and Pergamum,[3] Antony at Ephesus.[4] The new right of asylum was extended to Caesar's statues, probably by the *lex Rufrena* mentioned above;[5] this created additional security in places where there was no temple. In 30 B.C. the son of Antony fled at Alexandria to the statue of Divus Iulius, but was dragged away by Octavian and killed,[6] which was, of course, an offence. The same right of asylum was later granted to Augustus' statues at Rome as well as in the provinces,[7] then to those of his successors.[8] Caesar's idea was of the greatest importance. It strengthened the authority of Rome since her subjects, especially in the provinces, could turn for immediate relief not just to old-established sanctuaries but to the shrines of the emperors, dead or alive.

Caesar's birthday was to be celebrated annually.[9] This had already been decreed in 45[10] but was probably omitted in 44 and 43. Now the decree was renewed, but the celebration was moved on the advice of a Sibylline oracle from 13 to 12 July, in order to avoid a collision with the principal day of the *ludi Apollinares*.[11] It was an obligatory festival and people wore laurel wreaths; and it was observed all through the imperial period.[12] Its significance and its consequences have already been explained. By contrast, when Antony died in 30 it was decreed that his birthday should become a sinister day, a *dies vitiosus*.[13] He had been a public enemy whereas Caesar was judged to be a god. The 'birthday' of the temple was celebrated on a different day, 18 August, which was the day of its dedication in 29.[14] The day of the murder, on the other

---

[1] Cf. Latte, *Heil. Recht* 106 ff.; Schlesinger, *Die griech. Asylie* (1933), 71 ff.; Rostovtzeff, *Social and Econ. Hist. of the Hell. World*, passim; Nilsson 1. 77 f.; 84 f.; 2. 151; 154; 156; L. Robert, *Hellenica* 6 (1948), 34 ff.

[2] Tac. *A.* 3. 62. 2 f.; *Or. gr.* 473; Rehm, *Inschr. v. Didyma* 391 A II; L. Robert, op. cit., 37 and *Ant. Class.* 35 (1966), 416. 1.

[3] Tac. *A.* 3. 62. 4; L. Robert, op. cit., 37 ff.

[4] Strab. 14. 641.

[5] See above, p. 303. 9; Rufrenus, a supporter of Antony, was in the army of Lepidus in 43 (Cic. *fam.* 10. 21. 4) and as author of this law he could have been *tribunus plebis* in 42: Münzer, *RE* 1A. 1200 f.

[6] Suet. *Aug.* 17. 5; Dio 51. 15. 5.

[7] Tac. *A.* 3. 36. 1; 4. 67. 6; 3. 63. 3; Suet. *Tib.* 53. 2; 58.

[8] Mommsen, *StR* 2. 760. 1; *Strafr.* 460; 585. [9] Dio 47. 18. 5 (above, p. 207. 1).

[10] Dio 44. 4. 4. [11] Dio 47. 18. 6; above, p. 157.

[12] See above, pp. 206 f.

[13] Dio 51. 19. 3; *F. Praen.*; *F. Verul.* 14 Jan. (Degrassi 397); cf. Plut. *Cic.* 49. 6; Leuze, *Bursians Jahresber.* 227 (1930), 110; above, p. 209. 7.

[14] Dio 51. 22. 2; *F. Ant. min.* (Degrassi 497).

hand, was called the Parricidium and became a *dies nefastus*;[1] it was commemorated with a gruesome sacrifice in 40 at Perusia.[2]

Another Caesarian innovation was confirmed by the clause about the supplications.[3] They were to be held in his honour whenever a victory was reported, as decreed in 45. This meant that all victories were Caesar's victories because he alone was the supreme commander. With his death such supplications naturally came to an end. And yet Antony renewed them in September 44[4] clearly with the intention of uniting the various Caesarian factions and of assuring continuity, which was the purpose of the confirmation of Caesar's acts as well. The renewal by the *triumviri* in 42 will have had the same aim: all three were bound to conduct Caesar's war against the conspirators. This scheme did not last; after the victory at Philippi supplications were held only in honour of the *triumviri*.[5] But later Caesar's privilege was renewed for Augustus and his successors.[6]

3. THE CULT IN ROME

It is probable that nothing further was undertaken until the battle of Philippi. Antony then remained in the East, Octavian returned to Rome, and both began to organize the cult in their territories.[7] But the concord was shattered by the Perusine War, of which two incidents are relevant here. Octavian fought in the name of the new god: during the siege of Perusia the missiles of his eleventh legion bore the inscription 'Divom Iulium'.[8] After the surrender he slaughtered many senators and knights,[9] but certainly not as many as three hundred,[10] at the altar

---

[1] Dio 47. 19. 1; Suet. *Caes.* 88: 'placuit Idusque Martias Parricidium nominari, ac ne umquam eo die senatus ageretur'; cf. Cic. *fam.* 12. 3. 1; Val. Max. 1. 8. 8; Flor. 2. 17. 1; Degrassi 423; above p. 190. 3.　　　　　　　　　　　　　　　[2] See below, p. 399.

[3] Dio 47. 18. 4: εἴ τε νίκη τις ἠγγέλθη ποθέν, χωρὶς μὲν τῷ κρατήσαντι, χωρὶς δὲ ἐκείνῳ καὶ τεθνεῶτι τιμὴν ἱερομηνίας ἔνεμον; cf. the supplications held by Tiberius in A.D. 16 after the suppression of the conspiracy, and the death, of Scribonius Libo, Dio 57. 15. 5: καὶ θυσίας ἐπ' αὐτῷ οὐχ ἑαυτοῦ μόνον ἕνεκα ἀλλὰ καὶ τοῦ Αὐγούστου τοῦ τε πατρὸς αὐτοῦ τοῦ 'Ιουλίου, καθάπερ ποτὲ ἐδέδοκτο, ψηφισθῆναι ἐποίησε; cf. 54. 3. 8.

[4] Dio 43. 44. 6; 45. 7. 2; Cic. *Phil.* 1. 12; 5. 19; above, p. 107. 9.

[5] Dio 48. 3. 2. A further festival, which had been vowed for the completion of the war, was held in 40 after the peace of Brundisium by the consuls L. Cornelius Balbus and P. Canidius Crassus, Dio 48. 32. 4. No details are given.

[6] Dio 54. 3. 8; 57. 15. 5; above, n. 3.　　　　　　　　　[7] See below, pp. 401 ff.; 407 ff.

[8] *Eph. Epigr.* 6. 59, no. 64 = Degr. 1116.

[9] Suet. *Aug.* 15: 'scribunt quidam trecentos ex dediticiis electos utriusque ordinis ad aram Divo Iulio extructam Idibus Martiis hostiarum more mactatos'; Sen. *clem.* 1. 11. 1: 'Perusinas aras'; Dio 48. 14. 4; App. *BC* 4. 48. 203 (does not mention the altar); cf. Vell. 2. 74. 4; Drumann–Groebe 1. 475 ff.

[10] This figure is given by Suetonius and Dio. In fact 'trecenti' can mean, like 'sescenti' or 'mille', an indefinite large number. Exaenetus was followed by 300 youths into Acragas

of Divus Iulius on 15 March 40. This slaughter becomes credible[1] when
one reads Valerius Maximus' chapter *De crudelitate*:[2] how, for instance,
after the victory of Sulla in 82 M. Marius Gratidianus was slaughtered
at the tomb of Q. Lutatius Catulus by the son of the latter.[3] Later
Cicero claimed that the Catilinarians would have slaughtered him at
the tomb of Catilina had they been successful.[4] After Caesar's triumph
in 46 two rioting soldiers were executed and their heads set up at the
Regia.[5] The heads of Helvius and Cornelius Cinna fixed on a spear were
carried round Caesar's pyre;[6] Brutus' head was sent to Rome to be
cast at the feet of Caesar's statue,[7] and this was done by Dolabella with
Trebonius' head at Caesar's statue at Smyrna.[8] Thus the incident at
Perusia was not isolated. It was the survival of a human sacrifice in
honour of the dead. Achilles killed twelve Trojans at the pyre of
Patroclus,[9] Aeneas eight captives at the pyre of Pallas.[10] It was a practice
which the Romans learnt from the Etruscans but soon replaced with
gladiatorial combats at the funeral games.[11]

The concord was restored with the peace of Brundisium. Octavian
began to call himself officially 'Divi filius'[12] and Antony was inaugurated
as *flamen Divi Iulii* at his request.[13] The organization of the cult was
carried on, and the head of Divus Iulius appeared on coins issued in
Rome and elsewhere (pl. 30. 6–8).[14] Octavian began to build the temple
c. 36, which is the date of a coin showing its projected form.[15] At any
rate, after the Actian victory the building must have been accelerated,

(Diod. 13. 82. 7), Romulus left a guard of 300 men at Fidenae (Dion. Hal. 2. 53. 4), Catullus
speaks of 300 adulterers and of 300 verses (11. 18; 12. 10, with Kroll's notes), Horace of
300 persons on a ship (*sat.* 1. 5. 12), Vergil of 300 temples dedicated by Augustus after
Actium (*Aen.* 8. 716); cf. *Georg.* 1. 15; *Aen.* 4. 510; 7. 275; 9. 370; 10. 182; Wölfflin, *Arch.
Lat. Lex.* 9 (1896), 188 ff.

[1] The evidence is rejected by Reid, *JRS* 2 (1912), 42 ff.   [2] Val. Max. 9. 2. 1.
[3] Cf. Münzer, *RE* 14. 1827.   [4] Cic. *Pis.* 16 (with Nisbet's note).
[5] Dio 43. 24. 3 (above, p. 79. 1).   [6] Val. Max. 9. 9. 1.
[7] Suet. *Aug.* 13. 1.   [8] Dio 47. 29. 2.
[9] Hom. *Il.* 18. 336; 21. 26; 23. 174; 180.
[10] Verg. *Aen.* 10. 517 ff.; 11. 81 f.; inspired, according to Heinze, *Virgils epische Technik*
210. 2, by the incident at Perusia.
[11] Serv. Dan. *Aen.* 3. 67 (Varro); Serv. *Aen.* 10. 519; Tert. *spect.* 12; Schwenn, *Menschenopfer*
173; Malten, *Röm. Mitt.* 38/9 (1923/4), 317; 330.
[12] *F.Triumph.* (Degrassi, *Inscr. It.* 13. 1. 87): 'Imp. Caesar Divi f. (C. f.) IIIvir r.p.c. ovans an.
DCCXIII quod pacem cum M. Antonio fecit'; Mommsen, *StR* 2. 756. 1. He would already
have done this three years earlier, if Alföldi, *Nederlands Kunsthist. Jaarboek* 5 (*Festschr. A. W.
Byvanck*), 1954, 163 ff., were right in attributing the coins of Ti. Sempronius Gracchus and
Q. Voconius Vitulus (Sydenham 184 f.) with the legend 'Divi f.' to 43 B.C. But he has not
proved his case, so that the traditional date of the coins after the peace of Brundisium remains; cf. Crawford, op. cit., Table XV.
[13] Plut. *Ant.* 33. 1: Ἀντώνιος ... Καίσαρι χαριζόμενος ἱερεὺς ἀπεδείχθη τοῦ προτέρου Καίσαρος.
[14] See above, pp. 299; 378; and below, pp. 408; 410.
[15] Sydenham 208; Grueber, pl. 122. 4; above, p. 378.

and the temple was dedicated immediately after the triumph on 18 August 29, which recalls the synchronization of Caesar's triumph in 46 with the dedication of the temple of Venus Genetrix.[1]

The temple consisted of two parts, a rectangular platform and the temple proper.[2] This platform had two unusual features. In the centre at the front there was a niche and within it a round altar.[3] That is to say, the altar of 44 was preserved[4] and incorporated in the building in this fashion. Secondly, the platform was decorated with beaks of ships captured at Actium:[5] it thus became the Rostra Iulia, a new platform for the orators,[6] which did not replace the old republican Rostra but was used in addition to it. The question naturally arises of why it was done. The probable answer is that it took the place of the Tribunal Aurelium, another platform where speeches were delivered to an audience assembled on the Gradus Aurelii nearby.[7] It had probably been built by M. Aurelius Cotta (cos. 74); it is mentioned a few times by Cicero[8] and then never again; it will have been demolished when the temple of Divus Iulius was built on its site, and reappeared finally as the Rostra Iulia. This Rostra cannot have been planned or even erected by Caesar.[9] It was he who transferred the old Rostra to its present place when he began to build the Curia Iulia[10]; he sat there at the memorable Lupercalia of 44, and Antony delivered his funeral oration there.[11] Nor did Augustus intend to replace it; on the contrary, he enlarged it, and it remained the principal Rostra of the imperial period.[12] Thus we need not search further. The temple of Divus Iulius was the only temple in Rome which had a Rostra, the importance of which was in turn enhanced by this connection; it was used, naturally, at the funerals of the family, but also on other occasions. But however

[1] See above, pp. 76; 82.

[2] Platner–Ashby 286 f.; Stucchi, *I monumenti della parte meridionale del Foro Romano* (1958), 11 ff.; B. Andreae, *Arch. Anz.* 72 (1957), 158 ff.; Nash 1. 512 ff.

[3] See n. 2; also Lugli, *Monumenti minori del Foro Romano* (1947), 58 f.

[4] See above, pp. 364 ff.

[5] Dio 51. 19. 2: τήν τε κρηπῖδα τοῦ Ἰουλιείου ἡρῴου τοῖς τῶν αἰχμαλωτίδων νεῶν ἐμβόλοις κοσμηθῆναι.

[6] Frontin. *aqu.* 129: 'in Foro pro Rostris aedis Divi Iulii' (9 B.C.); Dio 56. 34. 4 (A.D. 14): ἀπὸ δὲ τῶν ἑτέρων Ἐμβόλων τῶν Ἰουλιείων; cf. Suet. *Aug.* 100. 3; Dio 54. 35. 4; Strack, op. cit. 2. 114. 247; Lugli, op. cit. 54 ff.

[7] Platner–Ashby 539 f.; Lugli, op. cit. 74 ff.; Welin, *Studien z. Topographie des Forum Romanum* (1953), 104 ff.; Romanelli, *Gnom.* 26 (1954), 259; Nash 2. 478.

[8] Cic. *p. red. Quir.* 13; *dom.* 54; *Sest.* 34; *Pis.* 11.—Gradus Aurelii: Cic. *Cluent.* 93; *Flacc.* 66.

[9] This would have been the case if Livy were right, *Per.* 116: 'Caesaris corpus . . . a plebe ante Rostra crematum est'; accepted by Platner–Ashby 287; for a different view see Stucchi, op. cit. 76 ff. The reference cannot, of course, be to the republican Rostra.

[10] Dio 43. 49. 1; cf. Ascon. *Mil.* 12 (p. 37 St.); Diod. 12. 26. 1; Dio 44. 5. 1.

[11] See above, pp. 331; 350 f.   [12] Cf. Platner–Ashby 452; Nash 2. 276 ff.

singular it was, it hardly had any extraordinary or even religious significance.

The temple had its proper place in public life after its dedication. A new *flamen Divi Iulii* was appointed in place of Antony, Sextus Appuleius, Augustus' brother-in-law.[1] It had its festivals, priest, privileges. Augustus deposited spoils there in 29 B.C.[2] and probably transferred the *quadrigae* of 46 to it from the Capitol;[3] a marble statue of L. Volusius Saturninus (*cos.* A.D. 56) stood in the temple,[4] and the Arvals had their meeting there in A.D. 69.[5] There is evidence about it in the age of Hadrian,[6] but there is no doubt that it existed, and was cared for, until the end of antiquity.

4. THE CULT IN ITALY AND THE PROVINCES

It will be recalled that the first moves towards a cult were made after the victory at Pharsalus.[7] Coins were issued with Caesar's image and statues were set up in his honour; he was styled on inscriptions a founder, saviour, benefactor, even a god; and he was associated with the Dea Roma. The colonies founded by him were particularly prominent in spreading his cult, and he himself took the initiative by building Caesarea at Alexandria, Antiochia, and no doubt elsewhere. A great deal will have been achieved while he was still alive; he may have planned more, but a systematic organization had certainly not yet been started.

The cult was officially decreed at Rome in 44, if not already in 45, which implies detailed plans.[8] Caesar himself as *pontifex maximus* had appointed Antony as his *flamen*, so that probably Antony would have been in charge of the organization of the cult. But he was not inaugurated[9] until October 40 when peace was restored between him and Octavian at Brundisium.[10] And yet he had begun the organization in the East earlier, soon after the victory at Philippi. At Philippi itself he and Octavian together created a colony and instituted the cult of

---

[1] *ILS* 8963; M. W. H. Lewis, *The Official Priests of Rome under the Julio-Claudians* (1955), 37; 77; cf. *JRS* 47 (1957), 151.

[2] *Mon. Anc.* 21. 2; Dio 51. 22. 3.   [3] See above, p. 59. 2.

[4] Inscription from Lucus Feroniae, M. Moretti, *Autostrade* 10. 8. 1968, 10.

[5] Henzen, *AFA* 151.

[6] Mattingly 3. 433; pl. 81. 10; Strack, op. cit. 2. 114; pl. 9. 599; Bernhart, *Handb. z. Münzkunde d. röm. Kaiserzeit*, pl. 78. 2; Stucchi, op. cit. 43, fig. 16; 80, fig. 34. It is probably also represented on one of the 'Plutei Traiani'(e.g. Nash 2. 176); *contra*, Platner–Ashby 454; Stucchi, op. cit. 80 ff. The difficulty is the sloping steps at the back of the platform, which are not possible for the temple of Divus Iulius.

[7] See above, p. 296.   [8] See above, pp. 287 ff.

[9] Dio 44. 6. 4; Cic. *Phil.* 2. 110.   [10] Plut. *Ant.* 33. 1; above, p. 392.

Divus Iulius (pl. 29, 12).[1] He then remained in the East and undertook a great deal of administrative work.[2] He was at Ephesus in 41, and a fragment of a precious document, found at Ephesus,[3] shows what he did there. He must have done it at that time, because he was not at Ephesus again until 33/32 B.C.

$$
\begin{array}{lll}
 &]\theta\acute{\epsilon}\lambda\epsilon\tau\epsilon\ \kappa\epsilon\lambda\epsilon\acute{\upsilon}\epsilon\tau\epsilon,\ \acute{\iota}\nu\alpha\ M\hat{\alpha}\rho\kappa\sigma s\ \mathring{A}\nu\text{-} \\
[\tau\acute{\omega}\nu\iota\sigma s &]\epsilon\mathring{\iota}\tau\epsilon\ \tau\iota\ \acute{\upsilon}\pi\grave{\epsilon}\rho\ \tau\alpha\acute{\upsilon}\tau\eta s\ \langle\tau\hat{\eta}s\rangle\ \acute{\iota}\epsilon\rho\omega\sigma\acute{\upsilon}\nu\eta s\ \tau\epsilon\text{-} \\
[\lambda\epsilon\hat{\iota}\nu\,? & \acute{\iota}\epsilon\rho\sigma\mu]\nu\eta\mu\sigma\nu\acute{\iota}\alpha\nu\ \theta\epsilon\sigma\hat{\upsilon}\ \mathring{I}\sigma\upsilon\lambda\acute{\iota}\sigma\upsilon\ \mu\epsilon\tau\grave{\alpha}\ \pi\sigma\text{-} \\
 &]\tau\epsilon\ \pi\sigma\hat{\eta},\ \mu\acute{\eta}\tau\epsilon\ \tau\iota s\ \tau\sigma\acute{\upsilon}\tau\omega\nu\ \tau\iota\nu\grave{\alpha}\ \tau\hat{\omega}\nu \\
5 &]\omega\nu\ \pi\rho\grave{\sigma}s\ \tau\alpha\acute{\upsilon}\tau\eta\nu\ \tau\grave{\eta}\nu\ \acute{\iota}\epsilon\rho\sigma\mu\nu\eta\mu[\sigma]\text{-} \\
[\nu\acute{\iota}\alpha\nu & \pi\alpha]\rho\acute{\epsilon}\chi\epsilon\iota\nu\ \tau\sigma\acute{\upsilon}\tau\omega\nu\ \tau\hat{\omega}\nu\ \delta\iota\delta\acute{\sigma}\nu\tau\omega\nu\ \mathring{\eta}\ \upsilon\text{-} \\
 &]\mathring{\eta}\nu\ \tau\grave{\eta}\nu\ \acute{\epsilon}\rho\acute{\omega}\tau\eta\sigma\iota\nu\ \pi\sigma\acute{\eta}\sigma\eta\ \mathring{\eta}\ \gamma[..]\text{-} \\
 & \sigma\omega\tau\hat{\eta}]\rho\iota\ \mu\acute{\sigma}\nu\eta\ \tau\epsilon\ \alpha\mathring{\iota}\tau\acute{\iota}\alpha\ \pi\acute{\alpha}\nu\tau\omega[\nu\ \tau\hat{\omega}\nu] \\
[\mathring{\alpha}\gamma\alpha\theta\hat{\omega}\nu\ \theta\epsilon\hat{\omega}\ \mathring{I}\sigma\upsilon\lambda\acute{\iota}\omega\ldots]
\end{array}
$$

The first words in l. 1 $\theta\acute{\epsilon}\lambda\epsilon\tau\epsilon\ \kappa\epsilon\lambda\epsilon\acute{\upsilon}\epsilon\tau\epsilon$ stand for the frequent Latin phrase 'velitis iubeatis'[4] and suggest that we are dealing with an official document, probably a letter from the Senate. Its bearer is Antony and the addressee cannot have been the Ephesians alone but the whole League, the Koinon of Asia, because in l. 3 $\acute{\iota}\epsilon\rho\sigma\mu\nu\eta\mu\sigma\nu\acute{\iota}\alpha$[5] refers to the delegates of its constituent cities. The suggestions of the Senate concern a priesthood, $\acute{\iota}\epsilon\rho\omega\sigma\acute{\upsilon}\nu\eta$, and the cult of Divus Iulius; $\tau\epsilon\lambda\epsilon\hat{\iota}\nu$ (?) in ll. 2 f. and $\delta\iota\delta\acute{\sigma}\nu\tau\omega\nu$ in l. 6 seem to indicate financial contributions by the members. The rest is not clear, except the end: the common cult and the festival was to be established in honour of the Saviour and Benefactor, Divus Iulius.[6]

The Romans found free cities, leagues, and kingdoms in the East which had their own individual traditions and organizations, and also the cult of the Hellenistic rulers.[7] Roman rule brought some changes. There were now client kingdoms, leagues, free and federated cities, and

---

[1] A coin of Philippi, issued after 27 B.C., shows the head of Augustus on the obv., Augustus and Caesar standing on a *cippus*, with an altar before it and the legend 'Divo Iulio Aug. Divi f.', on the rev., Grant, op. cit. 275; pl. 9. 22; Vittinghoff 128. According to Collart, *Philippes*, 238 it is the emperor crowned by the Genius of the city (not convincing).

[2] Cf. *Or. gr.* 454–6; E.–J. 300; H. Buchheim, *Die Orientpolitik des . . . M. Antonius* (1960), 11 f.; Deininger, *Die Provinziallandtage d. röm. Kaiserzeit* (1965), 16.

[3] J. Keil, *Forsch. aus Ephesos*, 4. 3 (1951), 280 f., no. 24, with full supplements *exempli gratia* in order to help the understanding of the inscription; above, only those supplements are adopted which seem to be certain. The inscription is briefly mentioned by Latte 302. 3.

[4] See, e.g., Gell. 5. 19. 9; Cic. *dom.* 44; *Pis.* 72; Mommsen, *StR* 3. 312. 2.

[5] This term, the office of the $\acute{\iota}\epsilon\rho\sigma\mu\nu\acute{\eta}\mu\sigma\nu\epsilon s$, has not yet been found elsewhere.

[6] Cf. *IGR* 4. 982 (Samos, Livia's father): $\mu\epsilon\gamma\acute{\iota}\sigma\tau\omega\nu\ \mathring{\alpha}\gamma\alpha\theta\hat{\omega}\nu\ \alpha\mathring{\iota}\tau\iota\sigma\nu\ \gamma\epsilon\gamma\sigma\nu\acute{\sigma}\tau\alpha\ \tau\hat{\omega}\ \kappa\acute{\sigma}\sigma\mu\omega$.

[7] See above, p. 314.

Roman colonies and *municipia*.[1] Roman supremacy had found its religious expression in the gradual creation of the cult of the Dea Roma in the cities and Koina since the beginning of the second century B.C., with statues, altars, and temples, priests, and games.[2] Ephesus too will have had an early cult of the Dea Roma, at least since the creation of the province of Asia in 134 B.C. A priest, ἱερεύς, is recorded for 94/93 B.C.[3] and games, 'Ρωμαῖα, on an undated inscription of the imperial period.[4]

Caesar, the 'manifest god', was represented at Ephesus with a statue as early as 48 B.C.[5] There is relevant evidence of later date. In 29 Augustus allowed the dedication of a shrine to Dea Roma and Divus Iulius at Ephesus for the use of the resident Roman citizens.[6] In 19/18 a coin was issued with a hexastyle temple bearing the inscription 'Rom(ae) et August(i)' and with the legend 'Com(mune) Asiae' (pl. 29. 13);[7] in 5 B.C. Augustus authorized the building of a wall round the temple of Artemis and the Augusteum.[8] The following sequence of events may be suggested on the basis of this evidence. There was first a temple of Dea Roma at Ephesus, which received a statue of Caesar in 48 and his cult after 40; it may also have been renamed a Caesareum or replaced by one. In 29 the Roman citizens either were allowed to have a share in this cult of the Koinon or built their own temple. In 19/18 the Koinon either built a new temple for Roma and Augustus and called it Augusteum, or rebuilt and renamed the old one, incorporating, however, the cult of Divus Iulius. The cult will have had a similar history in many other places. This suggestion rests on some odd fragments, on the popularity of the cult in the colonies, which will be discussed presently, and on an inference from the widespread cult of Augustus, which may have had Caesarian roots in some places. Of the odd fragments one, a passage in Pausanias, refers to a temple at Sparta;[9] another passage and an inscription suggests that Smyrna, which possessed the earliest temple of Dea Roma, was also one of the first to adopt

---

[1] Larsen, *Representative Government in Greek and Roman History* (1955), 106 ff.; Deininger, op. cit. (with bibliography).

[2] Smyrna, 195 B.C. (Tac. *A.* 4. 56. 1); Antiochia-on-Maeander, soon afterwards (inscr. from Samos, Habicht, *Ath. Mitt.* 72 (1957), 242. 1. 6; cf. 250); Lycian Koinon, *c.* 189 B.C. (inscription from Araxa, Bean, *JHS* 68 (1948), 46 ff. [= *SEG* 18. 570]; for later mentions of priests of Roma in the Lycian Koinon see *IGR* 3. 474; 490; 595); Caunus, *c.* 189 (*SEG* 12. 466); Cibyra, *c.* 189 (*Or. gr.* 762. 14 f.); Alabanda, 170 (Livy 43. 6. 5; Head, *HN* 607); Ephesus (below, nn. 3–5); cf. Richter, *Myth. Lex.* 4. 131 f.; Larsen, *Mél. Piganiol* (1966), 1635 ff.

[3] *Or. gr.* 437. 89 f. (*IGR* 4. 297); cf. *Ephesos* 2. 153, no. 30 (first cent. B.C.).

[4] *IGR* 4. 1262.   [5] *Syll.* 760 (above, p. 296. 9).

[6] Dio 51. 20. 6.

[7] Mattingly 1. 114; pl. 17. 13; cf. the Claudian coins, ibid. 196; pl. 34. 4.

[8] *ILS* 97.   [9] Paus. 3. 11. 4.

the cult of Divus Iulius;[1] lastly, a coin with the legend θεός (pl. 30. 1-2), testifies to an early cult at Thessalonica, another, already mentioned, with the legend 'Divo Iulio', to a cult at Philippi.[2]

As to the organization of the cult, later evidence helps again. It proves that the priesthood, ἱερωσύνη, mentioned in the letter of the Senate was that of an ἀρχιερεύς.[3] This was an anomaly. The priests of the Greek kings, Roman generals, and even Dea Roma, were always ἱερεῖς:[4] an ἀρχιερεύς existed only in Cyprus[5] and in the kingdom of the Seleucids.[6] Unless we assume a borrowing from either of these countries, the conclusion to be drawn is that ἀρχιερεύς was the translation of the Roman *flamen* right from the beginning, as in fact it was later.[7] If so, the further conclusion is unavoidable that Antony and the Ephesians were executing Caesar's plans. The decree of 44 for his *flamen*[8] became the model on which the later *flamines* depended. Consequently, his chief priest for the Koinon will have had the same or similar privileges as his *flamen* at Rome had, comparable to those which were, as we shall see, explicitly granted later to the provincial *flamen* of Gallia Narbonensis.[9] There was, however, one great difference from Rome: as a rule it was an annual, not a perpetual, priesthood.[10] These priests were elected by the delegates, ἱερομνήμονες,[11] of the constituent cities of the Koinon. They were, later at least, always distinguished citizens who often enjoyed the patronage of the imperial family: of the seventy or so known chief priests of Asia twelve had the name Iulius and eighteen Claudius.[12]

---

[1] A statue is mentioned by Dio (47. 29. 2) at which Dolabella hurled Trebonius' head in 42 B.C.; *ILS* 74: 'Divo Iulio civit(as) Zmyrnaeorum'; see above, pp. 314; 403. 2.

[2] *BMC Macedonia* 115; Kraft, l.c. 9; pl. 1. 5. (Octavian's head on obv., Caesar's head with the legend θεός on rev.). For Philippi see above, p. 402. 1; cf. also for Sandainae in Lydia *IGR* 4. 1155: ... ἱερατεύσαντα τά τε πρὸς τὸν θεὸν Καίσαρα; Oenoanda, *IGR* 3. 482: ἐπιστατήσας τοῦ Καίσαρος ναοῦ ... καὶ ἱερατεύσας Καίσαρος, τῷ Καίσαρι καὶ δήμῳ. It is, however, not certain whether these inscriptions refer to Caesar or Augustus.

[3] Cf. Brandis, *RE* 2. 471 ff.; on the related offices of Asiarches, Lyciarches, and the like, which are not relevant here, see Kornemann, *RE* Suppl. 4. 936; Magie, *Roman Rule* 1298 ff.; Nilsson 2. 386 f.; Deininger, op. cit., 43 ff.

[4] Plaumann, *RE* 8. 1424 ff.

[5] *Or. gr.* 56. 73; 140. 6; 148. 3; 152. 2; 155. 5; 158. 3; 159. 3, etc.; Brandis, *RE* 2. 471 ff.

[6] *Or. gr.* 224. 22; 230; Wilcken, *Sitz. Ber. Berl.* (1938), 318 f.; Nilsson 2. 168 f.

[7] Greek inscriptions call Q. Trebellius Rufus, the provincial *flamen* of Gallia Narbonensis, ἀρχιερέα πρῶτον ἐπαρχείας τῆς ἐκ Ναρβῶνος (*IG* 2². 4193; McCrum–Woodhead 129. 1 f.; 14 f.).

[8] See above, p. .   [9] See below, pp. 305 ff.; 409.

[10] One could hold the office more than once (*Or. gr.* 509; 767. 4; *IGR* 3. 364 f.; 831; *IG* 12. 3. 1119; more in F. Geiger, *De sacerdotibus Augustorum municipalibus* (1913), 55 f.) and, as an exceptional honour, for life (*Syll.* 790; *IGR* 4. 468; West, *Corinth*, no. 68), more often in the West (*Thes.L.L.* 6. 857. 43 ff. *flamen perpetuus*; Geiger, op. cit. 46 ff.).

[11] Hepding, *RE* 8. 1490 ff.

[12] See the list in Magie, *Roman Rule* 1601 ff.

The assemblies of the Koinon will have remained as they were before, with all their administrative and other tasks;[1] but the cult was now set within the framework. The financial contributions were also needed for this cult, especially for the organization of the games. These have already been discussed and were, it is important to note, equally connected with a decree issued in Rome in 44, this time about the *ludi quinquennales*.[2]

Colonies were always the strongholds of Roman power and influence, also of Roman cults. Accordingly, one would expect the Caesarian colonies not to lag behind the Greek Koina in promoting the cult of Divus Iulius. We have seen that some of them issued coins with Caesar's image while he was alive as did many more after his death.[3] For two of these, Alexandria in Troas and Corinth, there is also evidence about a local *flamen Divi Iulii*, which implies a cult in a temple or at least at an altar. The evidence is not of Caesarian date, but this fact does not exclude a Caesarian origin. A base set up in honour of C. Antonius Rufus, who was a *flamen Divi Iulii* at Alexandria in Troas, is decorated with an *apex* (pl. 31. 2),[4] the cap of a *flamen*, which suggests that he was not only dressed like the Roman *flamen* but also had some of his privileges. He was a distinguished citizen: he was also *flamen* of Augustus at Alexandria, Apri, and Philippi, and in addition the *princeps* of these colonies.[5] As we have seen, the cult in Corinth dates from the lifetime of Caesar;[6] the first priest was probably not yet a *flamen*, but those after Caesar's death certainly were. An important personality of the Neronian age, C. Iulius Spartiaticus, was the *flamen Divi Iulii* at Corinth and at the same time the first *archiereus* of the Domus Augusta for life in the Koinon of Achaea.[7] He thus had the same function both in the Roman colony and the Greek Koinon. The term 'Domus Augusta' clearly stands for the cult of the successive Divi: Caesar(?), Augustus, and Claudius. Spartiaticus was not the first high priest but

---

[1] Kornemann, *RE* Suppl. 4. 918 ff.; Habicht, 138 ff.; cf. Busolt, *Gr. Staatskunde* 1280–1575.

[2] See above, p. 316.   [3] See above, pp. 296 f.

[4] A. H. Smith, *Cat. of Greek Sculpture in the Brit. Mus.* 3. 427, no. 2621; Daremb.-Sagl. 2. 1179, fig. 3108. In the age of Augustus games were held at Alexandria in honour of Apollo and Paullus Fabius Maximus, the Σμίνθεια Παύλεια, *IGR* 4. 244; cf. *Prosopogr.* 2. 48, n. 38.

[5] *CIL* 3. 386 (*ILS* 2718): 'Divi Iuli flamini, C. Antonio M. f. Volt. Rufo, flamini Divi Aug. col. Cl. Aprensis et col. Iul. Philippens., eorundem et principi, item col. Iul. Parianae ...' On a *sacerdos Caesaris* at Parium see above, p. 299. 1.

[6] See above, p. 299.

[7] A. B. West, op. cit. 50, no. 68: 'C. Iulio ... Spartiatico ... flam. Divi Iuli, pontif. IIvir. quinq. iter. agonothete Isthmion et Caesa. Sebasteon, archieri Domus Aug. in perpetuum primo Achaeon ... tribules tribus Calpurniae patrono'; *Syll.* 790 (Athens): Γάιον Ἰούλιον Σπαρτιατικόν, ἀρχιερέα θεῶν Σεβαστῶν καὶ γένους Σεβαστῶν ἐκ τοῦ Κοινοῦ τῆς Ἀχαίας διὰ βίου πρῶτον τῶν ἀπ' αἰῶνος ...; Larsen, op. cit. 220. 16.

PLATE 30

1. Bronze of Thessalonica (*BMC Macedonia* 115), Oxford; *obv.*: head of Octavian, legend Θεσσαλονικέων; *rev.*: head of Caesar, legend θεός; p. 404.

2. The same, but legend of *rev.* on r.

3. Aes of Octavian, *c.* 38 B.C. (Sydenham 208. 1335), Oxford; *obv.*: head of Octavian, legend 'Caesar Divi f.'; *rev.*: head of Caesar, legend 'Divos Iulius'; p. 407.

4. Aes of Octavian, *c.* 38 B.C. (Sydenham 208. 1336), Oxford; *obv.*: head of Octavian, legend 'Divif.'; *rev.*: legend 'Divos Iulius' within laurel wreath; p. 407.

5. Denarius of Agrippa, 38 B.C. (Sydenham 207. 1330), London; *obv.*: heads of Caesar and Octavian facing each other, legend 'Divos Iulius, Divif.'; *rev.*: legend 'M. Agrippa cos. desig.'; p. 408.

6. Denarius of Q. Voconius Vitulus, *c.* 40 B.C. (Sydenham 185. 1132), Oxford; *obv.*: head of Caesar with lituus, legend 'Divi Iuli'; *rev.*: calf (*vitulus*), legend 'Q. Voconius Vitulus'; p. 399.

7. 'Denarius of Q. Voconius Vitulus, *c.* 40 B.C. (Sydenham 185. 1133) Oxford; *obv.*: head of Caesar; *rev.*: calf, legend 'Q. Voconius Vitulus, q(uaestor) design.'; p. 399.

8. Denarius of Ti. Sempronius Graccus, *c.* 40 B.C. (Sydenham 185. 1129), Oxford; *obv.*: head of Caesar, legend 'S.C.'; *rev.*: two military standards, plough, sceptre, legend 'Ti. Sempronius Graccus q(uaestor) desi(gnatus)'; p. 399.

9. Bronze from Arelate(?), *c.* 38 B.C., Oxford; *obv.*: head of Caesar, legend 'Divos Iulius'; *rev.*: Ceres with torch and plough, legend 'ex d(ecreto) d(ecurionum) Col(oniae) Iul(iae) Pat(ernae)'; p. 408.

10. Bronze of Paestum, *c.* A.D. 20 (Grant, *Aspects of the Principate of Tib.* 3), London; *obv.*: laureate head, legend 'P(aesti) s(ententia) s(enatus) [c(. . .?)]; *rev.*: apex of a flamen, legend 'L. Cael. Clem. fla(men) Ti. Caesar(is)'; p. 409.

11. Bronze from Africa, *c.* 37 B.C. (Grant, *FITA* 50 f.), Copenhagen; *obv.*: head of Caesar, legend 'Divos Iulius'; *rev.*: prow with star over it, legend 'Caes[ar] dictator perp.'; p. 409.

12. Bronze of Achulla, *c.* 37 B.C. (Grant, *FITA* 230), London; *obv.*: head of Octavian, legend 'Caesa[r Divi f.], Achulla'; *rev.*: head of Caesar, legend 'Divos Iulius', all in laurel wreath; p. 409.

PLATE 30

1

2

3

4

5

6

7

8

9

10

11

12

the first to hold that office for life in the province of Achaea; it was an exceptional honour, although it was granted elsewhere too.[1]

The progress in the West was more gradual and took much longer. Octavian was in charge, but here again the first moves were made under Caesar. It will be recalled that a close relationship had existed between Caesar and the *municipia* of Gallia Cisalpina since his first consulate.[2] That is no doubt why a *flamen* of Divus Iulius is more often attested there than anywhere else in the West, at Ateste, Brixia, Industria, and the city where later Gemona was built;[3] there is also evidence for a Caesareum at Ateste and Mutina.[4] At Ameria, a Roman *municipium*, the cult of the Victoria et Felicitas Caesaris was instituted in 46 or soon afterwards with a *flamen* in charge:[5] such a *flamen*, so named probably only after Caesar's death, was possible because of the connection of the cult with the person of Caesar. There is further evidence of the cult, though without reference to a priesthood, from Perusia,[6] Ocriculum,[7] an unidentified town in Picenum,[8] Minturnae,[9] Herculaneum,[10] Aesernia,[11] perhaps also from Puteoli (pl. 30. 3–4).[12]

In Gaul proper we meet a puzzling situation. The Tres Galliae had had from 12 B.C. a provincial assembly at the Ara Romae et Augusti at Lugdunum, and this was always presided over by a *sacerdos*, never by a *flamen*.[13] One is therefore inclined to conclude that these provinces did

---

[1] See above, p. 404. 10.   [2] See above, p. 299.

[3] *CIL* 5. 1812 (*ILS* 1122, Gemona); 2536 (Ateste); 4386 (Brixia); 4459 (*ILS* 6715, the same); 7478 (Industria); cf. 4966 (Vallis Camonica): '... sacerdoti Caesaris'; 9. 2598 (Teruentum): '... [sacerdot?]ibus Divi Iu[li...]' is doubtful.

[4] *CIL* 5. 2533; 11. 948. Other Caesarea in Italy, at Volcei (10. 415) and near Volsinii (*Röm. Mitt.* 18 (1903), 336), may have been built later, as was that of Beneventum under Augustus c. 15 B.C. (*CIL* 9. 1556 = *ILS* 109).

[5] *ILS* 6631: '... pontifici, flamini Victoriae et Felicitatis Caesaris perpetuo ... sacerd. Victoriae (et) Felicitatis Caesaris ...' (another *sacerdos Victoriae Felicitatis*, ibid., *CIL* 11. 4367). It is possible that in the first part of the inscription only a *flamen Caesaris* is meant, and 'Victoriae et Felicitatis' is due to an error of the lapicide.

[6] It is to be inferred from the altar of Divus Iulius at which Octavian killed Roman senators and knights in 40 B.C., Suet. *Aug.* 15; Sen. *clem.* 1. 11. 1; Dio 48. 14. 3; above, p. 399.

[7] *ILS* 73 (Degr. 409): 'Divo Iulio iussu populi Romani statutum est lege Rufrena.'

[8] *ILS* 73a (the same wording).

[9] J. Johnson, *RE* Suppl. 7. 478; 487: 'Deivo Iulio iussu populi Romani e lege Rufrena' (with the suggestion that temple B at Minturnae could have been Caesar's); Degrassi, *Mem. Linc.* 13. 8. 1 (1967), 12 ff. (*Scritti* 3. 102 ff.).

[10] *CIL* 10. 1411 (*ILS* 74a): 'Divo Iulio Augustales'; cf. 1412: 'Divo Augusto Augustales.'

[11] *ILS* 72 (Degr. 410): 'Genio Deivi Iuli, parentis patriae, quem senatus populusque Romanus in deorum numerum rettulit.'

[12] Grant, op. cit. 47 ff., ascribes coins with or without Caesar's head and with the legend 'Divos Iulius' (Sydenham 208. 1335 f.; Grueber, pl. 105. 9; 11), formerly ascribed to Gaul, to Puteoli(?).

[13] Livy, *Per.* 139; Dio 54. 32. 1; Mattingly 1. 92 ff.; *ILS* 7013 ff., etc.; Deininger, op. cit. 21 ff. (with bibliography); A. J. Christopherson, *Hist.* 17 (1968), 357 ff.

not possess a cult of Caesar; and that Augustus, when creating the provincial cult, proposed to avoid the Caesarian form.[1] But this conclusion cannot apply to the individual cities of the province. It was Lugdunum itself, the Colonia Copia Felix, planned by Caesar and founded by L. Munatius Plancus in 43,[2] that issued coins with the heads of Caesar and Octavian and with the legend 'Divi Iuli, Imp. Caesar Divi f., Copia',[3] to some extent imitating Agrippa's coins of 38 (pl. 30. 5; 28. 3–4);[4] a few of these even place a star over Caesar's head.[5] On the reverse there is the prow and the star over it which we also met on coins of Rome and Africa.[6] Thus there was an early cult in Lugdunum and possibly in other places in the province also; but there is no evidence that it was supervised by a *flamen*.

The case of Gallia Narbonensis is different. There is definite evidence from Arelate and Reii. Arelate, the Colonia Iulia Paterna since 46, issued a bronze coin with the wreathed head of Caesar and the legend 'Divos Iulius' on the obverse, Ceres in a *biga* with snakes and the legend 'ex d(ecreto) d(ecurionum) Col(oniae) Iu(liae) Pat(ernae)' on the reverse (pl. 30. 9).[7] The reverse, which derives from much earlier Roman coins,[8] is not relevant here. The obverse closely follows the pattern of a bronze coin issued by Octavian in Italy *c.* 37.[9] That will have been the approximate date of our coin too, but not that of the cult; doubtless it was created much earlier. Later a T. Iulius was Augustalis and *flamen Romae et Divi*(?) *Caesaris* at Arelate;[10] the name points to a Julian patronage, either by Caesar or by Augustus. Further, excavations at the local temple of Augustus brought to light a column decorated with a comet, the *Caesaris astrum*.[11] This means that the temple replaced an earlier temple of Caesar and incorporated his cult. Reii, the Colonia Apollinaris Reiorum, was probably founded before Caesar, but was in his debt because it had received Latin rights from him: it had a *flamen Divi Iuli* and later a *flamen Romae et Augusti*, who was also the *pontifex coloniae*.[12] One might assume that the cult also existed in other Caesarian colonies, especially at Valentia and Narbo. Narbo, the Colonia Iulia Paterna Narbo Martius Decimanorum since 46, may have issued the coin attributed

---

[1] The relation between *flamen* and *sacerdos* has never been properly explained, cf. Hirschfeld, *Kl. Schr.* 490 f.; Bickel, *BJ* 133 (1928), 22; Latte 319. 4; Deininger, op. cit. 148 ff.

[2] Dio 46. 50. 5; *ILS* 886; Grant, op. cit. 206; Vittinghoff 67 f.

[3] Grant 207; pl. 7. 23 (rev. only).

[4] Sydenham 207; pl. 30. 1330 (legend: 'Divos Iulius, Divi f.').

[5] Grant, pl. 7. 22 (Berlin).   [6] See above, p. 378.

[7] In the Ashmolean Museum, unpublished. I am indebted for the information to Dr. Kraay.

[8] It is found on the coins of C. Vibius Pansa, *c.* 48 B.C., Sydenham 158; pl. 26. 946.

[9] Sydenham 208. 1335; Grueber, pl. 105. 9 f.   [10] *AE* 1954, 104.

[11] F. Benoit, *Gallia* 11 (1953), 109, fig. 11 (Neronian (?) age).   [12] *CIL* 12. 370; 983.

above to Arelate.[1] But even if it did not, Narbo's later importance for
the imperial cult strongly suggests an early beginning. From A.D. 11 there
was the Ara Numinis Augusti, an unusual form of cult, and a temple of
Augustus after his death;[2] nothing is known about the forms of this cult.
It was Vespasian who created the provincial cult there, and chance has
preserved details about it, recorded in the *lex Narbonensis*.[3] A *flamen* was
in charge and had many privileges. He was entitled to a lictor, had a
special seat in the theatre, was a member of the provincial council,
wore the *toga praetexta* and could set up his statue at the end of his tenure
of office; his wife was entitled to wear a purple or white robe, etc. Some
of these privileges were no doubt later accretions and of local character,
but the essential matter must be old, conceived in the age of Caesar,
and accepted everywhere (pl. 30. 10).[4] The question as to why this provincial cult was not created before could be answered with the suggestion that the local cult in the various cities of the province was found
sufficient until then.

A similar development can be observed in Africa. The provincial
cult of Africa Proconsularis also dates from the reign of Vespasian.[5] But
Achulla on the east coast, which had received some privileges from
Caesar on his African campaign, issued a bronze coin *c.* 37 B.C. with the
head of Octavian on the obverse, and that of Caesar, 'Divos Iulius', on
the reverse (pl. 30. 12):[6] it points to the existence of a local cult at an early
date. Another coin ascribed to 37/36 B.C. and to Africa, perhaps
Carthage, the Colonia Iulia Concordia, shows the head of Caesar,
a *lituus*, and the legend 'Divos Iulius' on the obverse, a galley and the
legend 'Caesar dictator per(petuus)' on the reverse (pl. 30. 11).[7] The
galley must refer to some naval enterprise which is of no consequence
here; the legend is surprising though not unique. It was used by the
moneyers of 44, but also in 43 by Octavian on an *aureus*.[8] At Rusicade,

---

[1] See above, p. 408. 8; cf. Vittinghoff, 66.

[2] *ILS* 112; *CIL* 12. 392. 6: '... templi Divi [Aug. quod est Nar]bone.'

[3] *ILS* 6964 (McCrum–Woodhead 128); Hirschfeld, *Kl. Schr.* 489 ff.

[4] This conclusion is supported by the fact that the cap of the *flamen* is found on a coin
issued in Paestum *c.* A.D. 20 with the legend 'L. Cael(ius) Clem(ens) fla(men) Ti. Caesar(is)'
(Grant, *Aspects* 3; pl. 1. 11; Mattingly, *Roman Coins*, pl. 48. 4) and on the frieze of the temple
of Augustus at Tarraco (pl. 31. 1 = R. Étienne, *Le culte impérial dans la péninsule ibérique*
(1958), pl. 3).

[5] Fishwick, *Herm.* 92 (1964), 342 ff.; T. Kotula, *Mél.* 79 (1967), 207 ff.; R. P. Duncan-
Jones, *Epigr. Studien* 5 (1968), 151 ff.

[6] Grant, *From Imperium to Auctoritas* 230 f.; Vittinghoff 84 n.; Mr. G. K. Jenkins kindly
drew my attention to the specimen of this rare coin in the British Museum.

[7] Sydenham 214. 1368; Grant, *From Imperium to Auctoritas* 50; pl. 2. 12; on Carthage see
Vittinghoff 81 f.; C. Van Nerom, *Hommages à M. Renard* (1969), 2. 767 ff.

[8] Sydenham 177 f.; 206. 1321 (above, pp. 394 f.).

which belonged to Cirta, the Colonia Iulia Honoris et Virtutis since 46 or 44,[1] a C. Caecilius Gallus who lived in the first century A.D. was both the *flamen Divi Iuli* and the *flamen provinciae*:[2] clearly the former applies to the local cult of the colony, the latter to that of the provincial assembly of Africa.[3] It should be added that the cult of Rusicade implies the existence of a similar cult at Cirta. Fragmentary as this evidence is, it suggests that in Africa too the provincial cult instituted by Vespasian rested on foundations gradually laid in the cities from the time of Caesar onwards.

Some of the other provinces had their provincial cult and *flamen* long before Vespasian,[4] but further inferences are seldom possible. The provincial cult of Hispania Citerior, for instance, dates either from *c.* 26 B.C., when an altar of Augustus was set up at Tarraco,[5] or from A.D. 15, when a temple was built after his death;[6] but it would be surprising if in this Caesarian colony no cult of Caesar had ever existed.

To sum up. The first move was made by the Greeks: they honoured Caesar as they did their kings and later the Dea Roma and Roman generals. Caesar intervened early with the building of Caesarea in provincial cities and probably in his colonies. His intention must have been to transform the isolated and more or less improvised honours into a comprehensive cult. The last decrees of 44 were intended to sanction and extend to Rome and Italy what was being done in the East. His first *flamen* was created, temples were to be built, games to be instituted. This plan was fully realized after his consecration; and it was the cult of Divus Iulius that served later as the model at the creation of the imperial cult.

---

[1] Mommsen, *Ges. Schr.* 5. 474; *contra*, and for the foundation by Octavian, Vittinghoff 112 f.; cf. also Grant, op. cit. 232. [2] *CIL* 8. 7986 (*ILS* 6862); 7987.

[3] For a different interpretation see Fishwick, *Herm.* 92 (1964), 361 f.; Deininger, op. cit. 31. 2. But see *CIL* 2. 4223 (*ILS* 6932): 'sacerdos Romae et Augusti Conventus Asturum' and 'flamen Augustalis' of the province of Hispania Citerior. At Bulla Regia L. Iulius Cerialis was 'flamen Aug. perpetuus municipii sui' and 'flamen Aug(usti or -alis) provinciae Africae' *c.* A.D. 110, T. Kotula, *Mél.* 79 (1967), 207 ff. A provincial *flamen* of Gallia Narbonensis was also *flamen* of the Colonia Aug. Nemausensium (*CIL* 12. 3212, with addenda).

[4] For the full evidence see *Thes.L.L.* 6. 855 ff.; Dessau, *ILS* 3, pp. 571 ff.; F. Geiger, op. cit. 21 ff.; Larsen, op. cit. 126 ff.; Deininger, op. cit. 107 ff.

[5] Quintil. 6. 3. 77; *Anth. Pal.* 9. 307; Étienne, op. cit. 372; pls. 12. 1. 6; 13. 3 (coins); cf. the altar in the theatre dedicated 'Numini August(i)', *AE* 1924, 6 = 1946, 198; Étienne 309.

[6] Tac. *A.* 1. 78. 1; Étienne, 405 ff. (with bibliography); for coins with the legend 'Deo Augusto' ibid. pls. 12. 8 f.; 13. 4 (also Grant, *Aspects*, pl. 6. 8), and with the temple, pl. 12. 7–9 (Grant, pl. 7. 2); Deininger, op. cit. 121 ff. Its frieze was decorated with the cap of a *flamen* (Étienne, pl. 3); the earliest known *flamen* (*ILS* 1393) belongs to the age of Claudius or Nero (Étienne 132). In Lusitania the cult was founded under Tiberius (Étienne 122 ff.; Fishwick, *AJP* 91 (1970), 79 ff.), in Hispania Ulterior under Vespasian (Deininger, *Madr. Mitt.* 5 (1964), 167 ff.).

PLATE 31

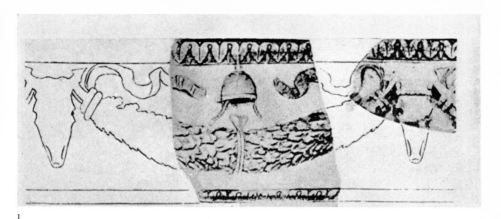

I

2

1. Temple of Augustus at Tarraco: part of the frieze decorated with the *apex* of a *flamen* (From Étienne, *Le culte impérial dans la Péninsule Ibérique*, pl. 3); p. 409. 4.

2. Base in honour of a *flamen Divi Iulii* from Alexandria in Troas in the British Museum: the *apex* of the *flamen* on the top of it (Photograph: British Museum); p. 405.

XIX

EPILOGUE

In this book we have been concerned with Caesar as an imaginative and daring religious reformer, who created and planned new cults, accepted extraordinary honours, and died when he was about to become a divine ruler—a reformer, moreover, who did not want to appear as an innovator, nor to spread a new philosophy of life, but to be guided by tradition; and yet one who in the end radically broke with it. This portrait is remote and unfamiliar; to some it may seem unconvincing or irrelevant. It is certainly incomplete, and that is why it has been drawn as part of a wider picture in which Caesar appears as the founder of the empire. This view of Caesar, too, is unusual; it is not new,[1] but it has been too seldom presented.

His plan was not an old one, conceived in his youth: he was not a prodigy. He certainly did not think of seizing power at the age of nineteen as Augustus was to do; nor, in contrast to Pompey, was he fascinated in his early twenties by the example of Alexander. In fact his political rise was not an easy one. At the time of his consulate and in his first years in Gaul he did not aspire further than to be honoured for his achievements as Pompey had been. Even after his break with the Senate he did not conceive a far-reaching plan. He vowed to cultivate some of the gods who had helped Pompey, in the hope that now they would help him to become victorious. But the right to decide about his honours—and that is what matters most here—rested not with himself, but with the Senate. How then did the Senate come to its decisions?

The Senate did not have a plan either; it was not at first guided by political theory, nor had it a clear idea of what its aim should be. There were precedents in the heroes of the past, Romulus, L. Brutus, Camillus, Scipio. Their honours, real or fictitious, had been exceptional, more fitting for a king or a god than for a citizen of the Republic. Some of these honours were genuinely Roman, odd relics of the regal period; others were created in imitation of Greek examples, above all of Alexander and, strangely enough, Demetrius Poliorcetes. The immediate

---

[1] It is discernible in the pages of Mommsen's *StR*, presupposed rather than fully argued. That is one of the reasons why Mommsen is the most quoted author in this book.

precedent was Pompey, who had but recently joined the ranks of the heroes. The Senate first granted to Caesar the honours which Pompey had received; but when it had to look for more, it turned directly to the example of the earlier heroes. Contemporary political ideas too, in the first place those of Cicero, began to exert their influence. Since his consulate Cicero had never ceased to speak and write about the virtues of the true statesman and the honours due to him. Some of these honours the Senate decreed for Caesar, at first probably against Cicero's wishes, later with his active co-operation.

Caesar was not a passive recipient. The decrees often fulfilled his expectations; if not, he made changes or refused. The result was complex and has been analysed in the individual chapters of this book. These chapters are arranged as far as possible chronologically; but their primary aim is to bring order into the substantial and often confusing evidence and to deal with related matters under common headings. They do not represent the single stages of a pre-conceived plan.

The honours of his predecessors had proved to be temporary, his own were to be lasting; and he received more of them than anyone before him. Moreover, he always gave a new turn to them, even to the cults. Pompey, too, had founded a temple of Venus; but Caesar's also honoured the ancestress of the Gens Iulia. Victoria Caesaris ranked him with the victorious generals of the past; at the same time she became his companion and represented his claim to be the permanent Imperator. There was thus a special significance in his representation as the conqueror with the globe on the Capitol, at first sight a new version of a Pompeian honour. Fortuna Caesaris and Felicitas Caesaris also became his permanent companions in war and peace. These new deities were to be joined by others similarly attached to his person, Salus Caesaris, Genius Caesaris, and the personifications of his political virtues. Their significance may be assessed by the fact that their archaic precedents, Lua Saturni, Maia Volcani, Moles Martis, and the like, had been attached to gods only, while their successors, the numerous deities with the epithets Augustus or Augusta, lost much of their force through the attempt to make their attachment less personal. The titles 'Saviour' and 'Liberator' had had a long history before Caesar; yet few were so vital for him as that of 'Liberator', which placed him at the side of L. Brutus. As a new 'Founder' he was a successor of Romulus, Camillus, and their Greek models; hitherto an honour without any consequence, it now implied that Caesar would rebuild the State. As *parens patriae* he had been anticipated by Cicero. But in Caesar's case it indicated a new relationship to his fellow-citizens: they were bound to him by *pietas*, prayed for his welfare, swore by his name, and took an oath of allegiance.

It was probably on his Eastern campaigns that Caesar conceived the plan of a Roman version of the ruler cult. There it was a political and religious necessity to claim for himself what had been due to the kings of the East; Dea Roma as a religious bond no longer sufficed to hold the parts of his empire together. In Rome itself his new position was to be prepared in the Roman fashion by the honours mentioned above. In the past the gods had represented a continuity, a never-changing authority, in contrast to that of the annual magistrates. Now their authority was to be shared by Caesar, who therefore required religious backing. These preparations were intensified when the Parthian campaign became imminent. In Parthia Caesar meant to appear as a legitimate king, the heir to all its political and religious traditions, and he wished to be honoured accordingly. It may well be that he drove into Rome in his triumph of 46 in a chariot with white horses precisely because that was how the Persian kings used to appear. Later he wore, or planned to wear, the Eastern tunic and wanted to wear the diadem. In Rome his house received a pediment; he wore the shoes of the Alban kings and rode like a king into Rome on horseback. His cult was decreed and a priesthood created. During his long absence his cult was to become established in Rome and Italy and perhaps to prepare for more. The Parthian victory would have consolidated his empire in the East, and the West would have followed suit.

His plan was taken up again soon after his murder: the cult of Divus Iulius inherited most of its features. It was established everywhere, and his priests had special privileges in the communities as well as in the provincial organizations. After long hesitation Augustus began to apply the conception to himself.[1] Tacitus reports that he wanted to have his own cult, temples, and priests,[2] and there is evidence from many places to show that this was true,[3] even if he was more restrained with regard to Rome. But what was achieved under him and later was a partial failure. One could say that Caesar's spell was no longer effective; or that the failure was due to Tiberius who resisted the idea of a divine

---

[1] Caesar has not yet been given his due share in the development of the imperial cult. Hirschfeld, *Kl. Schr.* 476 ff., suggested that it developed from local cults in the provinces and by local initiative; Bickel, *BJ* 133 (1928), 5 ff., that it was conceived and mostly executed by Augustus.

[2] Tac. *A.* 1. 10. 5: 'nihil deorum honoribus relictum, cum se templis et effigie numinum per flamines et sacerdotes coli vellet'; cf. Mommsen, *Ges. Schr.* 4. 268. 2; *StR* 2. 757. 1.

[3] e.g. the appointment of a *flamen* during his lifetime: see the list in Geiger, op. cit. 8 f.; *Thes.L.L.* 6. 855. 39 ff.; L. R. Taylor 270 ff.

ruler right from the beginning;[1] or to Caligula who in his attempt to wear Caesar's mantle discredited it. Yet the ruler cult was there to stay and was one of the pillars of Roman rule for centuries. It is difficult, however, to believe that this was all that Caesar wanted to achieve.

[1] Cf. *Ath. Mitt.* 77 (1962), 327.

ADDENDA AND CORRIGENDA

Bibliography.   The typescript of this book was completed in the summer of 1968. Minor additions and corrections were subsequently made in the text and notes on the basis of recent publications up to 1970. But unfortunately Miss Gesche's monograph (1968) could not be taken into account, as this would have involved more substantial changes than were possible at so late a stage.

pp. 10. 6; 315. 8; 379. 5.   Add to the list of forgeries: fragment of a painting formerly in Berlin, showing Caesar with the diadem: K. Zimmermann, *Wiss. Zeitschr. Rostock* 17 (1968), 9/10. 803 ff.; pl. 64 f.

p. 102.   On Parthian coins Nike is held by King Orodes I (40/39 B.C.), Head, *HN* 820; *BMC Parthia* 73. 34 ff.; pl. 15. 1 f., and by Phraates IV (33/2–28/7 B.C.), ibid. 100 ff. 8–10; 13–17; pl. 18. 17; 19. 3 (cf. also King Artavasdes I of Armenia, *BMC Galatia* 101. 1; pl. 14. 2); T. Hölscher, *Victoria Romana*, 26. If it is right to assume that these kings follow Caesar's example at the time of their great successes against the Romans rather than earlier native tradition, the argument above, p. 102, receives fresh support.

p. 124. 5.   Mr. Crawford kindly draws my attention to a coin of Aristarchus, dynast of Colchis, issued in 52 B.C. (G. K. Jenkins, *Num. Chron.* 1959, 32; pl. 6. 13; Head, *HN* 496): the *rev.* shows Tyche, with the mural crown, seated, a rudder at her side. It is thus certain that Tyche in fact had a rudder as her attribute. Yet the rest of what has been said above about Caesar's innovation need not be revised.

p. 271. 1.   Add: T. Adam, *Clementia Principis* (1970), 9 ff.; 82 ff.

p. 299. 1.   Dr. Kraay kindly draws my attention to the article of Seyrig, *Rev. num.* 66. 10 (1969), 149 ff., who attributes the coin (our pl. 21. 10) not, as Grant, to Alexandria but to Ninica (Cilicia).

p. 330.   Jesus' entry into Jerusalem is now discussed in a valuable monograph by Dinkler, *Der Einzug in Jerusalem* (1970), 47 ff. (with bibliography); on the rites of *adventus*, epiphany, and the like, see ibid. 42 ff.

INDEX I

NAMES AND SUBJECTS

G g

INDEX II

GREEK AND LATIN WORDS

(a) GREEK

(b) LATIN

INDEX III

SOURCES

An asterisk indicates a passage where the reading of the text is queried or discussed.

(a) LITERARY

(b) NON-LITERARY

1. Inscriptions